AMERICA'S
Wonderful
LITTLE
HOTELS
& INNS
Fourteenth Edition

The Middle Atlantic

States Covered in This Edition

Delaware
District of Columbia
Maryland
New Jersey

New York
Pennsylvania
Virginia
West Virginia

Also in This Series

America's Wonderful Little Hotels & Inns, U.S.A. and Canada
America's Wonderful Little Hotels & Inns, The Midwest
America's Wonderful Little Hotels & Inns, The Rocky Mountains and The Southwest
America's Wonderful Little Hotels & Inns, New England
America's Wonderful Little Hotels & Inns, The South
America's Wonderful Little Hotels & Inns, The West Coast
Europe's Wonderful Little Hotels & Inns, Great Britain & Ireland
Europe's Wonderful Little Hotels & Inns, The Continent

AMERICA'S
Wonderful
LITTLE
HOTELS
& INNS
Fourteenth Edition

The Middle Atlantic
Edited by Sandra W. Soule

Associate Editors:
Nancy P. Barker, June C. Horn,
Betsy Nolan Sandberg,
Abby Humphrey, Amy Phillipps

Contributing Editors:
Suzanne Carmichael, Rose Ciccone, Betty Norman,
Susan Schwemm, Diane Wolf

Editorial Assistants:
Sarah Phillipps, Jeffrey Soule

St. Martin's Press
New York

This book is dedicated to the people who take the time and trouble to write about the hotels and inns they've visited, and to my children—Hilary and Jeffrey—my husband, and my parents.

ISBN 0-312-13421-5

10 9 8 7 6 5 4 3 2 1

Maps by David Lindroth © 1995, 1993, 1992, 1991, 1990, 1989, 1988, 1987 by St. Martin's Press.

Contents

Acknowledgments

I would like again to thank all the people who wrote in such helpful detail about the inns and hotels they visited. To them belong both the dedication and the acknowledgments, for without their support, this guide would not exist. If I have inadvertently misspelled or omitted anyone's name, please accept my sincerest apologies.

I would also like to thank Hilary Rubinstein, who originated the concept for this series. Also thanks to my helpful and supportive editors Anne Savarese and Helen Packard; to my wonderful colleagues Nancy Barker, June Horn, Betsy Sandberg, Mary Ann Boyle, Abby Humphrey, Amy Phillipps, Suzanne Carmichael, Rose Ciccone, Nancy Debevoise, Gail Davis, Linda Goldberg, Betty Norman, Pam Phillips, Susan Schwemm, and Diane Wolf; and to faithful respondents Peg Bedini, Bruce Bilmes, John Blewer, Donna Bocks, Chrys Bolk, Pat Borysiewicz, Elaine Bounds, Judith Brannen, Sherrill Brown, James and Pamela Burr, April Burwell, Marjorie Cohen, Nancy Cohn, Happy and Ernie Copley, Dianne Crawford, Ann Christofferson, Brian Donaldson, Sally Ducot, Ellie and Robert Freidus, Connie Gardner, Alan Hay, B. J. Hensley, Stephen Holman, William Hussey, Linda Intaschi, Keith Jurgens, Arleen Keele, Al and Lauren Kenney, Shirley Lieb, Bradley Lockner, Bill MacGowan, Esther and Jack Magathan, Myra Malkin, Celia McCullough, Mark Mendenhall, Michael and Dina Miller, Lou Moriconi, Carolyn Myles, Bill Novack, Julie Phillips, Adam Platt, Penny Poirier, Jill Reeves, Stephanie Roberts, Glenn Roehrig, Mary Louise Rogers, Duane Roller, Marion Ruben, Betty Sadler, Lori Sampson, Joe and Sheila Schmidt, B. J. and Larry Schwartzkopf, Robert Sfire, Fritz Shantz and Tara O'Neal, Nancy Sinclair, Mary Jane Skala, Jeanne Smith, Mary Jane Southwick, Ruth Tilsley, Lee Todd, Susan Ulanoff, Wendi Van Exan, LuAnn and Steve Weiner, Hopie Welliver, Tom Wilbanks, Beryl Williams, Rose Wolf, Karl Wiegers and Chris Zambito, Susan Woods, and the many others who went far beyond the call of duty in their assistance and support.

Introduction

Each entry generally has three parts: a description of the inn or hotel, quotes from guests who have stayed there, and relevant details about rooms, rates, location, and facilities. Please remember that the length of an entry is in no way a reflection of that inn or hotel's quality. Rather, it is an indication of the type of feedback we've received both from guests and from the innkeepers themselves.

Wherever a location is of particular tourist interest, we've tried to include some information about its attractions. If we have only one listing for a town, this description usually falls within the body of the entry. If there is more than one inn or hotel listed for a town, the description of the town and information about its location precede the individual entries.

In some areas the magnet is not a particular town but rather a compact, distinct region. Travelers choose one place to stay and use it as a base from which to explore the area. But because this guide is organized by town, not by region, the entries are scattered throughout the chapter. When this applies, you will see the name of the region noted under the "Location" heading; check back to the introduction for a description of the region involved. When an inn is located in a small village close to a better-known town, cross-references are provided to make the process easier.

The names at the end of the quotations are those who have recommended the hotel or inn. Some writers have requested that we not use their names; you will see initials noted instead. *We never print the names of those who have sent us adverse reports, although their contributions are invaluable indeed.*

Although we have tried to make the listings as accurate and complete as possible, mistakes and inaccuracies invariably creep in. The most significant area of inaccuracy applies to the rates charged by each establishment. In preparing this guide, we asked all the hotels and inns to give us their 1996–1997 rates, ranging from the least expensive room in the off-season to the most expensive peak-season price. Some did so, while others just noted the 1995 rate.

Some of the shorter entries are marked "**Information please:**" or "**Also recommended:**" The former usually refer to establishments which have just come to our attention, as well as those that were listed in past editions. The latter are sometimes too big or small for a full entry, or those that have been recommended just as we were going to press.

1

Please remember that the process of writing and publishing a book takes nearly a year. *You should always double-check the rates when you make your reservations; please don't blame the hotel or this guide if the prices are wrong.* On the other hand, given the current level of inflation, you should not encounter anything more than a 5% increase, unless there has been a substantial improvement in the amenities offered or a change of ownership. Please let us know immediately if you find anything more than that!

If you find any errors of omission or commission in any part of the entries, we urgently request your help in correcting them. We recognize that it takes extra time and effort for readers to write us letters or fill in report forms, but this feedback is essential in keeping this publication totally responsive to consumer needs.

The Fifteen Commandments of Vacation Travel

We all know people who come back from a vacation feeling on top of the world, and others who seem vaguely disappointed. Here's how to put yourself in the first category, not the second.

1. Know yourself. A successful vacation is one that works for the person you are, not the person you think you should be. Confirmed couch potatoes who resent having to walk from the far end of the parking lot will not find true fulfillment on a trek through the Himalayas. If privacy is a top priority, a group tour or communal lodge will turn fantasy into frustration. Acknowledge your own comfort levels. How important is it for you to be independent and flexible? Structured and secure? How essential are the creature comforts when it comes to sleeping, eating, and bathing? Would you rather have one week of luxury travel or two weeks of budget food and accommodation? And remember that while your personality doesn't change, your needs do. The type of vacation you plan for a romantic getaway is totally different from a family reunion.

2. Know your travel companions. Adjust your plans to accommodate your travel partners. Whether you are traveling with friends, spouse, children, and/or parents, you'll need to take their age, attention span, agility, and interests into account. If you're traveling with the kids, balance a morning at an art museum with an afternoon at the zoo; if you're spending time with elderly parents, make sure that they can stroll a country lane while you go rock-climbing; if your group includes skiers and non-skiers, pick a resort that has appealing shops and other activities.

3. Plan ahead: anticipation is half the fun. Enjoy the process. The more you know about an area you're going to visit, the more fun you'll have. Skim a guidebook; get a calendar of events; write to the local chambers of commerce and tourist offices; read a novel set in the region; talk to friends (or friends of friends) who have been there recently.

4. Don't bite off more than you can chew. Keep your itinerary in line with the amount of time and money available. Focus on seeing a smaller area well, rather than trying to cover too much ground and seeing nothing but interstate highways. Don't overprogram; allow yourself the luxury of doing nothing.

5. Avoid one-night stands. Plan to stay a minimum of two nights everywhere you go. A vacation made up of one-nighters is a prescription for exhaustion. You will sleep poorly, spend most of your time in transit, and will get only the smallest glimpse of the place you're visiting. If it's worth seeing, it's worth spending a full day in one place.

6. Travel off-season. Unless your vacation dates are dictated by the school calendar, off-season travel offers many advantages: fewer crowds, greater flexibility, and a more relaxed atmosphere. Learn to pick the best dates for off-season travel; typically these are the weeks just before and after the rates change. Off-season travel offers big savings, too; for example, most ski areas are delightful places to visit in summer, and offer savings of 50% or more on accommodations.

7. Book well ahead for peak season travel. If you must travel during peak periods to popular destinations, make reservations well in advance for the key sites to avoid aggravation, extra phone calls, and additional driving time.

8. Take the road less traveled by. Get off the beaten path to leave the crowds behind. Instead of booking a room in the heart of the action, find a quiet inn tucked in the hills or in a neighboring village. If you visit the Grand Canyon in August, at the height of the tourist season, stay at the North Rim, which attracts 90% fewer visitors than the South Rim.

9. Ditch the car. Sure you need a car to get where you're going. But once you're there, get out and walk. You'll see more, learn more, experience more at every level, while avoiding crowds even at the most popular destinations. We promise. Car travel is an isolating experience, even when you're in bumper-to-bumper traffic.

10. Hang loose. The unexpected is inevitable in travel, as in the rest of life. When your plans go astray (and they will), relax and let serendipity surprise you. And keep your sense of humor in good working order. If possible, travel without reservations or a set itinerary.

11. Carpe diem—seize the day. Don't be afraid to follow your impulses. If a special souvenir catches your eye, buy it; don't wait to see if you'll find it again later. If a hiking trail looks too inviting to pass up, don't; that museum will wait for a rainy day.

12. Don't suffer in silence. When things go wrong—an incompetent guide, car troubles, a noisy hotel room—speak up. Politely but firmly express your concern then and there; get your room changed, ask for a refund or discount, whatever. Most people in the travel business would rather have you go away happy than to leave grumbling.

13. Remember—being there is more than seeing there. People travel to see the sights—museums and mountains, shops and scenery—but it is making new friends that can make a trip memorable. Leave a door open to the people-to-people experiences that enrich travel immeasurably.

14. Don't leave home to find home. The quickest way to take the wind out of the sails of your trip is to compare things to the way they are at home. Enjoy different styles and cultures for what they are and avoid comparisons and snap judgments.

15. Give yourself permission to disregard all of the above. Nothing is immutable. If you find a pattern that works for you, enjoy it!

Inngoer's Bill of Rights

We've read through a lot more brochures for inns and hotels than the average bear, and can attest to the fact that not one makes mention of its possible drawbacks, however slight. Furthermore, unlike this guidebook, *which accepts no fee of any kind for an entry,* many inn guidebooks charge a listing or membership fee of some kind, making them basically paid advertisements. Despite brochure promises and glowing listings in other books, we all know that perfection isn't possible in this world, but we feel that (despite the irate reactions of some innkeepers) complete and honest reporting will give readers *reasonable* expectations, ones that are often surpassed in the best of hostelries.

On the other hand, travelers have the right to expect certain minimum standards. These rights are especially important in hotels and inns at the top end of the rate scale; we don't expect as much from more modestly priced places, although good service is often received.

So, please use this Bill of Rights as a kind of checklist in deciding how you think a place stacks up on your own personal rating scale. And, whether an establishment fails, reaches, or exceeds these levels, be sure to let us know. We would also hope that innkeepers will use this list to help evaluate both the strong points and shortcomings of their own establishments, and are grateful to those who have already done so.

The right to suitable cleanliness: An establishment that looks, feels, and smells immaculate, with no musty, smoky, or animal odors.

The right to suitable room furnishings: A firm mattress, soft pillows, fresh linens, and ample blankets; bright lamps and night tables on each side of the bed; comfortable chairs with good reading lights; and adequate storage space.

The right to comfortable, attractive rooms: Guest rooms and common rooms that are as livable as they are attractive. Appealing places where you'd like to read, chat, relax.

The right to a decent bathroom: Cleanliness is essential, along with reliable plumbing, ample hot water, good lighting, an accessible electric outlet, space for toiletries, and thirsty towels.

The right to privacy and discretion: Privacy must be respected by the innkeeper and ensured by adequate sound-proofing. The right to discretion precludes questions about marital status or sexual preference. No display of proselytizing religious materials.

The right to good, healthful food: Fresh nutritious food, ample in quantity, high in quality, attractively presented, and graciously served in smoke-free surroundings.

The right to comfortable temperatures and noise levels: Rooms should be cool in summer and warm in winter, with windows that open, and quiet, efficient air-conditioning and heating. Double windows, drapes, and landscaping are essential if traffic noise is an issue.

The right to fair value: Prices should be in reasonable relation to the facilities offered and to the cost of equivalent local accommodation.

The right to genuine hospitality: Innkeepers who are glad you've come and who make it their business to make your stay pleasant and memorable; who are readily available without being intrusive.

The right to a caring environment: Welcoming arrivals with refreshments, making dinner reservations, providing information on activities, asking about pet allergies and dietary restrictions, and so on.

The right to personal safety: A location in a reasonably safe neighborhood, with adequate care given to building and parking security.

The right to professionalism: Brochure requests, room reservations, check-ins and -outs handled efficiently and responsibly.

The right to adequate common areas: At least one common room where guests can gather to read, chat, or relax, free of the obligation to buy anything.

The right of people traveling alone to have all the above rights: Singles usually pay just a few dollars less than couples, yet the welcome, services, and rooms they receive can be inferior.

The right to a reasonable cancellation policy: Penalties for a cancellation made fewer than 7-14 days before arrival are relatively standard. Most inns will refund deposits (minus a processing fee) after the deadline only if the room is rebooked.

The right to efficient maintenance: Burnt-out bulbs and worn-out smoke detector batteries are the responsibility of the innkeeper—not the guest. When things go wrong, guests have the right to an apology, a discount, or a refund.

Of course, there is no "perfect" inn or hotel, because people's tastes and needs vary so greatly. But one key phrase does pop up over and over again: "I felt right at home." This is not written in the literal sense—a commercial lodging, no matter how cozy or charming, is never the same as one's home. What is really meant is that guests felt as welcome, as relaxed, as comfortable, as they would in their own home.

What makes for a wonderful stay?

We've tried our best to make sure that all the hotels and inns listed in this guide are as wonderful as our title promises. Inevitably, there will be some disappointments. Sometimes these will be caused by a change in ownership or management that has resulted in lowered standards. Other times unusual circumstances will lead to problems. Quite often, though, problems will occur because there's not a good "fit" between the inn or hotel and the guest. Decide what you're looking for, then find the inn that suits your needs, whether you're looking for a casual environment or a dressy one, a romantic setting or a family-oriented one, a vacation spot or a business person's environment, an isolated country retreat or a convenient in-town location.

We've tried to give you as much information as possible on each hotel or inn listed, and have taken care to indicate the atmosphere each innkeeper is trying to create. After you've read the listing, request a copy of the establishment's brochure, which will give you more information.

Finally, feel free to call any inn or hotel where you're planning to stay, and ask as many questions as necessary.

Inn etiquette

A first-rate inn is a joy indeed, but as guests we need to do our part to respect its special qualities. For starters, you'll need to maintain a higher level of consideration for your fellow guests. Century-old Victorians are noted for their nostalgic charms, not their sound-proofing; if you come in late or get up early, remember that voices and footsteps echo off all those gleaming hardwood floors and doors. If you're going to pick a fight with your roommate, pull the covers up over your head or go out for a walk. If you're sharing a bath, don't dawdle, tidy up after yourself, and dry your hair back in your room. If you've admired the Oriental carpets, antique decor, handmade quilts, and the thick fluffy towels, don't leave wet glasses on the furniture, put suitcases on the bed, or use the towels for removing makeup or wiping the snow off your car. After all, innkeepers have rights too!

Hotels, inns . . . resorts and motels

As the title indicates, this is a guide to exceptional inns and hotels. Generally, the inns have 5 to 25 rooms, although a few have only 2 rooms and some have over 100. The hotels are more often found in the cities and range in size from about 50 to 200 rooms.

The line between an inn or hotel and a resort is often a fine one. There are times when we all want the extra facilities a resort provides, so we've added a number of reader-recommended facilities. We've also listed a handful of motels. Although they don't strictly fall within the context of this book, we've included them because readers felt they were the best option in a specific situation.

Although we do not provide full coverage of hotel chains, we do want to point out that the Four Seasons and Ritz-Carlton hotels are almost impossible to beat at the luxury end of the spectrum. Readers consistently rave about their unbeatable combination of unparalleled service and plush accommodation; weekend rates make them an exceptional value.

What is a B&B anyway?

There are basically two kinds of B&Bs—the B&B homestay and the B&B inn. The homestay is typically the home of an empty nester, who has a few empty bedrooms to fill, gaining some extra income and pleasant company. B&B inns are run on a more professional basis, independently marketed and subject to state and local licensing. Guests typically have dedicated common areas for their use, and do not share the hosts' living quarters, as in a homestay. We list very few homestays in this guide. Full-service or country inns and lodges are similar to the B&B inn, except that they serve breakfast and dinner on a regular basis, and may be somewhat larger in size; dinner is often offered to the public as well as to house guests. The best of all of these are made special by resident owners bringing the warmth of their personalities to the total experience. A B&B is *not* a motel that serves breakfast.

Rooms

All hotel and inn rooms are not created equal. Although the rooms at a typical chain motel or hotel may be identical, the owners of most of the establishments described in this book pride themselves on the individuality of each guest room. Some, although not all, of these differences are reflected in the rates charged.

More importantly, it means that travelers need to express their needs clearly to the innkeepers when making reservations and again when checking in. Some rooms may be quite spacious but may have extremely small private baths or limited closet space. Some antique double beds have rather high footboards—beautiful to look at but torture for six-footers. Most inns are trading their double-size mattresses in for queens and kings; if you prefer an oversize bed, say so. If you want twin beds, be sure to specify this when making reservations and again when you check in; many smaller inns have only one twin-bedded room.

Some rooms may have gorgeous old bathrooms, with tubs the size of small swimming pools, but if you are a hard-core shower person, that room won't be right for you. Many more others have showers but no baths, which may be disappointing if you love a long, luxurious soak in the tub. If you are traveling on business and simply must have a working-size desk with good lighting, speak up. Some rooms look terrific inside but don't look out at anything much; others may have the view but not quite as special a decor. Often the largest rooms are at the front of the house, facing a busy highway. Decide what's important to you. Although the owners and staff of the hotels and inns listed here are incredibly hard-working and dedicated people, they can't read your mind. Let your needs be known, and, within the limits of availability, they will try to accommodate you.

Our most frequent complaints center around beds that are too soft and inadequate reading lights. If these are priorities for you (as they are for us), don't be shy about requesting bedboards or additional lamps to remedy the situation. Similarly, if there are other amenities your room is lacking—extra pillows, blankets, or even an easy chair—speak up. Most innkeepers would rather put in an extra five minutes of work than have an unhappy guest.

If your reservation is contingent upon obtaining a particular room, make this very clear to the innkeeper. Some inns will not accept such reservations, feeling that they are too difficult to guarantee. Those that do accept them have an obligation to meet their guarantee; if circumstances prevent them from following through on the promised room, make it clear that you expect some sort of remuneration—either the return of your deposit or a reduction in the price of another room.

If you really don't like your room, ask for another as soon as possible, preferably before you've unpacked your bags. The sooner you voice your dissatisfaction, the sooner something can be done to improve the situation. If you don't like the food, ask for something else—since you're the guest, make sure you get treated like one. If things go terribly wrong, don't be shy about asking for your money back, and be *sure* to write us about any problems.

What is a single? A double? A suite? A cottage or cabin?

Unlike the proverbial rose, a single is not a single is not a single. Sometimes it is a room with one twin bed, which really can accommodate only one person. Quite often it is described as a room with a standard-size double bed, in contrast to a double, which has two twin beds. Other hotels call both of the preceding doubles, although doubles often have queen- or even king-size beds instead. Many times the only distinction is made by the number of guests occupying the room; a single will pay slightly less, but there's no difference in the room.

There's almost as much variation when it comes to suites. We define a suite as a bedroom with a separate living room area and often a small kitchen, as well. Unfortunately, the word has been stretched to cover other setups, too. Some so-called suites are only one large room, accommodating a table and separate seating area in addition to the bed, while others are two adjacent bedrooms which share a bath. If you require a suite that has two separate rooms with a door between them, specify this when you make reservations.

Quite a few of our entries have cabins or cottages in addition to rooms in the main building. In general, a cabin is understood to be a somewhat more rustic residence than a cottage, although there's no hard-and-fast rule. Be sure to inquire for details when making reservations.

Making reservations

Unless you are inquiring many months in advance of your visit, it's best to telephone when making reservations. This offers a number of advantages: You will know immediately if space is available on your requested dates; you can find out if that space is suitable to your specific needs. You will have a chance to discuss the pros and cons of the available rooms and will be able to find out about any changes made in recent months—new facilities, recently redecorated rooms, nonsmoking policies, even a change of ownership. It's also a good time to ask the innkeeper about other concerns—Is the neighborhood safe at night? Is there any renovation or construction in progress that might be disturbing? Will a wedding reception or bicycle touring group affect use of the common areas during your visit? If you're reserving a room at a plantation home that is available for public tours, get specifics about the check-in/out times; in many, rooms are not available before 5 P.M. and must be vacated by 9 A.M. sharp. The savvy traveler will always get the best value for his accommodation dollar.

If you expect to be checking in late at night, *be sure to say so;* many inns give door keys to their guests, then lock up by 10 P.M.

We're often asked about the need for making advance reservations. If you'll be traveling in peak periods, in prime tourist areas, and want to be sure of getting a first-rate room at the best-known inns, reserve at least three to six months ahead. This is especially true if you're traveling with friends or family and will need more than one room. On the other hand, if you like a bit of adventure, and don't want to be stuck with cancellation fees when you change your mind, by all means stick our books in the glove compartment and hit the road. If you're traveling in the off-season, or even midweek in season, you'll have a grand time. But look for a room by late afternoon; never wait until after dinner and expect to find something decent. Some inns offer a discount after 4:00 P.M. for last-minute bookings; it never hurts to ask.

Payment

The vast majority of inns now accept credit cards. A few accept credit cards for the initial deposit but prefer cash, traveler's checks, or personal checks for the balance; others offer the reverse policy. When no credit cards are accepted at all, you can settle your bill with a personal check, traveler's check, or even (!) cash.

When using your credit card to guarantee a reservation, be aware that most inns will charge your card for the amount of the deposit, unlike motels and hotels which don't put through the charge until you've checked in. A few will put a "hold" on your card for the full amount of your entire stay, plus the cost of meals and incidentals that you may (or may not) spend. If you're using your card to reserve a fairly extended trip, you may find that you're well over your credit limit without actually having spent a nickel. We'd suggest inquiring; if the latter is the procedure, either send a check for the deposit or go elsewhere. If you have used American Express, Diners Club, MasterCard, or Visa to guarantee your reservation, these companies guarantee if a room is not available, the hotel is supposed to find you a free room in a comparable hotel, plus transportation and a free phone call.

Rates

All rates quoted are per room, unless otherwise noted as being per person. Rates quoted per person are usually based on double occupancy, unless otherwise stated.

"Room only" rates do not include any meals. In most cases two or three meals a day are served by the hotel restaurant, but are charged separately. Average meal prices are noted when available. In a very few cases no meals are served on the premises at all; rooms in these facilities are usually equipped with kitchenettes.

B&B rates include bed and breakfast. Breakfast, though, can vary from a simple continental breakfast to an expanded continental breakfast to a full breakfast. Afternoon tea and evening refreshments are sometimes included as well.

MAP (Modified American Plan) rates are often listed per person and include breakfast and dinner. Only a few of the inns listed serve lunch, although many will prepare a picnic on request for an additional charge. Full board rates include three squares a day, and are usually found only at old-fashioned resorts and isolated ranches.

State and local sales taxes are not included in the rates unless otherwise indicated; the percentage varies from state to state, city to city, and can reach 20% in a few urban centers, although 10–15% is more typical.

When inquiring about rates, always ask if any off-season or special package rates are available. Sometimes discounted rates are available *only* on request; seniors and AAA members often qualify for substantial discounts. During the week, when making reservations at city hotels or country inns, it's important to ask if any corporate rates are available. Depending on the establishment, you may or may not be asked for some proof of corporate affiliation (a business card is usually all that's needed), but it's well worth inquiring, since the effort can result in a saving of 15 to 20%, plus an upgrade to a substantially better room.

A number of companies specialize in booking hotel rooms in major cities at substantial discounts. Although you can ask for specific hotels by name, the largest savings are realized by letting the agency make the selection; they may be able to get you a discount of up to 65%. **Hotel Reservations Network** (800–96–HOTEL) offers discount rates in over 20 U.S. cities plus London and Paris; **Quikbook** (800–789–9887) is a similar service with competitive rates. **Express Reservations** (800–356–1123) specializes in properties in New York City and Los Angeles, and **Capitol Reservations** (800–468–3500) covers Washington, D.C.

Another money-saving trick can be to look for inns in towns a bit off the beaten path. If you stay in a town that neighbors a famous resort or historic community, you will often find that rates are anywhere from $20 to $50 less per night for equivalent accommodation. If you're travelling without reservations, and arrive at a half-empty inn in late afternoon, don't hesitate to ask for a price reduction or free room upgrade. And of course, watch for our ¢ symbol, which indicates places which are a particularly good value.

If an establishment has a specific tipping policy, whether it is "no tipping" or the addition of a set service charge, it is noted under "Rates." When both breakfast and dinner are included in the rates, a 15% service charge against the total bill—not just the room—is standard; some inns are charging 18–20%. A number of B&Bs are also adding on a service charge, a practice which sits poorly with us. If you feel—as many of our readers do—that these fees are a sneaky way of making rates seem lower than they really are, let the innkeeper (and us) know how you feel. When no notation is made, it's generally expected that guests will leave $1–3 a night for the housekeeping staff and 15% for meal service. A number of inns have taken to leaving little cards or envelopes to remind guests to leave a tip for the housekeepers; most readers find this practice objectionable. If you welcome a no-tipping policy and object to solicitation, speak up.

While the vast majority of inns are fairly priced, there are a few whose rates have become exorbitant. Others fail to stay competitive, charging top weekend rates when a nearby luxury hotel is offering a beautiful suite at a lower price. No matter how lovely the breakfast, how thoughtful the innkeepers, there's a limit to the amount one will pay for a room without an in-room telephone, TV, or a full-size private bathroom. We recently learned about a B&B that has the nerve to charge $125 for a room with shared bath, and asks you to bring your own pool towels during the summer!

Deposits and cancellations

Nearly all innkeepers print their deposit and cancellation policies clearly on their brochures. Deposits generally range from payment of the first night's stay to 50% of the cost of the entire stay. Some inns repeat the cancellation policy when confirming reservations. In general, guests canceling well in advance of the planned arrival (one to four weeks is typical) receive a full refund minus a cancellation fee. After that date, no refunds are offered unless the room is resold to someone else. A few will not refund *even if the room is resold,* so take careful note. If you're making a credit card booking over the phone, be sure to find out what the cancellation policy is. We are uncomfortable with overly strict refund policies, and wish that inns would give a gift certificate, good for a return visit, when guests are forced to cancel on short notice.

Sometimes the shoe may be on the other foot. Even if you were told earlier that the inn at which you really wanted to stay was full, it may be worthwhile to make a call to see if cancellations have opened up any last-minute vacancies.

Minimum stays

Two- and three-night minimum weekend and holiday stays are the rule at many inns during peak periods. We have noted these when possible, although we suspect that the policy may be more common than is always indicated in print. On the other hand, you may just be hitting a slow period, so it never hurts to call at the last minute to see if a one-night reservation would be accepted. Again, cancellations are always a possibility; you can try calling on a Friday or Saturday morning to see if something is available for that night.

Pets

Very few of the inns and hotels listed accept pets. When they do we've noted it under "Extras." On the other hand, most of the inns listed in this book have at least one dog or cat, sometimes more. These pets are usually found in the common areas, sometimes in guest rooms as well. If you are allergic to animals, *we strongly urge that you inquire for details before making reservations.*

Children

Some inns are family-style places and welcome children of all ages; we've marked them with our 👪 symbol. Others do not feel that they have facilities for the very young and only allow children over a certain age. Still others cultivate an "adults only" atmosphere and don't even welcome children at dinner. When inns and hotels do not encourage all children, we've noted the age requirement under the heading "Restrictions." If special facilities are available to children, these are noted under "Facilities" and "Extras." If an inn does not exclude children yet does not offer any special amenities or rate reductions for them, we would suggest it only for the best-behaved youngsters.

Whatever the policy, you may want to remind your children to follow the same rules of courtesy toward others that we expect of adults. Be aware that the pitter-patter of little feet on an uncarpeted hardwood floor can sound like a herd of stampeding buffalo to those on the floor below. Children used to the indestructible plastics of contemporary homes will need to be reminded (more than once) to be gentle with antique furnishings.

State laws governing discrimination by age are affecting policies at some inns. To our knowledge, both California and Michigan now have such laws on the books. Some inns get around age discrimination by limiting room occupancy to two adults. This discourages families by forcing them to pay for two rooms instead of one. Our own children are very clear on their preferences: although they've been to many inns that don't encourage guests under the age of 12, they find them "really boring"; on the other hand, they've loved every family-oriented place we've ever visited.

Porterage and packing

Only the largest of our listings will have personnel whose sole job is to assist guests with baggage. In the casual atmosphere associated with many inns, it is simply assumed that guests will carry their own bags. If you do need assistance with your luggage, don't hesitate to ask.

If you're planning an extended trip to a number of small inns, we'd suggest packing as lightly as possible, using two small bags rather than one large suitcase. You'll know why if you've ever tried hauling a 50-pound oversize suitcase up a steep and narrow 18th-century staircase. On the other hand, don't forget about the local climate when assembling your wardrobe. In mountainous and desert regions, day- and nighttime temperatures can vary by as much as 40 degrees. Also, bear in mind that Easterners tend to dress more formally than Westerners, so pack accordingly.

Meals

If you have particular dietary restrictions—low-salt, vegetarian, or religious—or allergies—to caffeine, nuts, whatever—be sure to mention these when making reservations and *again* at check-in. If you're allergic to a common breakfast food or beverage, an evening reminder will ensure that you'll be able to enjoy the breakfast that's been prepared for you. Most innkeepers will do their best to accommodate your special needs, although, as one innkeeper noted tartly, "we're not operating a hospital."

In preparing each listing, we asked the owners to give us the cost of prix fixe and à la carte meals when available. An "alc dinner" price at the end of the "Rates" section is the figure we were given when we requested the average cost of a three-course dinner with a half bottle of house wine, including tax and tip. Prices listed for prix fixe meals do not include wine and service. Lunch prices, where noted, do not include the cost of any alcoholic beverage. Hotels and inns which serve meals to the public are noted with the ✕ symbol.

Dinner and lunch reservations are always a courtesy and are often essential. Most B&B owners will offer to make reservations for you; this can be especially helpful in getting you a table at a popular restaurant in peak season and/or on weekends. Some of the establishments we list operate restaurants fully open to the public. Others serve dinner primarily to their overnight guests, but they also will serve meals to outsiders; reservations are essential at such inns, usually eight or more hours in advance.

A few restaurants require jackets and ties for men at dinner, even in rather isolated areas. Of course, this is more often the case in traditional New England and the Old South than in the West. Unless you're going only to a very casual country lodge, we recommend that men bring these items along and that women have corresponding attire.

Breakfast: Breakfast is served at nearly every inn or hotel listed in this guide, and is usually included in the rates. Whenever possible we describe a typical breakfast, rather than using the terms "continental" or "full" breakfast.

Continental breakfast ranges from coffee and store-bought pastry to a lavish offering of fresh fruit and juices, yogurt and granola, cereals, even cheese and cold meats, homemade muffins and breads, and a choice of decaffeinated or regular coffee, herbal and regular tea. There's almost as much variety in the full breakfasts, which range from the traditional eggs, bacon, and toast, plus juice and coffee, to three-course gourmet extravaganzas.

We've received occasional complaints about breakfasts being too rich in eggs and cream, and too sweet, with no plain rolls or bread. A dietary splurge is fun for a weekend escape, but on a longer trip we'd advise requesting a "healthy breakfast" from your innkeeper. You can be sure that they don't eat their own breakfasts every day! Equally important to many guests are the timing and seating arrangements at breakfast. As one reader put it: "We stayed at a B&B where breakfast is served at one large table, promptly at 8:30 A.M. This is a mixed blessing. The breakfast was lovely and fresh, and the setting encouraged a convivial meal with the other guests. But there are those who consider any conversation prior to a second cup of coffee to be barbaric. More importantly, this doesn't allow for different time schedules." *(William Hussey)*

Lunch: Very few of the inns and hotels listed here serve lunch. Those that do generally operate a full-service restaurant or are located in isolated mountain settings with no restaurants nearby. Quite a number of B&B inns are happy to make up picnic lunches for an additional fee.

13

Dinner: Meals served at the inns listed here vary widely from simple home-style family cooking to gourmet cuisine. We are looking for food that is a good, honest example of the type of cooking involved. Ingredients should be fresh and homemade as far as is possible; service and presentation should be pleasant and straightforward. We have no interest in the school of "haute pretentious" where the hyperbolic descriptions found on the menu far exceed the chef's ability.

Drinks

With a very few exceptions (noted under "Restrictions" in each listing), alcoholic beverages may be enjoyed in moderation at all of the inns and hotels listed. Most establishments with a full-service restaurant serving the public as well as overnight guests are licensed to serve beer, wine, and liquor to their customers, although "brown-bagging" or BYOB (bring your own bottle) is occasionally permitted, especially in dry counties. Bed & breakfasts, and inns serving meals primarily to overnight guests, do not typically have liquor licenses, although most will provide guests with setups, i.e., glasses, ice, and mixers, at what is often called a BYO (bring your own) bar.

Overseas visitors will be amazed at the hodgepodge of regulations around the country. Liquor laws are determined in general by each state, but individual counties, or even towns, can prohibit or restrict the sale of alcoholic beverages, even beer.

Smoking

The vast majority of B&Bs and inns prohibit indoor smoking entirely, allowing it only on porches and verandas; a few don't allow smoking anywhere on the grounds. Larger inns and hotels usually do permit smoking, prohibiting it only in some guest rooms, and dining areas. Where prohibitions apply we have noted this under "Restrictions." We suggest that confirmed smokers be courteous or make reservations elsewhere. If there is no comment about smoking under "Restrictions," non-smokers should ask if smokers are in residence.

Physical limitations and wheelchair accessibility

We've used the well-known symbol ⅋ to denote hotels and inns that are wheelchair accessible. Where available, additional information is noted under the "Extras" heading. Unfortunately, what is meant by this symbol varies dramatically. In the case of larger hotels and newer inns, it usually means full access; in historic buildings, access may be limited to the restaurant and public rest rooms only, or to a specific guest room but not the common areas. *Call the inn/hotel directly for full details and to discuss your needs.*

If you do not need a wheelchair but have difficulty with stairs, we urge you to mention this when making reservations; many inns and small hotels have one or two rooms on the ground floor, but very few have elevators. Similarly, if you are visually handicapped, do share this information so that you may be given a room with good lighting and no unexpected steps.

Air-conditioning

Heat is a relative condition, and the perceived need for air-conditioning varies tremendously from one individual to the next. If an inn or hotel has air-conditioning, you'll see this listed under "Rooms." If it's important to you, be sure to ask when making reservations. If air-conditioning is not available, check to see if fans are provided. Remember that top-floor rooms in most inns (usually a converted attic) can be uncomfortably warm even in relatively cool climates.

Transportation

A car is more or less essential for visiting most of the inns and hotels listed here, as well as the surrounding sights of interest. Exceptions are those located in the major cities. In some historic towns, a car is the easiest way to get there, but once you've arrived, you'll want to find a place to park the car and forget about it.

If you are traveling by public transportation, check the "Extras" section at the end of each write-up. If the innkeepers are willing to pick you up from the nearest airport, bus, or train station, you'll see it noted here. This service is usually free or available at modest cost. If it's not listed, the innkeeper will direct you to a commercial facility that can help.

Parking

Although not a concern in most cases, parking is a problem in many cities, beach resorts, and historic towns. If you'll be traveling by car, ask the innkeeper for advice when making reservations. If parking is not on-site, stop at the hotel first to drop off your bags, then go park the car. In big cities, if "free parking" is included in the rates, this usually covers only one arrival and departure. Additional "ins and outs" incur substantial extra charges. Be sure to ask.

If on-site parking is available in areas where parking can be a problem, we've noted it under "Facilities." Since it's so rarely a problem in country inns, we haven't included that information in those listings. Regrettably, security has become an issue in most cities. Never leave anything visible inside the car; it's an invitation for break-in and theft.

Christmas travel

Many people love to travel to a country inn or hotel at Christmas. Quite a number of places do stay open through the holidays, but the extent to which the occasion is celebrated varies widely indeed. We know of many inns that decorate beautifully, serve a fabulous meal, and organize all kinds of traditional Christmas activities. But we also know of others, especially

15

in ski areas, that do nothing more than throw a few token ornaments on a tree. Be sure to inquire.

Is innkeeping for me?

Many of our readers fantasize about running their own inn; for some the fantasy will become a reality. Before taking the plunge, it's vital to find out as much as you can about this demanding business. Begin by reading *So You Want to be an Innkeeper*, by Pat Hardy, Jo Ann Bell, and Mary Davies. Hardy and Bell are co-directors of the Professional Association of Innkeepers, International (PAII—pronounced "pie") which also publishes *Innkeeping Newsletter*, various materials for would-be innkeepers, and coordinates workshops for aspiring innkeepers. For details contact PAII, P.O. Box 90710, Santa Barbara, CA 93190; 805–569–1853. Another good book is *How to Start and Run Your Own Bed & Breakfast Inn* by long-time innkeepers Ripley Hotch and Carl Glassman, covering everything from financing to marketing to day-to-day innkeeping responsibilities ($14.95; Stackpole Books, P.O. Box 1831, Harrisburg, PA 17105; 800–732–3669). Another excellent source, especially in the East, are consultants Bill Oates and Heide Bredfeldt. Contact them (P.O. Box 1162, Brattleboro, VT 05301; 802–254–5931) to find out when and where they'll be offering their next seminar entitled "How to Purchase and Operate a Country Inn." Bill and Heide are highly respected pros in this field and have worked with innkeepers facing a wide range of needs and problems; his newsletter, *Innquest*, is written for prospective innkeepers looking to buy property.

For more information

The best sources of travel information in this country and in Canada are absolutely free; in many cases, you don't even have to supply the cost of a stamp or telephone call. They are the state and provincial tourist offices.

For each state you'll be visiting, request a copy of the official state map, which will show you every little highway and byway and will make exploring much more fun; it will also have information on state parks and major attractions in concise form. Ask also for a calendar of events and for information on topics of particular interest, such as fishing or antiquing, vineyards or crafts; many states have published B&B directories, and some are quite informative. If you're going to an area of particular tourist interest, you might also want to ask the state office to give you the name of the regional tourist board for more detailed information. You'll find the addresses and telephone numbers for all the states and provinces covered in the Appendix at the back of this book.

You may also want to contact the local chamber of commerce for information on local sights and events of interest or even an area map. You can get the necessary addresses and telephone numbers from the inn or hotel where you'll be staying or from the state tourist office.

If you are one of those people who never travel with fewer than three guidebooks (which includes us), you will find the AAA and Mobil regional guides to be helpful references. The Mobil guides can be found in most bookstores and Mobil gas stations, while the AAA guides are distributed free on request to members. Both series cover hotels, restaurants, and sightseeing information, although we find the AAA guides to offer wider coverage and more details. If you're not already an AAA member, *we'd strongly urge you join before your next trip*; in addition to their road service, they offer quality guidebooks and maps, and an excellent discount program at many hotels (including a number listed here).

Guidebooks are published only once every year or two; if you'd like to have a more frequent update, we'd suggest one of the following:

Country Inns/Bed & Breakfasts (P.O. Box 182, South Orange, NJ 07079; 800–877–5491), $20, 6 issues annually. You know what they say about a picture being worth a 1000 words. A must for inngoers.

The Discerning Traveler (504 West Mermaid Lane, Philadelphia, PA 19118; 800–673–7834 or 215–247–5578), $50, 6 issues annually, $8 single copy. Picks a single destination in the New England, Mid-Atlantic, or Southern states and covers it in real depth—sights, restaurants, lodging, and more. The authors have published three delightful books on the subject as well

Guidebook addict? Consider a subscription to *Travel Books Review* (P.O. Box 191554, Atlanta, GA 31119) covering guidebooks for the U.S. and abroad, plus travel information on CD-ROM disks as well. Four sixteen-page issues annually, $19.95; single issues, $5.95.

Where is my favorite inn?

In reading through this book, you may find that your favorite inn is not listed, or that a well-known inn has been omitted from this edition. Why? Two reasons, basically: In several cases, establishments have been dropped because our readers had unsatisfactory experiences. Feel free to contact us for details. Other establishments have been omitted because we've had no reader feedback at all. This may mean that readers visiting these hotels and inns had satisfactory experiences but were not sufficiently impressed to write about them, or that readers were pleased but just assumed that someone else would take the trouble. If the latter applies, please, please, do write and let us know of your experiences. We try to visit as many inns as possible ourselves, but it is impossible to visit every place, every year. So please, keep those cards, letters, and telephone calls coming! As an added incentive, we will be sending free copies of the next edition of this book to our most helpful respondents.

Little Inns of Horror

We try awfully hard to list only the most worthy establishments, but sometimes the best-laid plans of mice and travel writers do go astray. Please understand that whenever we receive a complaint about an entry in our guide we feel terrible, and do our best to investigate the situation. Readers occasionally send us complaints about establishments listed in *other* guidebooks; these are quite helpful as warning signals.

The most common complaints we receive—and the least forgivable—

are on the issue of dirt. Scummy sinks and bathtubs, cobwebbed windows, littered porches, mildewed carpeting, water-stained ceilings, and grimy linens are all stars of this horror show.

Next in line are problems dealing with the lack of maintenance: peeling paint and wallpaper; sagging, soft, lumpy mattresses; radiators that don't get hot and those that make strange noises; windows that won't open, windows that won't close, windows with no screens, decayed or inoperable window shades; moldy shower curtains, rusty shower stalls, worn-out towels, fluctuating water temperatures, dripping faucets, and showers that only dribble, top the list.

Food complaints come next on this disaster lineup: poorly prepared canned or frozen food when fresh is readily available; meals served on paper, plastic, or worst of all, styrofoam; and insensitivity to dietary needs. Some complaints are received about unhelpful, abrasive, or abusive innkeepers, with a few more about uncaring, inept, or invisible staff. Complaints are most common in full-service inns when the restaurant business preoccupies the owners' attention, leaving overnight guests to suffer. Last but not least are noise headaches: trucks and trains that sound like they're heading for your pillow, and being awakened by the sound of someone snoring—in the next room. More tricky are questions of taste—high Victorian might look elegant to you, funereal to me; my collectibles could be your Salvation Army thriftshop donation. In short, there are more than a few inns and hotels that give new meaning to the phrase "having reservations"; fortunately they're many times outnumbered by the many wonderful places listed in this guide.

Pet peeves

Although we may genuinely like an inn, minor failings can keep it from being truly wonderful. Heading our list of pet peeves is inadequate bedside reading lights and tables. We know that there is not always room for a second table, but a light can always be attached to the wall. For reasons of both safety and comfort, a lamp should be at every bedside. Another reader is irked by inadequate bathroom lighting: "I think it must be an innkeepers' conspiracy to keep me from ever getting my makeup on properly." *(SU)* Equally annoying is the addition of fancy amenities when the basics are inadequate. As one reader put it: "Brandy by the bed and chocolates on the pillow are no excuse to overlook all other aspects of an enjoyable stay. When everything else is perfect, the small touches make a hotel magical, but in the absence of solid comfort the extras are mostly jarring." *(Robert Freidus)* Other readers object to overly friendly innkeepers: "The innkeeper chatted with us all during breakfast, and was disappointed that we didn't plan to go in to say goodbye after we loaded up the car. Innkeepers should remember that the guests are customers, not long-lost relatives." *(Karl Weigers & Chris Zambito)* Another common gripe concerns clutter: "Although pretty and interesting, the many collectibles left us no space for our personal belongings." And: "Instructions were posted everywhere—how to operate door locks, showers, heat, air-conditioning, and more." Anything you'd like to add?

Glossary of Architectural and Decorating Terms

We are not architectural experts, and when we started writing *America's Wonderful Little Hotels & Inns*, we didn't know a dentil from a dependency, a tester from a transom. We've learned a bit more since then, and hope that our primer of terms, prepared by associate editor Nancy Barker, will also be helpful to you.

Adam: building style (1780–1840) featuring a classic box design with a dominant front door and fanlight, accented by an elaborate surround or an entry porch; cornice with decorative moldings incorporating dentil, swag, garland, or stylized geometric design. Three-part Palladian-style windows are common.

antebellum: existing prior to the U.S. Civil War (1861–1865).

Arts and Craft movement: considered the first phase of the Modern movement that led to the Prairie style (1900–20) of Frank Lloyd Wright in Chicago, and the Craftsman style (1905–30) of the Greene brothers in Southern California. In the Arts and Craft style, historical precedent for decoration and design was rejected and ornamentation was "modernized" to remove traces of its historic origins. It features low-pitched roofs, wide eave overhangs, and both symmetrical and asymmetrical front façades.

beaded board: simple ornamented board, with a smooth, flat surface alternating with a half-round, rod-like carving (bead) running the length of the board. Common wainscoting or panelling in Victorian-era homes.

carpenter Gothic: *see* country, folk Victorian.

chinoiserie: imitation of Chinese decorative motifs; i.e., simulated Oriental lacquer covering pine or maple furniture. See also Chinese Chippendale below.

Chippendale: named for English furniture designer, Thomas Chippendale, of the Queen Anne period (1750–1790); the style varies from the Queen Anne style in ornamentation, with more angular shapes and heavier carving of shells, leaves, scrolls. Chinese Chippendale furniture employs chiefly straight lines, bamboo turnings, and as decoration, fluting, and fretwork in a variety of lattice patterns.

Colonial Revival: building style (1880–1955) featuring a classic box design with a dominant front door elaborated with pilasters and either a pediment (Georgian-style) or a fanlight (Adam-style); double-hung windows symmetrically balanced.

corbel: an architectural member that projects from a wall to support a weight and is stepped outward and upward from the vertical surface.

Corinthian: column popular in Greek Revival style for support of porch roofs; the capitals are shaped like inverted bells and decorated with acanthus leaves.

cornice: projecting horizontal carving or molding that crowns a wall or roof.

country, folk Victorian: simple house form (1870–1910) with accents of Victorian (usually Queen Anne or Italianate) design in porch spindlework and cornice details. Also known as carpenter Gothic.

Craftsman: building style (1905–1930) with low-pitched, gabled roof and wide, unenclosed eave overhang; decorative beams or braces added under gables; usually one-story; porches supported by tapered square columns.

dentil: exterior or interior molding characterized by a series of small rectangular blocks projecting like teeth.

dependencies: buildings that are subordinate to the main dwelling; i.e., a detached garage or barn. *See* also garçonnière.

Doric: column popular in Greek Revival style for support of porch roofs; the simplest of the three styles, with a fluted column, no base, and a square capital.

Eastlake: architectural detail on Victorian houses, commonly referred to as "gingerbread." Typically has lacy spandrels and knob-like beads, in exterior and interior design, patterned after the style of Charles Eastlake, an English furniture designer. Eastlake also promoted Gothic and Jacobean Revival styles with their strong rectangular lines; quality workmanship instead of machine manufacture; and the use of varnished oak, glazed tiles, and unharmonized color.

Eclectic movement: architectural tradition (1880–1940) which emphasized relatively pure copies of Early American, Mediterranean, or Native American homes.

eyebrow dormer: a semi-circular, narrow window over which the adjoining roofing flows in a continuous wave line; found on Shingle or Richardsonian Romanesque buildings.

faux: literally, French for "false." Refers commonly to woodwork painted to look like marble or another stone.

Federal: *See* Adam.

Franklin stove: metal heating stove which is set out into the room to conserve heat and better distribute it. Named after its inventor Benjamin Franklin; some designs resemble a fireplace when their front doors are open.

four-poster bed: variation on a tester bed but one in which the tall corner posts, of equal height, do not support a canopy. Carving of rice sheaves was a popular design in the Southern states, and signified prosperity.

gambrel roof: a two-slope, barn-style roof, with a lower steeper slope and a flatter upper one.

garçonnière: found on antebellum estates; a dependency housing unmarried male guests and family members.

Georgian: building style (1700–1830) featuring a classic box design with a dominant front door elaborated with pilasters and a pediment, usually with a row of small panes of glass beneath the crown or in a transom; cornices with decorative moldings, usually dentil.

Gothic Revival: building style (1840–1880) with a steeply pitched roof, steep gables with decorated vergeboards, and one-story porch supported by flattened Gothic arches. Windows commonly have pointed-arch shape.

Greek Revival: building style (1825–1860) having a gabled or hipped roof of low pitch; cornice line of main and porch roofs emphasized by a wide band of trim; porches supported by prominent columns (usually Doric).

half-tester bed: a bed with a low footboard and a canopy projecting from the posts at the head of the bed. Pronounced "half tee'-stir."

Ionic: column popular in Greek Revival style for support of porch roofs; the caps of the column resemble the rolled ends of a scroll.

Italianate: building style (1840–1885) with two or three stories and a low-pitched roof with widely overhanging eaves supported by decorative brackets; tall, narrow windows arched or curved above with elaborate crowns. Many have a square cupola or tower.

keeping room: in a Colonial-era home, the equivalent of a modern family room; it was usually warm from proximity to kitchen, so infants and the ill were "kept" here.

kiva: stuccoed, corner beehive-shaped fireplace common in adobe homes in Southwestern U.S.

latillas: ceiling of unpeeled, rough sticks, supported by vigas (rough beams); seen in flat-roofed adobe homes.

Lincrusta (or Lincrusta-Walton): an embossed, linoleum-like wallcovering made with linseed oil, developed in 1877 in England by Frederick Walton.

lintel: horizontal beam, supported at both ends, that spans an opening.

mansard roof: having two slopes on all sides with the lower slope steeper than the upper one.

Mission: building style (1890–1920) with Spanish mission-style parapet; commonly with red tile roof, overhanging, open eaves, and smooth stucco finish. In furniture, the Mission style is best represented by the work of designer Gustav Stickley. Using machine manufacture, he utilized simple, rectangular lines and favored quarter-sawn white oak for the rich texture of the graining.

Palladian window: typically a central window with an arched or semicircular head.

Pueblo Revival: building style (1910 to present) with flat roof, parapet above; corners and edges blunted or rounded; projecting vigas, stepped back roof lines, and irregular stucco wall surfaces. Influenced by the flat-roofed Spanish Colonial buildings and Native American pueblos; popular in Arizona and New Mexico; common in Santa Fe and Albuquerque.

Pewabic (tile): glazed tiles made in the Detroit, Michigan, area, in the first half of the 1890s, whose unique manufacturing process has been lost.

pocket doors: doors that open by sliding into a recess (pocket) in the wall.

portal (or portale): in Spanish-style homes, the long, narrow porch that opens onto an internal courtyard; it functions as a sheltered passageway between rooms.

post and beam: building style based on the Medieval post-and-girder method, where upper loads are supported by heavy corner posts and cross timbers. In contemporary construction, the posts and beams are often left exposed on the interior.

Prairie: building style (1900–1920) with low-pitched roof and widely overhanging eaves; two stories with one-story wings or porches; façade detailing that emphasizes horizontal lines; massive, square porch supports.

Queen Anne: building style (1880–1910) with a steeply pitched roof of irregular shapes; an asymmetrical façade with one-story porch; patterned shingles, bay windows, single tower. In furniture design the Queen Anne style was prevalent from 1725 to 1750, characterized by a graceful, unadorned curve of the leg (known as cabriole) and repeated curve of the top crest and vase-form back (splat) of a chair.

quoin: wood, stone, or brick materials that form the exterior corner of a building and are distinguishable from the background surface because of texture, color, size, or material.

rice-carved bed: *See* four-poster bed.

Richardsonian Romanesque: building style (1880–1900) with massive masonry walls of rough, squared stonework and round-topped arches over windows, porch supports, or entrances; round tower with conical roof common.

Second Empire: building style (1855–1885) with mansard roof adorned with dormer windows on lower slope; molded cornices above and below lower roof, and decorative brackets beneath eaves.

Shaker: style of furniture which represents the Shaker belief in simplicity. The finely crafted pieces are functional, without ornamentation. Chairs have ladder backs, rush seats, and simple turned legs; tables and cabinets are angular, with smooth surfaces.

Sheraton: named for English furniture designer, Thomas Sheraton, of the Federal period (early 1800s); style marked by straight lines, delicate proportions, wood inlays, and spare use of carving; characteristically tapered legs.

Shingle: building style (1880–1900) with walls and roofing of continuous wood shingles; no decorative detailing at doors, windows, corners, or roof overhang. Irregular, steeply pitched roof line and extensive porches common.

shotgun: simple 19th century house form suited to narrow urban lots, featuring a single-story, front gable building one room wide. Rooms and doorways are in a direct line, front to back; theoretically, a bullet fired through the front door would travel through the house unobstructed.

spandrel: decorative trim that fits the top corners of doorways, porches, or gables; usually triangular in shape.

Santa Fe: *see* Pueblo Revival.

Spanish Colonial: building style (1600–1900) of thick masonry walls, with low pitched or flat roof, interior wooden shutters covering small window openings, and multiple doorways. Pitched roof style often has half-cylindrical tiles; flat style has massive horizontal beams embedded in walls to support heavy roof of earth or mortar. Internal courtyards or cantilevered second-story porches are common.

Stick: building style (1860–1890) with a steeply pitched, gabled roof, usually with decorative trusses at apex; shingle or board walls interrupted by patterns of boards (stickwork) raised from the surface for emphasis.

Territorial: a variation of the Spanish Colonial building style found in New Mexico, western Texas, and Arizona. The flat roof and single story are topped by a protective layer of fired brick to form a decorative crown.

tester bed: a bed with a full canopy (the tester), supported at all four corners by tall posts. Pronounced "tee'-stir."

transom: usually refers to a window placed above a doorway.

trompe l'oeil: literally, French for "to trick the eye." Commonly refers to wall paintings that create an optical illusion.

Tudor: building style (1890–1940) with steeply pitched roof, usually cross-gabled; decorative half-timbering; tall, narrow, multi-paned windows; massive chimney crowned with decorative chimney pots.

vergeboard: decorative trim extending from the roof overhang of Tudor, Gothic Revival, or Queen Anne-style houses.

vernacular: style of architecture employing the commonest forms, materials, and decorations of a period or place.

viga(s): exposed (interior) and projecting (exterior) rough-hewn wooden roof beams common in adobe homes in Southwestern U.S.

wainscoting: most commonly, narrow wood paneling found on the lower half of a room's walls.

widow's walk: a railed observation platform built above the roof of a coastal house to permit unobstructed views of the sea. Name derives from the fate of many wives who paced the platform waiting for the return of their husbands from months (or years) at sea. Also called a "captain's walk."

Windsor: style of simple chair, with spindle back, turned legs, and usually a saddle seat. Considered a "country" design, it was popular in 18th and early 19th century towns and rural areas.

For more information:

A Field Guide to American Houses (Virginia and Lee McAlester, New York: Alfred A. Knopf, 1984; $19.95, paperback) was an invaluable source in preparing this glossary, and is highly recommended. Its 525 pages are lavishly illustrated with photographs and diagrams.

Clues to American Architecture (Marilyn W. Klein and David P. Fogle, Washington, D.C.: Starrhill Press, 1985; $6.95, paperback) is a handy, affordable 64-page pocket guide to over 30 architectural styles, from the Colonial period to contemporary construction. Each is clearly described in easy-to-understand language, and illustrated with numerous detailed sketches. Also in the same style and format is *Clues to American Furniture* (Jean Taylor Federico, Washington, D.C.: Starrhill Press, 1988; $6.95), covering design styles from Pilgrim to Chippendale, Eastlake to Art Deco. If your bookstore doesn't stock these titles, contact Starrhill directly at P.O. Box 32342, Washington, D.C. 20007; 202–387–9805.

Regional itineraries

Contributing editor Suzanne Carmichael has prepared these delightful itineraries to lead you from the best-known towns and cities through beautiful countryside, over less-traveled scenic highways to delightful towns and villages, to places where sights both natural and historic outnumber the modern "attractions" which so often litter the contemporary landscape. To get a rough idea of where each itinerary will lead you, take a look at the appropriate map at the back of this book. But to really see where you'll be heading, pull out a detailed full-size map or road atlas, and use a highlighter to chart your path. (If you're hopeless when it comes to reading maps, ask the AAA to help you plan the trip with one of their Triptiks). Some of our routes are circular, others are meant to be followed from one end to another; some are fairly short, others cover hundreds of miles. They can be traveled in either direction, or for just a section of the suggested route. You can sample an itinerary for a weekend, a week, or even two, depending on your travel style and the time available. For information on what to see and do along the way, refer to our state and local introductions, and to a good regional guidebook. For a list of places to stay en route, see the list of towns at the end of each itinerary, then refer to the entries in the state chapters for full details.

Finger Lakes Loop: A contemporary haven for travelers who like quiet towns and top-notch wineries, the Finger Lakes region was shaped both by ancient glaciers which carved out eleven skinny lakes, and local 19th century events which left their mark historically. Begin the tour in Syracuse, where you can see the country's most comprehensive collection of American ceramics at the Everson Museum. Head west on Route 175, then follow Route 20 to Skaneateles (pronounced Skinny-atlas) to the tip of its namesake lake. Continue west on Route 20 through Auburn, where the Republican Party was founded and escaped slave Harriet Tubman helped other slaves flee to Canada. Skirting the top of Cayuga Lake, Route 20 next passes through Seneca Falls, where the women's rights movement was born during an 1848 suffragist convention. Recommended are the Women's Rights National Historical Park and the National Women's Hall of Fame.

Route 20 next goes through Waterloo, where the Mormon Church was organized, to Geneva, situated on the northern shore of Seneca Lake. Known for its South Main Street Historic District, Geneva is surrounded by vineyards and farmland. From here head south on Route 14 along the lake, then jog west at Dresden on Route 54 to follow the shore of Keuka Lake into the heart of upstate wine country. Tour the Wine and Grape Museum in Hammondsport, then detour north on Route 54A for more lake views and winery tours.

From Hammondsport take Route 54 south to Bath, then Route 415 (or speed along Route 17) southeast to Corning, the U.S. glass capital. Families will enjoy the Corning Museum of Glass and tours of the Steuben Glass Factory. Head towards Seneca Lake on Route 414 north to Watkins Glen, known for its auto racing and multi-waterfalled state park. Cross over to Cayuga Lake on Route 227, then follow Route 89 south, stopping at Taughannock Falls, and continue to Ithaca, home of Cornell University.

Time to stop lake hopping and see some of the area's rolling farmland. Head east from Ithaca on Route 13, north at Dryden along Route 38 to Groton, then east on Route 222 to Cortland. Continue northeast on Route 13 through small sleepy towns such as Sheds, and on to Cazenovia, situated at the south end of yet another picturesque lake. From here return to Syracuse via Route 92, turning west at Fayetteville on Route 5.

Suggested overnights included in this region (in order of their appearance above): Geneva, Penn Yan, Branchport, Hammondsport, Corning,

Rock Stream, Trumansburg, Ithaca, Dryden, and Cazenovia. See entries for full details.

Marvelous Delmarva: Get away from metropolitan stress for a week or a weekend by visiting what locals call the Delmarva peninsula. Taking its moniker from the letters of *DEL*aware, *MAR*yland and *Virgini*A, this three-state peninsula is surrounded by the Chesapeake Bay and the Atlantic Ocean. Our route takes you through historic towns and small Chesapeake villages, across lush farmland and to popular ocean beaches. Try the region's famous crabcakes or, in season, softshell crabs. And bring along your bicycle—the flat but scenic back roads are a perfect way to explore the peninsula. For an introduction to the area from pre-European settlement to modern times, read *Chesapeake* by James Michener.

Begin your sojourn from Washington, D.C., or Baltimore by driving to Annapolis to watch Naval Academy pomp and see 18th-century colonial architecture. Follow Route 50 east across the Chesapeake Bay Bridge, through Stevensville on Kent Island and on to the peninsula. Turn north on Route 213 to Chestertown, a genteel town with historic riverfront brick homes, then wend your way north on Route 213 with a possible detour to bayside Betterton (Route 292, just after Kennedyville).

Continue to explore the upper peninsula by driving north on Route 213, stopping at Chesapeake City to see an 1832 canal still used by boats traveling between Chesapeake Bay and Delaware Bay. In Elkton, turn east on Routes 40, then 13 and 273 to New Castle, Delaware, where William Penn first arrived to explore his colonial lands. Preserved rather than restored, New Castle is a charming 17th century town, centered around The Green laid out in 1655 by Peter Stuyvesant. If time permits, a recommended detour is to drive north on Route 9 to Wilmington and the Brandywine Valley in Pennsylvania to see DuPont family homes, gardens, and other treasures at Winterthur, Hagley, and the Nemours Museums.

If you crave ocean beaches and the hoopla of busy vacation villages, head south along Routes 13, 113 and 1 to bustling Rehoboth Beach or quieter Lewes; then continue south on 528 to Ocean City. From here take Route 50 west to Route 113 and Snow Hill, a sleepy river town not far from Chincoteague Bay. If you prefer quieter environs for the whole trip, go directly from New Castle to Snow Hill on Routes 13 and 113. During the fall, scan the sky and fields for huge flocks of migrating Canadian geese.

Continuing on Route 113 south to Pocomoke City, you can extend your explorations by driving south on Route 13 to Virginia's Cape Charles near the peninsula's tip, or turn north on Route 13. If you choose Route 13, jog south on Route 413 to Crisfield. Sample local oysters here, or board a boat to visit Smith Island, a virtually unsullied Bay retreat. Back on Route 13 stop by Princess Anne's historic district, then turn northwest onto Route 50 at Salisbury.

As you drive through evergreen forests, farms and marshlands, turn towards the Bay on Route 333 to visit 17th-century Oxford, then cross the Tred Avon River on the country's oldest continuously operating, privately-owned ferry. A few miles farther (turn left on Route 33) is isolated St. Michaels, a haven for sailing enthusiasts and home to the Chesapeake Bay Maritime Museum. Another option is to leave Route 50 at Easton, and head up Route 328 to Denton, a quiet town near the Choptank River. Complete your trip by following Route 50 north and back across the Chesapeake Bay Bridge.

A slew of great accommodations can be found in this area including those in (in order of their appearance above): Annapolis, Stevensville, Rock Hall, Chestertown, Betterton, and Chesapeake City (Maryland); New Castle, Wilmington, Lewes, and Rehoboth Beach (Delaware); Snow Hill (Maryland); Cape Charles (Virginia); Princess Anne, Easton, Oxford, St. Michaels, McDaniel, Tilghman, and Denton (Maryland).

Shenandoah Sojourn: Nature outdoes herself in the 200-mile-long Shenandoah Valley: majestic Blue Ridge Mountains, glittering limestone caverns, and lush green valleys. Scattered through the area are important historical sites, small inns and posh resorts. Only a short drive from Washington, DC, the area can be explored in a series of weekend jaunts or on a leisurely loop as we suggest here.

Leave DC on Route 50 going south, then go west through Aldie, where you can visit one of James Monroe's homes, or continue on to Middleburg, near three of the state's finest wineries. Follow Route 50 west, then Routes 340 and 277 west to Route 11 which will be your path south into Shenandoah country. Consider stopping first in Middletown, where there is another winery as well as Belle Grove, an unusual 1794 limestone-fronted mansion.

Route 11 now heads south through numerous small towns including Woodstock (great summer music festival), Edinburg (another winery here), Mt. Jackson, and historic New Market with its nearby caverns (Endless and Shenandoah). Route 11 next passes through Harrisonburg, known for its great river fishing; Mt. Crawford; and on to Staunton, birthplace of Woodrow Wilson. Stop by Staunton's Chamber of Commerce for a map outlining a self-guided walking tour of the town's 19th-century architecture.

Turn west on Route 250 into the state's Highland Country, the heart of the Allegheny/Shenandoah Mountains. Pass through forests and small river valleys to Monterey, a center for maple syrup production. Go south on Route 220, along the Jackson River, to Warm Springs and Hot Springs, towns known for their medicinal springs and pampering resorts.

From Warm Springs, take Route 39 east to Lexington, home of Washington and Lee University. Go north on Route 11, past Vesuvius to Steeles Tavern, then east on Route 606 to the Blue Ridge Parkway. A 470-mile scenic road that starts in Asheville, North Carolina, the Parkway joins Virginia's Skyline Drive north of Afton, winding through pristine forests and along mountain crests.

We suggest you follow the Parkway/Skyline Drive north to its terminus in Front Royal, stopping at overlooks which double as perfect picnic sites. Optional diversions include a detour on Route 664 east, passing through Nellysford and on to Charlottesville to visit both Ash Lawn-Highland, James Monroe's home, and Thomas Jefferson's Monticello. Return to the Parkway on Route 250 and continue north. Another detour, which children will especially enjoy, is Route 211 west to Luray to explore the east coast's largest caverns. From here you can return to Washington on Routes 211 east, 522 and 29, or complete the Skyline Drive to Front Royal, taking I-66 back to town.

Overnight options along this route include (in order of their appearance above): Aldie, Middleburg, Middletown, Woodstock, New Market, Mt. Crawford, Staunton, Swoope (just west of Staunton), Monterey, Warm Springs, Hot Springs, Raphine, Lexington, Goshen, Nellysford, Charlottesville, Luray, and Stanley (just south of Luray).

Criteria for entries

Unlike some other very well-known guidebooks, *we do not collect a membership or listing fee of any kind from the inns and hotels we include.* What matters to us is the feedback we get from you, our readers. This means we are free to write up the negative as well as the positive attributes of each inn listed, and if any given establishment does not measure up, there is no difficulty in dropping it.

Free copy of *INNroads* newsletter

Want to stay up-to-date on our latest finds? Send a business-size, self-addressed, stamped envelope with 55 cents postage and we'll send you the latest issue, *free!* While you're at it, why not enclose a report on any inns you've recently visited? Use the forms at the back of the book or your own stationery.

Key to Abbreviations and Symbols

For complete information and explanations, please see the Introduction.

¢ Especially good value for overnight accommodation.
👪 Families welcome. Most (but not all) have cribs, baby-sitting, games, play equipment, and reduced rates for children.
✗ Meals served to public; reservations recommended or required.
🎾 Tennis court and swimming pool and/or lake on grounds. Golf usually on grounds or nearby.
♿ Limited or full wheelchair access; call for details.
Rates: Range from least expensive room in low season to most expensive room in peak season.
Room only: No meals included; European Plan (EP).
B&B: Bed and breakfast; includes breakfast, sometimes afternoon/evening refreshment.
MAP: Modified American Plan; includes breakfast and dinner.
Full board: Three meals daily.
Alc lunch: À la carte lunch; average price of entrée plus nonalcoholic drink, tax, tip.
Alc dinner: Average price of three-course dinner, including half bottle of house wine, tax, tip.
Prix fixe dinner: Three- to five-course set dinner, excluding wine, tax, tip unless otherwise noted.
Extras: Noted if available. Always confirm in advance. Pets are not permitted unless specified; if you are allergic, ask for details; *most innkeepers have pets.*

We Want to Hear from You!

As you know, this book is effective only with your help. We really need to know about your experiences and discoveries. If you stayed at an inn or hotel listed here, we want to know how it was. Did it live up to our description? Exceed it? Was it what you expected? Did you like it? Were you disappointed? Delighted? Have you discovered new establishments that we should add to the next edition?

Tear out one of the report forms at the back of this book (or use your own stationery if you prefer) and write today. *Even if you write only "Fully endorse existing entry" you will have been most helpful.*
Thank You!

Delaware

The Lord and Hamilton Seaside Inn, Rehoboth Beach

Delaware is a small but historic state. The Brandywine Valley, overlapping both Delaware and Pennsylvania, is particularly rich in sites of cultural interest such as Winterthur, the Hagley Museum, and the Nemours Mansion. Wilmington, Delaware's major city, has restored many of its historic areas in recent years. History buffs will also enjoy the 18th- and 19th-century houses of Odessa (including a Muskrat Skinning Shack), and the Victorian architecture of Dover's Historic District. If you're traveling through on I-95, be sure to stop in lovely, historic New Castle for at least an hour or preferably overnight.

The beaches of Rehoboth and Lewes are favorite escapes from the heat and humidity of summertime Washington. They are 120 miles (approximately 3 hours) from Washington, Baltimore, and Philadelphia. If you're coming from New York or New Jersey, take the New Jersey Turnpike over the Delaware Memorial Bridge, then take Route 13 to Route 1 to Lewes and Rehoboth. An alternate route (recommended for the trip home) is to take the 70-minute ferry ride from Lewes to Cape May to the Garden State Parkway (call 800–64–FERRY for details); it's about a 5-hour drive to New York City. A recommended short detour is the Bombay Hook National Refuge (northeast of Dover) where migrating ducks and geese stop by in spring and fall, and herons, egrets and other wading birds spend the summer.

Peak rates generally run from June 15 to September 15; off-season rates are considerably less. Rehoboth is a favorite family resort, combining all

29

the boardwalk stuff kids love with chic shops and gourmet restaurants; Lewes is a bit more sedate.

Worth noting: Delaware has no sales tax, so outlet malls have sprung up in tourist areas faster than mushrooms after rain.

CLAYMONT

Darley Manor Inn ¢   *Tel:* 302–792–2127
3701 Philadelphia Pike, 19703   800–824–4703
                                             Fax: 302–792–2127

Dating back to the 1700s, Darley Manor was later home to Felix Darley, a popular illustrator of books by Edgar Allan Poe, James Fenimore Cooper, and other famous 19th-century authors. When Ray and Judy Hester purchased the house in 1991, the yard was overgrown, layers of paint and paper covered the windows and walls, and garbage was piled high. Today the interior of this Dutch Colonial home is completely renovated, decorated with antiques, reproductions, and many charming collectibles; restoration of the exterior is planned for the future. Ray has drawn upon years of personal experience to create an inn ideal for the business traveler: convenient location, efficient phone service, good working space, modern amenities, and flexible breakfasts. Breakfast is served at the guests' choice of time, from 7 to 9 A.M. weekdays, 8 to 9:30 on weekends; guests select cereal, yogurt, eggs, pancakes, or quiche, with grits or hash browns, bacon or sausage, biscuits or toast; coffee is ready in the kitchen by 6:30 A.M. on weekdays.

"Comfortable antiques, with soft quiet music permeating the house." *(John Morris)* "Paintings, prints, and books represent Felix Darley's influence and the rich history of the house." *(Mary Jane Darrow)* "Comfortable recliners, good reading lights, and more. The charming North-South Suite has a Civil War theme, with a railing salvaged from the Confederate White House in Richmond." *(Martha & Charles Fisher)* "Real grits and melt-in-your-mouth biscuits; attention to dietary needs." *(James Thompson)* "Ice, tea and coffee, and homemade cookies were always available in the kitchen. Good selection of videos." *(Tim & Elizabeth Tierney)* "Ray and Judith are helpful, considerate hosts." *(Robert & Cheryl Fehn)* "Convenient location, close to the Philadelphia airport and Brandywine Valley attractions." *(Bill Gothorpe)* "Firm, comfortable bed; efficient, quiet air-conditioning system. A just-cut rosebud and chocolates awaited on the turned-down bed. Excellent sound-proofing. A pleasure to stay in such a guest-oriented B&B." *(SWS)*

Open All year.
Rooms 3 suites, 2 doubles—all with private bath and/or shower, telephone, radio, clock, TV/VCR, desk, air-conditioning, fan, hair dryer. 3 with refrigerator, 1 with fireplace.
Facilities Dining room, 2 parlors with fireplace, piano; library with books, videos; guest pantry. Off-street parking, rose garden with gazebo, arbor. Off-street parking. Golf nearby.
Location N DE, 10 min N of Wilmington, 15 min. S of Philadelphia Airport, 30

min S of Philadelphia. From I-495, Exit 5, go S 1 block on Rte. 13 (Phila. Pike) to inn on right.
Restrictions No smoking. Children 10 and over.
Credit cards Amex, MC, Visa.
Rates B&B, $79–99 suite, $69–79 double. Extra person, $10. 2-night holiday/special events minimum. Business packages.

DOVER

Inn at Meeting House Square ¢
305 South Governors Avenue, 19904

Tel: 302–678–1242

Built in 1849, the Inn at Meeting House Square is owned by Sherry and Carolyn DeZwarte, and is listed on National Register of Historic Places. Breakfast is served weekdays from 7–9 A.M., weekends from 8–10, and might include fruit with vanilla yogurt, your choice of omelets with toast or perhaps blueberry pancakes, hash browns or grits, bacon or sausage, and homemade peach pastry.

"The rooms remind me of the home of a favorite aunt—cozy, neat and comfortable. Breakfast was wonderful, cooked and served by a woman who obviously enjoys every minute of it." *(John King)* "Warm, friendly innkeeper; clean, comfortable, homey inn. Two guest rooms are small, but all had some seating, with bedside lamps on both sides of the bed. Robes are provided for guests whose private baths are down the hall. Ideal for a person traveling alone." *(Diane Wolf)* Comments welcome.

Open All year.
Rooms 5 doubles—all with private shower bath, telephone, TV, air-conditioning, desk.
Facilities Living room, dining room, sun room with swing, guest pantry. Terrace, barbecue grill. Off-street parking. Golf, swimming nearby.
Location Central DE. Approx. 40 m S of Wilmington. Meeting House Sq., across from State Museum. Walk to shops, restaurants, Legislative Hall.
Restrictions Areas permitted for smoking.
Credit cards Amex, DC, Discover, MC, Visa.
Rates B&B, $48–68 double, $40–60 single. Corporate rates.

LAUREL

Spring Garden B&B ¢
Delaware Avenue Extended, Rte. 1, Box 283A, 19956

Tel: 302–875–7015

"This 18th century brick and frame country manor is listed on the National Register of Historic Places. Owner Gwen North welcomed us with wine, cheese and crackers. Gwen grew up in the house; her parents restored it and started collecting the 18th and 19th century antiques which adorn every room. There are beautiful wide-planked floors, original woodwork, a gorgeous staircase and tall windows. Guest rooms have antique brass or four-poster beds; plenty of hot water in the bathroom. Breakfast was served at an antique wooden table, from 8 to 9:30 A.M., and included granola with fresh fruit and a toasted bagel with ham, cheese and tomato one day; warm coffee cake, seasoned scrambled eggs, thick-sliced toast and orange juice, the next. Our energetic hostess was friendly and enthusiastic about the house's restoration, the history of Laurel, and area attractions. She steered us to Trap and Trussum Ponds, whose stands of bald cypress give them the look of a Louisiana bayou. Most people rush through southern Delaware on their way to the beach; they miss a lot when they do." *(Lori Sampson)*

Gwen founded the "Biking Inn to Inn Delaware" specializing in safe, scenic bicycle touring. She notes that with "the best wilderness canoe trails in the state nearby, I am happy to provide parking space for canoes or boats."

Suggestion box: "Stronger lighting in the upstairs shared bathroom."

Open All year.

Rooms 1 suite with private bath, 4 doubles—2 with private bath and/or shower, 2 with a maximum of 4 persons sharing bath. All with clock, air-conditioning. 4 with desk, 2 with fireplace, 1 with whirlpool tub.

Facilities Dining room, living room with 2 fireplaces, library with TV/VCR. Barn with artist studio, antique shop. 3 acres with gardens, lawn games, stream. 4 m to canoeing (rentals), 30 min to Atlantic beaches.

Location SW DE. 15 m N of Salisbury MD, 20 m W of Rehoboth. From Rte. 13, turn right in Laurel, at 2nd traffic light (Delaware Ave. Ext). Go 2/10 m to inn on right.

Restrictions No smoking in guest rooms; innkeeper is trying to quit. Some traffic noise in front rooms. Children 10 and over.

Credit cards None accepted.

Rates B&B, $85 suite, $65–75 double. $5 surcharge for single night-stays. 10% senior discount. 3-night bike tour, MAP, $540–560 double. Artists creative workshops.

LEWES

Founded by the Dutch in 1631, Lewes offers much of historic interest. Visit Shipcarpenter Square to see restored buildings dating back 300 years; tour the harbor on a ship departing from Fisherman's Wharf. It's a short drive to Cape Henlopen State Park for wide ocean beaches and nature trails. Lewes is located 2 ½ hours south of Philadelphia and east of Washington, DC.

Information please: A good choice for families is the **Blue Water House** (407 East Market Street, 19958; 302–645–7832) at Lewes Beach, just a short walk from the bay beach and a quick drive to the ocean at Cape Henlopen. Built in 1993, the six guest rooms open onto a wrap-around veranda, each with a private bath and air-conditioning. The upper level offers spectacular views, board games and TV. Breakfast includes home-baked breads with fresh fruit and cereal. Guests are welcome to borrow the inn's beach balls, boogie boards, and bicycles. Furnishings are casual, the rates moderate, $60–100 double.

Not far from the canal, in the old market section of town, is the **New Devon Inn** (2nd and Market Streets, P.O. Box 516, Lewes 19958; 302–

645–6466 or 800–824–8754). A 1926-era hotel turned boarding house in its later years, it was restored in 1988 in the style of a small European hotel. The breakfast room is decorated in Depression-style furnishings, while the guest rooms have antique beds, fine linens and other collectibles. Double rates of $65–130 include a continental breakfast.

Reader tip: "Rosa Negra is a great little Italian restaurant." *(Joan Stankiewicz)* Also: "Good restaurants in town, especially Kupchiks." *(Kathryn Falk)*

For an additional area entry, see **Milton.**

Inn at Canal Square 🏃 ♿

Tel: 302–645–8499
800–222–7902

122 Market Street, 19958

Built in 1988, most rooms at the Inn at Canal Square overlook the harbor and are furnished with Queen Anne reproductions, including a king- or queen-size bed, wing chair, fabric-covered bench, brass lamps on either side of the bed, and coordinating floral print fabrics. The suites are individually decorated with antiques or Caribbean decor. Breakfast includes a variety of juices, coffee, tea, Danish, muffins, homemade breads, yogurt, and fruit, and can be eaten in the common area or taken back to your room on a tray.

"Beautiful morning view." *(Cherilynn Glascoe)* "Rooms are spacious and attractive. Walking distance to shops, restaurants, and historical attractions." *(Susan Friday)* "Clean and quiet." *(Kathryn Falk)* Reports welcome.

Open All year.
Rooms 1 2-bedroom, 2-bath houseboat with kitchen, TV, stereo, fireplace; 3 suites, 19 doubles—all with private bath and/or shower, telephone, radio, clock, air-conditioning, balcony, hair dryer. Suites in adjacent building.
Facilities Lobby/living room with books; conference rooms. Off-street parking. Tennis, golf, swimming, boating, fishing nearby.
Location Follow Savannah Rd. (Rte. 9) into Lewes. Go left at traffic light for 1 block to inn on right. On harbor front; 1/4 m from Delaware Bay, 1/3 m from Cape May/Lewes ferry.
Restrictions No smoking in some guest rooms.
Credit cards Amex, DC, Discover, MC, Visa.
Rates B&B, $175–225 houseboat; $65–155 suite, double. Corporate rate midweek $65–135, single. Extra person, $15. Children under 12, free. 2-night weekend minimum summer, holidays.
Extras Wheelchair access. Crib, babysitting. Boat slips.

Wild Swan

Tel: 302–645–8550
Fax: 302–645–8550

525 Kings Highway, 19958

As antique collectors and old house addicts, Mike and Hope Tyler have achieved their goal of creating "more than simply a place to stay at the beach." The beautifully restored 1910 Victorian home which they bought in 1991 is complete with original gingerbread trim, gable-end barge boards and finials, and wraparound porch. Rooms are furnished with eclectic Victorian flair, including authentic brass chandeliers and gasoliers. Music is an integral part of the Wild Swan. Mike gives impromptu concerts on the player piano—their collection includes hundreds of pieces—or he may play the Edison cylinder record phonograph. Early morning fresh-ground coffee is ready at 7 A.M.; a typical heart-healthy breakfast buffet, set out between 8:30 and 9 A.M., might include juice, poached pears Amaretto, Belgian waffles or breakfast burritos, and honey banana bread or tomato muffins.

"A wonderful little B&B. Nice touches included extra towels and bicycles. Everything in town is within walking distance." *(Joan Stankiewicz)* "Mike and Hope Tyler are gracious innkeepers offering warm hospitality. Breakfast is a delicious experience." *(Anne & Ken Roth)*

Open All year.
Rooms 3 doubles—all with private bath and/or shower, radio, clock, air-conditioning.
Facilities Dining room, living room with player piano. Guest refrigerator, wraparound porch. Swimming pool, gazebo, garden. Ample on-street parking. State park, beaches nearby. Bicycles, beach chairs, umbrellas, coolers.
Location From Rte. 9 (Savannah Rd), turn right onto Manila. Inn is one block ahead at intersection with Kings Highway. 10 min. walk to town.
Restrictions No smoking. No children.
Credit cards None accepted.
Rates B&B, $85–120 double, $80–115 single. 2-3 night weekend/holiday minimum; 2-night minimum Aug.
Extras Local airport, ferry pickup.

MILFORD

Reader tip: "Milford has a lot of potential. Restored Victorian homes sit side-by-side with decaying houses. Our exceptional dinner at The Banking House included roast duck with almond sauce and Key lime pie." *(DW)*

Milford is located about 90 miles east of Washington DC, southeast of Baltimore, and south of Philadelphia; it's about one hour south of Wilmington, and 30 minutes northwest of Lewes and Rehoboth.

Causey Mansion Bed and Breakfast ¢   *Tel:* 302–422–0979
2 Causey Avenue, P.O. Box 675, 19963

Originally built in 1763 as the Georgian-style manor house of a 1000-acre plantation, Delaware Governor Peter Causey purchased the estate in 1849, added a third floor, and changed the architectural style to Greek Revival. In 1986, Ken and Fran Novak bought the home, listed on the National Register of Historic Places, and began its renovation as a B&B. Breakfast is served from 8:00–9:30 A.M., includes juice, fresh fruit, and a different entrée each day—perhaps an egg and sausage casserole, crispy French toast, or scrambled eggs with bacon and biscuits.

"Our favorite is the Sunroom, with windows on three sides (nine in all), and a huge bathroom with both a stall shower and a clawfoot tub." *(Katherine Carangelo)* "The Novaks are gracious, kind, and intelligent, without being stuffy. Breakfasts are large, well-presented and delicious." *(Sally Smith)* "Extremely clean and well-maintained." *(Tara Calaman)* "This appealing mansion, painted a soft yellow, is set far back from the street, just outside the downtown shopping area. The spacious common areas are furnished with antiques and interesting pieces." *(Diane Wolf)*

Open All year.
Rooms 1 suite, 4 doubles—all with full private bath. All with desk, air-conditioning, ceiling fan. 1 with TV.
Facilities Dining room, breakfast room, living room with fireplace, library with TV/VCR, books; screened porch. 3 acres with gazebo, boxwood garden. Golf, swimming, tennis nearby. 30 minutes to ocean, 10 minutes to Delaware Bay beaches.
Location From Philadelphia take U.S. Rte. 13 to Dover. Then U.S. Rte. 113 to Milford. Turn left at Rte. 14 onto NW Front St. Go to Walnut & turn right. Go 3 blocks and turn right on Causey Ave. at the Old Theater building. The first driveway on left is the inn; turn in between large white posts.
Restrictions Smoking only on screened porch. "Well-behaved children accepted."
Credit cards MC, Visa.
Rates B&B, $95 suite, $75 double, $60–70 single. Extra person $10.

The Towers   *Tel:* 302–422–3814
101 Northwest Front Street, 19963   800–366–3814

Victorian architecture buffs may find it worth a trip to Milford just to see The Towers, purchased by Dan Bond in 1992. This magnificent mansion was originally built as a simple Colonial home in 1783, but elaborately remodeled in 1891 in the Steamboat Gothic style, with quantities of gingerbread, towers, gables, fans, and ornamental frills. Restored in 1985, it took three years of work plus over a 100 gallons of paint to complete. The outside is painted with 12 shades of soft lavender, pink, and mauve with accents of blue and yellow; inside, the original walnut and cherry woodwork and the stained glass windows glow again.

"Furnished with charming, quality antiques. In the evening we relaxed by the fire, sipped good sherry, listened to classical music, and read poetry by the Milford bard who lived and wrote in the Towers." *(William May)* "Dan is a masterful chef; breakfast was delicious and beautifully presented with attention to every detail. Wonderful ricotta pancakes with strawberry rhubarb sauce." *(Robert Hunt)* "Enjoyed conversations with the other guests and innkeepers." *(Donna Baumgartner)* "Excellent host; excellent breakfast, beautifully presented. Nearby are quaint beach villages for shopping, dining, and swimming." *(Terri Striso)*

Open All year.
Rooms 2 suites, 4 doubles—all with private bath, air-conditioning, ceiling fan.
Facilities Dining room with fireplace, parlor, music room with grand piano and fireplace. Formal garden, small swimming pool, gazebo, fish pond, bicycles. Off-street parking.
Location Take Rte. 113 into Milford. In Milford, go E on N.W. Front St. (Rte. 14) to inn on left.
Restrictions No smoking. No children under 12. No pets.
Credit cards MC, Visa.
Rates B&B, $95–125 suite, double.

MILTON

Captain William Russell House   *Tel:* 302–684–2504
320 Union Street, 19968

Built in the mid-1800s by one of Milton's shipbuilding families, the Captain William Russell House is a mix of pre-Victorian and modern architectural styles with bay windows and a center gable. A nautical theme accents the decor, and many of the pictures and antique furnishings are English. Husband-and-wife team Tony Boyd-Heron and Carol Gillie opened their home as a B&B in 1993. Tony serves an afternoon tea of homemade scones, shortbread, or sweet English biscuits. Breakfast is served at the dining room table and includes fresh fruit, Carol's quiche, homemade bread or muffins, and English jams. Rates also include fresh towels both in the morning and as part of the evening turndown service for the inn's queen-size beds. Milton is a small historic town at the head of the Broadkill River, only minutes from the Prime Hook National Wildlife Refuge, and a short drive from Lewes and Cape Henlopen.

"Tony is a warm and friendly host with a charming British style. Afternoon tea was delicious. The next morning we fetched early morning coffee from the sun room and enjoyed it on our private terrace." *(Gayle Lemke)* "Beautifully decorated home-away-from-home. Carol is a gracious hostess with a delightful sense of humor." *(Dorice Egerton)*

Open All year.
Rooms 3 doubles—all with private shower-bath, air-conditioning, ceiling fan. 2 with terrace, 1 with fireplace.
Facilities Dining room, living room with fireplace, books; sun room with books, deck. Off-street parking, swing set, lawn games. Tennis, water sports nearby.
Location S DE. 10 m W of Lewes. Historic area, 1 block from Broadkill River. From Rte. 16 E, turn right onto Union Street, right onto Broad Street, right onto Reed St. to the inn on right.
Restrictions Smoking only in sun room. Children 12 and over.
Credit cards None accepted.
Rates B&B, $65–90 double. Extra person, $15. 2-night weekend minimum, high season.
Extras Limited German, French spoken.

NEW CASTLE

New Castle is a delightful town, an ideal spot to stop for lunch or for the night if you're traveling along I-95 between Washington and New York. In the few minutes it takes to drive from the highway to the historic section, you can travel back 250 years to a living Colonial village.

The town was founded in 1651 by Peter Stuyvesant. It was claimed alternately by both the Dutch and the Swedish governments, until the Duke of York took it for the British in 1664 and renamed it New Castle. The town was Delaware's capital until the early eighteenth century, when it was shifted to Wilmington. Development stopped, and a lovely piece of history was preserved. The town is built right along the Delaware River, nearly under the Delaware Memorial Bridge. In the Colonial-era Battery Park, along the river, the modern bridge looms almost overhead—a strange but beautiful juxtaposition.

Reader tips: "Within easy walking distance are a magnificent 1732 Court House, Delaware's Colonial capitol, the home of George Read II, and a lovely and inspiring Presbyterian Church built in 1707. Be sure to see how the Dutch settlers lived by visiting the Amstel House and the Old Dutch House museums." *(Nancy Harrison & Nelson Ormsby)* "While in New Castle, be sure to stop for a leisurely meal at the **Newcastle Inn,** built as an arsenal in 1809—crab cakes and walnut rum pie are specialties." *(DW)*

Information please: The **Terry House** (130 Delaware Street, 19720; 302–322–2505) is an 1860s townhouse, furnished with antiques. "Spacious public rooms; the guest rooms are adequate and meticulously clean. Pleasant porch on the back of the house. Welcoming, enthusiastic hostess. Breakfast consisted of grapefruit, cereal, instant coffee." *(PA)* B&B double rates for the five guest rooms are $60–80. Comments?

William Penn Guest House ¢
206 Delaware Street, 19720

Tel: 302–328–7736

When you consider that the William Penn House is one of the oldest buildings listed in this guide, it seems especially appropriate that its owners, Irma and Richard Burwell, have been in the B&B business longer than almost any other innkeepers. Rates include a light breakfast, served at 8:30 A.M.

"This historic townhouse is where William Penn stayed the very first night after landing in America. The center section of the house is the oldest, consisting of just two rooms—one up, one down; you can see the original fireplace in the bedroom. In the 1700s, a front section was added, including the dining room and large guest sitting room. Our bedroom (William Penn's) had beige wallpaper and tiny closets on either side of the fireplace. The comfortable furnishings included a dried flower arrangement, some antiques, and twin beds, each with its own electric blanket." *(SC)* "The dining room is furnished with antiques and a particularly fine chandelier. Breakfast consisted of sweetened strawberries, orange juice, home-baked muffins, and good coffee. The guest rooms have queen- or twin-size beds with handmade spreads and shams; a shower ring was added over the clawfoot tub." *(Janet Murray)* "The Burwells are knowledgeable hosts, and New Castle is a lovely town." *(Mary White)* "Comfortable and well-appointed; convenient location." *(Burton Carlson)*

Open All year.
Rooms 4 doubles—1 with private bath, 2 with a maximum of 4 people sharing bath. All with TV, air-conditioning, fan.
Facilities Living room with fireplace.
Location Historic district. 1 m from I-95.
Restrictions No smoking in guest rooms. No children under 8.
Credit cards None accepted.
Rates B&B, $45–50 double.
Extras Italian spoken.

ODESSA

Cantwell House   *Tel: 302–378–4179*
107 High Street, 19730

Odessa was one of the principal trading ports on the Delaware River until
the 1890s. Its wealthy traders built houses in the latest architectural styles
and trends; there are many examples of Colonial, Federal and Victorian
design. When industrial progress bypassed Odessa, these fine homes were
left behind; several have now been restored as part of the Winterthur
Museum, while others have been privately refurbished.

The Cantwell House has been owned since 1982 by Carole Coleman,
an auctioneer, interior designer, architectural drafter, and antiques dealer.
Breakfast favorites include poached fresh pears, sugar-top oatmeal muffins,
and almond granola.

"Carole is a pleasant, unobtrusive hostess. The third floor is charming
and totally private." *(Judy Brookover)* "Beautifully renovated in period.
Carole provides every convenience, from bedside tissues to the hotpot for
early morning tea or coffee." *(Paula Keltner)* "Linen, silver, and lovely china
are used at breakfast, served on the screened porch, overlooking the
garden." *(Linda Cline)* "Firm, comfortable bed, lots of hot water and
towels." *(Nancy Calabretta)* "A cozy fire crackled in the living room
fireplace in a rainy day. Delicious caramel rolls at breakfast." *(Laura Shanks)*

Open All year.
Rooms 3 doubles—1 with private bath/shower; 2 with shared bath. 2 with radio,
desk, air-conditioning. 1 with whirlpool tub, TV, refrigerator. 1 with fireplace.
Facilities Dining room with fireplace, living room with fireplace, games; screened
porch. 1 block to tennis.
Location N DE, New Castle County. 25 m S of Wilmington, 25 m N of Dover.
1 block from historic district.
Restrictions No smoking in guest rooms. No children under 6.
Credit cards None accepted.
Rates B&B, $65–85 double. Extra person, $10.

REHOBOTH BEACH

Rehoboth is located on Delaware's Atlantic shore, 125 miles east of
Washington, D.C., and has been a mecca for Washingtonians escaping the
oppressive summer heat and humidity ever since the Chesapeake Bay
Bridge was completed in 1952. Rehoboth's beautiful white sands are
bordered in most areas by shady pine forests, offering a welcome respite
from the summer sun. Children love the mile-long boardwalk, complete
with snack bars alternating with miniature golf courses and video games
and capped with the rides at Funland. Those in search of more sedate
entertainment will prefer the weekend evening concerts at the bandstand
nearby on Rehoboth Avenue. Area activities center on the water, and
include swimming, surf-casting, sailing, windsurfing, clamming, and fishing, plus the favored indoor sport of the 1990s: the designer outlet mall.

As is the case in most beach towns, parking is a pain in season, when Rehoboth's population zooms from 3,000 to 90,000. Once you've found an unmetered parking space, just leave your car where it is, and walk or bicycle to in-town destinations. To avoid congestion, visit mid-week.

Information please: The ever-present sound of waves upon the beach inspired the name of **The Sea Voice Inn** (14 Delaware Avenue, 19971; 302–226–9435 or 800–637–2862), a circa-1910 home just ½ block from the boardwalk. Restored as a B&B in 1991, it is furnished simply to accommodate casual, quiet beach living. All of the ten rooms are air-conditioned and have double beds (some with an additional twin bed). Rates of $60–90 include a full breakfast; children over age 6 are welcome "as long as peace and quiet are maintained."

Barry's Gull Cottage
116 Chesapeake Street, 19971

Tel: 302–227–7000
Fax: 302–227–7000

Barry's Gull Cottage was built in 1962, and has been owned by Vivian and Bob Barry since 1976. This casual beach cottage is bright and airy, cheerfully decorated with white wicker, lots of flowers, rag rugs and patchwork quilts, contrasting with the natural wood walls and ceilings. Rates include a full breakfast, afternoon tea, and evening sherry and cake.

"Welcoming atmosphere; helpful directions, sightseeing, and restaurant advice." *(Abu Ameyaw, and others)* "Vivian and Bob are friendly and flexible, accommodating to our dietary needs. Rooms are comfortable, though on the small side." *(Kara Paul-Stern)* "Peaceful, relaxing, clean; great breakfast and afternoon tea." *(H. Stone, & others)* "Great waffles and coffee cake." *(Ginger Brown)* "Delicious food, almost all homemade; elegant presentation. The guest rooms are in a private wing, and you gather on the screened porch for breakfast and snacks." *(Gail Eisner)* "Beautifully landscaped with flower gardens and private nooks. Breakfasts are delightful and varied—banana and prune nut bread, egg soufflé or apple pancakes, honey bacon." *(Kathleen Dollins)*

Open April–Oct. 31.
Rooms 5 doubles—3 with private bath, 2 sharing 1 bath. All with air-conditioning.
Facilities Dining room, living room with TV/ VCR, screened porch with hot tub, deck, gardens, bicycles. 2 off-street parking spaces; more on street in front of inn. 1 block from Dewey Beach.
Location 1 m to boardwalk. Take Rte. 1 to Dewey Beach. Go left on Cullen St. Left on Bayard to right on Chesapeake St. to 116.
Restrictions No smoking. No children.
Credit cards None accepted.
Rates B&B, $85–$125 double. Senior, AAA discount. 2-3 night weekend/holiday minimum. Honeymoon packages.
Extras Station pickup. German spoken.

The Corner Cupboard Inn 🚶 ✕
50 Park Avenue, 19971

Tel: 302–227–8553

The Corner Cupboard Inn was built as a private home for Alice and Jess Gundry, aunt and uncle of the present innkeeper, Elizabeth Gundry

Hooper. An inn for over 50 years, Mrs. Hooper calls the Corner Cupboard the "inn that was in before inns were in." Mrs. Hooper describes her inn as a place where people are encouraged to gather for conversation and refreshments in front of the fire in the winter and on the patios in summer. Dinners feature home-style cooking, with lots of seafood dishes (crab is a favorite), plus a beef and chicken entrée, and home-baked desserts.

"A mere five-minute walk to the beach, the inn is located in the peaceful setting of a residential area. The inn itself is a charming clapboard house with muted pink shutters, entered through a living room decorated in antique furniture, including a corner cupboard filled with fine old ceramics. The dining room consists of a sizable screened porch on the ground level running the length of the house oceanside, and cooled by several ceiling fans. The food is traditional, preceded by chilled soup. Desserts include homemade pies and lighter fare. You are welcome to bring your own wine, which they will gladly serve for you." *(Louisa & Horst Huber)* Comments needed.

Open All year. Restaurant open Memorial Day weekend to mid-Sept.
Rooms 18 doubles—all with private bath and/or shower, air-conditioning. Some with desk, TV. 9 rooms in inn, 4 in annex, 5 in cottages.
Facilities Restaurant, living room with fireplace, breakfast room, patios. 1½ blocks to beach for swimming, fishing. Tennis, golf nearby.
Location 8 blocks from town center. Between 1st and 2nd sts.
Credit cards Amex, MC, Visa.
Rates B&B (Sept 15.–late May), $90–155 double; extra person, $25. MAP (Memorial Day–Sept. 15), $145–245 double; extra person, $50. Alc dinner, $25.
Extras Crib, babysitting. Airport/station pickups.

The Lord and Hamilton Seaside Inn ¢

Tel: 302–227–6960

20 Brooklyn Avenue, 19971

The Lord and Hamilton was opened in 1982 by Marge and Dick Hamilton after considerable restoration work. Marge says, "We named the inn the Lord and Hamilton because we need all the help we can get."

"The inn is painted cream and rose outside; inside, it's appealingly Victorian with roses and flowers everywhere. Marge and Dick suggested places to look for free on-street parking; after we found a space, we didn't use the car all weekend. They were extremely helpful in recommending restaurants and area activities. Our cheerful room had windows facing east and west, with lots of early morning sunshine. The backyard showers are large and comfortable and huge towels were provided; the backyard is small but secluded, with lines for drying towels and bathing suits. The fruit at breakfast was fresh and plentiful, with excellent muffins and coffee cakes." *(Kelly Bowers)* "Guests gather on the porch for a breakfast spiced by lively conversation, from political debates to restaurant reviews." *(Linda Long)* "The beach, shops, and restaurants are just a short walk on safe and friendly streets." *(Vivian Romano)* "Our first-floor room had comfortable stuffed chairs for sitting and reading, and a just-right queen-size bed." *(Rob & Susan Lamp)* "The wraparound veranda has plenty of sturdy, comfortable wicker furniture. The rooms have canopy beds with charming quilts, antiques, collectibles, and plenty of reading material."

(Victoria Berman) "Fully endorse existing entry. A wonderful place for single women, due to the inn's warm atmosphere and the safe feel of the Rehoboth community." *(Janet Collinge)* Note: At press time, we learned the inn was for sale; inquire further when booking.

Open Early May–late Sept.
Rooms 2 suites, 5 doubles—1 with private bath and/or shower, 2 with private half-bath, 4 with a maximum of 4 people sharing bath. All with desk; 2 with air-conditioning, 5 with fan.
Facilities Dining/living room, wraparound porch with hammock, grill, picnic tables, guest refrigerator. Beach, fishing ½ block away. Tennis, golf nearby. Unmetered parking 1 block away.
Location 3 blocks to center of town. 3 blocks S of Rehoboth Ave.
Restrictions No smoking. No children. Some evening boardwalk noise possible on busy weekends.
Credit Cards None accepted.
Rates B&B, $55–100 suite, double. Extra person, $20. 2–4 night weekend, holiday minimum. 7th night free (except Saturday).
Extras Bus station pickup.

The Royal Rose Inn ¢   *Tel: 302–226–2535*
41 Baltimore Avenue, 19971

The Royal Rose is a 1920s beach cottage, opened in 1989 as a B&B by school teachers Kenny and Cindy Vincent. Kenny chose the name after his mother's 600-piece china collection, and the rose theme is echoed in the inn's decor.

"Clean, quiet, and affordable, with a central location, just a block from the beach, shops, and restaurants. We forgot to pack our beach chairs, and before we knew it, the innkeepers had supplied us with two of their own." *(Carol Paolini)* "Kenny and Cindy Vincent, as well as their parents who help out, are delightful hosts who take pains to keep their guests happy. Our rose-themed room was simply furnished with antiques, embroidered linens, and fresh flowers." *(Connie Lew)* "We left our car in their parking lot (a real plus in Rehoboth), and walked or bicycled everywhere during our stay." *(Shirley Thorner)* "Kenny and Cindy let you park in their lot after check-out, so that you can spend the rest of the day on the beach. The self-service breakfast is served on Royal Rose china, offered on the porch or in the living room." *(Maura Angela Barry)* "Breakfast included fantastic coffee, fresh fruit kabobs, home-baked bread and cake, and an egg and bacon casserole." *(Dianne & Craig Failing)* "Kenny mapped out a cycling route through the most scenic part of Rehoboth." *(Steve & Bonnie Spivack)* "Loved the outdoor shower; a delightful combination of hot water, blue sky, and a warm breeze." *(Kate & Ron Merritt)* "So relaxing to sit on the porch, sipping a glass of wine, watching the people pass by." *(Kathy Wayment)* Comments appreciated.

Suggestion box: "A shelf in the bathroom for toiletries."

Open May through Oct. Other times by chance.
Rooms 7 doubles—3 with private shower bath, 4 rooms share 2 baths. All with air-conditioning. 3 with ceiling fan.
Facilities Living room, screened porch, guest refrigerator, outdoor enclosed hot/cold showers. Off-street parking. 1½ blocks to beach/boardwalk.

Location 1 block N of Rehoboth Ave., between First & Second Sts.

Restrictions No smoking. No children under 6. Occasional early morning noise from garbage pickup at restaurant across street.

Credit cards None accepted.

Rates B&B, $55–120 double. Extra person, $10–20. 2-night minimum stay some weekends. Off-season, mid-week, group rates. Weekend packages.

Extras Station pickups.

WILMINGTON

Also recommended: The famous **Hotel Dupont** (11th & Market Street, 19801; 302–594–3100 or 800–441–9019) re-opened in 1993 after a two-year renovation. The lovely rooms now showcase the latest Dupont products in baths, on walls, floors, and beds. Food and service in the hotel's famous restaurants is as good as ever. Double rates for the 216 rooms run from $110–220; weekend packages are a good value.

Information please: Four miles northwest of Wilmington is the village of Montchanin, a compound of modest Greek- and Gothic-Revival buildings, dating to 1870, that housed workers from the duPont powder mills and the Winterthur estate. Five generations and millions of dollars later, duPont descendants Missy and Daniel Lickle are restoring the eleven buildings to form the **Inn at Montchanin Village** (Route 100 at Kirk Road, Montchanin 19710; 302–888–2133) with 37 luxury suites and doubles, all with marble baths and state of the art amenities; a 55-seat restaurant will open in a renovated barn. Rates of $125–350 include a continental breakfast. Comments?

For additional area entries, see **Claymont**, and also **Mendenhall**, Pennsylvania.

The Boulevard B&B ¢   *Tel: 302–656–9700*
1909 Baynard Boulevard, 19802   *Fax: 302–656–9700*

The Boulevard is an imposing red brick house built in 1913, with neoclassical and Federal elements; Chuck and Judy Powell opened it as a B&B in 1986. Served from 8–9 A.M., breakfast includes fresh fruit and juice, cereal, eggs cooked to order or the daily special—perhaps apple pancakes, pecan waffles, or cinnamon French toast.

"Spacious home, eclectically furnished with traditional pieces and antique accents. Warm, inviting living room; the little library has an unusual tiled fireplace. Especially pretty is the second floor landing, with a comfy window seat. Our favorite room, tucked under the eaves on the third floor, is done in shades of rose and pink, with a queen-size bed, sitting area, and a Jacuzzi. Guest rooms are bright and sunny, comfortable but modest in decor." *(SWS)*

"Delicious breakfast beautifully served, either in the spacious and bright dining room in winter or the screened porch in warmer months." *(Elaine Bermas)* "Judy and Chuck readily accommodated my desire for a later breakfast." *(Dr. Victor Viser)* "The Powells were always available for conversation, dining suggestions, and area information." *(Pat & Nick*

WILMINGTON

Holden) "Lovely house, as described. Chuck and Judy were gracious and friendly." *(Steve Thomas)*

Open All year.
Rooms 6 doubles—4 with private bath and/or shower, 2 with maximum of 3 sharing bath. All with radio, TV, desk, air-conditioning. 4 with telephone, 3 with ceiling fan. 1 with whirlpool tub.
Facilities Dining room, living room with fireplace, stereo, organ; library with fireplace, TV/VCR; screened porch. Meeting room.
Location Historic district. 10 blocks from center. Take Exit 8 off I-95 onto Concord Pike (Rte. 202 S). Go right at 2nd light onto Baynard Blvd. B&B on right after 20th St.
Restrictions No smoking.
Credit cards Amex, MC, Visa.
Rates B&B, $60–75 double, $55–70 single. Extra person, $10.

Free copy of *INNroads* newsletter

Want to stay up-to-date on our latest finds? Send a business-size, self-addressed, stamped envelope with 55 cents postage and we'll send you the latest issue, *free!* While you're at it, why not enclose a report on any inns you've recently visited? Use the forms at the back of the book or your own stationery.

We Want to Hear from You!

As you know, this book is effective only with your help. We really need to know about your experiences and discoveries. If you stayed at an inn or hotel listed here, we want to know how it was. Did it live up to our description? Exceed it? Was it what you expected? Did you like it? Were you disappointed? Delighted? Have you discovered new establishments that we should add to the next edition?

Tear out one of the report forms at the back of this book (or use your own stationery if you prefer) and write today. *Even if you write only "Fully endorse existing entry" you will have been most helpful.*
Thank You!

District of Columbia

The Henley Park Hotel

Everyone needs to visit "DC" at least once in their lives. Early spring is the prettiest time, with cherry blossoms adding color and softness to a city that can seem rather cold and impersonal. In addition to the obligatory monuments, museums, and other famous tourist spots, add some less-visited stops to your itinerary: see hundreds of water plants at the Kenilworth Aquatic Gardens, wander through sprawling Rock Creek Park, stroll along the B&O Canal just west of Georgetown, or drive up MacArthur Parkway to Great Falls—a spectacular setting for picnics. If Congress is in session when you're in town, be sure to watch your lawmakers in action (night sessions are particularly intriguing). From late June to early July, join the throngs at the Festival of American Folklife. For a more sedate cultural experience, attend a performance at the Folger Shakespeare Theater (September to June).

Spring and fall are peak periods in Washington, when rates are high and space is tight. You can get the best deals on weekends year-round, and from December through February and during the summer, when Congress adjourns and many Washingtonians escape the city's infamous heat and humidity. When making reservations always ask if any special rates are in effect. To save money on hotel reservations, call **Capitol Reservations** (1730 Rhode Island Avenue N.W., Suite 506, 20036; 202–452–1270 or 800–VISIT–DC) which can book you into 75 local hotels (including Loew's L'Enfant Plaza described below) at a lower price than you could get by calling the hotel directly. A similar service is **Washington D.C. Accommodations** (1534 U Street, N.W., 20009; 202–289–2220 or 800–554–2220). Some of the properties listed here are represented by these free services; many are chain hotels.

Another option is a B&B reservation service called **The Bed & Breakfast League, Ltd./Sweet Dreams & Toast, Inc.** (P.O. Box 9490, 20016–9490; 202–363–7767). The accommodations have been inspected; the criteria for membership includes safe neighborhoods, comfortable bedrooms, immaculate baths, hearty continental breakfasts, and location within an easy walk of the public transportation system. A similar B&B reservation agency is **Bed & Breakfast Accommodations, Ltd.** (P.O. Box 12011, 20005; 202–328–3510).

Reader tips: "Washington is a busy, noisy city. In popular areas like Georgetown, street noise can continue into the wee hours, especially in summer. If you are a light sleeper, you might need to sacrifice a view for a quieter courtyard room." Also: "Staying in Georgetown is great if you have a car or can take taxis. There's no Metro stop, a definite problem for sightseers." *(Robin Clarke)*

In the interests of minimizing space and maximizing information, we abbreviated the listings for a number of Washington's small hotels.

Also recommended—budget: Although readers have checked in with minor complaints about housekeeping and furnishings, most agreed that the following inns still represent a good value because of their location and reasonable rates:

Within an easy walk of the Kennedy Center is the **Inn at Foggy Bottom** (824 New Hampshire Avenue, N.W., 20037; 202–337–6620 or 800–426–4455) with 95 spacious, well-equipped suites. The $79–109 weekday, $79–99 weekend rates include a modest breakfast, *Washington Post*, and evening chocolates and brandy. The location is close to the State Department, the Kennedy Center, and the Metro. "Although some sprucing up wouldn't hurt, it's hard to beat the rates and location." *(SR)*

Overlooking Pennsylvania Avenue is the **Hotel Lombardy** (2019 I Street, N.W., 20006; 202–828–2600 or 800–424–5486), within walking distance of the White House, Georgetown, and the Kennedy Center. Many of the 126 rooms and suites have kitchenettes, and the double rate is $130–165. Although the lobby is tiny, most rooms are quite spacious.

The closest you'll come to a real inn in DC is the **Tabard Inn** (1739 N Street, N.W., 20036; 202–785–1277), located on a quiet side street close to Dupont Circle and its Metro stop. Composed of three linked Victorian townhouses, the inn is furnished with well-used antiques, and offers idiosyncratic charm that will delight some, but not all, readers. B&B double rates range from $59–79 for the shared-bath rooms; $99–135 for rooms with a private bath. "Reminds me of the old hotels I used to stay at on the Left Bank in Paris—pleasantly down-at-the-heels, in a charming way. Excellent food in the restaurant, much of it grown on the owners' farm or obtained from local suppliers." *(EA)*

Next door to the Tabard is the **The Canterbury Hotel** (1733 N Street, N.W., 20036; 202–393–3000 or 800–424–2950). All 99 rooms have a stocked wet bar, separate sitting and work areas, and queen- or king-size beds; the rates ($79–125) include the morning paper, continental breakfast, bathrobes, evening turndown with chocolates, and fitness center. Rooms are furnished with eighteenth-century reproduction English furniture. "Convenient location three blocks from the Metro. Attractive furnishings, firm bed." *(KC)*

About five blocks from Dupont Circle is the **Windsor Inn** (1842 16th Street, 20009; 202–667–0300 or 800–423–9111), with modestly furnished rooms and B&B rates of $79–150 weekdays, $55 weekends, which includes continental breakfast, morning paper, and evening sherry and snacks; similar rates are offered at the nearby **Embassy Inn** (1627 16th Street, N.W.; 202–234–7800), done in 19th century Federalist style, located four blocks south and owned by the same company.

In an appealing neighborhood, ten minutes by Metro to the White House, Capitol, and the Mall is the **Kalorama** (1854 Mintwood Place, N.W., 20009; 202–667–6369). "Excellent value, homey atmosphere. Our room was comfortable, not fancy; the bathroom was small. Roomy breakfast/sitting area. Great neighborhood, with lovely streets of private house and plenty of good restaurants nearby." (*Bill Hussey*) B&B double rates range from $45–95.

Located in the Embassy District, the **Normandy Inn** (2118 Wyoming Avenue N.W., 20008; 202–483–1350 or 800–424–3729) was built as an apartment building and converted to a hotel in 1981. Double rates for the 80 guest rooms are $104 weekdays, $69 weekends, and include afternoon tea and cookies; continental breakfast is $4 additional. "Quiet, side street location; lots of great restaurants nearby; friendly staff." (*GR*)

Also recommended—moderate: Although certainly not a small hotel, an excellent choice for families and the cost-conscious is **Loew's L'Enfant Plaza** (480 L'Enfant Plaza East S.W., 20024; 202–484–1000), located within walking distance of the Holocaust Museum, the Air & Space Museum, and the Smithsonian. Underneath this office building/hotel complex are shops, snack bars, and a Metro stop; a rooftop pool and health club provide relaxation. Most of this luxury hotel's 370 well-equipped rooms have been recently renovated; top floor rooms have the best views. Regular double rates range from $190–230, with summer rates at $119, and weekend packages at $139 (including breakfast and parking); children stay free. "Our soothing, well-appointed room had two double beds with a desk, table, lounge chairs, (armoire holding the TV and refrigerator), with another TV and phone in the bathroom. Good restaurants; friendly service." (*KLH*)

The **Latham Hotel** (3000 M Street NW, 20007; 202–726–5000 or 800–LATHAM-1) offers a good location on busy M Street in Georgetown, an outdoor swimming pool, and 143 attractive well-equipped rooms with contemporary decor (light sleepers should ask for a courtyard room, especially in summer). Double rates range from $165–200, with a $99–129 weekend rate, and special AAA weekend/summer rates; children under 18 stay free. Excellent meals are offered in its Citronelle restaurant, where windows permit you to watch the chefs at work.

Also recommended—luxury: At the edge of Georgetown is the **Four Seasons Hotel** (2800 Pennsylvania Avenue, N.W., 20007; 202–342–0444 or 800–332–3442), with 200 luxurious guest rooms, an excellent restaurant, and a first-class fitness center. Double rates range from $275–320, with weekend packages starting at $225.

Based in two grand townhouses dating to 1864 plus a contemporary addition, the **Morrison-Clark Inn** (Massachusetts Avenue at 11th Street, N.W., 20001; 202–898–1200 or 800–332–7898) enjoys a top reputation for the creative international cuisine served in its charming dining rooms. Reports on the rooms vary, although the Victorian rooms in the original mansions seem to be the first choice. The location is convenient to the convention center, although some nearby streets are not appealing. Rates range from $125–185, with lower rates on weekends.

For additional area recommendations, see the **Virginia** chapter entries under **Aldie, Alexandria, Fairfax**, and **Leesburg.** Fairfax is closest to the city; the others are a short drive from Dulles International Airport.

Georgetown Inn ⅋

Tel: 202–333–8900
800–424–2979
Fax: 202–625–1744

1310 Wisconsin Avenue, N.W., 20007

In the heart of Georgetown, close to restaurants, shops, and the C&O Canal is the Georgetown Inn, built in 1962. The guest rooms are decorated with traditional mahogany furniture covered in silk and brocade fabrics. Rates include a continental breakfast, daily newspaper, robes, toiletries, and nightly turndown service.

"Busy area, fun for strolling. Attractive, cheerful room, with queen-size bed, spacious sitting area, and functional bathroom. Good reading lights. The rates include an adequate buffet breakfast, and you can order from the menu if desired. Extremely pleasant staff. The hotel's restaurant, the Georgetown Bar & Grill, was very lively at night with a young crowd and a piano player." *(Robin Clarke)* Comments appreciated.

Open All year.
Rooms 10 suites, 85 doubles—all with private shower or tub, telephone, radio, clock, TV, desk, air-conditioning.
Facilities Restaurant, breakfast room, lobby, meeting room, bar/lounge with jazz Wed–Sat. Health club. Off-street parking.
Location Central Georgetown historic district, at corner of Wisconsin Ave. & N St. (just N of M St.). 10 min. to Nat'l Airport, Kennedy Center.
Restrictions No smoking on 4th, 5th, 6th floors. "All rooms have soundproof windows." Light sleepers should request a room away from Wisc. Ave.
Credit cards All major.
Rates B&B, $195–250 suite, $119–159 double, $109–149 single. Extra person, $20. Children under 12 free in parents' room. Senior, AAA discount. Alc lunch, $15–20; alc dinner, $30–45.
Extras Wheelchair access; bathroom equipped for disabled. Crib. French, Spanish, German spoken.

Hay-Adams Hotel ♟ ✕ ⅋

Tel: 202–638–6600
800–424–5054
Fax: 202–638–2716

800 16th Street, 1 Lafayette Square, 20006

"Where nothing is overlooked but the White House," is the opening line of the Hay-Adams' brochure, a beginning unique among such publications. Built on the sites of the homes of John Hay and Henry Adams, this hotel dates back to 1927, when it was built in the Italian Renaissance style. Restored in 1983 to its original grandeur, and redecorated in 1995, it has developed a reputation for its luxurious atmosphere and excellent service. The lobby is decorated in shades of ivory and rose, punctuated by massive carved walnut pillars, polished brass, English antiques, and a seventeenth-century tapestry. The hotel's Lafayette restaurant serves light, creative American cuisine; flavors are enhanced with herbs and spices, rather than butter and cream. Possible entrées include Moroccan salmon with cous-cous, wild mushroom risotto, and Southwestern pork chops with apple-onion chutney.

"The lobby is lovely and used by guests for sitting, reading and relaxing. Guest rooms are furnished with antique reproductions and plush fabrics; many have elaborate plaster ceilings and gorgeous crystal chande-liers. Junior suites consist of one large room with a sofa bed (in addition to the regular bed), and a sitting area. The suites have the best views; the fourth floor and above have year-round views of the White House, while those lower down are blocked by trees in summer. The bathrooms have lots of big, heavy, fluffy towels and bathrobes, marble vanities, good lighting, and electrical outlets." *(Diane Wolf)* "Superb service in all areas; elegant room, completely refurbished." *(Gerald Bahr, also Sally Ducot)* "Decor, food, and service were excellent. We lingered at dinner for hours, enjoying the music, and were never hurried." *(Lynn Avenoso)*

Open All year.
Rooms 18 suites, 143 doubles—all with full private bath, telephone, radio, TV, desk, air-conditioning, hair dryer. Some with balcony, kitchenette.
Facilities Restaurant, grill, lounge with piano, lobby, library, fitness center. Valet parking, $15 daily.
Location Directly opposite White House facing Lafayette Square Park.
Credit cards All major cards accepted.
Rates Room only, $280–900 suite, $210–360 double. Children 16 and under free; extra adult, $30. Alc breakfast, $10–20; alc lunch, $30; alc dinner, $60. Weekend rates, packages.
Extras Wheelchair access; many bathrooms equipped for disabled. Airport/station pickups, for a fee. Pets permitted with approval. Crib, babysitting. Spanish, French, German, Italian, Japanese, Arabic, Chinese, Hebrew, Greek, Hungarian, Rumanian spoken. Member, Preferred Hotels; Historic Hotels of America.

The Henley Park Hotel ✗
926 Massachusetts Avenue, N.W., 20001

Tel: 202–638–5200
800–222–8474
Fax: 202–638–6740

A Tudor-style building constructed in 1918, the Henley Park's exterior is ornamented with 119 gargoyles and plaques. Restored in 1982, its com-mon areas include a spacious parlor where afternoon tea and scones are served. Rooms are traditionally furnished in soothing shades of beige, taupe, and mauve, with chintz floral bedspreads and matching drapes. Deluxe rooms have king- or queen-size beds; standard rooms are smaller with a double bed. The hotel's Coeur de Lion restaurant combines classic cuisine with a contemporary flair and attentive service. Menus change seasonally, but some recent entrées included pork tenderloin with cumin; salmon steak with coriander; lobster ravioli; and grilled eggplant with angel hair pasta.

"The room had two robes and lots of elegant brass towel racks. The furniture was gleaming wood, with beautiful painted ceiling trim, and a fabulously comfortable four poster king-size bed. The air conditioning and windows kept out street noise; the refrigerator was silent as well. At breakfast, I had a perfectly poached egg; my coffee cup was refilled each time I took a second sip." *(Maureen Banner)* "Fully endorse existing entry. An especially good choice if you have a car." *(BH)* "Even the entryway is elegant; you almost feel like you're walking into a private estate. Topnotch service; we ordered wine from room service, and it arrived in five minutes flat." *(Julie Irmischer)*

Open All year.
Rooms 7 suites, 89 doubles—all with full private bath, telephone, radio, TV, desk, air-conditioning. Some with four-poster beds, refrigerator.
Facilities Lobby, parlor with fireplace, restaurant with atrium, lounge with entertainment. Fitness center, valet parking. Concierge service. Limousine service to downtown & Capitol Hill.
Location Downtown. At intersection of 10th Street and Massachusetts Ave. 2 blocks from Convention Center; 6 blocks from Union Station; 4 blocks from Metro Center subway station.
Restrictions No smoking in some guest rooms. Some area streets not recommended for night-time walks.
Credit cards Amex, Choice, MC, Visa.
Rates Room only, $295–675 suite, $155–215 double. $99 weekend rate. Extra person, $20. Children free in parents' room. Senior discount. Alc breakfast, $9–15; alc lunch, $25–40; alc dinner, $45–70. Holiday, anniversary packages.
Extras Crib, babysitting available by prior arrangement. French, Spanish spoken. Member, The Classic Collection.

The Jefferson Hotel ♦️ ✕ ♿

Sixteenth & M Streets, 20036

Tel: 202–347–2200
800–368–5966
Fax: 202–331–7982

The Jefferson was built in 1923 as an apartment building for the wealthy. Totally renovated in recent years, it features elegant, individually decorated rooms, many with rich fabrics, canopy beds, original paintings, and antiques. The hotel has been popular for years with the rich and famous of the political, social, literary, and theatrical worlds. The Jefferson's restaurant was long a place for Washingtonians to see and be seen; it has developed a reputation for fine French cuisine, serving such entrées as rack of lamb, swordfish with couscous, and pheasant with carrot sauce.

"One of the best small hotels in America—a gem of class, sophistication and warmth—rare in our nation's capitol. Our wish was their command, cheerfully executed. Tuna tartare Sunday evening from room service, lunch at 10:30 A.M. before our plane departed—no problem for the Jefferson staff. All luxurious amenities and business services are provided. Public areas are spotless, the marble in the bathrooms shines like a mirror, even in the corners. The small intimate dining room and the cozy club lounge with fireplace are romantic settings when I travel with my wife and pleasantly comfortable when I am by myself." *(Ron Crider, also DLG)* Reports appreciated.

Open All year.
Rooms 32 suites, 68 doubles—all with full private bath, 2-line telephone, radio, TV/VCR, desk, air-conditioning, mini-bar, hair dryer, computer/fax hookups, stereo/CD player. 2 with balcony, fireplace. 12 rooms in annex.

Facilities Restaurant, breakfast room, bar/lounge, video/CD library. Health club with indoor swimming pool. Weekend jazz. Valet parking. Laundry service, 24-hour concierge, room service. Tennis, golf nearby.

Location Downtown. At corner of 16th & M Sts. 4 blocks N of White House.

Credit cards Amex, CB, DC, ER, MC, Visa.

Rates Room only, $330–975 suite, $245–285 double, $230–270 single. Weekend rates, $225–275 suite, $160–175 double. Packages. Alc lunch, $15–25; alc dinner, $50.

Extras Wheelchair access. Crib, babysitting. Some pets by prior arrangement. Lancaster Group, Small Luxury Hotels. Dutch, French, German, Italian, Spanish spoken.

Key to Abbreviations and Symbols

For complete information and explanations, please see the Introduction.

¢ Especially good value for overnight accommodation.

ℳ Families welcome. Most (but not all) have cribs, baby-sitting, games, play equipment, and reduced rates for children.

✕ Meals served to public; reservations recommended or required.

✵ Tennis court and swimming pool and/or lake on grounds. Golf usually on grounds or nearby.

& Limited or full wheelchair access; call for details.

Rates: Range from least expensive room in low season to most expensive room in peak season.

Room only: No meals included; European Plan (EP).

B&B: Bed and breakfast; includes breakfast, sometimes afternoon/evening refreshment.

MAP: Modified American Plan; includes breakfast and dinner.

Full board: Three meals daily.

Alc lunch: À la carte lunch; average price of entrée plus nonalcoholic drink, tax, tip.

Alc dinner: Average price of three-course dinner, including half bottle of house wine, tax, tip.

Prix fixe dinner: Three- to five-course set dinner, excluding wine, tax, tip unless otherwise noted.

Extras: Noted if available. Always confirm in advance. Pets are not permitted unless specified; if you are allergic, ask for details; *most innkeepers have pets.*

---

rian hotel has 25 guest rooms, a parlor with 14-foot ceilings and floor-to-ceiling windows, a breakfast room, and reading room. B&B double rates of $85–110 include in-room telephones, TVs, kitchenettes, plus a continental breakfast and evening sherry. "Friendly staff, eager to please. The evening aperitif included a nice selection of white and red wines served with cheese and crackers. Pleasant rooms in a convenient location." *(Ann Christofferson)*

Formerly the Peabody Court, the **Latham Hotel** (612 Cathedral Street, 21201; 410–727–7101 or 800–528–4261) is an elegant 104-room hotel, with both a casual and fine dining restaurant. Furnishings are traditional, with marble bathrooms (some with Jacuzzis), and nightly turndown service includes imported chocolates. Double rates are $150–170, with weekend packages available. "Beautiful location on Mt. Vernon Place, next to Walter Art Museum and one block from famous Charles Street. Lovely period furnishings, warm at-home feeling. Hot towel rack in the bathroom, plus a magnifying mirror mounted in the bathroom, great for applying makeup. Helpful friendly staff; elegant older hotel." *(Gloria King)*

Twenty minutes north of downtown is the **Gramercy B&B** (1400 Greenspring Valley Road, Box 119, Stevenson, 21153; 410–486–2405), a brick and half-timbered Tudor mansion. The common areas have the dark woodwork and leaded windows you'd expect from Tudor-style architecture, while the guest rooms are decorated with antiques, period furnishings, and flowered fabrics. Breakfast includes a choice of eggs, omelets, French toast, blueberry pancakes, cereals, and fruit, served at guests' convenience, and accented by herbs from the inn's own farm. There are five comfortable suites ($90–175) and five modest shared-bath singles ($50), plus a swimming pool and tennis court.

Information please: The **Admiral Fell Inn** (888 South Broadway 21231; 410–522–7377 or 800–292–INNS) is located near the waterfront in Fell's Point, among Market Square's historic townhouses. This 80-room hotel consists of several contiguous buildings, the oldest of which dates back to 1770. The interiors have been renovated to combine historic accuracy with modern comfort. The inn houses a pub serving drinks and casual food, and a restaurant providing more elaborate meals. B&B double rates of $165 include a continental breakfast and the morning paper. Request a courtyard room for weekend stays because of late night/early morning revelers.

Perhaps the Inner Harbor's most elegant hotel is the luxurious, beautifully furnished 203-room **Harbor Court Hotel** (550 Light Street, 21202; 410–234–0550 or 800–824–0076), with excellent harbor views from the fifth and sixth floors. The hotel has an exceptionally well-equipped fitness center, a fine restaurant (also with harbor views), Hampton's, and a more casual eatery. Doubles range from $220–270, suites are $375–650, and children under 18 stay free. Weekend packages are an excellent value at $150–300.

For a Fell's Point location, there's the **Inn at Henderson Wharf** (1000 Fell Street, 21231; 410–522–7777 or 800–522–2088), a converted 19th century tobacco warehouse, now home to 38 guest rooms (no smoking permitted). Continental breakfast is served in the lobby and can be taken to the attractive courtyard; spacious brick-walled guest rooms overlook the harbor or the courtyard. B&B double rates are $120–145, with weekend and package rates available.

In the Mt. Vernon district is the **Inn at Government House** (1125 North Calvert Street, 21202; 410–539–0566) built in 1889, and owned by the inventor of the bottle cap. Restored in 1983 (and previously known as a Society Hill Hotel), it is operated by students of the Baltimore International Culinary College. The 18 guest rooms have antique and reproduction furnishings, private baths, telephone, and TV; double rates are $125–150, and include free parking and a continental breakfast delivered to your room.

For an additional Baltimore area listings (and an outstanding reader favorite), see entry for **Twin Gates B&B** in **Lutherville,** 15 minutes north of downtown Baltimore.

Ann Street B&B ¢

804 South Ann Street, 21231

Tel: 410–342–5883

The town of Fell's Point was Baltimore's original seaport on the Chesapeake Bay, and dates back to the 1730s. Some of the earliest wharves, taverns, and shops are still in operation, and the area remains a working seaport today. The Ann Street B&B, two adjacent 18th-century houses in this historic waterfront district, has been Joanne and Andrew Mazurek's home since 1978; they opened it to overnight guests in 1988. Joanne notes that the inn "offers travelers the opportunity to enjoy the atmosphere of an authentic Colonial home. Our inn has 12 working fireplaces, including two in the suite, and one in a bathroom. Hardwood floors and antiques highlight the decor."

"A first-class B&B; Joanne made us feel at home immediately. Our accommodations were very spacious: a living room with comfortable couch, table and chairs, fireplace; a separate bedroom with comfortable bed, good reading lights and another fireplace laid ready to light. Breakfast was delicious with grilled grapefruit, a German pancake, orange juice, muffins, and coffee served in their antique-filled kitchen by a cozy fire." *(Mary Jane Southwick)* "Joanne is a thoughtful, friendly innkeeper who has thought of all her guests' possible needs and wants. From 7–10 A.M., she serves breakfast in the common room in cool weather, and in the walled courtyard in the summer months." *(Monna Hormel)* "Loved my room with fireplace, flannel sheets, and antique rope bed; the large bathroom had a great tub for soaking. Delicious fresh mushroom and cheese omelet." *(Janet Hinerfeld)*

Open All year.
Rooms 1 suite, 2 doubles—all with private shower and/or bath, radio, air-conditioning. 1 with desk.
Facilities Common room, garden. Boat dockage nearby.
Location Historic waterfront area.
Restrictions Smoking in designated areas only. Children over 10 preferred.
Credit cards None accepted.
Rates B&B, $95 suite, $85 double, $70–80 single. Extra person in suite, $15.

Celie's Waterfront B&B &

1714 Thames Street, 21231

Tel: 410–522–2323
800–432–0184
Fax: 410–522–2324

If your idea of the ideal B&B combines modern plumbing with historic ambiance, then visit the three-story inn Celie Ives built in 1989. Tucked into a narrow lot in the heart of Fell's Point, the inn's rooms are comfortably furnished, highlighted with antiques, collectibles, fresh flowers, down comforters, flannel sheets, and terry robes. In-room refrigerators are stocked with soda and juice, coffee makers with complimentary fresh-ground coffee (caf and decaf) and fine teas. The buffet breakfast of fruit and fresh-squeezed orange juice, just-baked breads and pastries can be enjoyed in the dining room, courtyard, or on the rooftop deck with its city skyline and harbor views.

"We enjoyed sitting on our private little balcony, reading books from the selection in our room, and sipping a soda or cup of coffee. Scrumptious breads for breakfast with fresh fruit, granola and yogurt. We ate in the lovely garden, listening to the water trickling through the fountain. Celie had discount tickets for the Aquarium and wonderful restaurant suggestions. She reserved theater tickets for us and even gave us a lift to the train station." *(Kelly Ann Connor)* "Celie is a gracious hostess, attentive to a business traveler's needs." *(Douglas Baxter)*

"The guest rooms have reading lamps on both sides of the bed and comfortable chairs. On each guest room floor is a display of sightseeing information and a basket of toiletries; the ground floor has a small but comfortable sitting room. We had dessert on the rooftop deck and breakfasted in the lovely garden." *(Diane Wolf)* "Our room was small but cozy with a comfortable bed and woodburning fireplace." *(Hal & Urve Landers)*

Open All year.

Rooms 2 suites, 5 doubles—all with full private bath, telephone (with modem capability), radio, TV, desk, air-conditioning, ceiling fan, refrigerator, coffee maker. 4 with whirlpool tub, 2 with fireplace, 3 with patio/balcony, 2 with microwave.

Facilities Dining room, living room with fireplace, roof deck. Garden, courtyard. Off-street parking.

Location Fell's Point. 9 blocks to Harborplace, business district.

Restrictions Street noise in harbor rooms on weekends. "White noise" radio for light sleepers. No smoking. Children over 10 welcome.

Credit cards Amex, Discover, MC, Visa.

Rates B&B, $135–160 suite, $90–135 double, $90–125 single. Tipping discouraged. 2-night minimum weekends, holidays, special events.

Extras Wheelchair access; 1 bathroom equipped for disabled.

Mr. Mole Bed and Breakfast

1601 Bolton Street, 21217

Tel: 410–728–1179
Fax: 410–728–3379

As you've probably guessed, Mr. Mole B&B is named for the character in Kenneth Grahame's *Wind in the Willows* who is always spring cleaning. As Paul Bragaw and Collin Clarke found out when they renovated this 1870 row house, an innkeeper's life involves constant "spring cleaning" too. Located in Bolton Hill, Mr. Mole B&B is set in a quiet, tree-lined neighborhood of spacious brick row houses, constructed by wealthy merchants of mid-19th century Baltimore to escape downtown congestion (some things never change). The house is decorated with great style and elegance with many 18th and 19th century antiques. The first floor rooms have 14-foot ceilings, bay windows, and non-working marble fireplaces. A Dutch-style buffet breakfast is served at 8 and 9 A.M., consisting of fresh fruit, sliced meats and cheeses, such home-baked breads as buttermilk-cheese or honey-oatmeal, and dessert, perhaps apricot-pecan cake or brown sugar-cream cheese pie, plus juice, coffee and tea.

"Careful attention has been paid to every decorating detail, with each guest room furnished with a different theme. The Garden Suite has a separate sun room, perfect for a spring or summer visit. The hosts were warm and friendly and offered excellent dining recommendations in Little Italy. A big plus is the garage parking, complete with your own remote control door opener for the length of your stay. A welcome convenience in this regentrified historic neighborhood." *(LuAnn & Steve Weiner)* "Creative, original decor, great charm and comfort, imaginative food, and marvelously interesting hosts." *(GR, also Susan Berry)*

Open All year.
Rooms 2 suites, 3 doubles—all with private bath and shower, telephone, radio, clock, desk, air-conditioning. 1 with sun room.
Facilities Dining room, living room with fireplace, parlor. Garage parking.
Location Bolton Hill. 1.5 m to center. 8 blocks to symphony hall, opera house. From I-95 N take Exit 53 to I-395. Go 0.8 m & bear right on Martin Luther King Jr. Blvd. After 2 m, go left on Eutaw St. At 4th stop light, go right on McMechen St. Cross Bolton St. intersection to inn on left. Call for directions from other areas.
Restrictions No smoking. No children under 10.
Credit cards Amex, Discover, MC, Visa.
Rates B&B, $150 suite (for 3), $95–130 double, $80–105 single. 2-night weekend/holiday minimum. "No tipping expected."
Extras French, German, Dutch spoken.

BERLIN

Berlin is located on the Eastern Shore, ten miles west of Ocean City and seven miles west of Assateague Island National Seashore.

Information please: For an elegant alternative to Ocean City's motels, consider a stay at the **Atlantic Hotel** (2 North Main Street, 21811; 410–641–3589 or 800–814–7672), built in 1895. Its guest rooms combine the charm of antique decor with all modern conveniences, including an elevator. A restaurant and lounge occupies the first floor, on the second, guests can relax in the parlor. The 16 guest rooms (on the second and third floors) are furnished with careful attention to detail; each has a private bath, telephone, and air-conditioning, and B&B double rates range from $55–135, depending on room and season, and include a self-serve continental breakfast.

Merry Sherwood Plantation
8909 Worcester Highway, 21811

Merry Sherwood Plantation is about six miles and 150 years away from the cacophony that is Ocean City. Kirk Burbage bought this Italianate Revival mansion in 1990, and opened his B&B in 1992 after extensive renovation. Built in 1859, it covers 8,500 square feet, with nine working fireplaces, and is completely decorated and furnished in authentic Victorian style. It sits on what was originally a 1,200-acre estate, and Kirk invites his guests to "experience the opulent lifestyle of wealthy landed gentry." Breakfast includes fresh fruit, juice, homemade muffins, breads, jellies, plus a hot entrée such as puffed apple pancakes.

"Our lovely suite had a marble bath with Jacuzzi; even the sheets were ironed for our antique double bed. It also had an antique wedding gown and photos." *(Kim Mast)* "Beautiful grounds, handsomely landscaped 19th century gardens. The guest rooms are lovely; each one is decorated with a different period theme, and is named after a significant person from the estate or area. It is evident that a great deal of research was involved in this inn's renovation. Excellent breakfast; thick, soft towels." *(Nancy Mitch)* "The innkeepers could not have been more accommodating; they were there whenever needed, yet made us feel as though we had the place to ourselves." *(Susan Richardson)* Reports appreciated.

Open All year.
Rooms 1 suite, 7 doubles—6 with private bath and/or shower, 2 with maximum of 4 people sharing bath. All with desk, air-conditioning. 4 with fireplace, 1 with whirlpool tub.
Facilities Dining room, parlor, library, ballroom, sunporch, verandas; most with fireplace. 19 acres with swing, lawn games. 6 m from ocean. Golf, tennis, water sports nearby.
Location Eastern Shore. Take Rte. 50 to Rte. 113 S. Go 2.5 m to entrance gate.
Restrictions No smoking. No children under 12.
Credit cards MC, Visa.
Rates B&B, $150–175 suite, $125–150 double, $85–115 single. Extra person, $15.

BETTERTON

Lantern Inn ¢
115 Ericsson Avenue, P.O. Box 29, 21610

Ann and Ken Washburn restored the Lantern Inn, built in 1904 as a guest house, and opened it as a B&B in 1987. While the guest rooms are decorated with country fabrics and period antiques, the common rooms have been modestly furnished with comfortable contemporary furniture.

"A sleepy town on the bay—wonderfully relaxing in the off-season, busy in the summer. Ken and Ann greet arriving guests with tea or wine. The inn has a comfortable front porch for reading or conversation. Guest rooms are decorated with Eastern shore accessories. Ann is an excellent cook; imaginative breakfasts." *(Frederick & Susan Krall)* "My spotless room had a brass bedstead and a beautiful old quilt. After I admired the lilies of the valley in the garden, a little vase of them was placed in my room." *(Henrietta Search)* "Ann and Ken do everything to make you feel at home, but do not bother you when you want to read or just sit." *(Harry Baernstein)* "Ken and Ann are well-informed about area sights and activities." *(George Ryan & Jane Rolfus)*

Open All year.
Rooms 13 doubles—4 with private shower, 9 with maximum of 4 people sharing bath. All rooms with air-conditioning; 1 with desk.
Facilities Dining room, 2 living rooms with TV, piano, books, games. $\frac{1}{2}$ acre with picnic table. 2 blocks to tennis. $1\frac{1}{2}$ blocks to sandy beach and pier on Chesapeake Bay for swimming, boating, fishing. Goose hunting (in season), hiking, bicycling nearby.
Location Upper Eastern Shore. $1\frac{1}{2}$ hrs. to Philadelphia, Baltimore, and Washington.
Restrictions Smoking on 1st floor only. Children 12 and over.
Credit cards MC, Visa.
Rates B&B, $68–85 double. 2-night holiday weekend minimum.

BUCKEYSTOWN

The Inn at Buckeystown   *Tel:* 301–874–5755
3521 Buckeystown Pike (Route 85),   800–272–1190
c/o General Delivery, 21717

The village of Buckeystown is listed on the National Register of Historic Places, and was founded before the American Revolution; because of the many battles fought nearby, it was greatly affected by the Civil War.

The Inn at Buckeystown is a restored Victorian mansion opened in 1982 by Dan Pelz, assisted by innkeepers Rebecca Shipman-Smith and Chase Barnett. Guest rooms are extensively furnished with period pieces, choice art, and collectibles; an additional suite is found in St. John's Cottage, a converted nineteenth-century church. Rates include complimentary port in the guest rooms, and wine served with dinner. Menus change daily, but a recent autumn dinner included Burgundy wine; fried Brie with fruit; cream of pumpkin soup; romaine lettuce with apples and blue cheese; pistachio-herb stuffed flank steak with oven-browned potatoes, acorn squash, and corn muffins; and pecan pie.

"The inn is located in a small village that has three streets and lovely Victorian homes. Excellent service; the delicious food is presented on a lovely collection of old china and antique silver." *(Sylvia & Martin Tulkoff)* "The church cottage has a wonderful outdoor hot tub, a fireplace, piano, microwave, refrigerator stocked with soda and wine, plus a huge library of videos. The bath was supplied with terry robes and plenty of towels. Dinner was delicious with brie, salad, soup, and baked salmon. Breakfast was equally excellent, and included French toast with maple syrup and sausage. Dignified, elegant service." *(Stephanie Roberts)* "Dan is a marvelous host, who has the knack of making all his guests feel at home."

(Leonora Welsher) "The atmosphere is informal, friendly, and warm. The grounds are well maintained and inviting." *(Ellen Stahly, also Carol Armel)*

Open All year.
Rooms 3 suites, 3 doubles, 1 cottage—all with private bath and/or shower. All rooms with air-conditioning; cottages, suites with TV/VCR, desk, fireplace, hot tub.
Facilities Library, 2 parlors with fireplaces, stereo, games; wraparound porch. 2½ acres, gardens, wooded grounds. Cross-country, downhill skiing, swimming, tennis, skating nearby.
Location W MD. 1 hr. W of Baltimore, NW of Washington, DC. 5 m S of Frederick, MD. Take Buckeystown exit off I-270 or I-70 to MD Rte. 85.
Restrictions No smoking. No children. "Admission by reservation or appointment only; no tours." Jacket & tie suggested at dinner.
Credit cards Amex, MC, Visa.
Rates MAP, $300 cottage, $250 suite, $225 double, *including* tax, gratuities. 2-night minimum Oct., holidays. Prix fixe dinner for outside guests with 24-hour notice, $38.
Extras Limited wheelchair access. Limo service to D.C. airports, $60 per party.

CHESAPEAKE CITY

Started in 1803, the Chesapeake and Delaware Canal was dug to connect these two major bays, saving ships the nearly 300-mile trip around the Delmarva peninsula. Chesapeake City, long known as Canal Town, first housed the workers who dug the canal, and was later home to the men who operated the canal's locks and engines. Widened and deepened many times over the years, the canal is now used by over 150 ocean-going ships monthly. When the locks and engines needed to operate the canal were eliminated in the 1920s, the town became a sleepy backwater, only recently rediscovered by tourists and boaters.

Reader tip: "Outstanding food and service at the Bayard House. I had a salad of shrimp with vegetables in a radicchio lettuce bowl, framed with melon and berries, and my husband had a grilled chicken and pasta dish with sun dried tomatoes and herbs." *(Rose Ciccone)*

Inn at the Canal   *Tel:* 410–885–5995
104 Bohemia Avenue, 21915   *Fax:* 410–885–3585

"Overlooking the Canal, the Inn at the Canal is owned by Al and Mary Ioppolo. Built by a 19th-century tugboat captain, the Ioppolos have restored its beautiful pine floors, and have furnished the inn with period decor. The common room has round oak tables with spindle back chairs, and the original ceiling has a classic design dramatically painted in shades of blue, gold, and green. The guest rooms have antique quilts hung on the wall, coordinating with quilts Mary has made for the queen-size beds; three rooms overlook the water. The spotless bathrooms are new, with the sinks installed in antique oak bureaus; one has the original bathtub, over six feet long and enclosed in a beaded board frame with oak railing. The inviting front porch has white wicker furniture, while the side porch has rocking chairs overlooking the water—the perfect place to sip an iced tea." *(NB)*

"Immaculate rooms with lovely quilts; lovely breakfast table with spotless linens. Mary and Al are gracious, down-to-earth, friendly, and are more than willing to talk about the inn, its history, and its restoration." *(Deborah DiSalvo)* "Mary and Al's delicious breakfasts include just-brewed coffee, freshly squeezed juice, homemade breads, and a hot entrée." *(Tom & Elena Murphy)* "Watch the ships pass by on the C & D Canal from the porch, or walk down the street in either direction to seafood restaurants and small shops." *(Mrs. Tanya Harris)* "Even the smallest room is charming, with a comfortable bed and lovely quilt." *(Sherrill Brown)* "Fully endorse existing entry." *(Rose Ciccone)*

Open All year.
Rooms 6 doubles—all with private bath, TV, radio, air-conditioning. 3 with desk.
Facilities Dining room with fireplace, living room with stereo, books, games; parlor, conference room, porches. Antique shop. Off-street parking.
Location NE MD. 30 min. S of Wilmington, DE. On Bohemia Ave., between 1st & 2nd St. On Chesapeake and Delaware Canal.
Restrictions No smoking. No children under 10.
Credit cards Amex, Discover, MC, Visa.
Rates B&B, $95–105 double. Extra person, $25. Corporate rates. Off-season packages.

CHESTERTOWN

A quiet Colonial town on the Eastern Shore, Chestertown's area attractions include walking tours of its historic homes, the Eastern Neck Island Wildlife Refuge and the Chesapeake Bay Maritime Museum, while birding, boating, fishing, crabbing, bicycling, hiking, hunting, golf, tennis, and swimming are among the favorite activities. Chestertown is located 90 miles east of Washington, DC; take the Chesapeake Bay Bridge to Route 301 north to Route 213 north.

Reader tip: "The Chestertown area is quiet and peaceful, but not isolated. Lots of historic buildings in town, and a wildlife refuge full of migrating waterfowl (in season), deer, and other creatures. Stay to watch the magnificent sunset from the little one-lane wooden bridge leading into the refuge." *(Brad Freden)*

Information please: For elegant American cuisine and guest rooms lavishly decorated in high Victorian style, try the **Imperial Hotel** (208 High Street, 21620; 410–778–5000). Dating to 1904, the inn was elaborately restored in 1984, and is listed on the National Register of Historic Places. Guest rooms are supplied with towel warmers, terry robes, in-room telephone and TV, and B&B double rates are $125 double, $200–300 suite. The Imperial's restaurant is highly regarded for its fine cuisine and desserts. Comments?

Brampton &   *Tel:* 410–778–1860
25227 Chestertown Road, 21620

Listed on the National Register of Historic Places, Brampton is a handsome red brick Italianate Greek Revival home, owned by Michael and

KEEDYSVILLE

Antietam Overlook Farm *Tel:* 301–432–4200
P.O. Box 30, 21756 800–878–4241

The best of old and new, in a secluded, breathtaking location convenient to major Civil War battlefields, state parks, antique shops, and more, is what you'll find at the Antietam Overlook Farm, built by John and Barbara Dreisch in 1988. This 19th-century reconstruction of a farmhouse and barn combines genuine historic ambiance with the advantages of modern construction, including sound- and fire-proofing and central air-conditioning. Breakfast is served family-style at 9 A.M., and a typically hearty menu includes fresh fruit and juice, just-baked breads and homemade jams, fried ham with Dijon mustard, herbed cheese omelet, home fries with paprika, and Bavarian apple torte.

"Almost every possible comfort (minus TV) for a relaxed getaway. When they built their B&B, Barbara and John anticipated their guests' needs and comforts. The spacious guest rooms have a remote-control gas fireplace, queen-size bed, comfortable chairs, reading lamps on each side of the bed, plus rough-hewn beamed ceilings and walls decorated in blues and greens with Civil War motif prints. Fabrics include beautiful floral print sheets, dust ruffles, comforters, and lace curtains. The dressing area, separated by a wooden trellis, contained a large soaking tub surrounded by plants. The pedestal sink was supplied with quality bath products, including a basket with hair dryer, curling iron, and shaving cream. The large bathroom had a walk-in molded shower with a seat, good water pressure, ample hot water, and a plentiful supply of ultra thick soft towels. Downstairs, Barbara and John have provided their guests with a wet bar, instant hot water for beverages, and a selection of sodas in a stocked full-size refrigerator. The dining area has two large tables, china cabinets with antique china and crystal, and a large array of after-dinner cordials for guests. The spacious sitting room is furnished with plush, comfortable sofas and has a large, beautiful stone wood-burning fireplace surrounded by shelves of books, magazines, and Civil War memorabilia. A wonderful porch, furnished with tables and chairs, overlooks the battlefield and mountains in four adjoining states. Barbara and John are charming and lovely people who keep this B&B incredibly neat and clean. They are delightful to chat with about local attractions and dining arrangements." *(Perri Rappel)*

Open All year.
Rooms 5 doubles—all with private bath and/or shower, gas fireplace, desk, air-conditioning, ceiling fan, porch.
Facilities Great room with breakfast area, fireplace, books, wet bar, guest refrigerator; screened porch. 95 acres with hiking. Canoeing, fishing, tubing, rafting, swimming, golf, skiing, bicycling, hiking nearby.
Location W MD, 1 1/4 hrs W of Washington, DC & Baltimore, MD. 4 m E of Sharpsburg, 8 m E of Shepherdstown, WV.
Restrictions No smoking. Children 13 and over.

Credit cards Amex, DC, Discover, MC, Visa.
Rates B&B, $112–155 double. Extra person, $35. 2-night weekend minimum.
Extras "Baltimorese" spoken.

LUTHERVILLE

Twin Gates   *Tel:* 410–252–3131
308 Morris Avenue, 21093   800–635–0370

A long-time reader favorite, Twin Gates is a Second Empire mansard-roofed Victorian, built in 1857, and owned and operated by Gwen and Bob Vaughan since 1985. Each room is decorated in the theme of one of the Vaughans' favorite locales: the California room, the Cape May room, the Sanibel room, and the Maryland Hunt room. Rates include a full *heart-healthy* breakfast, afternoon wine and cheese, and a warm robe, liqueur, and chocolates at bedtime. Lutherville is a Victorian village, a northern suburb of Baltimore.

"Our spacious room had a comfortable queen-size bed, good reading lights, stocked medicine cabinet, terry bathrobes, and a rubber duckie! The spring garden was fragrant with flowers; a spectacular magnolia tree bloomed outside the dining room window. Gwen's delicious breakfast was beautifully served on fine china. Bob's directions were flawless (maps included)." *(Rick & Janet McNerny)* "We loved the Cape May room, decorated in lavender and periwinkle with white wicker furniture and a beautiful quilt. Outside, the grounds were lush and numerous benches under massive chestnut trees beckoned one to relax." *(Marcia Hostetler)* "Gwen served us tea and chatted with us in the parlor when we arrived. Every possible amenity was provided from fluffy robes in the closet to a clock/radio/tape player with tapes; even our own little Christmas tree during the holidays." *(Rose Cicone)*

"The front porch is furnished with comfortable cushioned wicker furniture and hanging baskets of flowers. Inside, teddy bears line the stairway from the main hall. The Nostalgia Room had antique baby linens, window seats and twin headboards cleverly made from a baby's crib. Homemade oatmeal cookies were set on the bed with the evening turndown. My young sons found the Underground Railroad room on the third floor fascinating; the windows had been left painted over for authenticity. Breakfast was a highlight with baked glazed pears and French toast in the shape of bears." *(Betsy Sandberg)*

Open All year.
Rooms 6 doubles with private bath and/or shower, radio, air-conditioning, ceiling fans, cassette players.
Facilities Living room with fireplace, dining room, greeting room with TV, fireplace. 1½ acres with gardens, magnolia trees. Off-street parking.
Location Suburb 15 min. N of downtown Baltimore. From I-695 (Baltimore Beltway) take Exit 25N (Charles St.). Take immediate right onto Bellona Avenue. In 3 blocks turn left onto Morris Ave. 3 blocks to inn. Light rail transit to Oriole Park, National Aquarium, Harborplace.
Restrictions No smoking. No children under 12.

Credit cards Amex, MC, Visa.
Rates B&B, $95–135 double. 2-night weekend minimum.

NEW MARKET

National Pike Inn   *Tel: 301–865–5055*
9 West Main Street, P.O. Box 299, 21774

Founded in 1793, New Market once served as a stopover for drovers taking their herds to market. Today it's a destination for antiques collectors eager to explore the 30 or so shops of the "Antiques Capital of Maryland." Named for the first federally funded highway in the U.S., the National Pike Inn was converted to an inn by Tom and Terry Rimel in 1986.

"The inn consists of two joined houses: an 1802 Federal House and a smaller 1796 dwelling at the rear. The main sitting room is formally decorated in Wedgwood blue and deep rose with dark birch hardwood floors, an Oriental rug, and handsome reproduction furnishings. The kitchen is accessible to guests and has the original cooking crane in the fireplace. A full breakfast is served at 9 A.M., and consists of pancakes or French toast served with a breakfast meat, cereals, pastries, fruit, and muffins. The house is close to the sidewalk, as are all the houses in town, but the back lot is large and deep with big trees. The Brass Americana room has country pine furniture, bookshelves, a brass queen-size bed, and foot-wide pine floorboards. Two larger rooms are in the 1804 residence, at the front of the house. The Federal Room is decorated in burgundy and white, with a queen-size canopy bed. The pale pink and rose Victorian Room has puffed flower curtains matching the spread on the four poster spindle spool bed." *(SHW)* "Impeccably clean, warm, and cozy. A lovely table setting and tasty breakfast greeted us in the morning." *(Vicki Almond)* "Intelligent, accommodating, down-to-earth innkeepers. We enjoyed talking to Terry at breakfast and learning the history of the house and town." *(GR)* Comments appreciated.

Open All year.
Rooms 1 suite, 4 doubles—3 with full private bath and/or shower, 2 with maximum of 4 people sharing bath. All with air-conditioning. 1 with fan.
Facilities Dining, living room with fireplaces, sitting room with TV, games; courtyard. ½ acre with off-street parking, azalea garden, ice house, smoke house. Tennis nearby.
Location 35 m W of Baltimore on I-70, Exit 62. 6 m E of Frederick. Center of town.
Restrictions Weekday traffic noise in front guest rooms. No smoking. No children under 10 on weekdays, under 12 on weekends.
Credit cards MC, Visa.
Rates B&B, $130–180 suite (sleeps 4), $75–125 double, $65–85 single (weekdays only). 2-night minimum holiday/festival weekends.

OAKLAND

Information please: In western Maryland, 100 miles south of Pittsburgh, is the **Oak & Apple B&B** (208 North Second Street, 21550; 301–334–

9265), named for the handsome trees which shade this 1915 Colonial Revival home. Floral wallpapers, fresh paint, and gleaming woodwork are enhanced by period antiques and reproductions. Four of the simply furnished guest rooms have queen-size beds, while the fifth has a double and a twin; three have private baths. A typical breakfast includes orange juice, granola, strawberries, yogurt, lemon poppyseed bread, and blueberry muffins. Afternoon tea is served by the parlor fireplace or on the sunporch. B&B double rates range from $55–80.

OXFORD

Oxford is located on the Eastern Shore, on Chesapeake Bay, 80 miles southeast of Baltimore, and the same distance east of Washington, DC. From Easton take Route 50 south to Route 333. Go south on Route 333 eleven miles to Oxford. Area activities include tennis, golf, water sports, hunting, and bicycling, although a walking tour of this sleepy town, and an afternoon with a good book, and a sunset stroll along the water, is all most visitors seem to want. Oxford is also the home of one of the oldest ferries in the U.S. The line, which connects Oxford with Bellevue, was started in 1760 by Elizabeth Skinner, who collected her fares in tobacco, the currency of the time.

Information please: "The **1876 House** (110 North Morris Street, P.O. Box 658, 21654; 410–226–5496) is an immaculate and gracious Queen Anne Victorian home. Rooms are decorated in period, and most have Oriental carpets, ten-foot ceilings, and wide-planked pine floors. Breakfast included juice, fresh fruit cup, soft boiled eggs, muffins, and bread." *(Gail Davis)* B&B rates for the three guest rooms range from $81–97. Current comments?

Robert Morris Inn ✕ ⅋.
Morris Street, P.O. Box 70, 21654

Tel: 410–226–5111
Fax: 410–226–5744

The Robert Morris Inn is one of the oldest buildings in one of Maryland's oldest towns. The earliest part of the inn was built prior to 1710 by ships' carpenters using wooden pegged paneling, ships' nails, and hand-hewn beams. Robert Morris, Sr., moved into the house in 1738 and became prominent in the shipping business. His son, Robert Morris, Jr., achieved fame as the financier of the Continental Army during the Revolutionary War.

Long-time owners Wendy and Ken Gibson have expanded the inn to a number of buildings. The Sandaway, built in 1875, located one block away from the inn, offers larger and more luxurious rooms at correspondingly higher rates. The River Rooms overlook the Tred Avon River, and additional rooms are found in several other buildings.

"Our clean, spacious room in Sandaway had a queen-size canopy bed with an incredible view of the Chesapeake Bay. Friendly, accommodating staff; excellent crab cakes and shrimp-and-cheese cakes. Pleasant, quiet, old town with no traffic lights or through traffic." *(Mark Pritchard)* "Obvious care is taken by the owners and staff to keep up the inn and its grounds.

Our room in the original inn was wonderfully appointed and immaculate." *(Gary Cook)* "Beautiful, well-kept grounds, which lend themselves to walking and picnicking. Convenient parking. Our room (separate from the inn) was exceptionally comfortable: clean, well-lit, with two separate sinks, and a great view of the river. Great towels and shower, too." *(Lyman & Marilyn Cohen)* "We looked at the rooms in our price range. We chose one that was very small but comfortable and charming. The bathroom was tiny but had a new shower and tub which worked well. Some fine antiques, especially in the downstairs rooms. Excellent food, nicely presented. Picturesque location, a stone's throw from the Tred Avon River and the tiny ferry which enabled us visit St. Michaels easily. We relaxed on the lovely lawn and enjoyed the peaceful river view." *(Ann McLaughlin)*

Open All year. Restaurant closed mid-January–mid-March.
Rooms 34 doubles—26 with full private bath, 8 with private shower. All rooms with air-conditioning. 9 with porch, 4 with desk. 15 rooms in inn, 8 rooms at Sandaway, 10 rooms in 5 separate buildings.
Facilities 2 sitting rooms with TV, books. Dining room with fireplace. 2½ acres on Tred Avon River with private beach.
Location In town.
Restrictions No smoking. No children under 10.
Credit cards Amex, MC, Visa.
Rates B&B, $70–220 double. 2-night weekend minimum. Alc breakfast, $5–10; alc lunch, $10–20; alc dinner, $20–35. Children's menu.
Extras Wheelchair access to dining room.

ROCK HALL

Named for its once-rich oyster beds, Rock Hall was a typical Chesapeake Bay watermen's village, although its focus is shifting to yachting and tourism; it's known for its excellent seafood restaurants, including Waterman's Crab House Restaurant. Flat quiet roads are good for bicycling, and birders and hikers will enjoy the Eastern Neck Wildlife Refuge. Located on the Eastern Shore, Rock Hall is north of the Chesapeake Bay Bridge, about 12 miles southwest of Chestertown, and one hour from Annapolis.

Information please: Located on a 70-acre working farm, **Huntingfield Manor** (4928 Eastern Neck Road, 21661; 410–639–7779 or 800–720–8788) has been owned by George and Bernie Starkens since 1992. B&B double rates range from $75–105, including a breakfast of fresh fruit and juice, breads, muffins, and biscuits. Comments appreciated.

The Inn at Osprey ✕   *Tel:* 410–639–2194
20786 Rock Hall Avenue, 21661   800–720–8788
          Fax: 410–639–7716

Completed in 1993, the Osprey Point Yacht Club includes a 160-slip marina, the Inn at Osprey, and a restaurant. The inn is a reproduction of the Coke-Garrett House in Williamsburg, with shiplap wooden siding; Susannah Ford is the manager. Rooms are furnished with reproduction

Federal-style furnishings, cherry and pine floors, and Oriental rugs. Most rooms have queen-size four-poster beds, and all are fitted with 250-count pima cotton linens. Breakfast is served between 8 and 10 A.M. and includes bagels, muffins, Danish, fresh fruit, cereal, oatmeal, and tea or freshly ground coffee. Sample dinner entrées in the inn's restaurant include crab cakes (of course), beef tenderloin with onions, and duck with balsamic vinegar.

"Impeccably clean and cozy with a roaring fire in the sitting room fireplace to welcome guests. The grounds are tended with great care. Bicycles are available for a tour of Rock Hall, a friendly little town. Manager Susannah Ford does her job with real zest and caring for her guests. We stayed in the Cotton Blossom Room: comfortable bed, fine linens, good reading lights." *(Amy McAvaddy)* "Fine quality furnishings. Spotless bathroom with quality toiletries. Peaceful location; most guest rooms look out over the marina and the bay beyond. Impeccable service from the entire staff; always helpful and pleasant. We enjoyed a delicious dinner, exquisitely presented." *(Dick & Terry Colgan, also Bob Kenney)*

Open All year. Restaurant closed Jan.–March.
Rooms 1 suite, 6 doubles—all with private bath and/or shower, radio, clock, TV, air-conditioning. 3 with desk, 1 with fireplace, whirlpool tub.
Facilities Restaurant with fireplace, breakfast room with fireplace, pub, sitting area with TV; deck. 30 waterfront acres with off-street parking, swimming pool, lawn games, picnic tables/grills, laundry, nature walks, bicycles, boathouse, dock with marina services. Tennis nearby. Chesapeake Bay for water sports.
Location 1 m N of town. From I-95, take Rte. 896 S from Middletown. Turn right at Rte. 301 S to Chestertown/Galena exit to Rte. 290 S. At Chestertown, turn right onto 291. Go ¼ m to Rte. 20 S, & turn right. Go 12 m to inn on right (1 m past traffic light).
Restrictions Restaurant noise in one guest room.
Credit cards MC, Visa.
Rates B&B, $120–150 suite, $80–130 double. Extra person, $15. Alc dinner $28–32. 2-night minimum holiday weekends. January discount.
Extras Wheelchair access to restaurant. German spoken. Docking privileges.

ST. MICHAELS

Founded in 1632, St. Michaels was a noted shipping center throughout the 1700s. Under British attack during the War of 1812, the townspeople saved their homes by blacking out the town and hanging lanterns in treetops, causing the enemy to overshoot the town. Today, excitement in St. Michaels is more likely to ensue when a neophyte sailor overshoots a buoy, but visitors are attracted to its historic heritage, and the Chesapeake Bay Maritime Museum, devoted to the history of the Bay and its ships.

Reader tip: "A real restaurant find is '208 Talbot.' Subdued atmosphere, quaint, and charming with superlative food." *(Hopie Welliver)* "We were pleased with The Crab Claw, on the water, adjacent to the Maritime Museum." *(RC)*

Information please: The **Kemp House Inn** (412 Talbot Street, Box

638, 21663; 410–745–2243) is a stone house built in 1805. The seven guest rooms are decorated with period antiques, many with four-poster rope beds with trundle beds underneath, patchwork quilts and down pillows. Some have fireplaces, and others share a bath; B&B rates range from $65–90, and second floor rooms tend to be more quiet. Also available is a cottage ($105) with a queen-size four poster bed, cathedral ceiling, and a private terrace. A breakfast of fruit, pastry, and cheese, is brought to the room in a wicker basket between 8–10 A.M. The off-street parking is a plus, the lack of a guest parlor a minus.

For additional area entries, see **Easton, Oxford,** and **Tilghman Island.**

The Inn at Perry Cabin ✗	*Tel:* 410–745–2200
308 Watkins Lane, 21663	800–722–2949
	Fax: 410–745–3348

In 1989, Sir Bernard Ashley, co-founder of the Ashley decorating and clothing business, purchased The Inn at Perry Cabin, making it the first Ashley inn to debut on this side of the Atlantic (for another, see Charlottesville, Virginia). Originally an 18th century Georgian-style farmhouse, the inn sits right on the banks of the Miles River and is surrounded by country gardens. After a $6 million restoration and expansion, familiar Ashley patterns can be found throughout this elegant small hotel, decorating everything from the antique furnishings to the bathroom towels. Rates include a full breakfast, daily newspaper, afternoon tea, in-room mineral water and fresh fruit, and evening turndown service. In addition to fresh-baked croissants, brioches, and muffins, breakfast includes such selections as pancakes and strawberries or smoked salmon omelets with caviar. A typical menu for the five-course prix fixe dinners might be cream of wild mushroom soup, black currant sorbet, salmon with horse radish butter sauce, phyllo basket filled with chocolate mousse and raspberries, coffee and petit fours.

"If you want to be pampered (and can afford it) this is the place. Our room was small for the price, but charming, clean, and comfortable. Fresh flowers and fruit, cookies, mineral water, and a full ice bucket awaited our arrival; small pastries were placed at our bedside at night. The breakfast menu was extensive and the food delicious; and we were served an elegant high tea in one of the sitting rooms that overlook the gardens and river." *(Maryann DiMartino)* "Sprawling and elegant, from its splendid location at the end of a long road to the finest of china and silver in the dining room. Definitely at the top of its class, for which you pay dearly. Truly luxurious." *(Hopie Welliver)* "Warm and cordial reception, despite our somewhat informal attire." *(RC)*

Open All year.
Rooms 41 doubles—all with full private bath, telephone, TV, air-conditioning.
Facilities Restaurant, sitting room, veranda, conference room; indoor heated pool, sauna, steam room, exercise room. 27 acres with gardens, croquet, docking facilities, bicycles. Golf, tennis, hunting, swimming, sailing nearby.
Location Eastern Shore, 50 m E of Baltimore, Washington, DC. ¼ m from town. On Miles River.
Restrictions No children under 10.

Credit cards Amex, DC, MC, Visa.
Rates B&B, $400–500 suite, $150–475 double. Alc lunch, $15–30. Prix fixe dinner, $50.
Extras Docking privileges.

St. Michaels Harbour Inn & Marina ♦ ✕ ♿   *Tel:* 410–745–9001
101 North Harbor Road, 21663   800–955–9001
                                         Fax: 410–745–9501

Spread in a wide "V" right along the harbor, most guest rooms in this harbor-side hotel have wonderful water views of the Miles River and Chesapeake Bay beyond, and many have balconies from which to enjoy them. Built in 1986, the Harbour Inn is a three-story gabled structure with gray clapboard siding; Cynthia Long is the manager. The Lighthouse Restaurant has an equally good harbor view, and serves breakfast, lunch and dinner. Chesapeake Bay seafood and Eastern Shore specialties are featured, with crab-spinach tortellini, oysters Talbot, crab cakes, and Eastern Shore duck appearing on the dinner menu. "Attractive inn; appealing location; good, firm bed." *(Hope Welliver)* "Fine restaurant." *(RC)* Comments welcome.

Open All year. Restaurant closed Mon., Tues. from Dec.–Feb.
Rooms 38 suites, 8 doubles—all with full private bath, telephone, radio, clock, TV, desk, air-conditioning, fan. Most with refrigerator, balcony.
Facilities Restaurant, bar/lounge, lobby, fitness center, conference rooms, guest laundry, deck. Piano music in restaurant on weekends. Picnic area, off-street parking, swimming pool, bicycle rentals, marina with dock slips, marine services, boat rentals. On Chesapeake Bay for water sports. Tennis, golf nearby.
Location Eastern Shore, town center, 65 mi SE of Baltimore. Take Rte. 50 to Easton. Go E on Rte. 33 to St. Michaels. Walking distance to village.
Restrictions No smoking in restaurant, public areas, some guest rooms.
Credit cards All major.
Rates Room only, $159–375 suite, $149–299 double, $109–179 single. Extra person, $12. Children under 18 stay free in parents' room. 2-night weekend minimum May–Oct. Weekend packages. Alc breakfast, $6; alc lunch, $10; alc dinner, $25–35.
Extras Wheelchair access; bathroom equipped for disabled. Free local airport pickup; docking privileges. Crib. French, Portuguese spoken.

Wades Point Inn ♦ &   *Tel:* 410–745–2500
Wades Point Road, McDaniel, 21663
Mailing address: P.O. Box 7, St. Michaels, 21663

Bordered on three sides by the Chesapeake Bay, the Wades Point Inn is an old-fashioned Eastern Shore guest house with wonderful water views from most rooms. Thomas Kemp—a Baltimore shipwright known for his speedy clipper ships—built the original Georgian structure in 1819. In 1890, the Kemp family expanded the house to accommodate visitors fleeing the big-city summer heat for cooling bay breezes. The inn stayed in the Kemp family until 1984, when it was purchased by John and Betsy Feiler. Accommodations are available in the Main House, the 1890 Victorian Summer Wing, and the Mildred Kemp building. A buffet breakfast of fruit salad, juice, cheeses, fresh-baked rolls and muffins is served from 8 to 10 A.M.

"A porch wraps around the first and second floors of the main house, and has ample rocking chairs. After we checked in, we helped ourselves to the pitcher of ice water (tea was also available) in the beautiful, sunny, large breakfast room that faces the bay. The largest guest room has a lovely four-poster bed and a single sleigh bed, antiques, and beautifully restored hardwood floors. We also liked the two simply furnished rooms at the end of the hall; they share a bath, have beautiful water views, and are close to the door leading to the porch. You can hear the sound of the waves at night. The rooms in the main house are not air-conditioned, but there was a constant breeze off the bay." *(Lori Sampson)* "Wonderful location right on the bay." *(Donna Bocks)*

Open March–Dec.
Rooms 24 doubles—15 with private bath, 9 with maximum of 4 people sharing bath. Some with desk, air-conditioning, refrigerator, kitchenette, porch/balcony. 9 rooms in main house, 15 in 2 other buildings.
Facilities Breakfast room, lobby with fireplace, living room with piano, games, books; screened porches, balconies. 120 acres with 2,000-foot bay waterfront, tree swing, hammocks, lawn games, nature trail, fishing pond, dock for fishing, crabbing. Golf, boating, bicycling nearby.
Location Eastern Shore. Halfway between St. Michaels & Tilghman Island. Take Rte. 50 to Easton & exit onto Rte. 322 (Easton Pkwy). Follow sign to St. Michaels via Rte. 33. Continue on Rte. 33 for 5 m beyond St. Michaels to Wades Pt. Rd. Turn right & go to end.
Restrictions No smoking. Children over age 1.
Credit cards MC, Visa.
Rates B&B, $80–175 double. Children under 12 free in parents' room. Extra person, $10. 15% midweek senior discount or 10% discount for 3-night stay. 2-night weekend minimum. Tips appreciated.
Extras Wheelchair access; some rooms equipped for disabled. Crib.

SHARPSBURG

For an additional area entry, see **Keedysville** and **Shepherdstown, West Virginia**.

Inn at Antietam   *Tel:* 301–432–6601
220 East Main Street, P.O. Box 119, 21782   *Fax:* 301–432–5981

This turn-of-the-century Victorian home has been owned and run by Cal and Betty Fairbourn since 1984. "This large restored home with a wrap-around porch borders Antietam Cemetery and the historic Antietam Battlefield, site of the bloodiest day of the Civil War. The tiny town of Sharpsburg is just a short walk down the road. The inn is beautiful with wide-plank hardwood floors and antiques. There's a sun room at the side of the house supplied with coffee, homemade cookies and a fruit bowl. The sitting room had a decanter of brandy and glasses set out for guests to help themselves. We stayed in the Master Suite with attractive floral wallpaper, coordinated fabrics, and a beautiful high four-poster antique cherry wood bed. Chocolates were placed by the bed. A delicious break-fast of bacon, homemade waffles topped with fresh blueberries and powdered sugar, plus orange juice and coffee was served in the dining room on antique china and silverware." *(Lori Sampson)* "A basket of freshly picked apples waited at the door. The porch, brick patio, and backyard garden are quiet, peaceful spots to relax, providing views of the countryside and Blue Ridge Mountains beyond. We stayed in the Bluebird Suite, appropriately named for the charming bluebird wallpaper and down comforter on a four-poster bed piled with big fluffy pillows on a comfortable, firm mattress. Our private bath was immaculately scrubbed and supplied with an array of toiletries including an herbal bath that made mounds of bubbles. The Fairbourns provided pleasant conversation, charming anecdotes, and perfectly appropriate dining recommendations. They remained discreetly attentive yet completely unobtrusive." *(Alissa Lash)*

Open All year. Closed Dec. 20–Jan. 1.
Rooms 4 suites—all with private bath, 1 with tub only. All with air-conditioning, 1 with TV, 3 with desk.
Facilities Sitting room, sun-room, dining room, porches. 8½ acres with patio, gardens. Fishing, swimming, hiking, bicycling, cross-country skiing nearby.
Location W MD. 4 m E of Shepherdstown, WV. 13 m from intersection of I-70 and I-81. From Washington or Baltimore, take I-70 to Braddock Heights, Exit 49 & turn left to Alt Rte. 40 W. Go W through Middletown & Boonsboro to Rte. 34. Turn left onto Rte. 34, 6 m to Sharpsburg. Approaching Sharpsburg, the Antietam Battlefield Cemetery is on left; inn just past it.
Restrictions No smoking. "Well-mannered children over age 6 are welcome."
Credit cards Amex.
Rates B&B, $95–105 suite. Extra person, $25. No tipping. 2-night weekend, holiday minimum.
Extras Airport/station pickup, $25.

SNOW HILL

Snow Hill is located on the Eastern Shore, about 12 miles north of the Virginia border, 20 miles southwest of Ocean City, 90 miles south of Wilmington, Delaware, and 130 miles southeast of Baltimore.

Reader tips: "Founded in 1642, Snow Hill is a pretty, quiet little harbor town on the Pocomoke River, with over 100 historic homes; its sidewalks are made with bricks used as ballast in the early English sailing ships." *(Dr. Gunter Born)* "A fantastic area for canoeing, bicycling, and birding; ocean beaches within a ten-mile drive." *(Marilyn Stone)* "Best crab cakes ever at the Snow Hill Inn." *(BJ Hensley)*

Chanceford Hall
209 West Federal Street, 21863

Tel: 410–632–2231

Michael and Thelma Driscoll opened Chanceford Hall as a B&B in 1986, after completing a major restoration of their Georgian-style home, built in 1759 and now listed on the National Register of Historic Places. The inn is decorated with period antiques and reproductions, lots of comfortable wing chairs, canopied beds, and handmade quilts.

"Charming hosts. Mr. Driscoll is an amazing furniture and cabinet maker; each room has examples of his fine reproductions. The gracious hospitality included wine and hors d'oeuvres the evening of our arrival and a bounteous breakfast in the morning." *(Sally Truitt)* "The grounds are private and beautifully landscaped, the parking plentiful. The house is impeccably clean, with effective central air-conditioning and heating. The plumbing and wiring are all new, the lighting excellent." *(M.A. Filippino)* "The original paneling, moldings, mantels, and plank flooring have been renovated with a cabinet maker's skill." *(John Callander)*

"Our fireplace had a carefully laid fire ready to light. We settled into our room and were brought tea and cookies. The Driscolls recommended an excellent seafood place for dinner. We were most impressed with the flexibility of breakfast times, and their sensitivity to our dietary requests. The plumbing was in fine working order, the street silent, the bed firm with lighting on both sides. Parking is under cover, and we were given a map and ferry timetables for our trip north." *(Ellie & Bob Freidus)* "Our room had a four-poster canopy bed (made by Mr. Driscoll), a free-standing wooden mirror, and down comforter. Outstanding breakfast (served until 11 A.M.), of fresh fruit, muffins, eggs, potatoes, sausage, English muffins, bacon, honey butter, and coffee." *(Wendy Hancock)*

Open All year.
Rooms 1 suite, 4 doubles—all with private shower and/or bath, air-conditioning, desk. 4 with fireplace.
Facilities Dining room, kitchen, living room all with fireplace. Solarium/family room with TV/VCR, stereo, books, games. 1½ acres with lap pool, bicycles. Pocomoke River for canoeing. 6 m to Chincoteague Bay, 30 min. to Chincoteague, Assateague National Wildlife Refuge. Golf, tennis, swimming nearby.
Location Historic district.
Restrictions No children under 12.
Credit cards None accepted.
Rates B&B, $130 suite, $110–120 double. Extra person in suite, $15. Prix fixe dinner, $110 for 2 (prior notice required).
Extras Airport/station/dockside pickup.

The River House Inn ♠♠   Tel: 410–632–2722
201 East Market Street, 21863   Fax: 410–632–2866

A rambling white house with black shutters and elaborate gingerbread and wrought iron trim, The River House dates back to 1835, and was restored by owners Larry and Susanne Knudsen in 1991. While the house fronts on Snow Hill's main street, the back yard slopes down to the Pocomoke River, where herons, osprey, eagles, and hawks can often be spotted.

"A superlative B&B. Our cottage room overlooked the lawns and river. The Knudsens were most helpful with area information and dining suggestions." *(BJ Hensley)* "Guest rooms are lovingly restored and exquisitely appointed. Larry and Susanne are superb innkeepers and gracious hosts. Equally inviting are the gardens and lawns stretching down to the river, with deck chairs perfect for wine, cheese, and conversation." *(Rod & Sue Welles)* "The Little House next to the inn is ideal for families." *(Mindi Thalenfeld)* "Lots of wonderful porches. Two matching, well behaved standard poodles romp the grounds and greet the guests." *(Marilyn Stone)* "The rooms are of ample size, bright, clean, with good private baths. Adequate parking in an excellent location." *(Joan Heiss)*

"Breakfast was served in a beautiful room overlooking the rear lawn and the river. We watched the birds at nearby feeders, and chose our breakfast from a menu recited by Larry: our choice of eggs, French toast, waffles, or the daily special, accompanied by bacon or sausage, and home-baked eggs. Coffee (decaf and regular) was on the table, as well as hot water for tea. Juice and fruit compote waited on a corner buffet. Larry was attentive, introducing us to other guests seated at the next table, and was available to answer any questions. We returned around 5 P.M. after a day of exploring to find most guests in the library, enjoying wine and snacks, listening to Larry and Susanne explain the history of the house. All of the guests introduced themselves, and we felt we were in the company of friends; the conversation was lively, intelligent and informative." *(Michael Maloney & Carole DeSalvo)* "The inn is decorated in the Georgian, Federal, and early Victorian styles appropriate to its age. The Colonial Room has a fishnet canopy bed and fireplace. The bath has a pedestal sink and a clawfoot tub with a hand-held shower." *(Larissa & Michael Milne)*

Open All year.

Rooms 2 suites, 7 doubles—all with private bath and/or shower, clock, air-conditioning. Some with desk, ceiling fan, fireplace (gas or wood), porch. Rooms in Main House, Little House, and River Cottage.

Facilities Dining room, living room, library with TV/VCR, stereo; all with fireplace. Screened, unscreened porches. 2 acres with fish ponds, gardens, swings, hammock, off-street parking, lawn games; bicycles. On river for fishing, canoeing; 15 min. to ocean beaches. Golf, boating nearby. Canoeing, bicycling, birding packages.

Location 1 block from center. From Baltimore, take U.S. Rte. 50 E across Bay Bridge and down Eastern shore. Continue through Salisbury to U.S. Rte. 13. Go S on Rte. 13 about 2.5 m to MD Rte. 12 to Snow Hill. Go over bridge & turn left at light onto Market St.

Restrictions No smoking. Light sleepers should request back rooms.

Credit cards MC, Visa.

Rates B&B, $129 cottage, $89–129 suite and double, $59–119 single. Midweek business rate. Extra adult, $20; extra child, $10. 5% AAA, senior discount. 2-night minimum holiday or summer weekends.

Extras Wheelchair access to cottage; bathroom specially equipped. Crib, babysitting. Docking privileges.

SOLOMONS

Back Creek Inn   *Tel:* 410–326–2022
A & Calvert Streets, P.O. Box 520, 20688

With a fine deep water harbor, Solomons has long been known as a boating and fishing center. The Calvert Marine Museum is a good place to get a feeling for the region's maritime history.

The Back Creek Inn is a century-old waterman's home, restored as a B&B by Carol Pennock and Lin Cochran. Guest rooms are decorated with antiques, handmade quilts and fresh bouquets from the inn's herb and floral gardens. Rates include your choice of a full or continental breakfast.

"Solomon's Island is a picturesque town appealing to anyone who likes water, boats and the smell of the sea. The garden was a comfortable place to have coffee and read the newspaper or watch the procession of boats drift from Back Creek into the Patuxent River. Attention to detail included the freshly cut flowers, scented soaps, and terry robes in each room. Our hostess advised us on points of interest, then mapped out directions for us." *(Margaret Sullivan)* "Charming and clean, delicious breakfast. The Peppermint Suite has a stunning view of the pier and water." *(Gloria King)* "The beautiful garden provides a charming entrance to the inn. The decor is appealing, with a sun room with stenciled walls, exposed beams, and wicker furniture." *(Marci Spanitz)*

Open All year.
Rooms 1 cottage, 2 suites, 4 doubles—all with private bath and/or shower. 3 with TV, 2 with fireplace.
Facilities Breakfast room, sun room. Deck with hot tub, patio, gardens. On water with pier. Bicycles.
Location W shore of Chesapeake Bay. 90 min. S of DC. Take Rte. 4 S to Solomons. Go left just before Gov. Thos. Johnson Bridge. Go approx. 1/2 m, go left onto A St., just before Catholic Church. Inn at foot of A St.
Restrictions No smoking. Children 12 and over.
Credit cards Not accepted.
Rates B&B, $140 cottage, $120 suite, $85 double. Extra person, $15. Government, corporate rate. Discount for 3-night stay.
Extras Pier with 2 deep water slips; phone for availability.

TANEYTOWN

For an additional area entry (very different in style and price), see **Thurmont.**

Antrim 1844	*Tel: 410–756–6812*
30 Trevanion Road	800–858–1844
	Fax: 410–756–2744

When Richard and Dorothy Mollett first saw Antrim in 1988, this antebellum plantation house, built in 1844, had been deserted for 60 years and was in shambles. It scarcely resembled the house that General Meade used during the Civil War, when he ascended to the widow's walk to observe Confederate troop movements during the Battle of Gettysburg. Even less did it resemble the beautifully restored and refurbished Antrim of today. Combining antebellum grace with European style, the inn is elegantly furnished with Sheraton and Federal antiques dating from 1750 to 1840, set off by the Oriental rugs on the original pine floors, 14-foot ceilings with elaborate moldings and medallions, and tall windows.

Guests start the day with muffins, coffee, and the newspaper, set on a tray outside the door at 8 A.M., followed by formal breakfast served in the mansion dining room from 9 to 10 A.M.; Belgian waffles with fresh berries are a favorite. Rates also include afternoon tea, evening hors d'oeuvres, and turndown service with a fresh rose and chocolates. In fine weather, dinner may be offered on the veranda overlooking the formal gardens; during the cooler months, dinner is served in what was originally the smokehouse, summer kitchen, and slave kitchen, with rough brick floors and large fireplaces. The five-course prix fixe dinner includes a choice of three entrées and desserts.

"Beautifully restored, exceptional accommodations, convenient location. The guest rooms are lushly decorated with Laura Ashley and Waverly fabrics and wallcoverings; ours had a queen-size canopy bed with a featherbed." *(LuAnn & Steve Weiner)* "Fabulous dinner, excellent value, wonderful atmosphere. The restaurant is a separate building, so it doesn't detract from the marvelous common rooms in the inn." *(Diane Wolf)*

Suggestion: "If offered a brandy after dinner, inquire about the cost."

Open All year.

Rooms 5 suites, 9 doubles—all with private bath and/or shower, air-conditioning. Some with desk, double whirlpool tub, fireplace, balcony. Telephone, clock/radio on request. Suites in 3 outbuildings.

Facilities Restaurant, dining room, drawing rooms with fireplace, piano; library, pub with fireplace, games, TV; conference room/business services. Piano music Sat. nights. 24 acres with off-street parking, swimming pool, gardens, tennis court, putting green, gazebo, lawn games.

Location N central MD. Catoctin Mts. 12 m S of Gettysburg, PA, 40 m W of Baltimore, 70 m N of Washington DC. From Baltimore, take I-695 Beltway to Exit 19. Go N on Rte. 795. Exit onto Rte. 140 W. Go through Westminster to Taneytown. Turn left on Trevanion Road & go 150' to inn on right.

Restrictions No smoking. Children permitted in cottages.

Credit cards Amex, MC, Visa.

Rates B&B, $150–300 suite, double. Extra person, $50. MAP, prix fixe dinner, $50. Midweek packages. 2-night weekend minimum.

Extras Restaurant wheelchair accessible. Airport, station pickup, $50–100. Crib, babysitting with notice.

THURMONT

For an additional area entry *(very* different in style and price), see **Taneytown.**

Cozy Country Inn ♾
103 Frederick Road (Route 806)

Tel: 301–271–4301
Fax: 301–271–4301

Have you ever wondered where the press stays when the President of the U.S. helicopters from the White House to Camp David in the Catoctin Mountains? At the Cozy Inn, that's where. Since its founding in 1929 by Willie Freeze, the Cozy (as it is known) has grown from a gas station and 12-stool lunch counter to a sizable industry, encompassing a 700-seat restaurant, the inn, and a village of antique, specialty, and craft shops. Still family owned and operated, the inn's guest rooms and cottages are decorated to commemorate the style of the Presidents and dignitaries who have visited nearby Camp David or the inn itself. On weekdays, rates include a breakfast of juice, fruit, cereal, homemade breads and hot beverages; on weekends, the restaurant serves an extensive breakfast buffet.

"Our room was comfortable and spotless; the staff friendly and attentive." *(Carol Berman)* "The handsome Franklin Roosevelt room has a king-size bed, gas fireplace, and a sitting area. The bath had a whirlpool tub, towel warmer, makeup mirror and separate shower." *(Karen & David Hagins)* "Check-in was fast, friendly and efficient. Great buffet dinner in the restaurant." *(Richard & Deborah Miller)* "Our executive suite had a fireplace, 25-inch TV/VCR, and refrigerator." *(Rolland Artel)* "Not your usual country inn, but an excellent value for food and lodging." *(MW)*

Open All year.
Rooms 5 cottages, 4 suites, 11 doubles—all with private bath and/or shower, telephone, radio, clock, TV, air-conditioning, refrigerator. Some with desk, deck, gas fireplace, whirlpool tub, kitchen, VCR.
Facilities Restaurant, bar/lounge with fireplace, breakfast room, game room, conference rooms, arboretum dining area. 4 acres with swimming pool, off-street parking, village of shops. Tennis, golf, lake, cross-country skiing, hiking nearby. 14 m to downhill skiing.
Location W MD. Catoctin Mts. 60 mi NW of Washington DC. Town center. From Washington, take Rte. 270 N to Frederick. Take Rte. 15N to first Thurmont Exit. Go 5 blks on Rte. 806 to inn.
Restrictions No smoking in lobby, some guest rooms. No children in Executive rooms. Traffic noise in one room.
Credit cards Amex, DC, MC, Visa.
Rates B&B, $85–135 suite, $50–75 double. Extra person, $4. Children under 12 stay free. 10% Senior, AAA discount. Weekend breakfast, $6. Alc lunch, $6; alc dinner, $18. 15% service charge. Children's menu.
Extras Limited wheelchair access. Pets allowed in some guest rooms with approval. Crib. Sign language, German spoken.

TILGHMAN ISLAND

Reader tips: "We had a good dinner at Harrison's, right on the drawbridge." *(Hope Welliver)* "Excellent dinner at Bay One Hundred, right by the drawbridge as you approach the island, with large windows overlooking the water." *(RC)*

Information please: For complete R&R, consider the **Black Walnut Inn** (P.O. Box 308, 21671; 410–886–2452) overlooking Chesapeake Bay, with a wildlife sanctuary to explore and a swimming pool and tennis court to enjoy. Dating back to the mid-1800s, the inn has seven guest rooms, with double rates of $110–160, including a continental breakfast.

Chesapeake Wood Duck Inn	*Tel:* 410–886–2070
Gibsontown Road, P.O. Box 202, 21671	800–956–2070
	Fax: 410–886–2263

Those of you who aren't finished exploring until you've come to road's end will enjoy the location of Tilghman Island, a picturesque Chesapeake Bay island offering the charm of a 19th century waterman's village. Built as a boarding house in 1890, the inn functioned as a bordello during the steamboats' heyday, then later as a waterman's family residence. In 1991, its restoration was completed by owners Dave and Stephanie Feith, who decided it was time to leave their Atlanta home and jobs as Fortune 500 company executives to start new lives as innkeepers.

The Wood Duck overlooks Dogwood Harbor, home of the Skipjacks (oyster boats), the last commercial sailing fleet left in America. You can watch them from the screened porch at breakfast, from the deck in the afternoon, or from your room. Breakfast is an event at the Wood Duck; a recent menu included fresh berries and melon topped with Sabayon sauce; a ham omelet enclosed in puff pastry, topped with mustard sauce; corkscrew bacon; and lemon poppyseed muffins.

"While David showed us around, Stephanie made us some mint ice tea to go with David's cookies. Our lovely room was done in pinks and greens, with a view of the water and skipjack docks. It had a painted iron double bed, an antique oak dresser, small wing chair, and was accented with lovely dried and fresh flower arrangements, small antique china pieces, and prints. The bathroom had a variety of toiletries, along with plenty of towels, and an unusually pretty medicine cabinet. We had access to snacks and cold drinks; coffee and tea were always available. Breakfast included fresh fruit, David's just-baked low-fat raisin bran muffins, and crab quiche." *(Rose Ciccone)*

"Our breakfasts were served elegantly in the dining room or on the porch overlooking the harbor." *(Carol & Wayne Petty)* "Dave and Stephanie are as much a reason to return as the lure of the Chesapeake, the wonderful food, the charming decor, and the relaxing atmosphere. Dave and Stephanie arranged for us to sail on a skipjack, a memorable experience." *(Maureen Achey)* "Exceptional cleanliness and attention to detail by innkeepers who are directly involved in all aspects of running their inn. At my husband's request, Dave arranged for him to go crabbing with some of the local watermen, the highlight of his vacation." *(Julie Davis)*

Suggestion box: "A reading lamp and table for my side of the bed."

Open All year.

Rooms 6 doubles—all with private bath and/or shower, clock, air-conditioning, ceiling fan.

Facilities Dining room, living room with fireplace, family room with TV/VCR, stereo, books. Screened, unscreened porches, deck. 1 acre on harbor with off-street parking, lawn games, fishing, boat ramp. Bicycles (1 tandem), fishing gear. Privileges at Harbourtowne Country Club for swimming, tennis, fitness center, golf. Fishing, hunting, charters; horseback riding. Kayaking, sunset sails.

Location Eastern Shore. 80 m E of Baltimore/Washington DC; 140 m S of Philadelphia. 15 min. to St. Michaels. From Rte. 50 E, take Rte. 322 to Rte. 33. Follow Rte. 33 through St. Michaels to Tilghman Island. After bridge, go left on Gibsontown Rd. Walking distance to shops, restaurants.

Restrictions No smoking. Children over 13.

Credit cards MC, Visa.

Rates B&B, $115–135 double. 2-night weekend minimum in season.

New Jersey

The Queen Victoria, Cape May

Those who have seen New Jersey only from the turnpike have given the state a bad reputation. Others, familiar with Atlantic City and the more raucous beach towns, assume that it simply is not their sort of place. In truth, the state has quite a lot more to offer. Gracious beach resorts are found from Bay Head to Spring Lake to Cape May; many pleasant country towns along the Delaware River invite you to relax and explore; and shoppers may find Nirvana in the bargain shops of Flemington. To the south, the Pine Barrens include lush marsh and woodlands, in the northwest, New Jersey shares the impressive Delaware Water Gap National Recreation area with Pennsylvania. Since this is the "Garden State," be sure to stop by one of the region's most impressive horticultural centers: Leaming's Run Gardens in Swainton (5 miles north of Cape May) has 25 different gardens spread over 50 acres.

Most inns at beach resorts provide beach badges or passes to guests, which eliminates the need for guests to buy expensive nonresident passes; a deposit is commonly charged to ensure their return. Two- and three-night minimums are the rule in most beach towns and resorts.

ABSECON HIGHLANDS

White Manor Inn ¢   *Tel: 609–748–3996*
739 South Second Avenue, 08201   *Fax: 609–652–0073*

In 1932, Howard Bensel, Sr. built a sturdy, spacious four-square farmhouse
with nine-foot ceilings and a six-foot wide hallway running the length of
the house. The house was moved in the 1950s to accommodate the
Garden State Parkway; it later was used as a preschool, and in 1993, was
purchased and remodeled as a B&B by Howard Bensel, Jr. and his wife
Anna Mae. Howard reports that "our guests are amazed at how quiet our
B&B is given its convenient location. Extensive renovations, inside and
out, have made the inn quiet, cozy, and comfortable. We are very flexible
about check-in times and make every effort to accommodate our guests'
schedules and needs." Howard learned his carpentry skills from his father
and was able to do much of the renovation work himself. A breakfast of
garden-fresh fruit and juice, cereal, and such home-baked treats as blueberry buckle or strawberry muffins is served at guests' choice of time.
Rates also include an afternoon or evening treat of home-baked cookies
or cake.

"The inn is just off the Garden State Parkway, in a convenient location
for 'country gamblers.' Howard and Anna Mae are friendly folks who
made us feel relaxed and comfortable. They are know the area and keep
current on local points of interest. The well-lit sitting room has plenty of
reading material; guest rooms are simply furnished with traditional pieces
and wall-to-wall carpeting." *(John & Lillie Galvin)* "Spacious room, comfortable bed. Delicious sour cream coffee cake with chocolate chips and
walnuts." *(Michele Forsythe)* "The rooms, bathrooms and grounds of the
inn were impeccable. Just wish I'd been here during strawberry season."
(Daniel Birch)

Open All year.
Rooms 1 suite, 6 doubles—5 with private bath, 2 with shared bath with a
maximum of 4 people sharing bath. All with air-conditioning. 5 with ceiling fan,
2 with bath. Telephone, radio, clock on request.
Facilities Dining room, living room, family room with TV/VCR, guest refrigera-
tor. 1 acre with off-street parking, flower & vegetable gardens, lawn seating. 10
min. to beach. Golf nearby.
Location SE NJ, 10 m W of Atlantic City. From Garden St. Pky. S, take Exit 40.
Go 2 blks, make U-turn at 3rd Ave. Go W 1 block & turn right on 2nd Ave. Go
1/2 blk to inn on left.
Restrictions No smoking.
Credit cards None accepted.
Rates B&B, $120–160 suite (sleeps 4), $48–85 double. 2-3 night weekend/holi-
day minimum.
Extras Free airport/station pickup.

ALLOWAY

Josiah Reeve House Tel: 609–935–5640
P.O. Box 501, 08001 Fax: 609–935–5640
North Greenwich Street

Inland from the Delaware Bay and the old Quaker settlement of Salem lies the little village of Alloway, amid wetlands that enabled it to play a part in the shipping boom of the early 19th century. In 1836 Josiah Reeve, engineer and shipbuilder, designed a grand home in the Greek Revival style, just across the street from his boatyard; he built it of red brick, with white trim, massive double chimneys, and an unusual free-standing spiral staircase. In 1988, Paul and Judith D'Esterre restored the home and, to illustrate those earlier days, hand painted scenes of the village on the hallway walls. Breakfast is served in the dining room or on the patio; a recent menu included fresh-squeezed orange juice, cantaloupe and strawberries, herbed egg souffle, and sweet potato muffins.

"Warm hospitality from Paul and Judy; charming, beautifully appointed rooms. Delicious hors d'oeuvres and breakfast." *(Doris Ackerman)* "We enjoyed a reasonably priced dinner at Newport House, an old fishing shack near the Delaware River." *(Mary Chamberlin & Mark Commander)* "No stuffiness or stiff formality, despite the beautiful antiques. The pets in residence are delightful: two dogs, a cat, and a pot-bellied little pig named 'Truffles.'" *(Kathy Kerr & Sheldon Coad)* "Our bathroom had a free-standing claw-foot tub, various toiletries, a shower with brass fittings, soft terry robes, and even a hair dryer. We spent a delightful day exploring the nearby historic town of Odessa." *(Maryann & Tony DiMartino)* "The French Suite was elegant and romantic; furnishings are antique, but lighting and plumbing work like new. Classical music, stacks of books, and a beautiful garden terrace with a fountain all added to the ambience. Although the house sits right next to the road, tall boxwood hedges block the sight of traffic." *(Brenda Lepley)*

Open All year.
Rooms 1 suite, 3 doubles—2 with private bath, 2 with a maximum of 4 sharing bath. All with radio, air-conditioning, fireplace.
Facilities Living room with TV, 2 fireplaces, piano, books; dining room with fireplace, unscreened porch. Gardens with patio, fountain. Bicycles. Golf nearby. Lake nearby for fishing; pedal boat, rowboat.
Location SE NJ. Salem County. In village. From Woodstown, go S on Woodstown-Alloway Rd. to stop sign at Rte. 581. Turn right to light at center of town. Turn right to inn at bottom of hill. From DE Memorial Bridge, take last exit before toll on NJ Tpke (Atlantic City exit). Bear right at light on Rte. 540. Follow Rte. 540 to Alloway. Inn on left before going up hill to traffic light in center of town.
Restrictions No smoking. Children 16 and over.
Credit cards MC, Visa.
Rates B&B, $95 suite, $80–85 double. Corporate rates midweek. No tipping.

AVON-BY-THE-SEA

For additional area entries, see **Belmar** and **Spring Lake.**

Information please: Built at the turn of the century, the **Cashelmara Inn** (22 Lakeside Avenue, P.O. Box 223, 07717; 908–776–8727 or 800–821–2976) overlooks a swan lake on one side and the ocean on the other. Guest rooms are decorated with Laura Ashley prints and period antiques. Breakfast favorites include omelets, scrambled eggs, French toast, or fruit-filled pancakes, accompanied by bacon or sausage. B&B rates for the twelve doubles range from $75–105.

BAY HEAD

Only an hour away from New York City, Bay Head offers a quick trip back to the turn of the century. The town was developed in 1879 by a group of wealthy Princeton men as a summer retreat for their families; many homes are still owned by these families. Bay Head has no neon signs, no supermarkets, no movie theaters, no parking meters, and no fast-food restaurants. It does have beautiful, uncrowded beaches and Victorian summer "cottages" and gardens. Some find it relaxing, others think it dull; nearly all agree that it's pretty. Area activities include swimming, fishing, sailing, windsurfing, tennis, and golf.

Bay Head is located 60 miles south of New York City via the Garden State Parkway, and 65 miles east of Philadelphia.

Reader tips: "Families will enjoy visiting nearby Point Pleasant, with a wonderful boardwalk and amusement area." *(CM)* Also: "Most of Bay Head's inns are on Main Avenue, a busy thoroughfare in peak season; ask for a quiet room if you are a light sleeper."

Information please: Bay Head's first B&B, **Conover's Bay Head Inn** (646 Main Avenue, 08742; 908–892–4664) has been operated by Carl and Beverly Conover since 1970. They describe it as "a small place where we can pay attention to detail. We try to equip the twelve rooms, all with private bath, as you would a guest room in your own home. Everything is home-baked for a hearty breakfast each day, and during the winter, afternoon tea is served." One reader described it as "beautifully decorated with antique furnishings, canopied beds, flowers, ruffles, and hand-stenciled walls, with attentive innkeepers and delicious food." *(Mrs. Michael Cromis).* Double rates range from $90–210.

Bay Head Gables	Tel: 908–892–9844
200 Main Avenue, 08742	Fax: 908–295–2196

An elaborate Georgian-style cedar-shake "cottage," the Gables has been owned by Don Haurie and Ed Laubusch since 1984. Built in 1914 and attributed to architect Stanford White, the three-story inn has Art Deco furnishings; guests are welcome to relax on the overstuffed chairs and couches of the art-filled living room. Guest rooms in the front have ocean views; rear ones overlook the lake. Breakfast is served on the enclosed porch, or in the formal dining room in the cooler months; one morning there might be poached pears with pistachio sauce, Norwegian salmon omelet with potatoes Murphy; on another, warm grapefruit sections with honey and blueberries, and apple-walnut, orange-banana, raspberry, blueberry or plain buttermilk pancakes.

"The innkeepers have made a dramatic design statement, with each room done in a different style. The Art Deco living room contrasts with the period dining room. Guest rooms range from the Southwestern Room to the Paisley room, with paisley wallcoverings, spread, curtains, and towels. Another room is painted in Oriental yellows and reds—magnificent with lacquer pieces. The largest room on the second floor was Art Deco, in black and chrome with mirrors and its own porch. The Victorian Room is done in laces and flowers with a half-canopy over the bed." *(Rose Ciccone)* "Don was great when I called for reservations, describing each room's decor and location; the confirming letter was clear and personal. Don, Ed, and Eileen were helpful and welcoming innkeepers." *(Wilma & Jack Schloerb)* "Ample privacy, yet the owners were always available when we needed a restaurant recommendation or advice. Wonderful breakfasts of cinnamon French toast, and spinach quiche. The main street was right out front, but the traffic wasn't heavy." *(Timothy Wry)* "While not large, every room has a good reading chair, contemporary decor, and lots of art." *(LP)*

Open All year. Weekends only, Jan.–March.
Rooms 11 doubles—all with private shower and/or bath, air-conditioning. Some with private deck.
Facilities Breakfast room, living room with fireplace, piano, TV; dining room, wraparound porch. Lawn, gardens, on-site parking, beach passes, beach chairs & towels.
Location On Rte 35S. 75 yards from beach.
Restrictions No smoking. "Not suitable for children under 14." Light sleepers should request rooms away from street.
Credit cards Amex, Discover, MC, Visa.
Rates B&B, $85–195 double. 2–3 night weekend, holiday minimum. Off-season, midweek specials.

BELMAR

For additional area entries, see **Avon by the Sea, South Belmar,** and **Spring Lake.**

Reader tip: "We relaxed in lawn chairs on a starry night listening to Disney tunes played by a string quartet in an elegant gazebo near the town's centerpiece lake. We also enjoyed the quaint honky-tonk mood of the main strip where lone walkers on the beach at night are not uncommon." *(Michele Frank)*

Inn at the Shore ¢ ♥   *Tel:* 908–681–3762
301 Fourth Avenue, 07701   *Fax:* 201–945–2822

A turreted Victorian home built in 1880, The Inn at the Shore has been welcoming guests since 1910. Owned by Rosemary and Tom Volker since 1994, the inn has contemporary living room decor, and guest rooms furnished with Victorian antiques (and not-so-antiques), floral fabrics and wallcoverings, ruffled curtains, and quilts. The inn welcomes children, who love the seasonally dressed teddy bears set up to greet them on the stairway and the saltwater aquarium in the dining room. A breakfast of fresh fruit and juice, cereals, home-baked breads, croissants, and bagels is served from 9 to 11 A.M. at individual tables in the dining room.

"Stepping onto the huge wraparound porch, the summer breeze invites you to relax on the glider or porch rockers with a cooling drink and a good book. Rosemary and Tom take time to get to know you and to help with information on restaurants and activities." *(Grace Halliwell)* "Family photos add to the warmth of the sitting area." *(James Venezia)* "Convenient location on a quiet tree-lined street within walking distance of the train station. Comfortable rooms, simply furnished. Warm, welcoming owners. Home-baked cookies are a welcome evening treat." *(Michele Frank)* "Warm, friendly atmosphere. Attractive, comfortable living room with good entertainment facilities. Pleasing garden setting." *(Kathleen Huntingford)*

Open All year.
Rooms 10 doubles, 2 singles—3 with private bath and/or shower; 9 rooms, each with in-room sink share 3 baths. All with telephone, radio, clock, fan. 2 with TV, 1 with air-conditioning.
Facilities Dining room, living room with fireplace, TV, stereo; books, guest kitchen; wraparound porch. Patio with barbecue grill, lawn. Ample on-street parking. Bicycles, beach chairs. 2 blocks from river, ocean.
Location Central NJ shore. 65 m S of NYC. From NYC; take Garden State S to Exit 98, then Rte. 138 E to Rte 35 N. At 1st traffic light turn right onto 16th Ave. to end. Turn left on Ocean Ave. Go to 4th Ave & turn left. Go 2 blks to inn on left. From NJ Turnpike, take Exit 7A to Rte 195/138 East. Continue as above. Walking distance to train.
Restrictions No smoking.
Credit cards All major.
Rates B&B, $55–95 double, $45–65 single. Children free in same room. 10% senior/AAA discount. 2-3 night weekend/holiday minimum.
Extras Free bus/train station pickup. Crib.

The Seaflower ¢

Tel: 908–681–6006

110 Ninth Avenue, 07719

Pat O'Keefe and Knute Iwaszko have owned this B&B since 1986. A Dutch Colonial built in 1907, the Seaflower is furnished with a casual seaside mixture of antiques and wicker. Pat notes that "our guests are becoming more and more health conscious—and so are we. Low cholesterol and low fat breakfasts with lots of fresh fruits and vegetables seem to suit us all." Typical menus might include baked apples, omelets with tomatoes and cheese, toasted homemade herb bread, and raspberry chocolate chip muffins; or strawberries and Chantilly cream, whole grain waffles with fresh fruit sauce, and cranberry orange bread.

"Knute quickly made us feel welcome and at home. Room seven is the most popular, decorated with pretty flowered wallpaper and a canopy bed; ocean breezes wafted in through the open windows. The inn is exceptionally clean, cozy and comfortable. Reading lights were wonderful, and a magnifying mirror was thoughtfully provided for applying makeup. Pat accommodated our request for a strict vegetarian meal with a delicious hot breakfast of ratatouille-stuffed pitas, while Knute skillfully kept the conversation flowing." *(Gail Davis)* "The living room has two cozy love seats and a window seat filled with board games. The dining room is decorated with the sun, moon and stars (ask Pat why) and has a small blackboard with a saying of the day, and a listing of local events." *(Mark Rinis)*

"Clean and bright, with a safe, private parking area. Pat serves breakfast until 10:30 A.M., allowing plenty of time for a leisurely start. With soft classical music playing, the table was beautifully set with flowers from the garden and a chilled pitcher of juice, a thermal carafe of hot coffee, and a platter of fresh fruit." *(Mr. & Mrs. Paul Lustig)* "Over a pre-dinner wine, Pat and Knute advised us on the local restaurants and night spots." *(James Bovaso)*

Open All year.
Rooms 2 suites, 6 doubles, 1 single—7 with private bath and/or shower, 2 with maximum of 4 people sharing bath. All rooms with fan.
Facilities Breakfast room, parlor with TV/VCR, movies, games; porch, deck, off-street parking. Beach passes, bicycles. ½ block to beach for swimming, fishing.
Location Central NJ shore. From NYC, take Garden State S to Exit 98, then Rte. 138 E to Belmar. From Philadelphia take NJ Turnpike to Exit 7A, then go E on I-195 to Rte. 138 E into Belmar. From Belmar, go left on Rte. 35 N to 4th light. Go right on 10th Ave., left on Ocean Ave., left on 9th Ave. to inn on right.
Restrictions No smoking. Children 10 and over.
Credit cards Amex.
Rates B&B, $110–150 suite, $75–105 double, $55–65 single. 5% senior discount. 2-3 night minimum summer weekends. Winter weekend, special event packages.
Extras Station pickup.

CAPE MAY

Cape May has so many Victorian gingerbread houses that the town has been designated as a National Historic Landmark. Cape May's heyday as a beach resort stretched from 1850 to 1900, when thousands of visitors arrived by train or steamer each summer from Philadelphia and points farther south. Many of today's guest houses date from a disastrous fire in 1878. From the ashes rose this extraordinary collection of elaborate beach "cottages" designed by Philadelphia's best architects, built by the town's master carpenters, and paid for by the millionaires of the day. These "cottages" actually come in three sizes: cottage, villa, and mansion, or big, bigger, biggest.

Cape May has an unusually large number of high-quality owner-operated inns. When calling for reservations you may find that your first choice is full; inn owners are good about referring you to a nearby establishment of equal appeal, and you'll do well to follow their suggestions. Almost none of Cape May's inns serves dinner; there are so many good restaurants within an easy walk that there's no need. One respondent did note that "many of Cape May's best restaurants do not have liquor licenses, a fact which we were dismayed to learn after we'd been seated." Ask when making reservations, and, if necessary, stop by a liquor store on your way to dinner.

Activities in Cape May include swimming, fishing, birding, and bike riding on the town's flat roads, and, of course, touring the Victorian mansions. The Mid-Atlantic Center for the Arts sponsors walking tours, summer theater, and special Victorian programs. The walking tours are a special treat; many are guided by the innkeepers of the establishments listed below. A number of the most famous inns serve afternoon tea along with an afternoon tour; we recommend that you give it a try. Many special events are sponsored at Christmas time; call the Chamber of Commerce (609–884–5404), or ask your favorite inn for details.

Most guest houses require a two- to three-night minimum stay on weekends and holidays during the spring, summer, and fall. Most inns restrict smoking because of strict state fire regulations and guest preference. Be prepared for parking problems during the summer; once you find a spot, leave the car and forget it until it's time to go home. Peak season crowds also create noise, as people walk around this crowded town at night, and buildings are set close to the street; if you want a more peaceful visit, visit before Memorial Day or after Labor Day. Keep in mind that a few inns are not air-conditioned. Although ceiling fans and the ocean breezes are normally cool enough for comfort, if you hit a real heat wave, you will be hot. Most inns in Cape May provide an outside shower, and refrigerators for guest use.

Cape May is at the southernmost tip of New Jersey, 3½ hours from New York and Washington, 2 hours (90 miles) from Philadelphia, and 38 miles south of Atlantic City. To get there, follow the Garden State Parkway to the end, when it becomes Lafayette Street. From the south, take the ferry from Lewes, Delaware; call (302) 645–6313 for information.

Reader tip: "Kitchens close early in Cape May—after enjoying the entertainment at a great piano bar, the only thing we could get to eat at 10:15 P.M. was a cold sandwich, which wasn't our preferred choice." *(CM)* Also: "Buildings—inns, tiny beach cottages, mansions, hotels, private homes—in Cape May are very close together, despite sometimes misleading brochures which give an impression of spaciousness." *(DAP)*

Worth noting: A number of Cape May's best known inns acquired new owners in 1995; high selling prices are reflected in the rates you'll be asked to pay. A number of others remain on the market, so do inquire before booking.

Also recommended: Received just as we were going to press was an enthusiastic report on the **Hotel Macomber** (727 Beach Avenue, 08204; 609–884–3020), a grand shingle-style 1911 mansion a few steps from the beach. Most rooms have private baths, and double rates range from $45–175, depending on room size and season. "Central location at the corner of Howard Street, this four-story hotel has been carefully restored by the Czworkowski family. Rooms are comfortable, and guests also enjoy the first floor living room and solarium, but best of all is the front porch, the true center of Macomber life. Inviting wooden rockers and cool ocean breezes combine to creat a casual, friendly atmosphere. Reasonable rates, too." *(Frank Perch, III)*

The **Abigail Adams B&B** (12 Jackson Street, 08204; 609—884—1371) is a casual, comfortable B&B, just 100 yards from the beach; B&B double rates for the five guest rooms (three with private bath) range from $85—155, including breakfasts of fresh fruit and juice, quiches and scones, plus afternoon refreshments.

Information please: Listed in many previous editions, we'd like current reports on **The Abbey** (34 Gurney Street at Columbia Avenue, 08204; 609—884—4506). This striking Victorian home was built in 1869 and has been authentically restored and decorated in period. Easy to find because of its 60-foot tower, the inn's original stenciled and ruby glass windows have been complemented by high Victorian antiques, ornate glass fixtures, 12-foot mirrors, tall walnut beds, and marble-topped dressers. B&B double rates for the 14 suites and doubles range from $95—200.

Under new ownership is an old favorite, **The Brass Bed Inn** (719 Columbia Avenue, 08204; 609—884—2302 or 800—884—2302), a Carpenter Gothic cottage. The eight guest rooms are decorated in period, with you-know-what kinds of beds; B&B double rates of $75—165 include a private bath, full breakfast, and afternoon tea.

A long-time reader favorite, **The Manor House** (612 Hughes Street, 08204; 609—884—4710) has new owners, Nancy and Tom McDonald. Built in 1906, this classic Colonial revival/American shingle style inn has nine guest rooms, furnished with late Victorian pieces and decorated with period reproduction wallpapers and burnished oak trim. The B&B double rates of $79—160 include a full breakfast and afternoon refreshments.

One of the original "seven sisters" designed by Stephen Decatur Button, **Springside** (18 Jackson Street, 08204; 609—884—2654) is located just ½ block from the beach and the mall. Built in 1891, the comfortable guest rooms have king-size beds, ceiling fans, and shared baths; some have partial ocean views. The double rates of $60—75 include a breakfast of homemade muffins and breads, coffee and tea.

Another previously recommended inn with new owners is **The Summer Cottage Inn** (613 Columbia Avenue, 08204; 609—884—4948), built in the Italianate style in 1867. Located on a quiet, tree-lined street one block from the Mall and the beach, the inn offers air-conditioned guest rooms with private baths and country Victorian decor. B&B double rates of $85—160 include a full breakfast and afternoon tea and treats.

The **Wilbraham Mansion** (133 Myrtle Avenue, 08204; 609—884—2046) was built in 1840 and expanded in 1900, but remained a private residence until 1988. Some of the original furnishings of the John Wilbraham family, wealthy Philadelphia industrialists, still remain. The indoor heated swimming pool is open year round. Guest rooms have private baths and air-conditioning. Double rates of $95—185 include a full breakfast served in the formal dining room.

Thirteen miles north of Cape May is the **Doctors Inn at Kings Grant** (2 North Main Street, Cape May Court House, 08210; 609—463—9330), a handsomely restored Italianate Victorian mansion built in 1854, and restored as an inn in 1994. A health spa with a large lap jacuzzi and exercise equipment are available for the guests to use. B&B double rates for the six guest rooms range from $115–150 and all rooms feature working gas fireplaces and private marble baths with whirlpool tubs and steam showers. A full breakfast is served each morning and dinners are served in the inn's Bradbury Restaurant.

Angel of the Sea
5-7 Trenton Avenue, 08204

Tel: 609–884–3369
800–848–3369

Next time you take a long pull on an icy gin and tonic, think of William Weightman, a Philadelphia businessman who made a fortune from the manufacture of quinine for medicinal use. In 1850, Weightman built himself a "summer cottage" in Cape May. His son cut the building in half in 1888 and moved it to a location closer to the shore. The inn arrived at its present destination in 1962, and was abandoned in the 1980s. What is now the Angel of the Sea was rescued by Barbara and John Girton in 1989. A $3.5 million restoration has resulted in all new heating, plumbing, electrical, and fire protection systems. Guest rooms are furnished with period reproductions, including four-poster, sleigh, wicker, or canopied beds, Victorian floral fabrics and wall coverings, and handsome beaded board ceilings. The exterior is a cream and mauve Victorian fancy, complete with lacy gingerbread trim, layers of porches, and three turrets. A multi-course breakfast is served at your leisure in the dining room; rates also include afternoon tea and sweets and evening wine and cheese.

"Efficiently run by staff, beautifully decorated, congenial atmosphere. Breakfast, tea, wine and cheese were all delicious and interesting. Wide variety of guest rooms, some with ocean views. Our bed was firm and comfortable. Ample, convenient parking. The staff was knowledgeable and helpful with area information and dinner reservations." *(Linda McCreedy)* "Our beautifully decorated room had a four-poster bed and a porch with an ocean view. A buffet of cereal and fresh fruit serves as an introduction to the breakfast, with a choice of two entrées. Everyone socializes in the living room when the hosts serve wine and cheese—a nice way to meet the other guests." *(Greg Rohrer & Veronica Farmer)* "Light, airy, Victorian-style decor. Prices are high for rooms with a view, but well worth it." *(Lynn Avenoso)*

Open All year.
Rooms 26 rooms in 2 adjacent buildings—all with private bath and/or shower, ceiling fan. Some with balcony or porch.
Facilities Dining room, living room with fireplace. Off-street parking, bicycles, beach equipment, beach tags (with deposit). ½ block from ocean.
Location 1 m from center. As enter town, turn left at Sidney St., left at Washington St. then right at traffic island. Follow Pittsburgh Ave. (Ocean Dr.) to Beach Dr., turn right. Turn right on Trenton to B&B on right.
Restrictions No smoking. 50% deposit with reservation; "balance due at check-in payable in CASH."
Credit cards Amex, MC, Visa.
Rates B&B, $95–275 double. Extra person, $50. Package rates. 2–3 night weekend, holiday minimum.

Barnard-Good House   *Tel:* 609–884–5381
238 Perry Street, 08204

Nan and Tom Hawkins have owned and operated the Barnard Good House since 1980, and have combined period decor with modern comfort. Nan says "our hallmarks are our warm, friendly attitude and our breakfasts, which are an event in themselves. We cater to allergies and dietary restrictions; just let us know in advance." A typical breakfast menu includes cranberry-grape juice, broiled nectarines and pecans, seafood roulade, corn custard, whole-grain bread, and blackberry tarts.

"Nan's breakfasts are elaborate three-course affairs, always outstanding, creative, and unusual. The Victorian furnishings mix the formal and funky, so guests feel comfortable putting their feet up. The bathrooms are small, but adequate; one has a wonderful copper tub for relaxing soaks. Parking is tight, but sufficient." *(Barbara Pressman)* "Outstanding features are the friendly atmosphere, delicious food, and the cleanliness." *(Tomi Deutsch-Berney)* "The location is convenient to the beach, shopping and numerous fine restaurants. Nan and Tom provided helpful advice and menus from local restaurants for review. During the afternoon, iced tea was available—a different flavor each day—in a small guest refrigerator." *(Karen Trommelen)* "Afternoon refreshments are served on the wraparound porch, which is furnished with comfortable wicker furniture." *(Monna Hormel)*

Open April 1–Nov. 1.
Rooms 2 suites, 3 doubles—all with private bath and/or shower, clock, air-conditioning.
Facilities Dining room, living room, parlor, guest refrigerator, veranda. Beach chairs, beach passes, off-street parking.
Location 2 blocks from beach, at corner of Perry & Lafayette.
Restrictions No smoking. Children 14 and over.
Credit cards MC, Visa.
Rates B&B, $125 suite, $89–120 double, 10% less for single. 2–3 night weekend, holiday minimum.
Extras Airport/station pickups.

Carroll Villa B&B ¢ 🏃 ✕   *Tel:* 609–884–9619
19 Jackson Street, 08204   *Fax:* 609–884–0264

Adjacent to the well-known Mad Batter restaurant is the Carroll Villa, one of the original small Victorian hotels of Cape May, built in the Italianate style complete with cupola. Harry Kulkowitz and Vickie Seitchik, and innkeeper Mark Kulkowitz have spent years renovating the hotel, reducing the room count from 34 to 21 rooms, adding floral wallpaper and carpeting to complement the period antiques, upgrading the beds, installing air-conditioning, and more. There's a wicker-filled living room and garden terrace for relaxing. Breakfast is served at the Mad Batter, and except midweek off-season, the tempting entrée choices include orange-almond French toast, oatmeal pancakes, and Swiss rösti potatoes with eggs and Gruyere cheese, accompanied by juice, homemade fruit breads and muffins, coffee, tea, espresso, or cappuccino. Service is leisurely, the atmosphere relaxed. Lunch and dinner is also served, and the creative menu has an eclectic international flavor, with such dishes as tuna with seafood salsa, rack of lamb with mushroom flan, and veal with balsamic vinegar and goat cheese.

"Exceptionally clean room, especially the bath; mercifully quiet air-conditioner. Although it was described to us as being small, we had ample room. Friendly staff." *(GR)* "We were made to feel welcome, pampered, and valued from check-in to check-out. Our room was spacious, elegant, and comfortable. Scrumptious breakfast; adequate service." *(BK)* Comments appreciated.

Open All year.
Rooms 21 doubles—all with private shower bath, telephone, fan, air-conditioning.
Facilities Restaurant with fireplace, sitting room, living room with TV, books; garden terrace. 5 blocks to off-street parking. 1/2 block to beach. Beach, off-street parking tags provided.
Location In center of historic district. Follow Lafayette St. through town to end at Jackson St. Turn left & go 1 1/2 blocks to inn on left.
Restrictions No smoking. Street noise in front rooms. Least expensive rooms quite small.
Credit cards MC, Visa.
Rates B&B, $55–127 double, $50–105 single. Extra person, $20. Reduced rates for children. 2–3 night weekend/holiday minimum in season. 10% discount for 6 days. Alc breakfast, $7–10; alc lunch, $8–12; alc dinner, $30. BYOB.
Extras French, German spoken.

Chalfonte ¢ 🏋 ✕

301 Howard Street, 08204

Tel: 609–884–8409
Fax: 609–884–4588

The oldest hotel in Cape May, the Chalfonte has accommodated guests since 1876. Despite ongoing restoration work, not a lot has changed since then. Students from the University of Maryland still come every spring to work on the hotel as part of an architecture course! You can come too—for a $15 registration fee—and spend a May or October weekend painting and plastering, sewing or gardening, to help get the hotel in shape.

The Chalfonte is known for its traditional family-style Southern cooking, served in the enormous dining room. Breakfast often consists of eggs, biscuits, fried fish, bacon or sausage, and a big bowl of spoon bread. Dinners offer a choice of either of three entrees: the fish of the day in a lemon sherry sauce; a scallop or crab dish; and a meat dish, typically roast beef, turkey or lamb, fried chicken, or country ham. The supervised children's dining room is open for both breakfast and dinner; children age 6 and younger are especially accommodated but any kids under age 15 enjoy special meal rates—and parents are welcome too. Many of the common rooms are decorated with furniture original to the building. Guest rooms are spare—a bed, a dresser, a chair—but no one spends much time in their room.

"Not just a hotel, but a way of life. Laid back, friendly, and most of all, wonderfully civilized." *(Penny Reeves)* "The place rings with happiness. The food is fantastic, the guest mixture is fun, and the relaxed air of guests and staff is a wonderful treat in these rushed times." *(W. Richard Sattler)*

"Charmingly evocative of the Victorian era during which it was built, The Chalfonte is a terrific place to rendezvous with old friends. Breakfast and dinner are unfailingly ample and delicious. Unlike many modern hotels and motels, it feels perfectly natural to chat with a perfect stranger while sitting in a rocker on the wraparound porch or in a Victorian armchair in the comfortable, unpretentious lobby. Each year we plan our vacation to coincide with one of the two 'children's weeks' with special activities for kids. The hotel also provides adult entertainment most nights: vintage movies, cabaret, and concerts by candlelight. Virtually unchanged since it was built, it lacks many modern amenities, but ocean breezes and muscular ceiling fans make all but the hottest summer weather bearable. The management team is experienced, professional, and genuinely interested in showing the hotel's guests a good time; the waitstaff, desk clerks, and so on are pleasant and obliging college students, though not too speedy. Then again, the Jersey Cape is no place to be in a hurry." *(Peter Howell)*

Open May through Oct.
Rooms 67 doubles, 5 singles—11 with private bath and/or shower, 61 with maximum of 6 people sharing bath. All with ceiling fan. 21 rooms in 3 separate cottages.
Facilities Dining room, main lobby, solarium, library, reading room, bar, TV room with VCR, playroom, children's program, porches, garden with swings. Concerts and cabaret weekends; painting, craft, personal growth workshops. 2 blocks to ocean. Outside bath house. Beach tags on first-come, first-served basis.
Location 2 blocks from ocean and town center. From Lafayette, turn left on Madison, right on Columbia (at water tower), left on Howard.
Restrictions Smoking in public rooms only. Children 6 & under eat in separate supervised dining room.
Credit cards MC, Visa.
Rates MAP, $76–154 double, $54–75 single, plus $6 per person daily service ($4 per child). Extra person over 15, $25; under 15, $3–15. Weekly rates. 2-night weekend minimum. Theme workshops, programs. Prix fixe breakfast, $7.50; dinner, $20. 15% service added to beverage checks.
Extras Limited wheelchair access. Crib, babysitting. French, German spoken.

The Mainstay   ♿ 🛉

Tel: 609–884–8690

635 Columbia Avenue, 08204

Although Cape May is full of inns, The Mainstay is really in a class by itself. It's one of those "velvet rope" inns—the kind with furnishings you'd normally only see, and not touch, in a museum. Although the environment is a bit intimidating at first, the owners' goal is to offer a relaxing, fun vacation experience. Innkeepers Tom and Sue Carroll were pioneers in Cape May's redevelopment, having opened The Mainstay in 1971.

The Mainstay was built in 1872 as a private club for wealthy gentlemen gamblers. They spared no expense; the villa was complete with 14-foot ceilings, ornate plaster moldings, and lavish furnishings, many of which are still in place today. Advance reservations are imperative at The Mainstay, at least several months ahead for summer weekends. A full breakfast is served in spring and fall (continental in summer); guests are also invited to join the Carrolls for afternoon tea. In 1994 the Carrolls opened "The Officers' Quarters," a 1910-era frame building which once housed naval officers during World War I. Just opposite the Mainstay, this carefully redesigned building has four luxury suites, fully soundproofed and wheelchair accessible; continental breakfast is delivered to guests' doors.

"The crown jewel among Cape May's many Victorian gems, with airy rooms elegantly appointed with period furniture, a spacious veranda for snoozing or conversation, and a cupola that commands a breathtaking vista of this unique seaside resort. What truly sets The Mainstay apart is the relaxed hospitality and cheerfulness of its hosts, Sue and Tom Carroll, whose exquisite taste and love of innkeeping show in every gracious detail." *(J.I. Merritt)* "Our very private suite in the Officers' Quarters included our own porch with rocking chairs. It was beautifully decorated, in a more simple, contemporary style than the inn. A breakfast of juice, fruit, and baked goods was left outside our door; we made our own coffee. Our only contact with the staff and other guests was at tea-time, when we were also joined by outside visitors who paid an extra fee to attend." *(Judy Schwartz)* "The innkeepers and staff are genuinely warm and friendly people, responsive to the needs of their guests." *(Bernie Schultz)* "The Inn is breathtaking, from its beautifully manicured gardens to its fifteen-foot windows." *(Jessica Ciandella)* "Each of the elegant and immaculate rooms have been lovingly decorated by Tom and Sue. All are furnished with lovely antiques, including marble-topped dressers, tall wardrobes, and huge Victorian beds. Delicious, homemade food." *(Susan Goebel)*

Open Mid-March–mid-Dec.

Rooms 7 1-2 bedroom suites, 9 doubles—all with private shower and/or bath, fans. 10 with desk, 2 with balcony or deck. 6 rooms in Cottage. 4 suites in Officers' Quarters—all with private bath, double whirlpool tub, telephone, TV/VCR, air-conditioning, gas fireplace, kitchenette, off-street parking.

Facilities Dining room, library, music room, parlor, veranda. Flower garden with fountain, croquet, swings. 13 off-street parking spaces. Beach passes.

Location Historic district, 3 blocks to center, 2 blocks to beach. Turn left at 1st light after Canal Bridge, go 3 blocks & turn right on Columbia.

Restrictions No smoking. "Young children generally find us tiresome; children over 6 in Officers' Quarters; over 12 in inn." On-street parking tight in summer. Occasional street noise in summer. Common rooms locked at 11 P.M.

Credit cards None accepted.

Rates B&B, $120–205 suite, $105–185 double, $95–175 single. Extra person, $25. 3-night minimum stay, June–Sept., also some weekends. Weekend packages, early spring & late fall; off-season midweek promotions. 4 P.M. tea & tour, Sat., Sun., Tues, Thurs.: $5–8.

Extras Wheelchair access; some suites specially equipped.

The Mooring
801 Stockton Avenue, 08204

Tel: 609–884–5425
Fax: 609–884–1357

Built in 1882 in the Second Empire style, The Mooring is one of Cape May's original guest houses, and was restored as an inn in 1993 by Leslie Valenza. A wide entrance hall opens onto the parlor and dining room and a wide spiral stairway leads to the guest rooms, furnished in period. Breakfast is served from 8:30 to 10 A.M. in the dining room at tables for two, or on the front veranda. Breakfast specialties include baked cinnamon French toast, Mexican fritatta, and Swiss muesli with fresh fruit and homemade muffins. In cooler months, afternoon tea is served on fine Czechoslovakian china and features fine teas, coffee, and cakes. In summer months, a more casual assortment of finger foods and iced tea are available.

"Always a refreshing ocean breeze. Leslie made me feel comfortable from the moment I walked in the door. The house is well-cared for and clean; guest rooms are spacious, each decorated with a different color scheme. Meals were delicious, the portions generous, with lots of conversation among the guests. Homemade cakes and cookies were served for tea. Parking is ample and we didn't use our car at all. The center of Cape May is within walking distance." *(Sue Hartman)* "Leslie has a great personality and a constant smile." *(Donald Brandi)*

Open Early April–Jan 1.
Rooms 12 doubles—all with private bath and/or shower, clock. Most with ceiling fan, air-conditioning. 2 with balcony, 1 with TV, refrigerator.
Facilities Dining room, parlor with books, stereo; guest kitchen, porch. Outdoor showers, beach tags, towels. Off-street parking. 1 block to beach.
Location 5 blks from town center. From Garden State Parkway S, continue straight over bridge to Rte 109, which becomes Lafayette St. At first traffic light, turn left onto Madison. Go 10 blocks, turn right onto Stockton. Go 4 blocks to inn on right at corner of Howard.
Restrictions No smoking. Children over 6.
Credit cards Discover, MC, Visa.
Rates B&B, $80–175 double, $70–165 single. Extra person, $10. 2-3 night summer/weekend/holiday minimum.
Extras Some French spoken.

The Queen Victoria ♿   *Tel:* 609–884–8702
102 Ocean Street, 08204

The Queen Victoria is a complex of three neighboring Victorian homes and two carriage houses from the 1880s, restored a century later as a B&B inn by Dane and Joan Wells. Rooms are decorated with authentic Victorian furnishings, attractive wallpapers and quilts, and antique iron, brass, and four-poster beds. In 1995, the Wells family opened **The Queen's Hotel**, just across the street, offering small hotel privacy in a restored Victorian commercial building; all guest rooms are equipped with air-conditioning, television, telephones, hair dryers, coffee makers, refrigerators, and of course, private baths.

"Joan and Dane are experts in the field of Victoriana, but our questions were treated as though it was the first time someone had ever asked and they were pleased to answer." *(Mary Ann Carey)* "Small things stand out—always a bowl of fruit and a supply of club soda, well stocked bookshelves, and a journal where guests can record their experiences at local restaurants. Guests are welcome to use the inn's facilities (including a shower) throughout the day they check out." *(Arthur Fink)*

"Rooms have fresh flowers, fluffy color-coordinated towels, and an excellent information packet. Breakfast hours are flexible, and served buffet-style with wonderful breads, hot dishes, cereal, and fruit. They try

101

hard to accommodate special diets, and if you need to leave early, they will see that you get fed. In the evening you return to a turned-down bed, fresh towels, empty wastebasket, and a welcoming bedside light." *(Gene Kubal)*

"The Westminster Room is large and airy, with a four-poster queen bed. The weather was wet and cool so we sat in the parlor reading and playing dominoes, with classical music playing in the background. Tea was served, including little sandwiches, making the day very civilized. On a previous visit we had stayed in the Gilbert & Sullivan room, which has a small bathroom, but the airy sitting room and pristine housekeeping more than compensated." *(Carolyn Myles)* "We had the carriage house, which was perfect for our family. The downstairs had a large living room, while upstairs was a large bedroom with an alcove area for a cot." *(Marie Dropkin)* "Perfectly located—equally close to the beach, the historic mall area, and excellent restaurants." *(Mr. & Mrs. Thomas Grealy)* "We turned in for the night to the muffled sounds of jovial conversation and the player piano in the parlor downstairs. On a second visit, we had the Balmoral Room in the cottage—with a whirlpool tub for two, illuminated by a Victorian stained glass window." *(Janice & Kennedy O'Brien)* "Breakfasts were delicious, highlighted by an eggs and salsa one day, and crêpes à l'orange the next." *(LuAnn & Steve Weiner)*

Open All year.

Rooms 7 suites, 16 doubles—all with private bath and/or shower, refrigerator, air-conditioning, clock-radio; some with desk, fan, Jacuzzi tub, porch. Suites in adjacent carriage house & cottage with telephone, TV, air-conditioning. 1 with gas fireplace.

Facilities Dining rooms, "quiet" parlor with fireplace; parlor with player piano, TV, library, games, 6 porches. Victorian flower garden, beach passes, chairs, towels; beach shower with changing room, bicycles. On-site parking for handicapped only; free parking 5 blocks away. Tennis, golf nearby.

Location Historic district, 1 block to beach, 2 blocks to shops. Turn left at 2nd stoplight on Lafayette St. onto Ocean St. Go 3 blocks to inn on right.

Restrictions No smoking. Children in suites only. "Toddlers usually aren't happy here."

Credit cards MC, Visa.

Rates B&B, $145–270 suite, $90–220 double, $80–170 single. Extra person, $20. Winter packages; off-season midweek rates. 2–4 night weekend minimum.

Extras 1 suite equipped for disabled. 3 blocks to bus. Crib, babysitting, beach toys. French, Spanish spoken.

Virginia Hotel 🍴 ✗

25 Jackson Street, 08204

Tel: 609–884–5700
800–732–4236
Fax: 609–884–1236

The Virginia Hotel, built in 1879 by Alfred and Ellen Ebbit, was fully restored 110 years later by Curtis Bashaw as a small, elegant hotel. The restaurant, named after the Ebbits, offers seafood and regional American cuisine. A continental breakfast is served from 8–10:30 A.M. on the veranda, or brought to guests' rooms.

"Offered the privacy unavailable at most B&Bs. Exceptional service, comfortable room. Our pre-season visit was quiet and romantic." *(Deirdre*

Nesko) "Upon arrival, our luggage was quickly taken to our room, and our car whisked away by valet parking. Our immaculate room was elegantly decorated with both contemporary and antique furnishings, as were the lobby and lounge." *(Carol Middendorf)* "We were delighted with the spare elegance of the Virginia. Our room was decorated in cream and ivory tones, with a cherry headboard and accent pieces, and a down comforter on the queen-size bed. Plush terry-cloth robes were supplied for the well-equipped bathroom." *(MA)*

Open Feb. through Dec.
Rooms 24 rooms—all with full private bath, telephone, TV/VCR, air-conditioning. Two with porch.
Facilities Lobby with fireplace, piano. Room service. Book, video library. Porch, garden, valet parking weekends/peak season. Pianist most evenings. Beach tags, towels, chairs.
Location Historic District. 1/2 block from Beach Ave. and Washington St. Mall.
Restrictions Smoking restricted.
Credit cards Most major credit cards accepted.
Rates B&B, $80–260 double. Extra person over 5, $20. 2–3 night weekend/holiday minimum. Midweek, weekend, kayaking, family packages. Corporate rates. Children's menu.
Extras Crib. Babysitting by arrangement.

White Dove Cottage
619 Hughes Street, 08204

Tel: 609–884–0613
800–321–DOVE

The White Dove was built in 1866 in the Second Empire style, with a mansard roof faced with hand-cut octagonal slate. It was renovated as a B&B in 1987, and was bought by Frank and Sue Smith in 1990. The house is furnished in American and European antiques, accented with period wallpapers. An antique music box sets the atmosphere for breakfast, served around a banquet table set with crystal and china. Breakfast entrées, fruits and juice, homebaked breads and desserts are all chosen to match the season; quiche and blintzes are two popular dishes.

"High marks in all categories. Charmingly decorated house on a tree-lined, quiet street. Excellent breakfasts with good food, beautifully presented. Friendly hosts were well informed about area activities and helpful with restaurant recommendations and reservations." *(Peter Albert)* "The water pressure is fine, even on the third floor, and there was plenty of hot water. Hallways are well lighted." *(Rosemary & John Robinson)* "In the afternoon tea and hot chocolate, homemade cookies or cake, are served in the parlor, which is highlighted by Frank's teddy bear collection (wall-to-wall and floor-to-ceiling), and a wonderful old player piano complete with a variety of music rolls. Frank Smith is a personable host who looks out for your comfort, and a creative cook who makes breakfast a special event." *(Iris Fernandez)*

Open All year.
Rooms 1 suite, 5 doubles—all with private bath and/or shower, radio, air-conditioning, hair dryer. Suite with private entrance, refrigerator, TV.
Facilities Dining room; parlor with player piano, books; veranda; off-street parking. Beach passes, beach chairs and towels.

Location Historic district, 2 blocks from beach. From Lafayette St. turn left on Franklin, right on Hughes.
Restrictions No smoking. Children 10 and over.
Credit cards None accepted.
Rates B&B, $125–185 suite, $75–130 double, $65–135 single. Extra person, $25. 2-night weekend minimum, also mid-June–Labor Day. Tipping encouraged. 10% weekly discount. AAA, senior discount midweek off-season. 3-night off-season discount.
Extras Airport/station pickup.

The Wooden Rabbit ♦♦

Tel: 609–884–7293

609 Hughes Street, 08204

The Wooden Rabbit is one of the few Cape May inns to welcome families with children, and has been owned by Greg and Debby Burow since 1988. The inn takes its inspiration from Beatrix Potter's storybook characters, and whimsical rabbit touches are found throughout the inn, along with collectibles and folk art. The inn is also unusual in that it was built by a sea captain in 1838; Robert E. Lee spent summers here, and the house was also used by the Underground Railroad. The buffet breakfast is served from 8:30–9:30 A.M., and includes fresh fruit, an egg casserole, homemade granola, muffins, and breads; home-baked treats and refreshments are offered on the sun porch from 4 to 5 P.M.

"Although accommodating to children, the inn was peaceful and quiet." *(Robin Koslo)* "Greg is a friendly, down-to-earth innkeeper who made us feel right at home. We parked in the driveway and left our keys in case our car had to be moved when we weren't around." *(Madeline & Joe Bradley)* "Delicious cherry crisp and applebread pudding at breakfast." *(Judy & Russ Evans)* "Central location, close to everything." *(Bruce Damasio)* "Cheerily decorated with rabbit collectibles throughout. Our room was spacious and spotless, decorated in small country prints with coordinating borders. Handmade accents—quilts, pillows, and wall hangings—highlight the decor; the furnishings are mainly wicker, except for the beds and bureaus." *(Beverly Lang)* "Great cat, Oscar, who spent most of the night purring with us." *(Tina Chapman)* "We learned about local history and the best restaurants during the tea-and-treats gathering. Greg's sticky buns, cookies, and nut breads were the best." *(Stephanie Lesiga)* "The living room has a variety of reading materials, including children's books and a child-size rocker." *(Arlette & Gary Braman)* "Our third floor attic suite was perfect for our family. The private outdoor shower was a pleasure after a day at the beach." *(Susan Lammie)*

Open All year.
Rooms 1 suite, 2 doubles—all with private bath and/or shower, TV, air-conditioning, fan.
Facilities Dining room with fireplace, living room with fireplace; sun porch. Outside shower. Beach passes, chairs. Off-street parking. Tennis, playground nearby.
Location In historic district, 2 blocks from beach. From Lafayette St., turn left on Franklin St., then right onto Hughes St.
Restrictions No smoking. Sept.–mid-May, children over 6 & under 1 welcome. All ages welcome Mem. Day through Oct.

Credit cards MC, Visa (for deposits only).
Rates B&B, $90–175 suite, $85–165 double. Extra person, $15. 3-4 night summer minimum.
Extras Nanny service.

FLEMINGTON

Peaceful rural relaxation is well and good in its place, but there are days when nothing gets the adrenalin going like a serious round of bargain hunting. Flemington, with over 150 outlet shops in two Colonial-style shopping centers, fits the bill perfectly. When you're all shopped out, you'll awake to notice that you're in an appealing National Historic District town with a self-guided tour of its varied Victorian and Greek Revival architecture. You can view the peaceful farms on a historic steam train ride, or visit in mid-September for the New Jersey State Agricultural Fair. Flemington was famous in the early 1900s for its cut glass, and you can stop by the Flemington Glass Company, one of the companies still in operation, for a free demonstration.

Flemington is located in west central New Jersey, about 60 miles southwest of New York City, and the same distance northeast of Philadelphia. It's about 20 minutes northeast of New Hope, Pennsylvania, and budget travelers might do well to make it their base of operations, since rates are lower than they are in New Hope, or even Lambertville.

Reader tip: "We had a terrific dinner at the Sargentville Inn." *(Lynne Batlan)*

For an additional area entry, see listing for **Whitehouse Station**, 10 miles to the north.

The Cabbage Rose Inn
162 Main Street, 08822
Tel: 908–788–0247

Named for its prevailing decorative motif, the Cabbage Rose Inn was bought by Pam Venosa and Al Scott in 1988. Gallons of paint, uncounted rolls of wallpaper and fabric, and unending quantities of elbow grease were needed to restore a shine to this former restaurant's oak floors and carved staircase. From the stained glass window that illuminates the foyer, to the antique-filled parlor, to the sun room furnished with white wicker, to the numerous collectibles scattered throughout the rooms, Pam and Al take pride in the old-fashioned Victorian charm of their inn. The inn's exterior combines a dozen angles, and includes porches and gables with gingerbread trim, highlighted by a "painted lady" color scheme of rose, pink, and burgundy with lots of white accents. Other projects included the addition of queen-size beds in most rooms, and a guest pantry where sparkling water, cider, lemonade, ice, and cookies are always available. In the dining room, or brought to your room, the weekday breakfast consists of fruit salad with granola and yogurt, cereal or oatmeal, and home-baked breads and muffins. On weekends, a hot entrée such as bacon cheddar quiche or buttermilk waffles is included.

"Terrific location, close to hot air ballooning, shopping, theater and

New Hope nightlife." *(Lynne Batlan)* "Pam served refreshing lemonade and cookies in the afternoon; breakfasts were varied, delicious and plentiful. Al was helpful with information on area activities and restaurants." *(M. Cromis)*

Open All year.
Rooms 5 doubles—all with private tub and/or shower, radio, telephone, desk, air-conditioning, fan. 1 with gas fireplace.
Facilities Dining room with piano, parlor with fireplace, TV, stereo; sun-room, porch. Near river for canoeing, rafting, and tubing. Golf nearby.
Location Midway between NYC and Philadelphia. In center of town.
Restrictions No smoking. Some traffic noise in front rooms. Children 10 and over.
Credit cards Amex, MC, Visa. "Cash or checks preferred."
Rates B&B, $80–120 double. Extra person, $15. 2-night weekend minimum. Midweek, corporate rates. Romance package.
Extras Station pickup.

Jerica Hill
96 Broad Street, 08822

Tel: 908–782–8234
Fax: 908–782–8234

After a hard day of shopping, you may feel the need to get a new perspective on things, and how better to do so than from the basket of a hot-air balloon? Innkeeper Judith Studer, owner of Jerica Hill since 1984, will happily make all the arrangements for your flight; all you have to do is hope for good weather. Of course, you don't have to leave terra firma to enjoy the relaxing atmosphere of this B&B. A turn-of-the-century Victorian home painted gray with dark red trim, the interior features a beautiful center hall staircase; surprisingly, the antique decor is Colonial, not Victorian. Breakfast includes fruit, yogurt, cereal, homemade pastry and breads, with fresh fruit and flowers provided in the guest rooms. The guest pantry is always available for snacks, ice, cookies, mixers, coffee, tea, and cocoa.

"Judith is a warm, caring innkeeper who makes us feel as though the inn was our own. Room One is bright, cheery, and clean, equipped with a personal welcome note, bottles of sparkling water, and a basket of fruit and chocolate mints. The bathroom is supplied with soaps, shampoo, conditioner, travel tooth brushes, toothpaste, shaving cream, and a hairdryer. The guest pantry is always open for snacks and beverages. We love the inn cats, Mookie and Binkie." *(Raymond Farreny)* "In the morning, we had breakfast on the plant-filled screened porch, cool and inviting with white wicker furniture and a flagstone floor." *(MW)* "We were welcomed with cider and cookies. Breakfast favorites included homemade apple muffins, banana bread, and apricot scones." *(Peter & Tessie Nolan)*.

"On a quiet side street, with big backyard. In cooler weather, curl up in the casual living room with one of Judith's many books; the dining room is large and more formal, with a large table and several smaller ones. The original front parlor is now an inviting bedroom with a lace-canopied reproduction Shaker bed, bay windows with adjustable shutters, a hand-woven coverlet, an old-fashioned wooden rocker, and an antique upholstered chair. Another favorite room is located at the front of the house on the second floor. Done in hunter green and white, it has a desk, a wingback chair and an antique wooden chair flanking a little table with a reading lamp, and a pineapple four-poster bed." *(SWS)*

Note: The inn was for sale as we went to press, so inquire further when booking.

Open All year.
Rooms 5 doubles—all with private shower and/or bath, radio, telephone, air-conditioning, fan. TV on request.
Facilities Living room with fireplace, library, TV; guest pantry; screened porch. Off-street parking. Bicycle rentals from inn. Tennis, golf nearby. River nearby for tubing, rafting, bicycling.
Location 2 blocks E of Main St.
Restrictions No smoking. Limited facilities for children.
Credit cards Amex, MC, Visa.
Rates B&B, $90–105 double. Extra person, $20. Corporate, midweek rate. 2-night minimum most weekends. Senior discount. Ballooning, winery, bicycle touring packages.
Extras Station pickup.

HOPE

Inn at Millrace Pond ✗ ⅃
Route 519, P.O. Box 359, 07844

Tel: 908–459–4884

For the mood of Bucks County without the crowds, head out Interstate 80 to the historic hamlet of Hope, founded in 1769 by Moravian settlers, and listed on the National Register of Historic Places. During the Revolutionary War, grain from the mill in Hope was hauled over Jenny Jump Mountain to Washington's troops in Morristown. In 1985, the long-vacant complex of cut limestone buildings was restored as a country inn, combining authentic period detail with modern comforts; in 1994 the inn was purchased by Charles and Cordie Puttkammer. Guest rooms are found in the restored miller's and wheelwright's houses, while the original mill building is home to the restaurant, tavern, and additional guest rooms. Some rooms are done in a mix of formal and "country" Colonial styles, and are accented with antique and reproduction furnishings, and Williamsburg colors of blue, soft reds, grayish green, and cream. "Food in the restaurant was delicious, the atmosphere charming and romantic. The tavern (on the ground floor) has a rustic European feeling to it. Our second floor room in the miller's house was well appointed and comfortable." *(Frank Perch)* "On arrival we were given a packet that included a walking tour of the area, and information on local wineries and places of interest. Our room (#8) in the Millwright House had wide pine floors, a canopy bed with open-work crochet top, and a comfortable chair. Most interesting of all is the way these buildings have been restored. You can walk along the original mill race, and see where the water was diverted to run the mill wheel; from the restaurant you can see the mill wheel. The town itself is two blocks away, and is pleasant, truly historic, and unspoiled." *(SC)* "The wrought iron table and chairs overlooking the brook was the perfect spot for having coffee. My favorite room is #4, with a little bay window and reddish color scheme. Great lighting—dimmer switches made the lamps perfect for reading or fine as a night light." *(Mary Ann Boyle)* Comments appreciated.

Suggestion box: "Carpet the hallways and stairs for quieter guest rooms."

Open All year. Restaurant open for dinner daily, Sunday lunch; closed Dec. 25.
Rooms 17 doubles—all with full private bath, telephone, desk, air-conditioning. 5 with whirlpool tubs; 9 with TV. Rooms in 3 separate buildings.
Facilities Dining room with weekend music, tavern with fireplace, TV, games, parlor with fireplace, TV, books; porch. 23 acres with tennis, picnic areas, paths, brook. 10 m to Delaware River for canoeing, rafting, swimming, fishing. Golf, downhill and cross-country skiing, wineries, Waterloo Village nearby.
Location NW NJ, Skylands Region, Warren Cty. 50 m W of NYC, 70 m N of Philadelphia. In center of town. From Rte. 80, take Exit 12 to Rte. 521 S. Go 1 m to blinker light in town, then left on Rte. 519 1 block to inn.
Credit cards Amex, DC, MC, Visa.
Rates B&B, $85–140 double, $75–120 single. Extra person, $25. 2-night weekend minimum. Senior, AAA discount. Corporate rates. Alc dinner, $37.
Extras Restaurant has wheelchair access.

LAMBERTVILLE

A five-minute walk across the river from New Hope, Lambertville was settled in 1705, and grew into an industrial center with the development of the Delaware & Raritan Canal. After years of neglect, its many fine homes are being restored, and its factories reused as artists' studios, shops, and restaurants.

Reader tips: "A lively, interesting little town, just as historic as New Hope, but not so 'tarted up'—real people live here. Lambertville's shops have lots of personality, and our favorites were Phoenix Books, with shelves crammed with used books, and the trendy Fran Jay Antiques, overflowing with collectibles from Depression glass to rediscovered Fiesta Ware." *(Linda Phillipps)* "Great dinner at Hamilton's Grill—casual atmosphere and interesting American cuisine; bring your own wine." *(Linda Intaschi)*

Information please: A Georgian Revival mansion built in 1909 by a local coal baron as an anniversary present for his wife, the **York Street House**, (42 York Street, 08530; 609–397–3007) was featured in *House and Garden* magazine in 1911. Today, this B&B offers quiet lodging to travelers who prefer the more relaxed atmosphere of Lambertville over the bustle of New Hope. A full breakfast is served in the dining room; in the evening sherry and port are available in the library. Double rates range from $55–100.

For additional area entries, see **Stockton**.

The Inn at Lambertville Station � ✕ & Tel: 609–397–4400
11 Bridge Street, 08530   Outside NJ: 800–524–1091
                                            Fax: 609–397–9744

Right on the Delaware River, just across from New Hope, is The Inn at Lambertville Station, comprising both a hotel and a restaurant. The former is a contemporary hotel with river views from all of its guest rooms, while the latter is a restaurant housed in a restored 19th century train station. Each of the antique-filled guest rooms feature a decor inspired by a different city, from London to New Orleans, Paris to San Francisco. Rates include a continental breakfast of muffins or croissants, delivered to the room, and a copy of *The New York Times*. The appealing restaurant menu includes a number of low-cholesterol and vegetarian choices, from tuna with balsamic vinegar, spinach, and roasted peppers to potato pancakes with grilled vegetables and tomato jam; of course, hearty steaks also await hard-core carnivores.

"The New York Suite has some lovely antiques, a comfortable sitting area, fun period prints on the wall, a gas fireplace and interesting blue wallpaper." *(LI)* "A new but charming hotel, with an active conference business, and a welcoming staff. Spacious guest rooms with dressing areas and superb bathrooms supplied with English toiletries." *(Margaret Pilgrim)* "Enjoyed a spacious room with a wonderful view of the Delaware. The 'Sunset' menu in the charmingly restored station restaurant is an excellent value." *(Betty Norman)* "Well appointed rooms, all different. Friendly staff, good value. Excellent area restaurants." *(Ilene & Gerald Bahr)*

Open All year.
Rooms 8 suites, 37 doubles—all with full private bath, telephone, TV, radio. Suites with gas fireplace, whirlpool tub. Refrigerator on request.
Facilities Restaurant, bar/lounge. Lobby with fireplace, conference facilities, deck. Off-street parking. Swimming, boating, fishing nearby.
Location On Rte. 518 (Rte. 179 in PA), at Rte. 29. On river, next to "Free Bridge."
Restrictions Some non-smoking rooms.
Credit cards Amex, CB, DC, MC, Visa.
Rates B&B, $150–225 suite, $75–170 double. Extra person, $15. Corporate, weekly rates. Off-season getaway packages. Early bird "Sunset" dinner midweek, $10. Alc lunch, $8; alc dinner, $20–30.
Extras Crib. Wheelchair access; some rooms specially equipped.

MAYS LANDING

Also recommended: In the southern part of the Pine Barrens, about 20 miles west of Atlantic City, is the **Inn at Sugar Hill** (5704 Mays Landing-Somers Point Road [Country Road 559]; 609–625–2226) with water views of Great Egg Harbor from the restaurant and some of the six guest rooms. Most have private baths, and several have fireplaces; the suite also has a canopied private sunporch overlooking the water. B&B double rates range from $70–90, including a continental breakfast; the rate for two including dinner is $135–200. "Great lunch on porch overlooking the river; friends who live in the area say the restaurant is one of the best around. Beautifully landscaped grounds." *(J. Cary)*

MILFORD

Chestnut Hill on the Delaware ¢   *Tel:* 908–995–9761
63 Church Street, P.O. Box N, 08848

Long-time owners Linda and Rob Castagna invite guests to their romantically decorated Victorian home, built in 1860. Rob repainted Chestnut Hill and its neighboring cottage as "painted ladies;" the main house is a pale shade of green, with accenting shades of darker green, plus gold leaf and cranberry red, while the cottage is a rich cream with ocher trim and five accent colors. In warm weather, guests love to sit on the antique rockers of the wraparound veranda overlooking the Delaware, sipping a glass of iced tea.

The breakfast menu varies daily, and might include fresh fruit salad, juice, German apple pancakes, and home baked muffins. It is served on the front veranda during fine weather, and inside on the candle lit table in the dining room during the cooler months. Each guest room has individual charm; several have spindle spool beds, braided or Chinese rugs, or river views.

"Linda's concern for her guests' well being keeps us coming back. Our favorite room is the private Teddy's Place, with over 170 bears in residence, many sent by past guests. Crisply ironed, white cotton, lacy, designer sheets and monogrammed toothbrushes are typical special touches." *(Linda & David Glickstein)* "Milford is just big enough to enjoy by itself, yet is close to other scenic towns with great restaurants, shopping, antiquing, and bicycling. It is clear from the well-furnished rooms that Linda loves to decorate and does a great job. The third floor suite is our favorite; it is private and has a bathroom overlooking the river—a great way to shower. Linda and Rob are friendly, knowledgeable hosts who are never overbearing. Linda's breakfasts are a delicious way to start the day." *(Joe Waldo)*

"A meticulous restoration. The parlor has ornate moldings, period furniture, and an antique drugstore cabinet displaying Victoriana. The dining room has Anaglypta wallcovering below the chair rail, and an ornate floral Bradbury & Bradbury wallpaper above. Our room was spacious, with a tiny private bath well supplied with plush towels and hot water. Delicious dinner of grilled swordfish with red pepper at the Oyster House nearby." *(NB)*

Open All year.
Rooms 1 cottage, 2 suites, 3 doubles—3 with private bath, 2 with maximum of 4 sharing bath. Some with desk, TV, air-conditioning, ceiling fan. Telephone on request. Cottage with kitchen.
Facilities Dining room, parlor with fireplace, drawing room with gift gallery, library, fireplace, piano, pump organ; wraparound veranda. River tubing, canoeing, hiking, cross-country skiing nearby.

Location W central NJ, Hunterdon Cty. 70 min. W of NYC, N of Philadelphia. Approx. 20 min. NW of Flemington, 30 min. N of New Hope, PA. From I-78, take Exit 11 to Rte. 614 S (toward Pattenburg). Go 7.9 m to Rte. 519. Go left, 2.3 m to Bridge St. & turn right. Follow Bridge St. to Church St., turn right to inn facing river.
Restrictions No smoking. Children 12 and over.
Credit cards None accepted.
Rates B&B, $135 cottage, $80–105 double. Extra person, $10. 2-night weekend minimum.
Extras Bus station pickup.

NEWTON

The Wooden Duck   *Tel:* 201–300–0395
140 Goodale Road, 07860   *Fax:* 201–300–0141

Set in the rolling hills of rural Sussex County, The Wooden Duck is a Colonial-style country home built in 1978, and opened as a B&B in 1995 by Bob and Barbara Hadden. Deer and wild turkeys frequent the open fields and woodlands surrounding the inn. Guests are invited to curl up by the double hearth fireplace in the living room on chilly evenings or relax by the swimming pool on lazy summer days. Furnished with antiques and reproductions, the decor is highlighted (but not overwhelmed) with Bob and Barbara's collections of duck decoys (the source of the B&B's name) and pewter ice cream molds. Breakfast is served at guests' convenience at the dining room table or on the patio, and includes home-baked breads and muffins, fresh fruit, juices, yogurt, cereals, tea and coffee. Homemade cookies and beverages are available throughout the day.

"Beautiful, peaceful setting. Only the sounds of chirping birds to wake us in the morning." *(Rachael & Kevin Detwiller)* "Friendly hosts providing lively conversation, yet were sensitive to guests' needs for privacy." *(Sylvia & Robert McTague)* "Impeccably clean; beautiful, just-picked wild-flowers. Delicious blueberry muffins, served in the dining room with a view of flowering trees and gardens." *(Gail Vigra)* "Comfortable, spacious guest rooms with large modern baths." *(D.O. McCloskay)*

Open All year.
Rooms 1 suite, 3 doubles—all with private bath, telephone, radio, clock, TV, desk, air-conditioning. Suite in carriage house.
Facilities Dining room, living room with fireplace, game room with fireplace, TV/VCR, video library, pool table, games; guest pantry. 17 acres with swimming pool, garden. Adjacent to state park for fishing, hiking, biking; golf nearby. 20 min. to Great Gorge, Vernon Valley, Action Park.
Location NW NJ, Sussex Cty. 50 m W of NYC. From I-80, Exit 25 to Rte 206 N. Go N 6.2 m to Andover Center. Continue N 1.6 m to Goodale Rd. (just past Holiday Motel). Turn right on Goodale Rd. Go 1.5 m to inn on left.
Restrictions No smoking. Children over 12.
Credit cards Amex, MC, Visa.
Rates B&B, $150 suite, $85 double. Extra person, $30.

NORTH WILDWOOD

Reader tip: "Unlike Cape May, the Wildwoods have lots of busy hotels and motels but very few B&Bs. The beaches have long, white sands, and Cape May and Stone Harbor are within driving distance for shopping and exploring. Numerous good restaurants nearby." *(Evelyn Sloat)*

Candlelight Inn ¢
2310 Central Avenue, 08260

Tel: 609–522–6200
Fax: 609–522–6125

An imposing four-story Queen Anne Victorian home awaits visitors to this residential section of the Wildwoods. Central Avenue is a broad tree-lined boulevard, with wide borders and a landscaped center island. Built by Leaming Rice at the turn of the century, it remained the family home until it was restored as a B&B in 1985 by Paul DiFilippo and Diane Buscham. They've decorated the inn in period, with a 1855 sofa and Eastlake piano in the parlor, and the original built-in oak breakfront and chestnut pocket doors in the dining room. Guest rooms are furnished with brass or antique wooden beds, period pieces in oak, mahogany, walnut, and pine, accompanied by Oriental rugs, old prints, and lace. Rates include a full breakfast, afternoon refreshments; and in-room evening sherry, chocolates, and fresh flowers.

"Diane and Paul are the best part of the inn, and are responsive to guests' needs. They're always ready with touring suggestions and ideas, and send you on your way with ideas, maps, reservations and whatever else is needed for a pleasant excursion. Hammocks entice you to laze away the afternoons. The hot tub is available anytime, with plenty of extra towels on hand. The rooms are bright and airy with fresh flowers; the atmosphere is comfortable and relaxing. The delicious breakfasts include eggs Benedict, blueberry pancakes, French toast with strawberry sauce, or crepes, accompanied by a bacon, sausage, or ham." *(Evelyn Sloat)* "Romantic atmosphere. Paul and Diane are always accomodating to special dietary needs and no request is a problem. Afternoons bring fresh lemonade, hot tea, homemade cookies and breads." *(Michelle McCaffrey)*

Open Feb.–Dec.
Rooms 1 suite, 7 doubles—all with private bath and/or shower, ceiling fan. 4 with air-conditioning, 1 with whirlpool tub; suite with TV, refrigerator, microwave.
Facilities Dining room, parlor with piano, wraparound porch, deck, hot tub, hammocks, outside shower. On-site parking. Short walk to beach, tennis. Bicycling, fishing, boating, golf nearby.
Location Jersey Shore. 40 m S of Atlantic City, 6 m N of Cape May. Take Garden State Pkwy. S to Exit 6 (Rte. 147.) Go E on 147 to 24th Ave. Turn left on 24th. From Garden State Parkway N take Exit 4. Turn left on New Jersey Ave. Go to 24th Ave. to inn on left.
Restrictions No smoking. Not suitable for children.
Credit cards Amex, Discover, MC, Visa.
Rates B&B, $125–235 suite, $80–125 double. 2-3 night minimum July, Aug., holiday weekends. 10% senior discount midweek. Murder mystery weekends off-season.
Extras Station pickup. French spoken.

OCEAN CITY

Ocean City is located 30 miles north of Cape May and eight miles south of Atlantic City. The Lake brothers (who were all ministers) established the town as a Christian summer resort in 1879, and prohibited the sale of liquor. Ocean City has remained a dry town, and a family atmosphere prevails. Good fishing, an eight mile long beach with amusement and music piers, and a pleasant climate also account for its popularity. Tennis and golf are available as well. To reach Ocean City, go south on the Garden State Parkway to Exit 30. Follow signs for Ocean City, and go around traffic circle to Route 52 which becomes 9th Street in Ocean City.

Reader tip: "Ocean City has a lovely beach and boardwalk. Since it is a 'dry town' it does not attract a rowdy crowd of teenagers as do many New Jersey beach resorts." *(Judy Hayes)*

Northwood Inn
Tel: 609–399–6071
401 Wesley Avenue, 08226

Among Ocean City's leading historic restoration projects was the Northwood Inn, a 1894 Queen Anne Victorian house. John Loeper, along with his wife Marj, used his experience as a builder of wooden boats and custom homes to restore the Northwood in 1989. Once peeling clapboards are now distinctively painted in cream, with soft green and salmon accents. The interior, including the original oak and plank pine floors, has been totally restored. The furnishings are antique, with Victorian brass or wrought iron headboards in the guest rooms and some pieces from a Connecticut island once owned by showman Billy Rose. Two guest rooms are built into the inn's turret, giving them an uncommon shape. All window treatments, spreads, and ruffles have been custom made with designer fabrics. A "continental-plus" breakfast is served on weekdays; on weekends, a typical meal might include baked apples, French toast or blueberry pancakes, bacon, banana muffins, fresh fruit, juice, coffee, tea, and decaf.

"The aroma of just-baked cake greeted us, along with a warm welcome from Marj and John. Comfortable beds and a bright, cheerful interior. The Loepers are knowledgeable; they are willing to meet the special needs of their guests." *(Joann Montagna & Trish Roche)* "Located in the 'gardens' section of town, close to the nicest beaches. After a day out on the sand, the wide sweeping porch lined with rockers is most inviting. We awoke to the smell of Marge's fresh-baked muffins, anticipating another delicious breakfast, served on the sun porch. Beautifully decorated guest rooms, notably clean." *(Sandra & Michael Sexton)*

Open All year.
Rooms 1 suite, 7 doubles—all with private bath and/or shower, radio, clock, air-conditioning, ceiling fan. 2 with TV.
Facilities Dining room, living room with stereo; billiard room with pool table; library with TV/VCR, guest refrigerator. Limited off-street parking. Beach shower, dressing room; beach tags. 3 blocks from beach.

Location 4 blocks from center. Follow Rte. 52 to 9th St. Bridge. At 5th light, go left on Wesley Ave. to inn at corner of 4th St. & Wesley.
Restrictions No smoking. Children 10 and over.
Credit cards MC, Visa.
Rates B&B, $135–145 suite, $75–105 double. Extra person, $15. 2-night holiday, summer weekend minimum. Discount for 3-night midweek stay. 7th night free.
Extras Airport/station pickup.

Serendipity B&B ¢   *Tel: 609–399–1554*
712 Ninth Street (Route 52), 08226

Here are five good reasons to stay at the Serendipity B&B: the guest rooms are clean and comfortable; the location is close to the beach, shops, and restaurants; the food is good and good for you; the owners are welcoming; and the price is right. Built in 1912, the inn has been owned by Clara and Bill Plowfield since 1991. Rates include a copy of the *Philadelphia Inquirer* and a breakfast of fresh-baked muffins, juice, coffee, and herbal tea. For an additional charge, hot vegetarian entrées may be ordered from 8:30–9:30 A.M., including omelets, whole-grain waffles and pancakes.

"The guest rooms are furnished for comfort and rest—a large chair, magazines, bottled water, terry robes, immaculate bathrooms, superb mattresses, colors in seashore blues, greens, and mauve, and sparkling clean windows. At high tide you can hear the surf pounding the beach." *(Judith Bonifacino)* "Innkeepers are attentive to every detail, accommodating and friendly. Excellent dinner, carefully prepared with quality vegetarian ingredients." *(M. McDonald)* "It's fun to visit during the Indian Summer Weekend with boardwalk sales and a block party, including food and crafts." *(Kathryn Lindenfeld)* "The guest rooms are small with cheerful, colorful linens and bedspreads; some have canopy beds or cozy window seats." *(Judy Hayes)* "Clara and Bill have notebooks filled with information on the area restaurants, shops, and activities." *(Elizabeth Kaufman)*

Open All year. Dinner Oct.–May by reservation.
Rooms 6 doubles—2 with private bath, 4 with a maximum number of 4 people sharing bath. (2 with half-bath, 2 with in-room sink). All with clock, air-conditioning. 2 with ceiling fan. Oscillating fans on request.
Facilities Dining room, living room with fireplace, TV/VCR, stereo, books; sitting room, porch. 2 beach showers, dressing rooms. 1/2 block to beach. Bicycle rentals nearby.
Location 2 blocks from center. Take Rte. 52 across bridge. Rte. 52 becomes 9th St. Inn on right, ½ block before boardwalk.
Restrictions No smoking. Children over 10.
Credit cards Discover, MC, Visa.
Rates B&B, $48–80 double. Full breakfast, $3–4 additional. 2-night weekend minimum. Off-season weekend packages; dinner $15.

PEMBERTON

Information please: If you'd like to rent a canoe to explore the Pine Barrens, or have family or business at Fort Dix or Deborah Hospital, consider the **Isaac Hilliard House** B&B (31 Hanover Street, 08068; 609–894–0756), dating back to the 1850s. Each of the four guest rooms have a private bath, and the B&B double rates of $50–85 ($125 for the suite) include hearty breakfast with homemade preserves. Guests can relax in the gardens, or cool off in the swimming pool.

PRINCETON

Despite the fact that Princeton is the home of Princeton University and numerous large companies, we have no B&Bs or inns to recommend. Though fairly well known, reader reports on the establishments described have been *mixed*. Suggestions most welcome.

Information please: The **Nassau Inn** (Palmer Square, 08542; 800–862–7728 or 609–921–7500) is the best-known hotel in Princeton. Members of the Continental Congress came here to eat in 1783. Now a 217-room hotel, rooms have been refurbished with handmade quilts and period furnishings. One recent report noted that "the location is great; the guest rooms are beautiful and quiet with thick walls and carpeting; the lounge areas are also warm and inviting." Another reader complained: "Twice during a one-night visit we overheard loud arguments between the guests and staff when we walked through the lobby. Although our room was fine, we thought the price was too high." *(AH)*

A small hotel alternative is the **Peacock Inn** (20 Bayard Lane, 08540; 609–924–1707). Built in 1775 as a private home, the popular Le Plumet Royal restaurant occupies the main floor. Double rates for the seventeen guest rooms (most with private bath) range from $90–125 and include a buffet breakfast. Every night except Saturday overnight guests are offered a three-course prix fixe dinner for $28, an excellent value. Comments?

SPRING LAKE

Spring Lake is one of New Jersey's most pleasant shore towns. It offers a 2-mile-long boardwalk (with no commercial facilities) for strolling along the ocean; wide, tree-lined streets, with many turn-of-the-century houses; and, in the center of town, a lovely lake, surrounded by a park. Outdoor activities include golf, tennis, horseback riding, and canoeing. Joggers will enjoy the path around the lake or the boardwalk. Peak season in Spring Lake extends from Memorial Day through mid- to late September. The town is located in Monmouth County, 1½ hours south of New York City, 1½ hours north of Philadelphia and Atlantic City. Take Exit 98 off Garden State Parkway to Route 34. Go 1½ miles to traffic circle and go left on Route 524 (Allaire Rd.). Go east on Route 524 for 3 miles into town.

Reader tip: "Wonderful dinner at The Old Mill Inn. Fantastic swordfish with crabmeat in a macadamia crust. Entrées are pricy but the fixed price three-course menu is a super value at $30." *(Rose Ciccone)*

Information please: Additional reports are needed for two of Spring

Lake's first B&B inns. The **Ashling Cottage** (106 Sussex Avenue, 07762; 908–449–3553 or 800–237–1877) is a mansard-roofed Victorian built in 1877, and offers sunken bathrooms, private porches, lace curtains, and cool ocean breezes. The cottage is just one block from the ocean, and guests are delighted with the warm hospitality of owners Jack and Goodi Stewart. Rates for the ten rooms (eight with private bath) range from $75–150 double, and include a full breakfast.

Built in 1888, **The Normandy Inn** (21 Tuttle Avenue, 07762; 908–449–7172) is located just four houses from the ocean. White wicker tables and chairs furnish the wraparound porch; antique clocks, stained-glass lamps, and gilded mirrors grace the parlor; and beautiful Victorian brass, walnut, and mahogany beds can be found in the guest rooms. The breakfast menu includes eggs to order, omelets, Irish porridge, French toast, or pancakes. B&B rates for the 17 guest rooms range from $92–170 double, $215–265 suite, with 2-3 night minimums most of the year.

For additional area entries, see **Belmar.**

Hollycroft   *Tel:* 908–681–2254
506 North Boulevard, South Belmar
P.O. Box 448, Spring Lake 07762

Along a shoreline where motels and bungalows predominate, a country lodge like Hollycroft comes as a surprise. Built by a prosperous lumber baron in 1908 as a private summer retreat, this inn seems transplanted from the Adirondacks, with its whole log beams and columns, knotty pine walls, and floor-to-ceiling stone fireplace. Linda and Mark Fessler have owned the inn since 1985 and have furnished the guest rooms with country Victorian wallpapers and antique and reproduction beds. Most recently, they completed a luxurious suite, complete with cathedral ceiling and a stone fireplace with a soaking tub opposite.

"Furnishings are substantial and comfortable. The buffet breakfast includes a nice variety of hot and cold offerings, fruit, and freshly squeezed orange juice." *(Fred Best)* "Original brick and mahogany floors, and a double-sided staircase. The Windsor Rose room has a brass queen-sized bed, white wicker furniture, private screened-in porch, and immaculate large bathroom. The rose and green color scheme is complemented by hand stenciling, lace curtains, flowers, pictures, lamps, and all sorts of whimsical accessories. Linda and Mark are always available to offer tips on dining, sightseeing, shopping, recreation and local lore. We explored the public rooms, admiring the collection of handmade dolls, miniature English cottages, ceramic tea pots, antique beaded bags, and the old-time player piano." *(Stephen & Marsha Meyers)*

"Towering oak, pine, and holly trees dominate the view from the sitting area. Breakfast favorites include chocolate-cranberry muffins, scones, and baked apples. Guests can dine outside under the trees, or on the enclosed patio. The guest rooms are large, airy, and comfortable; most afford a wonderful view of Lake Como, situated directly below the house, with the Atlantic shimmering in the distance." *(Erich Rupprecht)* "Delightful inn cats, Pip and Bouncer." *(Joan Rodano)*

Open All year. Closed Christmas.

Rooms 1 suite, 7 doubles—all with private bath and/or shower, air-conditioning. 2 with ceiling fan, balcony or porch, fireplace. Suite with desk, soaking tub, TV/VCR, balcony.

Facilities Dining room, sun-room, living room with fireplace, player piano; breakfast patio. Bicycles, beach passes. 1 acre with hammock, off-street parking. 2 blocks from ocean swimming. Lake/ocean fishing, golf, tennis nearby.

Location NE NJ, on Jersey Shore. 50 m S of NYC, 50 m N of Atlantic City, 70 m N of Philadelphia. From Garden State, take Exit 98. Follow Rte. 34 S to traffic circle. Go around circle to Rte. 524 E (Allaire Rd.). Go 3.3 m to 3rd traffic light (Rte. 71) & turn left. Make quick right on Church St. Go to 3rd Ave., turn left. Go 2 blocks, turn right on North Blvd. Go 2½ blocks to inn on left.

Restrictions No smoking. Children 12 and over.

Credit cards Amex.

Rates B&B, $275 suite, $95–150 double. 2-3 night weekend/holiday minimum in season. Midweek discounts.

Extras Station pickup by arrangement.

La Maison

Tel: 908–449–0969

404 Jersey Avenue, 07762

The name of this B&B will give you your first clue to its owner's love of things French. Built as a guest house in 1870, Barbara Furdyna has owned La Maison since 1982, restoring it to its present charm and elegance when she started innkeeping full-time a decade later. Furnishings include Louis Phillippe furnishings, French-style queen-size sleigh beds, and other treasures Barbara has found during her European travels. Barbara is assisted at the inn by Peter Oliver and Paula Jordan, both artists whose paintings adorn the inn, along with works by other local painters.

Breakfast is an event at La Maison, and is served from 8:30 to 10:30 A.M. at your choice of tables, in the dining room or on the spacious front porch. Oversized French coffee cups are filled with cappuccino, tea, regular coffee, or espresso, accompanied by freshly squeezed orange juice or Mimosas, fruit, muffins, French bread or pastries, plus Belgian waffles, French toast, or quiche.

"The front hall and stairwell walls are covered with paintings and prints which change periodically as they sell. The dining room has a country French look, and is decorated with pine ladderback chairs flanking a large table, and soft red wallpaper with a small floral print with matching draperies. The cozy bedrooms are charming yet not fussy, with delicate pastel wallpapers, bedside tables with reading lamps on both sides of the beds, one or two prints or paintings on the walls, fresh flowers, and balloon shades on the windows. The suites sleep three comfortably in two rooms. The bathrooms are supplied with glycerin soaps, bath gels, and shampoos; some have clawfoot tubs." *(Rose Ciccone)*

"Barbara is an exceptional hostess who made us feel at home in her beautiful house." *(Judy Torello)* "The ample staff accounts for the impeccably clean rooms and deliciously filling breakfasts." *(Chris Young)* "The dining area was lovely with Villeroy & Boche plates and French country figurines; tasty spinach quiche with blue cheese." *(Susan Stelmach)* "Fabulous poached pears and waffles. The town and beach are easily reached on foot or bicycle. The porch is great for relaxing with a good book in the seaside air. The refrigerator of complimentary soda and beer is a thoughtful touch." *(Robert Green)* "Our serene bathroom had a Jacuzzi tub, with white European tiles and a skylight." *(Kenneth Friedman)*

Open All year.
Rooms 2 suites, 4 doubles, 1 cottage, 1 single—all with private bath and/or shower, telephone, TV, air-conditioning. Cottage with kitchen, living room, porch. 1 with whirlpool tub.
Facilities Dining room, living room with fireplace, stereo, books; wraparound porch, guest refrigerators. Garden, off-street parking, bicycles. Beach passes. 4 blocks to ocean. Tennis, golf nearby.
Location 1 block to town center. Take Rte. 524 E to Spring Lake. Cross railroad tracks, turn right on 5th Ave. Go 5 blocks, turn left on Jersey Ave. to inn on left.
Restrictions No smoking. Children over 12 in inn; any age in cottage.
Credit cards Amex, DC, Discover, MC, Visa.
Rates B&B, $130–220 suite, $100–175 double. Extra person, $35. Senior, AAA discounts off-season. 2-3 night weekend/holiday minimum in season.
Extras Wheelchair access, cottage. Free train/bus station pickup. Some French, Spanish spoken.

Sea Crest by the Sea   *Tel:* 908–449–9031
19 Tuttle Avenue, 07762

John and Carol Kirby chose early retirement from high-pressure careers in northern New Jersey to move south to the Jersey shore, where they had long vacationed. Their 1880s Victorian home, Sea Crest, had been a guest house for 25 years, and when they bought it in 1989, it was sorely in need of refurbishing. Now hardwood floors gleam throughout the house, accented by French and English antiques. Guest rooms are individually decorated: the Yankee Clipper has memorabilia from John's days as an officer in the Merchant Marines, while the Velveteen Rabbit room has reminders of Carol's favorite childhood story. The luxurious Teddy Roosevelt suite has a soaking tub for two, placed just right for enjoying the warmth of the room's fireplace. Breakfast, served from 9 to 10 A.M., features the Kirby's special blend of coffee, accompanied by fresh fruit salad, yogurt, buttermilk scones with orange marmalade and clotted cream, and such daily specials as honey walnut French toast, spicy cheese toasting bread, and old-fashioned breakfast pudding; afternoon tea is served to the tunes of a player piano in the background.

"Beautiful inn, great location. The Victorian Rose room, one of the larger guest rooms, has a fainting couch set near the windows to take advantage of the ocean view. Carol and John Kirby are delightful hosts; there when you need them, absent when you don't. Delicious buffet breakfast of herb scrambled eggs, roasted potatoes with sausage, butterscotch muffins, and more. At each place was a small bowl with a peach and blueberry cobbler topped with whipped cream. The entire staff goes of their way to be helpful." *(Rose Ciccone)* "The 100% cotton sheets and duvets accented with lace, the fresh flowers, thick towels, Caswell-Massey bath amenities, and antique furniture create a pampering atmosphere." *(Annette Curnyn)* "An easy walk to the beach, with on-site parking." *(Sheila Morrison)* "John helps with luggage, dinner reservations, and is a fount of local lore. Carol keeps breakfast surprises coming from the kitchen and the rooms neat and spotless." *(Robert Rodriquez)*

Open All year.
Rooms 1 suite, 10 doubles—all with private bath and/or shower, air-conditioning, TV. 7 with remote-control gas fireplace. Suite with gas fireplace, soaking tub for 2, mini-refrigerator, private porch.
Facilities Parlor with player piano, living room with fireplace, dining room, porch. Bicycles, croquet. On-site parking. ½ block from beach, boardwalk. Tennis, golf nearby.
Location 6 blocks from center. From traffic circle, take Rte. 524 E (right), go 1 block. Turn right on Tuttle Ave. to inn.
Restrictions No children. No smoking.
Credit cards MC, Visa.
Rates B&B, $195–239 suite, $110–179 double. 2–3 night weekend minimum; 2-night midweek minimum July, Aug.
Extras Station pickup.

White Lilac Inn ¢   *Tel: 908–449–0211*
414 Central Avenue, 07762   *Fax: 908–295–3796*

Porches are made for summers and ocean breezes, and the White Lilac Inn, built in 1888, has them in abundance, with triple-tiered southern-style verandas wrapping around one end of the house. A guest house since the 1920s, the inn was renovated and reopened in 1995 by Mari and Chuck Slocum, who furnished it with some Victorian antiques and wicker furnishings. Breakfast is served from 8:30 to 10 A.M. at tables for two in the garden room or on the enclosed porch; coffee is available for early birds at 6:30 A.M. On a recent morning, the meal included cantaloupe, orange juice, coffee and tea, crullers and Danish pastry, and a hot entrée such as French toast with sausage, asparagus quiche, or waffles topped with blueberries.

"Thoughtful touches like current magazines and a variety of newspapers, snacks in the kitchen, and a personal note upon arrival. Mari seemed to always have a smile and time for each guest's needs. Friendly fellow guests." *(Dorothy Merryman)* "Decorated with soothing colors and patterned wallpapers. We enjoyed looking through the Slocums' album of 'before and after' photos. The White Lilac Suite has a claw foot tub right in the bedroom, a tiny bathroom, and a door opening to the second floor porch with a view of the pond. Our favorite rooms are the Mary Chess, Jessica's Garden, and the Room at the Top. The garden room has lots of fresh flowers, white lace, soft blue colors, French doors and big windows. The Slocums were gracious, attentive and enthusiastic about their new B&B venture." *(Barbara Ponter)*

Open All year.
Rooms 2 suites, 6 doubles—all with private bath and/or shower, radio, clock. 4 with balcony, 2 with fireplace, 1 with TV, fan.
Facilities Dining room, parlor with fireplace, library with stereo, guest refrigerator, porch. Garden with off-street parking. 1/2 blk to Wreck Pond; 4 1/2 blks to ocean. Tennis, golf nearby.
Location 1/2 to town center. From Rte. 524 E, cross RR tracks. Turn right onto 4th Ave. Continue to Wreck Pond, turn right onto Ocean Rd, quick left onto Shore, quick right onto Central Ave. to inn.

Restrictions No smoking. No children under 14.
Credit cards Amex, MC, Visa.
Rates B&B, $90–110 suite, $55–110 double, $45–100 single. 2-3 holiday/week-end minimum.
Extras Free local train/bus station pickup.

STANHOPE

Information please: Listed in past editions, we need current reports on the **Whistling Swan Inn** (110 Main Street, 07874; 201–347–6369), 1905 Queen Anne Victorian home. The ten guest rooms are decorated in different themes—Oriental, Art Deco, "Forties Swing," and white iron. A typical buffet breakfast includes cold fruit soup, cereals, yogurt, spinach pie, vanilla muffins, with bagels and oatmeal bread for toasting, plus a selection of coffees, teas, and juices. B&B double rates range from $85–110. Stanhope is close to I-80, one hour west of New York City.

For an additional area entry, see **Newton**, twelve miles north.

STOCKTON

Information please: Known as the inspiration for the Rodgers and Hart song, *There's a Small Hotel (with a Wishing Well)*, **The Stockton Inn** (One Main Street, Route 29, P.O. Box C, 08559; 609–397–1250) was originally built as a private home in 1710, and became a stagecoach stop in 1796. Recognized for its fine food served in three dining rooms, the inn also offers eleven guest rooms in four Main Street buildings. B&B rates range from $60–165, and include a continental breakfast. Andy McDermott is the longtime manager. Reports?

The Woolverton Inn ♿   *Tel:* 609–397–0802
6 Woolverton Road, 08559

The Woolverton Inn is a stone manor house built in 1792, set on a hill above the village of Stockton and the Delaware River Valley. It gained its present appearance in the 1850s, when Maurice Woolverton remodeled the building, adding a mansard roof, elaborate scrollwork on the arcaded front porch, fanlight transom, tall windows, and wrought iron cresting. Opened as a B&B in 1983, the inn was bought and refurbished by Elizabeth and Michael Palmer a decade later. Furnishings include antiques, family heirlooms, and Elizabeth's teddy bear collection; terry robes and fresh flowers are among the guest room amenities. Breakfast is served from 9 to 10 A.M. at your choice of tables in the dining room or on the inn's porches, and includes fresh fruit and juice, just-baked muffins, and such entrées as strawberry French toast, fruit crepes, or perhaps orange waffles.

"The Palmers' hard work is paying off on this beautiful inn. It's set on a peaceful knoll with century-old oaks, apple trees, and formal gardens.

Breakfast both mornings was delicious and well presented." *(Gwen & Bob Vaughan)* "Lovely rooms with Victorian touches. The plumbing was up-to-date and all was clean. The location is perfect for a restful sleep." *(TL)* "Excellent service, charming hosts, and outstanding breakfasts." *(Michael & Barbara Scott)*

Open All year.

Rooms 2 suites, 8 doubles—8 with private bath, 2 with a maximum of 4 people sharing bath. All with radio, clock, air-conditioning, 2 with fireplace, 1 with desk, whirlpool tub, deck. 2 in carriage house.

Facilities Dining room with fireplace, living room with fireplace, piano; porches. 10 acres with gardens, croquet, horseshoes, orchard, sheep. Delaware River for fishing, tubing, canoeing.

Location Central NJ, 15 m N of Trenton, 5 m N of Lambertville, NJ & New Hope, PA. From NYC, take NJ Turnpike to Exit 14, to Rte. 78 W. Take Exit 29 to Rte. 287 S to Rte. 202 S. Take 2nd Lambertville exit before Delaware River Bridge. Take Rte. 29 N to Stockton. Bear right onto Rte. 523. Go $^2/_{10}$ m, turn left on Woolverton Rd. to 2nd drive on right. From Philadelphia, take Rte. I-95 N to Exit 31 to Rte. 32 N through New Hope to Rte. 263. Cross Center Bridge over Delaware River to "T" in Stockton; turn left. Bear right at fork onto Rte. 523, then as above.

Restrictions No smoking. Children over 12.

Credit cards Amex, MC, Visa.

Rates B&B, $115–160 suite, $75–120 double. Extra person, $20. 2-night weekend minimum.

Extras Limited wheelchair access.

SUMMIT

Information please: The **Grand Summit Hotel** (570 Springfield Avenue, 07901; 908–273–3000 or 800–346–0773) is just 15 minutes from Newark Airport and 45 minutes from Manhattan. The hotel dates back to 1868, when New Yorkers traveled by train to what was then a resort area. In 1929, the present hotel was built in Tudor style, with detailed brick work, a vaulted beamed ceiling and leaded glass in the lobby, and elaborate detailing. Restored in 1986, the 145 guest rooms are furnished in period decor, some with four-poster beds and cherrywood armoires. The hotel's Hunt Club restaurant has an excellent reputation. Facilities include a fitness center and outdoor swimming pool. Midweek rates include a complimentary morning newspaper and coffee delivered to your room after your wakeup call, plus free shuttle service to Newark airport (by reservation). Rates are $125–185, with corporate and weekend rates available.

Another nearby option is the **Marlboro Inn** (334 Grove Street, Montclair 07042; 201–783–5300 or 800–446–6020) about five miles north of Summit. Set in a residential neighborhood, the Marlboro is an English Tudor-style structure, restored to a 1920s ambience. Original exposed beams and several antiques add to the atmosphere of the lovely public areas. B&B double rates for the 32 guest rooms range from $110–125.

WHITEHOUSE STATION

Holly Thorn House ♿   *Tel:* 908–534–1616
141 Readington Road, 08889   *Fax:* 908–534–9017

Once a cow barn, Holly Thorn has been rebuilt as a replica of an English manor house by Anne and Joe Fosbre. Guest rooms are furnished with antiques and queen- or twin-size beds. Breakfast is served by the fire in the dining area, or outside on the terrace, adjacent to the herb garden.

"Spotless inn, decorated with a myriad of fascinating collectibles. Our handsome room looked fresh and new, with forest green walls, a four-poster bed with a fluffy comforter and lots of pillows, good bedside lights for reading, and matching window treatments. There was an antique desk with writing paper and books, a wingback chair, and basket of magazines. The room was very quiet and the bed exceptionally comfortable. The guest pantry was stocked with hot and cold beverages and homemade cookies. Breakfast was delicious, with cereal, fruit, muffins, coffee, tea, and a choice of omelets. The Fosbres are friendly; we spoke with them at breakfast and they were helpful in directing us to area activities. Great ambience and housekeeping; a wonderfully lovable big old dog, too." *(Pamela Carafello)*

Open All year.
Rooms 4 doubles—all with private bath and/or shower, air-conditioning, clock/radio.
Facilities Gathering room with fireplace, TV/VCR, books, games, puzzles, guest pantry; exercise room with hot tub; billiard room with wet bar. 3 acres with terrace, herb garden, swimming pool, horseshoes. Golf, skating, ballooning nearby.
Location Approx. 40 m W of NYC, 10 m NW of Flemington, 3 m S of Rte. 22. From I-78, take Exit 26 toward North Branch to end. Go left for 700 yards & turn right on Orr Rd. Cross Rte 22; you are now on Readington Rd. Go S on Readington 3 m to end & turn right at church. Go 300 yds. to inn on left. From Somerville Circle, go S on Rte. 202, approx. 4 m & go right at bank. Go 1³⁄₁₀ m to inn on left.
Restrictions No smoking.
Credit cards Amex, Discover, MC, Visa.
Rates B&B, $80–90. Extra person, $25. Corporate rates.
Extras Wheelchair access; 1 room specially equipped.

WOODBINE

Henry Ludlam Inn   *Tel:* 609–861–5847
1336 Route 47, 08270

The homestead of a prominent local family—active in the area since the 1700s—the Henry Ludlam Inn is an early 19th-century farmhouse owned since 1983 by Ann and Marty Thurlow. Hand-stenciled walls, plank doors, wide-board floors, and Colonial-era antiques convey a sense of the past. Marty's four-course breakfast includes homemade breads, seasonal fruits and creative, heart-healthy vegetarian entrées. It is served family-style, around a long table by the common room fireplace, or on the porch in warm weather. Wine, sherry, coffee, and tea are available in the late afternoon. Birdwatchers will want to visit in spring or fall; this area is on the north/south flyway, and several nature sanctuaries are just a short drive away.

"Spacious, clean room full of fascinating decor in a handsome building, no more than a half hour's drive to most places of interest in South Jersey. Best of all is its friendly, concerned owners, and the extraordinary breakfasts—filling, scrumptious, and good for you." *(Ruth Segal)* "Delightful lake for canoeing." *(Lee Gates)* "Ann and Marty welcomed us warmly. Our room was supplied with thick towels, night-time mints, and a fluffy featherbed on the queen-size mattress." *(LS)* "Delightful stories about the inn's ghosts." *(GR)*

Open All year.
Rooms 5 doubles—all with private shower and/or bath, air-conditioning, fan. 3 with desk, fireplace.
Facilities Common room with wood-burning stove, TV, games; screened porch; guest refrigerator. Lakeside gazebo. On lake (canoes available); bird-watching, fishing, bicycling, beach tags. All water sports, golf, tennis, hiking, horseback riding nearby.
Location S NJ, Cape May Cty. 18 N of Cape May, 40 min S of Atlantic City.
Restrictions No smoking. Traffic noise in front rooms. Children 12 and over.
Credit cards Amex, Discover, MC, Visa.
Rates B&B, $85–120 double. Extra person, $20. 2–3 night holiday, weekend minimum in season. Picnics, $35 for 2. Midweek corporate rate.
Extras Airport pickup.

We Want to Hear from You!

As you know, this book is effective only with your help. We really need to know about your experiences and discoveries. If you stayed at an inn or hotel listed here, we want to know how it was. Did it live up to our description? Exceed it? Was it what you expected? Did you like it? Were you disappointed? Delighted? Have you discovered new establishments that we should add to the next edition?

Tear out one of the report forms at the back of this book (or use your own stationery if you prefer) and write today. *Even if you write only "Fully endorse existing entry" you will have been most helpful.*

Thank You!

New York

Onteora Mountain House, Boiceville

Although to some people, New York is synonymous with New York City, the state is an exceptionally diverse one. In fact, the New York State Tourism Council divides the state up into the following distinct regions (not counting the Big Apple, which most consider a region unto itself): Long Island, the Hudson Valley, the Catskills, the Capital (Albany), Saratoga, the Adirondacks, Thousand Islands Seaway, Central/Leatherstocking, the Finger Lakes, the Niagara Frontier, and Chautauqua/Allegheny. The New York State Tourism Division publishes first-rate materials on all these regions; see the appendix for the address and telephone.

If you don't belong to the "see-everything-in-one-visit" club, you might want to design a trip, even within a single region, around a specific theme. Possibilities abound but might include: New York gardens (branch out from the Brooklyn Botanic Garden to the sculpture gardens in Harrison or the formal Sonnenberg Gardens in Canandaigua); craft museums (begin with New York City's American Craft museum for contemporary work, Old Chatham's superb Shaker Museum, or East Aurora's historic Roycroft crafts community); historic architecture (from Manhattan's many landmarks to the Adirondack "Great Camps" and FDR's Hyde Park mansion); ethnic New York (in addition to the Big Apple's myriad ethnic neighborhoods, seek out Albany's Dutch heritage, and sample some of the ethnic food in Buffalo's Polish and German communities); New York's Native Americans (visit the Iroquois Museum in Schoharie, and Niagara Falls's outstanding Native American Center for the Living Arts, housed in a turtle-shaped building).

For those of you looking for inns in the **Finger Lakes,** here is a town-by-town list, to assist in your search: Alpine, Auburn, Branchport, Burdett, Canandaigua, Corning, Dryden, Elmira, Geneva, Hammondsport, Ithaca, Penn Yan, Rock Stream, Skaneateles, Trumansburg.

ADAMS BASIN

For an additional area entry, see **Brockport.**

Canalside Inn B&B ¢   *Tel: 716–352–6784*
425 Washington Street, 14410

The Canalside Inn, listed on the National Register of Historic Places, is a post-and-beam-construction building that dates back to the early 1800s. The Greek Revival–style north portion of the house was added in 1858, when the house was converted to an inn and tavern. In those days, the bar and card rooms were for men only; women and children had to wait in the "Loafing Room" while the men refreshed themselves. The inn was closed to the public in 1916, when the canal had fallen into disuse because of the railroads. In 1972, Bud and Elsie Nichols purchased the house and began a 12-year restoration effort. Each guest room is furnished with a different type of wood—walnut, chestnut, tiger maple, and pine—and is named accordingly.

"A perfect experience. The inn is located beside the old Erie Canal and towpath, now a walking trail. Great care and attention to detail in the restoration. A delectable breakfast of orange juice, poached pears in strawberry sauce, apple pancakes with sausage, muffins, sweet bread, and lots of coffee was served from 8–9:30 A.M. Bud and Elsie Nichols were ideal hosts." *(Judith Brannen)*

Open All year.
Rooms 1 suite, 4 doubles—all with private shower. 1 with desk, 1 with air-conditioning.
Facilities Living room with TV, piano; dining room, porches. ½ acre with fish ponds. Hiking, bicycling on canal towpath. Golf, tennis, swimming, cross-country skiing nearby.
Location W NY, on Erie Canal. 20 m W of Rochester; 3 m N of Ogden. Take Rte. 31 W from Rochester. Turn N on Rte. 36 to town on canal.
Restrictions Smoking permitted in tavern rooms. Children 12 and over.
Credit cards None accepted.
Rates B&B, $65 double, $50 single. Extra person, $10. 2-night weekend minimum.
Extras Airport/station pickup.

ALBANY

For an additional area entry, see **Averill Park,** 15 miles east of Albany.

Mansion Hill Inn 🛉 ✕ �&   *Tel: 518–465–2038*
115 Philip Street, 12202   *Fax: 518–434–2313*

Built in 1861 for brush-maker Daniel Brown, Mansion Hill Inn was used as a tavern for many years. In 1984, Maryellen and Steve Stofelano restored it as a restaurant and inn, and have gradually expanded to four nearby buildings. The inn's popular restaurant offers an appealing and creative menu: a recent dinner included lamb broth with wild rice; red pepper pasta with mushrooms; veal medallions with tart cherries; and chocolate walnut mousse. Breakfast choices include banana French toast, blueberry buttermilk pancakes, frittata, and hot oatmeal, accompanied by fresh fruit and juice.

"In a hilly area with lots of brownstone houses, many in the process of being renovated. It's a good location for walking, with the Governor's Mansion right up the street. My room had reproduction furnishings, wall-to-wall rose carpeting, ruffled rose curtains, and a quilted floral bedspread." *(Kathie Desmond)* "My room was large, nicely decorated and scrupulously clean. Ample hot water and plenty of good reading lamps and drawer space. Dinner was packed with local residents and friends of guests, but Steve makes sure that overnight guests are taken care of. A good choice for business travelers; messages were taken and promptly relayed." *(SF)* "The lovely courtyard was inviting for reading and sharing a drink. Excellent restaurant." *(Nancy Cohn)* "Service by proprietors exceptional; food at dinner and breakfast beautifully prepared and delicious." *(Karen Burstein)* "Outstanding inn, but best of all are the Stofelanos." *(Richard Killun)*

Open All year.

Rooms 8 doubles—all with private bath and/or shower, clock/radio, TV, desk, air-conditioning. Suites with kitchen, deck. Rooms in 3 buildings.

Facilities Dining/breakfast rooms with fireplace. Room service; fax/modem service. 1 acre with off-street parking, garden courtyard. Hiking, boating, fishing nearby.

Location South End; Mansion Neighborhood, around the corner from the Governor's Mansion. From NYS Thruway or I-787, exit at Madison Avenue; follow Rte. 20 (Madison Ave.) through 4 traffic lights; turn left onto Philip St.; continue to 2nd blinking light and inn on right at corner of Park Ave.

Credit cards Amex, DC, MC, Visa.

Rates B&B, $115–155 double, $95 single. 10% service. Extra person, $10. Reduced rates for families. Weekend packages. Senior/AAA discount. Alc lunch, $8–13; alc dinner, $28–35.

Extras Wheelchair access. Station pickup. Pets by prior arrangement. Crib, babysitting. Spanish, German, Italian, French spoken.

ALPINE

Information please: The **Fontainebleau's** (2800 State Route 228, 14805; 607–594–2008) lovely rural setting offers rolling lawns, wooded hillsides, and expansive views of Cayuga Lake. Built in 1814 by Congressman Samuel Lawrence, it stayed in the family's hands until the 1920s. Now renovated as a B&B, it offers three attractive rooms with queen- and king-size beds, hand-stenciling, Laura Ashley prints, and lake views. A full breakfast is served on the porch, overlooking the lake in good weather and is included in the $75 double rate.

AMENIA

Also recommended: *Rose Ciccone* wrote us about her visit to the **Inn at Palmer House** (Cascade Road, 12501; 914–373–7870), offering two spacious suites at B&B double rates of $110; a three-course dinner costs $20–30. "In addition to the bedrooms, the comfortable suites have well-appointed sitting rooms and large handsome wood-paneled bathrooms. The two dining rooms were beautifully done, one a Colonial red with a cozy fireplace, the other decorated in a pearl gray. Our delicious dinner included onion soup, filet mignon with sun-dried tomatoes and shiitake mushrooms and duck with blackberry sauce, and homemade apple pie. Breakfast is taken at a little cafe across the street."

Troutbeck ✕ 木
Leedsville Road, 12501

Tel: 914–373–9681
Fax: 914–373–7080

Once a gathering place for the literati and liberals of the 1920s, Troutbeck has a dual personality: it's a gracious country estate on weekends and an executive retreat for conferences and seminars during the week. It had been vacant for 35 years when James Flaherty and Robert Skibsted bought and restored it in 1979. The main house is a slate-roofed, leaded-windowed Tudoresque manor built from 1918 to 1920, and houses the common areas and some guest rooms; additional accommodations are located in the Farmhouse and the Garden House. Both the common and the guest rooms are furnished traditionally, with pleasing colors and consciously comfortable chairs and sofas. The inn is known for its sumptuous five-course dinners, with a half-dozen appealing entrées.

"We took the train from New York on a snowy weekend; the inn sent a car to meet us, so we wouldn't have to cope with icy roads. We were warmly welcomed by the innkeeper. We went cross-country skiing, followed by a swim in the indoor pool. Dinner was good, the atmosphere delightful; it's clearly a popular choice with locals. Wonderful Sunday breakfast and leisurely morning." *(Amy Blau)* "Every room is different, many with bright sun porches; we like the old-fashioned feel of the ones in the main house best. The inn is filled with books—it was a private residence for years and the main house still feels much like one. In the winter all the cozy common rooms have blazing fires in beautiful stone fireplaces." *(JC)* "The decor and staff give a warm and cozy feel to this large, imposing mansion. The fireplace in our charming, comfortable room was ready for us to light. Of the many common areas, we were especially taken with the card room, with its wonderful poker table." *(Phyllis Stimler)* "No one tells a more amusing story than Jim Flaherty. He makes the whole place work and your stay both relaxing and fun." *(Carl & Judy Stewart)*

Open All year.
Rooms 6 suites, 27 doubles—most with full private bath, radio, desk, air-conditioning. Some with canopy bed, fireplace, deck. 18 rooms in farmhouse, 3 in garden house.

Facilities Dining room; living room with fireplace, piano; bar/lounge with fireplace; library with fireplace, TV/VCR. 442 acres with gardens, indoor and outdoor swimming pools, hot tub, sauna, tennis courts, exercise room, greenhouse, hiking, jogging, cross-country skiing, lake for fishing. Golf nearby.

Location SE NY; Dutchess County, on NY/CT border, near Sharon, CT. 2½ hrs. N of NYC, 1½ hrs. N of White Plains & W of Hartford, 1½ hrs. E of Albany, 3½ hrs. SW of Boston. Take I-684 W to Rte. 22. In Amenia, go right (E) on Rte. 343 2.4 m to inn driveway on right.

Restrictions No children between the ages of 12 mos. and 13 yrs. No smoking in dining room.

Credit Cards Amex.

Rates Full board and open bar, $375–475 per couple, plus tax and 12% service. 2-night stay, $575–790. Lower rates for 2 couples sharing one bath. Prix fixe lunch, $26; dinner, $40. Weekend packages.

Extras Spanish, Portuguese, Italian, some French spoken. Station pickup. Cribs, babysitting.

ATHENS

The Stewart House ¢ ♦ ✗   *Tel:* 518–945–1357
2 North Water Street, 12015

Kim McLean and Yura Adams spent the first half of the 1980s in New York City's trendy SoHo district—Kim as a chef, and Yura as an artist. In 1986 they moved upstream—about 120 miles up the Hudson River to the center of Athens, a relatively unchanged Victorian river town, where their goal was to restore The Stewart House, built in 1883. The dining room has an air of old-fashioned formality, with chandeliers, restored pressed tin ceiling, and white tablecloths; more casual is the equally popular bar/bistro area. Kim's "new American cuisine" has won kudos all around from local reviewers, and many guests come from Albany just for dinner. Although the menu changes frequently, recent dinner entrées included bouillabaisse, herb-crusted pork, and grilled shrimp with Thai peanut sauce, with burgers, fajitas, or sandwiches available in the bistro.

On the inn's second floor is a small sitting room and the guest rooms, most with river views. The innkeepers live on the third floor with their young daughter Mabel. The guest rooms are simply furnished with a few antiques and Oriental rugs; most popular is Room 8, where Meryl Streep "died" in the movie *Ironweed*, still decorated as it appeared in the movie.

"Comfortable, tasteful, and clean guest rooms. Our outstanding dinner combined modern American cuisine with French and Asian influences. Helpful, understanding owners." *(Jon Melnick)* Reports welcome.

Open All year.

Rooms 5 doubles—all with private bath and/or shower, air-conditioning. 1 with fan.

Facilities Restaurant, bar/lounge, sitting room. Parking in front of hotel; park across street. Bicycling, boating, fishing, hiking, cross-country skiing nearby.

Location Hudson River Valley. W side of Hudson River, in center of town. 30 m S of Albany, 120 m N of NYC, 4 m N of Catskill (town). From I-87, take Exit 21.

Turn left at stop sign, go ½ m, then left onto Rte. 23 E. Go 2 m to 1st stoplight & turn left on Hwy 385 N. Go 4 m into Athens. Take 3rd right on 2nd St. to hotel ½ block.

Restrictions Street, bar/restaurant noise possible in summer; light sleepers should inquire. No smoking in guest rooms.

Credit cards Amex, MC, Visa.

Rates B&B, $60–85 double. Extra adult, $15; child under 12, $8; under 3, free. Alc dinner, $25; prix fixe dinner (except Sat.), $19; bistro, $10.

AUBURN

The Irish Rose ¢
102 South Street, 13021

Tel: 315–255–0196
Fax: 315–255–0899

The well-known quote "Living well is the best revenge" is a key element of both the Irish Rose's brochure and its guest philosophy. Pat and Frank Fitzpatrick have owned this 1872 mansion since 1990, and have complemented its original woodwork and hand-carved cherry staircase with antiques and period furnishings. History buffs can walk to Seward Mansion, museums, or the Harriet Tubman Homestead.

"Dried roses form a decorating motif throughout the inn. Pat brought us a basket with fresh towels and fancy soaps matching the colors of our room." *(Donna Bocks)* "The full, eye-appealing candlelit breakfast was a great start to the day. Patricia and her staff are well-informed about area attractions; their professional attitude assured a memorable stay." *(G.L. Stafford)*

Open All year.

Rooms 1 suite, 4 doubles—3 with full private bath, 2 rooms share 1 bath. All with radio, clock, desk. 1 with fireplace, balcony.

Facilities Breakfast room, parlor with fireplace, TV/VCR, stereo, books; guest refrigerator, guest laundry, porch with swing. Swimming pool, croquet. Tennis, golf, water sports, downhill skiing nearby.

Location Finger Lakes. 24 m SW of Syracuse, N end of Oswasco Lake. In historic district. Take Exit 40 off NYS Thruway (I-90) & go S on Rte. 34 to inn on left, S of Auburn.

Restrictions No smoking in guest rooms.

Credit cards Amex, Discover, MC, Visa.

Rates B&B, $65–95 suite, $65–85 double. Extra person, $10. Tipping encouraged. Reduced rates for children. AAA, mid-week discounts. Certain weekend/holiday minimum. Murder/mystery weekends.

Extras Small pets with prior approval. Airport/station pickups, $20. Crib, babysitting.

AVERILL PARK

The Gregory House ✕ ♿ ¢
Route 43, P.O. Box 401, 12018

Tel: 518–674–3774

The Gregory House was built by Elias Gregory around 1830 and remained in the family for three generations. In 1964 it was purchased by

129

the Jewell family and served as their residence until 1976 when they converted it into a restaurant, expanding it into an inn in the early 1980s. Although they leased the inn to Chris and Melissa Miller from 1991–1994, Bob Jewell informs us that he and his wife Bette are back at the helm, "going full steam." At dinner, chef (and grandson) Rob Jewell offers such entrées as rack of lamb, Wienerschnitzel, and salmon with pink peppercorn sauce.

"Bette and Bob Jewell handled complex logistics for our group with unending good humor and skill. Guest rooms were clean and comfortable and the living room nicely furnished, often with a welcoming fire." *(Benjamin McAlpin)* "Bette and Bob are exceptionally kind and caring innkeepers." *(Nancy Lewis)* "A sitting room separates the cozy bar and restaurant from the guest rooms. Furnishings are country-style and traditional; dark woods prevail. My favorite room (the most romantic) is the first room on the second floor, with a four-poster bed with lace hangings and a bay window. Otherwise, the pleasant rooms are quite similar—all with comfortable beds, a dresser, two chairs, a night table, off-white walls, stenciling along the ceiling, and wooden floors with scatter rugs." *(Nancy Cohn)* Comments welcome.

Open All year. Restaurant closed Mon.
Rooms 12 doubles—all with full private bath, telephone, radio, desk, air-conditioning; 2 with balcony.
Facilities Restaurant, bar, common room with fireplace, TV, books. 1 acre with swimming pool, off-street parking. Nearby lake for swimming, windsurfing. Golf nearby; 20 min. to cross-country, downhill skiing.
Location E central NY; Hudson Valley. 15 m E of Albany, 10 SE of Troy. In center of village on Rte. 43.
Restrictions Traffic, hall noise in some rooms. Limited smoking. Children over 12.
Credit cards All major.
Rates B&B, $85–95 double, $80–90 single. Extra person, $5–10. Alc dinner, $30.
Extras Limited wheelchair access. Station pickups.

BERLIN

The Sedgwick Inn ¢ ♖ ✕
Route 22, P.O. Box 250, 12022

Tel: 518–658–2334
800–845–4886
Fax: 518–658–3998

Edie Evans left her career in hospital management in 1981 for the "retirement" career of running a country inn. The Sedgwick Inn was built as a stagecoach stop in 1791, and was originally part of the Van Rensselaer estate. Guests enjoy a full breakfast, served from 8 to 9 A.M. on the airy sun porch. Lunch and dinner are also available in the coach tavern dining room. The menu changes weekly, with a choice of five entrées at dinner; Viennese-style desserts are a specialty.

"A warm and comfortable inn, with an interesting collection of art and objects (including Edie's sculptures). Our comfortable room was well ventilated and charmingly decorated. Excellent food and atmosphere at dinner. One Saturday evening, four generations of a family were celebrating a 50th wedding anniversary and, after dinner, sang along to the accompaniment of the piano. The warmth and joy of the scene was wonderful; we felt privileged to be present. Edie, a gracious hostess, said that the music is often contagious; she's delighted when guests join in." *(William Hussey)*

"The Colonial-style rooms in the motel wing are clean and quiet, most with two double beds, a black and white TV, and ceiling fan. We have visited in the heat of summer and cold of winter and have always been comfortable. The charming Carriage House shops have wonderful antiques, edibles, cookware, one-of-a-kind stuffed toys, pottery, and jewelry." *(Mary Kraushar)*

"The inn is old—the slightly canted floors and doors and windows out of plumb add to its charm—yet every last nook and cranny is scrupulously clean and in good repair. Each bathroom has a supply of toiletries and luxurious towels; old-fashioned tubs hold hot water in abundance. The food is accompanied by a backdrop of quiet music, either from a tape, or on weekends, from Charlie playing the piano in the corner. Breakfast includes fresh orange juice, copious quantities of aromatic coffee, freshly baked buns or rolls, and eggs to order, all served with more music and the morning papers, including the *New York Times*." *(Kathleen Ober)*

Open All year. Restaurant closed Mon., Tues.
Rooms 1 suite, 10 doubles—all with private bath and/or shower, telephone, radio, fan. Many with desk, TV. 6 rooms in annex.
Facilities Dining rooms, 2 sitting rooms, with fireplace, TV, books, video discs; antique/gift shops. Dinner pianist weekends. 12 acres. Hiking, skiing, swimming, fishing, cross-country skiing nearby. 12–14 m to downhill skiing at Jiminy Peak, Brodie.
Location E central NY. Approx. 30 m E of Albany, 15 m W of Williamstown, MA, 25 m NW of Tanglewood. On Rte. 22, 5 m S of intersection with Rte. 2.
Restrictions No smoking in inn guest rooms; no cigars in dining room. Children in motel only. Traffic noise in front rooms.
Credit cards Amex, DC, MC, Visa.
Rates B&B, $100–125 suite, $65–95 double, $55–75 single. Extra person, $12. Alc lunch, $6–10; alc dinner, $20–25. 2-night minimum summer, fall weekends. Children under 6, free.
Extras Limited wheelchair access. German, French spoken. Pets in motel by arrangement.

BINGHAMTON

For an additional area entry, see **Deposit.**

Strawberry Hill Bed and Breakfast   *Tel: 607–785–5058*
564 Jones Hill Road, Vestal 13850

An 1824 farmhouse filled with antiques and situated among quiet meadows, Strawberry Hill was opened as a B&B in 1994 by Hope Cormack. Breakfast is served on trays, allowing guests the choice of dining location—perhaps the wraparound veranda or by the fireplace. "A bit of

Europe and a dash of Americana surrounded by beautiful scenery." *(Edward Morris)* "Breakfast included assorted fruits, teas and coffees, pastries, cakes, warm home-baked breads, and more. Hope also provided afternoon punch, cheese and crackers, and other snacks." *(Michael Grotti)* "Hope's fine selection of antiques, her homey touches, and her respect for our privacy coupled with friendly conversation, all combine to make one feel pampered but not smothered. Delicious pancakes with fresh strawberries and whipped cream for breakfast; dietary requests graciously accommodated. Charming gift shop." *(Linda Kent)* "Our guest room was quaint, comfortable, and appealing, with a view of green lawn and magnificent trees." *(June Betty DeBolt)*

Open All year.
Rooms 1 suite, 4 doubles—with private and shared baths. Suite with double Jacuzzi, fireplace, balcony.
Facilities Living room with fireplace, library with fireplace, wraparound porch. Four acres with gift shop, swimming pool.
Location S central NY. 9 m W of Binghamton. From Rte. 17 take Exit 67 S. Follow Rte. 26 S to blinking light at Pierce Hill Rd. & turn right. At stop sign turn left on Main St. (Vestal). Cross over bridge and turn right on Glenwood Rd. Take 2nd right onto Jones Rd. Go 1 m to inn (pass house to upper driveway).
Restrictions Smoking porch available. Children by arrangement.
Credit cards None accepted.
Rates B&B, $95–125 suite, $75–85 double, $60–80 single.

BLUE MOUNTAIN LAKE

In the heart of the Adirondacks, Blue Mountain Lake is a good base for hiking and canoeing in the area's many mountains and lakes; it's also home to the Adirondack Museum, devoted to the history, culture, and geography of this region. You can easily spend a full morning or afternoon wandering the exhibits—from guide boats, to paintings, to a custom railroad car. Another possibility is the Blue Mountain Lake Arts Center, with daily classes and special night programs.

Information please: Listed in past editions is **Hemlock Hall** (Route 28N, 12812; 518–352–7706 or, in winter, 518–359–9065), owned by Paul and Susan Provost. This old-fashioned summer resort offers 23 rustic accommodations in motel units, lodge rooms, and 1- and 2-bedroom cottages, with private or shared bath; some have kitchens, porches, and/or fireplaces. Guests are summoned to the family-style meals by a large bell on the porch of the lodge (usually rung by one of the visiting kids). Activities include free use of canoes, sailboats, paddle boats, and rowboats, plus numerous hiking trails. Rates range from $110–130 for two in a cottage, including breakfast and dinner, lodge rooms are less, and children are warmly welcomed.

We also need current reports on **The Hedges** (Blue Mountain Lake, 12812; 518–352–7325 or in winter, 518–761–3115), a relaxing, old-fashioned lakeside inn, long owned by the Van Yperen family. Rustic lodges and cabins are furnished with simple oak antiques and traditional Adirondack furniture. The double rates of $128–148 include breakfast and dinner (single entrée, salad bar, homemade breads, and dessert), tea and coffee throughout the day, and evening coffee or cocoa, cake, and cookies. "The two lodges (circa 1880 and 1920) feature the requisite reading room with fireplace and deep, upholstered chairs, plus a porch with tree trunk posts. Even though it rained, we enjoyed sitting in the Adirondack chairs, reading, listening to the loons, and gazing out on the glassy water. Buffet-style meals are served in the dining hall, and guests are assigned a particular table for their stay." *(DB)*

BOICEVILLE

For additional area entries, see **Fleischmanns** and **Lake Hill.**

Onteora, The Mountain House ♿   *Tel:* 914–657–6233
96 Piney Point Road, Box 356, 12412   *Fax:* 914–657–6233

Onteora is the house that mayonnaise built. In 1929, Richard Hellmann cashed in his recipe for mayonnaise and retired to the mountain retreat he had designed. For the site, he chose a pine-studded promontory with views of the Ashokan Reservoir, the valley of Esopus Creek (famous for its trout), and the valley the Mohawk Indians called Onteora (on-tay-OR-ah)—"The land in the sky." In 1992, Bob McBroom and Joe Che bought Onteora and restored it as a B&B. The inn's great room is highlighted by a 15-foot picture window, cathedral ceiling, stone fireplace, and comfortable contemporary furnishings.

"Art Deco mixes with an Emersonian ambiance in this transcendental Catskill retreat. Engaging hosts suffused the sharp mountain air with seductive musical rhythms and enticing aromas. The monumental grace of the setting is complemented by elegantly styled distractions—backgammon, chess, and billiards. Walk amid rich foliage and deer habitat. Visit the nearby time warp known as Woodstock." *(Gina Gold & Richard Horton)* "The rooms are beautifully furnished, especially the antique dressers and pottery collection. We played billiards on a perfectly maintained 1920s pool table in a room designed like a Spanish wine cellar. The superb breakfast included fresh juice, coffee, our choice of pancakes (including caviar), or an omelet, with bacon or sausages, and ripe melon." *(Louis Milgrom & Naomi Gamorra)* "Congenial innkeepers. Arts and Crafts interior is accented by Joe's Korean influence. Well-appointed guest rooms are adjacent to the great room where a tremendous fire keeps guests warm. One is lured to the screened porch by tremendous views of the Catskills and the inventive breakfasts, served from 8:30–10:30 A.M." *(Livia Cowan & Mark Glovsky)*

Open All year.
Rooms 1 suite, 3 doubles—1 with private bath, 3 with sink in room & a maximum of 4 people sharing bath. 1 with fireplace, porch.
Facilities Dining porch, great room with fireplace, stereo; game room with billiards, library, sun deck, observation deck. 25 acres with gazebo, swing set, lawn games, pond. Tennis, canoeing, tubing, swimming, cross-country skiing, hiking nearby.

Location Catskill Mts. 18 m W of Kingston, 100 m N of NYC. From I-87, exit at Interchange #9 (Kingston). Go right at rotary (Rte. 18, Pine Hill), 15 m to Boiceville. Go right on Piney Point Rd.
Restrictions Smoking in game room only. Children 12 and over.
Credit cards MC, Visa.
Rates B&B, $135 suite, $95 double, $80 single. 2-night weekend minimum. 10% discount for 4-night stay.
Extras Pets by prior arrangement. Japanese, Korean spoken.

BRANCHPORT

Branchport is located in the Finger Lakes, 11 miles north of Hammond-sport, on the west side of Keuka Lake, about 60 miles south of Rochester. Water sports are popular of course, along with wine touring, hiking, and birding.

For an additional area entry, see **Penn Yan.**

Gone With the Wind
453 West Lake Road, 14418

Tel: 607—868—4603

A 1887 stone building with broad white porches overlooking Keuka Lake, Gone With the Wind has been owned by Linda and Robert White since 1989. Breakfast, served from 8:30–10 A.M., might include banana, blue-berry, apple, or pumpkin pancakes, Ashley's stuffed French toast, or Scarlett's Scrambled Eggs, plus Rhett's Rhubarb Rave, Melonie's Muffins, fruit, freshly baked pastries, and cereal. After breakfast, guests may feel like quoting Scarlett themselves: "I'll never go hungry again."

"We enjoyed the cozy fire in the living room, followed by a delightful soak in the hot tub while watching the falling snow. A walk around the grounds and through the woods whetted our appetite for the leisurely, delicious, and elegant breakfast. Memorable pumpkin pancakes with freshly whipped cream." *(Lucia Reed)* "Friendly, pleasant innkeepers; wel-coming Christian atmosphere." *(MW)* "A beautiful house built on the side of the high ridge that runs along the lake's west shore. First choice is Scarlet and Rhett's Hideaway, a well-decorated king-bedded room, which opens onto a veranda, with a beautiful view of the lake and far shore. Rhett's Room, while small, was furnished with a comfortable canopy bed. Robes were supplied for the bathroom, which was well equipped with toiletries. Excellent breakfast with delicious local grape juice, coffee cake, warm fruit compote, Amish French toast, and flavored coffee. Inviting front veranda. Built onto the back of the adjoining garage is a skylit hot tub, surrounded by windows and overlooking the woods and garden. Only one room's occupants use it at a time; a small gate closes off the access hallway when it is in use." *(Fritz Shantz)*

Open All year.
Rooms 6 doubles with maximum of 4 people sharing bath. All with radio, clock, fan. 3 with air-conditioning, 1 with refrigerator, deck.
Facilities Dining room, living room with fireplace, library with fireplace; porch, hot tub. 14 acres with gazebo, private beach cove. Boating, tennis, golf, cross-country skiing, hiking nearby.

Location From Rte. 17 in Bath, turn N on Rte. 54A to Hammondsport. Continue on Rte. 54A to inn.
Restrictions No smoking. Children age 6 and over.
Credit cards None accepted.
Rates B&B, $70–125 double. Extra person, $20.
Extras Airport/station pickups. Some Spanish spoken.

10,000 Delights ¢
1170 West Lake Road, 14418

Tel: 607–868–3731

Delights come in abundance at this 1850 Greek Revival mansion overlooking Keuka Lake. Filled with antiques and original art, the main house offers eight theme rooms from the romantic Lavender and Lace Room to the Native American Room. Outbuildings include a three-bedroom house on the beach, a cathedral-ceilinged luxury apartment, a studio-cum-herb shop, and a Japanese teahouse set at the top of a 60-foot waterfall—a stream flows under the glass-paneled cypress floor. Owner Vera Van Atta writes us, "I don't believe that any guest leaves who has not been touched by wandering through our gardens and woods, meditating in the Japanese teahouse or the tipi tucked away in the pines, or sitting among the twelve 14-foot banners honoring Native Americans. Mine is not so much a business as it is a mission." "Breakfast is a three-course affair (one does not need lunch), served on the veranda of the circa 1850 house. The food is always delicious and beautifully presented, including a dessert topped with a whimsical Gummi Bear. Be sure to try the fresh grape juice from a neighbor's vineyard. Owner, chef, and chief decorator Vera Van Atta joins guests for coffee and conversation. The inn is convenient to Corning, the other Finger Lakes, as well as towns and restaurants located on Keuka Lake." *(Donna Kluegel)*

Open May 1–Oct. 31. Lakeside House open all year.
Rooms 1 suite, 10 doubles, 1 single—2 with full private bath. 10 with a maximum of 4 sharing a bath. Most with clock, fan. 2 with desk. 3 rooms in Lakeside house; 1 in carriage house suite with whirlpool tub.
Facilities Dining/breakfast room, living room with fireplace, library, guest refrigerator, porches/patios. 50 acres with gardens, walking paths, stream & waterfall, Japanese teahouse, beach/dock for swimming; canoe, sailboat, paddleboat.
Location 2½ m S of Branchport on Rte 54A. Watch for a mailbox that looks like a small cottage with a blue roof, on side of road opposite lake.
Restrictions No smoking. No children Fri., Sat., Sun.
Credit cards None accepted.
Rates B&B. $110 suite, $70–90 double, $60 single. Extra person, $20.
Extras Crib.

BROCKPORT

For an additional area entry, see **Adams Basin** and **Hamlin.**

The Portico B&B ¢
3741 Lake Road, 14420

Tel: 716–637–0220

In 1850, John Bowman built this imposing Greek Revival red brick mansion—complete with three porticos, massive white columns, pediments, and a cupola—for his fiancé, Kate Bellinger. Just before the wedding, John disappeared on a trip to New York, and never returned. Kate dressed in black and stood vigil in front of the house as a sign of her grief; we assume she was mourning her absent lover, but no doubt her grief was tinged with sadness for the house she would never have. These days, things are happier at The Portico, a warm and hospitable B&B owned by Anne and Ronn Klein since 1989. Framed by mature sycamores, maples, and blue spruces, it's located in a neighborhood of historic homes, and is a short drive from a growing antique market. The Klein's breakfast will surprise and delight you: a recent menu included orange juice; strawberries in cream, smoked salmon with capers and lemon, quiche, mushrooms with bacon and chutney, gingered cantaloupe, and pound cake with chocolate curls.

"The Kleins are doing a wonderful job in this on-going restoration. Our large front bedroom was tastefully decorated with a dark floral wallpaper and dark green trim, and furnished with a reproduction desk, a wonderful antique dresser, wicker chairs, and a comfortable queen-size brass bed, smothered in pillows. A vase of fragrant lilacs and lilies-of-the-valley was a nice touch. The new private bath was clean and bright. Anne offered good, candid dinner recommendations, and when we returned, our room had been straightened, the bed turned down, and we had been left ice water, almond cookies, and a charming note from the Kleins. The house is remarkably quiet. Delicious, if unusual breakfast, served at my convenience: broiled grapefruit, pumpkin roll, chicken in Dijon sauce, cheese soufflé, and raspberry sorbet. Welcoming, yet unobtrusive hostess." *(Fritz Shantz)* "Tea and snacks upon arrival, coffee whenever desired, fruit and candy to munch on." *(Nancy & Ed Olivo)* "Outstanding food—fresh seasonal ingredients and herbs, beautifully presented. Poached pears with mulberry sauce a favorite." *(Jan Stephens)* "The Kleins are down-to-earth, warm, likable, and friendly." *(Joann Scotty)*

Suggestion box: "A bedside table and light for my side of the bed."

Open All year.
Rooms 3 doubles—1 with private bath, 2 with maximum of 4 people sharing baths. All with fan. 1 with desk, fireplace.
Facilities Dining room; living room; drawing room with piano; library with fireplace, TV/VCR, games, books; cupola sun room; laundry facility; porch. 1.2 acres with picnic area. Tennis, golf, swimming, boating, fishing nearby.
Location W NY. 15 m E of Rochester. Clarkson district, 2 m from Brockport. 7 m S of Lake Ontario. From I-90, take Exit 47 (Leroy) & go N on Rte. 19 to Brockport. Watch for inn on left after passing Rte. 31-Brockport/Spencerport Rd., just S of Rte. 104.
Restrictions No smoking. Children 12 and over. Possible traffic noise in summer.
Credit cards None accepted.
Rates B&B, $70, private bath. $60, shared bath. Tipping "not necessary."

CANANDAIGUA

Information please: Built in 1900, the **Thendara Inn and Restaurant** (4356 East Lake Road, 14424; 716–394–4868) is a 14-room Victorian 'cottage' set on a bluff on Canandaigua Lake. Its five guest rooms are furnished in turn-of-the-century antiques, and have lake views, private baths, TVs, and air-conditioning. The B&B rate of $110–165 includes a continental breakfast. Two of its three dining rooms are highlighted by the spectacular scenery of the lake; from mid-May through mid-September the inn also operates The Boathouse restaurant, offering light fare. Reports welcome.

Acorn Inn
Tel: 716–229–2834

4508 Route 64 South, Bristol Center
Mailing address: P.O. Box 334, Canandaigua, 14424

In 1795, when stagecoaches were the only mode of public transportation, this Federal-style inn began hosting travelers; 55 years later it became a private home. In 1990 paying guests were welcomed once again: Joan and Louis Clark opened the renovated Acorn Inn with all the amenities modern travelers expect. The inn is decorated with 18th and early 19th century antiques, and reflect Joan's expertise in the decorative arts; many are for sale. In the dining room, Windsor armchairs surround the table, and simple linen tieback curtains accent the windows.

"On a cold night, our bed was turned down and warmed. Our room had an inviting sitting area, perfect for reading one of the inn's hundreds of books." *(BB)* "The charming antiques, fine china and silver are complemented by perfectly functioning plumbing, firm beds, and more. Peaceful breakfast in the garden, with their lovely dog Sasha lying quietly at my feet." *(Suzanne Findley)* "Warm, country charm. The beautiful Hotchkiss Suite is decorated in masculine colors, with a sitting area with a beautiful view to the garden, and various bird feeders. We sat and watched finches and hummingbirds flock in front of our window. Spotless bathroom, luxurious towels, inviting whirlpool tub. Incredible breakfasts of fresh fruit cup, fresh-squeezed orange juice, hazelnut coffee, blueberry egg soufflé, and sausages, accompanied by delightful conversation among the guests. John and Louis were pleasant, cordial, and talkative, yet respected our privacy when needed." *(Catherine Kubitz)* "Acorn-shaped chocolates were left to sweeten our dreams when the bed was turned down." *(Linda DeLorm)*

Open All year.
Rooms 4 doubles—all with private bath and/or shower, radio, clock, air-conditioning, fan. Some with fireplace, soaking or whirlpool tub, TV/VCR. Telephone on request.
Facilities Living room with fireplace, books; dining room. 1 acre with gardens, lawn games, nature trails. Golf, hiking, lake for water sports, downhill skiing nearby.
Location NW NY, Finger Lakes. 8 m S of Canandaigua. From I-90, take Exit 43 (Manchester) & go S on Rte. 21. In Canandaigua, take Rtes. 5/20 to Rte. 64. Go S on Rte. 64 to inn on right
Restrictions No smoking. Children over 10.
Credit cards Discover, MC, Visa.
Rates B&B, $75–175 double. Extra person, $25. 10% senior, AAA discount. 2-night weekend minimum, July-Nov. Off-season midweek discounts.

Morgan-Samuels Inn
2920 Smith Road, 14424

Tel: 716–394–9232

"This 1810 historic stone mansion has the appearance of an English manor house. Innkeepers Julie and John Sullivan serve meals to guests only—and do they know how to cook. We like the Victorian Room, with its private balcony, fireplace with slate mantel, and 19-foot garret-style bath with Jacuzzi, surrounded by marble, wood, brick and stone. The Garden Room, off by itself in old servants' quarters, is surrounded by greenery." *(Eloise Daniels)* "Delightful place, quiet setting, friendly hosts; breakfast was a treat." *(Debbie Mosiman)* "Beautiful, rural setting, within ten minutes of a comprehensive shopping area. Lovely grounds; inside are elegant antiques and well-furnished guest rooms with wide-plank hardwood floors and Oriental rugs." *(FS)*

Suggestion box: "Stronger lighting in bedroom and bath."

Open All year. Closed Christmas.
Rooms 1 suite, 5 doubles—all with private bath and/or shower, air-conditioning, fireplace. Suite with whirlpool tub, TV, fireplace. Some with balcony.
Facilities Dining room, breakfast room, living room—all with fireplace; library with fireplace, games, TV/VCR, video library, screened porch. 46 acres with patios, gardens, tennis court, pond, cross-country skiing, wagon/sleigh rides. Downhill skiing nearby.
Location NW NY, Finger Lakes region. From I-90, take Exit 43 (Manchester). Go S on Rte. 21 to Chapin. Turn left on Rte. 488. Turn right on East Ave. At 1st stop sign (Cty. Rte. 4) proceed ¾ m to inn on right.
Restrictions No smoking. Children under 3 or over 10. BYOB. Cancellation policy.
Credit cards Discover, MC, Visa.
Rates B&B, $195–225 suite, $110–195 double. Extra person, $20. Midweek off-season business rate, $70–100. Dinners by reservation Sept.-June. 2-night weekend minimum.
Extras Airport pickups.

CASTILE

For an additional area entry, see **Wyoming**, 15 miles northwest of the park.

Information please: In Letchworth State Park, known for the dramatic beauty of the gorges and waterfalls created by the Genesee River, is the **Glen Iris Inn** (7 Letchworth State Park, Castile 14427-1124; 716–493–2622), an 1828 Federal-style house with Victorian modifications. After preservationist-humanitarian William Pryor Letchworth deeded his home and estate as a permanent park in 1910, the Glen Iris became a restaurant, with overnight accommodations opening in 1914. Today, the 15 guest rooms, and well-known restaurant, are open from Easter until early November (rates range from $70–$135). A succession of readers were delighted with the inn's extraordinary setting, atop the waterfalls, but were discouraged by the crowds of people and traffic.

CAZENOVIA

Founded in 1793, lakeside Cazenovia became a summer retreat for wealthy big-city families after the Civil War, and many of its finest mansions date from this period. The lake remains a focus of activity to this day, with fishing, swimming, and sailing leading in popularity, along with golf, hiking, tennis, and horseback riding. Winter favorites include ice-skating, hockey, ice-fishing, sleigh rides, downhill and cross-country skiing. Cazenovia is in central New York state, 20 miles southeast of Syracuse.

Brewster Inn ✕ ⴲ

6 Ledyard Avenue, P.O. Box 507, 13035

Tel: 315–655–9232
Fax: 315–655–2130

The Brewster Inn is a typical little country cottage—typical, that is, if you were a prosperous business associate of John D. Rockefeller, Sr., in the late 1800s. Benjamin Brewster worked closely with Rockefeller in establishing Standard Oil, and was instrumental in the construction of New York City's elevated railroads. When completed in 1890, the Brewster Inn had nine master bedrooms with baths, eight servants' rooms, and fourteen fireplaces.

Dick and Cathy Hubbard purchased the inn in 1984. The decor combines numerous antiques (some original to the house), cheery floral wallpapers, hand-stitched quilts, burnished hardwood floors, and Oriental rugs. The common rooms feature the original oak and mahogany woodwork, leaded glass windows, and a curving main stairway. Dinner at the Brewster—an area favorite—offers an award-winning wine list to accompany such entrées as salmon with sesame, beef with artichoke hearts, or veal with tarragon butter sauce.

"Staying in the elegant home of a real oil baron was an experience; accommodations were warm, comfortable and cheerful. Richard and Kathy Hubbard attentive to guests' every wish." (George & Haley Garrison) "We stayed in room #4, with a king-sized brass bed and Jacuzzi tub (in the room), with plenty of windows overlooking the lake; there was an old-fashioned tub in the bathroom, plus plenty of thick, fluffy towels. Breakfast was buffet-style, nicely presented: cereal, juices, coffee or tea, a selection of pastries, English muffins, and homemade banana bread." (Jenny Caspar) "We enjoyed the cozy fireside atmosphere in the lounge, nibbling finger food, sipping hot chocolate, playing cards, and watching a basketball game." (Mary Kent) "Delightful setting for a lovely dinner, calm and peaceful with beautiful lawns sweeping down to the lake. Our charming third floor room under the eaves had two double sleigh beds and coordinated wallpaper and fabrics. The guest sitting room on this floor is a good spot for reading—quiet and away from the busy reception area." (Mary Beth O'Reilly)

Open All year. Closed Christmas.
Rooms 2 suites, 15 doubles—all with private bath and/or shower, telephone,

radio, clock, TV, air-conditioning. Most with desk, 4 with fireplace, 4 with whirlpool tub. 8 rooms in annex.

Facilities Restaurant with fireplace, bar/lounge with TV, lobby with fireplace, sitting room. 5 acres with lakefront/dock for swimming, boating, fishing; gardens.

Location Central NY. 3 blocks from center. From I-90, take Exit 34 to Rte. 5, then left (S) onto Rte 13. Go to Cazenovia, turn onto Rte. 20 (W) to inn.

Restrictions Traffic noise from Rte. 20 possible in some rooms. No smoking in dining rooms.

Credit cards DC, MC, Visa.

Rates B&B, $90–225 suite, $60–160 double. Extra person, $10. Alc dinner, $25–35.

Extras Crib, babysitting (by prior arrangement).

CHAUTAUQUA

Although this far western corner of New York state attracts visitors to its lakes, wineries, and antique shops for nine weeks during the summer, a key attraction is the Chautauqua Institution, a century-old National Historic Landmark offering an extensive program of music, opera, dance, theater, lectures and education courses, religious services, and extensive recreational opportunities—golf, tennis, and water sports. Special activities for children are also on the list. For more information, call 800–836–ARTS.

Also recommended: For accommodations within the Institution, a classic choice is the **Athenaeum Hotel** (Box 66; 800–821–1881), a 160-room classic Victorian hotel, built in 1881 and restored 103 years later. All rooms have a private bath and air-conditioning, and double rates range from $208–296, including three meals a day (plus two desserts at dinner, a long-standing tradition)."We relaxed on the verandas overlooking the lake, had a simple but satisfactory room, adjusted to the leisurely pace of meal-time, dressed for dinner, and enjoyed the wonderful activities." *(EKP)*

For additional area entries, see **Westfield.**

Plumbush B&B *Tel: 716–789–5309*
Route 33, Mayfield
Mailing address: P.O. Box 864, Chautauqua, 14722

Less than a mile from the Chautauqua grounds, Plumbush is an Italianate villa built in 1865 and laboriously restored as a B&B in 1988 by Sandy and George Green. Painted in the inn's theme colors of mauve, pink, burgundy, and green, the inn's tower offers a wonderful view of the countryside. The house is handsomely decorated in period, highlighted by a wonderful collection of curios and collectibles. Breakfast includes yogurt, fruit, cheese, granola or cereal, and home-baked goods—perhaps blueberry muffins and applesauce cake.

"Beautiful inn, appealing location, warm and caring owners. Plumbush is exquisitely furnished with antiques and Victorian-style wallpapers. One of the original side porches is now a glassed-in sunroom overlooking acres of meadows and woods; you can snuggle by the stove while the snowy wind blusters, or watch the hummingbirds feed in summer. Breakfast is served here, and you are always welcome to help yourself to an afternoon or evening cup of tea and homemade cookies. Guest rooms range from spacious to small, but all are attractive and comfortable, with extra blankets and pillows, reading lamps by each side of the bed, armoires and dressers for storage, and thick, soft towels for the small but spotless baths." *(Patricia Belcastro)* "The Greens are well informed about area activities, from bird-watching to the Chautauqua program. Fresh flowers from Sandy's garden are found throughout the house." *(Myrna & Earl Lewis)* "Whenever we wandered into the family room, with its floor-to-ceiling windows, George was there to start a fire for us." *(Lois Holino)*

Open All year.
Rooms 5 doubles—all with private bath and/or shower, ceiling fan.
Facilities Dining room, living room with TV, music room with piano & organ, enclosed porch with fireplace, screened & unscreened porches, bicycles. 125 acres with picnic area, hiking trails, cross-country skiing. Tennis, golf, boating, fishing, skiing nearby.
Location W NY. Chautauqua County. 15 m NW of Jamestown, 10 m S of Westfield. 1 m from Chautauqua Institute. From Rte. 17, take Exit 7. Take Cty. Rte. 33 N 3 m, to inn on left. From Rte. 394 at Chautauqua, go S on Cty. Rte. 33 for ³/₄ m to inn on right.
Restrictions No smoking. Children 12 and over.
Credit cards MC, Visa.
Rates B&B, $90–110 double, $80–100 single. 2-3 night weekend/holiday minimum.

CHESTERTOWN

Chestertown is located in the Adirondacks of northeastern New York, 72 miles north of Albany, and 18 miles northwest of Lake George.

Information please: One of the area's best known inns, the **Balsam House** (Atateka Drive, 12817; 518–494–2828) closed after a kitchen fire in 1994, and was due to re-open after renovations for the 1995-96 ski season. The original inn was built in 1891, and was restored in 1981 by Frank Ellis. Unchanged is its lovely setting on Friends Lake, and its location, ideal for fishing, boating, canoeing, rafting, hiking, downhill and cross-country skiing. In the past, B&B double rates ranged from $75–120; the inn is also well-known for its restaurant. Good luck to owners and staff; reports most welcome!

The Chester Inn B&B (Main Street, Box 163; 12817; 518–494–4148), a classic Greek Revival home built in 1830, is owned by Suzanne and Bruce Robbins. Situated on 13 acres with 19th century barns, carriage stalls, and its own smokehouse, the inn offers five guest rooms, each with a private bath and air-conditioning; most with double beds. The rates of $65–125 include breakfasts of fresh fruit and juice, oatmeal, and baked French toast with local maple syrup. For lunch or dinner, the Robbinses invite you to their century-old Coca-Cola soda fountain and restaurant, one block away. "Beautiful rooms, especially the Victorian Suite; great breakfast, helpful owner, restful stay." *(Beth Kientzle)* Additional comments welcome.

Friends Lake Inn (Friends Lake Road, 12817; 518–494–4751), well-known for its creative restaurant, offers everything from blue corn pancakes at breakfast to grilled duck with apple coulis for dinner. The 16 guest rooms, all with private bath and some with Jacuzzi, have double rates of $155–225, including breakfast and dinner. Guests can use the private dock and beach, canoes, and 25 kilometers of groomed cross-country ski trails; the inn runs its own Nordic ski center and rents mountain bikes. Reports please.

CLARENCE

Asa Ransom House ✕ &

10529 Main Street (Route 5), 14031

Tel: 716–759–2315
Fax: 716–759–2791

Longtime owners Robert and Judith Lenz have decorated the Asa Ransom House with antiques and period reproductions, country wallpapers and Colonial motifs. The inn's restaurant is extremely popular with visitors and locals alike for its good country cooking. Among the many house specialties are a variety of tempting deep-dish pot pies—chicken and leek, and salmon and vegetable topped with cheese pastry. As might be expected from an inn located in a wine-growing region, the cellar features New York's finest labels.

"Peaceful, comfortable, beautiful setting. Judy, Abby, and Bob provide friendly, caring service, taking special care with respect to cleanliness." *(Bruce Dyer, also DM)* "Beds are excellent, lighting is good for reading in bed, the bathrooms are spotless. The food is consistently well prepared and delicious. Particularly outstanding are the desserts and breads." *(Mr. & Mrs. David McConnell)* "The sitting room invites both restaurant and overnight guests with its blazing fire, jigsaw puzzles, and comfortable chairs for reading." *(Ronald & Shirley Martin)* "Our attractive room was provided with an appealing fruit and cheese basket, along with sparkling mineral water and ice. At checkout, we were treated to delicious chocolate chip-peanut butter cookies. At breakfast, we had a choice of apple oatcakes, blueberry and strawberry crepes, soufflé, and quiche, plus coffee, juice, a fruit plate, toast and bran muffins with three kinds of butter, and peach puff pastries." *(Karl Wiegers & Chris Zambito)*

Open Feb. through Dec.
Rooms 3 suites, 6 doubles—all with private bath and/or shower, radio, TV, desk, air-conditioning. 7 with fireplace, 5 with balcony. Telephone on request.
Facilities Restaurant with fireplace, library with fireplace, games; gift shop. 2 acres with herb & flower gardens, gazebo, picnic area, pond. Swimming pool, tennis, golf nearby. 25 m to skiing.
Location W NY. 18 m NE of Buffalo, 28 m SE of Niagara Falls. Take Exit 49 from I-90. Go N on Rte. 78 (Transit Rd.) to Rte. 5. Go E 5 m to inn at corner of Main and Ransom Rd.
Restrictions No smoking.
Credit cards Discover, MC, Visa.
Rates B&B (midweek), $145 suite, $85–120 double, $75 single. Extra person, $15. MAP, $195–245 suite, $145–220 double. Off-season packages. Alc lunch, $10; alc

dinner, $20–35; children's, early-bird menu. Afternoon tea by reservation. Children's, Braille menu. Tipping encouraged.
Extras Wheelchair access. Station pickup.

COLD SPRING

Just 90 minutes north of New York City is the charming Hudson River village of Cold Spring. Its main street runs steeply downhill from Route 9D to the river, and is lined with charmingly restored (for the most part) 19th-century buildings and intriguing shops. The bandstand overlooking the river offers beautiful views of the Hudson Highlands. Do come here for a delightful escape from Manhattan. Good restaurants abound—and there's a long list of sights worth seeing: Boscobel Restoration, FDR's home and library and the Vanderbilt Mansion in Hyde Park; the quiet little village of Garrison's Landing; and across the river, West Point and Storm King Art Center. For a breath of fresh air, hike the stream-side trails at Manitoga, on Route 9D just south of the Garrison turn-off. But don't come to this area looking for bargains. Room rates are high (and climbing) for what you get, and parking in Cold Spring is inconvenient at best.

Reader tip: "Cold Spring's picturesque Main Street runs about six blocks down to the river and is wall-to-wall antique, gift, and craft shops."

Information please: We need reports on the **Pig Hill B&B** (73 Main Street, 10516; 914–265–9247), right in the middle of town. Stunningly decorated with antiques, nearly all of which are for sale, the inn has a small, formally decorated parlor. Guests tend to relax in the lovely backyard garden, or in their rooms. Breakfast—which might include soufflé rolls, egg pot pies, fresh fruit and juice, and homebaked breads—is served at the dining room table or brought to your door. Each guest room has a different decor, from Adirondack cottage to flowered chintz; most have a fireplace or woodstove. B&B double rates range from $100–$150.

For additional area suggestions, see **Garrison** and **West Point.**

Free copy of *INNroads* newsletter

Want to stay up-to-date on our latest finds? Send a business-size, self-addressed, stamped envelope with 55 cents postage and we'll send you the latest issue, *free!* While you're at it, why not enclose a report on any inns you've recently visited? Use the forms at the back of the book or your own stationery.

We Want to Hear from You!

As you know, this book is effective only with your help. We really need to know about your experiences and discoveries. If you stayed at an inn or hotel listed here, we want to know how it was. Did it live up to our description? Exceed it? Was it what you expected? Did you like it? Were you disappointed? Delighted? Have you discovered new establishments that we should add to the next edition?

Tear out one of the report forms at the back of this book (or use your own stationery if you prefer) and write today. *Even if you write only "Fully endorse existing entry" you will have been most helpful.*

Thank You!

COOPERSTOWN

Cooperstown was founded in 1786 by William Cooper. His son, James Fenimore Cooper, became world famous as the author of a series of books known as the Leatherstocking Tales. Cooperstown is also the place where Abner Doubleday invented the game of baseball in 1839, and is the home of the National Baseball Hall of Fame. The Glimmerglass Opera Theater, noted for its original productions, has a beautiful opera house, right on the lake. Other attractions include the Leatherstocking Theater; the Farmer's Museum, a working museum depicting 18th- and 19th-century life; Fenimore House, with a collection of American folk art and Cooper memorabilia; and nine-mile-long Otsego Lake, with three areas for public swimming, boating, and good fishing. There's plenty of hiking, bicycling, golf, and tennis in summer, and cross-country skiing, skating, and snow-tubing in the winter.

Cooperstown is in New York's Central/Leatherstocking region, 30 miles south of the NY State Thruway (I-90), 20 miles north of Oneonta, and 70 miles west of Albany. From the west, use Thruway Exit 30 at Herkimer (Route 28); from the east, Thruway Exit 25A at Route I-88.

Reader tip: "Wonderful dinner at the Squires Restaurant." *(Ruth Schultz)*

Information please: Once part of the largest cattle farm in Otsego county, the **Brown-Williams House** (Route 28, R.R. #1 Box 337, 13326; 607–547–5569) is a circa 1825 Federal-style home offering five bedrooms (with private bath), a continental breakfast, and a warm welcome to families. Rates range from $60–95. **Evergreen** (Route 33, RD 2,

Box 74, 13326; 607–547–2251) is an 1867 brick home accented by 100-year-old pines, with one two-bedroom suite, one double room, and one single, at rates ranging from $60–150 including a deluxe (and delicious) continental breakfast. Current reports welcome.

Creekside B&B 👫   *Tel: 607–547–8203*
Fork Shop Road, RD 1, Box 206, 13326

Although all are welcome, musically oriented travelers will especially enjoy the Creekside B&B, owned by Fred and Gwen Ermlich, founders of and performers with the Glimmerglass Opera. Cooperstown residents since 1970, the Ermlichs opened their Colonial-style home to B&B guests in 1983. Fred prepares breakfast—perhaps scrambled eggs with herbs or cinnamon French toast—and refreshments are served in the afternoon. Gwen reports that recent improvements to the bridal suite and honeymoon cottage have made them even more delightful for special occasions.

"Peaceful and secluded. The stream that runs through the property is perfect for trout fishing and swimming. Gwen and Fred were friendly and accommodating, offering advice and directions." *(Leigh Hoffman)* "Thought the least expensive, we were delighted with the comfortable Green Room, with a comfortable queen-size bed and spacious bathroom." *(Ellen Simon)* "The Ermlichs make you feel like family, yet treat you like royalty." *(Pat McDermott, and others)* "Gwen and Fred welcome children with open arms and are kind and generous to them." *(Diane Russo)* "The Bridal Chamber was quiet and private with a wonderful view of the mountains and water." *(JMP)* "Ample grounds with plenty of chairs and tables by the creek. Our breakfast feast consisted of homemade cakes and breads, eggs Benedict and fresh fruit." *(Bunny & Max Meister)* "The ample towels were thick, fluffy and color coordinated. Loads of parking. Fred and Gwen fixed us no-fat, no-cholesterol breakfasts, served on a different china each morning." *(Shan Ellentuck)* "Gwen and Fred set my kids up in another room with a TV so that peace and quiet prevailed during breakfast." *(Fred Eng)* "Gwen and Fred told us the history of the opera; we bought tickets and enjoyed seeing them perform—it added a special dimension to our stay." *(Gigi & Steve Shanes-Hernandez)* "We were treated to wonderful after-dinner homemade brownies, a cold drink, and warm conversation on the lovely back porch." *(Ruth Schultz)*

Open All year.
Rooms 1 cottage, 1 suite, 4 doubles—all with private bath and/or shower, TV. Some with ceiling fan, balcony. Cottage with living room, dining room, bedroom, bath.
Facilities Dining room, living room, guest refrigerator, deck. Creek for swimming, fishing.
Location 3 m from town. From Cooperstown, turn right onto Rte. 26. Go 2.5 m and turn left on Fork Shop Rd. Inn is 1st house on left.
Restrictions No smoking.
Credit cards Amex, MC, Visa.
Rates B&B, $145 cottage, $85–135 suite, $80–100 double. Extra person, $10. 2-3 night weekend/holiday minimum. Off-season discount for extended stay.
Extras Crib. French, German spoken.

The Inn at Cooperstown ♙ ♿.
16 Chestnut Street, 13326

Tel: 607–547–5756
Fax: 607–547–8779

Michael Jerome restored and reopened The Inn at Cooperstown in 1985. Built in 1874 as the annex to the Fenimore Hotel (then across the street), the building has a mansard roof and detailing typical of the Second Empire style. The architect, Henry J. Hardenbergh, was also responsible for New York City's Plaza Hotel, Dakota apartments, and Waldorf-Astoria Hotel. Guest rooms are simply furnished with period reproductions; most have white chenille bedspreads, ruffled sheer Priscilla curtains, good lighting, two comfortable chairs or a couch, white or pastel painted walls, and a few framed prints.

"Personal service, attention to detail, and congenial hospitality. Straightforward and spotlessly clean, the inn lacks the calculated cuteness of many Victorian inns." *(Mark Rysor)* "Guest parking is convenient and well lit. A large porch at the front of the inn is inviting on warm summer evenings. Our room was spacious and clean, with two comfy chairs in the sitting area. Fresh linens dressed the comfortable bed. High-quality hand lotion and shampoo were provided. Breakfast consisted of corn muffins, date bread, bananas, apples, juice, coffee, and tea." *(Maria Posella)* "The yellow Victorian inn looked beautiful against the snow. My husband and I had a cozy room with a double bed, two chairs, and a small table, while our sons' comfortable room was furnished with three single beds and a bath." *(Nancy Brower)*

Suggestion box: "A guest pantry to fix an afternoon cup of tea."

Open All year.
Rooms 17 doubles with private shower, fan.
Facilities Dining area; 2 sitting rooms with TV, books, fireplace; conference room; veranda with swings.
Location Cooperstown Historic District, on W side of Rte. 80. 3 buildings N of the traffic light.
Restrictions No smoking in public areas, some guest rooms. Minimal interior soundproofing.
Credit cards Amex, DC, Discover, MC, Visa.
Rates B&B, $98 double. Extra person, $15. Reduced winter rates.
Extras Wheelchair access; 1 room specially equipped. Bus station pickup. Crib, babysitting.

The J.P. Sill House
63 Chestnut Street, 13326

Tel: 607–547–2633

The J.P. Sill House is a 19th-century Italianate Victorian home, built of brick and cut stone, with handcrafted woodwork, marble fireplaces, and etched glass. Restored in 1985, it was purchased in 1990 by Laura and Angelo Zucotti, and is listed on the National Register of Historic Places.

"Restored with extraordinary attention to historic accuracy. Samples of the original wallpaper were found in the attic under five layers of paper; it was reproduced by Bradbury and Bradbury, blocked and printed in the original process. The Peacock room, which has a lavish peacock motif on the wallpaper, is highlighted by real gold leaf. The original gaslight fixtures and chandeliers are complemented by period furnishings, inlaid wood floors, ornate mirrors, and valances.

"Every bathroom amenity—cotton balls, lotions, bubble bath, soaps, and shampoos. Laura's delicious breakfast included melon, fresh-squeezed orange juice, crêpe-like buttermilk pancakes, and Irish soda bread." *(Rebecca Carón)* "Our suite had a delightful private porch and luxurious bathroom. Exceptional breakfasts; Laura is a gifted cook." *(Myra Malkin)* "Charming, comfortable accommodations; impressive housekeeping." *(Catherine Heneghan)* "Laura is a wonderful hostess who made our stay pleasant and comfortable. She encouraged us to use the downstairs parlor where we could drink port or sherry and munch on cookies and chocolates. She recommended local restaurants and called for reservations, and even gave us snacks for the trip home." *(Anne Samuels)*

Open All year.
Rooms 1 suite, 4 doubles. Suite with private Jacuzzi tub, TV/VCR, stereo. 4 doubles share 2 baths.
Facilities Dining room, parlor with games, books, fireplace; porches. 1 acre with lawn, carriage house, off-street parking.
Location Historic district. State Rte. 28 becomes Chestnut St. 2 blocks from center, Otsego Lake.
Restrictions No smoking. No children.
Credit cards Amex, MC, Visa.
Rates B&B, $150–155 suite, $85–105 double. 2-night weekend minimum, June–Oct.
Extras Station pickup.

Thistlebrook B&B ⅃

Tel: 607–547–6093

County Route 28, RD 1, Box 26, 13326

An architecturally dramatic B&B, Thistlebrook is a handsome 1866 barn that Jim and Paul Bugonian converted into a luxurious inn in 1990. The spacious living room is elegantly done in French and English furnishings, with a staircase leading up to a cozy landing containing books, magazines, and periodicals. The deck off the living room is ideal for bird-watching. Surrounded by windows, the garden room offers views of the pond and acres of fields and meadows. In addition to fruit salad, yogurt, granola, cereals, bread and muffins, and juice, breakfast includes such entrées as orange pancakes, French toast, omelets, and frittatas. "When we drove up to the barn it was truly hard to believe that the interior could be anything like the pictures we had seen in a magazine; once inside, we were speechless. The exceptionally lovely interior is an eclectic mix of English, French and Chinese furniture, Oriental rugs, wicker, and chintz. One of the Gothic-style doorways in our master suite led to a huge bathroom, complete with separate bath and shower units, commode, bidet, and a ten-foot-long double-sink vanity. Well-stocked with amenities, the bath also had a walk-in closet with padded hangers and a double dresser. Delicious breakfast of broiled grapefruit with brown sugar, warm zucchini bread, and pancakes with sautéed apples and cinnamon sugar." *(Rose Ciccone)* Comments appreciated.

Open Open May–Oct.
Rooms 1 suite, 5 doubles—all with private bath/shower, radio, clock, air-conditioning, fan. 1 with desk.

147

Facilities Dining room, living room with fireplace, library; deck, garden room with small indoor pool. 5 acres with pond.

Location Otsego County. Leatherstocking Region. 70 m W of Albany. From traffic light in village (corner Chestnut & Main), take Chestnut across Main one block to stop sign (Lake St. Rte. 80). Go left onto Rte. 80 for 2.1 m past golf course, Farmers' Museum. Bear left up hill on Otsego Cty. Rte. 28 for 1.1 m to inn on right. Note: Cty. Rte. 28 is *not* same as state Rte. 28.

Restrictions No smoking. Well-behaved older children.

Credit cards None accepted.

Rates B&B, $125 suite, $105 double. Extra person, $10. 2-night minimum weekend/holiday minimum.

Extras Wheelchair access; 2 rooms specially equipped. Bus station pickups.

CORNING

Located just south of the Finger Lakes, Corning is best known for the Corning Glass Center, covering the history, art, and science of glass making. In addition to several other worthwhile museums, a full range of outdoor recreation is available: tennis, golf, swimming, boating, fishing, hiking, and cross-country skiing.

Information please: Just ten minutes south of Corning is the **Addison Rose B&B** (37 Maple Street, Addison 14801; 607–359–4650), a beautifully restored Queen-Anne-style "painted lady." Rates for the three guest rooms (each with private bath) range from $65–85, and include a full breakfast and afternoon tea.

Rosewood Inn   *Tel:* 607–962–3253
134 East First Street, 14830

Built in 1855 as a Greek Revival home, and then redone in English Tudor style in 1917, the Rosewood was purchased by Stewart and Suzanne Sanders in 1992. Stewart does all the cooking and baking; breakfast is served from 8:30–9:30 A.M., and a recent one included orange-banana juice; fresh fruit salad with honey and vanilla; banana chocolate chip muffins and strawberry rhubarb bread; granola and yogurt; and apple French toast.

"Perfect location just two blocks from Main Street, on a quiet, tree-lined street. The Victorian decor in the living room is striking, from the rust-colored velvet swag curtains to a proper (for Victorians, that is) velvet and lace mantel drape. The rooms are furnished with period antiques; the Frederick Carder suite has beaded board panelling and a marble sink built into a rosewood bureau." *(NB)* "Suzanne and Stewart are terrific, funny, and outgoing. Suzanne has redecorated the inn, keeping the Victorian atmosphere, but lightening things up with cheery floral prints and crisp white linens." *(SWS)*

"Our room was quiet, private, and comfortable with plenty of storage space. The sitting area on the second floor is a great place to visit with fellow guests, and to browse through the menu basket." *(April Burwell)*

"Stewart is a wonderful cook, from the delicious breakfast to the home-baked cookies and fresh lemonade at teatime." *(Diane Wolf)*

Open All year.
Rooms 2 suites, 5 doubles—all with private bath and/or shower, air-conditioning. Some with telephone, TV. 1 with fireplace, private entrance.
Facilities Dining room, living room with piano, sitting room with TV, laundry privileges. Limited off-street parking. Golf nearby.
Location Central NY, Finger Lakes Region. Town center. 1 m from Corning Glass center. Follow Rt. 17 to downtown Corning. Turn S on Chemung St., go 1 block, turn right on First St. to inn.
Restrictions No smoking. Children over 11.
Credit cards Amex, DC, MC, Visa.
Rates B&B, $100–125 suite, $70–105 double. Extra person, $20. 2-night minimum some weekends June–Oct.
Extras Station pickup.

DEPOSIT

Chestnut Inn at Oquaga Lake ¢ 🛅 ✕ 🛫 ⅙ *Tel:* 607–467–2500
498 Oquaga Lake Road, 13754   800–467–7676
                                                                              Fax: 607–467–5911

Although the wood used to built the Chestnut Inn in 1927—North American chestnut—is virtually extinct, we're pleased to report that the inn itself is alive and well—unlike many similar summer resorts of the era. Restored in 1992 by two local businessmen, the inn is just a few feet from the shores of Oquaga Lake; James Gross is the manager. Dinner entrées include chicken with sherry and chives, pork with applejack gravy, and fettucine with shrimp in lime butter.

"Rooms are furnished with lovely country Victorian antiques, and overlook the lake or woods. Relaxing atmosphere, comfortable setting, attentive service, excellent food." *(Marcia Hartz)* "From the innkeeper to the parking lot attendants, the staff is top-notch, well-groomed, sincere, willing to do whatever they can to make your stay memorable. Dinner menus are varied and reasonably priced. Guest rooms comfortably furnished." *(Stephen J. Smith, and others)* Comments welcome.

Open March–Dec. 31.
Rooms 3-bedroom cottage, 6 suites, 30 doubles—10 with full private bath, 20 with maximum of 6 sharing bath. 6 with TV, 10 with desk; fan on request.
Facilities Restaurant, lobby with fireplace, library; game room; tavern with piano, weekend entertainment; dining terrace, patio. Business services. 5 acres on Oquaga Lake for swimming, boating; lawn games. Bicycling, golf, tennis, hiking, cross-country skiing nearby.
Location Southern Tier. 3 hrs. W of NYC. 30 m E of Binghamton. From Rte. 17, take Exit 82, & go S to inn on lake.
Restrictions No smoking in guest rooms, some areas of dining room.

Credit cards Amex, DC, Discover, MC, Visa.
Rates Room only, $99–189 suite, $69–109 double. MAP, $32 per person additional. 15% service. Extra adult, $15; children under 12, free. Alc lunch, $8; dinner, $30. AAA discount. Cottage, $1000–1250 weekly. Packages. Children's menu.
Extras Wheelchair access; some rooms specially equipped. Crib, $5.

DOVER PLAINS

Old Drovers Inn ✗
Old Route 22, 12522

Tel: 914–832–9311
Fax: 914–832–6356

Named for the professional middlemen or "drovers" who purchased herds of cattle and swine from New England farmers and "drove" them down the post roads to New York City's markets, this inn has been welcoming travelers for 250 years. It is well known for its restaurant, the Tap Room; the second floor has guest rooms furnished with antiques and double beds. The breakfast room is decorated with hand painted murals by artist Edward Paine, depicting Hudson Valley landmarks. Weekend breakfasts offer such choices as oven pancakes with apple compote, an omelet with cheddar cheese and spinach, or turkey hash with poached eggs; a continental breakfast is offered weekdays. Chef Francois de Melogue has been winning rave reviews for such dinner entrées as Thai spiced lobster, and rack of veal with roasted shallots and wild mushrooms.

"The real atmosphere of Old Drover rests in proprietors Alice Pitcher, Kemper Peacock, and long-time host Charlie Wilbur. They are professional, elegant, witty, and fun. They're knowledgeable about Dutchess County and can direct visitors to the many charms of the countryside as well as the best spots for antiques." *(Nora Kennington)* "Lovely rooms, terrific food, quiet and relaxing location." *(Linda & Michael Rogalski)* "Ample places to relax inside and out. Dinner was top-notch with creative twists on hearty tavern fare." *(Donna & David Kmetz)* "Although the rates are high, we were delighted to find such an appealing escape so close to New York City. As you would expect from the inn's age, bathrooms are modest, though the toiletries and towels are not." *(MW)*

Open All year. Restaurant closed Wed.
Rooms 4 doubles—all with private bath and/or shower, radio, desk, air-conditioning. 3 with fireplace.
Facilities Restaurant, breakfast room, sitting room, library—all with fireplace. 12 acres. Tennis, golf, skiing, boating, swimming nearby. Croquet, badminton.
Location E NY, Dutchess County. 15 m E of Poughkeepsie. From New York City, take Hutchinson River Pkwy to I-684. Take I-684 N to Brewster. Turn N on Route 22 and continue 21 m N to inn. Watch for sign.
Restrictions Traffic noise possible in some rooms.
Credit cards MC, Visa, Diners.
Rates B&B weekdays, $150–230. MAP weekends, $320–395, including tax and service. 2-night weekend/holiday minimum. Alc lunch $25, alc dinner, $35–60.
Extras Station pickup. Small dogs by prior arrangement. Member, Relais et Châteaux.

DRYDEN

Candlelight Inn ¢   *Tel:* 607–844–4321
49 West Main Street, NY Route 13, 13053

Purchased by Doris and Sam Nitsios in 1995, the Candlelight Inn (formerly known as Sarah's Dream) is a Greek Revival home built in 1828 and listed on the National Register of Historic Places. Rooms are furnished primarily with Victorian antiques, including marble-topped tables, wicker chairs, and elaborately carved canopy beds. Breakfasts vary daily, but might include melon with raspberries and kiwi, granola, egg casseroles, and quiche. Refreshments available throughout the day include hot and cold beverages, fruit, cheese and crackers, cookies and fruit breads. Tea is served midweek (by reservation), with an array of goodies, from cucumber sandwiches to Greek delicacies.

"The candlelit windows create a welcoming impression. The gracious innkeeper treats you like family. Convenient parking and location." *(Darlene Casey)* "Comfortable queen-size brass bed. With Mozart playing softly in the background, we savored delicious cranberry scones, apricot bread, and a breakfast frittata of cheeses, peppers, bacon, and potatoes." *(Patricia Mason)* "Each room has an interesting collection of furnishings, pictures, and books, combining cleanliness and comfort with Victorian charm." *(Ethel & Marshall Weiss)* "An excellent base for touring the Cayuga Lake wine trail." *(Karl Wiegers, and others)*

Open All year.
Rooms 2 suites, 3 doubles—all with private bath and/or shower, air-conditioning, fan. 2 with TV.
Facilities Dining room, living room, library with fireplace, TV/VCR, deck. Tennis, golf nearby. 9 m to Cayuga Lake for water sports. 3 m to cross-country, 8 m to downhill skiing.
Location Finger Lakes region. 9 m NE of Ithaca on Rte. 13. 9 m SW of Cortland. From I-81, exit at Whitney Point and take Rte. 79 W to Richford. Then take Rte. 38 N to Dryden & Rte. 13. 2 blocks to center.
Restrictions Traffic noise in one room. No smoking.
Credit cards Amex, DC, Discover, MC, Visa.
Rates B&B, $85–120 suite, $65–85 double, $55–80 single. Corporate rate. 2-night minimum some weekends. Afternoon tea, $9.50.
Extras Airport/station pickup.

EAGLE BAY

Information please: In the heart of the Adirondacks is the **Big Moose Inn** (Big Moose Lake, 13331; 315–357–2042 or e-mail at bmi@aao.win.-net), a turn-of-the-century Adirondack inn with sixteen guest rooms and a popular restaurant (reservations strongly recommended). Guests are welcome to hike the many trails near the inn, or borrow the inn's canoes to explore the lake, ideal for swimming and birdwatching. Most guest rooms have lake views and queen- or king-size beds, and rates include a continental breakfast weekdays, full on weekends and holidays. Prices range from $40 for a room with shared bath off-season, to $150 for the lakeview room with double Jacuzzi and fireplace on weekends in season.

For an additional area inn, see **Thendara.**

EAST HAMPTON

Although known best for its beaches and fashionable restaurants and shops, East Hampton actually has many historic homes dating back to the eighteenth century. If you're visiting on a rainy day, stop by to see the Mulford House, dating back to 1680, now a museum of architectural history. East Hampton is 96 miles from New York City, on the South Fork of eastern Long Island, reached via the Long Island Expressway or the Southern State Parkway to Route 27.

Reader tips: "The Hamptons are best enjoyed off-season, either in the late spring or early autumn. My favorite time is September, when the weather is usually good and the ocean temperature is still relatively high. July and August can be a nightmare on weekends, with unbelievable traffic jams and mobs of trendy people everywhere, although things are much quieter during the week." *(RSS)* And: "The Hamptons are expensive. Just because you're spending $200 does not mean you'll be staying in a palace." *(MW)*

Typical for a resort town, two- and three-night weekend minimums are the rule in season, with four or five nights required for July 4th and Labor Day weekend. Rates range from high to astronomical, so discuss your requirements with the innkeeper, to be sure you'll get the room you want. Read the fine print and be sure of your plans before booking; in season, many East Hampton inns refund payments only if the room is re-rented, *regardless of the date of cancellation;* refunds are subject to 15-25% processing fees.

Information please: The **Centennial House** (13 Woods Lane, 11937; 516–324–9414), an 1876 summer cottage, has marble bathrooms adjoining elegant bedrooms and a formal parlor which boasts two crystal chandeliers and an Italian marble hearth. Breakfast is served buffet-style in an equally lovely setting. B&B rates range from $100 midweek off-season to $325 weekends in season, with 3-night minimums weekends in season.

Under the same ownership are the **Hedges Inn** (74 James Lane 11937; 516–324–7100) and the **Huntting Inn** (194 Main Street, 11937; 516–324–0410). Both of these historic inns offer comfortable common areas and simple but comfortable guest rooms. The Huntting is also home to the Palm Restaurant, while the Hedges features the James Lane Café. B&B rates range from $125–275, with a continental breakfast. The 1850s-era **Pink House** (26 James Lane, 11937; 516–324–3400) is decorated with a light country touch, without stinting on the luxuries. Breakfast includes fresh fruit, juice, granola, homemade breads and a main dish: perhaps sourdough French toast with sautéed apples and pears. B&B double rates for the four guest rooms range from $135–285 double, including use of the swimming pool.

A charming 1870 Victorian farmhouse, the **Lysander House** (132 Main Street, 11937; 516–329–9025) just opened in 1995. The sunny parlor is decorated with folk art, primitive paintings, and Mexican and Indonesian masks, while the dining room is highlighted by Japanese wood block prints. The two spacious guest rooms have private baths and queen- or king-size beds. The B&B double rates of $100–225 include a gourmet breakfast (served on the brick patio in summer) and afternoon refreshments.

About two miles east of East Hampton is the **Bluff Cottage** (266 Bluff Road, P.O. Box 428, Amagansett, 11930; 516–267–6172), a shingled Dutch Colonial inn built in 1892. Restored as an inn in 1991 by Clem Thompson and John Pakulek, it is handsomely furnished with French and English antiques. This impeccably maintained inn, only a short walk from the beach, is open from April through November. Rates for the four guest rooms, each with a new private bath, air-conditioning, and a water view, range from $185–210, including a light continental breakfast of pastries from fine local bakeries and afternoon lemonade (3–4 night summer weekend minimum).

For additional area entries, see **Shelter Island, Southampton,** and on the North Shore, **Greenport.**

Maidstone Arms ✕

207 Main Street, 11937

Tel: 516–324–5006
Fax: 516–324–5037

The Maidstone is set across from the town pond and village green in East Hampton's National Historic District. Originally built as a private home around 1750, it was converted to a hotel in the 1870s. In 1992, it was purchased by Coke Anne Saunders, and has been carefully renovated and redecorated. Most rooms have Colonial or Shaker-style reproduction furnishings, soothing color schemes, and hand-stitched quilts; especially appealing for special occasions are the private cottages.

A breakfast of freshly squeezed juice, coffee or tea, and a basket of muffins, pastries, and breakfast breads with homemade preserves and honey is served on the plant-filled wicker sun porch; a la carte specialties include sourdough cinnamon raisin pecan French toast and strawberry ricotta griddle cakes. The inn's popular restaurant serves such entrées as roast free-range chicken with semolina gnocchi; grilled sea bream with braised fennel and clam vinaigrette; and rack of lamb with grilled ratatouille and mashed potatoes.

"This New England–style inn has inviting common rooms, and a popular restaurant. Dinner is conducted with style, close attention, and gently self-confident humor." *(JL)* "Charming atmosphere, beautiful decor." *(Julie Irmischer, also LDG)* "Superb food, superior service in both restaurant and inn." *(Harold Greenwald)* Reports appreciated.

Open All year. Restaurant closed 2 weeks in March.
Rooms 3 cottages, 4 suites, 12 doubles—all with full private bath, telephone, TV, desk, air-conditioning. 3 cottages with fireplace, patio, 1 with kitchen.

Facilities Restaurant with fireplace, bar with fireplace, sun room, Water Room with games. 2 acres with lawn furniture, valet parking. Golf, tennis, riding, beaches nearby.

Location 15 min. walk to town. Take Rte. 495 E from NYC to Exit 70. Continue E on Rte. 27 to East Hampton. ¼ m from center.

Restrictions Some traffic noise in front rooms. Smoking only in Water Room.

Credit cards Amex, MC, Visa.

Rates B&B, $295–325 cottage, $275–295 suite, $165–250 double. 5% service. 2-3 night weekend/holiday minimum. Discount midweek, off-season. Full breakfast, $10; alc lunch, $18; alc dinner, $40.

Extras Crib, babysitting.

The Mill House 🏃 ♿.

33 North Main Street, 11937

Tel: 516–324–9766

It's a good idea to renovate your house every 100 years or so, whether it needs it or not, right? Built in 1790, the Mill House Inn was expanded to its present shingled Dutch Colonial style in 1898, and was extensively renovated in 1994 by owners Katherine and Dan Hartnett. Fireplaces and whirlpool or soaking tubs were added to many of the guest rooms, making them especially inviting for a quiet off-season getaway. To further tempt visitors during quiet times, Katherine uses her professional culinary training to entice her guests with hearty full breakfasts—perhaps corn-meal waffles or made-to-order omelets—plus afternoon tea. Breakfast is served from 9 to 10 A.M. in the dining room or on the porch overlooking Windmill Green, and can also be brought to your room between 7 and 10:30 A.M. A typical summer breakfast includes fresh fruit and juice, perhaps a berry cobbler with fresh whipped cream, cereal, and just-baked muffins and breads. Guest rooms have quality linens, thick towels, and featherbeds, with inviting decor. The Hampton Breezes room has cheerful floral prints and a pink and green color scheme, with a pine queen-size bed and antique armoire, while the Dominy Mill Room is done in deep greens, red checks, and flowers, with a white iron full-size bed, and a striking view of the historic windmill.

"During our spring visit, we took long walks along the beaches, then returned to the inn's cozy living room, snuggled up before the fire with hot cups of tea. Convenient location, easy walking distance of the town center." (MW) Reports needed.

Open All year.

Rooms 8 doubles—all with private bath and/or shower, radio, clock, air-conditioning, fan. Telephone, TV on request. 6 with gas fireplace, 3 with whirlpool tub.

Facilities Dining room, living room with fireplace, books; guest refrigerator, porch. ¾ acre with off-street parking, hammock, gardens; beach passes. 1 m to beaches, fishing.

Location Historic district, across from Hook Windmill. 1 block from shops, restaurants.

Restrictions Traffic noise possible in front rooms during summer. No smoking.

Credit cards Amex, MC, Visa.

Rates B&B, $125–225. Extra person, $25. Tipping envelopes. 2-3 night weekend/holiday minimum in season. Off-season cooking workshops.

Extras Wheelchair access; bathroom specially equipped. Station pickups. Crib, babysitting by arrangement. Spanish spoken.

ELIZABETHTOWN

For an additional area entry, see **Westport.**

Stony Water Bed and Breakfast ¢ 🏃 ♿
Roscoe Road, RR #1 Box 69, 12932

Tel: 518—873—7125
800—995—7295

Lovers of books and the outdoors will find kindred spirits waiting at Stony Water. Reputed to have been a stop on the Underground Railroad, this 1870 Italianate farmhouse was once home to author Louis Untermeyer, and was visited frequently during the 1930s and '40s by poet Robert Frost. Curl up before the six-foot library fireplace when the weather is chilly; when the sun shines, explore the inn's grounds and the many Adirondack attractions within an easy drive. Set amid fields and woodlands by a babbling brook, Stony Water was restored as an inn in 1990 by Winifred Thomas and Sandra Murphy. Wake-up coffee or tea is brought to your room, and breakfast is served from 7 to 9:30 A.M.; in addition to orange juice and fresh fruit, it might include cranberry apple muffins, eggs to order (compliments of the chickens in the barn), bacon, and homemade toast; blueberry pancakes and sausage, or vegetable frittata. No mixes are used, and sugar and salt are kept to a minimum. Afternoon tea is available in the library.

"We were warmly welcomed by the innkeepers and their lovely little dog, and offered tea and cookies. Inside is a huge library/great room, filled with endless books and comfortable chairs. The immaculate exterior boasts a broad veranda and beautiful landscaping." (*Anne Turcot*) "Each room is immaculate and well-appointed with thick towels, good reading lights, and interesting reading material. Breakfast is delicious; individual tastes and dietary needs are met with ease." (*Barbara & Mark Kronman*)

Open All year. Sometimes closed in April or Nov. Dinner by reservation, Sept.–June.
Rooms 2 cottages, 1 suite, 2 doubles—all with private bath and/or shower, radio, clock, fan. 2 with desk, balcony/deck; 1 with refrigerator.
Facilities Dining room, living room; library with fireplace, books, games, TV/VCR; music room with grand piano, guest refrigerator, screened/unscreened porches. 87 acres with swimming pool, streams, gardens, hammock. Hiking, bicycling, cross-country skiing nearby; 30 min. to downhill skiing; 15 min. to Lake Champlain.
Location N NY; Adirondacks. 2 hrs. N of Albany; 1½ hrs. S of Montreal; ½ hr. E of Lake Placid. 2 m to town. 10 min. from I-87, Exit 31. Call for directions.
Restrictions No smoking.
Credit cards Amex, MC, Visa.
Rates B&B, $85 cottage, suite, $75 double, $65 single. Extra person, $15. Picnic lunch, $6. Prix fixe dinner $20; children under 12, $8. 2-bedroom cottage, $500 weekly.
Extras Wheelchair access; 1 room specially equipped. Crib. French spoken.

FLEISCHMANNS

For additional area entries, see **Boiceville** and **Lake Hill.**

River Run B&B ¢ 🏃

Tel: 914–254–4884

Main Street, Box D-4, 12430

Attention dog lovers! In contrast to most inns, your dog is warmly welcomed—not rejected, not just tolerated—at River Run, a rambling Victorian house, built in 1887 and renovated as a B&B a century later. Owner Larry Miller describes the B&B he's owned since 1992 as the "Inn for Pet Lovers," and notes that all are welcome at River Run, whether or not they're traveling with a pet. He's taken care to establish a 'Code of Conduct for Canines' to ensure that the B&B experience is equally pleasant for both two- and four-legged guests. Guest rooms are named for rivers of the Catskills, and are simply furnished with king-, queen-, and twin-size beds. Stained glass borders the windows of the living and dining rooms, where breakfast served from 8:30 to 9:30 A.M. The menu includes fresh fruit and juice, sausage or bacon, such baked goods as Irish soda bread, blueberry muffins, or cranberry bread, and such entrées as whole wheat banana pancakes, cinnamon French toast, or cheddar omelets.

"Larry is an extremely outgoing, charming, gracious host who appears to love being an innkeeper. The 'country comfortable' rooms are cozy, cheerful, and immaculate, with no doggie odors anywhere. A pretty backyard with many large trees completes the scene." *(Gail Davis, also Meg Ruley)*

Open All year.
Rooms 1 2-bedroom apartment, 7 doubles—4 with private bath and/or shower, 3 with maximum of 3 people sharing bath. All with fan, 4 with TV, 1 with desk. Apartment with kitchen, TV.
Facilities Dining room, living room with fireplace, piano; den with TV/VCR, stereo, books; guest refrigerator. 1 acre with stream, lawn games. Swimming, tennis, golf, hiking, hunting, float trips nearby.
Location Catskills. 135 m NW of NYC, 25 m W of Woodstock. Take I-87 to Exit 19 in Kingston, then Rte. 28 W to Fleishmanns.
Restrictions Smoking in ground-floor apartment only.
Credit cards MC, Visa.
Rates Room only, $75–90 apartment. B&B, $50–95 double, $45–85 single. Extra person, $15. 10% AAA discount. 2-3 night weekend/holiday minimum. Tips appreciated.
Extras Limited wheelchair access. NYC bus stops at door. French, German spoken. Crib.

FREDONIA

Fredonia is a small college town in western New York, about 45 miles east of Buffalo, and about 20 miles east of Westfield and Chautauqua. Strong music and theater departments at the college provide a wealth of cultural opportunities during the academic year.

The White Inn ⊄ ♔ ✗
52 East Main Street, 14063

Tel: 716–672–2103
Fax: 716–672–2107

Despite its classic white exterior accented with black shutters, the White Inn was not named for its appearance, but for its founder, Dr. Squire White. He built the original dwelling on this site in 1809; the current building dates to 1919. Rooms are furnished with antiques and quality reproductions. Kathleen Dennison and Robert Contiguglia—both with extensive experience in the hotel and restaurant business—leased the inn since 1993, and plan to purchase it this year.

The inn's restaurant is an established local favorite. Breakfast choices include Belgian waffles with fresh berries, eggs with cheese and herbs, and buttermilk pancakes; the lunch options are convenient, tasty, and reasonably priced; dinnertime brings such entrées as lamb stuffed with spinach and garlic; shrimp with shallots and cream; and filet mignon glazed with peppercorns and lemon.

"Our long-time favorite is even more pleasant under the new management. Helpful front desk; super housekeeping." *(MRW)* "Our large room had two brass beds, antique bureau, and a renovated bathroom; a vanity with sink was unobtrusively tucked away in the corner of our bedroom." *(Nancy Barker)* "The Presidential Suite has a fireplace, Jacuzzi, firm king-size mattress, and TVs in both rooms—the perfect mix of old-fashioned charm and modern elegance." *(Marilyn & Dave Lamb, and others)* Reports needed.

Suggestion box: "A guest sitting room."

Open All year.
Rooms 11 suites, 12 doubles—all with full private bath, telephone, cable TV, air-conditioning. Most with desk; 2 with whirlpool tub, gas fireplace, refrigerator.
Facilities Restaurant, lobby, bar/lounge, meeting rooms. Herb, flower gardens. 1 acre with off-street parking. Golf, playground, vineyards, Lake Erie beaches nearby. 20 min. to cross-country, downhill skiing.
Location W NY, Chautauqua County. Center of town & historic district. 48 m SW of Buffalo. From I-90, take Exit 59 and go S on Rt. 60. At Rt. 20, turn right and continue 1.3 m to inn on right.
Restrictions Some traffic, interior noise. Smoking permitted in 5 guest rooms, some dining sections.
Credit cards Amex, DC, Discover, MC, Visa.
Rates B&B, $89–169 suite, $59–99 double. Extra person, $5. Children under 12 free. Alc lunch, $7; alc dinner, $28. Children's portions. Dinner packages.
Extras Limited wheelchair access. Crib. Babysitting with notice. French spoken.

GARRISON

Information please: Established in 1761, **The Bird & Bottle Inn** (Old Albany Post Road, R2 Box 129, 10524; 914–424–3000 or 800–782–6837) pre-dates the Revolutionary War. Originally known as Warren's Tavern, it was an important stagecoach stop along the old Albany Post Road, now Route 9. Today, the inn retains the ambience of the Colonial era, with woodburning fireplaces, beamed ceilings, wide plank floors, and authentic antiques. Each of the four beautifully restored guest rooms has a working fireplace and antique furnishings, including a canopy or four-poster bed. The double rate of $210 includes a full English country breakfast and a credit of $37.50 towards the four-course gourmet dinner. Husband-and-wife team, chefs Loren Centrello and Robert Carpino, offer such entrées as roast pheasant with truffle sauce, salmon with lemon vinaigrette, or duck with balsamic vinegar. Ira Boyar has owned the Bird & Bottle since 1982.

GENEVA

Set at the head of Seneca Lake, one of the larger Finger Lakes, Geneva makes a good base for visits to the many excellent area vineyards. It's also home to Hobart and William Smith Colleges, and to Rose Hill, a restored Greek Revival mansion. Geneva is located in the Finger Lakes region of western New York, 50 miles west of Syracuse, and 35 m southeast of Rochester.

For additional area entries, see listings for **Branchport** and **Penn Yan**, about 10 miles south.

Information please: A slightly scaled-down replica of the Lancellotti villa of Frascati, Italy, **Geneva-on-the-Lake** (1001 Lochland Road, P.O. Box 929, 14456; 315–789–7190 or 800–3–GENEVA) was built from 1910 to 1914, and was restored as an inn and restaurant in 1980. Rates for the 29 suites range from $160–465 suite, including a continental breakfast. "Opulent pampering, some suites with in-room kitchenettes and Jacuzzis. There's a private, stationary houseboat below the bluff where you can sunbathe; it's reached by a secluded path. The swimming pool in the formal gardens is great fun, too." *(Eloise Daniels)* Comments welcome.

Over a century ago, 50 craftsmen labored for four years to construct a mansion of red Medina stone at a cost of $475,000—in 1885 dollars. The result, a castle built in the Richardsonian Romanesque style, was the private home of Mrs. Carrie Collins until 1926. In 1975, it was transformed into **The Inn at Belhurst Castle** (Lochland Road, P.O. Box 609, 14456; 315–781–0201). All the original leaded glass, marble fireplaces, and hand-carved woodwork were well preserved, and needed only a thorough cleaning to restore them to their original beauty. The eleven guest rooms are decorated with period antiques, including canopied four-poster beds and leather wingback chairs. The restaurant serves hearty portions of prime rib, and a variety of Italian-style veal and seafood entrées. Double rates range from $65–295 and do not include breakfast.

GREENPORT

Information please: Just two blocks from the harbor is the **White Lions Inn** (433 Main Street, 11944; 516–477–8819), with five guest rooms, two with cathedral ceilings and private balconies, and most with private bath. Rates of $65–110 include a home-cooked breakfast.

Bartlett House Inn   *Tel: 516–477–0371*
503 Front Street, 11944

While fast-track types head for the Hamptons in Long Island's South Fork, those who prefer a more relaxed pace are discovering the quieter, slower paced North Fork, now home to award-winning wineries, antique shops, and appealing restaurants. Built in 1908, the Bartlett House is a large, shingled Victorian house with Corinthian columns and stained glass windows. It served as a family home for over 60 years, then became a convent for the nearby Catholic church. In 1982, John and Linda Sebatino restored it as a B&B, furnishing the rooms with brass beds, oak chests, and period antiques. The buffet-style breakfast typically contains orange juice, fresh fruit, cereals, quiche, sausage, scones, blueberry muffins, and granola bran muffins; you can eat in the dining room or take a tray to your room.

"Convenient yet quiet location, a few blocks from the heart of town. John and Linda are friendly, helpful, and knowledgeable, but never intrusive. Our room was scrupulously clean, with a good shower." *(Mary Acker)* "Shaded porch and comfortable chairs for relaxing. The lighting in our room was romantically soft; the bed was comfortable with a warm quilt." *(Donald & Elizabeth Albinson)* "The atmosphere is conducive to reading, conversation, and relaxation. Breakfast is served between 8–10 A.M., with soft music (mostly Mozart) playing in the background." *(Peter Dominic Pecere)* "Exceptional breakfast: hot cornbread muffins, excellent coffee, and a light, tasty egg/cheese soufflé." *(Mary Frances Hatfield)*

Open All year.
Rooms 1 suite, 9 doubles—all with private bath and/or shower, air-conditioning. 4 with desk, 1 with fireplace.
Facilities Dining room, living room with fireplace, books; porch. Gardens, off-street parking. Beach at end of block; 2 blocks to harbor.
Location Long Island, North Fork, Suffolk County. 2 blocks from village, Shelter Island ferry, LIRR. 8 m W of Orient Pt./New London ferry. Take Long Island Exwy E to end at Cty Rd. 58. Go E to Rte. 25 E to Greenport. Inn is at corner of Front St. (Rte. 25) & 5th St.
Restrictions Traffic noise in front rooms. No smoking in dining room. Children 10 and over.
Credit cards Amex, MC, Visa.
Rates B&B, $75–100 suite, $62–100 double, $57–95 single. Extra person, $10. 2–3 night summer weekend/holiday minimum.
Extras Station pickups.

GREENVILLE

Greenville Arms ✕   *Tel: 518–966–5219*
Route 32, South Street, 12083   *Fax: 518–966–8754*

Greenville Arms sits amid lush lawns and gardens dotted in spring with daffodils, tulips, and lilacs. Built in 1889 by William Vanderbilt, this turreted Queen Anne inn has floor-to-ceiling brick fireplaces, chestnut woodwork and wainscotting, original art, lace curtains, antiques, and fresh flowers; it's been owned by Eliot and Tish Dalton since 1989. In buying the inn, Eliot forfeited his position as a tugboat captain, and Tish readjusted her life style as a graphic designer; the whole family helps to run the inn, including their school-age children, Anne Marie and Woody.

Breakfast is served from 8:30–9:30 A.M., and consists of juice, fruit, yogurt, cereals, eggs any style, pancakes, French toast, and a daily special. A set dinner menu is offered for midweek, with a buffet on weekends; the focus is on healthy food, and chef Scott Van Aker, a CIA graduate, is also a certified chef of nutritional cuisine.

"Eliot and Tish welcome their guests with a sincere homey manner. The grounds surrounding the inn are spacious and restful with a large pool and a picturesque creek in front of the carriage house. Tasty meals, friendly atmosphere." *(Marion and Frankie Becker)* "Well-kept rooms and grounds; ample, convenient parking. Eliot is always there to greet the guests and help with their luggage. Excellent art workshops that draw me going back every year." *(Pat Rutigliano)* Comments welcome.

Open All year. Closed Christmas.
Rooms 14 doubles—all with private bath and/or shower, clock, fan. 3 with deck. 5 in main house, 9 in carriage house.
Facilities Restaurant with fireplace, dining room with fireplace, living room with TV/VCR, books; family room with TV/VCR, guest refrigerator. 6 acres with gardens, swimming pool, swing set, lawn games, stream. Tennis, golf, hiking nearby. Art workshops.
Location Hudson Valley/N Catskills. 25 m SW of Albany. From I-87, take Exit 21 (Catskill). Take Rte. 23 W 9 m. Go N (right) on Rte. 32, 9 m to Greenville.
Restrictions No smoking. Children over 12.
Credit cards Discover, MC, Visa.
Rates B&B, $115–150 double, $85–115 single. Extra person, $30. 2-night holiday weekend minimum. Prix fixe, single entrée dinner, $20; weekend dinner buffet, $20.

HAGUE

Trout House Village Resort ¢ ♠ ✕
Lake Shore Drive (Route 9 N), 12836

Tel: 518–543–6088
800–368–6088

Those underwhelmed by the overdeveloped town of Lake George should head directly north to Hague, where the natural beauty of the lake is not obscured by dozens of tacky T-shirt shops. Trout House is an old-fashioned family resort, owned by Lynn and Bob Patchett since 1971, and managed by son Scott and daughter Alice Patchett. Furnishings are modest, although some guest rooms in the main lodge have four-poster and brass beds. Although no organized children's programs are offered, kids will keep busy with all the area has to offer; save a day to visit nearby Fort Ticonderoga.

"Spread out along the lake front, the resort consists of the comfortable old lodge, basic motel rooms and new log cabins. We stayed in the Library Room with a spectacular view of the lake, shelves of great books, and good lighting. We spent a pleasant summer evening in rocking chairs on the big veranda." *(Gladys & Jim Gilliland)* "Beautiful to see the sun come up over the lake." *(Scarlet Gorton)* "Our three-generation family ranged in age from 9 to 80, and all enjoyed themselves thoroughly. Best of all, the owners live right on the property, and it shows." *(Michael Halloran)* "Alice and Scott Patchett are exceptionally caring hosts." *(Horst Buehler)* Reports needed.

Suggestion box: "Brighter lights for reading." Also: "A ceiling fan in the bedroom and a screen for the window."

Open All year. Restaurant closed July, Aug.
Rooms 13 1–3 bedroom cabins, 16 suites, 11 doubles—most with private bath. 3 rooms share 1 bath. All with TV, fan. 12 cabins with kitchen, porch; 9 with gas- or wood-burning fireplace; 4 with whirlpool tub.
Facilities Dining room, living room, TV/game room, lounge. 5 acres with putting green, lawn games, bicycles. 400-foot beach/lake front for swimming, canoeing, kayaking, sailing, fishing, paddle boats; boat docking. Cross-country skiing, snowmobiling, hiking. Golf, tennis nearby.
Location NE NY. N end of Lake George. 8 m S of Ticonderoga. From I-87 take exit 25 and follow Rte 8 to Hague. Turn left onto Rte. 9. Resort on right.
Credit cards Amex, Discover, MC, Visa.
Rates Room only, $95–257 cabin, $39–139 suite, double. Extra person, $5. Weekly rates. 2-night minimum summer holiday weekends.
Extras Airport pickups. Crib, $7 setup charge; babysitting.

HAINES FALLS

Information please: Listed in past editions, we understand that the **Huckleberry Hill Inn** (Route 23A, P.O. Box 398, 12436; 518–589–5799) has reopened with new owners. This turn-of-the century summer boarding house has 18 guest rooms with B&B double rates of $40–80 with shared or private bath. "Innkeepers Carvin and Colleen greeted us at the door with their lovable golden retriever, and helped us up to our cozy room, furnished with antiques. A small bottle of wine was provided in the room. After dinner in town, we enjoyed a nice conversation with the innkeepers and other guests in front of the roaring fire and visited the game room, complete with darts, backgammon, pool, and more. Other activities in the area include downhill skiing and horseback riding." *(Robin Miesemer)*

HAMLIN

For an additional area entry, see **Brockport.**

Sandy Creek Manor House ¢   *Tel:* 716–964–7528
1960 Redman Road, 14464   800–594–0400

Owners Shirley Hollink and James Krempasky urge their guests to explore the wooded acres surrounding the 1910 English Tudor home they bought in 1987. Shirley is a master gardener, maintaining over 25 perennial gardens on the property. This homestay B&B is furnished traditionally, with a few antiques and crafts; feather pillows and Amish quilts highlight the guest rooms. The antique player piano, which has over 1,600 piano rolls, prompts sing-alongs, and guests are often inspired to share tales of their grandparents' player pianos. Breakfasts of fresh fruit and juice, a hot egg dish, breakfast meats, muffins, fruit breads, and coffee cake are served as early as 4:00 A.M. (if necessary), until 9:30 A.M.; tea is offered in the evening.

"Lovely ambience and great hospitality; plenty of friendly outdoor cats, with a cat motif throughout the house." *(Neil & Hazel Hobbs)* "Have no fear that permitting pets also means allowing dirt or fur; this B&B is very clean. Delicious breakfast. We felt like guests in the owners' own home." *(Jim Richards)* "Comfortable rooms; detailed, helpful area information. The location is convenient to Hamlin and Brockport as well as all the antique stores in between. Hamlin Beach State Park is nearby—an extra bonus in the summer." *(Jean Terry)*

Open All year.

Rooms 4 doubles—2 with private bath and/or shower, 2 with maximum of 4 people sharing bath. All with radio, clock, TV, air-conditioning, fan.

Facilities Dining room, living room with fireplace, TV/VCR; family room, music room with player piano, stereo, books; porch. 6 acres with perennial gardens, lawn games, creek for fishing. 5 m to Lake Ontario for swimming, boating. Skiing, hiking, golf nearby.

Location N NY. 25 m NE of Rochester. From Hamlin Beach State Pkwy E, go S (right) on Rte. 272. Go left on Moscow Rd.; take 1st right on Redman Rd. to inn on left.

Restrictions No smoking.

Credit cards Amex, Discover, MC, Visa.

Rates B&B, $55–65 double, $35–45 single. Extra person, $15. Weekly, monthly discounts.

Extras Airport/station pickups. Pets welcome by arrangement.

HAMMONDSPORT

Hammondsport is located on Keuka Lake, in the Finger Lakes region, and is the center of New York's wine-growing region, and is an ideal base for touring local wineries. Keuka Lake is inviting for all water sports, while the Finger Lakes Trail offers a network of cross-country and hiking trails.

Hammondsport is located 30 minutes northwest of Corning, and approximately two hours south of Rochester. Take Route 17 to Bath, then go seven miles north on Route 54. Turn off onto Route 54A, and go ½ mile further into town.

Blushing Rosé ¢   *Tel:* 607–569–3402
11 William Street, 14840   607–569–3483
                                                 800–982–8818

The Blushing Rosé is an Italianate Victorian home built in 1843, painted just the shade of pink you'd expect, given this B&B's name. Ellen and Bucky Laufersweiler opened it in 1986, decorating with Victorian antiques and country decor, including handmade quilts, ruffled curtains, grapevine wreaths, braided rugs and period oak furnishings. Guests enjoy a breakfast of fresh fruit and juice, homemade granola, jams and jellies, and a hot entrée, perhaps baked French toast or cheese strata.

"Great location for wine touring. The spacious Burgundy Room has a king-size lace canopy bed with a handmade quilt (with good reading lamps and bedside tables), pine dresser and cupboard, and country touches from the eucalyptus swags over the windows to the grapevine wreathes and baskets. A radio/tape player with music tapes rested on a desk. A wicker loveseat and table, plus a steamer trunk completed the decor. In the upstairs hall a butler's table held a basket of 'forgetables,' from a toothbrush to contact lens cleaner. The large bathroom was well-stocked with full, fluffy towels; the makeup/shaving mirror on a swing-out arm was particularly useful. Ellen and Bucky were very helpful with directions and dinner suggestions. We opted for the Village Tavern right on the corner and were very pleased. Homemade chocolate chip cookies, plus the fixings for coffee, tea, or hot chocolate were alwasys available." *(Rose Ciccone)*

"Individual thermostats allowed us to control our room's temperature. It had a four-poster, queen-sized bed, a sitting room, and a spotless bathroom. Excellent breakfast of muffins, juice, egg souffle, sausage, and apple butter, served on fine china and crystal." *(Mr. & Mrs. J. Knoetyen)*

Open All year.
Rooms 4 doubles—all with private bath and/or shower, clock/radio, air-conditioning, coffee maker. 2 with fan.
Facilities Dining room, living room with TV/VCR, stereo, books, guest refrigerator; porch. 1/2 block to beach, boat launch.
Location Center of town. 1/2 block to Village Sq.
Restrictions No smoking. No children.
Credit cards None accepted.
Rates B&B, $75–95 double, $65–75 single. Extra person, $20. 2-night weekend minimum late May–Oct.

Park Inn Hotel ✕ ¢   *Tel: 607–569–9387*
37 Sheather Street, 14840

Built in 1828 and operating as an inn since 1861, the Park Inn Hotel overlooks the Village Square, the location of various events, including old-fashioned band concerts weekly in summer.

"Innkeeper and entrepreneur John Jensen and his buddies bought and renovated this historic site in 1978. He also owns the restaurant downstairs where we had our choice of breakfast entrées (omelets, French toast, and pancakes), served from 6:30–11:30; a local tavern, and the Crooked Lake Ice Cream Company. Before breakfast, fresh coffee, doughnuts, and the local paper were set outside our room." *(Zita Knific)* "Suite 4 has a small sitting area with a daybed, two chairs, a table, and an antique dry sink holding the TV; a small bedroom with a double bed and floorlamp; and a large, recently renovated bathroom. Dried floral arrangements, yellow floral spreads on the bed and couch, and the yellow walls made the room quite cheery. The other rooms are similar with different color schemes. My favorite was Room #2, the largest, with a desk, wing chairs, and an armoire." *(Nancy Cohn)*

Open All year. Restaurant closed Sun. in winter.
Rooms 4 suites—all with private bath and/or shower, radio, clock, TV, air-conditioning, fan. 1 with desk, refrigerator.
Facilities Restaurant, bar/lounge with TV, stereo. Limited off-street parking. 1 block from Keuka Lake.
Location Center of town.
Restrictions No smoking in large dining room. Bar noise in some rooms.
Credit cards Discover, MC, Visa.
Rates B&B, $55–75 suite. MAP, $85–105 suite. Extra person, $10–25. Senior discount. 20% business discount midweek. Alc lunch, $6; alc dinner, $16.

HEMPSTEAD

Country Life B&B ¢ ♙
237 Cathedral Avenue, 11550

Tel: 516–292–9219

To experience an inviting side of Long Island life rarely enjoyed by travelers, consider a stay at the Country Life B&B. This shingled Colonial house was built in 1929 and has been owned by Richard and Wendy Duvall since 1972; it opened as a B&B in 1982. Guest rooms are furnished with antiques and traditional decor, including twin four-poster beds and a marble-topped antique dresser in one room, and Queen Anne furniture in another. In good weather, the Duvalls give you a tour in one of their 1929 Model A Fords. Breakfast includes Dutch baby pancakes, cheese strata, or perhaps stuffed French toast; afternoon soda and cheese are also served.

"As a woman traveling alone, it was great to have a safe, inviting, welcoming place to come back to each night." *(Kate Germond)* "The Duvalls' immaculate home is highlighted by Wendy's lovely needle craft. Pleasant, quiet neighborhood." *(Bonnie Sweeney)* "The rooms are cozy with little knick-knacks—lace pillows, family photos, plus comfortable chairs with reading lamps." *(Pierre & Lalor Ferrari)* "Breakfasts were creative, tasty, with outstanding coffee. Never a shortage of hot water. Pleasant location for walking; close to the village and station." *(Lora Stenard)* "The Duvalls are knowledgeable about the area, and are always thinking of ways to make their home more comfortable for their guests." *(Helen & Al Levi)*

Open All year.
Rooms 1 suite, 3 doubles—2 with private bath, 2 with shared bath. All with radio, clock, TV, air-conditioning. 2 with desk.
Facilities Living room with fireplace, stereo, books; dining room. ¼ acre with off-street parking, swing set, lawn games, patio. Golf nearby; 20 min. to ocean beach.
Location Long Island, Nassau Cty. On Garden City border; 1 m to village of Garden City. 20 min. to Kennedy Airport. 7 blocks to NYC train. From CT & NYC, take Northern State Pkwy. Take Exit 26S (New Hyde Park Rd.), continue 2.9 m to Stewart Ave. & turn left. Go 1.9 m, turn right at Middle School. At light, turn left; at next light turn right onto Cathedral Ave. Go through 2nd light; #237 is 3rd house on right after 1st St.

Restrictions Absolutely no smoking.
Credit cards None accepted.
Rates B&B, $150 suite (for 4), $60–95 double. Extra person, $15; infant, $10. No tipping. 2–3 night weekend/holiday minimum in season.
Extras Airport/station pickups, $20 plus parking. Limited German, Spanish, French. Crib, babysitting.

HIGH FALLS

Captain Schoonmaker's B&B ¢   *Tel:* 914–687–7946
County Route #213 West, R.D. #2, Box 37, 12440

Sam and Julia Krieg are both educators—he is an animal behaviorist at SUNY New Paltz, and she is a third grade teacher—who got into the B&B business in 1981. Their B&B occupies three historic landmark buildings—a 1760 Revolutionary War hero's home, a converted barn/carriage house, and the old lock tender's house on the 1840 Delaware Hudson Canal.

"Welcoming warmth and hospitality. Our immaculate room was charmingly decorated with antiques. Throughout the 1760 inn, one finds historic quilts, paintings, and pottery. Our outstanding breakfast consisted of poached pears with raspberry sauce and whipped cream, orange juice, spinach souffle, sausage, homemade bread and jam, blueberry walnut strudel, apricot Danish, and lemon poppyseed cake." *(Kay & James Black)* "Full of antiques, plants, books, pictures, and interesting artifacts. All guests are invited to wine and cheese on Saturday evening before going off for dinner; everyone gathers in front of roaring log fires in the winter or the flower-filled solarium in summer. Guests linger after breakfast just to chat with each other and with Sam and Julia. Although Route 213 runs directly behind the main house, traffic noise was not a problem. Several good restaurants and antique shops are within easy driving distance." *(Patrick & Sarah Swan)*

Open All year.
Rooms 2 suites, 11 doubles, 1 single—2 with full private bath, 12 with maximum of 4 people sharing bath. All with fan. Some rooms with desks, fireplaces, private verandas. 3 guest buildings with 4 rooms and 2 baths in each.
Facilities Dining room; family room with TV, solarium, canopied patio, decks. 11 acres with flower gardens, croquet, woodlands. Remains of 1760 grist mill. Stocked trout stream for fishing and "country dipping." Hiking, cross-country skiing nearby. 5 m to Mohonk Preserve.
Location SE NY; Hudson River Valley. 80 m N of NYC, approx. 10 m N of New Paltz. ½ m to village.
Restrictions Smoking discouraged. No children on weekends; infants and children over 5 permitted Sun.–Thurs. Two rooms in 1760 house very small.
Credit cards None accepted.
Rates B&B, $90 suite, $80 double, $50 single. Extra adult, $20; no charge for children staying in parents' room. Extra charge for fireplace rooms in season.
Extras Bus station pickup.

HILLSDALE

Hillsdale is an attractive resort area, located on the New York/Massachusetts border, 100 miles north of New York City, and 45 miles southeast of Albany. The area is pleasant in winter for skiing at Catamount and Butternut, and popular in summer for golf, swimming, fishing, and hiking. It's also a 20–30 minutes drive to Tanglewood and the other Lenox area attractions.

Information please: Formerly L'Hostellerie Bressane, **L'Aubergine** (Corner Routes 22 and 23, P.O. Box 387, 12529; 518–325–3412) is a red brick Colonial house built in 1783, home to a restaurant downstairs and guest rooms on the second floor. Chef-owner David Lawson serves his guests French-inspired country cuisine. Double rates for the six guest rooms (two with private bath) are $75–95.

Inn at Green River ¢   *Tel:* 518–325–7248
9 Nobletown Road, 12529

The Inn at Green River is a restored 19th century farmhouse, set in a quiet spot above a meadow. Once a parsonage and then an inn of dubious distinction during Prohibition, the building was purchased in 1988 by Deborah Bowen and Andy Rosenzweig. White-washed walls are accented with painted woodwork; the original scrubbed pine doors are complete with ceramic door knobs and old latches. Breakfast is served on the screened porch or in the candlelit dining room, and might include fresh-squeezed orange juice, home-baked scones, and lemon ricotta pancakes, or perhaps baked apples, omelets with tomato, basil, and ham, and hot muffins.

"An eclectic mix of country antiques and quilts, Oriental rugs, Victorian accent pieces, and heirloom photographs; totally charming and mercifully devoid of country kitsch. Our first floor room, right off the living room, had a queen-size bed, with firm mattress, good bedside lighting, and a new bathroom. Deborah has compensated for the lack of closets (frivolous luxuries when this house was built), by adding antique coat racks to each room. We watched deer grazing among the headstones of the centuries-old cemetary behind the property. Breakfast was leisurely, delicious, and interesting; Deborah told us about the area activities." *(NB)* "Our delicious breakfast, served on beautiful china and monogrammed sterling, included eggs Florentine, served with fresh fruit and juice, and home-baked muffins. The Van Buren Room has huge arched windows overlooking the meadow, and a four-poster queen-size bed, plus soft terry robes." *(Carol & Allen Weintraub)*

Open All year.
Rooms 4 doubles—2 with private bath, 2 rooms share 1 bath. All with clock, fan. 2 with desk, 1 with air-conditioning.
Facilities Dining room, living room with piano, fireplace, TV/VCR; porch, terrace. 1 acre with orchard, croquet, cross-country skiing. 8 m to downhill skiing. Hiking, fishing, kayaking, Tanglewood nearby.
Location From I-90 take Exit B3. Go S on Rte. 22 for 9 m. Go left on Rte. 71

towards Great Barrington. At bottom of steep hill, not more than 200 yds. from Rte. 22, make hard right. Inn is 1st on left. From NYC, take Taconic Pkwy to Rte. 23. Exit for Claverack, Hillsdale. Go right (E). At light go left on Rte. 22 N. At fork go right on Rt. 71. House 3rd on right.

Restrictions No smoking. Children over 12.
Credit cards MC, Visa.
Rates B&B, $55–105 double. Extra person, $20. 2-night weekend minimum July, Aug., Oct., holidays.
Extras Babysitting. Some French spoken.

HOBART

Breezy Acres Farm B&B   *Tel: 607–538–9338*
Route 10, R.D. 1, Box 191, 13788

Too many B&Bs have joined the "amenities war" in recent years, offering guests increasingly greater luxury at rapidly rising rates, while neglecting the basics: the hands-on hospitality, comfortable accommodations, down-home cooking, and affordable rates that started the B&B boom in the first place. A visit to Breezy Acres Farm will remind you what B&B is really all about. This 1830s rambling farmhouse was purchased by Joyce and David Barber in 1972, and renovated as a B&B in 1984. The decor includes a solid oak bed made by Joyce's great-great-grandfather, as well as other antiques, hand-crafted pieces, and contemporary furnishings. You can curl up on the down sofa in front of the fieldstone fireplace in the living room, or watch satellite TV on the huge leather sectional couch in the TV room, with deer trophies mounted on the walls.

Joyce prepares all of her own jam, breads and muffins, while David is in charge of maple syrup production, raising the pumpkins, and making applesauce. You'll enjoy the results of their labors each morning between 8 and 9:00 A.M. via such menus as baked apples, chocolate chip muffins, scrambled eggs and bacon, and honey-oatmeal bread; or nutmeg muffins, pumpkin pancakes with maple syrup, sausages, and applesauce.

"The lovely farm setting offers pristine and comfortable rooms and baths, delicious breakfasts, and two charming owners. They even invited us to join them for a slice of most delicious homemade pie." *(Barbara Thompson)*

Open All year.
Rooms 1 suite, 2 doubles—all with full private bath, radio, clock, fan.
Facilities Dining room, living room with fireplace, stereo; family room with TV/VCR, books; porch, deck. 8–9 acres with pond, croquet, walking/ski/snow-mobiling trails; corn, hay, pumpkin fields. Tennis, golf, hiking, hunting, horseback riding, cross-country & downhill skiing nearby.
Location N edge of Catskills., Delaware Cty. 3½ hrs. NW of NYC. 30 E of Oneonta. Halfway between Stamford & Hobart. Take I-87 to Exit 19 (Kingston). Take 1st right off traffic circle—Pine Hill, Rte. 28 W to Rte. 42 N (at Shandaken). Go W on Rte. 23A (at Lexington). Go W on Rte. 23 (at Prattville). Go S on Rte. 10 at Stamford. Inn is 2.2 m from light on right.
Restrictions No smoking. Well-behaved children welcome. Some traffic noise in some rooms.
Credit cards Amex, MC, Visa.

Rates B&B, $60–75 suite, double; $40–50 single. Extra adult, $15; child, $10. Tips appreciated. Generally 2-night weekend minimum, July–Oct.
Extras Crib.

HUDSON

The Inn at Blue Stores
Star Route, Box 99, 12534

Tel: 518–537–4277

Many New Yorkers looking to escape the city head up the Hudson as far as the delightful town of Rhinebeck and stop, which could be a mistake. We'd suggest driving just a bit farther to the peaceful Inn at Blue Stores, a Spanish Mission-style home built in 1908 as a gentleman's farm. Although owner Linda Saulpaugh operates it as a B&B, the property still functions as a working farm. Linda invites her guests to explore the 100 acres of surrounding land with three duck ponds, and to wander the country roads, excellent for walking and bicycling. The clay tile roof, stucco exterior, and expansive porches typical of the Mission style are a pleasant change from the area's typical Colonial or Victorian styles; inside, period antiques, stained glass fixtures, leaded glass entryway, and handsome black oak woodwork complete the picture. Rates include afternoon tea, as well as breakfast, with such entrées as stuffed French toast, yogurt waffles, or baked apple pancakes.

"Spacious porch with a comfortable sitting area and pleasant country view." *(Mary Ann Fish)* "We had a huge bedroom and spacious bathroom. Linda greeted us at 8:00 A.M. with a wonderful egg dish, banana/orange muffins, fresh fruit, yogurt and granola, and a scrumptious lemon poppyseed cake." *(DMB)* "Lovely antiques and dried flower arrangements throughout. On a cold, wintry evening, I was welcomed with freshly baked brownies and hot tea." *(Gail Davis)* "Our daughters loved their room with lacy white bed trimmings and old dollhouse. The bathroom between our room and theirs had a beautiful old porcelain sink, a white tile floor, and a fiberglass modular shower." *(Kathryn Andersen & Stephen Tarnell)* "The water pressure was good, the bed comfortable, the room sunny and cheerful." *(JM)*

Open All year.
Rooms 1 suite, 4 doubles—3 with private shower and/or tub, 2 with maximum of 4 people sharing bath. All with radio, air-conditioning, fan, TV. 2 with desk.
Facilities Living room with fireplace, family room with TV, VCR, fireplace. Dining porch. Piano in hall. Off-street parking. Swimming pool, gardens, goldfish pond, cross-country skiing. Boating, fishing, nearby. 35 m to downhill skiing.
Location 115 m N of NYC. 15 m N of Rhinebeck. 10 m S of Hudson. From Rte. 9 N, inn is ½ m N of Stage Coach Inn, on left; from Rte. 9 S, inn is immediately after Keil Farm Equipment, on right.
Restrictions Smoking restricted. Children 10 and over.
Credit cards Amex, MC, Visa.
Rates B&B, $150 suite, $95–125 double. Extra person, $25. Reduced rates for children, seniors midweek. 2-night weekend/holiday minimum.

ITHACA

Known best as the home of Cornell University and Ithaca College, Ithaca is also a lovely place to visit in the summer months, when the students are gone and the pace slows down. Follow Route 89 north along the west side of Cayuga Lake, past the 400-foot falls at Taughannock Falls State Park, and on to visit the several wineries of the Cayuga Wine Trail. The same glaciers that created the Finger Lakes left the Ithaca area with a combination of steep hills and deep gorges, making for beautiful waterfalls and occasionally treacherous driving in the hilly sections. Ithaca is located at the southern tip of Cayuga Lake, in the Finger Lakes region of central New York, 55 miles south of Syracuse.

We'd love to have some additional Ithaca recommendations; while readers have been generally pleased with the listings below, all have come in for their share of "minor niggles."

Also recommended: Less than two miles from the campuses of both Cornell and Ithaca colleges, the **Elmshade Guest House** (402 South Albany Street, 14850; 607–273–1707) has been accepting paying guests since 1930. The eight rooms (with private and shared baths) rent for $40–60 double occupancy; they have air-conditioning and cable TV, and children are welcome. A continental breakfast is served (on the porch if weather permits) and the Ithaca bus service goes right by the front door. "Simple and affordable, right in the center of town, within walking distance of restaurants and shops. There is a little kitchenette with fridge and microwave, and the overall atmosphere of this B&B is lovely." *(Julia Tsalis)*

For additional area entries, see **Dryden** and **Trumansburg.**

Buttermilk Falls B&B   *Tel: 607–272–6767*
110 East Buttermilk Falls Road, 14850-8741

A sturdy Federal-style brick house built in 1820, Buttermilk Falls B&B has been owned by the Rumsey family for five generations; owner Margie Rumsey came to Grandfather Rumsey's home as a newlywed in 1948. "While just around the corner from a busy road, this B&B provides a totally private hideaway, tucked behind high hedges. Across the street is Buttermilk Falls State Park for swimming and hiking up the gorge to Pinnacle Rock. The falls, with a 500-foot drop, are dramatic as they cascade down various rock formations into a swimming hole. Our room was simply furnished with antiques; a small bathroom with stall shower and excellent lighting was tucked into the corner of the room. Other guest rooms had a variety of antiques and more contemporary furnishings. Breakfast is typically served around 9:00 A.M. at large plank table in the dining room. We had a choice of three juices, two kinds of melon, blueberries, fresh apple fritters, whole-oat oatmeal with raisins, cheese soufflé with salsa, sausage, bacon, and just-baked bread. We were delighted to linger at the table until 10:30." *(NB)* Reports needed.

Open All year.
Rooms 1 cottage, 4 doubles—all with private bath and/or shower, air-conditioning. 1 with double Jacuzzi tub, fireplace, TV/VCR. Cottage with TV.

Facilities Living room with fireplace, CD, games; library, kitchen, dining room, screened porch. 2 acres with croquet, picnic table, swing. Swimming, boating, hiking, cross-country skiing nearby.
Location N NY, central Finger Lakes region. 3.5 m from Cornell/Ithaca College. At foot of Buttermilk Falls, just off of Rte. 13.
Restrictions No smoking.
Credit cards Not accepted.
Rates B&B, $75–240 double. Extra person, $25–35. 2–3 night college weekend/holiday minimum.
Extras Limited wheelchair access in Arbor cottage. Airport/station pickups by prior arrangement.

The Hanshaw House
15 Sapsucker Woods Road, 14850

Tel: 607–257–1437
800–257–1437

With an address like "Sapsucker Woods Road," bird lovers won't have to be told twice to make The Hanshaw House their base of operations in Ithaca. The pond and woods behind this antique-filled 1830s farmhouse are home to a variety of birds, and deer can be seen in the fall, grazing on the fruit from the apple and pear trees. Just a short walk away is Cornell's Ornithology Lab and hiking trails in beautiful Cayuga Heights.

The inn has been owned by Helen and William Scoones since 1989; Helen is an interior designer, while William is a dean at Ithaca College. The rooms are decorated with simple elegance, in both antiques and period reproductions, with delicate floral patterns in soft pink and gray tones, plus down comforters and pillows. Breakfast is different each day, served in the dining room overlooking the garden, or on the patio. The meal might include juice, poached pears, broccoli frittata, and oatmeal raisin bread with homemade jam. Hot mulled cider is served each afternoon in cool weather along with a homemade snack; in warmer months iced tea is the beverage of choice.

"Magnificent breakfast of Swedish pancakes, apples and crème fraîche." *(BC)* "Elegant furnishings, country setting, advice on restaurants and sights of interest." *(PM)* "Immaculate, with comfortable beds and large plush towels. Breakfast is an event, served with concern for the tastes of the guests." *(Nancy Gould)* "Tastefully decorated and well maintained. The garden is a delight—lying in the hammock with a glass of iced tea was the high point of my stay." *(Julia Tsalis)* Reports welcome.

Open All year.
Rooms 2 suites, 2 doubles—all with full private bath, clock, air-conditioning. 3 with desk, 2 with fan.
Facilities Dining room, living room, TV room, guest refrigerator, porch. 2 acres with patio, gardens, pond, woods. Hiking, swimming, cross-country skiing nearby.
Location 4 1/2 m NE of downtown Ithaca, 2 m to Cornell, 6 1/2 m to Ithaca College campus. Just N of intersection with Hanshaw Rd.
Restrictions No smoking.
Credit cards Amex, MC, Visa.
Rates B&B, $72–117 suite, double, $65–95 single. Extra person, $35. Crib, $10. Midweek corporate/education rate, $60–65. 2-night weekend minimum. 5-night discount. Off-season package.
Extras Local airport pickups.

The Rose Inn
Route 34 North, P.O. Box 6576, 14851

Tel: 607—533—7905
Fax: 607—533—7908

Since opening the Rose Inn in 1983, Charles and Sherry Rosemann have worked hard to create an exceptionally luxurious and formal inn, with four diamond/star ratings from both AAA and Mobil. Charles, who was born in Berlin, is delighted to help guests plan tours of the Finger Lakes wineries; Sherry is an interior designer specializing in pre-Victorian 19th-century furniture.

"The inn is situated in beautiful farm country north of Ithaca, overlooking Lake Cayuga. The house was built by a wealthy farmer during the 1800s; a remarkable spiral staircase (completed in 1924) runs through the core of the building. Coffee is available at 7:00 A.M., and Charles's breakfast, served from 8—9:30 A.M. (8:30—10 A.M. on Sunday), features entrées such as French toast or eggs Benedict, accompanied by cider from the inn's orchard." *(William Bennett)*

"Delicious German apple pancakes for breakfast. Exceptionally clean and well-maintained surroundings." *(HC, also RC)* "While pricey for the area, the inn is delightfully decorated, with meticulous attention to detail—we especially like the individual thermostats, heavy terry robes, oversize towels, and good quality bath amenities. Our dinner was superb—great care was taken with its preparation and the presentation." *(Frederick Shantz & Tara Neal)*

Open All year. Restaurant closed Sun., Mon.
Rooms 5 suites, 10 doubles—all with full private bath, radio, fan. Suites with double Jacuzzi; 3 have fireplace. Some with desk.
Facilities Dining room, 3 public rooms with TV, stereo, library, games, guest refrigerator. 20 acres with lawns, fishing pond. 4 m to sailing, fishing, swimming. 15—20 m to cross-country, downhill, skiing.
Location 9 m from town, Cornell; 12 m from Ithaca College. From Ithaca, take Rte. 34 N for 5.7 m to a "T," turn right, go ½ m to fork, stay left. Go 3.5 m to inn.
Restrictions No smoking. Children 10 and over.
Credit cards Not accepted for deposit. MC, Visa.
Rates B&B, $185—250 suite, $100—160 double. Extra person, $25. 15% service. 2-3 night minimum weekend/holiday/spec. univ. events. Prix fixe dinner, $50; 24-hr. advance reservations required.
Extras Airport pickup. German, Spanish spoken.

JAY

The Book & Blanket B&B
Route 9N, P.O. Box 164, 12941

Tel: 518—946—8323

A Greek Revival house built in 1860, the Book & Blanket was opened in 1993 by Kathleen Recchia, who reports "every room has an abundance of books, even the bathrooms. Guests may borrow many of the books indefinitely. Hopefully on another visit they will leave a book for another guest." The guest rooms are simply decorated; the Jack London room has an Adirondack log bed, while the Jane Austen has a delicate pink floral wallpaper and comforter. Breakfast, served at the large dining table from 7 to 10 A.M., always includes home baked breads and muffins, a hot entrée such as French toast or an egg dish, fresh-ground coffee, juices, and cereal.

"A marvelous haven hidden in the Adirondacks, a quiet retreat after the tourist throngs of Lake Placid. Host Kathy Recchia (as well as basset hound Daisy) greeted us with warmth and enthusiasm. Something wonderful is always baking and anytime we entered the house we were offered tea, coffee, hot chocolate and wonderful muffins and breads. The literary theme carries into each room with plenty of books to browse or borrow, down pillows and comforters to snuggle into or under. A fire in the fireplace each night was heavenly. Delicious breakfasts of apple pancakes, cinnamon puffs, cheese souffles, and other fresh, wonderful delectables." *(Danita Hiles)*

Open All year.
Rooms 3 doubles—1 with private bath with whirlpool tub, 2 with a maximum of 5 people sharing bath. All with radio, clock, fan. 1 with desk.
Facilities Dining room, living room with TV/VCR, piano, porch. 2½ acres on Ausable River for swimming, fishing. 7 m to downhill skiing; 10 m to cross-country skiing, hiking.
Location N NY. 17 m E of Lake Placid. 5 min. walk to town. From I-87 (Northway) take Exit 30. Follow Rte. 73 to Keene. Bear right on 9N North. Follow through Upper Jay & on to Jay. Inn on right before Jay Town Square.
Restrictions Smoking restricted.
Credit cards Amex.
Rates B&B, $45–65 double. Extra person, $10. 2-night holiday weekend minimum.
Extras Crib.

JEFFERSONVILLE

Griffin House ¢
Maple Avenue; RD 1, Box 178, 12748

Tel: 914–482–3371

Built in 1895, the Griffin House features ornate American chestnut woodwork, oak floors, and stained glass windows. Irene and Paul Griffin opened the inn a century later, and offer their guests a breakfast of home-baked muffins, biscuits and scones with plenty of properly brewed tea and coffee.

"There aren't two more charming hosts to be found than Paul and Irene Griffin. Irene's English charm and Paul's winsome manner made me feel like an old family friend. The house has beautiful original furnishings, floor coverings, and wallpaper. Plenty of towels were supplied. Breakfast was a delightful array of baked goodies, including scones, plus fresh fruit salad and more." *(Gail Davis)* "A charming Victorian house, well-cared for and clean." *(Jeffrey Friedhoffer)* "Irene and Paul are a talented couple who travelled with the Fred Waring Band, she as a singer and he as a musician. The property is secluded yet not far from the southern Catskills with fine entertainment nearby." *(Kathy Levine)* "Comfortable, immaculate, with agreeable hosts." *(Elisabeth McLaughlin)*

Open All year.
Rooms 4 doubles—2 with private baths, 2 rooms sharing 1 ½ baths. 1 with desk.
Facilities Dining room, living room with TV/VCR, piano; library with fireplace, foyer with fireplace, porch. 1840s cottage with gift shop. 1 ½ acres with croquet. Golf, picnic area, canoeing, horseback riding, skiing nearby.
Location Sullivan County. 100 m NW of NYC. 90 m S of Binghamton. ¼ m from Main Street. From Rte. 17 take Rte. 52 west into Jeffersonville.
Restrictions No smoking. No children under 11.
Credit cards None accepted.
Rates B&B, $75–95 double. Extra person $15.

LAKE HILL

For additional area entries, see **Boiceville** and **Fleischmanns**.

Ivy Farm Inn
4262 Route 212, PO Box 51, 12448

Tel: 914–679–9045

"An 1875 farmhouse restored and expanded by Cindy and Steve Gamcsik, the Ivy Farm Inn sits among meadows, with a view to the south of Mt. Tobias. The lovely front porch has white wicker furniture, while the large back yard, with its oversized hammock, is quiet and peaceful. The inn is furnished with antiques; the long dining room table came from a French monastery. Delicious breakfasts of fresh melon, juice, muffins and breakfast breads, omelets or pancakes, and a selection of cereals, all kinds of teas, and coffee. Cindy is a wonderful baker, and makes incredible chocolate chip cookies for afternoon snacking.

"The guest rooms are immaculately clean and cozy, well-furnished with a mix of antiques and reproductions, with good lighting on both sides of the bed. The two smallish rooms have queen-sized beds while the others have king-size beds. Convenient access to Woodstock without the congestion; there are many good restaurants in the area and Cindy has a collection of menus for guests to peruse. She is a gracious and kind innkeeper, and is a rescuer of abandoned cats. Her small, but friendly feline population is kept out of the way of visitors unless otherwise requested. We had a fabulous visit, and felt like we were leaving a friend's home." *(Gail DeSciose)*

Open All year.
Rooms 1 suite, 3 doubles—all with private bath, radio, clock, air-conditioning. Suite with woodstove.
Facilities Dining room, living room with wood burning stove, books, TV; porch. 2 acres with terrace, heated swimming pool, hammock, garden.
Location Catskills. 20 m NW of Kingston, 10 m NW of Woodstock. From I-87, take Exit 19 (Kingston) to Rte. 28 W to West Hurley. Go N on Rte. 375 to Rte. 212. Go left (W) on 212 6 m through Woodstock to Lake Hill to inn on right.
Restrictions No smoking. Prefer children over 12.
Credit cards Discover, MC, Visa.
Rates B&B, $60–125 double.

LAKE LUZERNE

The Lamplight Inn   *Tel:* 518–696–5294
2129 Lake Avenue (Route 9N), P.O. Box 70, 12846   800–262–4668

In 1984, Gene and Linda Merlino left jobs in the textile printing business to renovate The Lamplight. Judging from the reactions of their guests, they made the right decision. We've received virtually unanimous raves on the Merlino's hospitality, the handsome decor, the immaculate housekeeping, and especially, the outstanding breakfasts.

The home was built in 1890 by Howard Conkling, a wealthy lumberman and summer resident. Conkling was an eligible bachelor, and his home was designed for entertaining. Five doors off the parlor lead out to the wraparound porch. The first floor has 12-foot beamed ceilings, with chestnut wainscotting, moldings, and a keyhole staircase all crafted in England. Linda reports that "we have tried to make our inn as comfortable as we can, with good mattresses, reading lights on both sides of the beds, individual thermostats, and modern baths. Flannel sheets and fluffy comforters are provided for winter warmth."

"Lovingly restored and furnished in high Victorian style, with antiques, reproductions, Oriental rugs, and lots of collectibles. The comfortably furnished living room has several sitting areas, magazines to read and candies to nibble. Guest rooms have queen or double beds (most with canopies), plush carpeting and nicely fitted bathrooms. Breakfast—served on the dining porch between 8:30 and 9:30 A.M.—included fresh fruit, granola, muffins, juice, coffee (decaf was plentiful) plus a hot entrée." *(Nancy Cohn)*

"Gene and Linda have all the activities of the town and region posted; they're familiar with area restaurants and are happy to set up dinner reservations." *(MB)* "A fire is usually roaring in the parlor fireplace; the TV is discreetly tucked away in an antique cabinet." *(Nancy Sosinski)* "Although the Merlinos must be tremendously busy, they have the rare talent of making you think they have all the time in the world for you." *(Barb Robinson)* "The dining room has small tables to allow couples to mingle with others, or to enjoy a romantic breakfast together. Our bath had a mirror and lighting that really enabled one to shave or apply makeup, plus a handy sewing basket." *(Martin & Linda Wallad)* "Heart-shaped cranberry muffins for breakfast on Valentine's Day, with heart-shaped cookies left on our bed that night." *(Donna Palermo)* "Superb food, from Linda's homemade granola to Gene's 'to-die-for' home fries. Spotlessly clean, too." *(Mark Corigliano)*

Open All year. Closed Christmas.
Rooms 2 suites, 10 doubles—all with private shower, air-conditioning, ceiling fan. 5 with gas fireplace. 1 with full bath, 2 with double shower.
Facilities Dining sunporch; living room with 2 fireplaces, TV, game tables; library with fireplace, chess table; dining sun porch; gift shop, wraparound veranda with porch swing. 10½ acres with perennial garden, picnic area, hiking/cross-country ski trails. 1 block to Lake Luzerne for swimming, fishing. Tennis, golf, horseback riding, white-water rafting, cross-country, downhill skiing nearby.

Location E central NY. S Adirondack Region. 45 min. N of Albany, 17 m NW of Saratoga Springs, 9 m SW of Lake George village. Take Northway/I-87 to Exit 21; go left & follow Rte. 9N S 11 m to inn on right. 1 block from town.

Restrictions Traffic noise in front rooms ("rarely a problem because of central air-conditioning"). No smoking in guest rooms or dining room. Children 12 and over.

Credit cards Amex, MC, Visa.

Rates B&B, $85–150 double. Extra person, $25. 2-night weekend minimum. 3-night minimum holidays, August race track season. Ski, dining packages.

LAKE PLACID

Best known as the site of both the 1932 and 1980 Winter Olympics, the town of Lake Placid is located in the Adirondack Mountains, about 2½ hours north of Albany. Summer offers a full range of sports: hiking, golf, tennis, and horseback riding, plus a full range of water sports on Lake Placid and Mirror Lake. Winter brings both cross-country skiing and downhill at nearby Whiteface Mountain, as well as toboggan, bobsled, and sleigh rides. The Olympic Center is open year-round with a range of activities and spectator sports.

Also recommended: Just 500 yards from Whiteface ski area, and 10 miles northeast of Lake Placid is **The Inn at Whiteface Mountain** (Route 86, Wilmington 12997; 518–946–2232). The 11 guest rooms are large, with two double beds, private bath, radio and TV. The restaurant features German-American cuisine. Double rates for the room only are $45–85; with breakfast and dinner included, double rates are $95–105. "Quiet, convenient location. Clean, friendly, interesting, inexpensive, comfortable. Cheery dining room with pretty china and good food (real maple syrup and real ham cut from a bone for breakfast)." *(Connie Gardner)*

For additional area entries, see **Elizabethtown,** 27 miles east of Lake Placid, and **Jay,** 17 miles east of Lake Placid.

Highland House ¢ 👣
3 Highland Place, 12946

Tel: 518–523–2377
800–342–8101
Fax: 518–523–1863

Ted and Cathy Blazer bought this 1910 Adirondack farmhouse in 1981 and opened it as an inn a year later. They've added a glass-enclosed porch for use year-round as a sunny spot for breakfast, and the large family room provides a comfortable lounging area with several different seating areas. Breakfast is served at individual tables from 7:30 to 9 A.M., and includes a choice of blueberry pancakes, French toast, eggs to order, cheese omelets, and sausage. A selection of cereals, oatmeal, breads, juices, coffee, tea, and hot chocolate rounds out the meal (and the guests). "A child-friendly inn with spacious common areas, a hot tub, and guest rooms comfortably furnished with quilt-topped beds and sturdy bunk beds for the kids. Comfortable and inviting. The location is quiet and convenient, just a few blocks from the village in a residential area." *(SWS)* "Attractive setting with mature trees, gardens, and window boxes. Rustic decor with dried flowers, wreaths, antique furnishings, and paintings. Clean rooms with all facilities in good working order. Our private bath was just across the hall from our room. Wonderful coffee for breakfast. Ted and Cathy are young and enthusiastic innkeepers." *(Buzz & Linda Maiuri)* "Excellent blueberry pancakes. The welcoming innkeepers gave us tons of ideas for things to do in the area." *(Kristen Sayers)*

Open All year
Rooms 1 cottage, 7 doubles—all with private bath and/or shower, radio, clock, TV, fan. 4 with desk. Cottage with kitchen, TV/VCR, stereo, fireplace, air-conditioning, deck.
Facilities Dining room, family room with TV/VCR, games, piano, library; deck, guest refrigerator. $3/4$ acre with hot tub. $1/2$ m to lake, beach, cross-country skiing. 8 m to downhill skiing.
Location $1/4$ m to center of town. From Northway, take Rte. 73 to intersection of Rte. 86. Turn left on Main St. & go past Olympic Center. Turn left on Olympic Dr. Turn right on Highland Pl. to inn on left.
Restrictions No smoking.
Credit cards MC, Visa.
Rates B&B, $55–105 double. Extra person, $15. Tipping encouraged. 2-night weekend, 3–5-night holiday minimum. 3rd night free off-season. Tips encouraged.
Extras Crib, babysitting.

Interlaken Inn 👫 ✗

15 Interlaken Avenue, 12946

Tel: 518–523–3180
800–428–4369

Innkeeping is a family business, and the success of the Interlaken Inn certainly illustrates the truth of this axiom. Built in 1906, the Interlaken has been owned by Roy and Carol Johnson since 1986. The Johnsons operate the inn with the help of their daughters Kathy and Karri, and son Kevin, a Culinary Institute of America graduate. It is decorated in period, with antiques and reproduction furnishings. Breakfast menus change daily, and might include three-berry muffins, lemon pound cake, juices, and your choice of fresh fruit with date bread and vanilla yogurt; blueberry buttermilk pancakes; or herb and cheese omelets. A typical winter dinner menu might offer mushroom strudel; spinach salad with hot bacon dressing; raspberry sorbet; a choice of veal with cranberry, steak with mustard horseradish sauce, salmon with orange butter, or chicken baked in puff pastry; and concluded with chocolate turtle tortes.

"The main floor of the house has an ample dining room, a living room with huge fireplace, and a bar/lounge area. All invite mingling with comfortable groupings of chairs and sofas. The Johnsons were quick to accommodate with an extra towel or pillow as needed. Roy runs a topnotch bar. His comfortable manner, quick wit, and good service make the cocktail area a welcoming place." *(Dave & Jean Dohman)* "Our spacious room was done in green and white, with a lace canopied queen-size bed and French doors opening to a deck. Tea was served in the late afternoon with a variety of freshly baked pastries and breads." *(Chris & Norma Price)* "Quiet but convenient location close to the center of Lake Placid. Plumbing is old but functional." *(R. Climie)* "Warm and welcoming, pleasant and homey. Guest rooms are spacious, with double, queen- or king-size beds. Most have a sink in the bedroom; bathrooms have Caswell-Massey toiletries and good, thick towels. My room had ample room for a king-size bed, armoire, dresser, and two wing-chairs flanking a table with a reading light." *(SWS)* Comments appreciated.

Suggestion box: "Reading lights on both sides of the bed."

Open May–March. Restaurant also closed May 1–15, Nov.
Rooms 1 suite, 10 doubles—all with private bath and/or shower, clock/radio, fan. Some with kitchen, desk, balcony/deck.
Facilities Living room with fireplace, restaurant, bar with TV/VCR, porches, deck. 1 acre with lawn games. Off-street parking. Boating, sailing, windsurfing 1 block. Swimming, fishing nearby. 7 m to downhill skiing.
Location 2 blocks from Main St. Take Main St. to Mirror Lake Dr. to Interlaken Ave.
Restrictions No smoking in guest rooms. Children 5 and over; all ages welcome in Carriage House. Flight of steps to front door. Minimal interior soundproofing.
Credit cards Amex, MC, Visa.
Rates B&B (Tues., Wed. & when dining room closed), $110 suite, $50–110 double. MAP, $180 suite, $110–170 double, $80 single. Extra person, $40. 15% service. 2–3 night weekend/holiday minimum. Prix fixe dinner, $30. Ski packages.
Extras Airport/station pickup. Babysitting.

Lake Placid Lodge ✕ &

Whiteface Inn Road, P.O. Box 550, 12946

Tel: 518–523–2700
Fax: 518–523–1124

For the splurge of all splurges, you'll want to stay at The Point, one of the country's most expensive inns (see listing under Saranac Lake). For a slightly more affordable experience and a more accessible location, reserve a stay at the Lake Placid Lodge. Point owners David and Christie Garrett purchased this turn-of-the-century Adirondack Lodge in 1993 and spent a year renovating and decorating it to meet their high standards. Both the public and private rooms feature pine panelling, rock fireplaces, and twig furniture; the Moose Room lounge has diamond-paned windows, boldly patterned fabrics on comfy chairs and couches, and of course, the requisite moose head mounted over the mantel. Guest rooms, which range in size from cozy (the Catamount, Panther, and Trout ground level rooms with queen-size or double beds) to sybaritic (the Pinnacle third-floor room with spectacular views, king-size bed, and massive stone fireplace). The same devotion to detail is evident in the dining room which features innovative Adirondack cuisine. Recent dinner entrées included white truffle pasta with asparagus, artichokes, and wild mushrooms; pepper-crusted tuna with spinach potato gnocchi; duck with leek risotto; and sirloin with carmelized onions, roasted garlic, and mashed potatoes.

"Exquisitely decorated with antiques and Adirondack art. It is almost impossible to pick a favorite room—each is different but appealing. The public rooms are just as beautiful, with fireplaces burning constantly. The dining room ceiling has a canopy of twigs which looked like they were actually growing there. This is a cozy getaway, with lots of romantic corners. The food is excellent, as was the service." *(Lauren & Al Kenney)* "Stopped by for a delightful lunch; reasonably priced, too." *(MW)* Comments appreciated.

Open All year. Restaurant closed Tues. (except summer months).
Rooms 2 cottages, 5 suites, 15 doubles—all with full private bath, telephone,

clock, desk, fan, deck. 17 with fireplace, 20 with air-conditioning. Some with soaking tub. Rooms in 4 buildings.

Facilities Restaurant, pub with fireplace, living room with fireplace, piano; game room with TV/VCR, billiards; porches. Weekly harp, folk guitar entertainment in summer. 2 acres with boathouse, canoes, bicycles, paddleboats, hiking/cross-country ski trails. Tennis, golf nearby. 15 min. to downhill skiing.

Location N NY. 1 1/2m from town.

Restrictions No smoking except in pub. Children over 10 preferred. "Appropriate attire requested at dinner." Ground-level rooms less quiet than others.

Credit cards All major.

Rates B&B, $375–425 cottage, $250–425 suite, $175–325 double. Extra person, $50. 2–3 night weekend, holiday minimum. Alc lunch, $18; alc dinner, $50. Writing, art workshops; theme dinners.

Extras 1 room with handicap access. Local airport pickups. Pets by prior arrangement. Crib, babysitting by arrangement. French spoken.

Mirror Lake Inn ♁ ✕ ⊼ ⟋

5 Mirror Lake Drive, 12946

Tel: 518–523–2544
Fax: 518–523–2871

Built in 1924, the Mirror Lake Inn is a five-building hotel complex, long owned by Ed and Lisa Weibrecht. In 1988, the main building was destroyed by fire and was completely rebuilt, combining traditional atmosphere with modern construction. The common areas have mahogany paneling and antique furnishings, and afternoon tea is served from 3:30–4:30 P.M. Most guest rooms have cherry furnishings and are decorated with old photographs of historic Lake Placid. Upgrading is a continuing process—recent projects include the replacement of all doubles with queen-size beds, and the refurbishing of rooms with Schumacher/Waverly wallcoverings, bedspreads, and drapes. Elegant dinners are served in the dining room, while casual lunches, suppers, and drinks are available in the Cottage Café. Dinner entrées include such dishes as beef tenderloin with green peppercorn sauce; pasta with smoked shrimp and trout; or venison with mushrooms and shallots. Those who wish to vacation guilt-free can select from the equally appealing (well, almost) "wellness menu."

"Inviting, spacious common areas, with a two-sided fireplace separating the parlor from the library. The large plant-filled dining room occupies two levels to maximize the views of the lake and mountains beyond. Downstairs is an exercise room, a beautiful indoor pool, and large hot tub. Most guest rooms have lake views, and even the least expensive ones are acceptable, if slightly dated in decor. Nice, personable, helpful staff." *(SWS)* "Our charming, spacious room had dark wood furnishings, two queen-size beds, and a balcony with a lake view. The attractive Cottage Café is right on the lake, and serves light meals and snacks." *(Robin & Christine Edwards)*

Open All year.

Rooms 124 1- and 2-bedroom suites, doubles—all with full private bath, telephone, radio, TV, air-conditioning, refrigerator, hair dryer. Most with balcony, 18 with whirlpool tub. Rooms in 5 buildings.

Facilities Restaurants, bar/lounge, library, living room with fireplace, piano. Conference facilities. 7 acres with heated indoor & outdoor swimming pools, sauna, hot tub, tennis court, fitness center, playground. On lake with 1/8m beach for swimming, canoeing, row boating. Ice skating, snowshoeing, cross-country skiing.

Location 1 block of Rte. 86.
Restrictions No shorts or T-shirts in dining room; "Gentlemen required to wear a collared shirt, preferably with jacket or sweater." Some non-smoking guest rooms.
Credit cards Amex, CB, Discover, MC, Visa.
Rates Room only, $170–330 suite, $74–222 double. Extra adult, $15; children under 18 free in parents' room. Rollaway, $10 per night. MAP, package rates. Service additional. 2–3 night weekend/holiday minimum. Children's menu.
Extras Wheelchair access. Crib, babysitting. French spoken.

LEW BEACH

Information please: Avid fly fishers seeking a remote, lovely setting on the renowned Beaverkill will enjoy the **Beaverkill Valley Inn** (Lew Beach 12753; 914–439–4844), built in 1893 and recently restored by Larry Rockefeller (yes, *those* Rockefellers). The twenty guest rooms have shared and private baths, and facilities include a game room, Victorian bar, sundeck, indoor swimming pool, and ice cream parlor, two tennis courts, pond, and miles of hiking/cross-country ski trails. All meals are included in the rates, and are prepared with fresh, local ingredients to satisfy hearty outdoor appetites. The all-inclusive rates range from $260–330, with reduced rates for children. There are no service charges, and tipping discouraged. The inn is located 120 miles from New York City.

MADISON

Abigail's Straw Hat B&B
Box 242, 13402

Tel: 315–893–7077

A circa 1830 home, Abigail's Straw Hat is owned by Gail and Don Hergert. Guest rooms are decorated with Victorian antiques, reproductions, and lace curtains; Mary-Patricia's Room has twin brass beds and a built-in sleeping nook, while Aunt Grace's Room has a handmade canopy and hand-crocheted bedspread. A candlelit country breakfast is served by the fireplace in the dining room until 10 A.M., and might include French toast, crepes, biscuits with honey butter, and fresh fruit; coffee and tea is available for early risers to take to their room, the living room, or out to the porch. "Most delightful—all newly done rooms, good breakfast, and nice hosts. Convenient for parents' day at Colgate University." *(Anne Perce)*

Open All year.
Rooms 4 doubles—all with private bath and/or shower.
Facilities Dining room with fireplace, living room, porch. Cross-country, downhill skiing nearby.
Location Central NY. 40 m SW of Utica. 15 m E of Cazenovia. 6 m north of Hamilton (Colgate Univ.). From I-90, take Exit 32. Follow Rte. 233 S to 12B. Take 12b S to U.S. 20 & turn right. Follow Rte. 20 W to Madison & inn.
Credit cards None accepted.
Rates B&B, $60 double, $50 single. Extra person, $10.

MALONE

Kilburn Manor ¢   *Tel:* 518–483–4891
59 Milwaukee Street, 12953   *Fax:* 518–481–5028

In the remote town of Malone, in northernmost New York, Paul and
Suzanne Hogan and their family welcome guests to their magnificent
Greek Revival home, once owned by a U.S. Congressman. Guests are
welcome to relax with a book from the Hogan's library in front of the
fireplace. A good night's sleep is assisted by fine linens and down comforters. Rates include afternoon tea and a hearty breakfast.

"Guest rooms are warmly finished and comfortable. The common areas
on the main floor deserve special mention, as the Hogans have recreated
the plush, library-like atmosphere of older gracious homes. Suzanne greets
guests as if old friends, and Paul adds a wry wit." *(James & Pamela Burr)*
"Warm and caring atmosphere. Tranquil garden and woodlands down at
the river's edge; inviting swimming pool. Suzanne and Paul attend to
every detail; the house is spotless, the beds great, the plumbing efficient."
(Mrs. B.E. Nichols)

Open All year.
Rooms 2 suites with private bath.
Facilities Dining room, library with fireplace. 3 acres on Salmon River for fishing,
with swimming pool, lawn. Golf nearby. 5 m to cross-country, 8 m to downhill
skiing.
Location N Adirondacks, 50 m N of Lake Placid, 11 m S of Quebec border.
Restrictions No smoking.
Credit cards None accepted.
Rates B&B, $65–75 suite. Weekly, family rates. Golf packages.
Extras French, Spanish, Australian spoken.

MILLERTON

Simmons' Way Village Inn ✗   *Tel:* 518–789–6235
Main Street (Route 44 East), P.O. Box 965, 12546   *Fax:* 518–789–6236

Originally built in 1854 as a modest home, this inn was transformed in
1892 into a Victorian showplace, complete with elaborate porches and
gingerbread trim. Owners Nancy and Richard Carter, who bought the inn
in 1987, have decorated in a country Victorian style, with lots of white
wicker, soft floral chintzes and wallcoverings, and white iron beds, com-
plementing the inn's original marble fireplaces, oak trim, stained glass, and
hardwood floors. Millerton's location, close to the Connecticut/Massa-
chusetts border, makes it convenient to a variety of activities, from visits
to the Roosevelt and Vanderbilt estates, to summer stock theater in
Sharon, to music at Tanglewood.

Menus at the inn restaurant change with the seasons; recent entrées
included saffron pheasant ravioli with pine nuts; baked salmon with artichokes and walnuts; pork tenderloin with sour cherries; or roast duck with
orange fennel sauce.

"High up on a hill away from the main street of town, the inn was delightfully cool and quiet. Common rooms include a cozy tea room with an impressive cappuccino maker, a gracious living room with overstuffed couches, and an inviting breakfast area. The airy restaurant occupies a sunny, cathedral-ceilinged addition at the back of the house. The guest rooms have good reading lights and tables on both sides of the bed, down pillows and quality linens, flowered chintz window treatments, and English, European and Asian antiques." *(SWS)* "Our cozy third floor room, done in English pine, was tucked under the eaves. The queen-size bed had an extra-firm mattress. Good water pressure, amenities, large towels. Breakfast included fresh fruit and juices, coffee and tea, yogurt, granola and great banana muffins; toast and croissants on request." *(NB)* "Outstanding dinner; efficient and pleasant service, charming hosts. The Carter's son Eric took charge after we were welcomed by his parents. He seated us, took us through the menu, and gave us a tour of the house after dinner." *(Rose Ciccone, also Ian Crawford)* Reports welcome.

Open All year. Restaurant closed Tues.
Rooms 9 doubles—all with private bath and/or shower, radio, desk, air-conditioning. 2 with private porch, 1 with fireplace.
Facilities Dining room; breakfast room; living/TV room with games, fireplace; lounge with fireplace. Conference facilities. 1½ acres. Taconic State Park nearby for swimming, boating, sailing, fishing, hiking. Tennis, golf, skiing nearby.
Location 60 m S of Albany, 100 m N of NYC, 55 m W of Hartford, CT. In center. From S, take Rte. 22 N to Rte. 44 E.
Restrictions No smoking in guest rooms, dining room.
Credit cards Amex, MC, Visa.
Rates Room only, $260 suite, $145–175 double. MAP, $220–250 double. 15% service. Extra person, $25. 2–3 night weekend/holiday minimum. Alc dinner, $35; Sunday brunch, $10; alc lunch, $10.95. Midweek/corporate rates/packages.
Extras Crib, babysitting. 2-block walk from bus station. Member, Great Inns of America, Independent Innkeepers Assoc. German, French, Spanish spoken.

MUMFORD

Genesee Country Inn
948 George Street, P.O. Box 340, 14511

Tel: 716–538–2500
Fax: 716–538–4565

The Genesee Valley was settled by Scots in the early 1800s; one of them, Philip Garbutt, built a plaster mill in 1833. It was later used for the manufacture of hub and wheel spokes, then for making paper. In 1982 this historic stone mill was converted into a bed and breakfast inn by owner Glenda Barcklow.

"Lovely and picturesque; beautifully kept and immaculate. Cheese, crackers, cookies, coffee and tea were set out in the living room for us to enjoy. Glenda was helpful with dinner suggestions and reservations; we were delighted with our dinner at the Village Inn in Caledonia. Our first-floor room was large, handsomely decorated with traditional furniture. A queen-size bed, end table, chest, desk with a Hitchcock chair, along with two upholstered club chairs, a wing chair, floor lamp, built-in bookcase, and lace tie-back curtains with chintz floral swags made the room most appealing. Although tables were set for two in the breakfast room, we were close enough to enjoy chatting with another couple; the view of the stream and grounds was outstanding. Breakfast consisted of a fresh fruit platter, porridge, and a choice of pancakes with vanilla syrup and bacon, or a ham and cheese omelet." *(Rose Ciccione)*

"The Genesee Country Village and Museum (not connected to the inn) just down the road was an unexpected delight. It's made up of over 50 19th-century farm and village buildings moved to the museum's 150 acres." *(KG)* "Our room was comfortable and delightful, though smaller than we expected from its photo in the brochure. Lighting was excellent—everything from table lamps to recessed fixtures to a little chandelier on a dimmer switch. Other welcome features included a little deck built around a pine tree—shady, cool, and private; little pluses were the full-length mirror, hair dryer, and disposable razor." *(FS)* "Delightful experience. Cat lovers will appreciate the resident felines; if not, Glenda will confine them to her quarters." *(WZ)* "Glenda is a gracious hostess; her assistant, Kim, spent a long time talking with us about the history of the area. Afternoon tea was pleasant, and the mill stream created an air of serenity." *(Peter & Mary Holmes)*

Open All year.
Rooms 9 doubles—all with private shower and/or bath, telephone, radio, clock, TV, air-conditioning. 3 with gas fireplace, 2 with balcony.
Facilities Living room, breakfast room, conference/card room, gift shop. 7.5 acres with gardens, waterfall ponds, trout streams, gazebo. Bicycling, tennis nearby. 20 min. to Letchworth State Park for swimming, cross-country skiing, hiking.
Location W NY. 13 m SW of Rochester. In center of town. From I-90, take Exit 47. Take Rte. 19 S to Le Roy, & go E on Rte. 5 to Caledonia, then Rte. 36 N to Mumford. At main intersection go left on George St. to inn on right.
Restrictions No smoking.
Credit cards DC, MC, Visa.
Rates B&B, $85–130 double. Extra person, $10. 2-night minimum some weekends. Weekend, celebration packages.

NEW PALTZ

Only 90 minutes from New York City, New Paltz sits between the Hudson River and the Shawangunk Mountains, and is a funky little town, home to the State University of New York at New Paltz. Area activities include hiking and rock climbing in the Shawangunks, and cross-country skiing in winter.

Also recommended: If you'd like to spend your days exploring the grounds at Mohonk, but your evenings in a more intimate (and less expensive) B&B setting, visit the **Jingle Bell Farm** (1 Forest Glen Road, 12561; 914–255–6588). This stone and shingle farmhouse was built in 1776, and is surrounded by 25 acres of grazing sheep and horses. Three fireplaces will keep you toasty warm in winter, and the swimming pool will refresh you in summer. Rates of $105–120 double include a full breakfast by candlelight. The inn is right across the street from Ujjala's (see page 184).

For an additional area entry, see **High Falls.**

Mohonk Mountain House 🛏 🏃 ♿
Mohonk Lake, 12561

Tel: 914–255–1000
914–255–4500
800–722–6646
Fax: 914–256–2161

"How can I recommend a hotel with 300 rooms for a book about 'little' hotels and inns? Once you've spent time at Mohonk you'll understand why. This venerable hotel on the mountain, sitting since 1869 on its perch alongside a beautiful glacial lake, is the perfect retreat from city life. Well over a century after its founding, the hotel still belongs to the Smiley family, descendants of the two brothers, Albert and Alfred, who started it all. The interior is full of comfortable places to sit, perfect places to catch a view of the lake or the valley. You can join in a full range of sports, sit at one of the gazebos that dot the property, or relax in the lounge with tea and cookies." *(Marjorie A. Cohen)*

"The perfect cure-all for stress: a big helping of Victorian ambience, lots of quiet and serenity, excellent food, spacious rooms, obliging staff, and a magnificent physical setting." *(Seymour Reit)* "To get there you drive to the top of a mountain, pass a guardhouse, then go two miles on a cliff-edge road. Suddenly, the gardens open up before you, and a Victorian castle appears at the far end like a movie set." *(James Owens)* "Staff, from front desk to food servers, were without exception, friendly, helpful, and attentive. Food was good and plentiful; dinner choices included lobster and filet mignon, served with a green salad made exclusively with home-grown vegetables." *(Lynne Batlan)*

Suggestion box: "They need to print better maps for their hiking trails and rock scrambles."

Open All year.
Rooms 273 rooms—228 with private bath, 45 with sink in room & sharing hall baths. Many with working fireplace, balcony.
Facilities 3 dining rooms, verandas, parlor, library with TV. 22,000-acre preserve with private lake for fishing, swimming, boating; gardens, greenhouses, picnic area, hiking trails, museum, stables, fitness center, game room, tennis, golf, ice-skating, cross-country skiing. Children's program mid-June–Labor Day; most weekends year-round. Special interest programs (foreign languages, fitness, nature, music, writing, tennis, cooking, photography, etc.).
Location SE NY, Hudson River Valley. 6 m W of New Paltz. Approx. 90 min. N of NYC. From NY Thruway, take Exit 18 and turn left on Rte. 299 and go through New Paltz. Take 1st right after bridge, go ¼ m and bear left at the fork in road. Continue up road to hotel.
Restrictions No smoking in common rooms. "Appropriate attire at dinner; gentlemen age 12 and over are required to wear jackets. Shirts and shoes in Mountain House at all times."
Credit cards Amex, DC, MC, Visa.
Rates Full board, $385–465 suite, $268–372 double, $171–287 single, plus 15% service. Child in room, age 4–12, $60; over age 12, $85. 2–3 night weekend/

holiday minimum. Rates include children's program, boating, tennis, ice skating, cross-country skiing. Extra charge for some activities.
Extras Airport/station pickups, fee charged. Cribs, babysitting. Historic Hotels of America.

Ujjala's B&B
Tel: 914–255–6360
2 Forest Glen, 12561

Part of the fun of bed and breakfasting is that no two inns are alike—it's just that some are more different than others. Ujjala Schwartz opened New Paltz's first B&B in 1984, painting her 1910 Victorian home a distinctive lilac, plum, and blue, and decorating it with skylights, stained glass, ceramics, real plants and fresh flowers. A former model and dancer, trained in stress management, deep-relaxation therapy, and holistics, Ujjala's name is Sanskrit for "brightest light." A vegetarian breakfast is served in the country kitchen, with large windows overlooking the orchard, between 8:30 and 9:30 (until 10 A.M. on Sundays), and includes fresh fruit, eggs, whole grain breads, and a variety of coffees and teas. The adjacent Longhouse Sanctuary is available to guests for exercise, yoga, or tai-chi, and is used for Native American teachings and workshops.

"Lovely Victorian home, with traditionally furnished guest rooms and an eclectic decor in the common rooms. Ujjala serves good, healthy food. She is well-informed about Native American culture, and has built a longhouse sanctuary for ceremonial activities and seminars. Ujjala's is popular with parents of students at SUNY New Paltz and rock climbers." *(Melinda Ross)*

Open All year.
Rooms 4 doubles—2 with private bath, 2 with maximum of 4 people sharing bath. All with air-conditioning, 1 with fireplace.
Facilities Kitchen/dining area, living room. 4½ acres with gardens, barn with climbing wall, Longhouse Sanctuary, sweat lodge.
Location Corner of Rte. 208 S. From I-87 (NYS Thruway), take Exit 18. Go left on Rte. 299 into town, about 1.5 m, & turn left at light onto Rte. 208 S. Go 3.5 m, passing Dressel Farms on right. Take 2nd right onto Forest Glen Rd. to house on left corner. Use 2nd driveway near sign.
Restrictions No smoking. No children.
Credit cards None accepted.
Rates B&B, $78–89 double, $68 single. Weekly rates. 2-3 night weekend/holiday minimum May–Oct. Exercise, relaxation therapy programs.

NEW YORK CITY

There are many wonderful things to be found in New York City, but little hotels are unfortunately not at the top of the list. Most hotels can't even be bothered to respond to our information requests, and change—both good and bad—seems to happen more quickly in the context of corporate ownership than in the case of long-term family-owned establishments. So *please*, keep those cards and letters coming; your reports are the heart of every entry in this guide.

In making our selections, we considered anything under 300 rooms small; more important was the attentiveness of the staff and the quality of the rooms and public areas. We have also tried to present a variety of locations: some midtown hotels are convenient for daytime appointments, but in neighborhoods which are deserted at night; others—on the Upper West or East Side, for example, are surrounded by inviting restaurants, shops, and night spots.

Due primarily to stringent space limitations, plus a minimum of positive reader feedback, we have listed most entries in abbreviated format, organized by neighborhood: Midtown (34th–57 Streets, east and west), Upper East Side, and Upper West Side). The "nuts and bolts" for each hotel is fairly standard—each has private baths, telephone, TV, and air-conditioning. For more details on facilities and rates, call the hotel directly. Most properties are wheelchair accessible with some rooms fully equipped for the disabled; verification and advance reservations are essential.

You may want to think of a visit to New York City as a lesson in assertiveness training. Particularly in the older hotels, the quality of the rooms is uneven, and you may be shown to a room that appears dirty or stained, or has sagging beds, or is in otherwise poor repair. Reject it, and ask to be shown one that has been more recently redecorated. Another decision in selecting a room is the choice of light or quiet. Ideally, a room on a top floor will provide both; if one is not available, front rooms will usually be noisier, back rooms darker. Don't be shy about making your preferences known. Before the bellhop leaves, check to make sure that the bed is firm, and that TV, air-conditioning, and shower are working well; if there's a problem, change rooms or have it repaired immediately.

When booking a room, expect to pay at least $100–150 for a single midweek; weekend, summer, and Christmas week rates offer considerable savings, so always ask about any promotional rates when booking. To further reduce the pain, *always* ask if any discounts rates are available: senior citizen, family, AAA, corporate, whatever. You'll always get a better deal by calling the hotel directly, rather than their central reservation service. Budget-conscious travelers will want to plan their NYC visits to spend the weekend in the city, when rates are lowest, and weekdays exploring the countryside, when country rates are lower. To further reduce costs, we'd suggest calling **Express Hotel Reservations** at 800–356–1123 weekdays between 9 A.M. and 6:30 P.M. Eastern time or 303–440–8481. Though they're based in Denver, they offer 20–50% discounts at a number of first-rate hotels (including many that we recommend) in all price ranges—and there's no fee.

If hotel prices are beyond your means (not at all difficult), we'd advise booking a room in a B&B through one of the half-dozen agencies available. One frequent contributor stayed in a pleasant, unhosted apartment that he found through **City Lights, Bed & Breakfast Ltd.** (P.O. Box 20355 Cherokee Station, 10021; 212–737–7049 or fax, 212–535–2755). If booking through an agency, try to get a building with a doorman or security guard, and ask for a room that is set up as a bedroom, with adequate storage space, rather than a den or at-home office.

Also recommended—Midtown, moderate: The beneficiary of a $3.5 million renovation in 1994, the **Shoreham** (33 West 55th Street, 10019; 212–247–6700 or 800–553–3347), within walking distance of Rockefeller

Center and the Museum of Modern Art, now gleams with imaginative Art Deco furnishings reflecting its 1927 construction. The 84 rooms and suites have wet bars, VCRs, CD players, and color schemes of off-white, taupe, and olive; rates of $195–245 include a continental breakfast. "Clean and stylish rooms, with innovative lighting (our bed had a silver mesh headboard lighted from behind). Good traditional lighting throughout, too. Pretty accents and flowers highlighted the decor; complimentary videos and CDs awaited at the front desk. The breakfast of croissants, muffins, juice, coffee and tea was ample and satisfying. Staff was friendly, courteous, and always accessible." (GD)

Also recommended—Midtown, luxury: The **Delmonico** (502 Park Avenue at 59th Street, 10022; 212–355–2500 or 800–821–3842) is relatively small, with only 120 rooms, including 30 two-bedroom suites, all with full kitchens. "This newly renovated, tastefully done apartment hotel has superb rooms that are spacious, airy, clean, well stocked with high quality soaps and shampoos. Our suite was perfect for a family, with a well-equipped small kitchen. The midtown location is ideal, yet quiet at night." (KLH) Rates range from $275–$450 double, with monthly and special promotional rates available.

Though on the large side, the **Essex House** (160 Central Park South, 10019; 212–247–0300 or 800–NIKKO–US) is enthusiastically recommended. This grand 1930s Art Deco hotel reopened in 1992 after a $75 million renovation that upgraded, restored, or redesigned everything in the building. Owned by Nikko Hotels International, its 596 rooms have all the amenities, including speaker phones, refrigerators, VCRs, and safes; some efficiencies have a microwave oven and a steambath. Midweek rates range from $285–460, with weekend rates of $198–280; children under age 18 stay free. "Meticulously maintained, thoroughly modern, attractively furnished, and staffed by people who genuinely want to get it right. An executive double is the size of a suite, for just $40 more. This chain hotel feels like a top-notch boutique hotel." (Adam Platt)

The Michelangelo (152 West 51st Street, 10019; 212–765–1900 or 800–237–0990) was built inside the gutted shell of the old Taft Hotel. The hotel now has a charming Italian accent, from the art that graces the elegant marble-lined lobby to the complimentary Italian mineral waters and European bath amenities, accompanied by international and American newspapers. Weekday rates for the 178 doubles and suites range from $250–915 double; weekend packages start at $165.

The **Ritz-Carlton** (112 Central Park South, 10019; 212–757–1900 or 800–241–3333), small by New York standards with 234 rooms ($275–550 double), overlooks Central Park and specializes in personal attention. The hotel features traditional 18th- and 19th-century reproduction furnishings, an extensive art collection, 24-hour room service, and complimentary limousine service to the Wall Street area. Rates for the 214 doubles and suites range from $275–4,000 weekday; weekend B&B rates start at $285.

Also recommended—Upper East Side, moderate: Brought out of dingy obscurity by the same owner who renovated the Hotel Wales (listed below), **The Franklin** (164 East 87th Street, 10128; 212–369–1000) now offers 53 rooms at reasonable rates of $145 double (queen-size bed) or $135 single (double bed), including parking and video rental. "Small rooms, but furnished with a canopy bed—a contemporary version with white fabric draped over brushed steel rods suspended from the ceiling. In addition, there was a cherry wood desk, another cabinet housing a TV/VCR, cedar-lined closet, charcoal-colored carpets, and ample lighting for bedside reading. The complimentary continental breakfast included croissants, pastries, rolls, and coffee. We appreciated the Franklin's location in a most delightful neighborhood, where we felt comfortable strolling Third Avenue after dark." *(GD)*

The **Hotel Wales** (1295 Madison Avenue, 10128; 212–876–6000 or 800–428–5252) is a 1901 Edwardian-style hotel which re-opened in 1990 after a $5 million restoration. The 95 suites and doubles (room sizes vary considerably) have original golden oak or mahogany moldings and many have ornate mantels over (non-working) fireplaces. The Wales is one of the few hotels to offer guests a well-appointed parlor on the second floor, called the Pied Piper, where the light breakfast of coffee, juice, and pastry, plus afternoon tea, is served. Rates range from $145–155 double to $170–250 suite.

Also recommended—Upper East Side, luxury: Once the site of a rundown old hotel, the **Hotel Plaza Athénée** (37 East 64th Street, 10021; 212–734–9100 or 800–477–8800) is now a luxury hotel, European in style and clientele. Guest rooms are elegantly and tastefully decorated, with many French touches, and are intended to look more like the rooms in a private home than a hotel. The hotel restaurant, Le Regence, serves fine French cuisine, and there's a lounge to repair to for afternoon tea and evening cocktails. Rates for the 153 rooms and suites range from $285–900 midweek to $260 for B&B weekend rate in a standard double. Exceptionally small for a New York hotel at 61 rooms, **The Lowell** (28 East 63rd Street, 10021; 212–838–1400 or 800–221–4444) is able to offer truly personalized service to guests. Built in 1928, the building was overhauled in 1984 in a no-expense-spared renovation. Rooms are individually and distinctively furnished, with an eclectic mixture of French and Oriental pieces, 18th- and 19th-century prints, and Art Deco light fixtures; all beds have down comforters. The Pembroke Room is open for breakfast and English-style afternoon tea. Rates range from $320–520 double.

Within easy walking distance of Museum Mile is **The Mark** (Madison Avenue at 77th Street, 10021; 212–744–4300 or 800–THE–MARK), a 180-room hotel combining an Italian Renaissance facade with totally rebuilt interior. The best (and most expensive) rooms or suites are those on the higher floors, offering views of Madison Avenue and Central Park, and antique-studded furnishings. The oversize bathrooms gleam with black and white tile, and rooms are equipped with all possible amenities. Double rates range from $310–860, but less expensive weekend packages are available. One of New York's most famous small luxury hotels is the 185-room **Carlyle** (Madison Avenue at East 76th Street, 10021; 212–744–1600 or 800–227–5737), with a classy upper East Side location. Some feel that its service and luxury are unmatched, and at double rates of $295–400, that seems appropriate. **The Stanhope** (995 Fifth Avenue, 10028; 212–288–5800 or 800–828–1123) is located across the street from the Metropolitan Museum of Art and from Central Park, a location ideal for vacation travelers. Rack rates for the 148 luxurious rooms start at $275 weekdays.

Also recommended—Upper West Side, moderate: Although a sizeable hotel of 375 rooms, there's a lot to recommend the **Radisson Empire** (44 West 63rd Street [at Broadway], 10023; 212–265–7400 or 800–333–3333). Its location is superb—just across the street from Lincoln Center, and within easy walking distance are Carnegie Hall and the dozens of restaurants and boutiques of Columbus Avenue. The hotel was fully renovated in 1990, and once drab and dingy rooms have been redone in flowered chintzes; its once cavernous lobby now looks like an neo-Renaissance castle, with tapestries and Oriental carpets. Some interior rooms and baths are minuscule, while street-side ones are noisy, and tour groups can throw check-in into chaos, but overall the consensus is positive. The reasonable double rates range from $140–200, with special rates and packages available.

Information please—Midtown: Very much a small hotel by New York City standards, the location of the **Doral Tuscany** (120 East 39th Street, 10016; 212–686–1600 or 800–22–DORAL) on a relatively quiet residential street is convenient to most city activities. Rooms are decorated with traditional furnishings, and vary considerably in size—but not in price. A nearby hotel under the same management and similarly recommended is the **Doral Court** (130 East 39th Street, 10016; 212–685–1100 or 800–624–0607) with oversize rooms, a family atmosphere, and a pleasant courtyard cafe for casual dining. Double rates range from $240–290, with a weekend rate of $175.

Built in 1929, **The Gorham** (136 West 55th Street, 10019; 212–245–1800 or 800–735–0710) is a European-style boutique hotel extensively renovated in the early 1990s. Rooms are decorated in an eclectic contemporary style with queen- or king-size beds and ultra-modern marble baths. Adorning the lobby are chandeliers, birds-eye maple paneled walls, floors of imported marble, mirror accents and Art Deco French furnishings. Rates for the 120 suites and doubles range from $170–375, and children under 16 stay free.

Extensively renovated in 1994 is the 99-room **Hotel Elysée** (60 East 54th Street, 10022; 212–753–1066 or 800–535–9733), with rooms decorated in country French decor and new bathrooms with Caswell-Massey amenities. Double rates of $225–245 include a continental breakfast, afternoon tea and cookies, and evening wine and cheese. Guests can relax in the sitting room or cozy library.

Known for its outstanding service is the **St. Regis** (2 East 55th Street, 10022; 212–753–4500 or 800–759–7550), with 320 luxurious rooms in a beautifully renovated and refitted turn-of-the-century building. Double rates range from $390–490 (weekend rates on request), and the spacious guest rooms and lavish bathrooms have French antique reproduction furnishings.

Information please—Upper East Side: One of New York City's few bona fide inns is **The Gracie Inn** (502 East 81st Street, 10028; 212–628–1700), just around the corner from the Mayor's mansion and the East River, in a lovely residential neighborhood. The 12 suites (on five floors, with elevator) offer fully equipped kitchens, continental breakfast, color

TV, air-conditioning, beds with down comforters and pillows, telephones, antique furnishings, hand-stenciled walls, and hardwood floors. Rates range from $100–200 daily, with weekly and monthly discounts.

Information please—Upper West Side: Just a few blocks from Lincoln Center is **The Mayflower** (15 Central Park West at 61st Street, 10023; 212–265–0060 or 800–223–4164), with beautiful views of Central Park. The guest rooms (376 in all) are quiet, good-sized, attractively decorated with traditional furnishings; many have refrigerators. The lobby is handsome and the staff quite friendly; the hotel restaurant offers a reasonable pre-theater dinner. Rates are $160–200 weekday, $148–170 weekend. In an attractive residential neighborhood is the luxurious **Inn New York City** (266 West 71st Street, 10023; 212–580–1900), offering four fully equipped suites at rates of $195–295 nightly.

Information please—Lower Manhattan: An affordable choice in Greenwich Village is the **Washington Square Hotel** (103 Waverly Place, 10011; 212–777–9515 or 800–222–0418) overlooking Washington Square Park. Built in 1902, it received a thorough renovation in 1994; its 160 rooms have been streamlined and updated with handy closet storage instead of bulky bureaus. A no-frill approach (no bellhops or room service) helps keep the rates at an appealing $99–130 double, including a continental breakfast. For Victorian ambiance at twice the price, the newly opened **Inn at Irving Place** (54 Irving Place, 10003; 212–533–4600) offers 12 guest rooms, all with plush private bath, in a 19th century townhouse in historic Gramercy Park district. Period antiques mix with 20th century amenities such as TV/VCRs, and upon request, in-room fax machines, laptop computers and Internet access. Rates, including a continental breakfast, are $200–275 single or double.

The Algonquin ♦ ✕
59 West 44th Street, 10036

Tel: 212–840–6800
800–548–0345
Fax: 212–944–1419

Though it dates back to 1902 and served as the gathering place for a famous group of American writers in the 1920s and 1930s, the Algonquin has remained a relatively friendly and unpretentious establishment. Much of the staff has been there for over 30 years; longtime owner Ben Bodne, who bought the hotel in 1946, sold it late in 1987, and the hotel is now part of the Westin Hotel chain. Over the past few years, the entire hotel was renovated, although the famous lobby looks just the same. The guest rooms are just as small and dark as ever, but now they're a lot more comfortable, decorated in neutral colors and mahogany period furnishings.

"The handsome wood-paneled lobby has the aura of a well-loved club. The room rate seemed well worth the comfort, tradition, and splendid location that it buys." *(Carolyn Mathiasen)* "Dorothy Parker's famous round table is no longer, but the Rose Room continues to serve delicious meals. The famous lobby has great charm and nostalgic value; drinks are served amidst club-type chairs and tables, lit by 1930s-era lamps, with piano music, and brass bells to summon elderly waiters." *(Ann Baxter)*

"We were delighted with our return visit. The beautiful lobby-cum-cocktail lounge with its dark wood paneling, old Oriental rugs and tapestried furniture is the same as always. Our bedroom was done in a peaceful blue flowered pattern, with a comfortable queen-size bed, window seat, small desk, bureau, TV cabinet and old etchings of the Brooklyn Bridge. There wasn't much floor space with that amount of furniture, and travelers who are looking for space rather than charm would do well to stay elsewhere. Similarly if a fancy bathroom is a must, the Algonquin isn't for you. The rate included a continental breakfast served buffet-style in the Rose Room and a free *New York Times*. 'It's like the roof, it's on the house,' one of the old bellhops told us." *(CM)* "Charming lobby for drinks, and café-style piano entertainment in the dining room." *(Eileen O'Reilly)* Comments appreciated.

Open All year.
Rooms 23 suites, 142 doubles—all with full private bath, telephone, clock radio, TV, desk, air-conditioning, hair dryer, in-room safe. Suites with refrigerator.
Facilities Lobby, restaurants, entertainment, laundry. Room service 7 A.M.–11:30 P.M. Parking garage across the street with special rates for guests; free weekend parking with 2-night stay (5 P.M. Fri.–10 A.M. Mon.).
Location Midtown. Between Fifth and Sixth Aves.
Restrictions Light sleepers should request rooms at back. No smoking in some guest rooms.
Credit cards All major cards.
Rates B&B, $350–500 suite, $230 double, $210 single. Extra person, $25.
Extras Wheelchair access; room equipped for the disabled. Some non-smoking floors. Crib, babysitting. French, Spanish, Italian spoken. Member, Westin Hotels & Resorts.

B&B on the Park
113 Prospect Park West, Brooklyn, 11215

Tel: 718–499–6115
Fax: 718–499–1385

If you're visiting friends or family in Brooklyn, or simply want to experience New York the way New Yorkers do, a stay here will give you a totally new perspective. A classic New York brownstone, built in 1895, B&B on the Park has beautiful stained-glass windows and richly detailed oak woodwork and floors. Owner Liana Paolella has furnished it with 19th-century Victorian antiques, Oriental rugs, original oil paintings, formally swagged drapes with lace curtains, brass or lace canopied beds, and down comforters. A breakfast of home-baked bread and rolls, homemade jams and jellies, bacon or ham, and German pancakes, quiche Lorraine, crêpes, or omelets, is served on Irish linens with period silverware and china.

"Wonderful atmosphere and ambience, with immaculate rooms, beautifully appointed. The dining room has glorious stained glass windows and magnificent fretwork and furnishings." *(Gerri Luther)* "Creative and plentiful breakfasts, served family style; we met many interesting fellow guests." *(Barbara & Norman Ford)* "Outstanding service, convenient location with a nice view, good lighting. Victorian splendor at its finest in every nook and cranny." *(Molly Ann & Steve Adams)* "Liana makes sure each guest is relaxed and comfortable; delicious, well-presented breakfast." *(Regine Bernkopf)*

Open All year.
Rooms 3 suites, 4 doubles—4 with private bath and/or shower, 2 with a maximum of 4 people sharing bath. All with telephone, radio, TV, air-conditioning, ceiling fan, refrigerator. Some with desk, fireplace. 1 suite with kitchen.
Facilities Dining room with fireplace, living room, TV room with VCR, stereo, books; guest kitchen, laundry, roof garden. Tennis, bicycle, canoe rental across street in Prospect Park. Parking garage 4 blocks away.
Location Brooklyn, Park Slope, 2 m from Manhattan. Across street from Prospect Park. From Manhattan: FDR Drive to Brooklyn Bridge, turn left on Atlantic Avenue. Turn right on 4th Avenue. Go 1 m, turn left on 5th Street, continue to end. Turn right on Prospect Park West, go 2 blocks to inn between 6th and 7th St.
Restrictions No smoking. Prefer children over 5.
Credit cards MC, Visa.
Rates B&B, $155–250 suite, $100–165 double. Extra person, $35. 10% service. $10 surcharge for 1-night stay midweek; 2–3 night weekend, holiday minimum.
Extras French, Finnish spoken.

Dumont Plaza 🚸 ✕ ♿ *Tel:* 212–481–7600
150 East 34th Street, 10016–4743 800–ME–SUITE
Fax: 212–889–8856

Nine family-owned hotels throughout midtown make up the chain of Manhattan East Suite Hotels, including The Dumont, built in 1987. The 2-bedroom suites are particularly recommended for families or for two couples traveling together; the extra space and the weekend rates make this a very good option. If the location of the Dumont isn't convenient, call their reservations number for the addresses of their other properties, with locations extending north to 76th Street.

"Well-equipped, immaculate, spacious suite with full kitchen, dining/living area with sofa bed, bedroom with comfortable king-size bed, and bath. Welcome touches included the ironing board, a retractable clothes line in the bath, and an abundance of towels, pillows, and blankets. More than ample closet space. Harold's, the restaurant located on the main level, provided us with a reasonably priced (by NYC standards) breakfast. The Summer Garden looked inviting for summer dining." *(BNS)*

"Our suite was refreshingly decorated in muted green, gray, and peach. The mattress was firm, the pillows comfortable. For the best view, I'd recommend a room above the 15th floor. The neighborhood is well lighted and feels residential because of its proximity to Park Avenue." *(Amy Peritsky)* "We saved money by walking to a little grocery two blocks away, and fixing breakfast in our little kitchen. Safe, convenient location. Staff was attentive and prompt." *(Marcia Hostetler)*

Bette Maxwell reported a similarly positive experience with a sister property, the **Shelburne Murrray Hill** (301 Lexington Avenue; 10016-3104; 212–689–5200 or 800–ME–SUITE), with 258 suites decorated in an attractive traditional style with floral and damask fabrics.

Open All year.
Rooms 250 suites—all with full private bath, telephone, radio, TV, desk/table. Some with kitchenettes.
Facilities Restaurant, lounge, health club, sauna, garden terrace. Concierge service.

Location Midtown, East Side. 5–10 min. walk from Grand Central, Penn Station.
Restrictions Light sleepers should request back rooms.
Credit cards All major cards.
Rates Room only, $225–455 suite. Extra person, $20. Children under 12 stay free in parents' room. Weekend rates, $130–295 double. Seasonal, promotional, monthly rates.
Extras Wheelchair access; some suites fully accessible. French, Spanish spoken. Crib, babysitting.

Fitzpatrick Manhattan Hotel ✕

687 Lexington Avenue, 10022

Tel: 212–355–0100
800–367–7701
Fax: 212–308–5166

The Irish-owned Fitzpatrick Manhattan is part of the Fitzpatrick family hotel group (which also owns hotels in Dublin, Bunratty, and Cork, Ireland). Its Gaelic management is evident not only in the Waterford crystal chandeliers, Irish prints, and green-and-cream color scheme but also in the elevator carpeting which is changed *daily* to reflect the day of the week woven into the fabric, in Gaelic.

"Small, clubby, and very Irish—from the brogue of the staff to the *Irish Times* sold at the front desk. The lobby is done in a lot of wood and dark colors and feels friendly; there is a little bar and a small restaurant. Our two-room suite had about all the amenities you could expect, including a working desk (no modified dresser-desk) with computer and fax hook-ups, two phone lines with voice mail, and in the bath, a pants press built in the wall, hair dryer, and a makeup mirror. We found the hotel to be comfortable, reasonably priced and nicely located—a pleasant walk to museums and shopping areas." *(Frederick Shantz & Tara Neal)*

Open All year.
Rooms 52 suites, 40 doubles—all with private bath with whirlpool tub, multi-line telephones, TV, air-conditioning, wet bar, refrigerator, hair dryer, fax & computer hookups.
Facilities Restaurant, bar/lounge, lobby. Meeting rooms. Health club privileges. 24-hour concierge. Room service. Valet parking.
Location Midtown. Between 56th and 57th sts.
Restrictions No smoking rooms available.
Credit cards All major.
Rates Room only, $250–290 suite, $220–240 double. Extra person, $20. Children under 12 free in parents' room. Weekend, corporate rates.

Hotel Beverly ✕

125 East 50th Street at Lexington Avenue, 10022

Tel: 212–753–2700
800–223–0945

Although so-called European-style hotels are springing up faster than mushrooms after the rain, the Beverly has been one for many years. Built in 1927 and owned by the Dreier family since 1967, it has an inviting wood-panelled lobby with traditional furniture and crystal chandeliers.

"Exceptional value, excellent location. The lobby has lots of old-world charm, and the suites are unbelievably spacious, with closets everywhere. Upper floor suites have their own terraces with spectacular views of midtown Manhattan. Although the furnishings are unobtrusive, I liked the tapestry-covered sofa and the Impressionist prints on the walls of our room; the individually controlled central air and heat was a plus. We enjoyed the convenience of a 24-hour pharmacy/gift shop and the services of a knowledgeable and friendly concierge. Breakfast at the coffee shop, in conventional New York style, had quick, friendly service." (Gail Davis) "We had a huge room on the third floor (a junior suite), with a queen-size bed (great mattress), seating area with reading light, walk-in closet (tons of hangers), and a walk-in kitchen with a little refrigerator, sink, hot plate, dishes, coffee maker with coffee supplies. The bathroom was spotless, old but well cared for, with lots of towels and soaps. The highlight was the tub—deep and long—and the shower was the best, with lots of pressure." (WVE)

Open All year.
Rooms 85 suites, 101 doubles—all with full private bath, telephone, radio, clock, TV, desk, air-conditioning, refrigerator. All suites with kitchenette. 15 with balcony.
Facilities Restaurant, lounge with piano bar, lobby, coffee shop, pharmacy/gift shop, hair stylist, concierge. Room service. Laundry, valet service.
Location Midtown.
Restrictions Smoking restricted to some guest rooms.
Credit cards Amex, CB, DC, JCB, MC, Visa.
Rates Room only, $169–229 suite, $149–189 double, $129–159 single. Extra person in suite, $10. Weekend rates, $109–139 double (seasonal). Senior discount.
Extras Cribs, babysitting facilities. Spanish, French, Italian, Arabic, Portuguese spoken.

Roger Smith Hotel 👫 ✕
501 Lexington Avenue at 47th Street, 10017

Tel: 212–755–1400
800–445–0277
Fax: 212–319–9130

If asked to picture a typical New York City hotel owner, you'd probably imagine some gray-suited corporate type, right? But not at the Roger Smith, owned by accomplished sculptor and painter James Knowles. After the death of his father-in-law in 1988, Knowles took over as president of the hotel and soon put his signature on its renovation, both literally and figuratively. The inviting public rooms feature monthly art exhibitions by contemporary New York artists, while Knowles has created the exuberant murals that cover the walls of Lily's, the hotel restaurant. The guest rooms have been totally redecorated with traditional decor, and some even have canopy beds for a "country inn in the city look."

"The brilliant orange Matisse-like banners hanging from the hotel's facade attracted our attention immediately; bronze sculptures adorn the front entrance and lobby. Our ninth floor room was beautifully decorated, well lit, and comfortable. The granite-walled bathroom was complete with hair dryer, heated towel rack and whirlpool tub. Artwork that excited the eyes and imagination covers the restaurant's walls; unlike most city restaurants, there was plenty of room. Friendly, professional staff throughout." (Julie Irmischer & Michael Hagadorn) "Great little hotel with attractive rooms, excellent service." (Barb Bogdanski) Comments needed.

Open All year.
Rooms 134 suites, doubles—all with full private bath, telephone, TV, refrigerator,

coffee maker. Some with whirlpool tub. Fireplace, kitchen in penthouse suite. VCR on request.

Facilities Restaurant, bar/lounge, lobby, videotape library. Business services, concierge. Valet parking.

Location Midtown, East Side.

Restrictions Traffic noise in some rooms.

Credit cards Most major cards.

Rates B&B, $225–300 suite, $195–210 double, $180–195 single. Children under 16 free in parents' room. Weekend, corporate rates.

NIAGARA FALLS

In spite of an abundance of fast food restaurants, T-shirt shops, and outlet malls, the town of Niagara Falls can still claim one of the most beautiful and breathtaking natural wonders in the world, Niagara Falls (technically called the Canadian—also known as Horseshoe— Falls and the American Falls). A popular tourist attraction almost since its discovery in 1678, the rush of over 3 million liters of water *per second* down a 54-meter cliff still thrills the millions of visitors that come each year to see the Falls.

Reader tips: "Unchanged over the years is the all-pervasive roar of rushing water, which can be heard over the highway and tourist noise, and the heavy mist that engulfs the beauty of Queen Victoria Park (on the Canadian side) at dusk." *(NB)* "To really get a close-up feeling for the falls' power, be sure to take a ride on the *Maid of the Mist.* It's well worth it. If you have time, sign up for one of the guided walking trips down the wooden staircases and into the water-carved tunnels along the falls." *(RSS)*

Also recommended: The **Cameo Manor North** (3881 Lower River Road, Route 18-F, Youngstown 14174; 716–745–3034) is a restored English manor-style home eight miles north of Niagara Falls on the historic Seaway Trail. "Our large room had a rose-colored decor, a queen-size bed, marble fireplace, and French doors opening to a private screened porch. The tiled bath has an old-fashioned tub and a new shower. Innkeepers Carolyn and Greg Fisher are friendly and helpful; homemade muffins, fruit, cereal, and a scrumptious oven-baked French toast were served with terrific coffee." *(Happy Copley)* B&B rates for the five guest rooms with private and shared baths are $65–130. The Fishers also own the **Cameo Inn** (4710 Lower River Road, Lewiston 14092; 716–745–3034), a stately Queen Anne-style Victorian, four miles north of the Falls. It has three guest rooms, and a three-room suite overlooking the Niagara River. "Beautifully decorated, gracious hosts, delicious full breakfasts. Immaculately clean, comfortable rooms; the common area includes a fireplace, board games, reading materials. Convenient to all Niagara attractions; knowledgeable host." *(Dorothy Hoversen)*

Excellent accommodation choices at reasonable prices, given the favorable exchange rate, are found in **Niagara-on-the-Lake,** 20 miles north, in Ontario, Canada. Some possibilities are noted here; for more details, see the Ontario chapter of our *Midwest* edition (all prices quoted in Canadian dollars). The **Oban Inn** (160 Front Street, Box 94, L0S 1J0; 905–468–2165) dates back to 1824, but was rebuilt after a fire in 1992, combining the charm of the old and the convenience of the new, with lovely, flower-filled grounds. Rates for the 21 guest rooms range from $125–155. The **Kiely House Heritage Inn** (209 Queen Street, P.O. Box 1642, L0S 1J0; 905–468–4588), a gracious inn originally built as a private home in 1832, has four gorgeous suites ($150–168) with eight smaller double rooms ($75–98). The **Moffatt Inn** (60 Picton Street, L0S 1J0; 905–468–4116) was built as an inn in 1834 and has 22 guest rooms, plus a tea room and bar.

OLEAN

Old Library Inn B&B ✕ ♿
116–120 South Union Street, 14760

Tel: 716–373–9804
Restaurant: 716–372–2226
Fax: 716–373–2462

The Old Library Inn is an exciting example of architectural recycling at its best. The inn consists of two buildings: the library and an adjacent mansion. The library was constructed in 1910, on land donated by a wealthy local oilman; the building costs were contributed by Andrew Carnegie. When the library moved to larger quarters, the Louis Marra family purchased the building in 1982 and converted it to a restaurant, preserving its classic architectural features. Although the handsome woodwork and bookshelves were generally left intact, the Governor Higgins Lounge features an elaborate wooden back bar from Chicago's Cattlemen's Restaurant, once known for the notorious figures who frequented it in the 1920s and 30s. Listed on the National Register of Historic Places, the restaurant is open for lunch, dinner, and Sunday brunch. Next door is the "pink house," an elaborate Victorian mansion built in 1895. Restored by the Marrases in 1988 as Olean's first B&B, it features a towering brick chimney, beautiful bay windows, ornate cupolas, stained glass windows, rich woodwork, and parquet floors. Deborah Lanning is the innkeeper.

"A stylish mansion now converted to a spacious and welcoming B&B. The rooms have oversized furniture (some antique and some reproduction) and shiny, polished woodwork everywhere. The bathrooms are adequate, the towels plentiful. The full breakfast is served in the formal dining room, as well as in the charming nook off of the busy kitchen. One great advantage here is the accompanying restaurant, a sumptuous eatery with excellent food and congenial bar." *(Dennis & Shannon Picard)* Comments appreciated.

Open All year. Closed Christmas.
Rooms 7 doubles—all with private bath and/or shower, telephone, clock/radio, TV, air-conditioning.
Facilities Restaurant, bar/lounge; sitting room, dining room, meeting room. Off-street parking. Golf, skiing nearby. 10 m to Allegany State Pk.
Location W NY. 80 m S of Buffalo; 50 m E of Jamestown, just N of PA border. Center of town. From Rte. 17, take Exit 26 to N. Union St. & go S. Cross intersection with E. State Rd. to inn on right.
Restrictions Smoking restricted.

Credit cards Amex, Discover, MC, Visa.
Rates B&B, $65–125 double. Extra person, $20. Off-season weekend packages.
Extras Restaurant wheelchair accessible.

OLIVEREA

Information please: In the Catskills, 35 miles west of Kingston, the **Mountain Gate** (212 McKinley Hollow Road, 12410; 914–254–6000 or 800–733–0344) has 14 guest rooms with private baths and B&B double rates of $69–89. "I was wandering in the Catskills, contemplating a hike, when I saw a billboard in Big Indian, New York, advertising an Indian restaurant. I thought it was a joke, but soon found myself at the end of a road, near a trail head, eating exquisite Indian food on a beautiful deck under a spruce tree. The guest rooms were small and simply furnished, but there's a large swimming pool." *(KMC)*

ONEIDA

The opening of the Oneida Nation Casino has dramatically changed the availability of accommodations in the Oneida area, spurring the opening of several new motels, and affecting business at area B&Bs.

Also recommended: Received just as we were going to press was an enthusiastic report on **The Governor's House** (50 Seneca Avenue, Routes 5 and 365, Oneida Castle, 13421; 315–363–5643 or 800–437–8177). "A lovely four-story mansion with four appealing guest rooms. Thoughtful touches included the guest pantry and the full video library. One wall is filled with framed photographs of all of the guests who have stayed with the charming innkeeper, Dawn Andrews." *(Kim Barber)* Double rates of $75–115 include a full breakfast, afternoon tea, and evening snack.

Information please: Five miles east in Vernon is the **Taylor Creek Inn** (4604 State Route 5, Vernon 13476; 315–829–HOME), a restored 1810 farmhouse with three guest rooms, private and shared baths, and rates of $60–90. Innkeeper Debbie Gaiser runs an in-home bakery, so the full breakfast includes hot-from-the-oven cinnamon rolls, English muffins, and bagels; afternoon refreshments feature a fruit cobbler or pie. Not surprisingly, the nature trail behind the house is a popular before-and-after meal activity.

The Pollyanna Bed & Breakfast ¢   *Tel:* 315–363–0524
302 Main Street, 13421

The Pollyanna is a turn-of-the-century brick Italianate mansion with the original woodwork, crystal chandeliers, high ceilings, eclectic furnishings and lots of collectibles. Breakfast is served between 7:30–9:30 A.M., and typically includes scrambled eggs, waffles or pancakes, sausages, Swedish coffee and fine tea. "Ken and Doloria made our stay most enjoyable. Delicious breakfast, pretty table setting, and truly personal service." *(Ju-*

dith Brannen) "Comfortable queen-size bed, modern bath. Large, comfortable rooms, high ceilings, and lots of light. Don't miss the tiny Japanese garden—complete with lantern, Zen pond, and Window of Heaven." *(Jeanette Lurier)* "Ken is always open to a game of chess and Doloria will gladly show you her lace or play her dulcimer for you." *(Trudy Staples)*

Note: Ken and Doloria have decided it's time to retire and start traveling. As we go to press, the inn was still on the market, so inquire for details when booking.

Open All year.
Rooms 5 doubles—all with private bath and/or shower, air-conditioning. 4 with telephone, 2 with Jacuzzi tub.
Facilities Parlor, dining room, common room with TV/library, games, organ. Laundry facilities. Perennial, rose, Japanese gardens, off-street parking.
Location N NY, Leatherstocking region. 25 m E of Syracuse, 23 m W of Utica. Historic district. From Utica, take I-90 to Exit 33. Turn right on Rte. 365A. At 3rd light turn left and go 2 blocks to inn at corner of Stone & Main Sts. From Syracuse, take Exit 34 and turn left on Peterboro. Go to Rte. 5 and turn left. Go 5 m to Rte. 46 and turn left. Go through 1st light to end of block to inn on left.
Restrictions No smoking. Limited traffic noise on summer weekend evenings. "Well-mannered children welcome."
Credit cards Amex, Discover, MC, Visa; preferred for deposit only.
Rates B&B, $50–125 double. Extra person, $10. 10% discount for 4-day visit. 2-night college, holiday weekend minimum.
Extras Some pets permitted, off-season, by prior arrangement. Airport/station pickups, $10–25. Playpen.

PENN YAN

Information please: A stately Greek Revival home built in 1820, **The Fox Inn** (158 Main Street, 14527; 315–536–3101 or 800–901–7997) is named for the Fox family, who have owned the estate since 1888. The house is furnished with antiques, with the formal rose garden to enjoy in the summer. There are five guest rooms, each with private bath, and the rate includes a full breakfast. An even older home in the area, the **Wagener Estate B&B** (351 Elm Street, 14527; 315–536–4591) was built in the 1790s by one of the founding families of Penn Yan. Some of the early hand-hewn wood framing and the original brick fireplace and oven can be seen in the family room. There are four guest rooms, with private and shared baths; the rates of $60–70 include a full breakfast. Comments?

Heirlooms B&B ¢
2756 Coates Road, 14527

Tel: 315–536–7682

Once a stop on the Underground Railroad, this 1822 country manor house is owned by Kathy and Dan Disbrow. Set atop a hill overlooking Keuka Lake, the Heirlooms offers rolling hills, country lanes, a creek, stables, and pastured horses. The wide pine floors have been carefully preserved; Kathy's handmade quilts adorn the antique beds, and Disbrow family heirlooms are scattered throughout the house. A typical breakfast might include baked apples stuffed with dried fruit and drizzled with maple syrup; corn muffins with honey and Catawba grape jelly; asparagus on toast with egg, bacon, and Hollandaise; and scones with raspberry jam and cream.

"Quiet, relaxing atmosphere. Little treasures decorate the rooms, most with an interesting story behind them. The clean, comfortable guest rooms have individual thermostats, and ample storage space. Breakfast was different each day with concern for each guest's preferences. The owners are warm, personable, and welcoming, providing information and recommendations for area activities." *(Ron & Laura Smith)* "Dan and Kathy are congenial, but not intrusive." *(Leisa Noll)* "Our room had a king-size bed with adequate reading lights and a newly renovated bathroom." *(Bonnie & Ron Casper)* "Convenient location for touring the wine country, close to Hobart College too." *(Kathleen Lockyer)*

Open All year.
Rooms 4 rooms—1 suite, 3 doubles—all with private bath and/or shower, fan.
Facilities Living room with fireplace, dining room, patio. 18 acres with cross-country skiing. Golf, lake for all water sports, downhill skiing nearby.
Location W NY, Finger Lakes region. N end of Keuka Lake. 5 min. from downtown Penn Yan. From intersection of Rte. 54A & 14A, go 3 m on Rte. 54A towards Keuka College. Watch pull-off lane for Merritt Hill & turn right. Go to end; inn is at intersection of Merritt & Coates Rd.
Restrictions No smoking. "Older children preferred."
Credit cards Visa, MC.
Rates B&B, $55–75 suite, double. Extra person, $15. 2-night weekend minimum Memorial Day–Oct. 31.
Extras Local airport pickup. Pasturage for horses.

PINE CITY

Rufus Tanner House ¢ 🏇   *Tel:* 607–732–0213
60 Sagetown Road, 14871

Readers concerned about the rising costs of B&B travel will do well to seek out inns just a short drive from the beaten path, where excellent value can often be found. One such B&B is the Rufus Tanner House, owned by Bill Knapp and John Gibson since 1990. This 1864 Victorianized Greek Revival farmhouse holds a commanding position on a small knoll, surrounded by century-old sugar maples that are still tapped each March to provide syrup for guests' breakfast.

"Our room on the second floor was huge, with two beds (one a Murphy-type Victorian bed), the other a regular Victorian double; the private bathroom was a step down the hall and immaculate. John and Bill couldn't have been nicer or friendlier, and got along just as well with our teenagers. Breakfast was delightfully informal, as we sipped coffee in the kitchen before sitting down around the long table to eat." *(NB)*

"The spacious first-floor Master Bedroom has a double bed with a huge, elaborate headboard, marble-topped dressers, a portable stereo, and several 'Tranquil Mood' CDs to set the mood. The thoroughly modern bathroom was done in a black, white, and gray motif and featured a fabulous two-person Jacuzzi, a tiled double-head shower, track lighting, marble floor, and an old pedestal sink. The house was immaculate, and had an appealing blend of contemporary lighting and antique decor. The wainscotted dining room had upscale antiques and big house plants; and the breakfast room was decorated in a more rustic style. Our upstairs bedroom had a wide plank floor and pencil-post double bed; another was smaller but looked just as comfortable and had a queen-size bed." (*Karl Wiegers & Chris Zambito*) Reports appreciated.

Open All year.
Rooms 4 doubles—all with private bath and/or shower, radio, clock, fan. 2 with desk. 1 with Jacuzzi tub, stereo.
Facilities Dining room with fireplace, living room with fireplace, grand piano, TV/VCR, stereo, books; sun room with weight machine, guest refrigerator, hot tub, guest laundry; porch. 2½ acres with lawn games, hiking, orchard.
Location Central NY, Finger Lakes Region. 6 m S of Elmira. Follow Rte. 14 S through Elmira. At junction with Rte. 328, follow Rte. 328 for 5 m to Sagetown-Caton sign & turn right. Go ¼ m to Bartholomew Rd. on right, to inn on corner on the right. (While on Rte. 328, do not turn off into Pine City).
Restrictions No smoking. "Well behaved children welcome."
Credit cards MC, Visa.
Rates B&B, $55–95 double. Extra person, $5. Children under 12 free in parents' room. Tips accepted. 10% discount, 4-night stay; midweek, 5th night free. Weekend packages. Dinner by prior arrangement.
Extras Airport/station pickup. Crib, babysitting.

PITTSFORD

Also recommended: For a comfortable resort atmosphere, try the **Lodge at Woodcliff** (Route 96, Pittsford; mailing address, Woodcliff Drive, Box 22850, Rochester, 14692; 716–381–4000 or 800–365–3065), a contemporary hotel with indoor/outdoor swimming pools, golf, and tennis. Rates for the 125 guest rooms are $115 weekdays, $99 weekends, with appealing packages available. "Large modern buildings. Popular Sunday brunch, nice views, good golf, lovely walking trails. Beautiful sunsets, live jazz often at dinner." (*Eloise Daniels*)

Oliver Loud's Inn ✕ ♿
1474 Marsh Road, 14534

Tel: 716–248–5200
Fax: 716–248–9970

Oliver Loud's Inn was originally located in the village of Egypt, on a busy stagecoach route. When the Erie Canal was completed, the stagecoach business died out, and the once busy tavern lost much of its trade. In 1985, the inn was scheduled for demolition, but Vivienne Tellier, owner of Richardson's Canal House restaurant, decided to move it next door to provide luxury lodgings in a historic setting. Menus in the restaurant change seasonally, and a recent winter dinner included chicken Gallantine with Cumberland sauce; salad with Dijon vinaigrette; and paupiettes of sole with scallop mousse; and hazelnut cheesecake.

"We were warmly welcomed into a beautifully furnished sitting room, decorated with historic mementos relating to the history of the inn, and offered tea and cookies." *(George & Myra Trautman)* "Our room had a private porch facing the canal, good reading lamps on either side of the bed, a well-conceived closet with built-in dresser, and a clean and efficient bathroom, and good soaps." *(Judith Turner, and others)* "We brought our bicycles along and went for an enjoyable ride along the canal bike path; I'd love to follow the same route in winter on cross-country skis. Our room had a king-size canopy bed, a dressing table with mirror, a round table, and comfortable, good-looking chairs. At night, our bed was turned down and fresh bath towels (of excellent quality) had been delivered to our room. Breakfast was delivered promptly and discreetly at the specified time, and included muffins, rolls, juice, and coffee, plus the day's *Wall Street Journal*." *(Susan Earshen)* "Thoughtful touches included fresh fruit and cookies, crackers, mineral water, and a night light in bathroom." *(Joan Cohn)*

"Just as pleasant on a return visit, thanks to owner Vivienne Tellier." *(Brian Donaldson)* "Our room had two double beds with great mattresses. Attentive service, from a late-night cup of tea to an emergency hair dryer in the morning." *(SWS)* "Food at the Canal House was outstanding, the waitress informative and fun, and decor lovely." *(Rose & Frank Ciccone)* "Light suppers can be enjoyed at modest cost in the charming pub. The stencilled walls show fanciful trees, brick houses, farmers, and Colonial soldiers." *(Mary Raferty)*

Open All year. Restaurant closed New Year's Day, Memorial Day, 4th of July, Labor Day, Christmas Day.
Rooms 8 doubles—all with full private bath, telephone, desk, air-conditioning. 1 with deck. Radio, TV on request.
Facilities Common room with fireplace, books, games; restaurant with adjacent porch; pub. 4 acres on Erie Canal, with towpath for walking, bicycling, cross-country skiing, fishing. Bicycle rentals on request. Tennis, golf, boating nearby.
Location NW NY. Finger Lakes region. 12 m SE of Rochester, 3½ m from Pittsford. From I-90, take I-490 W to Bushnell's Basin exit. Turn right on Rte. 96 N & go 400 yds. to Richardson's Canal House Village at Marsh Rd. (on right) to inn.
Restrictions No smoking in public areas, some guest rooms. Children 13 and over.
Credit cards Amex, CB, DC, MC, Visa.
Rates B&B, $125–145 double, $115–135 single. Extra person $10. Alc dinner, $38 restaurant; $5–10, pub weekdays only.
Extras 1 room wheelchair accessible. Airport/station pickups $25. French, Spanish spoken; menus in French, Spanish, German, Japanese, Mandarin.

POTSDAM

The Clarkson Inn ♿
1 Main Street, 13676

Tel: 315–265–3050
Fax: 315–265–3050

Readers have frequently complained that pleasant places to stay are few and far between in the "North Country," so we were delighted when a frequent contributor wrote to us about the Clarkson Inn, built in 1985 and managed by Rita Manning. "Great place to stay while touring Clarkson and nearby St. Lawrence University. The rooms—both common areas and .guest rooms—are furnished with period reproductions, and are clean, spacious, and attractive. A light breakfast buffet is served from 6:30–10 A.M. in a dining area off the lobby. Staff was efficient and friendly. We had a fine dinner at Uncle Max's; good salad bar, superb meat and desserts in an informal, log cabin-like interior." *(DS)* "Just as good on a return visit: clean, efficiently run; simple, perfect breakfast." *(DS)*

Open All year.
Rooms 40 doubles—all with full private bath, telephone, clock, TV, air-conditioning.
Facilities Dining room, lobby with fireplace, books, magazines. Off-street parking; Winter plug-ins. Public beach nearby.
Location N NY, 10 m N of Adirondack Park, 20 m S of St. Lawrence River, 11 m NE of Canton. Potsdam center; corner of Main and Market Sts.
Restrictions Smoking only in specified guest rooms; no smoking in breakfast room, 1st floor lobby.
Credit cards Amex, MC, Visa.
Rates Room only, $78–100 double. Extra person, $8.
Extras Wheelchair access. Airport/station pickups; small fee. Crib.

RHINEBECK

Rhinebeck combines the charms of a beautifully preserved historic village with the modern-day appeal of first-class craft shops and galleries, and innovative restaurants. The village celebrated its 300th birthday in 1988, and dozens of its buildings, ranging in style from Dutch Colonial to Federal to Gothic and Greek Revival, are listed on the National Register of Historic Places. A key annual event in Rhinebeck is the Dutchess County Fair, held since 1919 during the third week of August; it's a real old-fashioned country fair, with ox-pulling contests and flower and vegetable displays (expect rate surcharges). From May through October, there's some kind of festival on the calendar nearly every month—crafts, antiques, and others. Be sure to catch an air show at the Old Rhinebeck Aerodrome, highlighting aircraft from World War I and earlier. Other area activities include bicycling, golf, and boating on the Hudson.

Rhinebeck is about 100 miles north of New York City, and is easily accessible by train from Grand Central Station. By car, take the NY State Thruway (I-87) to Exit 19 (Kingston-Rhinecliff Bridge). Continue to light. Right onto Rte. 9G to light. Right onto Route 9 to Rhinebeck. Another route is the Saw Mill Parkway to the Taconic to Route 199 west to Route 308 west into Rhinebeck.

Note that you pay a premium for the town's proximity to New York; rates are high and climbing. Let us know if you think it's worth it!

For an additional area entry, see listing for the **Inn at Blue Stores**, in Hudson, about 12 miles north of Rhinebeck.

Reader tip: "In addition to the highly recommended Le Petit Bistro, we ate at Calico, a tiny restaurant with fine service, good food, and excellent desserts." *(Amy Blau)*

Information please: An expansive contemporary home set on 15 acres, **Aunt Sally's Farm** (66 Cedar Heights Road, 12572; 914–876–8340) offers five guest rooms with private and shared baths; the Deerfield Suite has a four-poster bed, sitting room with fireplace, and a bath with whirlpool tub. Double rates of $95–175 include a full breakfast and afternoon tea.

Beekman Arms ¢ **ℎ ✕ ㅋ**
4 Mill Street, 12572

Tel: 914–876–7077
Delamater House: 914–876–7080

Founded in 1766, the Beekman Arms is one of the oldest inns in America; Revolutionary War soldiers held drills on the front lawn, William Jennings Bryan orated here, and Franklin Roosevelt spoke from the porch steps. The Beekman's well-known restaurant is now under the supervision of renowned chef Larry Forgione; seafood and game dishes are emphasized.

"The inn is impeccably landscaped and maintained with a profusion of flowers. Downstairs is the Colonial-style restaurant, the historic tap room, and an enormous parlor, filled with elegant yet comfortable couches and easy chairs, both beautiful antiques and quality reproductions. The guest rooms upstairs have an authentic 'old inn' feeling to them. Additional accommodations are found in the motel wing and another building in the back parking lot, and at the Delamater House and Courtyard one block away. The motel rooms are adequate but uninspired, while the rooms at the Delamater Courtyard are furthest from the road. Built in the 1980s, these neo-Victorian townhouses are set around a grassy common, and have Shaker-style pencil post beds, a comfortable sitting area, and country decor. The Delamater House, built in 1844, is a fine example of Gothic Revival architecture, and has been beautifully decorated with bright, airy colors, textures, and patterns." *(SWS)*

"Our room in the original building was in excellent condition, pleasantly wallpapered and curtained. The canopy bed with two pillows for each of us, was well-lit for reading." *(Emily & Jeff Clements)* "Our corner, second-floor Courtyard room was quiet, pleasantly furnished, large and well-arranged. Food at the Tavern was delicious." *(LI)* "We were delighted with our accommodations at Delamater House." *(Trudy Selib)*

Open All year.
Rooms 59 doubles—all with private shower and/or bath, telephone, TV, desk. Most with air-conditioning; some with fireplace, fan, refrigerators. 13 rooms in main inn; 43 in 5 buildings nearby.
Facilities Restaurant, bar/lounge with fireplace, library with TV, books, parlor, meeting rooms. Cross-country, downhill skiing nearby.
Location In town, at intersection of Rtes. 9 & 308.
Restrictions *Traffic, restaurant, guest noise in some rooms.* No smoking in public areas, some guest rooms.
Credit cards Amex, DC, MC, Visa.
Rates Room only, $80–140 double. Midweek corporate rates. 2-night weekend minimum, May–Oct. 31, holidays. Alc dinner, $35–50.
Extras Limited wheelchair access. Station pickups. Crib, babysitting. Spanish spoken.

Veranda House B&B ¢   *Tel:* 914–876–4133
82 Montgomery Street, 12572   *Fax:* 914–876–6218

Built in 1845, the Federal-style Veranda House has been a farmhouse, then a parsonage, and then a private home. Current owners Linda and Ward Stanley, found a compatible mix of opportunities in 1993 when they bought Veranda House and became innkeepers. Linda, retired from the medical library field, is an artist and amateur gourmet cook, while Ward, a semi-retired professor of architectural history, knew just what was important to preserve in the renovation of their home. The inn is furnished with an eclectic mix of old and new pieces, enhanced with contemporary American paintings and drawings. Guest rooms, each with a four-poster Shaker queen size bed, antique brass and iron double bed, or old-fashioned wood twin beds, are decorated with floral wallpapers and simple swag or lace curtain panels. Breakfast, served at the dining room table from 8 to 10 A.M., includes a fresh fruit plate, juice, plum strudel or perhaps apple walnut muffins, and such entrées as breakfast burritos, French toast, or herb mushroom omelets.

"Ward and Linda are helpful and available but unobtrusive." *(Mr. & Mrs. Herbert Church, Jr.)* "Perfect location, within walking distance of shops and restaurants." *(Ron Richardson)* "Lively conversation among hosts and guests, at breakfast or by the fire in the evening, ranged from art to politics. We soon felt like old friends. Charming, inviting ambience, with lots of fresh flowers and plants." *(Paul & Sheila Crone)* "Rooms are immaculate, charming and comfortable. Convenient setting yet removed and tranquil. You can just relax in a big, soft chair, listen to Vivaldi, and read one of hundreds of books. Breakfasts are imaginative and delicious." *(Jerry Lanning)* "Impeccably maintained. Ward and Linda are a great source of knowledge about local history." *(James McConkey)*

Open All year.
Rooms 4 doubles—all with private shower and/or bath, clock, air-conditioning, fan.
Facilities Dining room, living room with fireplace, den with TV/VCR, stereo; porch. 1 acre with parking, croquet.
Location 3 blocks from center. From town, go N on Rte. 9 (Montgomery St.) 3 blocks (²⁄₁₀ m). Turn left on Locust Grove Rd. & then turn right into inn's driveway.
Restrictions No smoking.
Credit cards None accepted.
Rates B&B, $75–100 double. Extra person, $10. No tipping. 2-night weekend minimum May through Oct.
Extras Station pickups. Cot, $10. Some German spoken.

Whistle Wood Farm   *Tel:* 914–876–6838
11 Pells Road, 12572   *Fax:* 914–876–5513

"Maggie Myer has had horses as guests on her little ranch since she bought Whistle Wood in 1975; in 1982, she decided people could come too. She has rarely stopped feeding one or the other ever since.

"Guests follow the long drive up to the house, past pastures of grazing horses, to Maggie's contemporary ranch-style home. Coming in through the sun porch, past oversized rockers, we tried hard not to track any barn mud into the house. From there you enter the sunken living room, with ample comfortable seating, quilts hung on the walls, and a cozy fire burning in the woodstove. A delightful collection of antique quilts, farm primitives, and collectibles is found throughout the house.

"Our spacious room had a rough-hewn queen-size canopy bed made by Maggie herself, a beautiful blue and white quilt serving as a partial canopy at the head of the bed, and luxurious blue and white linens and pillow shams. An armoire, desk and chair, day bed, table and chairs completed the decor, along with an old poster for an 1884 farm journal, and a rustic barrel bedside table. After dinner in town, we gathered with the other guests to sing around the player piano in the dining area, and savor Maggie's delicious homemade almond cake and deep-dish apple pie. In the morning we went for an early walk on the country road, returning in time for a hearty breakfast of fresh fruit salad, cereal, blueberry corn muffins, and egg/cheese strata. The food was set out on an antique cookstove, and we took our dishes out back to the sunny deck to enjoy." (SWS)

"Wonderfully adorned with country antiques and odd items collected over the years." (Keren Deere) "Rustic hideaway, with stone fireplace, wide plank floors, buffalo head on the wall." (Ronald Rubinstein) "Wonderful pies and cakes awaited after a day of sightseeing. The enclosed porch and open deck were gathering spots for friendly conversation among the guests." (John & Kathy Hefner) "We watched wild turkeys foraging for food as a gentle snow fell. The informal charms of the house and its owner made us feel relaxed and welcome." (Matt & Sally Kowalski)

Open All year.
Rooms 2 suites, 2 doubles—all with private bath and/or shower, radio, ceiling fan. 3 with desk. 1 with bath across hall.
Facilities Living room with fireplace, dining area with wood cookstove, family room with TV/VCR, player piano; sun porch, decks, gardens. 13½ acres with barns, paddocks, horses. Lakes nearby for swimming, boating, fishing.
Location 2 m E of town. From Taconic Pkwy, exit at Rte. 199 (Rhinebeck/Red Hook) and go W for 3 m to Rock City (traffic light). Bear left on Rte. 308 and continue for 3 m. Look for caboose on right, then turn right on Pells Rd. to inn (5th driveway on right). From Rhinebeck, take Rte. 308 3 miles to Pells Rd. & turn left.
Restrictions Smoking in common rooms only.
Credit cards Amex.
Rates B&B, $110–165 suite, $85–125 double; $65–85 single (weekdays only). Extra person, $25. 10% discount 4-day stays, seniors. Midweek discounts. 2-night weekend minimum.
Extras Limited wheelchair access. Airport/station pickups. Pets with approval; boarding kennel, $15 daily. Horses boarded.

ROCHESTER

For additional area recommendations, see **Adams Basin, Brockport,** and **Pittsford.**

"428 Mt. Vernon"   *Tel: 716–271–0792*
428 Mt. Vernon Avenue, 14620   800–836–3154

What "428 Mt. Vernon" may lack in the creativity of its name is more than compensated for by its lovely location adjacent to acres of trees, wildflowers, and birds, and the gracious hospitality extended to guests. Built in 1917, Claire and Philip Lanzatella have owned this B&B since 1986. Breakfast is served between 7 A.M. and 9:00 A.M., and offers guests their choice of eggs any style, sourdough pancakes, French toast, sausage or bacon, fresh fruit, homemade whole wheat bread, white bread, muffins, granola, cereals, or oatmeal. Light eaters can opt for a breakfast of hard-boiled eggs, cheese and fruit, muffins or toast. Wake-up coffee is available on request.

"Furnishings beautifully suit the house, which is filled with natural wood and large, sunny windows in its common rooms. The old but serviceable elevator made our third floor room accessible to those who have trouble with stairs. Our charming room was shady and cool, the brass bed was firm and comfortable. All was impeccably clean. Cookies, a carafe of ice water, and fresh flowers were thoughtfully placed in our room. Ample soaps, shampoos, and toiletries were placed in baskets outside the rooms. Wonderful breakfast of omelets with scones and home-baked breads. Convenient location just moments from downtown Rochester." *(Fritz Shantz)* "First-rate hospitality, service, comfort and food. Claire and Philip went out of their way to be helpful; no request went unanswered." *(CS)* Reports appreciated.

Open All year.
Rooms 7 doubles—all with private shower bath, telephone, radio, clock, TV, air-conditioning, ceiling fan. 5 with fireplace. 4 with desk.
Facilities Dining room, living room with books, fireplace; family room, guest refrigerator; porch. 2 acres with off-street parking. 155-acre Highland Park adjacent for hiking. 20 miles to downhill skiing.
Location Rochester center. From I-490, take Goodman exit going S. Go right on Rockingham, left on Mt. Vernon Ave.
Restrictions Smoking permitted in some common rooms, some guest rooms. Children 13 and over.
Credit cards Amex, MC, Visa.
Rates B&B, $99 double, $90 single. Advance notice: prix fixe lunch, $17.50, prix fixe dinner, $40; 17% service.

ROCK CITY FALLS

The Mansion   *Tel: 518–885–1607*
801 Route 29, 12863

Only in America could a man go from rags to riches as the inventor—of all things—of the folding paper bag. In 1866, George West used a portion of his profits to build an elegant 23-room Venetian villa-style mansion across the street from his paper mill. Thanks to the hard work of owner Tom Clark and innkeeper Alan Churchill, you too can savor 19th century elegance, along with modern plumbing, firm beds, and down comforters. In addition to Victorian antiques, The Mansion's decor includes original brass and copper chandeliers, 13-foot mirrored marble fireplaces, distinctive woodwork, and ornate plaster moldings.

"Stunning Italianate mansion, beautifully and unfussily restored. Good breakfasts; delightful porch with rocking chairs, handsome common rooms. Friendly, relaxed innkeeper who greeted us with iced tea when we arrived." *(MM)* "Alan Churchill welcomes guests with the unassuming warmth of a man who truly wishes to share this inn's wonderful Victorian treasure. He and Tom Clark have worked since 1986 to restore the house, retaining as much as possible of its original details. The parlor to the right of the central hall has a Tiffany chandelier, a magnificent fireplace and mantel, and wooden pocket doors reaching almost to the ceiling. The parlor to the left is more intimate for reading and listening to classical music." *(Judith & Allen Mossman)*

"Although he never intrudes, Alan has a knack for appearing just at the moment you want something; a drink, a corkscrew, or light conversation. The spacious guest rooms are beautifully decorated with antique furniture and fresh flowers. The front atrium on the second floor is our favorite sitting room, where we always find ourselves sipping wine and browsing through unlimited magazines and books." *(Steven Sitek)* "Breakfasts are served at individual tables with fresh linens, English china, and lead crystal. There is fresh-squeezed orange juice, fruit (warm homemade applesauce one day and sliced fresh fruit the next), wonderful coffee, fresh home-baked breads, and eggs Benedict, herb omelets, or Grand Marnier French toast." *(Sue & Peter Commanday)*

Open All year.
Rooms 1 suite, 4 doubles—all with private bath and/or shower, air-conditioning.
Facilities Dining room, 2 parlors with piano, stereo, books; sitting room. 3 acres of lawns, gardens with swimming pool, gazebo, picnic area. Tennis, golf, swimming, boating, fishing, skiing nearby.
Location Saratoga County. 7 m W of Saratoga Springs on Rte 29. From I-87 N, take Exit 13N (Rte. 9). Proceed on Rte. 9 (Broadway) to Rte. 29 W. Turn left & go 7 m to inn.
Restrictions No smoking in dining room. No children under 12.
Credit cards None accepted.
Rates B&B, $120–210 suite, $95–185 double. Extra person, $25. 2-night weekend minimum in July, Aug.

WATKINS GLEN

Reading House B&B ¢   *Tel:* 607–535–9785
4610 Route 14, Rock Stream 14878
Mailing address: P.O. Box 321, Watkins Glen 14891

Named for the hometown of its builder, Reading House is an 1820 Federal-style farmhouse later embellished with Greek Revival and Victorian details. Rita and Bill Newell opened it as a B&B in 1990, and report that "our B&B has been restored to its 19th century character, complete with antiques, but it is a comfortable home, not a museum. There are fresh flowers in season, and on chilly days, the warmth of a roaring fire; we have a wealth of good books on almost any subject. Breakfast is communal, enjoyed for good conversation as much as good food; the main course features French toast, pancakes, omelets, or frittatas. Special diets are happily accommodated with advance notice."

"A well-restored old farmhouse with a homey, welcoming atmosphere and a wonderful view of Seneca Lake. It is beautifully decorated with wide floorboards, lovely quilts, and old prints on the walls. Coffee, tea, and shortbread are available, along with a library of menus. Our room had a view of the lake from a little window; the autumn sunrise was brilliant. The king-size bed was firm, with tables and lamps on either side. There was no closet, but the wall pegs fit well with the style. The modern bath was small but well-appointed, with a night light, fresh soaps, and adequate towels; the medicine cabinet had a wide variety of shampoos and conditioners. Delicious breakfast in a convivial atmosphere: sliced grapefruit and oranges, cold cereal, and orange juice to start, followed by fresh muffins with a variety of jams (rhubarb-ginger a favorite). This was followed by pancakes, baked pears (from their own trees), and sausages." (Frederick Shantz & Tara Neal)

Open All year.
Rooms 4 doubles—all with private bath and/or shower, clock, fan.
Facilities Dining room, guest refrigerator, 2 living rooms (1 with fireplace) with books, puzzles, games. 3 acres overlooking Seneca Lake, with gardens, 2 ponds.
Location Central NY, Finger Lakes. 60 m SE of Rochester, 30 m S of Geneva, 5 m N of Watkins Glen. On W side of Seneca Lake, E side of Rte. 14.
Restrictions No smoking. Children over 10 preferred. Traffic noise in front rooms.
Credit cards None accepted.
Rates B&B, $50–70 double, $45–65 single. Extra person, $10. 2-night holiday minimum; 2-night weekend minimum May through December.

ROUND TOP

Winter Clove Inn ✗ ♠ ☂ ♿
Winter Clove Road, Box 67, 12473

Tel: 518–622–3267
Fax: 518–622–3299

Few resorts in North America have been family-owned for five generations, but the Winter Clove dates back to 1838, when H. B. Whitcomb opened his 400-acre farm to summer guests visiting the newly popular Hudson River and Catskills region. A family tradition began, continuing to the present. Winter Clove was named by an 18th century surveyor who found the north-facing "clove" or valley retained its winter snow long after spring came to the surrounding area. Breakfast, served from 8 to 9 A.M., includes the old favorites: pancakes, French toast, and eggs to order. Lunch and dinner menus vary daily, but include two entrée choices at each meal. A recent dinner included an artichoke appetizer; salad with raspberry vinaigrette; broccoli, potatoes, and a choice of roast beef with mushrooms or salmon with tomato-basil butter; and strawberry pie and coffee.

"The inn sits in the mountains with a wonderful veranda full of rocking chairs. Rooms in the main building are individually decorated with lovely wallpaper and antique furnishings. Meals are delightful, with enough choices for all ages to enjoy. Many of the guests have been returning for 10 to 20 years, and have formed friendships that are renewed on each visit. The Whitcomb family is friendly and courteous, and enjoy sharing their home with you. We are looking forward to our return visit—to hike, read, wade in streams, and spend time together, with activities to interest each generation, and no worries about preparing meals." *(Mary Dema)*

Open All year.

Rooms 1 suite, 51 doubles—all with full private bath, fan. 20 with desk, 7 with air-conditioning. Suite with fireplace, kitchen. 14 rooms in adjacent Oaks building.

Facilities Restaurant with fireplace, living room, 5 family rooms, summer entertainment (music, bingo, movies); porches. Conference facility. 400 acres with gardens, heated indoor swimming pool, 6 bowling lanes (fee charged), outdoor swimming pool, tennis court, 9-hole golf course, children's swing set, gazebo, lawn games, cross-country skiing, hiking. 15 m to downhill skiing.

Location N Catskill region. 100 m N of NYC, 40 m S of Albany. 10 m from town. From NYC, take Exit 20 on I-87. Turn left on Rte. 32, continue for approx. 11 m. Just beyond Round Top/Purling sign, turn left on Heart's Content Rd. Continue approx. 3 m & turn left on Winter Clove Rd. to inn at end.

Restrictions No smoking in dining room.

Credit cards Amex, DC, Discover, MC, Visa.

Rates B&B, $110 suite (for 2 people), $100 double, $55 single. Full board, $150 suite or double, $75 single. Extra person, $50. 15–20 service suggested. Family rates. Picnic lunches.

Extras Wheelchair access via ramp; some rooms equipped for disabled. Station pickups. Cribs, babysitting facilities.

SARANAC LAKE

Information please: Another Adirondack "Great Camp" turned luxury getaway is **Land's End** (Route 30 & Kimpton Road, HCR-1, Box 4C, 12983; 518–891–4059 or 800–859–9224), built in 1932 for Wilhelmina DuPont Ross and renovated in 1993 by Susan and Scott Yeaw. Decor throughout the inn and its twelve guest accommodations (two are in the Boathouse, one in the Gardener's Cottage) is handsome designer Adirondack rustic; the Boathouse rooms sport a nautical motif. Double rates include a full breakfast and three-course dinner, and range from $225–360. Initial reader reports expressed great enthusiasm for the lodge and its setting, but indicated ample room for improvement in the food, attention to detail, and the level of innkeeping professionalism; when rates are high, so are expectations. We also believe the inn may be for sale. Reports please.

The Point 🏕   *Tel:* 518–891–5674
HCR1, Box 65, 12983   800–255–3530
         Fax: 518–891–1152

If you've always wanted to live like a Rockefeller, The Point is the place to do it. This Adirondack camp was built in the 1930s by William Avery

Rockefeller, as a place to "modestly" entertain the elite during the summers. Today, The Point accepts paying guests in an elegant, yet relaxed house party atmosphere. Most guests feel that the experience is well worth the considerable expense, and The Point is consistently rated among the country's top resorts. The Point has been owned by David and Christie Garrett since 1986, and is hosted by Bill and Claudia McNamee.

"Each day begins with a light knock on the door announcing the arrival of morning coffee. About an hour later a rolling breakfast cart arrives, loaded with freshly squeezed orange juice, homemade muffins and rolls, and assorted fruits. Guests are seated together for lunch and dinner; the host and hostess each head one table and interject interesting trivia on the area and keep the conversation stimulating. Evening cordials and conversation around the twin floor-to-ceiling stone fireplaces cap off a wonderful and romantic day." *(Susie & Robert Preston)* "The main lodge has all the marvelous twiggy, woodsy and warm Adirondack atmosphere you could want. The rooms range from cozy and comfortable with a little stone fireplace, to huge, with a walk-in fireplace and picture window overlooking the lake." *(Julia & Coleman Walker)* "The soups are incredible; outstanding smoked salmon mousse; desserts to die for. Bathrooms are well supplied with hot water, stacks of giant towels and thick terry robes, although the facilities themselves are fairly basic." *(Dave & Cheri Kendall)*

"Guests gather for cocktails at seven; dinner is served at eight. Complete strangers are friends by the time coffee is served. If you don't feel like socializing, the friendly and unobtrusive staff will happily serve you in your room. Special dietary needs and preferences are handled with ease and imagination." *(J. Michael Flatt)* "Wonderful vegetarian dishes at my request." *(Pamela Munroe)* "From arrival to departure, the hospitality of Claudia, Bill, and their staff was warm and genuine." *(Susan & John Whitmore)* "A lakeside luncheon picnic, complete with linen, china and silver, was highlighted by a piping hot pot-au-feu, the perfect entrée for a crisp autumn day." *(SSM)* "Spectacular. We're saving up for our next visit." *(S. Kowalski)*

Open Closed 4 weeks in early spring.
Rooms 11 doubles—all with private bath and/or shower, fireplace. 4 rooms in main lodge, 7 in 3 adjacent buildings.
Facilities Living/dining room with two fireplaces, piano, bar; pub with billiards, games, TV/VCR. 10 acres with sailing, fishing, canoeing, boating, waterskiing, badminton, croquet, hiking, horseback riding, ice-skating, cross-country skiing, snowshoeing, including equipment. Downhill skiing, tennis, golf nearby.
Location NE NY, Adirondack region. 6 hrs. N of NYC. 200 m N of Albany, 150 m S of Montreal. 150 m W of Burlington, VT. 20 min. to Lake Placid. Directions with confirmation.
Restrictions No smoking at dinner. No children (call for information on exceptions). Jacket & tie at dinner.
Credit cards Amex.
Rates Full board, $775–1025 double, including liquor, sports equipment. 15% service. $150 reduction for singles. Extra person, $150. No tipping. 2–3-night weekend/holiday minimum.
Extras Airport pickups. Pets by arrangement. Some French spoken. Member, Relais et Chateaux.

SARATOGA SPRINGS

"Queen of the Spas," and one of the most popular and fashionable resorts of late Victorian America, the heritage of Saratoga Springs was nearly destroyed by the wrecker's ball in the 1960s. Fortunately, the voice of the preservationists was heard before all was lost, and the town has not only restored much of its past glory, but has added some important new attractions as well. In August, horse lovers head early in the morning for the 127-year-old track to watch the horses work out, return in the afternoon for the races, then move on to the polo fields at 6 P.M. for world-class matches. Culture buffs are equally delighted with the summer program at the Saratoga Performing Arts Center (SPAC), with the Philadelphia Orchestra and the New York City Ballet in residence during much of July and August. Open most of the year are the town's museums, including the country's first dance museum, the National Museum of Racing, and the Casino in Congress Park, with exhibits depicting the town's heyday. Last but certainly not least are the famous waters—sample them in town at Hathorn Spring No. 1, or head to Saratoga Spa State Park for a soak or a swim in the baths or swimming pools. Contact the Chamber of Commerce (494 Broadway; 518–584–3255) for more details. Another good source of information is the Preservation Foundation (6 Lake Avenue, P.O. Box 442, 12866; 518–587–5030) which sponsors walking and house tours, and workshops.

Of course, Saratoga also offers a full range of outdoor recreation, with golf, tennis, swimming, boating, fishing, cross-country and downhill skiing, and antiquing within an easy drive.

August is the season in Saratoga Springs, when room rates *triple*. Unless you expect to make up the difference at the track, consider staying in a neighboring town, where prices are somewhat more reasonable (see suggestions below). Another alternative, if you are something of a gambler, is to not make reservations and just see which hotels still have rooms available after six o'clock; we have heard that the Adelphi drops rates on unbooked rooms in the evening.

Saratoga is in eastern New York, about 35 miles north of Albany and about 30 south of Lake George via I-87. Take Exit 13 to South Broadway.

Reader tips: "Dinner at Eartha's Kitchen was good, with a great house salad. First choice for casual dining is The Olde Bryan Inn." *(SWS)*

Also recommended: The **Adelphi Hotel** (365 Broadway, 12866; 518–587–4688) is the only remaining grand hotel in Saratoga. It's been restored, starting with the piazza overlooking Broadway, to the three-story columns supporting a maze of Victorian fretwork and airy verandas, to the grand lobby and spacious guest rooms. Cafe Adelphi is open for desserts, coffees, teas, and cocktails all season; dinner is served from July to the end of August. A breakfast of homemade pastries, coffee, tea, and fresh fruit is brought to your room; rates for the 35 suites and doubles—all with private bath, telephone, TV, and air-conditioning—range from $90–295. "Charming Victorian decor—each room is different but well-done. Breakfast on the porch overlooking the main drag of Saratoga is fun." *(Nancy Bernard)*

For additional Saratoga area listings, see listings under **Rock City Falls, Schuylerville**, and **Lake Luzerne**.

Batcheller Mansion Inn
20 Circular Street, 12866

Tel: 518—584—7012
800—616—7012
Fax: 518—581—7746

A profusion of towers, chimneys, turrets, balconies, and porches was the hallmark of high Victorian architecture; the Batcheller Mansion exemplifies it. Designed by its owner, George Batcheller, the house was considered the most costly and elegant in Saratoga; its elaborate plans were patented before ground was broken in 1873. As the fortunes of Saratoga declined in 20th century, so did the Batcheller Mansion, ending up as a trash-filled boardinghouse slated for demolition in 1971. Rescued and restored as a B&B by Bruce Levinsky, and managed by innkeepers Lorena Lund and Stuart Williams, the Batcheller Mansion Inn opened its doors in 1994. Victorian decor highlights the large, airy rooms, and bathrooms have been upgraded to modern standards. Guests are welcome to visit the light-filled kitchen—a more contemporary space with two-story high windows from a bank in Boston—which also serves as an art gallery for Stuart's reproductions of famous paintings. Breakfast is served at individual tables in the dining room or kitchen from 8:30 to 10 A.M. in summer and 8 to 9:30 A.M. in winter, and includes freshly squeezed orange juice, fruit, cereals, home-baked pastries, cheeses, and meats.

"Exquisitely furnished and sparkling clean. Breakfast was beautifully served, with fresh fruit and muffins baked to accommodate our diet." *(Janice Gelfand)* "Our bedroom was large, quiet, and comfortable; the modern bath had plenty of towels, good water pressure, and thick, cozy bathrobes." *(S. Harberry)* "Warm, friendly innkeepers. Our room, #4, had a little balcony with white wicker furniture; the bath had a huge tub and even a scented candle. We walked to wonderful shops and restaurants, and a lovely park." *(Annabelle Smith)* "Fresh raspberries and warm muffins for breakfast with classical music in the background." *(Robert Joy)* "Impressive restoration. Comfortable rooms with good mattresses, interesting magazines, thick plush towels. Breakfast was served at lace-topped tables, with silver and fine china; the orange juice was freshly squeezed." *(MR)* "Immaculately clean. Stuart and Lorena were welcoming and accessible but not bothersome." *(Gina Ventre and others)*

Open All year.
Rooms 9 doubles—all with private bath and/or shower, telephone, radio, TV, desk, air-conditioning, refrigerator. 3 with fireplace, 3 with whirlpool tub, 1 with balcony.
Facilities Dining room, living room, library, billiard room—all with fireplace; kitchen, TV room, porches. 1 acre with off-street parking.
Location Historic district, 1/2 m from center of town. From exit 14 on I-87, go W 2 m on Rte. 9P (Union Ave.). At end of Union, turn left on Circular St. Go 1 block to inn at stop sign.

Restrictions No smoking. Children over age 14 preferred.
Credit cards Amex, MC, Visa.
Rates B&B, $70–380 double. Extra person, $25. 2–4 night minimum during holidays, racing weekends.
Extras French spoken.

Six Sisters B&B
149 Union Avenue, 12866

Tel: 518–583–1173
Fax: 518–587–2470

Kate Benton named the B&B she and husband Steve Ramirez opened in 1989 in honor of her siblings. Built in 1880, the house has "Saratoga porches" with basketweave railings on the first and second floors and an unusual scalloped-edge roof. The breakfast menu might include French toast with honey-nut bread, apple crisp, and maple sausage; or quiche with fresh vegetables, cheese, and bacon, accompanied by apple biscuits, juice, and a variety of fresh fruit.

"Kate greeted me with a choice of cold drinks—she and Steve are caring but unobtrusive hosts. My first floor room, the Katherine Lee, had a nice, firm bed, and the decor is Victorian but not fussy." *(Nancy Cohn, also Rosamond Brady)* "The Maureen Anita is our favorite room, with a fireplace, sitting area, and private porch. The bathroom is large, storage space ample. Thoughtful touches include a night light, clock radio, extra blankets and pillows, even a neck pillow for the tub and a jar of bubble bath. Each room has a detailed list of restaurants and local attractions. Although the B&B is on a busy street, we had no noise problems. It's right across the street from the racetrack, four houses away from the National Museum of Racing, and within walking distance of Congress Park, downtown shops and restaurants, the SPAC, and the mineral baths.

"Kate and Steve are warm, funny and full of suggestions for things to do and see. Having grown up in Saratoga, Kate knows much about the area. Thanks to her, early morning walks took us to the training track, where, binoculars in hand, we watched the horses at their morning workouts. The food and company at breakfast are equally satisfying." *(Martha & William Poole)* "Dried flowers, interesting photos, and books are found throughout the inn." *(Kirstin O'Rielly)* "Hardwood floors and Chinese rugs are fastidiously kept. Excellent recommendations for dining and activities." *(TM)* "They loaned us lawn chairs for an outdoor concert. Vegetable omelets were a breakfast favorite." *(Erica Breskin & Greg Leshé)*

Open All year.
Rooms 2 suites, 2 doubles—all with private bath and/or shower, clock/radio, desk, refrigerator, air-conditioning, fan. 2 with balcony, 2 with TV.
Facilities Dining room, parlor with fireplace, verandas, gardens. Off-street parking.
Location In town, walking distance to downtown, racetrack, colleges. Take I-87 to Exit 14. At 3rd light turn right onto Nelson Ave. and an immediate right onto Morton Place. First white house on right.
Restrictions Traffic noise in downstairs room during racing season. No smoking. Children 10 and over.
Credit cards Amex, MC, Visa.
Rates B&B, $90–225 suite, $60–200 double. Extra person, $20. Senior, corporate, military, extended stay discount. 4-night minimum in Aug. Off-season mineral bath/massage package.

Union Gables B&B   *Tel:* 518–584–1558
55 Union Avenue, 12866   800–398–1558

When this Queen Anne-style house was built in 1901, it had all the details the Victorians loved—a turret, gables, bays, windows of varying shapes and sizes, interesting shingle patterns, and a multi-colored exterior achieved through use of brick, stone, and painted wood. Jody and Tom Roohan bought Union Gables in 1992 and began an extensive renovation, creating a B&B with all the amenities today's travelers love—modern plumbing, comfortable beds, and air-conditioned comfort. The bow-windowed dining room is the place for breakfast, where guests sit at the long, lace-covered table and enjoy a meal of juice, fresh fruit, cereal, yogurt, and bakery-fresh croissants, bagels, and coffee cake.

"A gorgeous renovation. Each guest room is done quite differently—one in white and periwinkle blue, accented with crisp floral and striped fabrics; another on the third floor has skylights and a rustic, Adirondack theme with twig chairs, white-painted beaded-board walls, and lively red and white striped curtains draped over real branches used as brackets." *(SWS)* "My room offered beauty, comfort, and convenience; it was impeccably clean, fresh, and well-lit. Impressive details: a hand-crafted sign with directions on the operation of the shower; an ample supply of bottled water in the refrigerator. Jody is available to her guests but sensitive to their privacy." *(Martin Goldfine)* Comments appreciated.

Open All year.
Rooms 1 suite, 9 doubles—all with private bath and/or shower, telephone, clock, TV, air-conditioning, refrigerator. 2 with desk or balcony.
Facilities Foyer with fireplace, dining room with fireplace, living room with piano, wraparound porch. Off-street parking. Lawn games.
Location 3 blocks from Broadway.
Restrictions No smoking in guest rooms.
Credit cards Amex, MC, Visa.
Rates B&B, $80–200 suite, double. Extra person, $15.
Extras Station pickups. Pets permitted by prior arrangement. Crib, babysitting.

The Westchester House   *Tel:* 518–587–7613
102 Lincoln Avenue, P.O. Box 944, 12866

Almeron King, a local carpenter, built this gracious Queen Anne Victorian for his family in 1885; his skill and imagination can be seen in the architectural details of the house, enhanced by its repainting in subdued shades of heather, teal, burgundy, green, and gold. The hand-crafted chestnut moldings and elaborately carved fireplace mantels reflect a strong Eastlake influence. Stephanie and Bob Melvin, owners since 1986, have decorated with lace curtains, Oriental carpets on gleaming wood floors, antique clocks and furnishings; firm queen- and king-size mattresses, luxury linens, tiled baths, and ceiling fans. In 1994 they purchased the Greek Revival house next door to provide additional guest accommodations.

"The inn is located in a quiet neighborhood, yet is convenient to Saratoga's attractions. Bob and Stephanie are available when you need help with logistics, but otherwise leave you free to pretend the house is

213

your own." *(Laurent & Enid Hodes)* "Exquisite antiques are arranged to provide a homey feeling rather than a museum-like atmosphere. Stephanie happily lent our group extra blankets for our visit to the performing arts center." *(Paulette Bruno)* "The mahogany dining room table is the scene for a light breakfast of fresh fruit and juice, bakery muffins and pastries, honey, assorted spreads and jellies." *(Allan Stone)* "The lovely rooms have been decorated with exceptional attention to detail, from the night light in the bathroom to the good bedside lighting to the quality hangers in the armoire." *(SWS)* "Immaculately clean, quiet and relaxing, with cordial and helpful owners." *(Marge & Tom Dean)*

Open Feb. through Nov.
Rooms 7 doubles—all with private shower and/or bath, radio, air-conditioning, ceiling fan.
Facilities Dining room, front parlor with books; back parlor with piano, stereo, games. Off-street parking, gardens, terrace.
Location ½ m from center. From Exit 13N on I-87, go 4 m N to 5th traffic light, right on Lincoln.
Restrictions No smoking. "Well-behaved children only."
Credit cards Amex, Visa, MC.
Rates B&B, $75–250 double. Senior, AAA discount midweek. 2-night weekend minimum racing season. Spring, opera, autumn, holiday packages.
Extras German, French spoken.

SCHUYLERVILLE

The Inn on Bacon Hill   *Tel: 518–695–3693*
200 Wall Street, 12871
Mailing address: P.O. Box 1462, Saratoga Springs 12866

If you're looking to combine the excitement of Saratoga with a quiet country getaway, The Inn on Bacon Hill, opened in 1987 by Andrea Collins-Breslin, may fit the bill perfectly. Her Victorian home was built in 1862 by a prominent New York state legislator, and was fully restored by Andrea and her mother, Millie. Original features include the high ceilings, chestnut woodwork, ceiling moldings and border wallpaper, marble fireplaces, and kerosene chandelier. One parlor is furnished primarily with Victorian antiques, the other with Queen Anne reproductions, while the guest rooms have a few antiques, plus fresh flowers and an amenities basket. The breakfast menu includes French toast, blueberry pancakes, quiche, or egg casseroles, with juice, fruit, muffins, jams, coffee, and tea.

"Andrea is friendly, considerate, available when necessary, and unobtrusive. We were welcomed with cheese, crackers, and Saratoga mineral water when we arrived." *(Caran Kelsey)* "Our request for an earlier than usual breakfast was cheerfully accommodated." *(Bob Schmidt)* "Immaculately restored, exceptionally clean. Friendly golden retriever, too." *(Marla & Larry Sugarman)* "Provides solitude yet only a 15-minute drive to excellent restaurants. Lovely flower gardens." *(Robert Beers)* "The Parlor Suite has a baby grand piano, antique gas chandelier, and Victorian accents. The book collection provided good reading during our stay. Breakfast was outstanding and so was the conversation with other guests." *(Adele Morgan)* "Andrea has thought of everything, down to a book of local restaurants into which guests add their comments. Good water pressure; plenty of hot water." *(Eloise Kay)* "The Tulip Room has beautiful early morning light, a wonderfully comfortable four-poster bed, and a reading light that you could really read by." *(Judith Pratt)*

Open All year.
Rooms 1 suite, 3 doubles—1 with full private bath, 1 with private shower, 2 sharing 1 bath. Suite with piano.
Facilities Breakfast room, 2 parlors with fireplace, piano, library, stereo, games; porch. 5 acres with gazebo. 15–30 min. to cross-country/downhill skiing.
Location E Central NY. Saratoga County. 10 min. E of Saratoga Springs, 45 min. N of Albany. Take NY State Thruway to I-87 (Northway) Exit 24. Take I-87 N to Exit 14 (Rtes. 9P and 29). Follow signs for Schuylerville/Rte. 29 and go E on Rte. 29. At sign for Grangerville, turn left and go 1.3 m N to inn, opposite a red barn.
Restrictions No smoking. No children under 16.
Credit cards MC, Visa for final payment.
Rates B&B, $85–135 suite, $65–125 double. 2-night weekend minimum in August. Extended stay discounts.

SHELTER ISLAND

With over ⅓ of Shelter Island set aside as a nature preserve, the area has maintained a more peaceful mood than the more frantic Hamptons, yet is still convenient for such activities as bicycling, walking, tennis, horseback riding, and all water sports.

Shelter Island is located in Suffolk County, 100 miles east of New York City. It's 1½ hours by ferry from Boston to Orient Point, then an eight mile drive to the ferry to Shelter Island. From the Hamptons, go N on Rte. 114 to the ferry.

Information please: Under new ownership and recently restored, the **Chequit Inn** (23 Grand Avenue, P.O. Box 292, Shelter Island Heights 11965; 516–749–0018) has been providing meals and accommodations for vacationers for 120 years. The restaurant serves breakfast, lunch and dinner either on the covered veranda or under an enormous maple tree on the terrace. Guest rooms are in the Cedar House and Summer House; rates are $80–125 double, $95–195 suite. Reports?

Ram's Head Inn 🏃 ✕
Ram Island, 11965

Tel: 516–749–0811
Fax: 516–749–0803

The short ferry ride to Shelter Island will take you back to a quieter era; even more peaceful is the causeway leading to Ram Island. The Ram's Head Inn is set on a hill overlooking the water. Most guest rooms have flowered wallpapers, white-painted furniture, wall-to-wall carpeting, and old-fashioned bathrooms; the furnishings are clean and adequate, and the grounds are lovely, with plenty of big trees, lounge chairs, and hammocks.

Unless you have the stamina to deal with Long Island summer weekend traffic (or can get away during the week), we recommend a visit during the inn's off-season, from May to mid-June, or after Labor Day through October (excepting Columbus Day and Memorial Day weekends), when you and the locals may have the island to yourselves.

"A charming inn, in a pleasant, quiet, romantic location. We ate outdoors on the terrace, overlooking the hotel lawn. Delicious dinners of duck, fish, rack of lamb, and filet mignon, with wonderful desserts. Breakfast features freshly baked breads and muffins. Guest rooms are attractive, compact, and basic. One can spend hours on the rolling lawns that lead to the water and beach—Adirondack chairs and hammocks invite you to snooze." *(Philip Meade)* "Delightful location off the beaten track. The new sun room and patio are especially well done. Immaculate, excellent food." *(William Hussey, also LDG)* Reports needed.

Open All year.
Rooms 4 suites, 13 doubles—13 with private bath, 4 sharing 2½ baths. Most with telephone, ceiling fan.
Facilities Bar, restaurant with occasional entertainment, sun room, roof deck, patio. 4 acres with 800-foot waterfront, 10 boat moorings, swimming, tennis, sailboats, pedalboats, hammocks, play equipment, gazebo. Bike rentals, golf nearby.
Location Take Rte. 27 to Exit 8 (1 m past Southampton College) and follow Rte. 52 to Rte. 38 and turn right. Continue to Rte. 114 N to ferry. On Shelter Is., continue on Rte. 114 N to traffic fork and go straight on Cartright Rd. to stop sign. Turn right on Ram Is. Dr., then right turn over causeway to inn.
Restrictions Smoking permitted in lounge only.
Credit cards Amex, MC, Visa.
Rates Room only, $140–195 suite, $65–125 double. Extra person, $15. 2–3 night weekend, holiday minimum. Alc dinner, $45. 10–20% midweek discount.
Extras Ferry pickups. Crib, babysitting.

SKANEATELES

Also recommended: Among many 19th century experiments in utopian living was the Community Place, organized in 1843, which rejected religion, government, and individual ownership of property, prohibited the use of meat, narcotics and alcohol, and advocated free love. Perhaps its proximity to the Finger Lakes wine region doomed the experiment, but over 150 years later one of the original buildings is now **Frog Pond B&B** (680 Sheldon Road, 13152; 315–685–0146). Too small for a full entry, with only two guest rooms, this historic 175-year old stone home is recommended by *Fran Harris and Hans Wriedt.* "Delightfully decorated, with fresh flowers, sherry and chocolates at bedside, plus a comfortable bed, TV/VCR, and large bath overlooking the pond. Hosts Kathy and Jack Gordon have created a relaxing haven and a not-to-be missed breakfast."

Information please: Long listed in the guide is **The Sherwood Inn** (26 West Genesee Street, Skaneateles 13152; 315–685–3405), dating back to 1807. Although readers remain delighted with its lakeside location, and generally pleased with the food and service in both the tavern and dining room, some feel that the guest rooms are in need of renovation and refurbishing, and also noted significant traffic noise in front of the inn. Double rates range from $60–85 and include a continental breakfast.

SOUTHHAMPTON

Mainstay   *Tel:* 516–283–4375
579 Hill Street, 11968   516–287–6230

This restored Colonial-style house, built in the 1870s and once a country store, was renovated as a B&B in 1985. It was renamed the Mainstay by Elizabeth Main when she purchased it in 1992. One favorite guest room, tucked under the third floor eaves, has cloud-like, blue sponge-painted walls and a delicate flowering vine painted on the woodwork and built-in bureau; its furnishings include a wrought iron bed, fitted with pale pink linens. A larger room on the second floor has floral striped wallpaper, a crisp white duvet on a large brass and iron bed, lace curtain, Victorian dressing table, and a bath with clawfoot tub, outfitted with a shower ring. Homemade muffins, cereals, juice, and coffee are served from 9 to 10:30 A.M. at the country pine table in the dining room or can be taken outside to comfortable chairs scattered about the grounds.

"Clean, charming, and convenient. Guests are upscale and diverse. Ambience is quaint and Elizabeth is friendly and helpful. Wonderful muffins. Gardens are in constant bloom, and the house is full of flowers." *(Paul Siman)* "Fat-free, nutritional, and often lush buffet breakfasts. The 'do-it-yourself' waffles with various toppings are my favorites." *(Joseph Kremer)* "Beautifully restored, on a lovely piece of property." *(SB)* "The added touches make a difference, such as sherry-filled crystal decanters in each room. Elizabeth knows when to leave you be, and when to share a cup of coffee." *(Jonas Holmes)*

Open All year.
Rooms 1 suite, 7 doubles—4 with private bath and/or shower, 4 with maximum of 6 sharing bath. 2 with TV, 3 with fan, 1 with fireplace.
Facilities Dining room, sitting room with fireplace, deck. 1 acre with swimming pool. Off-street parking. Tennis, golf nearby. 1¼ m to ocean.
Location 80 m from NYC. ¾ m from town. On the corner of Hill St. & Bishops Lane.
Restrictions No smoking. Well-behaved children welcome. Traffic noise possible in some rooms.
Credit cards MC, Visa.
Rates B&B, $120–215 suite, $60–180 double. Extra adult, $40; extra child, $20. 2–3 night weekend, holiday minimum June–Oct. 1. 20% midweek discount in summer.
Extras Station/airport pickup.

STEPHENTOWN

Mountain Changes　　　　　　　　　*Tel:* 518–733–6923
RR1, Box 124, Wyomanock Road, 12168　　　800–497–0176
Mailing address: 12 Warren Court,　　　　*Fax:* 518–733–6997
Northport, NY 11768

"Mountains, fields, woods and water, ever ancient and ever changing," is how owners Walter and Charlotte Zloczower and manager Kirk Mitchell describe the panoramic views that inspired their inn's name. Mountain Changes is a spacious contemporary lodge, with broad decks and walls of glass offering great views of the Berkshires. A hearty breakfast is served from 8–9:30 A.M. at two large tables indoors, or at umbrella-covered tables on the deck; in addition to granola, yogurt, cottage cheese, fruit, juice, toast, muffins, or popovers, breakfast includes eggs and bacon, French toast, pancakes, or omelets.

"Short drives took us to fine music at Tanglewood, art and theater in Williamstown, dance at Jacob's Pillow, and many fine restaurants." *(George Slover)* "The grounds are well-kept and bordered with flowers. The atmosphere is friendly and informal; owners are courteous and attentive but not obtrusive." *(BS)* "Enjoyable walking trails; inviting decks." *(George & Adelia Williams)* "The large, comfortable living room, with good magazines and music, and a fire going during chilly evenings, was inviting for conversation with the interesting guests. Guest rooms are attractively decorated, with comfortable beds, and good reading lights." *(Susan Laskowski)* "Spotlessly clean, good lighting and plumbing, with hot, powerful showers, and ample parking near the front door. Walter, Charlotte, and Kirk are warm and welcoming." *(Grace & Frank Welch, and others)* "The guest rooms, while not large, are well-appointed. The shared baths are immaculate—I never had to wait." *(Rick Karl)* "Ever-present, soft classical music set a relaxing and peaceful mood." *(Evelyn Krell)*

Open All year.
Rooms 1 2-bedroom cottage, 1 suite, 9 doubles, 1 single—5 with private bath and/or shower, 7 with a maximum of 4 people sharing bath. All with clock, 8 with fan, 2 with deck, 2 with air-conditioning. Cottage with kitchen, 2 baths, living room; suite with kitchenette.
Facilities Dining room, living room with fireplace, stereo; family room with fireplace, TV/VCR; decks. Recreation cottage with darts, Ping-Pong. 50 acres with swimming pond, hiking trails, cross-country skiing.
Location E NY, Berkshires. 12 m NW of Pittsfield, MA. 4 m N of New Lebanon. From I-90, take Exit B3 & go N on Rte. 22 to New Lebanon. Go 3 m N on Rte. 22 from junction of Rtes. 20 & 22. Look for Stephentown sign ¾ m before a blue Mountain Changes sign. Take 1st left (Wyomanock St.) & go ¾ m. Turn right at 2nd Mountain Changes sign & follow dirt road ½ m to inn.
Restrictions No smoking.
Credit cards MC, Visa.
Rates B&B, $125–160 suite or cottage, $75–110 double, $65–90 double. Extra person, $15. Family, senior rates. 2-night weekend minimum July-Aug., Oct. foliage, winter holidays. Midweek rates.
Extras Airport/station pickups, $15–35. Cribs.

SYRACUSE

Bed & Breakfast Wellington
707 Danforth Street, 13208-1611

Tel: 315–471–2433
800–724–5006
Fax: 315–474–2557

Built in 1914 in the Tudor Revival style, B&B Wellington is named for its architect, Ward Wellington Ward, who designed the house with an Arts and Crafts interior considered to be one of the era's finest. A variety of woods highlight the interior, Mercer tiles surround the living room fireplace, and cozy porches and alcoves offer intimate seating areas. Owners Wendy Wilber and Ray Borg restored the house as a B&B in 1986. Breakfast is served at the dining room table from 7:30 to 9:30 A.M., and includes such entrées as an egg casserole with turkey sausage or French toast with pear Hawaiian sauce.

"A northside neighborhood close to restaurants and local attractions, convenient to the university, yet quiet at night. Plenty of hot water and tons of towels. Breakfasts are healthy and creative, scheduled to guest needs. Off-street parking, well-lit at night." *(Joyce Harvey)* "Charming innkeepers who make you feel relaxed; privacy when you wish and companionship when you prefer." *(Judy Fedele)* "Our room was huge, with a screened porch and comfortable beds. Wendy is gracious, thoughtful, and kind." *(Astrid Swain)* "Our room had many large windows and a small but functional bathroom. Delicious breakfasts of fresh fruit with yogurt, apple turnovers, multi-grain pancakes with granola, herb quiche with salsa, light golden home fries. When we came in at night there was a plate of chocolate chip cookies." *(Stef & Mar Petryszyn)*

Open All year.
Rooms 1 suite, 4 doubles—all with private bath and/or shower, radio, clock, TV, desk, fan. 3 with deck, 1 with refrigerator. Suite with fireplace, TV/VCR.
Facilities Dining room, living room with fireplace, TV/VCR; guest laundry, porches. Off-street parking. 5 min. from Syracuse Univ.
Location N central NY. 3 m from airport. From I-87, take Exit 36 (airport) & go S on I-81. Take Exit 22, Bear St. & continue 1 block past the light to Court St. Turn left on Court St. Go to 3rd light (Park St.) & turn right. Go 1 block to Danforth St. & turn left. Go 2 blocks to inn on left.
Restrictions No smoking. "For safety of children, over age 12 preferred."
Credit cards Amex, MC, Visa.
Rates B&B, $105 suite, $65 double or single. Extra person, $15. 2-night minimum on peak weekends.
Extras Airport/station pickups, $5.

TANNERSVILLE

Eggery Inn ¢
County Road 16, 12485

Tel: 518–589–5363
Fax: 518–589–5774

Founded in the early 1800s, Tannersville was named after its first major industry, leather tanning; hemlock bark was an essential ingredient in the tanning process, and hemlocks grew in profusion throughout the area. Later in the century, elaborate resort hotels were built. When the railroads allowed the wealthy to vacation farther north, the grand hotels were replaced by boardinghouses offering a mountain vacation for the working classes. The Eggery, once one of these boardinghouses, was converted into a country inn in 1979 by innkeepers Abe and Julie Abramczyk. Breakfast includes your choice of hot or cold cereal, yogurt and fresh fruit, eggs, French toast, or pancakes with bacon or sausage.

"Situated opposite Hunter Mountain, our room overlooked a varicolored panorama of fall foliage. The inn's 1900s Dutch Colonial-style architecture is enhanced with country furnishings and knick-knacks to complement the homey atmosphere." *(Joseph Giffuhl)* "Spectacular views of the northern Catskills. The Victorian parlor has lovely wood wainscotting, a wood-burning Franklin stove on a brick hearth, and an antique player piano." *(Michael Spring)* "Immaculate housekeeping, warm country atmosphere." *(Carol & Dan Alesandro)* "Great eggs, delicious coffee, warm room, fresh air." *(MPG)* "Abe and Julie are enthusiastic guides to local attractions and restaurants." *(Ralph Saviano)* "Friendly innkeepers who care about their guests' comfort. Excellent country breakfast—the pancakes are a must." *(Paula Perreault)*

Open All year.
Rooms 1 suite, 13 doubles—all with private shower and/or tub, telephone, TV, fan. 9 with air-conditioning. 6 rooms in annex.
Facilities Dining room with fireplace; living room with fireplace, TV, games; bar/lounge; wraparound porch. 13 acres. Lake swimming, trout fishing, golf, tennis, downhill cross-country skiing nearby.
Location SE NY, Northern Catskills, Greene County. 125 m N of NYC, 50 m S of Albany, 18 m Woodstock. 1 m from village. From I-87, take Rte. 23 to 23A to Tannersville traffic light. Go left (S) 1½ m to inn.
Restrictions Smoking in bar area of dining room. "Well-supervised children welcome."
Credit cards Amex, MC, Visa.
Rates B&B, $75–120 double. Extra person, $20–30. 2–3 night weekend, holiday minimum. Off-season rates. Tips appreciated.
Extras Limited wheelchair access. Spanish, Yiddish spoken. Station pickups sometimes.

THENDARA

Information please: Close to great hiking, the Moose River, and Fulton Chain of Lakes is **Van Auken's Inne** (Box 206, Thendara 13472; 315–369–3033), a few miles west of Old Forge. Built in 1891 in the heyday of the Adirondack camp period, it has a restaurant on the first floor, with a long veranda for relaxing. The 12 modestly furnished guest rooms vary in size, and have private baths, TV, and telephone. The $50–70 rates include a breakfast of juice, coffee, and choice of pancakes, French toast, or eggs. The restaurant also serves lunch and dinner. Reports?

For an additional area inn, see **Eagles Bay**.

TRUMANSBURG

Taughannock Farms Inn 🛶 ✗   *Tel:* 607–387–7711
2030 Gorge Road, Route 89
Taughannock Falls State Park, 14886

High above the shores of Lake Cayuga is the Taughannock Farms Inn, built in 1873 by a wealthy Philadelphian, John Jones, and decorated with furnishings imported from England and Italy. This lavish summer mansion stayed in the Jones family until the 1930s and 1940s, when the land was deeded to New York State for the creation of Taughannock Falls State Park, and the house was sold to Merritt and Maude Agard. Long-standing traditions continue to this day under the management of their grandchildren, current owners Keith and Nancy (Agard) le Grand. Rooms are furnished with Victorian antiques, some original to the house, and the inn is well known for its restaurant. Most tables are on the glassed-in porch, tiered to maximize the lake views for diners. Specialties include orange date bread, a long-time tradition at the inn, roast duck with black raspberry sauce, pork loin with apples, prime rib, or fresh fish. Dessert favorites include peppermint ice cream pie or chocolate mousse torte.

"The views of the forests of Taughannock, the waters of Lake Cayuga and the hills of the Finger Lakes region are breathtaking. The Garden Room is a large, charming room furnished with antiques and a queen-size canopy bed that requires a small step stool to reach. The Victorian-themed rose-patterned wallpaper is enhanced by drapes of matching fabric." *(Marion Fay)* "Tranquil, tasteful, uncluttered. Huge, lovely old windows that really open. Furniture is elegant, sturdy and comfortable; everything in good repair. Original woodwork is stunning. Staff are courteous and resourceful; owners are visible and cordial. Dining room service is folksy and the menu is classic American cuisine, with homemade relishes, freshly baked breads, and well-prepared vegetables. Breakfast breads and cakes absolutely delicious, with real butter and homemade jam, local grape juice and fresh-squeezed orange juice. Hiking trails lead from the front door to spectacular waterfalls." *(CG)*

Area for improvement: "Our king-size bed seemed to be two twins pushed together; the mattresses were soft, with a ridge down the middle."

Open All year.
Rooms 2 cottages, 5 doubles—all with private bath, radio, fan. 1 cottage with telephone, air-conditioning, kitchen.
Facilities Restaurant, lounge, sitting room. 7 acres with gardens, on Lake Cayuga. In state park with hiking, wildlife sanctuary, swimming, boat launch.
Location N Central NY, Finger Lakes region. 9 m NW of Ithaca. On Rte. 89 at entrance to state park.
Restrictions No smoking in guest rooms. "Well-behaved children welcome."
Credit cards Amex, MC, Visa.
Rates B&B, $190 cottage (sleeps 3–4), $95–125 double.
Extras Train station pickups. Babysitting by special arrangement. Dutch, German, French spoken.

TUPPER LAKE

Wawbeek ♦ ✕ ⴕ

Tel: 518–359–2656
553 Panther Mountain Road, 12986   800–953–2656

Wawbeek means "Big Rock" and is the name of this Great Camp, built on the shores of Upper Saranac Lake in 1907. The two original buildings are the main lodge and the Mountain House; the other buildings and cabins date to the 1970s. The Wawbeek restaurant occupies the main lodge, with the restaurant on the first floor and the bar-lounge on the second. Focal point of the restaurant is an unusual stone fireplace, flanked by stone benches, and framed by a split staircase. Upstairs, an enormous moose head supervises the goings-on in the bar. The shingled Mountain House is paneled in knotty pine, and has its own great room with stone fireplace; two-story porches, furnished with rockers, offer views of the lake and mountains through the tall pines. The resort is owned by Nancy and Norman Howard, who with several local partners, purchased the resort in 1994. Nancy has a background in publicity and a family history of country innkeeping; Norm's recent experience was as senior vice-president of the Cunard Line, in charge of the *QE2*. Rates include a full breakfast in summer, continental off-season, as well as use of the boating equipment and recreational facilities.

"Both Nancy and Norm were gracious and professional." *(William Orthwain)* "Outstanding food, service, and atmosphere in the restaurant. The all-inclusive recreation plan was great for us." *(Lori Piccirilli)* "The entire staff made us feel right at home." *(Clare Moore)* "Our room in the Mountain House was spacious, carpeted, and paneled in random-width knotty pine, with French doors opening to the second-floor porch. Our bath was large, well-furnished and modern. The views are exactly what tourists come to the Adirondacks to see." *(Dave & Cheri Kendall)*

Open All year. Cottages closed late Sept.–May.

Rooms 6 doubles in Mountain House; 4 doubles in Carriage House; 9 1–4 bedroom cottages/cabins—all with private bath and/or shower; 7 with kitchenette. Some with fireplace, deck.

Facilities Restaurant with fireplace, bar/lounge, living room with fireplace, TV; game room, screened porches. Lakefront with beach, swimming platform & slide, dock, boat launch, canoes, rowboats, sunfish; mt. bikes, basketball court, tennis court, cross-country skiing, hiking. Golf, horseback riding nearby.

Location Adirondack Park. 30 m W of Lake Placid, 10 m from village of Saranac, 5 m from town. From I-87, take Exit 30. Go W on Rte. 73 through Lake Placid to Saranac Lake. Go W (left) on Rte. 3, then N (right) on Rte. 30. Go 1 m to inn.

Credit cards Amex, Discover, MC, Visa.

Rates B&B, $75–215 cottage (sleep 2–5), $65–120 double. MAP, family rates. 2-3 night weekend minimum, except Carriage House. Weekly rates. Extra adult, $20, child under 18, $15.

Extras Station/airport pickup. Pets with approval. Cribs, babysitting by arrangement.

WARRENSBURG

Information please: Listed in past editions, **The Merrill Magee House** (2 Hudson Street, 12885; 518–623–2449) consists of an early 1800s Greek Revival building, housing the restaurant, tavern, parlor, and one guest suite, plus a recently built guest house, about 100 yards away, containing the ten guest rooms and a sun room with a hot tub. The rooms are spacious and comfortable, most with canopy or four-poster queen- or king-sized beds and country-style furnishings. B&B double rates of $95–105 include a full breakfast. Dinner favorites in the restaurant include duck with green peppercorns, shrimp with wine and garlic, and Wiener schnitzel.

House on the Hill B&B
Route 28, Box 248, 12885

Tel: 518–623–9390
800–221–9340
Fax: 518–623–9396

If sincere hospitality and a warm welcome are your top priorities in a B&B, then you'll be delighted with your stay at the House on the Hill. Longtime owners Joe and Lynn Rubino used to vacation in Warrensburg when they lived in New Jersey. They often hosted guests, so when Joe retired in 1989, they decided to restore this old farmhouse as a B&B. The house has an original section dating back to 1750; the main part of the house was built in 1890, and a new addition in 1988. The furnishings include antiques and contemporary art, collected over the years when Joe worked with a graphic arts company. Breakfast is served at guests' convenience, and might include Belgian waffles or Adirondack omelets.

"My favorite place is the Sun Room, a two-story addition with lots of windows and comfortable seating. It's a perfect place for breakfast, and for lingering and chatting with the Rubinos and the other guests. Joe and Lynn are well informed about area activities, and love to pamper their guests." *(SWS)* Comments appreciated.

Open All year.
Rooms 1 suite, 4 doubles—all with in-room sink; suite with private shower, 4 with a maximum of 4 people sharing bath. All with telephone, radio, clock, desk, air-conditioning, fan.
Facilities Dining room, living room, family room with TV/VCR. 176 acres with lawn games, hiking, cross-country skiing.
Location E central NY, Adirondack region. 3 m N of town. From NYC, take I-87 N to Exit 24 (2nd Albany Eixt). Go N on Northway 87 to Exit 23, Warrensburg. Go N on Rte. 9 for 4 m to Rte. 28. Go left on 28 for 500 yds. to B&B on left.
Restrictions No smoking. Children over 12 preferred.
Credit cards CB, DC, Discover, MC, Visa.
Rates B&B, $179–199 suite, $75–95 double, $55–75 single. Extra person, $15–20. 2–3 night weekend, holiday minimum. Off-season specials.
Extras Airport/station pickups; fee charged. French, Italian, German spoken.

WARWICK

Also recommended: Just two miles north of the New Jersey border is the **Peach Grove Inn** (205 Route 17A, 10990; 914–986–7411), an 1850s Greek Revival house owned by Lucy and John Mastropierro. The house is furnished with antiques collected from Lucy's days as an antiques dealer. Common areas include a double parlor and large dining room. Double rates for the four guest rooms, each with a private bath, are $95–110. This enthusiastic recommendation was received just as we were going to press: "Our spacious room was furnished with an antique French bed, a working fireplace, and a private bath. The inn has immense eleven-foot ceilings and is decorated attractively in a light Victorian style, with an eclectic collection of antiques. Delicious breakfasts with fresh fruit and muffins, an omelet made with fresh herbs from the garden one day, and orange French toast the next. John and Lucy Mastropierro were friendly innkeepers, always willing to talk or provide advice on area restaurants and attractions." *(Peter & Mary Holmes)*

WESTFIELD

Westfield is home to a number of excellent antique shops, and is 10 miles from the Chautauqua Institution, offering a full summer program of concerts, theater, opera, and lectures. The self-proclaimed grape juice capital of the world, it is also home to seven wineries and many antique shops. Lake Erie and Chautauqua Lake are nearby for swimming, boating, and fishing; hiking, golf, tennis and skiing are also easily accessible.

For an additional area entry, see **Chautauqua**.

Westfield House ¢   *Tel:* 716–326–6262
East Main Road, Route 20, P.O. Box 505, 14787

Westfield House is an 1840s-era brick home with a later Gothic Revival addition, restored as a B&B in 1987 by Betty and Judd Wilson.

"The Wilsons provided restaurant menus, brochures on nearby attractions, and excellent directions. At Betty's suggestion, we visited the local beach to watch a spectacular sunset over Lake Erie; we returned to sit on the porch for several hours in good conversation with other guests. Our breakfast of fresh fruit, homemade muffins, eggs and toast, was served at 9 A.M." *(Mary & Jim Rafferty)* "This charming B&B is set well back from busy Route 20, sheltered behind a double row of stately shade trees. Our first-floor room was equipped with a firm four-poster queen-size bed and a lovely fireplace." *(Beth & Geoff Eggert)*

"Fourteen-foot ceilings on the first floor are accented by the pointed arch windows; the grand foyer was furnished with an enormous antique mirror. The crisp blue and white decor of the Captain's Quarters was simply accented by a boat model and several other nautical accents. Breakfast—served in the dining room or on the patio—was well-done and filling; a fresh fruit salad followed by Betty's special French toast and sausage." *(NPB)* Comments welcome.

Open All year.
Rooms 3 suites, 4 doubles—all with private bath and/or shower, radio, clock, ceiling fan. 5 with air-conditioning, 3 with desk. Telephones available upon request. 1 suite with TV.
Facilities Dining room with fireplace, living room, parlor, porch. 1.7 acres with carriage barn. Golf, boating, fishing, skiing, tennis nearby.
Location W NY, 2 ½ hrs. NE of Cleveland, OH. 1 hr. SW of Buffalo, 45 min. NE of Erie, PA. 2 m E of town center on Rte. 20.
Restrictions No smoking. Children over 12 preferred.
Credit cards MC, Visa; discount for cash, check.
Rates B&B, $80–135 suite, $65–80 double. Extra person, $15. 2-night weekend minimum July, Aug. Off-season senior discount, mid-week.
Extras 1st floor room wheelchair accessible, equipped for disabled. Crib.

The William Seward Inn
6645 South Portage Road, 14787-9602

Tel: 716–326–4151
Fax: 716–326–4163

The original section of the William Seward Inn was built in 1821, and was bought by William Henry Seward soon afterward. Seward, at that time the agent for the Holland Land Company in Westfield, later became famous as the secretary of state under Abraham Lincoln and Andrew Johnson when he arranged the purchase of Alaska from Russia—known at the time as Seward's Folly. Seward made several additions to the house, including the distinctive two-story Greek pillars. In the 1840s the house was sold to George Patterson, who became lieutenant governor of New York, and remained in that family for over 100 years. It was moved from town to its present location about 25 years ago, and was bought by Jim and Debbie Dahlberg in 1991.

Meals are a highlight of a stay at the William Seward. Breakfast includes fresh juice, home-baked muffins, fresh fruit, and a hot entrée—perhaps Amaretto-flavored French toast; a four-cheese and tarragon omelet; or a vegetable quiche with nutmeg and curry. The dinner might start with homemade spinach ravioli with basil sauce; followed by salmon with pinot noir sauce; beef au poivre with wild mushrooms; or veal tenderloin with mustard sauce.

"Our room had a view of Lake Erie in the distance and was furnished with a four-poster bed, period antiques, and ample storage space. The comfortable bed had an abundance of blankets and numerous fluffy pillows to lounge on. The sink was in the bedroom, while the commode and shower were in a closet-size room off the sitting area." *(Jim & Cathy Sirianni)* "A successful marriage of 19th century authenticity and 20th century amenities, including king-size beds and double Jacuzzis." *(Robert McClain)* "Our first inn, and still our favorite. Comfortable, enfolding silence in the sunny library, with subdued classical music playing in the background, and a large (unguarded) bowl of M&Ms. Comfortable perfection." *(Donna Bocks)* "Jim and Debbie are a charming couple whose goal is to make your stay memorable. Good service; outstanding meals." *(Margaret Room)*

Open All year. Dinner served Thurs.–Sun.
Rooms 14 doubles—all with private bath and/or shower, radio, air-conditioning. Telephone on request. 4 rooms in carriage house with double Jacuzzi.

Facilities Living room with fireplace, library; dining room. 2 acres.
Location W NY, 2½ hrs. NE of Cleveland, OH. 1 hr. SW of Buffalo, 45 min. NE of Erie, PA. 3 m to town. 4 m S of I-90, on Rte. 394.
Restrictions No smoking. Children 13 and over. Check-in between 2–8 P.M.
Credit cards Discover, MC, Visa.
Rates B&B, $85–165 double, $75–155 single. Extra person, $15. 2-night minimum most weekends, holidays. Prix fixe dinner, $36, by reservation Thurs.–Sun.
Extras 1 room in Carriage House fully handicap accessible, also 1st floor of inn.

WEST POINT

Also recommended: On the grounds of the U.S. Military Academy at West Point is the imposing, castle-like **Hotel Thayer** (West Point, 10996; 914–446–4731 or 800–247–5047). The large lobby has stone arches, carved wood balconies, wrought iron chandeliers, and state flags mounted on each stone column. The restaurant offers seating in the dining room or on the terrace, with a spectacular panorama of the Hudson Valley. The 200 guest rooms vary in size, with typical hotel furnishings; those on the river side offer good views of the Hudson River for a slight premium. The $70–155 rates offer an excellent alternative to the pricey B&Bs on the other side of the Hudson, especially if traveling with children.

Information please: Five miles north of West Point is the **Cromwell Manor Inn** (Angola Road, Cornwall-on-Hudson 12518; 914–534–7136), a Greek Revival-style house built in 1820. Recently renovated and furnished with period antiques, the fourteen guest rooms have private baths and air-conditioning. Double rates of $120–175 include a full breakfast.

WESTPORT

Traveling the Northway (I-87) up the west side of Lake Champlain will bring you to Route 22 and the resort community of Westport, with all the lakefront activities you would expect.

Information please: Right on the village green is **The Inn on the Library Lawn** (1 Washington Street, Westport, 12993; 518–962–8666), where concerts are held in summer. "A comfortable, well-maintained inn. The first floor has an antique/crafts shop and a small parlor; the ten guest rooms (with private bath and air-conditioning) are on the second floor, many with views of the lake, but also overlooking Route 22. If you want to sleep late, ask for a room in the rear. My room was nicely furnished with a double bed, two chairs for reading, good lights, and a TV." *(Nancy Cohn)* The double rates of $55–95 include breakfasts of fresh fruit and juice, bagels and muffins, and souffles, pancakes, French toast, or waffles.

For an additional area entry, see **Elizabethtown.**

All Tucked Inn ¢   *Tel:* 518–962–4400
53 South Main Street, P.O. Box 324, 12993

With a name like "All Tucked Inn" you won't be surprised to learn that guests at this B&B are delighted with its coziness and warmth. When nights are chilly, innkeepers Claudia Ryan and Tom Haley make sure that beds have flannel sheets, fireplaces are ready to blaze, and steaming hot mugs of coffee are ready before breakfast. The house, overlooking Ballard Park and Lake Champlain, was built in 1872 in the Dutch Colonial style with a gambrel roof and a long porch across the front; Tom and Claudia restored it as an inn in 1993. The decor is an eclectic mix of antiques and more contemporary pieces. Tom serves breakfast at individual tables in the dining room from 8 to 10 A.M.; his homemade breads and muffins are guest favorites.

"The aroma of freshly brewed hazelnut coffee enticed us from our comfortable queen-size brass bed." *(Bernd & Bärbel Ettrich)* "Comfortable common areas. Tom and Claudia, and their two gentle collies, make their guests feel right at home. Good lighting, and considering the age of the inn, very quiet." *(Dr. & Mrs. S. Amleis)* "Our room was beautifully lit by a warm fire, with windows overlooking Lake Champlain." *(Helen & Eric Ross)* "Lace pillows and handmade quilts covered our king-size bed. The bathroom was well supplied with fresh towels, soaps, and linens. The innkeepers are pleasant and cheerful, helpful yet respecting guests' privacy. We enjoyed delicious breakfasts of warm blueberry muffins, cranberry nut bread, freshly squeezed juice, eggs and bacon, accompanied by lovely views of the frozen lake and drifts of snow." *(Sheila Suerig)* "We had dinner on the enclosed porch overlooking the lake, and thoroughly enjoyed the hearty turkey soup, lemon chicken, crisp string beans, roasted potatoes, and salad; dessert was a warm brownie topped with ice cream." *(Ed & Patty Taylor)*

Open All year.

Rooms 1 suite, 8 doubles—all with private shower and/or tub, fan. 4 with clock, 4 with desk, 3 with fireplace. Suite with fireplace, porch.

Facilities Dining room, living room with fireplace, TV/VCR, stereo; family room, library, porch. Across street from Lake Champlain for water sports. 5 min. to cross-country skiing, 45 min. to downhill skiing.

Location N NY, Adirondack region. 2 hrs. N of Albany, 2 hrs. S of Montreal. In town. From I-87 (Northway) take Exit 31. Go S on Rte. 9N for 4 m to Westport. Bear right on Rte. 22 through village to inn on right.

Restrictions No smoking. Children over age 6 preferred.

Credit cards None accepted.

Rates B&B, $85–95 suite, $55–85 double. Extra person, $15. No tipping. Getaway package. Prix fixe dinner, $15–18.

Extras Station pickups.

WINDHAM

Albergo Allegria
Route 296, P.O. Box 267, 12496

Tel: 518–734–5560
800–6–ALBERGO
Fax: 518–734–5570

Leonore and Vito Radelich, originally from Veneto Province (once part of Italy), ran a restaurant on Long Island before they moved to Windham and opened La Griglia, a restaurant specializing in Northern Italian cuisine. In

1986, the Radelichs created Albergo Allegria from two cottages of the Osborn House, a summer boardinghouse complex built in 1876. Rooms are decorated with period wallpapers and Victorian furnishings, complemented by the original woodwork, trim, and moldings. In 1989 the Radelichs, and their daughter and son-in-law, Marianna and Leslie Leman, left the restaurant business in order to devote their full attention to innkeeping. But they haven't forgotten the importance of serving good food in a welcoming atmosphere—the sunny breakfast room has handsome reproduction Victorian oak tables and chairs, lace placemats, and floral centerpieces. Breakfast is served from 8–9:30 A.M. in summer and 7:30–9:30 in winter; a buffet of fresh fruit, homemade croissants, cereals and juices awaits on the sideboard, followed by the daily entrée—perhaps omelets with mushrooms and cheese, Belgian waffles, or ginger peach pancakes.

"When we arrived, the huge fireplace was roaring, and a table filled with hot drinks and tempting snacks created a welcoming atmosphere." *(Donna Netschert)* "The high mineral content of the tap water reminded me of a hot springs spa—good for skin and hair." *(MD)* "Leslie and Marianna (along with their dog, Shalom) are friendly and helpful, yet unobtrusive. Guest rooms vary in size, but all are immaculate, romantic, and well decorated." *(Lynne Batlan, and others)* "Our dinner at La Griglia was first rate, with excellent food and service." *(Judith Pilbat)* "Surprisingly quiet for an inn filled to capacity." *(Lucille Kennedy)* "Delicious omelet Florentine and waffles for breakfast." *(Randi Schneweiss)*

Open All year.
Rooms 4 suites, 16 doubles—all with full private bath, telephone, TV, fan. 6 with deck, 3 with desk. Suites with VCR; 1 suite with double Jacuzzi. 4 rooms in motel annex.
Facilities Living room with fireplace, family room with fireplace, TV/VCR, video library; breakfast room, guest refrigerator, porches. 4 acres with lawn, deck, creek with swimming hole, children's swing set. 1 m to Ski Windham, 7 m to Hunter Mt. Golf, tennis, cross-country skiing across street.
Location SE NY, Northern Catskills, Greene County. 1 hr. S of Albany, 2½ hrs. N of NYC. ½ m to town. From I-87, take Exit 21 (Catskill) & go W on Rte. 23. Turn left at sign "Ski Windham Mt." & then left to inn.
Restrictions Smoking permitted in some guest rooms only. "Well-behaved children welcome."
Credit cards MC, Visa.
Rates B&B, $95–175 suite, $55–105 double, $50–105 single. Extra person, $15. Tipping encouraged. 2–3 night weekend, holiday minimum. Midweek packages.
Extras 1 room with wheelchair access. Station pickups. Crib, babysitting by advance reservation. Italian, Croatian, Afrikaans, Australian spoken; American, Australian sign language.

Point Lookout Mountain Inn ♁ ✗ ♿
Route 23, Box 33, East Windham 12439

Tel: 518–734–3381
Fax: 518–734–6526

The first travelers to enjoy the view from Point Lookout were the Mohican Indians, who stopped here to rest as they made their way to the summer hunting grounds in the mountains. Later, it became a stagecoach stop, and in the 1920s, a snack bar was built with a tower to enhance the five-state view. The current structure dates to 1965, built after a disastrous fire. In 1980, Rosemary Jensen and Mariana and Lucio DiToro bought the inn, and have worked non-stop to renovate and upgrade the property. Future plans include a separate entrance and parking for overnight guests, four disabled access guest rooms, and a new cafe. Rosemary notes that "we remodeled our breakfast room to provide an even cozier setting for our 'raid the refrigerator' breakfast. Now guests just help themselves to coffees, teas, Danish, cookies, tea breads, donuts, hot and cold cereals, fresh fruit, juices, and more." An extensive menu is offered at lunch and dinner; the owners will gladly cater to special dietary requirements. Rosemary reports that "our atmosphere is casual and comfortable, to reflect the lifestyle of the mountains."

"The dining room, with its huge fireplace, has a comfortable atmosphere, excellent service, a menu to suit most tastes, and a magnificent view. Our room was large, airy, clean, simply but adequately furnished with a motel-style layout, and offered the same memorable view as the dining room. The bathroom was modern and clean with an excellent shower." *(KH)* "Breakfast is quick, convenient, and nutritious." *(Deborah Robertson)* "Food is wholesome, delicious, ample in quantity and reasonable in price; the staff is friendly, funny, and accommodating." *(Joyce O'Connell & Irene Portice)* Reports appreciated.

Open All year. Restaurant hours vary with season.
Rooms 14 doubles—all with full private bath, radio, TV, desk, ceiling fan.
Facilities Dining room, breakfast room with books, fireplace; game room with pool table, deck. 4 acres with gazebo, picnic area, birdwatching. Tennis, golf, swimming nearby. 2 m to cross-country, 5 m to downhill skiing.
Location Catskill Mountains. 2½ hrs. north of New York. From I-87 take Exit 21 to Rte. 23. Go west 16 m to inn.
Credit cards Amex, DC, Discover, MC, Visa.
Rates B&B, $60–125 double. Extra child in room, $10–15; extra adult, $15–25. 10% senior discount. Alc lunch $8, alc dinner $18. Midweek non-holiday ski packages.
Extras Pets by prior arrangement, $10 plus $50 security. Italian spoken.

WYOMING

Reader tip: "The little town of Wyoming is a wonderful surprise, with over 70 buildings listed on the National Register of Historic Places; we found it far more charming than other, better-known Finger Lakes towns. We had a delightful lunch at a beautifully renovated luncheonette from the 1800s, with a brass and copper espresso machine that turns out the real stuff. And it's a convenient distance from spectacular Letchworth State Park." *(Eloise Daniel)*

Hillside Inn ✕   *Tel:* 716–495–6800
890 East Bethany Road, P.O. Box 300, 14591   800–544–2249

Although one expects to find grand mansions in Newport, Rhode Island, or Bar Harbor, Maine, it's always a surprise to discover one in a quiet agricultural community. A 40-room Classic Revival mansion built as a health spa in 1851, the Hillside Inn still uses its abundant mineral springs to provide water for its guests. Many notables stayed here, including Susan B. Anthony, John Muir, and the Roosevelts. The gardens were laid out in 1912 by Bryant Flemming, who founded Cornell's horticultural school. The mansion was bought by Bill and Nancy Squier in 1989; after decades of neglect, extensive renovation was needed. Rates include a full breakfast and afternoon tea. Dinner is served to both inn guests and the public; dinner entrées include pork chops with peach salsa; veal with walnuts in lemon butter; Cornish game hen with apple raisin chutney.

"Antiques abound without Victorian clutter. Beds have firm mattresses and cozy down comforters; our four-poster was so tall we used the step stool provided. The bathrooms are modern, with ample hot water and bright lighting. Afternoon tea included cucumber sandwiches, and a creamy cheese-cinnamon dip for sliced apples. Breakfast treats included freshly baked German raspberry coffee cake, omelets, and corn pancakes topped with a homemade peach sauce. At dinner, our rainbow trout was perfectly cooked, garnished with nasturtiums." *(EDM)* "Nancy is a friendly hostess who takes time with everyone." *(Pat Boprey)* "Beautiful setting on a hill removed from town. Large, comfortable rooms with beautiful antiques. Spacious sitting rooms with crackling fires at night." *(Jeffrey Meadowcroft)* "Our room in the cottage was Victorian in color and decor—even the sheets had lace edging." *(EB)*

Area for improvement: "Reading lights and tables on both sides of the bed."

Open All year. Restaurant closed Mon., Tues.
Rooms 2 suites, 10 doubles—all with private bath and/or shower, clock. Most with radio, desk, air-conditioning, fireplace. 4 with whirlpool tub. Some with TV, refrigerator, balcony. 6 rooms in cottage. VCR on request.
Facilities Restaurant, living room, bar/lounge, breakfast room, family room, library, all with fireplace; library, bar with TV; unscreened porch. Guest refrigerator. 48 acres with gardens, gazebo, hiking, cross-country skiing. Tennis, golf nearby.
Location NW NY. 45 m SW of Rochester, 45 m E of Buffalo. 15 m N of Letchworth State Park. 8/10 m from Rte. 19. From Buffalo, take I-90 E to Batavia, Exit 48. Go S on Rte. 98 to Rte. 63. Turn left on Rte. 63, go to E. Bethany. Turn right East Rd. (becomes E. Bethany Rd.) to inn on right. From Rochester, go W on I-90 to LeRoy, Exit 47. Go S on Rte. 19 to Wyoming, then turn right at Gaslight Village on East Bethany Rd. to inn on left.
Restrictions Smoking in bar only. "Well supervised children welcome."
Credit cards Discover, MC, Visa.
Rates B&B, $150–175 suite, $60–175 double. Extra adult, $25; child, $15. 15% service on food. Breakfast, $6.50 for non-resident guests. Alc lunch, $7.50, alc dinner, $15–30. Off-season packages.
Extras Wheelchair access; some bathrooms specially equipped. Babysitting. German, Spanish, French spoken.

Pennsylvania

The Thomas Bond House, Philadelphia

From the ridges of the Appalachian mountains which cut diagonally across the state to softly rolling farmlands, dense northern woods and quiet river valleys, Pennsylvania offers visitors a wide palette of urban and rural landscapes. Anchoring the southeastern and southwestern corners are the state's cultural and urban centers, stately Philadelphia and a revived and lively Pittsburgh.

Eastern Pennsylvania has several distinct geographic areas, all of them with varied cultural and natural attractions and history. These include Bucks County, Chester County, Lancaster County, and the Poconos. Because the listings for each area are scattered throughout this chapter (we list them alphabetically by town), here are a few background notes on the different regions:

Bucks County: Although only 1½ hours from New York, and 45 minutes from Philadelphia, Bucks County is a peaceful rural retreat of rolling green meadows dotted with cows and deep forests, with the beautiful Delaware River running through. New Hope, its best-known town, was founded in 1681. Many of its inns and hotels date back to the 1850s, when the Delaware Canal was in full operation. After the railroad made the canal's mule-drawn barges obsolete, nothing much changed until the end of the century, when some New York artists discovered its charms. Its reputation as an artists' colony really grew during the 1930s, when it was rediscovered by some of New York's most well-known artists and writers.

Although it has its overtouristed side, Bucks County offers fine-quality food and lodging, excellent antique and craft shops, a wide river for

231

canoeing and rafting, lovely walking and hiking trails, and numerous historical sites relating to the Revolutionary War. Rates in Bucks County do not vary with the seasons, but are generally lower midweek and higher on weekends.

For additional area listings, see the New Jersey chapter, where you'll find descriptions of inns just on the other side of the Delaware.

Here's a list of towns with recommended inns in **Bucks County**: Doylestown, Erwinna, Gardenville, New Hope, Point Pleasant, Wrightstown.

Chester County/Brandywine Valley: Only 30 miles southwest of Philadelphia, this area of rolling hills and pastures is known for the 350-acre Longwood Gardens, the Wyeth Collection at the Brandywine River Museum, and the collection of American decorative arts and furniture at the Winterthur Museum.

Here's a list of towns with recommended inns in **Chester/Brandywine**: Avondale, Chadds Ford, Kennett Square, Kintnersville, Landenberg, Oxford, Valley Forge, West Chester.

Lancaster County: Also called Pennsylvania Dutch country, this area of rich rolling farmland is known for the Amish people, a religious group that eschews much of the twentieth-century world, including most modern conveniences we take for granted. We are able to learn much about their way of life through the Mennonites, who follow many of the same religious precepts, but feel that it is all right to have contact with the outside world, and are willing to adopt some modern ways. Calling this area "Pennsylvania Dutch" is confusing to some; the word "Dutch" here derives from the German word *Deutsch*, or German, and most Amish and Mennonite settlers originally came from Germany, not Holland.

Although Lancaster County has some tacky tourist traps, the area offers many attractions of genuine historic and cultural interest; if you saw the movie *Witness* you know how beautiful the region is. Accommodations in this area range from historic and elegant inns to working farms with guest rooms—nothing fancy, but they're clean and inexpensive. Most area innkeepers can arrange for you to have Saturday night dinner with an Amish family; readers often find this experience to be a highlight of their trip, so be sure to inquire.

Here's a list of towns with recommended inns in **Lancaster County**: Airville, Akron, Churchtown, Columbia, Ephrata, Gordonville, Intercourse, Lancaster, Lititz, Manheim, Mount Joy, Oxford, Paradise, Strasburg, White Horse.

The Poconos: Although some may know the area only by the heart-shaped beds featured in ads for the "honeymoon capital of the East," there is a great deal of natural beauty to be found in the Poconos, from the Delaware Water Gap, at the entrance to the Poconos, to the areas further north, around Canadensis.

Here's a list of towns with recommended inns in **The Poconos**: Beach Lake, Canadensis, Cresco, Hawley, Skytop, Stroudsberg.

Endless Mountains: Trailblazers will head for the pastoral rolling hills of northeastern Pennsylvania, just south of Binghamton, New York. The uncrowded roads are ideal for exploring, and the area is home to dozens of sparkling mountain lakes, along with hiking in the Endless Mountains.

Here's a list of towns with recommended inns in the **Endless Mountains**: Dallas, Eagles Mere, Harford, and Union Dale.

ADAMSTOWN

Adamstown Inn ¢   *Tel:* 717–484–0800
62 West Main Street, 19501-0938   800–594–4808

It's no wonder that Adamstown, home to more than 2,500 antiques dealers in the spring, summer, and fall, is called the "antiques capital of the world." Aficionados no longer have to break the mood when it comes to lodging, thanks to the Adamstown Inn. Although the original house dated back to the early 1800s, the yellow brick home you see today was largely constructed in 1925. It remained a private home until 1988, when Tom and Wanda Berman bought it and converted it into a B&B. They added bathrooms, refinished the floors and the chestnut woodwork, and wallpapered the rooms in reproduction papers. Highlights include the elaborate leaded glass doors, added in 1925. Guest rooms are beautifully furnished with antiques, lace and balloon curtains, Oriental rugs, handmade quilts, and marble-topped dressers.

"Immaculate rooms, careful attention to detail. The innkeepers made reservations for us at a great restaurant." *(Bonnie Garraux)* "Each morning, our choice of coffee, tea, or hot chocolate was waiting outside the door of our spacious, elegant room. Tom and Wanda are friendly and accommodating, well informed about area activities. The town is quiet and quaint." *(Heather Phillips)* "The Sunroom is decorated in shades of green with floral accents; a multitude of windows kept it filled with sunlight. Delicious breakfast of homemade muffins and bread, fresh fruit, and wonderful raspberry hot chocolate." *(Victorian Huntress)* "Our tiled bathroom had a Jacuzzi, shower, and pedestal sink. Well-lit parking behind the house." *(Marie Pavlik)* "We enjoyed antiquing in Adamstown and outlet shopping in Reading." *(Mary Lou Paratore)*

Open All year.
Rooms 4 doubles—all with private bath and/or shower, radio, air-conditioning. 2 with double Jacuzzi, 2 with desk. TV on request.
Facilities Breakfast room, living room with fireplace, library, games. ³/₄ acre with barbecue pit. Tennis, swimming pool, golf nearby. 20 m to downhill skiing.
Location PA Dutch Country. 20 m NE of Lancaster, 10 m SW of Reading. Approx. 3 m N of junction of I-76 & Rte. 222. From PA Tpke. (I-76), take Exit 21 to Rte. 222 and go N. Turn S at Rte. 272 and continue to town. Turn right at Broad St., then left on Main St. to inn on right.
Restrictions Smoking in library only. Children over 12.
Credit cards MC, Visa.
Rates B&B, $65–105 double. Extra person, $20. Reduced rate for 4 nights. 2-night holiday/weekend minimum.

AIRVILLE

Information please: Thirty miles west of Lancaster is the **Spring House** (1264 Muddy Creek Forks Road, 17302; 717–927–6906), built in 1798 by a Pennsylvania legislator, and beautifully restored and furnished with country antiques, hand-stenciling on walls, quilts, and hand woven rugs. Four guest rooms are available, each with private bath, and a creative full breakfast is included in the B&B double rates of $60–85. Reports appreciated.

AKRON

Information please: About two miles south of Ephrata and ten miles north of Lancaster is **The Boxwood Inn** (P.O. Box 203, 17501; 717–859–3466), a 1768 stone farmhouse graced by 150-year-old boxwoods. Owners June and Dick Klemm will gladly point out the handwritten 1850 deed in the front hallway or the original root cellar with its arched stone ceiling. The four guest rooms, decorated with a blend of country and Pennsylvania Dutch antiques, have modern private baths and king-, queen-, or twin-sized beds, while the Carriage House provides guests with a sitting area, fireplace, whirlpool tub, and balcony overlooking Amish farms. A full breakfast and afternoon tea are included in the double rates of $75–135.

ALLENTOWN

Information please: A small European-style hotel created from five townhouses in downtown Allentown, the **Coachaus Inn** (107–111 North Eighth Street, 18101; 610–821–4854 or 800–762–8680), has high ceilings and tall windows that give a light, airy feeling to rooms individually furnished with reproductions and antiques. Business travelers and transferees with children will appreciate the fully furnished kitchens in the suites. The double rate of $74 includes a full breakfast with eggs, bacon, sausage or ham, toast, and cereal, and early evening refreshments.

AVONDALE

B&B at Walnut Hill ¢   *Tel:* 610–444–3703
541 Chandler Mill Road, 19311

Part of the fun of B&B travel is discovering places you would never find on the beaten path. B&B at Walnut Hill, a mill house built in 1840, is just such an inn. Sandy and Tom Mills bought this house in 1962, opening it to guests in 1985. Sandy reports that "horses graze in our pasture, and a great blue heron fishes in the stream; deer, Canada geese and an occasional red fox visit the meadow."

"We were greeted with hot cider and cookies by the friendly, welcoming owners. Our room had a Laura Ashley-style comforter and matching canopy. Delicious French bread topped with orange-peach sauce, accompanied by homemade applesauce and whipped orange juice. Sandy made reservations for us at an excellent local restaurant." *(Maria Elmiger)* "Charming antique furnishings and country accents. Sandy and Tom make you feel right at home." *(Nancy Schneider and others)* "Within an easy, beautiful drive of the famous area gardens and museums. Tom even drew up a covered bridge tour for us." *(Stephen Garber)*

Open All year.

Rooms 2 doubles, 1 single. Maximum of 4 people sharing bath. All with clock, air-conditioning, TV. 2 with desk.

Facilities Family room with TV/VCR, fireplace, books; porch. 2.6 acres with hot tub. Tennis, golf nearby. Walking, bicycling.

Location Brandywine region. 20 min NW of Wilmington, DE. 60 min SW of Philadelphia. 2 m W of Kennett Square. From Kennett Square, go S on Union St. 1.7 m through 3 traffic lights to Hillendale Rd. Go right ½ m, then left on Chandler's Mill Rd. 1.4 m to inn on left.

Restrictions No smoking. Children over 7.

Credit cards None accepted.

Rates B&B, $80 double, $65 single. Extra person, $25.

Extras Some French, Spanish spoken.

BEACH LAKE

Information please: Located in Wayne County in the northern Poconos, **The Beach Lake Hotel** (Main Street and Church Road, P.O. Box 144, 18405; 717–729–8239 or 800–382–3897) has housed overnight guests since the Civil War. The guest rooms are decorated with reproduction Victorian wallpapers, lace curtains, restored woodwork, brass or canopy beds, and antique furnishings. Breakfast favorites include apple-sausage pancakes, eggs Benedict, and two-cheese omelets, served with a variety of muffins and popovers. A recent dinner included apple-carrot soup, raspberry chicken, and pecan Kahlua pie. B&B double rates for the six guest rooms, all with private bath, are $95.

BEDFORD

Bedford House ¢ ♿   *Tel: 814–623–7171*
203 West Pitt Street, 15522

Bedford is a historic community, dating back to 1751; George Washington made the town his headquarters during the Whiskey Rebellion of 1794. Bedford House built as a log cabin during this period, although later expansions gave the house its current appearance—a substantial red brick Federal-style town home. Lyn and Linda Lyon renovated it as a B&B in 1989. Furnishings include oak, cherry, and mahogany queen-, king-, or twin-sized beds, Oriental rugs, and colorful quilts; in one room, the original 200-year-old log wall is exposed. Breakfast is prepared to order between 8 and 9 A.M.; a guest refrigerator is kept stocked with ice and soft drinks.

"Lyn and Linda know the area well; they make a dynamite breakfast." *(BF)* "Convenient location in the business section of town. Linda and Lyn respected our privacy, yet were sociable and down-to-earth. Our made-to-order breakfast included a choice of eggs and bacon, blueberry pancakes, or croissant French toast with wonderful apple cider syrup, plus scrumptious gingerbread muffins." *(Linda Chao)* "Our room was rustic and Colonial, complete with an old quilt and fireplace. The Jean Bonnet Tavern is outstanding for dinner, with great food, service, and atmosphere." *(Annette Katsaros)* "The inn is within walking distance of wonderful shops, the Fort Bedford Museum, and is a short drive to Old Bedford Village (a collection of 40 historic structures with exhibitions and demonstrations of blacksmithing, woodworking, and weaving)." *(Connie Lew)*

Open All year.
Rooms 8 doubles—all with private shower and/or bath, radio, clock, air-conditioning, fan, TV. 5 with gas fireplace. 3 with desk. Telephone on request.
Facilities Breakfast room, living room with fireplace, TV/VCR, stereo, books; guest refrigerator, screened/unscreened porch, reading room; off-street parking. Tennis, golf, lakes, hiking nearby.
Location SW PA, Allegheny Mts., Bedford Cty. Midway between Pittsburgh & Harrisburg, 2 m from PA Turnpike (I-70/76), Exit 11. National Historic District. From PA Tpke., take Exit 11. After tolls, go right at stop sign, then go 2 m to town. Go right at 2nd light. House on left corner after 2 blocks.
Restrictions Street noise in some rooms. No smoking. Children over 12.
Credit cards Amex, Discover, MC, Visa.
Rates B&B, $55–85 double, $45–70 single. Extra person, $15. 2-night minimum 1st 2 weekends in Oct.
Extras Wheelchair access; 1 bathroom specially equipped. Airport pickup.

BERNVILLE

Sunday's Mill Farm B&B ¢   *Tel:* 610–488–7821
Station Road at Christmas Village Road
Rte. 2, Box 419, 19506

For an affordable country getaway, a visit to the 1850s brick farmhouse owned by Sally and Len Blumberg since 1983 may be just the ticket. Sally notes that "our home is furnished with antiques and original art; I've handmade quilts for all the beds. Our guests are welcome to tour the 1820 grist mill on our property, to hike our trails, or to bicycle the quiet country roads." Breakfast includes fresh fruit and juice, breakfast breads, and perhaps a puffed baked pancake with fresh fruit and yogurt sauce, or French toast with sausage, served in front of the brick fireplace, its mantel topped by Sally's collection of pewter pitchers and jugs.

"A real homestay experience. The Blumbergs live in the same part of the house as the guests, and join you at breakfast. We learned a lot about what to see and do in the area, and discovered wonderful restaurants thanks to their advice. Sally is an avid history buff and Len is a native of the area. The rooms are spacious and the plumbing adequate. Although the setting is rural, it's convenient to outlet shopping in Reading and close to Lancaster County." *(Lilly Galvin)* "The main house is delightful, with a warm and friendly atmosphere. Outstanding breakfast of corn meal pancakes with a delicious hot cranberry topping." *(BN)* "Just as warm and welcoming on a return visit. The Blumbergs are well informed about local events and activities." *(LG)*

Open All year.
Rooms 1 3-bedroom apartment with 2 baths (also rented as 3 separate rooms), 2 doubles—1 with private toilet and sink, & maximum of 4 people sharing bath. All with radio, air-conditioning. Apt. with kitchenette, TV.
Facilities Dining room, living room with TV, books, kitchen with fireplace. 23 acres with patio. Pond, creek for canoeing, fishing. Horseback riding nearby.
Location SE PA, Berks County. 15 m NW of Reading; 4 m to Bernville. Call for directions.
Restrictions No smoking. "Carefully supervised children welcome."
Credit cards None accepted.
Rates B&B, $170 apt., $45–60 double, $35–50 single. Extra person, $10. Weekly rate.
Extras Horses boarded, $7 nightly.

BETHLEHEM

Bethlehem was founded in 1741 by the German Moravian sect, and is known as the home of Bethlehem Steel and Lehigh University, and for its Christmas celebration and Bach Festival in May. The area was industrialized early, and visitors will enjoy a visit to the city's restored eighteenth-century industrial area.

Bethlehem is in eastern Pennsylvania, one hour north of Philadelphia and two hours west of New York City.

Reader tip: "Bethlehem is a wonderful historic town. The visitors' center has a terrific staff and offers great walking tours; across the street is a shop to buy delicious Viennese pastries. We felt totally safe walking around at night in the festive atmosphere of this well-lighted district."

Also recommended: A classic old-fashioned commercial hotel, built in 1920, the **Hotel Bethlehem** (437 Main Street, 18018; 610–867–3711 or 800–545–5158) offers comfortable, spacious, clean, and reasonably priced guest rooms, furnished with generic hotel decor. "Great location. It has a hotel's virtues; privacy and the freedom to come and go as you please. The real plus for us was the service." *(Sherrill Brown)* A remodeling project in 1996 involves the conversion of the hotel's top floors to condominiums; comments are welcome.

Information please: Built in 1858 by Robert Heysham Sayre, the chief engineer of the Lehigh Valley Railroad, **The Sayre Mansion Inn** (250 Wyandotte Street, 18015; 610–882–2100) was restored as an inn by Norah and John Cappellano in 1993. The restored mansion offers nineteen antique-filled rooms and suites, two parlors with fireplaces, and pictur-

237

esque grounds. Double rates, including a continental breakfast, range from $100–170.

For an additional area inn, see **Allentown.**

Wydnor Hall   *Tel:* 610–867–6851
3612 Old Philadelphia Pike, 18015   800–839–0020
                                         Fax: 610–866–2062

Wydnor Hall is an imposing fieldstone manor house, built around 1810, and opened in 1988 after a two-year restoration. Owner Kristina Taylor is assisted by a capable staff. Rates include a breakfast of juice, coffee or tea, and homemade muffins and rolls, served in the room or the dining room. Available at an extra charge are homemade muesli with fruit and yogurt, bagels with cream cheese and smoked salmon, and oatmeal pancakes with lingonberries, and Mexican eggs with tortillas, salsa, and jalapeño cheese.

"Spotless rooms; attentive service. Breakfast was delicious, unusual, and elegantly served. Reading material was abundant, current, and varied. Service was unobtrusive." *(Marlene Wurzbach)* "The house is convenient to the main road, but set back and quiet. The interior is an attractive combination of antiques and family pieces. Our suite at the front of the house was clean and thoughtfully appointed. Heavy curtains kept light out while we slept in. Our private bathroom was just outside our room in the hall; good toiletries and ample towels were provided." *(Carla Hashagen)* "A quiet place with lots of light for reading. Our beautifully appointed room had a large bath, with two terry robes." *(Margaret Miglione)* Comments welcome.

Open All year.
Rooms 1 suite, 4 doubles—all with full private bath, air-conditioning, telephone, TV. 1 with steam shower.
Facilities Dining room, living room, conservatory. Conference room/services. Massage therapist on call. 2 acres with stream.
Location 55 m N of Philadelphia. 3 m from Bethlehem. From Bethlehem, follow Rte. 378 S to Black River Rd. Turn right onto Black River Rd. and left at Old Philadelphia Pike. Inn is ¼ m on right.
Restrictions No smoking in guest rooms. Children by arrangement.
Credit cards Amex, CB, DC, MC, Visa.
Rates B&B, $75–130. Corporate rates. Golf, off-season packages. Full breakfast, $6 additional; hot beverages, $2–3; afternoon tea, $8.
Extras French, Hungarian, Spanish spoken.

BLOOMSBURG

The Inn at Turkey Hill 🏃 ✕ &   *Tel:* 717–387–1500
991 Central Road, 17815   *Fax:* 717–784–3718

Located just off Exit 35 of Interstate 80, The Inn at Turkey Hill provides good food and lodging to travelers on this major east-west route. Part of the inn is a farmhouse dating back to 1839; most of the guest rooms are in a modern wing, built onto the back of the original structure, facing a landscaped courtyard with a gazebo and pond. Dinner menus change seasonally; recent summer entrées were scallops with tarragon and shiitake mushrooms, Wiener schnitzel, and stuffed quail.

"Beautifully maintained and landscaped grounds, complete with a gazebo and pond, ducks and rabbits. Spacious, immaculate room with European-style comforters, magazines, and plenty of fresh, fluffy towels. Best of all is the friendly, welcoming, yet unobtrusive service, from the cheery personal wake-up calls, to the overnight in-house laundry service, to the restaurant wait staff. The restaurant is the area's best, combining country atmosphere with European flair and quality wines." *(James Barritt, also James Schwartz)*

"Rooms are simply decorated with reproduction Shaker furnishings—stained Colonial blue or red—and original primitive paintings. The new rooms are very quiet, with triple-glazed windows and shutters." *(NB)* "We were delighted with Room 17 in the original inn—the bathroom alone was equal in size to some guest rooms we've stayed in, and the bedroom with separate dressing area had a queen-sized bed, comfortable easy chair and foot stool, and great reading lights. The breakfast buffet, served in the Greenhouse, included juices, assorted muffins, bagels, a fresh fruit salad, cereals, coffee, and tea, with a waitress to attend full-time to refills or special needs. Morning newspapers were provided, and the sun kept the room cozy." *(Peg & Ben Bedini)* "We enjoy window-shopping along Main Street and visiting the local antique shops. Parking is plentiful and well lit." *(Jennifer Amarein)* "Rooms in the new wing are built around a lovely pond, yet each is accessible directly from the parking lot." *(James Lamberti)*

Open All year. Restaurant closed Jan. 1.
Rooms 2 suites, 16 doubles—all with full private bath, telephone, radio, TV, desk, air-conditioning. Suites with fireplace, Jacuzzi.
Facilities Restaurant; living room; library with fireplace, TV, games; lounge. 2 acres with patio, gardens, pond, gazebo. Tennis, golf, fishing, swimming nearby.
Location 3 hrs. NW of Philadelphia & W of NYC. 2 m from center. From I-80, take Exit 35; turn left to inn on left.
Credit cards Amex, Discover, MC, Visa, Diners.
Rates B&B, $100–170 suite, $84 double, $74 single. Corporate rates. Extra person, $15. Children under 12 free. Alc dinner, $30.
Extras Wheelchair access. Crib, babysitting. Airport/station pickup. Pets by prior arrangement.

BRADFORD

Information please: In northwestern Pennsylvania, about 1½ hours south of Buffalo, and 4 hours northeast of Pittsburgh is **Glendorn** (1032 West Croydon Street, 16701; 814–368–9923), a family retreat of the Dorn family, recently opened to the public. The 1930s country retreat of oilman C. G. Dorn, Glendorn occupies 1,280 acres bounded by the Allegheny National Forest. The compound includes the massive redwood Big House, with a cathedral-ceilinged great hall with a two-story stone fireplace, a billiards room, and four guest rooms. Additional accommodations are available in the guest house and three one-bedroom cabins, each with a fireplace. Furnishings range from elegant to rustic. Recreational facilities include three tennis courts, a trap and skeet shooting range, hiking and cross-country ski trails, lake and stream fishing, canoes, bicycles, basketball court, archery range, and outdoor swimming pool. Double rates of $250–500 include all meals and use of all recreational facilities.

CANADENSIS

Canadensis takes its name from the Latin name of the hemlock, and is located in the Pocono Mountains of eastern Pennsylvania, 15 miles north of Stroudsberg.

Information please: About 10 miles north are two well-known inns, both owned by Ron and Mary Kay Logan. The **Sterling Inn** (Route 191, South Sterling, 18460; 717–676–3311 or 800–523–8200) offers old-fashioned charm, nature trails, and well prepared meals. The 56 guest rooms are found in a variety of buildings, and are traditionally furnished; facilities include an indoor swimming pool, tennis, lawn games, a nine-hole putting course, cross-country skiing and tobogganing. Children are welcome and MAP double rates range from $130–220. The Logan's other inn is **The French Manor** (Huckleberry Road, P.O. Box 39, South Sterling 18460; 717–676–3244 or 800–523–8200), a lavish summer mansion built in the 1930s of oak, cedar, pecky cypress, and field stone, topped with a slate roof imported from Spain. The oak-beamed vaulted Great Room seats 60 people for dinner, while a basement common room provides a casual setting in which guests can mingle. B&B rates range from $120 for the more modest Carriage House rooms to $225 for the elegant suites. Reports most welcome.

For an additional area recommendation, see listing under **Skytop**.

Brookview Manor B&B Inn ¢   *Tel:* 717–595–2451
Route 447, RR 1, Box 265, 18325

A sprawling Victorian summer cottage built in 1911, Brookview Manor was bought by Lee and Nancie Cabana in 1991. Country furnishings and antiques appoint the bright and airy guest rooms, which overlook woods, mountains, and a stream. Breakfast (served at individual tables from 8:30–10 A.M.) may include buttermilk pancakes with fruit, cinnamon French toast, frittata, or cheese and egg casserole, accompanied by juice, fresh fruit, homemade muffins, breads, coffee cake, homemade granola, coffee, tea, and hot chocolate.

"Be sure to take the short hike through the woods to the wonderfully romantic waterfall on the property." *(Gary & Kathy Cohen)* "Nancie provided a warm and enthusiastic introduction to Brookview and its surroundings. She offered us sample menus from local restaurants and brochures to local attractions. Wood and matches were thoughtfully provided for the fireplace in our room, as well as scrumptious cookies for late-night snacking. Breakfasts were excellent, especially Nancie's homemade granola." *(Cindy Kam & Rob Mikos)* "Proprietors are friendly, informative, and outgoing. The little girl who lives in the house is a delight. The breakfast room is bright and sunny; the quiche exceptional." *(Vicky Lysek)* "The piano music at breakfast, accompanied by great service and excellent food would bring me back to the inn again." *(Pamela Carafello)*

Open All year.
Rooms 3 suites, 3 doubles—all with private bath and/or shower, radio, clock, fan. 3 with desk. 2 with deck. 1 with fireplace, refrigerator. 2 in annex.
Facilities Dining room, living room with fireplace, piano, books; den with TV/ VCR, fireplace, books; recreation room with games; guest refrigerator; porch with swing. 4 acres with lawn games; 400 acres of surrounding woods. Golf, tennis, boating, downhill and cross-country skiing, hiking nearby.
Location Pocono Mountains, 15 m N of Stroudsburg. 1 m N to Canadensis. From New York, take I-80 W through Delaware Water Gap toll booth. Take Exit 52 (Marshalls Creek, Rtes. 209 & 447) and take 1st left onto Rte. 447 N. Go 16 m to inn on right.
Restrictions No smoking. Children 12 and over.
Credit cards Amex, DC, Discover, MC, Visa.
Rates B&B, $105–145 suite, $70–105 double, $60–105 single. Extra person, $20. 2-night holiday weekend minimum.

The Pine Knob Inn ¢ ✗ 🏃   Tel: 717–595–2532
Route 447, Box 275, 18325

The Pine Knob dates back to 1847, when Dr. Gilbert Palen built a home and started a tannery. In the process he renamed the town (originally called Frogtown—anything would have been an improvement) Canadensis, after the botanical name of the hemlock, whose bark was used in the tanning of leather. The building was turned into a guest house in 1886; Dick and Charlotte Dornich are the long-time owners. The dinner menu includes such entrées as rack of lamb with mustard and rosemary, stuffed pork chops, and duck with raspberry sauce.

"Dick Dornich is outgoing and friendly, a big plus for his pleasant inn. The parlor, furnished with overstuffed arm chairs, was comfortably lit for reading." *(John Blewer)* "The inn is surrounded by landscaped grounds, with a large swimming pool just across the street. The inn has a light and spacious parlor, hung with lovely watercolors by local artists (most of which are for sale), an airy dining room, and a cozy Victorian-style bar. The guest rooms are simply furnished with brass or carved oak beds, cheery wallpaper, and period antiques; the bathrooms are functional. Some rooms have been recently redone; ask for one of these. Ample porches run along the side of the inn, facing the flower gardens, and are well supplied with rocking chairs for sitting and chatting." *(SWS)* "While my husband was fly fishing in the creek, I was content to sit on the rocks, pretending to read." *(MW)* "Hospitable hosts who work hard at maintaining the inn." *(BNS)*

Open All year.
Rooms 2 suites, 20 doubles, 2 singles—19 with private bath and/or shower, 5 with sink in room and shared bath. 5 with fireplace. All with fan, 1 with desk. Rooms 4 buildings.
Facilities Bar, restaurant, living room with fireplace, TV, piano, books, games.

6½ acres with gardens, woods, swimming pool, shuffleboard, tennis court, frontage on Broadhead Creek for trout fishing. Golf, downhill and cross-country skiing nearby.

Location Poconos, Monroe County. ½ m S of center of town. From I-80 W, take Rte. 447 N to inn.
Restrictions Children over 7.
Credit cards MC, Visa.
Rates MAP, $116–180 suite, double, $55–80 single. Extra person, $69. B&B, $70–110. 15% service. 2–3 night holiday/weekend minimum. Family, weekly rates. Prix fixe dinner, $29. Alc dinner, $27.
Extras Bus station pickup.

CARLISLE

For additional area entries, see **Dillsburg** and **New Kingston**.

Pheasant Field Bed and Breakfast ¢
150 Hickorytown Road, 17013

Tel: 717–258–0717
Fax: 717–258–0717

Denise Fegan and Charles DeMarco welcome guests to the 1810 brick farmhouse which they restored as a B&B in 1994. Homey and comfortable, Pheasant Field's decor includes wall-to-wall carpeting, traditional furnishings and some antiques, and king- or queen-size beds topped with quilts or floral comforters. Breakfast is offered at guests' convenience, and is served at individual tables; it includes fresh fruit and juice, hot beverages, home-baked muffins or bread, an egg dish, and breakfast meat; rates also include afternoon refreshments.

"Our room was spacious, clean, beautifully decorated, with ample closet space, special toiletries, plenty of plush towels." *(Lisa Strassburger)* "You can wake to the rooster's crowing, take a hike before breakfast on the country roads past the corn and pumpkin fields, or play a game of tennis on the courts near the stone horse barn. Sculptures and paintings of pheasants grace the interior." *(Polly Fanus)* "Managed with guests' comfort in mind, from the well-stocked guest refrigerator, to the home-made cookies, to the guest phone for reaching the innkeepers if necessary at night." *(Betty Norman)* "The well-lit parking area is at the rear of the house; guests enter the house from a lovely brick patio." *(DS)* "Attentive, considerate, detail-oriented innkeepers." *(Richard Williams)* "Excellent area trout-fishing streams." *(James Wilson)*

Area for improvement: "A bedside table on my side of the bed."

Open All year.
Rooms 4 doubles—2 with private bath and/or shower, 2 with maximum of 4 people sharing bath. All with radio, clock, air-conditioning. 2 with fan, 1 with desk.
Facilities Dining room, living room with fireplace, piano, stereo; family room with fireplace, TV/VCR, books; guest refrigerator, porch, patio. 8.5 acres with horse barn, tennis court, lawn games. 1 m to Appalachian Trail. 25 min. to downhill skiing.
Location S central PA, Cumberland County. 12 m SW of Harrisburg, 6 m W of Mechanicsburg. 2.5 m to town. From I-81 S, take Exit 16. Go left (E) onto Trindle

Rd. (PA Rte. 641). Go 2.3 m to Hickorytown Rd. & turn left. Go $^3/_4$ m to inn on left. From I-76 (PA Tnpke) take Exit 16 (Carlisle). Go N on U.S. Rte. 11 for $^4/_{10}$ m (just past Western Sizzlin' Restaurant). Turn right onto S. Middlesex Rd. Go 2.3 m; turn left onto Ridge Rd. Take 1st right onto Hickorytown Rd. to inn on right.

Restrictions No smoking. Children over 8.

Credit cards Amex, MC, Visa.

Rates B&B, $65–95 double, $60–90 single. Extra person, $10.

Extras Airport/station pickups $10–15. Horses boarded.

CHADDS FORD

The town of Chadds Ford is the artistic heart of the Brandywine Valley, with a countryside that has provided inspiration to three generations of Wyeth painters—N.C., Andrew, and Jamie. The Brandywine River Museum houses the largest collection of their works in the U.S.

Also recommended: The **Brandywine River Hotel** (P.O. Box 1058, Route 1 and Route 100, 19317; 610–388–1200) is a recently constructed 40-room hotel with Queen Anne-style Thomasville reproduction furnishings, quilted bedspreads with matching draperies, and old-fashioned prints. In addition to a private bath, TV, and telephone, many of the rooms have a fireplace and double whirlpool tub. The $120–140 rates (AAA discount) include continental breakfast and afternoon cookies. The hotel is adjacent to a cluster of original Colonial buildings, called the Barn Shops, which sell crafts, clothing, food, flowers, and gifts, with a special emphasis on regional art. Readers have generally been fairly pleased with the accommodations, breakfasts, and staffing here.

A few miles east of Chadds Ford is **Pace One** (Thornton & Glen Mills Road, Thornton 19373; 610–459–3702), a converted 250-year-old barn, and one of the area's most popular restaurants. The decor is simple but elegant; the original stone walls and hand-hewn beams are highlighted with lots of plants. A typical dinner might include an appetizer of mushrooms stuffed with hot sausage, salad, duck roasted with cider vinegar and orange juice, and cream puffs filled with ice cream, topped with chocolate sauce and raspberries. "Guest rooms are several flights up, and are simply furnished with Colonial decor and queen-sized beds; bathrooms are adequate, with minimal lighting and quality toiletries. Delicious coffee cake, coffee, and juice are served by the friendly, helpful staff in the Tavern." *(Judy Rosen, also SWS)* The B&B double rate of $85 (a smaller double-bedded room is $65) is a good value in an expensive area.

Well-known **Sweetwater Farm** (Sweetwater Road, Box 50, Glen Mills, 19342; 610–459–4711) was built in 1734, and is surrounded by pastures and fields. Three of the guest rooms in the main house share *one* bath, and rent for $145 each; the other two have private baths and a double rate of $155. Rates for the five cottages range from $150 for the cramped Herb Cottage, with double bed and shower bath, up to $225 for the largest cottage. A full breakfast is included in the rates, and is served from 8–10 A.M. The house and its setting are exceptionally lovely, but the prices seem out of line with the furnishings and amenities." *(SWS)* No refunds

are offered, although you may re-book within a year of the reservation.
For additional area recommendations, see **Kennett Square** and **West Chester.**

CHAMBERSBURG

The Ragged Edge Inn ¢ ♿   *Tel: 717–261–1195*
1090 Ragged Edge Road, 17201   *Fax: 717–263–7913*

Decorated for Christmas all year long, The Ragged Edge Inn is a 13,000-square-foot Victorian mansion built in 1900 by the president of the Cumberland Valley Railroad. Named for the ragged rocks that drop 50 feet to the creek below, the inn was built in 1900, and is set on a limestone hilltop, providing a dramatic setting. A hand-carved chestnut staircase winds to the third floor; mahogany walls surround the living and dining rooms. "Scenic, quiet location. Darlene Elders, the warm and friendly proprietor, prepares wonderful breakfasts. Handsome period furnishings. Fully decorated Christmas trees are found throughout the inn." *(Barbara & Dennis Stack)* "Our huge room was decorated with a green and burgundy color scheme and the triple windows overlooked the well-tended gardens; a clean, modern private bath was across the hall." *(KK)* "Darlene is informative, entertaining, and a wonderful chef." *(Linda Savastano)*

Open All year.
Rooms 4 suites, 6 doubles—all with private bath and/or shower, telephone, radio, clock, TV, air-conditioning. 3 with whirlpool tub, 2 with fireplace, 1 with deck.
Facilities Dining room with piano, living room with fireplace, family room with TV/VCR, library with books, stereo; conference room, guest kitchen/refrigerator, wraparound porch. 6.5 acres with gardens, creek, forest, horseshoes. 15–30 min. from skiing.
Location 24 m W of Gettysburg. I-81 to Exit 6, Rte. 30 (Lincoln Way East). Go right towards Gettysburg. Turn left at Schier's on Ragged Edge Road. Inn 1.1 m on right.
Restrictions No smoking. Children 8 and over.
Credit cards Amex, MC, Visa.
Rates B&B, $55–150. Extra person, $12. Weekly rates. Murder mystery weekends.
Extras Limited wheelchair access; 1 bathroom specially equipped.

CHURCHTOWN

Information please: Listed in past editions is the **Churchtown Inn** (Route 23; mailing address: 2100 Main Street, Narvon, 17555; 717–445–7794), a handsome fieldstone house dating back to 1735. Its cozy rooms extensively furnished with antiques, handmade quilts, and collectibles. Guests are encouraged to meet in the parlor at 9:00 P.M. each night for refreshments, while breakfasts are served communally at 9:00 A.M. Many special theme weekends are offered, a fine way to meet people. B&B double rates for the eight guest rooms range from $50–105.

The Inn at Twin Linden ✕

2092 Main Street, 17555

Tel: 717–445–7619
Fax: 717–445–4656

Once the manor house of a circa 1850 estate, the white clapboard Inn at Twin Linden is shaded by the pair of 100-foot-tall linden trees planted as saplings when the home was built. Opened in 1990 as an inn, owners Donna and Bob Leahy have painted and polished every corner. The guest rooms have oak beds, some with a canopy, and Laura Ashley and Ralph Lauren linens.

The Hunt Club dining room menu changes weekly, but might include such entrées as rack of lamb roasted with basil pesto and pine nuts, shrimp and asparagus in champagne sauce, and veal chops with blueberries and thyme. Reserve well ahead, especially for Saturday night. Breakfast is served from 8:30 to 9:30 A.M., and guests can sit by themselves, or with others, as they choose. Rates include breakfast, afternoon tea and sherry, and evening turndown service with mints and liqueurs.

"Guest rooms are spotless, elegant, and mercifully uncluttered, with canopy beds locally made by Amish craftsman, and great lighting for reading in bed; the selection of fabrics, colors, and Bob's wonderful photographs of Maine, the Amish country, and the Caribbean make it warm and inviting. The back view of gardens and fields is peaceful and rural. The dining areas are simple but attractive with a gas fireplace; the five prime tables overlook the gardens. The living room is handsome but a bit more formal than the rest of the inn, with grey carpeting." (SWS) "Bob is a genial host, ensuring that everything runs smoothly and that his guests are happy. Bob and Donna are there to greet you and make you feel welcome, and seem to have a sixth sense of when to be around and when to leave their guests alone." (Virginia & Haig Goshdigian) "Nothing is overlooked: terry bathrobes, bubble bath, soaps, books and magazines. Wonderful 4 P.M. tea in the living room, a pleasant time to socialize." (Mr. & Mrs. William Clark) "Donna's fantastic breakfasts include fruit with raspberry sauce, lemon poppy seed muffins, blueberry cobbler, and perhaps salmon quiche or stuffed French toast." (Mark & Sheila Palladino) (JCS) "Fully endorse existing entry. A delightful place, wonderful hospitality." (Dee Gasser)

Open All year. Closed Christmas. Restaurant open for dinner Fri.–Sat.
Rooms 2 suites, 6 doubles—all with private bath and/or shower, air-conditioning, TV. 3 with desk. Suites with TV/VCR, stereo, double Jacuzzi, refrigerator, gas fireplace.
Facilities Restaurant, 2 living rooms, 1 with fireplace, library; porch. 2½ acres with off-street parking, hot tub, picnic area, garden.
Location Center of town. From PA Tpke., take Exit 22 (Morgantown) to Rte. 10 S. Go W on Rte. 23, 4 m to Churchtown & inn on left.
Restrictions Traffic noise in front rooms. No smoking.

Credit cards Amex, Discover, MC, Visa.
Rates B&B, $210 suite, $100–165 double. Extra person, $25. Alc dinner, $30 (byob). Holiday packages. 2-night Saturday/holiday minimum.

CLARK

Information please: A few miles north of I-80 near the Ohio border is **Tara** (3665 Valley View Road, Clark 16113; 412–962–3535 or 800–782–2803), an 1854 Greek Revival mansion, restored at a cost of over $2 million. Inspired by the movie *Gone with the Wind*, its rooms are named and luxuriously decorated with antiques in the style of a particular character from the story. Package rates for this AAA four-diamond property range from $255–430, including a fruit and wine basket, afternoon tea, weekend hospitality hour, dinner, full breakfast, twice daily maid service, and a tour of Tara.

COLUMBIA

The Columbian ¢ 🚶‍♀️
360 Chestnut Street, 17512

Tel: 717–684–5869
800–422–5869

A turn-of-the-century Colonial Revival brick mansion, The Columbian has a handsome wraparound porch and a multi-tiered staircase overlooking an enormous stained glass window. Chris and Becky Will, owners since 1994, live on the premises with their young daughter, Katie, and are pleased to assist guests with directions, restaurant recommendations, and sightseeing advice. Breakfasts of fresh fruit, homemade granola, cinnamon nut bread, fruit kuchen, quiche Lorraine, apple pancakes, or waffles is usually served between 8–9 A.M. Each of the antique-filled guest rooms is decorated in Victorian or English country style with handmade quilts, bedspreads, needlework, and queen-size beds. The historic town of Columbia, described by the Wills as a "porch sitting" town, was once a stop on the Underground Railroad.

"Outstanding hospitality. Our beautiful room had a comfortable bed, well-equipped bath, and fresh fruit." *(Jane Bird)* "Large bathroom, excellent plumbing. Lovely street with many historic mansions. Outstanding breakfast of fresh fruit, homemade granola, pineapple pudding, delicious quiche, and home-baked bread. Friendly, interesting innkeepers." *(Jackie Lewis)*

Suggestion box: "A reading light on my side of the bed."

Open All year.
Rooms 1 suite, 5 doubles—all with private bath and/or shower, radio, clock, TV, air-conditioning. 4 with fan. 1 with fireplace, balcony/deck.
Facilities Dining room with fireplace, living room with fireplace, books; porch. ½ acre with private parking. Golf, boating, fishing, swimming, hiking, skiing nearby.
Location PA Dutch Country. 8 m W of Lancaster; 8 m E of York. Take Rte. 30 W to Rte. 441, Columbia Exit. Go S on Rte. 441 to 1st light. Left on Chestnut St. to inn 1 block E on corner of 4th & Chestnut Sts.

Restrictions No smoking.
Credit cards MC, Visa.
Rates B&B, $70–85 double. Extra person $10. Tips appreciated. Reduced rates for children, seniors. 2-night minimum holiday weekends & Oct. Winter getaway packages. 10% discount 4-night stays.
Extras Airport/station pickups. Crib. Babysitting on request.

COOKSBURG

Information please: Country inns are relatively sparse in Western Pennsylvania; here are two well-known ones we'd like to hear more about, both located adjacent to the virgin pine and hemlock of Cook Forest State Park:

Clarion River Lodge (River Road, P.O. Box 150, 16217; 814–744–8171 or 800–648–6743) has a natural riverside setting. Built as a private estate, the dining area is highlighted by a massive fieldstone fireplace, log beams, and cherry paneling. A breezeway connects the lodge with the modern guest rooms, simply furnished with contemporary Scandinavian decor. The dinner menu includes a selection of steaks, seafood, and pasta dishes. B&B double rates for the 20 guest rooms range from $67–109.

The **Gateway Lodge & Cabins** (Route 36, Box 125, 16217; 814–744–8017 or 800–843–6862) is a 1934 rustic log lodge. Furnished comfortably with antiques, hand-hewn chestnut beds, and braided rugs, it has a heated indoor swimming pool. Three meals a day are served to the public, and entrées might include chicken and biscuits and barbecued ribs. B&B double rates for the eight guest rooms and cabins range from $105–150.

CRESCO

Information please: Located in the Pocono Mountains, **Crescent Lodge** (Paradise Valley, 18326; 717–595–7486 or 800–392–9400) offers guest rooms in the main lodge and in private cottages; most cottages offer in-room double Jacuzzi tubs, canopy beds, remote control color cable TV, fireplaces, and private sundecks. The inn has a cozy bar, and a popular restaurant for such classics as prime rib, beef Wellington, veal Cordon Bleu, and mountain trout stuffed with crabmeat. You can work off all that good food with a few laps in the heated outdoor swimming pool, on the tennis court, or hiking trails. Although families are welcome, the inn's focus is on providing a romantic escape for couples. Rates range from $70–145 for rooms at the inn; $110–265 for the cottages. Comments welcome.

DALLAS

Ponda-Rowland B&B ¢   *Tel:* 717–639–3245
R.R. 1, Box 349, 18612   800–654–3286
                                     Fax: 717–639–5531

There's an old-fashioned magic about a stay on an old-fashioned farm, visiting with a yard full of animals—dogs, sheep, goats, turkeys, horses, a pot-bellied pig, chickens, a ferret and rabbits. Cliff and Jeanette Rowland offer their guests just such an experience. Built in 1850 of plank construction with exposed interior oak and hemlock beams, their home is furnished primarily with American Colonial country antiques. Most of the guest rooms have king-size beds.

"The inn is perched on a hill, allowing cool night breezes to waft through our open bedroom windows." *(Margo Holm)* "Delicious, hearty breakfast of sliced fresh fruit, eggs, sausage, bacon, potato pancakes, homemade muffins, juices, a variety of teas, and coffee." *(Geralyn Neves)* "Jeanette's home cooked corn and blueberry pancakes were served by candlelight in immaculate surroundings." *(Paul & Carol Crompton)* "The location is convenient to the mountains, movies, and a variety of nearby restaurants." *(Randy Bowers)* "The entire inn was ours to enjoy; we were treated like family by the welcoming Rowlands. After sightseeing and shopping, we returned to the inn, where we spent the afternoon reading under a tree, and were served coffee and homemade cake." *(Mr. & Mrs. Henry Guellnitz)* "Sparkling clean, well-lighted, and comfortable. Our children love playing with the animals. Friendly fellow guests. Enjoyable hayrides and long walks with Matthew, their greyhound." *(Gerald Kolpan & Joan Weiner)* "Common areas are ample, so when the kids were watching a movie in the family room, the adults could read or chat in the living room or on the enclosed porch." *(Diane Wolf)*

Open All year.
Rooms 5 doubles—all with private shower and/or bath, fan. Some with telephone, air-conditioning, fireplace. Family room has bunk beds, double, and youth bed.
Facilities Dining room, living room, family room with fireplace, TV/VCR, stereo, books; sunporch; enclosed patio with fireplace; breakfast/snack room with refrigerator and microwave. 130 acres with ponds for canoeing, boating, ice-skating; sledding, cross-country skiing; lawn games; trout fishing in stream; 30-acre wildlife sanctuary with trails.
Location NE PA, Endless Mts. 10 m N of Wilkes-Barre. Follow Rowland Farm signs from Rte. 309.
Restrictions No smoking.
Credit cards Amex, Discover, MC, Visa.
Rates B&B, $65–85 double. Infants free.
Extras Airport/station pickup. Pets by prior arrangement. Crib.

DILLSBURG

Also recommended: A Flemish bond Federal brick home built in 1798, **The Peter Wolford House** (440 Franklin Church Road, 17019; 717–432–0757) was beautifully restored in 1990 by Ted and Loretta Pesano. "Warm and inviting exterior; equally appealing inside, handsomely furnished with simple Colonial charm, stenciling, country antiques and handmade quilts." *(Betty Norman)* Guests are served hot or cold beverages with cheese and fruit on arrival, cookies at bedtime, plus breakfasts of cranberry bran muffins, thick-sliced cinnamon French toast with apples and pecans, or perhaps blueberry peach muffins, followed by spinach, tomato, and feta cheese omelets with bacon and whole grain toast. B&B double rates for the three guest rooms are $70–75; two rooms share a bath.

DONEGAL

Information please: Offering views of the surrounding Laurel Mountains, the **Mountain View B&B** (Mountain View Road, 15628; 412–593–6349 or 800–392–7773) includes an 1850s farmhouse and barn restored as an inn in 1987. The farmhouse guest rooms are furnished with 18th and 19th century American antiques, many of which are for sale. The renovated barn houses three guest rooms and a formal dining room—where a full breakfast is served. B&B double rates are $95–150.

DOYLESTOWN

In the heart of Bucks County, Doylestown is just as historic and appealing as New Hope, with lots of well-preserved buildings and appealing shops. Plan to spend at least a day or two visiting the "Mercer Mile," composed of the Mercer Museum, Fonthill Museum, and the Moravian Tile Works; also of interest is the James Michener Arts Center, with its collection of Pennsylvania Impressionists. Doylestown is located in southeastern Pennsylvania, about 12 miles west of New Hope, and 25 miles northeast of Philadelphia.

Information please: Formerly in Quakertown, the **Sign of the Sorrel Horse Country Inn** (4424 Old Easton Road, 18901; 215–230–9999) has relocated to Doylestown. Owners Jon Atkin, a British-born chef and his wife, Monique Gaumont-Lavin, a French Cordon Bleu graduate, have chosen a 1714 stone gristmill as their new home (formerly The Pear and Partridge restaurant). The seven guest rooms are decorated with a combination of European and American antiques; B&B rates range from $85–175. The inn's two restaurants are the New York Paris Cafe, offering new American cuisine with a European influence, and the Escoffier Dining Room, serving French gourmet food, with two prix fixe menus at $42 and $62 per person. Reports please.

| **Inn at Fordhook Farm** | *Tel:* 215–345–1766 |
| 105 New Britain Road, 18901 | *Fax:* 215–345–1791 |

Fordhook is more than a type of lima bean, all you gardening enthusiasts. It is also the name of the Burpee family estate, still owned by the family of W. Atlee Burpee, who founded the famous seed company 100 years ago. The handsome 18th century stone manor house is filled with family heirlooms and you can even relax in the study where W. Atlee wrote his first seed catalog. The guest rooms are furnished with antiques, and the Atlee and Burpee rooms have private balconies for watching the sunset and sunrise, respectively. Rates include breakfast and afternoon tea, served on the old Burpee family china and silver: the morning menu, available from 8:30 to 10:00 A.M., might include strawberry-orange juice, baked crunchy apples, oatmeal buttermilk pancakes with Vermont maple syrup, and bacon; afternoon tea, served from 4–6 P.M., might bring lemon poppy seed pound cake, ginger scones with honey butter, and tea sandwiches.

"Carole Burpee, who now manages the inn, was a gracious hostess who regaled us with family history as she showed us through the beautiful rooms. Idyllic setting." *(Caroline Lloyd)* "The Burpee Room, the original master bedroom, was lovely with its fireplace and view of the back lawn. Breakfast, served in the dining room, was elegant but relaxed, with several entrée choices. Snacks were always available; cookies were freshly baked each day." *(Elaine Bounds)* "You turn off the busy road onto a quiet tree-lined lane, driving past lush fields to an English country manor, complete with ivy-covered stone and stuccoed walls. Lots of family pictures hang on walls, along with framed magazine articles and old Burpee advertisements." *(SWS)* "The innkeepers graciously accommodated our business needs, providing telephone lines for our computer modems." *(J. Bell)*

"We stayed in the Atlee Room, with an extremely comfortable king-size bed and lovely Laura Ashley decor. A basket filled with home-baked goodies, chocolates, crackers and cheeses, grapes, 'designer' water, and a packet of Burpee seeds was waiting for us." *(Margie Samuels)* "The inn has lots of brochures on local attractions and menus to browse. It was fun to read the dining diary in which guests review local restaurants." *(Diane Wolf)* "Although its decor has fewer antiques, our party of four was delighted with the two-bedroom carriage house, with an enormous private living area with a cathedral ceiling, Palladian window, and chestnut beams and wainscoting." *(A.K. Archibald)*

Areas for improvement: "The Curtiss Room has a tiny corner bathroom."

Open All year.
Rooms 1 2-bedroom carriage house, 5 doubles—3 with private bath and/or shower, 2 with a maximum of 4 sharing bath. 2 with balcony, desk, fireplace. All with air-conditioning.
Facilities Dining room, living room, library/study—all with fireplace. Patios, verandas. 60 acres with walking trails, lawn games, test gardens. Golf nearby.
Location From Doylestown, follow State St. S past hospital & over Rte. 611. Go 1/4 m & turn left on New Britain Rd. Entrance to Fordhook is 1/4 m on left through stone pillars.
Restrictions No smoking. Children over 13.
Credit cards Amex, MC, Visa.
Rates B&B, $200–300 carriage house; $100–200 double. Extra person, $20. 2-3 night weekend/holiday minimum preferred.
Extras Station pickup.

Pine Tree Farm 🏃

Tel: 215–348–0632

2155 Lower State Road, 18901

Although Bucks County offers endless activities, you may not want to leave the grounds of the Pine Tree Farm until dinner time, given its swimming pool and peaceful acreage. Ron and Joy Feigles converted this stone farmhouse—which dates back to 1730—into a B&B in 1987, decorating it with flowered chintzes, American antiques, crafts, and period reproductions. Breakfast is served at individual tables and includes such entrées as omelets to order, Grand Marnier French toast with homemade

German sausage, puffed apple pancakes with bacon, or lemon shirred eggs, accompanied by biscuits, muffins, coffee cake, and fruit.

"Exquisitely furnished. Joy cheerfully accommodated my special dietary needs." *(David Fehr)* "Ron and Joy are helpful, friendly innkeepers who suggested ideal activities and arranged for tours. Appreciated the guest pantry, stocked with snacks." *(Ellen Winter)* "Comfortable queen-size beds with fine linens; gorgeous pool, beautifully maintained property." *(Joan Stratton)* "Our room had a white-twigged canopy bed with an adjoining sitting area. I was up at 7 A.M., and enjoyed a cup of coffee in the solarium. Joy has a collection of books ranging from the classics to quilting." *(Patricia Ralph)* "Delicious breakfast, elegantly served." *(Paul Gottlieb)*

Open All year. Closed Christmas.
Rooms 3 doubles—all with private bath and/or shower, clock, air-conditioning. 2 with telephone, desk.
Facilities Dining room, 2 living rooms with fireplace; family room, library, solarium with TV; porch. 16½ acres with swimming pool, lawn games. Canoeing, tubing nearby.
Location From S, take I-95 N to Street Rd. Exit (Rte. 132). Go left on Street Rd. for 18 m to dead end. Go right on Lower State Rd. 4 m to farm. From the N & E, take Rte. 202 into Doylestown; do not take bypass. Go through traffic light, go left at 2nd light. 1¼ m on left is inn.
Restrictions "Noisy frogs in July." No smoking. Children over 15.
Credit cards None accepted.
Rates B&B, $135–155 double, $115–135 single. Tipping welcome. 2-3 night weekend/holiday minimum.
Extras Minimal French spoken.

EAGLES MERE

The town of Eagles Mere is a little gem in the Endless Mountains of northern Pennsylvania. Sullivan County is the least populated in the state (only one traffic light in the county!), and nearby World's End State Park is ruggedly beautiful. The lake was long a popular vacation spot for well-to-do Philadelphians, with 100-room hotels and Victorian "cottages" dating back to the 1870s. Although the hotels are gone, several of the boarding houses which accommodated their staff and workmen have been converted into inns. The lake and surrounding property are now owned by residents, and use of the lake is limited to residents and inn guests. The lake is also the town's water supply, so the water is extremely clean for swimming. Shore development has been banned, and much of the lake is accessible via public hiking trails. Area activities include swimming, canoeing, sailing, fishing, and hiking in summer, and cross-country skiing in winter, along with tobogganing on the "Slide," an icy chute which runs down Lake Avenue and sends riders zooming across the frozen lake.

Eagles Mere is 34 miles northeast of Williamsport, about 3½ hours' drive from New York City or Philadelphia.

Eagles Mere Inn ✕   *Tel: 717–525–3273*
Mary & Sullivan Avenues, Box 356, 17731   800–426–3273

A boarding house built in 1878, the Eagles Mere Inn originally catered to the craftsmen who built the grand hotels and "cottages" of this mountain resort. Susan and Peter Glaubitz, who bought the inn in 1991, offer a relaxing year-round escape to travelers looking for genuine hospitality, good food, and comfortable lodging in an old-fashioned, neon-free setting. They've worked extremely hard to improve their inn; each year has brought significant improvements, from the plumbing to the decor. Guest rooms are simply decorated with Victorian antiques, cheerful print wallpaper, and lacy curtains; white iron, Jenny Lind, or pencil post beds with firm mattresses and colorful, handmade quilts highlight the rooms. In the basement of the inn is the Pub, a cheerful collection of rooms that house a long bar and cozy booths, a stone fireplace, TV, board games, and puzzles; it's been a popular spot for generations of young adults vacationing with their parents. There are two dining areas: one stretches across the back of the building, the second is a bright and cheerful converted sun porch, with windows overlooking a flower garden where hummingbirds flit about. Menu choices vary frequently, but a possible five-course dinner might include Roquefort or onion soup; salad with orange walnut dressing; prime rib with horseradish sauce, chicken Dijon, or salmon with lime butter; and desserts of hummingbird cake, pecan pie, or Amaretto cheesecake. Breakfast options include omelets, French toast, and pancakes with real maple syrup. Coffee, tea, and lemonade are available throughout the day.

"Our suite had forest green carpeting and an iron and brass queen-size bed topped with a quilt in the double wedding ring pattern; the sitting room had a daybed with a quilt in a complementary pattern and color. The ceiling fans kept the temperature cool, though it was hot outside. The modest bathroom was spotless, updated with a glass shower enclosure and good lighting." *(NB)* "A delightful inn with friendly innkeepers, in a picture-perfect Victorian village. Walking and hiking seem to be everyone's past-time, a good antidote to the inn's tempting desserts; Eagles Mere has its own hiking trails as does nearby Ricketts Glen and World's End State Park." *(Lisa Binkley)*

Open All year.
Rooms 3 suites, 12 doubles—all with private bath and/or shower, clock, fan. 2 with desk, air-conditioning. 1 with refrigerator. 5 rooms in Garden House.
Facilities Restaurant, breakfast room, living room with fireplace, books, music; family room with stereo; pub with piano, TV, fireplace; porch. Occasional evening guitarist. Tennis court, swing set, beach passes.
Location From east, take I-80 W to Exit 34; Rte 42 N to Eagles Mere. Pass 3 shops and clock. Go right at 2nd st. (Mary Ave.) From W take I-80 E to Rte. 220 N, then Rte. 42 N to Eagles Mere. 1 block from main st.
Restrictions Smoking in pub only.
Credit cards MC, Visa.
Rates B&B, $135–165 suite, $99–129 double, $75–110 single. Extra person, $25. MAP, $165–195 suite, $129–159 double, $90–125 single. Extra person, $40. 15% service. Senior discount midweek. 2-3 night peak season weekend/holiday minimum. Prix fixe dinner, $19–25.

EPHRATA

Ephrata's key sight is the Cloister, a Protestant monastery for men and women founded in 1732 by Conrad Beissel. An early experiment in communal living, the Ephrata Cloister became renowned for its German medieval-style architecture. Known for its prose, poetry, and music, it was a famous Colonial printing and publishing center. Tours and craft demonstrations are offered year-round; a musical drama depicting eighteenth-century cloister life is offered summer weekends.

Ephrata is located in the Pennsylvania Dutch Country of southeastern Pennsylvania, 5 miles south of Pennsylvania Turnpike Exit 21, 12 miles northeast of Lancaster, and 15 miles southwest of Reading. It's 1½ hours northeast of Baltimore, MD, and 1 hour west of Philadelphia.

Reader tip: "Ephrata is a good base for exploring Pennsylvania Dutch country, away from the tourists, with a measure of charm and the interesting Ephrata Cloister." *(William Gerhauser, also SWS)*

Information please: One of Ephrata's best known inns is **The Smithton Inn** (900 West Main Street, 17522; 717–733–6094), built as an inn and tavern in 1763. It continued in use as an inn through the Civil War, and stayed in the same family for over 200 years; it has been owned by Dorothy Graybill since 1979. Guest rooms are furnished with antiques and furniture crafted with hand tools in the inn's cabinet shop, hand-decorated antique blanket chests, and original paintings and folk art pieces. Readers agree on the inn's handsome furnishings and good food, but are less impressed with the level of hospitality. The double rates of $65–150 include a full breakfast served in the dining room.

Clearview Farm ¢
Tel: 717–733–6333
355 Clearview Road, 17522

Clearview Farm B&B is a limestone farmhouse built in 1814, the home and working farm of Glenn and Mildred Wissler for over 30 years. Entering the farmhouse, past the flower gardens and pond with resident swans, may come as a surprise: the inn is elegantly decorated with formal Victorian antiques and detailed window treatments in every room but the cheerful den, which has a country motif, complete with antique farm tools, quilted and stenciled hearts, and braided rug. Despite the formality, the Wisslers have taken care not to place form over function. Comfort took priority over appearance when they searched the area for just the right antiques for each room, and the queen-size lace-topped canopy beds, brass and iron beds, and carved walnut double bed all have comfortable mattresses and quality linens. AAA has rewarded their efforts with a four-diamond rating, unusual for a B&B. Breakfasts are farm-hearty, and vary daily; ham and cheese soufflé, French toast with oatmeal apple bread, or waffles with fresh strawberry sauce are among the favorites, accompanied by fresh fruit, muffins or coffee cake.

"Warm and welcoming hosts, immaculate housekeeping, lovely country setting, elegant antique furnishings, and a lovely collection of various chinas. We breakfasted on deliciously thick waffles with homemade peach sauce in the formal dining room." *(Monna Hormel, also MA)* Comments requested.

Open All year.
Rooms 5 doubles—all with private bath and/or shower, air-conditioning.
Facilities Parlor, dining room, den with fireplace, TV/VCR; porch. 200 acres with pond.
Location From Lancaster take Rte. 272 N to Rte 322 W. Go thru Ephrata, and after passing Family Time Restaurant take 5th Rd. on right at Pine Tree Motors onto Clearview Rd. Inn is 1st farm.
Restrictions No smoking. Children over 12.
Credit cards Discover, MC, Visa.
Rates B&B, $95–115 double. Extra person, $15.
Extras Airport/station pickup.

The Inns at Doneckers ♁ ✕ �&

251 & 318-324 North State Street, 17522
301 West Main Street

Tel: 717–738–9502
Fax: 717–738–9554

The Inns at Doneckers opened in 1984 as an extension of Donecker's complex of retail fashion stores, artists' galleries, and restaurants. The Guesthouse was created by connecting and restoring three turn-of-the-century brick houses; a nearby historic property, built in 1777, was restored in 1988 and two multi-level loft suites were added in the carriage house in 1990. The Homestead, the Donecker's original family residence, opened in 1993 as a non-smoking inn with four suites. Rooms are individually decorated with hand-stenciled walls, handmade curtains, and European as well as local antiques. The breakfast buffet includes croissants, breads, cheese, fruit, cereals, sausage, juice, tea, and coffee.

The Restaurant at Doneckers is divided into two sections, the larger serving a less expensive casual menu, the smaller providing innovative and imaginative French cuisine. A possible dinner selection might include an appetizer of shiitake mushrooms stuffed with fresh sea scallops; an entrée of duck breast with green peppercorn sauce; and a dessert of white and dark chocolate mousse.

"Our room was pretty, sparkling clean, and comfy, with a canopy bed and modern bath. It had big sunny windows and little porch with a private stairway covered in wisteria." *(Pat Falk & Pete Schmidt)* "Our Carriage House suite was furnished with country-style antiques, and had a bedroom downstairs, huge Jacuzzi on the 'mezzanine,' and sitting room and bath on the second floor. Friendly, helpful service. Excellent cinnamon apple casserole at breakfast. Pretty perennial flower beds, plenty of off-street parking. We ate in the formal area of the restaurant with excellent food, fine service. Decent wine list, lovely table setting; quiet setting, even though the 'formal' area overlooks the larger, informal dining room." *(William Gerhauser)* "Although some may miss having a hands-on innkeeper, we much preferred Doneckers hotel-style privacy." *(MW)* "Demuth's Suite had an unmarked private street entrance and was furnished with a queen-sized bed, a fireplace, and a large separate Jacuzzi room." *(Bruce Bilmes)*

A word of advice: "The basement breakfast room is windowless and low-ceilinged; bring your tray upstairs to the patio, the pretty sunroom, or back to your room."

Open All year. Closed Christmas. Restaurant closed Wednesdays and Sundays Jan.–Nov.
Rooms 13 suites, 22 doubles—30 with private bath and/or shower, 2 with a maximum of 4 people sharing bath. All with telephone, radio, air-conditioning. Some with desk, Jacuzzi, fireplace. Rooms in 5 buildings.
Facilities Restaurant, parlor with TV, breakfast pantry; small meeting room, balcony/deck. Artists' studios, quilt galleries, farmers' market, off-street parking. Swimming pool, tennis courts, golf, cross-country skiing nearby.
Location Center of town. Just off Rte. 322/Main St.
Credit cards Amex, CB, DC, Discover, MC, Visa.
Rates B&B, $139–175 suite, $59–119 double, $51–81 single. Extra person, $10; crib, $8. Alc lunch, $6–12; early dinner, $17; alc dinner, $50. Children's menu at lunch.
Extras Wheelchair access. Crib, babysitting.

Hackman's Country Inn ¢

140 Hackman Road, 17522

Tel: 717–733–3498

A sturdy brick farmhouse, with gently fading whitewash, green shutters and trim, encircled by big old shade trees, set on a country road— Hackman's fits just about anyone's vision of a country B&B. Stepping inside, the spell is not broken; the central keeping room has a walk-in fireplace, handsome country antiques, braided rugs, and plain white walls, while upstairs, a similar decor is highlighted by hand stenciling and colorful quilts in traditional patterns.

"Though just a short distance from the main road, the setting overlooking the fields is still quite rural, although encroaching subdivisions mar the view in one direction. Before entering the house, we stopped to pet a litter of kittens frolicking in the (former) doghouse. Mrs. Hackman came outside to greet us. A petite, trim, older woman wearing a lovely quilted apron, she was friendly, helpful, and happy to show us around. The common area consists of a large keeping room with a big table where a full country breakfast is served, plus a small wicker settee; an adjacent small room has a huge original fireplace for cooking and an oven for baking. The guest rooms are light and airy, with hand-stenciled white walls and lovely quilts—a refreshing change from the Victorian excess of many inns, and perfectly appropriate to the Amish country." *(SWS)*

"The farmhouse was built by Mrs. Hackman's husband's ancestors in 1857, and is still a working farm. The plumbing is old but works well. All doors lead to the kitchen, a warm and comforting room where a breakfast of homemade muffins and jam, fresh fruit and juice, and coffee is served." *(Maxine Lee Booth)* "Food was plentiful, our coffee cups always filled, and homemade strawberry jam delicious. Spotlessly clean. Electric candles in every window were a welcoming touch." *(Fil & Chris Notaro)* "Our room had its own entrance from the front porch and was decorated with locally made quilts, a pineapple bed, braided rug, and stencils. Large vases filled with fresh flowers were everywhere. Mrs. Hackman makes great blueberry muffins and shares the recipe." *(Kathy Stewart)* "Just as described, right down to the kittens." *(Conrad Schilke)*

Open All year.
Rooms 4 doubles—2 with private shower, 2 sharing 1 bath. All with air-conditioning.
Facilities Keeping room/kitchen, porch. Shaded lawn, 90-acre farm.
Location Take Hwy. 222 to Ephrata Exit. Go W on Rte. 322 for 4½ m to Hackman Rd. Turn right on Hackman Rd. at the Agway store and go N to inn on left.
Restrictions No smoking. Children over 10. Early morning traffic noise in some rooms.
Credit cards MC, Visa.
Rates B&B, $55–70 double, $45–55 single. Extra person, $15.

ERIE

Reader tip: "Take time to visit Presque Isle State Park, a peninsula jutting out into Lake Erie, with miles of beautiful beaches and hiking trails." *(BNS)*

Spencer House ¢
519 West Sixth Street, 16507

Tel: 814–454–5984
800–890–7263
Fax: 814–456–5091

An architectural showpiece when it was built in 1876, the Spencer House is a brick and wood Queen Anne Victorian mansion restored in 1992 by Pat and Keith Hagenbuch; the elaborate wooden gingerbread trim of the bay windows and gables is highlighted in true 'painted lady' fashion. The house's original woodwork is enhanced with antique, but comfortable, decor. Pat's hearty breakfasts consist of omelets, waffles or blueberry pancakes, plus home-baked bread, sticky buns, muffins, or cinnamon rolls, and is served at guests' choice of tables from 8:30–9:30 A.M. (earlier by request). Afternoon tea is served in the pretty rose parlor with white lace curtains.

"Incredible woodwork, plus 12-foot ceilings and interior folding shutters. We stayed in the spacious Niagara Room, furnished with a queen-size canopy bed, sofa, plenty of good lighting, and a roomy private bath. Pat was consistently hospitable but not overbearing. The tasty breakfast was served on fine china, with silver settings and romantic candlelight." *(Martha Banda)* "Delightful ambience; the innkeeper has an artistic flair for coordinating fabrics and furnishings. The food is excellent and plentiful. A nice balance between enjoying the Hagenbuch's warm company and having personal space." *(Daniel Lucia)*

Open All year.
Rooms 1 apt., 5 doubles—all with private bath and/or shower, telephone, radio, clock, TV/VCR, desk, air-conditioning, fan. 5 with fireplace. Apt. over carriage house with balcony, kitchen.
Facilities Dining room, living room with fireplace, piano, games; library with fireplace, gift shop, sunporch, veranda. Off-street parking. Water sports, golf, skiing nearby.

Location NE PA, on Lake Erie. From I-90, take I-79 N into Erie. Inn is center of town, historic district.
Restrictions No smoking. Well behaved children welcome.
Credit cards Amex, Discover, MC, Visa.
Rates B&B, $65–110 double, $60–105 single. Extra person, $15. 2-night minimum special events, holidays.
Extras Crib.

ERWINNA

Evermay-on-the-Delaware ✕ ⟨   *Tel:* 610–294–9100
River Road, Route 32, 18920   *Fax:* 610–294–8249

Some people head for the country to spend the weekend lounging around in old cut-offs and a well worn T-shirt; others relish the chance to dress for afternoon tea and a special dinner with casual elegance, in a setting that takes them back to an earlier era. Evermay, dating back to the 1700s, is a place for the latter traveler. Extensively remodeled and enlarged in 1871, Evermay is listed on the National Register of Historic Places, and has been owned by Ron Strouse and Fred Cresson since 1981. The inn is best known for its fine cuisine; dinner is served at 7:30, beginning with aperitifs and hors d'oeuvres and followed by six courses. On a recent evening, the menu included pâté with green peppercorns; seafood soup; vegetable tart; Boston lettuce with feta balsamic vinaigrette; grilled tuna, or veal with lentils and wild mushrooms, accompanied by asparagus and gingered carrots; a selection of cheeses; and chocolate chestnut torte or Kahlua coffee almond ice cream. Rates include a breakfast of fresh fruit and juice, croissants and coffee, as well as afternoon tea.

"Our room was on the small side, but had a handsome carved Victorian bed and an Oriental rug. We enjoyed exploring the extensive gardens out back, and watching the deer come to feed at dusk." *(MA)* "Fred and Ron set a high standard—beautiful antiques, cozy rooms, unmatched food served at a leisurely pace, and lovely, well-kept grounds." *(Kathy Coates)* Reports appreciated.

Open All year. Closed Christmas Eve. Restaurant open Fri., Sat., Sun., holidays.
Rooms 1 cottage, 1 suite, 15 doubles—all with private bath and/or shower, telephone, air-conditioning. Rooms in manor house, carriage house, cottage.
Facilities Dining/breakfast room, living room, library/parlor with fireplace, piano, books; meeting room. 25 acres with gardens, picnic area. Delaware River nearby for boating. Cross-country skiing nearby.
Location Bucks County. 45 m NE of Philadelphia. 65 m SW of NYC. From New Hope, go N on Rte. 32 to inn 13.5 m from New Hope, 5.5 m N of Pt. Pleasant.
Restrictions No smoking in dining areas. Children over 13.
Credit cards MC, Visa.
Rates B&B, 2-bedroom suite (4 people) $220, $85–170 double, $55–80 single (weekdays only). 2-night weekend minimum. Prix fixe dinner $52. Tipping only at dinner.
Extras Limited wheelchair access. German spoken.

FOGELSVILLE

Glasbern 🏃 ✕
2141 Pack House Road, 18051-9743

Tel: 610–285–4723
Fax: 610–285–2862

Glasbern, a reconstructed barn, combines the original foundation, wood beams, and shale rock walls, with cathedral ceilings and a contemporary airy feeling. Beth and Al Granger opened the inn in 1985; since then, they have added a handsome swimming pool, and have added accommodations in the adjacent Carriage House, Farm House, Gate House, and Garden Cottage. Dinners are prepared by chef Drew Stichter, and a typical meal might include spinach-mushroom gnocchi, salad, veal medallions with herbed applesauce, and a French apple tarte.

"Set in a quiet valley surrounded by magnificent pine trees, huge windows cover the inn's southern face, hence the name Glasbern—'glass barn.' A country feel is evident in the dried flower arrangements, candles, baskets, and comfortable furniture. Our room was furnished with antiques and modern pieces, and had a queen-size four-poster bed." *(Jon & Kae Tienstra)* "We loved the gracious and elegant atmosphere of our Carriage House suite, along with the king-size bed, fireplace, and whirlpool tub." *(Mrs. Paula Stubbs)* "Skylights created the illusion of sleeping under the stars." *(Raymond Skinner)*

"In winter, a fire roars all day in the Great Room; in the evening, candlelight dinners and excellent food make it romantic. We always see some wildlife on the walking paths: deer, rabbits, and many birds; both ponds attract ducks and geese." *(Rob & Joy Stirling)* "Fully endorse entry. Enjoyed chatting with Beth. Our suite was furnished with a king-sized bed and double whirlpool tub, with lovely fall foliage views from the huge windows. Delicious dinner of lamb served with roast potatoes and pecan pie. Neweilers black-and-tan ale on tap was a big hit with my husband." *(Janeen LaFaver)* "Our private cottage had a beautiful view of the stream. A friendly, helpful staff." *(Debrah Mosin)*

Open All year.
Rooms 14 suites, 10 doubles—all with private bath and/or shower, telephone, radio, TV/VCR, desk, air-conditioning. 17 with whirlpool, 11 with fireplace. 1 suite with kitchenette. Rooms in 4 buildings.
Facilities Common room with fireplace, sun-room, meeting room. 100 acres with heated swimming pool, jogging, bicycling, cross-country skiing. Downhill skiing, lake for fishing, swimming nearby.
Location E central PA. 10 m W of Allentown; 5 min. from intersection of rtes. 22/78 & 100. 2 m from Iron Run Industrial Area. From Rte. 100 N, take 1st left after Rte. 22 onto Tilghman St. (unmarked), opposite Comfort Inn. Turn right at Church St. to Pack House Rd.
Restrictions Children in farmhouse only. Evening sounds from whirlpools and restaurant in some rooms.
Credit cards MC, Visa.
Rates B&B, $120–300 suite, $105–170 double, $90–100 single. Extra person, $20. 2-night weekend minimum. Alc dinner $35–50.
Extras Limited wheelchair access. Crib.

GARDENVILLE

Maplewood Farm B&B ¢   *Tel: 215–766–0477*
5090 Durham Road, 18926

"Wander down to our shady stream and let the water cool those tired feet, or hang around the barn and pick your own eggs from under the hen (where they're still warm!). We'll initial them for you and serve 'em up hot for breakfast," report innkeepers Cindy and Dennis Marquis. They have lovingly restored this 1792 plastered fieldstone farmhouse, adding hand stenciling to every guest room, and piling the beds with handmade quilts or fluffy comforters. The old summer kitchen has a comfortable sitting area and two walk-in fireplaces; breakfast is served in the dining room with its original random width pine floors, exposed stone wall and dark-beamed ceiling. In addition to fresh eggs, breakfast might include home-made granola, buckwheat pancakes with fresh blueberry or raspberry topping, freshly squeezed orange juice, fruit salad with yogurt, home-baked breads and cakes, spiced teas, and coffee. Cindy is happy to accommodate special dietary needs.

"Spotless, with lovely details everywhere you look, including Cindy's stenciling. While all the rooms are charming, the loft is especially pleasing with country chests, a lovely settee, down-filled comforters, and antique quilts. The living room, with its roaring fire and two sweet labradors, is a welcome place to relax. Cindy and Dennis happily assist with dinner plans, and sent us on a wonderful driving tour of covered bridges. The winter breakfast specialty is a baked apple with brown sugar and granola—filling and delicious." *(Sue Abraham, also Jordana Parker)* "Delicious afternoon cakes and cookies." *(April & Pat Judge)*

Open All year.
Rooms 2 suites, 5 doubles—all with private bath and/or shower, radio, air-conditioning. 3 with fan. 1 with fireplace.
Facilities Breakfast room, living room with fireplace, stereo, books; sunporch. 5 acres with gardens, picnic area; farm with chickens, sheep. Horseback riding, canoeing nearby.
Location SE PA, Bucks County. 20 m N of Philadelphia. 15 min. W of New Hope, 10 min. N of Doylestown. Take Rte. 202 to Rte. 413 N. Go 4 m to light; continue for ³/₄ m to farm on left.
Restrictions No smoking.
Credit cards Amex, Discover, MC, Visa.
Rates B&B, $100–140 suite, $70–95 double. Extra person, $25. 2-3 night weekend/holiday minimum.

GETTYSBURG

Founded in the 1780s, Gettysburg grew up around the intersection of four major roads and a number of secondary routes; its strategic location led to its involvement in the bloodiest battle of the Civil War in 1863. The battlefield virtually surrounds the town, and is now a National Military Park. There is much to see and do in the area, but don't expect to experience it alone, especially on weekends in good weather. Start early in the day, and stop first at the National Park Visitors Center for information; local B&B owners should also be knowledgeable about the battlefield and can arrange for battlefield guides.

Gettysburg is located in south central Pennsylvania, 50 miles northwest of Baltimore. It's 45 minutes south of Harrisburg, and one hour west of Lancaster. Downhill skiing at Ski Liberty is 10 miles away; golf, swimming, hiking, and bicycling are all nearby.

Reader tips: "When we made our reservations, we asked our innkeepers to arrange for a National Park Service guide to show us through the battlefield, and were delighted with the results. He brought history to life, and even our teenagers were fascinated. Well worth the price." *(Elisabeth McLaughlin, also Diane Wolf)* "We enjoyed meals at the Dobbin House Tavern, and the Farnsworth House, close to the battlefield. The entire town of Gettysburg was clean, with friendly and courteous citizens." *(Barbara Stack)*

Also recommended: For those who prefer hotel accommodation, readers are pleased with the **Gettysburg Hotel** (1 Lincoln Square, 17325; 717–337–2000), built in the 1920s. This Best Western hotel has 83 guest rooms, some decorated in period reproductions, with gas fireplaces and Jacuzzi tubs. Double rates range from $69–129, and several appealing packages are offered; children 16 and under stay free. "Congenial staff, Christmas cookies and coffee on arrival, beautifully furnished guest rooms and lobby." *(Betty Norman)* "Located right in the center of everything; room above average in comfort." *(Sherrill Brown)* Less favorably: "Our rather empty room had standard issue hotel furnishings, no desk or comfortable seating, and no sense of history." *(DR)*

Information please—in Gettysburg: Situated atop Oak Ridge, with panoramic vistas of the battlefield, **The Doubleday Inn** (104 Doubleday Avenue, 17325; 717–334–9119) has an extensive library devoted exclusively to the Battle of Gettysburg. On selected evenings guests may participate in discussions led by licensed battlefield guides, who bring the battle alive with accurate accounts. Recently redecorated in an English country look, guest rooms are individually decorated with Civil War accents and private baths. Double rates of $79–100 include a candlelit country breakfast.

Built in 1810 and located in the heart of Gettysburg's historic district, **The Historic Farnsworth House Inn** (401 Baltimore Street, 17325; 717–334–8838) was used as a Union headquarters during the battle; over 100 bullet holes remain lodged in the south wall of the inn. The four Victorian-style room are decorated with 19th century antiques and colorful carpets. Artifacts found during the restoration of the inn are displayed in the inn's restaurant, along with original letters written by Generals Pickett and Lee. Dinners feature such specialties as peanut soup, game pie, and pumpkin fritters.

The Old Appleford Inn (218 Carlisle Street, 17325; 717–337–1711 or 800–APLEFRD [275–3373]) is an Italianate Victorian mansion, built in 1867, and located adjacent to Gettysburg College. The inn is decorated with Victorian antiques and reproductions; elaborate swag draperies accent the tall windows in the living room and library, while stenciling adds a country feel to the dining room. A recent breakfast included hot spiced peaches, raspberry pancakes or apple-sausage ring, pastries and breads. B&B double rates for the 12 guest rooms range from $93–103.

Information please—nearby towns: About eight miles west of Gettysburg is **The Hickory Bridge Farm** (96 Hickory Bridge Road, Box 282, Orrtanna, 17353; 717–642–5261), with a well-known restaurant in the restored barn, and accommodations in the farmhouse and four private cottages. B&B double rates range from $79–89, and dinners are served family-style on weekends.

Eight miles west of Gettysburg is the **Mulberry Farm B&B** (616 Flohrs Church Road, Biglerville, 17307; 717–334–5827), an 1817 Georgian Colonial farmhouse, with a quiet country setting in the foothills of the Appalachians. The inn's four acres include a barn, a board-and-batten cottage, a main house, and a perennial garden. The main house and its five guest rooms have been restored by owners Mimi and Jim Agard (previously owners of the Brafferton Inn in Gettysburg) and are decorated with pine and cherry antiques, stenciled floor coverings, and Oriental rugs. The B&B double rates of $100–125 include breakfasts of crepes with applesauce or French toast with mulberries.

For an additional area entries, see **Dillsburg** and **Hanover**, plus **Taneytown** and **Thurmont, Maryland.**

Baladerry Inn   *Tel:* 717–337–1342
40 Hospital Road, 17325

Built in 1812, and located at the edge of the Gettysburg battlefield, the Baladerry Inn served as a field hospital during the Civil War. Today's visitors will find a more peaceful refuge in the home Caryl and Tom O'Gara restored in 1992. Breakfast is served from 8 to 10 A.M., and might include fresh fruit and juice, cereal, and poached eggs and bacon or apple pancakes with sausage.

"Arriving after dark, we were greeted by the sight of a stately Federal home, with chandeliers aglow. Guests were reading in the great room, an addition constructed by the O'Garas, housing a large hearth, comfortable seating, a farm table, and chandeliers made of wagon wheels. Our room was typically Federal, spotless, small-sized and simply furnished with period reproductions; the whirlpool tub was especially pleasing after a day of skiing at nearby Ski Liberty. The O'Garas provided us with information and advice about the area's attractions and restaurants. Mr. O'Gara is a wine connoisseur and Civil War historian, and our conversations with him were both enjoyable and educational. Delicious breakfast served on beautiful china; majestic grounds." *(Joey Willms)*

Open All year.
Rooms 8 doubles—all with private shower bath, radio, clock, air-conditioning. 2 with fireplace, balcony/deck. Telephone on request. 4 rooms in carriage house.
Facilities Breakfast room, living room, great room with fireplace, piano, stereo, books, games; library, guest refrigerator, sunporch, dining terrace, patio. 4 acres with tennis court, gazebo, gardens. Bicycling. Golf nearby.

261

PENNSYLVANIA

Location 2 m to historic district. From downtown Gettysburg, take Baltimore St. S & turn right at the sign for Nat'l. Park Vistor Center-Eisenhower Farm. Inn is on Hospital Rd. near intersection with Blacksmith Rd.
Restrictions No smoking inside (Caryl smokes on patio). Children over 14.
Credit cards Amex, DC, MC, Visa.
Rates B&B, $78–95 double, $68–85 single. Extra person, $15. 2-night weekend/holiday minimum.

The Brafferton Inn

Tel: 717–337–3423

44 York Street (Route 30), 17325

Built of stone in 1786, The Brafferton Inn is one of the oldest homes in Gettysburg and is listed on the National Register of Historic Places. A "new" brick wing was added before the Civil War and houses six guest rooms. Rooms are decorated with 18th-century stencils, primitive antiques, samplers, and quilts. Restored in 1986, the inn was bought by Sam and Jane Back in 1993. Breakfast is served in the dining room at separate tables; peaches and cream French toast, or apple cinnamon pancakes with stewed apples are specialties. This room is highlighted by a hand-painted mural of 18th-century Gettysburg.

"Jane recommended an excellent Civil War novel for us to read before our visit." *(Diane Wolf)* "Jane and Sam suggested the Blue Parrot and Food for Thought for enjoyable meals, and arranged a private battlefield guide; the tour was excellent and reasonably priced. They served our tasty breakfast of French toast and bacon early because we had to leave to catch our flight home." *(Stephanie Roberts)* "Our third-floor suite was furnished with a mixture of antiques and traditional furnishings, with comfortable chairs for relaxing, interesting books and magazines for browsing, and lots of storage space for our clothes and luggage. Although the inn was full, it was quiet, peaceful, and immaculate. The inn's common areas were equally appealing. Best of all were Jane and Sam, the ultimate innkeepers. No matter how busy they were, they always had time to chat or answer questions; both are extremely knowledgeable, and provided battlefield guides, tour tapes, directions, introductions to the other guests, and more." *(Jeanne & Eric Simko)* "While the Brafferton sits on a busy street, inside all is peaceful and homey. Jane and Sam related equally well to both my children and my parents." *(Heidi Fitz)* "Coffee, tea, and juice are always available; inviting reading material awaits in the comfortable library/sitting room." *(Anne Weston)* "Jane and Sam sense when guests want company, and when they need quiet." *(Maureen Sirhall)*

Open All year.
Rooms 2 suites, 8 doubles—all with private bath and/or shower, air-conditioning. Suites with TV. Some with desk.
Facilities Dining room, library, living room, atrium, back garden/deck. Limited off-street parking; municipal lot directly behind garden.
Location Just off square in center of town.
Restrictions Smoking only in garden/deck area. Children over 8. Traffic noise in 2 front rooms; occasional conversation on deck can disturb guests in Garden room; minimal interior soundproofing. Some rooms have limited storage space.
Credit cards MC, Visa.

Rates B&B, $110–125 suite, $75–95 double, $60–90 single. Extra person, $10.
Tips welcome. 2-night minimum July 4, some college weekends.
Extras French spoken.

GORDONVILLE

Osceola Mill House   Tel: 717–768–3758
313 Osceola Mill Road, 17529

Too many Pennsylvania Dutch Country lodgings are on busy roads
packed with vacationers and commercialized versions of Amish culture.
It's a special relief to discover a B&B set on a country lane, amid Old
Order Amish farms. Built in 1766, this sturdy miller's home, constructed
of fieldstone, is adjacent to the mill itself (circa 1757), on the banks of
Pequea Creek. Restored to its original 18th century appearance in 1985,
it has been owned by Robin and Sterling Schoen since 1989. Breakfast is
served promptly at 8:30, and might consist of cranberry poached pears,
a walnut fruit tart, and German apple pancakes with vanilla sugar, orange-
baked French toast, or quiche with fresh herbs, bacon, and cheese. All the
apple-wood smoked bacon and sausage are made by the Schoens' Amish
neighbors.

"This stone house is done in perfect taste, with wonderful antique
furniture and canopy beds in most rooms. Sterling went up the road to
pick fresh blueberries for our breakfast, and Robin made dinner reservations for us." (B.J. Hensley) "The Schoens do a superb job of making
everyone feel at home. An expert on the Amish, Sterling arranged a
dinner at an Old Order Amish family's farm house, a five-minute walk
away—a highlight of our trip." (RT)

Open All year.
Rooms 5 doubles—2 with private tub and/or shower; 3 rooms share 2 baths. 4
with clock. 3 with air-conditioning. 2 with fireplace. 2 with fan.
Facilities Dining room, living room, keeping room with TV, books; bicycle
storage.
Location 15 m E of Lancaster City; 1.6 m to Intercourse. Take 340 E to Inter-
course. Follow 772 E for 1.6 m, go right on Osceola Mill Rd. House on Pequea
Creek, ½ m from Rte. 772.
Restrictions No smoking. Children 12 and over.
Credit cards None accepted.
Rates B&B, $100 double. No tipping.
Extras Station pickups.

HANOVER

Beechmont Inn ¢   Tel: 717–632–3013
315 Broadway, 17331   800–553–7009

Restored to its 1834 Federal period elegance, Beechmont has been owned
by Susan and William Day since 1994. The antique and reproduction

furnishings, primarily of walnut and mahogany, and the rose, green, and cream color scheme create an elegant atmosphere. Each room is decorated individually, one with a door opening onto the formally landscaped courtyard, another reached by a winding staircase. Rates include breakfast and afternoon refreshments. The morning meal (served at 8 A.M. Monday–Saturday, 9 on Sunday) always includes homemade granola, assorted cereals, fruit and juice, followed by apricot puff pancakes, bacon, melon, banana muffins, or perhaps country eggs, baked apples, and chocolate chip coffee cake. Susan mentions that many guests opt to "enjoy one of life's little treasures—breakfast in bed."

"The aroma of homemade gingerbread scented the air when we checked in. Our room was warm and cozy, with a canopy bed and marble fireplace. although the inn is on a well-traveled road, we slept well." (*Nancy Santoro*) "The nights are quiet and comfortable, the breakfasts superb. Susan accommodated my work schedule with early breakfasts." (*Hershel Norwood*)

Open All year.
Rooms 3 suites, 4 doubles—all with private bath and/or shower, telephone, radio, clock, TV, desk, air-conditioning. 3 with fireplace, 2 with refrigerator, 1 with whirlpool tub, deck.
Facilities Parlor, dining room, library. Courtyard, gazebo, garden, off-street parking. Tennis, swimming pool nearby. 4 m to Codorus State Park for swimming, fishing, boating, hiking, cross-country skiing.
Location S central PA, York County. 13 m E of Gettysburg, 40 SW of Lancaster, 75 m NW of Washington, DC. From Rte. 30, go S on Rte. 94 (Carlisle St.) to Center Square. Turn left on Broadway, go 3 blocks to inn on right.
Restrictions No smoking. Children over 12.
Credit cards Amex, Discover, MC, Visa.
Rates B&B, $115–135 suite, $80–95 double. 2-night minimum some weekends. Weekend, honeymoon packages.

HARFORD

Nine Partners Inn ¢   *Tel: 717–434–2233*
1 North Harmony Road,   *Fax: 717–434–1233 Extension 23*
P.O. Box 300, 18823

Taking its name from a local settlement carved from the wilderness by pioneers from western Massachusetts, the Nine Partners Inn was built in 1794 and was opened as a B&B 200 years later by Rudy Sumpter and Jim DeCoe. Moved to a more scenic location when it was renovated, the inn is a New England-style post-and-beam home, with original maple floorboards, primitive woodwork, and six fireplaces.

"Set on a cool, breezy hillside overlooking the pastoral countryside." (*Robert & Alisa DelFreo*) "Warm welcome by Rudy. Rustic antiques; spotless, well-appointed modern bath." (*John Burke*) "Secluded, yet not too far from restaurants, antique shops, skiing." (*Charles DeGregorio*) "Our room had a queen-size poster bed with beautiful linens, an antique rocking chair, plus a welcoming dish of cheese and crackers, and a vase of fresh flowers.

The breakfast table was beautifully set with fine china and crystal; we were offered cereal, huge homemade muffins, yogurt with kiwi and strawberries, a featherlight cheese omelet, plus juice and coffee." *(Charles & Maria Jennings, and others)* "Rudy rescued me after my car died, and turned a near disaster into a delightful mini-vacation." *(Robert Rifkin)*

Open All year.
Rooms 3 doubles—all with private bath and/or shower, radio, clock. 1 with desk.
Facilities Dining room with fireplace, living room with fireplace, books; keeping room with fireplace; guest refrigerator, deck. 24 acres with lawn games, hiking, cross-country skiing trails. Hiking, bicycling, fishing, canoeing, golf nearby. 11 m to downhill skiing at Elk Mt. (22% discount tkts.)
Location NE PA, Endless Mts. Halfway between Scranton & Binghampton. From I-81, take Exit 65. Follow Rte. 547 S through Harford 2 1/2 m S to N. Harmony Rd., turn right to inn on left.
Restrictions No smoking. Steep, narrow stairs to rear bedroom. Children discouraged, unless family booking entire inn.
Credit cards Amex, Discover, MC, Visa.
Rates B&B, $55–85 double. 2-night minimum for advance reservations.

HARRISBURG

Although we have no Harrisburg recommendations, for additional area entries, see under **New Cumberland**, as well as **Hershey**, **Dillsburg**, **Carlisle**, and **New Kingston**.

HAWLEY

Information please: Near Lake Wallenpaupack in the Poconos is **The Settlers Inn** (4 Main Avenue, 18428; 717–226–2993 or 800–833–8527), an English Tudor manor house built in 1927 and opened as an inn in 1945. B&B double rates for the 20 guest rooms $75–110 include a full breakfast, chosen from a menu; in summer, guests are invited to sip cool lemonade on the inn's front porch, or cuddle before the living room fire in winter with a steaming mug of tea or cocoa. The restaurant highlights regional foods obtained from local farmers: organic produce in season, locally raised and grown meats, goat cheese, and maple syrup.

HERSHEY

Information please: Although kids of all ages will enjoy a visit to the well-known Hersheypark amusement park and Hershey's Chocolate World, adult visitors may prefer to tour the lovely Hershey Botanical Gardens and the Hershey Museum, with exhibits detailing the growth of Milton Hershey's chocolate empire. Although chain motels abound, and the Hotel Hershey is an elegant four-diamond resort property, with beautiful gardens and five golf courses, we need some inn recommendations. Some possibilities in nearby Elizabethtown (seven miles south) and Palmyra (two miles east) include:

Apples Abound-Inn (518 South Market Street, Elizabethtown 17022; 717–367–3018) is a 1907 Victorian home with stained glass windows, chestnut doors, shutters and trim. The guest rooms have brass and oak queen-size beds, wicker furnishings, and sitting areas. Owners Jennifer and Jon Sheppard display their apple collection throughout their home. A typical breakfast includes cinnamon apple muffins, egg salad croissantwich, and healthy apple cake. B&B double rates range from $65–75, and children are welcome. Comments?

The West Ridge Guest House B&B (1285 West Ridge Road, Elizabethtown 17022; 717–367–7783) has nine guest rooms—each with a private bath and decorated to reflect a different historic period, an exercise room, hot tub, and two fishing ponds; double rates of $60–90 include a full breakfast and children are welcome.

In Palmyra, the **Hen-Apple B&B** (409 S. Lingle Avenue, Palmyra, 17078; 717–838–8282), has six guest rooms with private baths and air-conditioning. This 1825 Georgian-style farmhouse is furnished with antiques, reproductions, and flea market finds. Guests can relax in the parlor, wicker room, or in the backyard hammock under old fruit trees. A full breakfast (perhaps cinnamon raisin French toast and lemon poppy seed bread) and afternoon refreshments are included in the $75 double rate.

HOLLIDAYSBURG

Information please: Just south of Altoona and about 100 miles east of Pittsburgh is the **Parris House** (RR 2, Box 650, 16648; 814–696–2849), a 200-year-old stone home restored as a B&B by Stacey Parris. Rates for the four guest rooms, each with private bath, range $65–75. "Charming home, hospitable innkeeper, tasty breakfast of orange juice, fresh fruit, quiche, coffee cake, and very good coffee." (*Janet Payne*)

INTERCOURSE

For another nearby entry, see listing for the **Osceola Mill House** in **Gordonville**.

Information please: A visit to the **Carriage Corner B&B** (3705 East Newport Road, P.O. Box 371, 17534–0371; 717–768–3059), is a perfect introduction to the original concept of B&B: affordable lodging, genuine hospitality, delicious food, and immaculate housekeeping. Built as a B&B in 1980, the four guest rooms are small and modestly furnished, highlighted by beautiful handmade quilts in traditional patterns. Double rates of $45–70 include a hearty country breakfast. Reports please.

JIM THORPE

Wedged into a narrow gorge rising up from the Lehigh River, this town was originally made up of three separate areas, Mauch Chunk, Upper Mauch Chunk, and East Mauch Chunk (*Mauch Chunk* means "Bear Mountain" in the language of the local Native Americans), which were renamed Jim Thorpe in 1954 in honor of the famous Olympic athlete. The town's numerous mansions and historic buildings date back to the second half of the 19th century, when the Lehigh Valley Railroad brought coal to the big cities, tourists to enjoy the mountain scenery, and considerable prosperity to the inhabitants. Mauch Chunk State Park, perfect for swimming, boating, fishing, and picnics, is 2 miles from town; it's a 3-mile drive to cross-country skiing and white-water rafting, and 8–20 miles to downhill skiing.

Jim Thorpe is located 25 miles northwest of Allentown, and 80 miles northwest of Philadelphia.

Reader tip: "Weekend parking can be a real headache in Jim Thorpe because the streets are narrow and hilly. There's talk in town of building a garage, but that will take a while." *(NH)*

Information please: We need additional reports on the **The Harry Packer Mansion** (Packer Hill, P.O. Box 458, 18229; 717–325–8566), set high on a hill in the Mauch Chunk historic district. Built in 1874 in the Second Empire style, of brick, stone, and sandstone, with cast iron trim. Furnishings include elaborately carved walnut, oak and mahogany woodwork, inlaid oak parquet floors, Minton tile floors, Tiffany stained glass windows, and hand-painted ceilings. Thirteen guest rooms at double rates of $75–110 include a full breakfast. "A quirky adventure—not an experience for everyone but fun for one night. The perfect setting for the murder mystery weekends held by the innkeepers. We chose to stay in the more modern carriage house. The innkeeper cooked a wonderful breakfast and entertained us with his zany tales." *(Elaine Bounds)*

A less adventuresome choice is the **The Inn at Jim Thorpe** (24 Broadway, 18229; 717–325–2599) built in 1848 and restored in 1990. The 22 guest rooms are furnished with Victorian touches, including swagged floral curtains, ornate headboards, period reproductions, and baths with pedestal sinks and marble floors; most have two double or queen-size beds. The B&B double rates of $65–100 include a generous Continental breakfast. Under separate ownership, the inn's restaurant, Emerald, serves Irish-American and Continental cuisine.

KENNETT SQUARE

Kennett Square is located in the Brandywine River Valley and is close to Longwood Gardens, the Winterthur Museum, and the Brandywine River Museum. It claims to be the "mushroom capital of the U.S.," and is also home to the Philips Mushroom Museum.

Reader tip: "We had a delicious lunch at the **Longwood Inn** (815 East Baltimore Pike, 19348; 610–444–3515), just a ½ mile from Longwood Gardens. My mushroom strudel was outstanding." *(Rose Wolf, also JC)*

Information please: On a quiet country road, yet still convenient to Route 1 is the **Flower Farm B&B** (453 Bayard Road, 19348; 610–444–5659). A beautifully restored fieldstone Quaker home, built in 1828 with foot-thick walls, it has a lovely old barn and eight acres of terraced gardens with over 250 varieties of trees, shrubs, and perennials. The four guest rooms have private baths, air-conditioning, and TVs, and are furnished with antiques. A full breakfast, often featuring local mushrooms, is included in the $75–125 double rate.

For an additional area entries, see **Avondale** and **Landenberg.**

Meadow Spring Farm ¢ ♯ ♿   *Tel: 610–444–3903*
201 East Street Road, 19348

A stone farmhouse built in 1836, Meadow Spring Farm has been in the Hicks family for over 50 years, and is now operated as a B&B by Anne Hicks and her daughter Debbie, with occasional help from one of eight grandchildren. Anne is an inveterate collector. After a lifetime of acquiring dolls of all kinds, many to inhabit the three-story dollhouse built by her father over 50 years ago, and then a more recently acquired interest in Holstein cows (she has over 200), a friend gave her a Santa figurine. Now she rotates collections during the Christmas season (December 1 through January 14) in order to display the 140 Santas from all over the world (while the cows go into their storage barns). Breakfasts are served family-style in the large dining room and usually include juice, apple pancakes or mushroom omelets, breads, and coffee. "Despite encroaching housing subdivisions, this farm still has cows grazing (even Belted Galloways), sheep, and a large duck pond. The living room, dining room, and sunporch are all homey, lived-in, and inviting; Ann's wonderful cow collection appears everywhere. The guest rooms are comfortable and appealing; one on the ground floor in a new wing of the house is more modern, but would be most comfortable for anyone who has difficulty with stairs." *(SWS)*

"Christmas trees were everywhere—decorated in every style from Victorian to modern." *(Lisa Romeo)* "Our room in the old section of the farmhouse had a four-poster bed, two bedside tables with lamps, and comfortable chairs. We watched Amish sheep shearers quickly fleece the farm's flock. Anne has a passion for gardening, and her tender care had the spring plants blooming profusely. The inviting country kitchen has a sunny seating area where guests can admire the fantastic orchids and other unusual plants." *(Pat & Jim Lee)* "My room was above a detached garage and had a double bed and a private bath; it was large, clean, and modern. Mrs. Hicks prepared a fine breakfast each day with apple/peach pancakes, sausage from her farm, omelets and juice. She is an interesting and friendly person." *(Cheryl Slater)*

Open All year.
Rooms 6 doubles, 1 single—5 with full private bath, 2 with a maximum of 3

sharing bath. All with TV, desk, air-conditioning. 1 with fireplace, kitchen. 3 rooms in annex.

Facilities Dining/breakfast room, living room with fireplace, game room with pool table, Ping-Pong; sun porch with hot tub. 2 acres (plus farm acreage) with unheated swimming pool, picnic area, perennial gardens, fishing pond, cross-country skiing, farm animals. Tennis, canoeing, golf nearby.

Location Brandywine Valley. 60 min. SW of Philadelphia, 20 min. N of Wilmington, DE. 25 minutes S of PA Tpke. Exit 23. On Rte. 926 between Rtes. 52 & 82. From Kennett Square, go N on Rte. 82 approx 4 m & turn right on E Street Rd. (Rte. 926) to inn on left.

Restrictions No smoking in guest rooms.

Credit cards None accepted.

Rates B&B, $75–85 double. Extra child, $10. 2-night weekend minimum.

Extras Wheelchair access. Airport/station pickup. Crib, $10; babysitting.

KINTNERSVILLE

The Bucksville House &.

Tel: 610–847–8948

4501 Durham Road, 18930-1610

This registered landmark dates to 1795, when Captain Nicholas Buck built several stone buildings. The property passed to his son, who built the Bucksville Hotel in 1840. It became a popular stagecoach shop, and what is now the dining room was probably the wheelwright's shop. The house was a speakeasy during Prohibition, and a tavern in the 1930s. The Bucksville House was restored by Joe and Barb Szollosi in 1984, and is decorated with quilts, baskets, queen-size canopy beds, antiques and country reproductions handcrafted by Joe. Breakfast is served hearthside in the dining room (floored in Mercer tiles) or in the gazebo, and might include fresh pineapple with kiwi, savory egg casserole, ham, fruit soufflé, scones, juice, and coffee.

"Our enchanting room was furnished with reproductions made by Joe and antiques collected by Barb over the years, with the original planked floor boards. After a full day of antiquing, we snuggled in our four-poster bed under a generous supply of handmade quilts and took in the warmth and glow of our fireplace. Wonderful breakfasts of baked apples, fruit and yogurt parfaits, raisin waffles, omelets, sausage and bacon, served on pewter plates, while Joe and Barb told stories of the inn and their adventures during restoration." *(Michele Hokien)* "We especially liked the sitting areas, filled with comfortable couches and romantic touches." *(Brenda Sulick)* "Impeccably clean. Bathrooms are supplied daily with large, fluffy towels and all the beds are comfy." *(Susan Frank)* "Thoughtful touches included a hair dryer, an iron, and an ironing board. The large bathroom had plenty of counter space for makeup and toiletries. Cider and cookies awaited our return in the afternoon, and a carafe of Joe's homemade wine was offered in the evening." *(Joanne Mullen)*

Open All year.

Rooms 1 suite, 4 doubles—all with private bath and/or shower, air-conditioning. Some with desk, fan. 3 with fireplace.

Facilities Dining room with fireplace, living room with fireplace, family room with fireplace, games, TV, library. 4 acres with gazebo, croquet. Nockamixon State Park nearby for water sports, cross-country skiing.

Location Upper Bucks County, 1 hr. N of Philadelphia, about 45 min. N of New Hope. Take Rte. 611 N through Doylestown. Go 14 m N to Rte. 412. Turn left, go 2 m to inn on right.

Restrictions No smoking. Children over 12. Some traffic noise in front rooms.

Credit cards Amex, MC, Visa.

Rates B&B, $130 suite, $100 double. Extra person, $35. 2-night weekend minimum.

Extras Wheelchair access.

LACKAWAXEN

Information please: Overlooking the Delaware River is the **Roebling Inn on the Delaware** (Scenic Drive, P.O. Box 31, Lackawaxen, 18435; 717–685–7900). Dating from 1865, it is listed on the National Register of Historic Places and was built by the Delaware & Hudson Canal Company. The B&B double rates ($70–85) for the five simply furnished guest rooms include a breakfast of fruit, juice, cereal, eggs or pancakes with bacon and muffins. Guests enjoy the nearby Zane Grey Museum a block away, plus of course the Delaware River for fishing, canoeing, and swimming. Railroad buffs will enjoy hearing the nearby train whistle at night.

LANCASTER

Lancaster is known as the heart of the Pennsylvania Dutch country, and has numerous attractions: Amish, Mennonite, Colonial, and historical—even an amusement park to educate and entertain visitors. No matter what your interests, the best place to begin is at the Pennsylvania Dutch Visitor Information Center on U.S. Route 30 at the Greenfield Road exit (501 Greenfield Road, 17601; 717–299–8901). On Tuesdays, Fridays, and Saturdays you'll see the largest covered market in the country at Penn Square, where local farmers bring in fruits, vegetables, meats, flowers, and baked goods; if you take your little piggies to market, don't dawdle as it opens at 6 A.M. Lancaster has also developed a name for itself in the factory outlet business, with over 100 stores located in and around the town.

Lancaster is located 65 miles west of Philadelphia and 37 miles south east of Harrisburg.

Note: Lancaster is a generally attractive city with much to offer, but if you'd prefer to experience the Pennsylvania Dutch country from a more rural perspective, check the chapter introduction plus the map at the back of this book for the names of nearby towns and villages.

Also recommended: If a genuine Amish experience is more important to you than creature comforts, consider a stay at the **Lincoln Haus Inn** (1687 Lincoln Highway East; 717–392–9412), owned by a member of the Old Order Amish Church—the inimitable Mary Zook, a font of genuine

Pennsylvania Dutch hospitality and faith. Although readers are delighted with Mary's generous, convivial, family-style breakfasts of baked apple oatmeal, fried mush, shredded wheat pancakes, sausage, breads, eggs, and homemade apple butter, most feel that the guest room furnishings and amenities are extremely basic—not surprising when you consider Amish beliefs. The best choice is the spacious suite (B&B, $75), built on to the back of the house, with a kitchenette and cathedral ceiling. The five doubles cost $43–63, and children are welcome.

Although too small for a full entry with only three guest rooms, the **Flowers & Thyme B&B** (238 Strasburg Pike, 17602; 717–393–1460) is recommended for its welcoming owners, clean and comfortable accommodations, and delicious meals. The B&B double rates of $65–95 include breakfasts of poached pears or fresh fruit, sausage or bacon, muffins or sweet rolls, and such entrées as French toast with orange apricot sauce, waffles with raspberry sauce, or eggs and asparagus with cheese sauce and croissants. Neither smoking nor drinking is permitted; rooms at the back are quieter.

Daniel and Erma Wenger of **Der Wengerhof** (86 Greenfield Road, 17602; 717–393–0325) will give you genuine insights into Amish culture and invite you to sample their Mennonite hospitality. Dan is an expert on local Mennonite/Amish history and culture and an experienced tour guide. Dinners can be arranged in Amish or Mennonite homes with advance notice. B&B double rates for the three guest rooms (one with private bath) are $45–60. "Warm hospitality, interesting hosts, lovely quilt collection." *(Anne & Al Coneen)* "Delicious breakfast of crisp waffles and rhubarb muffins." *(Esther Wenger)*

The King's Cottage ♿

1049 East King Street, 17602

Tel: 717–397–1017
Fax: 717–397–3447

It took a lot of work, courage, and vision for Karen and Jim Owens to restore a decaying flop house to its original elegance as a Spanish Mission Revival home, built in 1913. Guests can now fully appreciate this home's unusual mix of Victorian and Art Deco detailing: the traditional marble fireplace, the Art Deco brick fireplace, stained glass windows, crystal chandeliers, original wainscoting, and hand-crafted decorative moldings. Rates include fresh-squeezed orange juice, fresh fruit, homemade granola, and a hot entrée—perhaps peaches-and-cream French toast—as well as afternoon tea, evening sherry, plus pillow chocolates and turndown service. All guest rooms have queen- or king-size beds and private baths, although some bathrooms are across or down the hall.

"The inn's common areas include a formal living room with brocaded sofa, and an adjoining, more casual library; afternoon tea and home-baked cake is set out here from 4–7 P.M., plus sherry after dinner. There's plenty of travel information, a menu basket, plus a guest notebook with frank comments on local restaurants. At the front of the house is a beautifully restored and inviting sunporch. The dining room has two large tables, where breakfast is served family style at your choice of 8:30 or 9:30 A.M. (earlier on weekdays). Our breakfast included carafes of regular and decaf coffee, plus hot water for tea, orange juice, sliced bananas with kiwi, spinach pie, and locally made sausages; cereal and granola are set on the sideboard. The decor is light and airy throughout the inn. Most rooms are painted a creamy white, with color scheme of soft blue, green, and mauve reflected in the dhurrie rugs; the eclectic antique furnishings include some Victorian pieces. Thoughtful touches in our room included an ample supply of wooden hangers, good linens, four soft, fluffy pillows, thick towels and terry robes, good reading lights and tables on both sides of the bed, and a shelf of books." *(SWS)*

"After breakfast, Karen updated the guests on all the current local activities, providing individual attention as needed." *(Mr. & Mrs. Wade Harvey)* "Beautiful hardwood floors. The innkeeper built a fire for us at night, and set out a decanter of Amaretto." *(Mark Smith)* Reports appreciated.

Open All year.
Rooms 1 cottage with fireplace, TV, refrigerator, microwave. 8 doubles—all with private bath and/or shower, air-conditioning. 1 with balcony, private entrance. Telephone with prior notice.
Facilities Dining room; parlor with fireplace, library with TV, fireplace; sun porch, off-street parking.
Location S central PA. Lancaster Cty. Exit Rte. 30 at Rte. 23 W/Walnut St. exit. Turn right at end of exit ramp, then turn left at 2nd light at Ranck Ave. At 2nd stop sign, turn left onto E. Orange St. Go 1 block to Cottage Ave. & turn right. Inn is last bldg on right. Turn right into lane just before inn, then left again into parking area.
Restrictions No smoking. Children over 12. Traffic noise in front rooms.
Credit cards Discover, MC, Visa.
Rates B&B, $160–175 cottage, $80–135 double.
Extras Spanish spoken.

New Life Homestead B&B ¢ ♦♦   *Tel: 717–396–8928*
1400 East King Street, 17602

The New Life Homestead is a 1912 brick home decorated in Victorian, country, and farmhouse styles by innkeepers Carol and Bill Giersch. The guest rooms are furnished with family heirlooms, handmade quilts and crocheted bedspreads. A typical breakfast might include juice, bananas drizzled with honey, homemade granola, baked French toast made from home-baked bread, sausages, sautéed apples, and lemon herb bread.

"Warm hospitality; we were welcomed back from dinner with delicious chocolate chip cookies and coffee. Night tables on both sides of the bed with excellent lighting; the firm mattress made for a good night's sleep. Carol graciously served us an early breakfast when we had to leave early. The pretty backyard has a flower garden, picnic table and chairs." *(Betty Norman)* "Carol and Bill are a warm Mennonite couple who enjoy getting to know their guests, and introducing guests to the Amish and Mennonite communities of which they are a part. The Giersch's home has large sunny rooms with high ceilings and good lighting." *(Laurie Flint)* "Despite the inn's location on a busy street, we slept well." *(Cecile Plante)* "Ample hot water, efficient plumbing." *(Sheilah Johnson)* "After a delicious breakfast, Carol took us on a two-hour tour of Amish shops and the surrounding towns. That night we had a wonderful dinner with an Amish family." *(Lori*

Opdenaker) "Carol's wonderful collection of dolls and pillows (most of which she has made herself) can be found all over the house." *(MW)*

Open All year.
Rooms 4 doubles—all with air-conditioning, fan. 2 with private shower, 2 with a maximum of 4 sharing bath. 1 with balcony.
Facilities Breakfast room, living room with fireplace, TV/VCR, stereo, books; library, porch. 1/4 acre with off-street parking, children's play equipment, picnic area, garden. Boating, swimming nearby.
Location 1 hr. NW of Philadelphia. 3 hrs. SW of NYC. 1 1/2 m E of Lancaster. 1 1/2 m S of Route 30 to Route 462 (E King St.).
Restrictions Minimal traffic noise in front rooms. No smoking. No alcohol.
Credit cards None accepted.
Rates B&B, $50–75 double, $40–50 single. Extra person, $15. Family rates. 2-night holiday/weekend minimum. 7th night free.
Extras Airport/station pickups. Crib, high chair.

LANDENBERG

Cornerstone B&B
Newark & Buttonwood Roads, R.D. 1, Box 155, 19350

Tel: 610–274–2143

The Cornerstone B&B takes its name from the stone that marked the completion of this historic home in 1820. Records show that the property was granted to William Penn's son in 1704, and that the original house was built in the early 1700s. Quaker masons constructed the house of "plum pudding" fieldstone, while the elaborate fireplace mantels were carved by Hessian soldiers after the Revolutionary War. Now owned by Linda Chamberlin and Marty Mulligan, the Cornerstone is decorated with wing chairs, ruffled curtains, canopy beds, and hand-stitched quilts, with 18th century antiques. Rates include afternoon tea and a breakfast of juice, fresh fruit, homemade muffins, Amish jellies, jams and apple butter, and a hot entrée, perhaps creamed eggs with chives stuffed in a croissant and topped with Monterey Jack cheese, with bacon or sausage.

"Although the area is being developed, the inn sits on a quiet country road where wildflowers bloom. The Pineapple room is clean and pretty with antique decorative objects and a high four poster bed, and a window overlooking the countryside. The other guest rooms were equally clean and pretty. A good sit-down breakfast was served in the dining room." *(Maureen & Michael Banner)*

Open All year.
Rooms 1 2-bedroom cottage, 1 suite, 5 doubles—all with private shower and/or bath, radio, TV, air-conditioning. 3 apartments in renovated barn with kitchen, laundry. 2 with fireplace.
Facilities Country kitchen, living room with fireplaces, den with TV/VCR, veranda. 4 acres with greenhouse, swimming pool, hot tub, garden, goldfish pond. Bicycles, hiking trails.
Location Chester County, just W of Wilmington DE. From I-95, take Exit 4 to Rte. 7 N. Go 7.1 m to Little Baltimore Rd. (traffic light, nursery at corner). Turn left onto Little Baltimore Rd (name changes to Newark Rd. at PA state line). Go 2.7 m to Buttonwood Rd. & inn on far right corner.

Restrictions No smoking.
Credit cards MC, Visa.
Rates B&B, $110 suite, $75–95 double. Extra person, $15. Weekly rate.
Extras French, German spoken.

LEWISBURG

Lewisburg developed most rapidly in the mid-1800s, when a canal system linked lush farmland in the west with the big cities of the East Coast. Merchants, entrepreneurs, and farmers moved into town and built stately Federal-style brick residences and row houses. Now home to Bucknell University, this lovely college town is characterized by its red brick buildings, both on and off campus. Amish and Mennonite farmers reside on neat farms in the surrounding countryside and examples of their handicrafts can be found in local shops. Plan on reserving well in advance for college weekends in the spring and fall.

Lewisburg is located in the Susquehanna Valley of central Pennsylvania, 180 miles west of New York City, 140 miles northwest of Philadelphia, and 60 miles north of Harrisburg.

Also recommended: A 200-year-old limestone home, **The Inn at Fiddler's Tract** (Route 192, R.D. 2, P.O. Box 573-A, 17837; 717–523–7197 or 800–326–9659) has five guest rooms, with floral wallpapers and curtains, down comforters, dried flower arrangements, and reproduction four-poster and brass beds. On the hillside, a large redwood gazebo covers a hot tub and sauna. B&B rates for the five guest rooms ranges from $75–95. "New owners, Paula and Chi, were warm and welcoming. Attractive inn, pretty garden, quiet setting, attentive service. Breakfast was simple but good: fresh peaches and blackberries, blueberry muffins, and cereal." *(Peter & Mary Holmes)*

Information please: The Pineapple Inn (439 Market Street, 17837; 717–524–6200) is a Federal-style brick home, built in 1857, with common areas that are plushly Victorian while still light and airy, with twelve-foot ceilings and tall windows. Each guest room has a theme to its decor, utilizing hand-painted stencils, quilts, and other collectibles. B&B rates for the six guest rooms range from $65–90, including a full breakfast.

About ten miles south of Lewisburg is **The Inn at Olde New Berlin** (321 Market Street, New Berlin 17855–0390; 717–966–0321), a turn-of-the-century Queen Anne home with five guest rooms, each with private bath, air-conditioning, and antique furnishings. B&B double rates of $80–95 include a full breakfast, served in Gabriel's, the inn's fine dining restaurant.

LIGONIER

Ligonier is located in southwestern Pennsylvania, about 60 miles southeast of Pittsburgh and 20 miles southwest of Johnstown, and is known for Fort Ligonier, Idlewild Park, and the Compass Inn Museum in neighboring

Laughlintown, plus antique shops, white-water rafting, hiking, golf, and bicycling.

Also recommended: Owners Duff and Sharri Eckstein are just completing the renovation of the **Old Kiln Place** (219 East Main Street, 15658; 412–238–2524), and offer four guest rooms with private baths. The B&B rates of $90–110 include a full breakfast, served in the garden in good weather. "The Bridal Suite is bright and cheery, with a queen-size canopy bed, and a sitting room and bathroom with coordinated decor. We were served a scrumptious breakfast on the adjacent flower-filled veranda. Every need was anticipated and we were royally treated. Ligonier is a quaint town of Fiskes and Mellons, ideal for a short getaway." (*Martha Banda*)

Those nostalgic for Campbell's Soup will enjoy Patti Campbell's extensive collection of Campbell memorabilia, displayed along with a profusion of gifts and collectibles in the common room of the **Campbell House B&B & Gift Parlour** (305 East Main Street, 15658; 412–238–9812). Each of the three guest rooms has a private bath, and is decorated with florals and lace. The B&B double rates of $80 include evening turndown service, plus such breakfasts as bananas with marshmallow vanilla yogurt and granola, orange juice, baked eggs with chives, sausages, and honey wheat English muffins. Behind the inn is a five-unit motel building called the Strawberry Lane Efficiencies.

LITITZ

Lititz was founded in 1756 as a Moravian community and named after the town in Bohemia where the Moravian Church was founded. To ensure the high moral caliber of the town, all inhabitants were required to abide by strict regulations, which prohibited, among other things, all "dancing, taverning, feasting, common sports, and the playing of children in the streets." These regulations carried weight with the early residents as the entire town was long owned by the church. Behavior has changed in the years intervening, but not the buildings, as much of the town is a National Historic District, encompassing 18th century homes with architectural detail reminiscent of Germany's Rhine Valley. Lititz is located in Lancaster County, seven miles north of Lancaster.

Reader tip: "While in Lititz, be sure to visit the Wilbur Chocolate Company (and museum) and the Sturgis Pretzel factory (in 1861, when founded, it was the first pretzel bakery in the U.S.) Sundae Best is an ice cream parlor to die for." (*Dianne Crawford*)

For an additional area suggestion, see **Akron**.

The Alden House   *Tel:* 717–627–3363
62 East Main Street, 17543   800–584–0753

The Alden House is a stately 1850 Victorian brick townhouse in the historic district of Lititz, renovated as a B&B in 1988 and further spruced up with queen canopy and pineapple four poster beds when it was purchased by Joy and Fletcher Coleman in 1994. Fletcher does the cooking, and prides himself on tasty breakfasts of fresh fruit, bacon or sausage, home-fried potatoes, eggs any style, plus such entrées as cinnamon chip pancakes, blackberry preserve French toast, or heart-shaped cocoa waffles. Breakfast is served by candlelight in the dining room or outside on one of the inn's three porches, as are afternoon beverages and snacks. "Pleasant owners, lovely breakfast. In-town location close to everything, including a fascinating herb shop a few doors away. Friendly cats." *(Donna Bocks)* Comments appreciated.

Open All year.
Rooms 3 suites, 3 doubles—all with private shower, radio, clock, TV, air-conditioning. 1 with ceiling fan. 2 with porch.
Facilities Dining room, guest kitchen/refrigerator. 3 porches. 1/2 acre with off-street parking, garden, bicycle storage.
Location Take Rte. 30 to Rte. 501 N exit & go N for 5 m to Lititz. Turn right at square onto Main St. to inn 1/2 block on right.
Restrictions Street noise in front rooms. No smoking. Children 8 and over preferred.
Credit cards MC, Visa.
Rates B&B, $95–100 suite, $75–85 double, $65–75 single. Extra person $15. 2-night weekend minimum 6/1–11/15.

The Historic General Sutter Inn 🛉 ✕   *Tel:* 717–626–2115
14 East Main Street, 17543

Built in 1764 by the Moravian Church, and known as Zum Anker (The Sign of the Anchor) this inn was well-known in Pennsylvania for its good food and lodging, and for its prohibition of dancing, cursing, gossip, and bawdy songs. Expanded and rebuilt in 1803 and 1848, the inn was renamed in honor of John Sutter (of California 49er gold rush fame). In 1981, it was purchased and renovated by long-time owners Joan and Richard Vetter. Breakfast and lunch are served in the coffee shop, while dinner is served in the Zum Anker room.

"Spacious guest rooms decorated in antique country and Victorian furnishings, with quilt-topped sleigh beds, black and white TVs, and rotary dial phones. From the spacious, shady brick patio, you might see an Amish buggy drive by. Grilled sticky buns are a sweet treat at breakfast; at dinner there's a wonderful selection of seafood and beef in the old-time atmosphere of Zum Anker Room. The Vetters and their staff are kind and gracious." *(Donna West)* "Great soups, burgers, and salads in the coffee shop; relaxing atmosphere, courteous and friendly servers in the Zum Anker." *(Beth & Clare Boyer, also Donna Bocks)*

Open All year. Closed Christmas, New Year.
Rooms 2 suites, 10 doubles—all with private bath and/or shower, telephone, radio, TV, desk, air-conditioning.
Facilities Lobby with fireplace, coffee shop, restaurant, bar/lounge, library, patio, off-street parking.
Location On the Square, at corner of Main & Broad Sts.
Restrictions Non-smoking area in dining room; smoking permitted in guest rooms.
Credit cards Amex, Discover, MC, Visa.

Rates Room only, $75–100, suite, double, $60–85 single. Extra person, $4. Alc lunch, $6; alc dinner, $25–35.
Extras Cribs.

Swiss Woods Inn ♞
500 Blantz Road, 17543

Tel: 717–627–3358
800–594–8018
Fax: 717–627–3483

In a town founded by German settlers with many houses dating back to the 18th century, the Swiss Woods Inn is a delightful anomaly. It's a contemporary house, built as a B&B in 1985, and the atmosphere you'll enjoy at the inn is Swiss, not German. Owner Werner Mosiman is a native of Switzerland, and he has fashioned the inn after the chalets that dot the Swiss hillsides. The main common area, the Anker Stube, is dominated by a massive sandstone fireplace and is the heart of the inn's activities. Werner's wife Debrah is a Lancaster County native, expert in finding out-of-the-way quilt and woodworking shops and farmers' markets, and in arranging dinners with Old Order Amish or River Brethren families. The Mosimans cultivate large gardens to supply fruit, vegetables, and flowers for the breakfast table which may include cinnamon raisin French toast stuffed with berry cream cheese, lemon brandied apples, sausage, or egg sausage souflé, fresh fruit cup, lemon ricotta muffins, freshly baked croissants, and homemade jams and granola.

"A great way to experience a bit of Switzerland. We enjoyed the wooded setting overlooking rolling farmlands, the spotless home, natural wood beams, lace valances, and Swiss specialties and breakfast." *(Betty Norman)* "Charming views of Speedwell Forge Lake; flowers everywhere. Inside it is airy and light, with natural pine and oak, and simple, handsome Swiss furnishings. Debbie has learned to cook with European flair after years of living in Switzerland, including such treats as birchermuesli, herb quiche, and cherry muffins." *(Ina Gartenburg)* "A candle-lit Christmas tree welcomed us as we stepped into the rustic entryway to find a roaring fire and hot appetizers with mulled cider." *(Elinor Currie)* "Little touches included a piece of Swiss chocolate placed on our goose down comforter at night. Tea, coffee, cookies, and fresh fruit were available in the common room, the Ankerstube, named for the Swiss artist who painted scenes of village life in the 1900s; prints of his works are displayed throughout the inn. The Mosimans are attuned to meet the special needs of guests in a most natural and unobtrusive manner." *(Hans Fickenscher)*

Open All year. Closed Dec. 24, 25.
Rooms 1 suite, 6 doubles—all with private bath and/or shower, radio, clock, air-conditioning, deck. 2 with whirlpool tub, desk, 4 with balcony, patio, or deck. Telephone on request.
Facilities Dining room, common room with fireplace, TV/VCR, stereo, books; guest kitchen; patio. 27 acres with meadows, gardens. Hiking nearby.
Location 3 m N of Lititz. From PA Tpke., take Exit 21. Follow Rte. 222 S to the Rte. 322 W. Exit (Ephrata). Go left on Rte 501. Go right on Brubaker Valley Rd. for 1 m. Go right on Blantz Rd. B&B 1st on left.
Restrictions No smoking. Children over 12. "No children in rooms with whirlpools."

Credit cards Discover, MC, Visa.
Rates B&B $105–115 suite, $75–135 double. Extra person, $15. 2-3 night weekend/holiday minimum.
Extras Crib. German spoken.

MANHEIM

Information please: Families looking for an appealing getaway will enjoy **Penn's Valley Farm** (6182 Metzler Road, Manheim 17545; 717-898–7386), just six miles northeast of Lancaster. The 64-acre farm has been in the Metzler family since 1770, and guests are accommodated in an 1826 cottage, adjacent to the main farmhouse. The cottage has a living room with fireplace, and a winding stairway leading to the second floor bedroom. In addition to Colonial-style furnishings and hand-stenciled walls, it has a private bath, kitchenette, TV, and air-conditioning. The double rate of $65 includes a full breakfast served in the farmhouse; children under 12 stay free; over 12, $10. Another guest room is available (B&B, $50 double) in the farmhouse, with Victorian furnishings and a queen-size bed.

Herr Farmhouse Inn ¢
2256 Huber Drive, 17545

Tel: 717–653–9852
800–584–0743

While we love historic homes of all kinds, from the most extravagant Victorian to the plainest saltbox, we admit to a real soft spot when it comes to fieldstone houses—perhaps because they're so solid, stable, reassuring. Herr Farmhouse is just such a place. Built circa 1810, with foot-thick walls and blue-gray shutters and trim, its original sections date back to 1738.

Owned by Barry Herr since 1987, the farmhouse has simple white walls, painted wooden trim in Williamsburg colors, bright quilts, antiques and reproduction furnishings; Oriental carpets complement the soft gleam of the original wide-board pine floors. Breakfasts of fresh fruit and juice, cereal, a hot dish, plus scones, sweet rolls, or muffins, are served (8:30 on weekdays, 9 A.M. on weekends) in the dining room, in the kitchen before the huge walk-in fireplace, or in the brick-floored sun porch with wicker furnishings. One favorite guest room has a cherry-wood canopy bed, a perfect spot to cuddle up in the red flannel nightshirts provided by the inn, and watch the flickering flames of the fireplace illuminate the room.

"Barry Herr is a friendly, helpful innkeeper. The inn has a wonderful atmosphere and a quiet pastoral ambience. The third-floor suite has a beautiful view of the countryside; with a king-bedded room and another with twin beds, it's ideal for a family. Two friendly cats, too." *(MA)* "A crackling fire in the parlor made it an appealing gathering place. Barry offered detailed maps and good advice on area activities and restaurants. We appreciated the terry robes and ample reading material." *(Anne & George Bailey)* "Our well-cared for room had a fireplace and good reading lights on both sides of the bed." *(Doree Kluss)*

Open All year.
Rooms 1 suite, 3 doubles—2 with private bath, 2 share bath. All with air-conditioning, clock. Some with fan, desk. 2 with fireplace.
Facilities Dining, living, common rooms with fireplaces; living room with piano, family room with stereo, TV, VCR, fireplace, piano, library with books, game room, sun porch. 11 acres with barns. Tennis, golf nearby.
Location 9 m NW of Lancaster, 2 m N of Mt. Joy. From Lancaster, take Rte. 283 W to Mt. Joy/Rte. 230 Exit. Turn right onto Esbenshade Rd. & then immediately go right onto Huber Dr. to inn on left. From Harrisburg, take Rte. 283 E to Salunga Exit. Turn right onto Esbenshade & left onto Huber Dr. to inn on left.
Restrictions No smoking. Children 12 and over.
Credit cards MC, Visa.
Rates B&B, $100 suite (sleeps 4), $75–90 double. Extra person, $15. 2–night minimum holidays, some weekends.

MATAMORAS

Also recommended: For a stopover if you're traveling I-84, *Peggy Vaughn* recommends the **Best Western Inn at Hunt's Landing** (900 Rtes 6 & 209, 18336; 717–491–2400), for its good restaurant and location bordering the Delaware River with views of mountains, river, ducks, swans. There are 108 motel rooms; the rate is $65–125.

MENDENHALL

Fairville Inn   *Tel:* 610–388–5900
Route 52, P.O. Box 219, 19357   *Fax:* 610–388–5902

In the heart of the Brandywine Valley, halfway between Winterthur and Longwood Gardens, and convenient to the Brandywine River Museum, the Hagley Museum, and the Delaware Museum of Natural History, is the elegant Fairville Inn, owned since 1986 by Patricia and Ole Retlev. Rooms are decorated in light colors with antiques; breakfast includes juice, toast, English muffins and scones, strudel, or muffins—"whatever is freshly baked that morning"—plus afternoon tea and home-baked cookies.

"Gracious, accommodating hosts, immaculately maintained inn. Sumptuous afternoon tea." *(Linda Freeland)* "A lovely, well decorated home with comfortable, large rooms. Innkeepers were helpful with directions and dinner recommendations." *(Elaine Bounds)* "Elegant in feeling with comfortable rooms." *(Pam Phillips)* "Pretty setting and grounds. Our quiet suite in the carriage house had a queen-size canopy bed, and a private deck overlooking lawn and woods." *(RSS)* "The main building has a small breakfast room, and a comfy living room with fresh flower arrangements and a roaring fire at tea time. Our large room was beautifully decorated with a four poster bed and flowered chinoiserie wallpaper with softly coordinating plaid fabric; lots of fluffy pink towels." *(Robin Clarke)* "We had the only twin-bedded room, facing Route 52, but it was quiet at night on our weekend visit. Five antique shops are just a block away. The owners are too modest about their wonderful pastries, and share their

cookie recipes generously. We enjoyed our dinner at Buckley's Tavern."
(Jim & Anne Gould)

Open All year.
Rooms 2 suites, 13 doubles—all with full private bath, telephone, TV, air-conditioning. 7 with fireplace; 9 with desk. Rooms in main house, barn, carriage house.
Facilities Living room with fireplace, breakfast room. On 3.5 acres. Canoeing, walking, bicycling, polo nearby.
Location Brandywine Valley. 8 m NW of Wilmington, DE. From I-95 take Exit 7 and go N on Rte. 52. Cross PA state line. Inn on right.
Restrictions Children over 10. Traffic noise in front rooms.
Credit cards Amex, Discover, MC, Visa.
Rates B&B, $180–195 suite, 125–$180 double. Extra person, $10. Corporate rates.
Extras Swedish spoken.

MERCER

Information please: We need current reports on the **Magoffin Guest House** (129 South Pitt Street, Mercer 16137; 412–662–4611 or 800–841–0824) located just north of I-80 in Mercer, in western Pennsylvania. A Queen Anne Victorian built in the late 1800s, it is decorated with period furnishings. Food in the Magoffin's restaurant focuses on traditional favorites. A total of ten guest rooms are located in two adjacent buildings. Rooms in the Magoffin Inn all have working fireplaces, while those in the John Orr House have air-conditioning and TV; B&B double rates range from $95–105; there's one room with a shared bath at $55. The area is a favorite of antiquers, with shops in all directions.

MERCERSBURG

The Mercersburg Inn ✕   Tel: 717–328–5231
405 South Main Street, 17236   Fax: 717–328–3403

Today, when most people would consider a house of 2,500 square feet to be spacious and many make do with far less, it's hard to imagine a private home of *20,000 square feet*. But that's just what Harry Byron built in 1910. Harry's wife quipped that she knew the house had forty closets, but that she really wasn't sure of the number of rooms. The foyer alone could double as a ballroom, with its gleaming parquet floors, rose marble columns, and curving double staircase. This Georgian Colonial mansion, set on a hill overlooking the Cumberland Valley to the Tuscarora Mountains beyond, was converted into an inn in the 1950s. Fran Wolfe bought the inn in 1986, and has returned the home to its original glory, restoring the original baths, and furnishing the guest rooms with locally crafted king-sized canopied beds. A recent menu included butternut squash soup, fettucini Alfredo, lemon sorbet, grilled salmon with lime-jalapeno butter, mixed baby greens with herb vinaigrette, and a pear tart with crème anglaise and raspberry sauce.

"Our extraordinary bathroom was absolutely wonderful with an enormous free-standing bath with mighty taps, plus a huge hip-bath, an enormous wash basin and a separate shower. Ample towels added to the luxurious feeling. Our vast bedroom had a huge balcony, a working fireplace, and two enormous walk-in closets. Our king-size four-poster bed was very comfortable with night tables and bedside lights on each side." *(Ellie Friedus)* "Without question, the most dramatic, elegant inn I have ever seen, with what has to be a four-star restaurant." *(David Humphrey)* Comments welcome.

Open All year. Dinner served Fri., Sat.
Rooms 15 doubles—all with private bath and/or shower, telephone, air-conditioning. Some with desk, fireplace, balcony.
Facilities Restaurant, 2 sitting rooms with fireplaces, porches, game room with pool table, TV, games, fireplace; porches. 5 acres with gardens. Tennis, golf, swimming, fishing, boating, hiking nearby. 10 min. from Whitetail Ski Resort.
Location S Central PA. Cumberland Valley. 90 min. from Washington, D.C. 3 blocks from town center. 10 mins. from Whitetail Ski Resort.
Restrictions No smoking. Children by prearrangement.
Credit cards MC, Visa.
Rates B&B, $110–180 double. Extra person, $25. Fireplace rooms—2-night minimum on weekends, holidays. Prix fixe dinner, $35. Alc dinner, $34. Alc menu available. Golf package, $166–236. Ski packages.
Extras Restaurant wheelchair accessible. Airport/station pickups, $20. Babysitting by prior arrangement.

MERTZTOWN

Longswamp B&B ¢ 🏃
1605 State Street

Tel: 610–682–6197
Fax: 610–682–4854

A country home built in 1770, Longswamp B&B has been owned by Elsa and Dean Dimmick since 1984. Before the Civil War, two of its outbuildings were used as way stations on the Underground Railroad. Breakfast is served at guests' convenience from 6:30–10 A.M., and includes juice, fresh fruit, bacon, and perhaps whole grain waffles, crepes, omelets, or bread pudding. Elsa is a chef, and notes that "we grow many of our fruits, all our vegetables, herbs, and flowers, and bake all our own muffins, coffee cakes, and breads."

"Warm, welcoming hosts. Appealing guest rooms; those in the Hideaway and Cottage are quite romantic. A secluded but wonderful oasis, with lots of places to explore within a one-hour drive." *(Laurie Ford)* "Lovely countryside setting." *(Angela Wiegand)* "Cheerful rooms; attentive staff; two big Labrador dogs to pet." *(G. Moffolt)* "Tastefully furnished with an eclectic mix of comfortable and antique pieces." *(Laura Dempsey)* "Beautiful gardens on the hillside to stroll through; a leisurely breakfast when we were ready for it." *(Michelle Powell)* "Fully equipped for children: swings, toys, large enclosed yard. Outstanding breakfast. Our room was clean, well-decorated, and in good working order." *(Kim Unicume)*

Open All year.
Rooms 2 suites, 8 doubles—6 with private bath and/or shower, 4 with maximum of 4 people sharing bath. All with radio, clock, air-conditioning, fan. 2 with TV, desk, fireplace. 2 rooms in cottage, 1 in Hideaway, 1 suite in barn.
Facilities Dining room, living room/library with piano, fireplace, books, stereo; porch, courtyard. 5 acres with gazebo, lawn games, swing set. Downhill skiing, bicycling, horseback riding nearby.
Location E PA, Berks Cty. Approx. 10 m W of Allentown, 15 m NE of Reading. Call for directions.
Restrictions No smoking.
Credit cards Amex, MC, Visa.
Rates B&B, $75 suite, $70–75 double, $60 single. Extra person, $30. No charge for children under 6.
Extras French spoken.

MOUNT JOY

Mount Joy is located in Lancaster County—Pennsylvania Dutch Country—about 11 miles northwest of Lancaster. Mt. Joy is also known for its restaurants, including Groff's Farm and Bube's Brewery, a historic brewery now home to three restaurants. If you're traveling during a busy time, ask your innkeeper to make dinner reservations for you.

Information please: Listed in many past editions is the **Cameron Estate Inn** (1895 Donegal Springs Road, 17552; 717–653–1773), one of Pennsylvania's best known inns. Dating back to 1805, it was purchased in 1872 by Simon Cameron, Abraham Lincoln's Secretary of War, who transformed the estate into a magnificent mansion, and planted the grounds with flowers and hundreds of beautiful shade trees. The mansion was restored as an inn and restaurant in 1981 by the highly regarded restaurateurs, Abe and Betty Groff. Recent reader reports on the staff, service, and breakfasts have been less than enthused. Double rates are $60–110.

For an additional area entry, see **Manheim**.

Cedar Hill Farm ¢ ♣   *Tel: 717–653–4655*
305 Longenecker Road, 17552

Although many innkeepers leave city life to put down roots in the country, Russel Swarr's roots run deeper. He was born at Cedar Hill Farm, home also to his father and grandfather. Russel and his wife Gladys restored their stone farmhouse as a B&B in 1987, decorating it simply but elegantly with floral wallpapers and 19th century antiques, many of them family heirlooms. Built in 1817, this working farm overlooks Little Chickies Creek. Cedar Hill has the original white pine floors, an open winding staircase, a walk-in fireplace, and an Indian door. Breakfast consists of fresh fruit, cheese, muffins, breads, jams, cereals, juice, coffee, and tea, and is served in the inn's spacious kitchen.

"Friendly, homey, quiet, and unpretentious; convenient location for day trips to Hershey and Pennsylvania Dutch Country." *(Gerry Maynard)* "Safety features included smoke alarms, night lights, and grab bars in the shower. Our room had a private balcony overlooking lush, green meadows." *(Winnie Barrell)* "Our corner room (#1) offered a great view from its three huge windows, and had a modern bath. The inn was surprisingly quiet; all four rooms were full but we didn't hear any of the other guests. Breakfasts were charmingly served with classical music playing in the background. The numerous 'barn cats' added to the country appeal." *(Meg McCormick)* "Delectable baked oatmeal and lemon bread for breakfast; freshly picked lilacs from the yard; strolling along the stream that wanders through the property. Altogether a delightful country treat." *(Mary Ann Pires)* "The Swarrs joined us at the breakfast table and told us about the area and its attractions." *(Peggy Probst)*

Open All year.
Rooms 5 doubles—all with private bath and/or shower, air-conditioning, radio, clock. 1 with balcony, whirlpool tub.
Facilities Dining room, sitting room with chess table and books, TV room with stereo, VCR, computer; porch. 51 acres with picnic facilities, cross-country skiing, stream for fishing. Tennis, golf, swimming nearby.
Location From Rte. 283 take Mt. Joy exit to Rte. 230. Go to bridge at "Welcome to Mt. Joy" sign. Take next left at Longenecker Rd. Cross bridge then take immediate left.
Restrictions No smoking.
Credit cards Amex, Discover, MC, Visa.
Rates B&B, $65–70 double, $55–60 single. Extra adult, $20; extra child, $8.
Extras Station pickup. Play equipment, games.

The Country Stay ¢
2285 Bull Moose Road, 17552

Tel: 717–367–5167

The Country Stay is an 1880s brick house owned since 1970 by Lester and Darlene Landis, who opened it as a B&B in 1987.

"Congenial and pleasant hosts; Mr. Landis sat at the player piano and entertained us." *(Doris Sands)* "Our scrumptious breakfast consisted of baked oatmeal, followed by meat and potato quiche and a homemade apple dumpling." *(Tammy Nowell)* "Gorgeous flowers greet you as you enter this perfectly manicured Victorian home." *(Diana Briggs)* "The owners have done a beautiful job of decorating—antiques, greenery, and gorgeous floral arrangements. Darlene, dressed in period costume, serves a scrumptious breakfast on beautiful china. The Landis' daughter Katie gave our girls a wonderful tour of the stone barn." *(Randy & Debbie Boggs)* "Mrs. Landis is genuinely interested in the people who stay at her inn; it is obvious that she loves her work." *(Diana Martin)* "We read on the front porch rockers, looking out over the cornfields and neighboring farms. While the inn is secluded and quiet, it is just minutes from restaurants and shopping. Our room had a four-poster canopy bed with a handmade Lone Star quilt." *(Kathy McIntosh)* "Darlene was helpful with area information, and showed us a video about the Amish life style. Old-fashioned bathtub and tons of fluffy towels." *(Mr. & Mrs. Donald Coop)*

Open April 1–Nov. 30.
Rooms 1 suite, 2 doubles—1 with private bath, 2 rooms share 1 bath. All with clock, air-conditioning, fan. 1 with desk.
Facilities Dining room, living room, family room with player piano, TV/VCR; porches. 98 acres with swing set.

Location From Lancaster, take Rte. 30 W to Rte 441 N (Columbia Exit), then to Rte. 743 N. Go through Maytown and go right on Bull Moose Rd. (about 1.5 m from Maytown). 1st farm on left.
Restrictions No smoking. Children 10 and over.
Credit cards MC, Visa.
Rates B&B, $100 suite, $60 double, $50 single. Extra person, $10. 2-night minimum holiday weekends.

Hillside Farm B&B
607 Eby Chiques Road, 17552–8819

Tel: 717–653–6697
Fax: 717–653–6697

Built in 1866, Hillside Farm served as a dairy farm through the 1920s, 30s, and 40s. Though no longer a working farm, this 1863 brick farmhouse is still surrounded by peaceful farmland. Owned by Gary and Deb Lintner since 1976, and restored as a B&B in 1989, guests describe this homestay B&B with enthusiasm, reporting that Gary and Deb are friendly, helpful, and knowledgeable hosts, and that their simply furnished home is immaculately clean, neat, and comfortable. Breakfast, served at 8:30 A.M., might include maple baked apples, whole wheat buttermilk walnut waffles with blueberry sauce, and local ham and scrapple.

"An old farmhouse in a quiet setting, with spacious bathrooms. Deb Lintner's breakfasts are innovative and delicious. She even hand-pitted their homegrown cherries for the outstanding cherry cobbler." *(Phyllis Sullin, and others)* "Deb and Gary treated us like royalty. I felt totally at home because of the atmosphere and cleanliness. Even the outside barn cats got over their initial shyness and made us feel at home." *(Martha Beiter)*

Open All year.
Rooms 5 doubles—3 with private bath and/or shower, 2 with maximum of 4 people sharing bath. All with radio, clock, air-conditioning. 4 with fan.
Facilities Dining room, living room with piano, TV/VCR, stereo, books, games; guest refrigerator; porch, balcony. 2 acres with hot tub, lawn games.
Location 8 m W of Lancaster. From Philadelphia: (60 m) Go W on PA Turnpike (I-76) to Exit 21. Follow Rte. 222 S to 30 W to 283 W. Take Salunga exit & turn left. Continue for 1¼ m. Turn right on Eby Chiques Rd. to first house on right.
Restrictions Absolutely no smoking. Children 10 and over.
Credit cards None accepted.
Rates B&B, $50–62.50 double. Extra person, $10.

Olde Square Inn ¢
127 East Main Street, 17552

Tel: 717–653–4525
800–742–3533
Fax: 717–653–0976

Right on Mount Joy's historic Old Square is the eponymous Old Square Inn, a neoclassic house built in 1917 and restored as an inn in 1991. Owners David and Fran Hand have decorated the inn with antiques and period furnishings. The dining room is done in peach and teal, with leaded glass windows, while the guest rooms have gentle floral wallpapers or hand-stitched quilts. Recent renovations include the addition of private baths for each guest room, plus new wallpaper and fabrics in one room, and furniture hand-painted by a local artist in another. A typical breakfast might include orange juice, pineapple brunch casserole, baked oatmeal, sour cream apple coffee cake, and banana nut muffins; in good weather, guests enjoy eating on the front porch.

"Attractive room with Victorian furnishings, yet not overdone. The bath was wonderful—great lighting and plenty of fluffy towels." *(Betty Norman)* "Convenient location in the center of town; well-maintained." *(Michael Stora)* "Clean, well-kept, with fine food and cheery decor, but best of all is Fran's helpfulness, friendliness, and ability to make you feel right at home." *(Cathy Bumbaugh)*

Open All year.
Rooms 4 doubles—all with private bath and/or shower, radio, air-conditioning, telephone, TV/VCR. 1 with whirlpool tub.
Facilities Dining room, living room with fireplace; video library, computer, fax; porch. ¼ acre with off-street parking.
Location In center, on historic square, on Rte. 230.
Restrictions No smoking. Children over 10 unless entire B&B is rented by family. Cat in residence.
Credit cards MC, Visa.
Rates B&B, $65–88 double. Extra person, $10. Reduced rates for families.

MUNCY

The Bodine House ¢   *Tel: 717–546–8949*
307 South Main Street, 17756

"Antique furnishings" is a descriptive phrase often used with abandon in B&B writing ("attique" is often more like it), but at the Bodine House, you'll find the real McCoy—from the 1750s high chest in the dining room to the jelly cupboard dating from the 1840s. Long-time owners David and Marie Louise Smith have complimented their handsome antiques with hand-painted stencils, Waverly fabrics, and reproduction Williamsburg wallpapers. Built in 1805, the house is listed on the National Register of Historic Places. Breakfast served from 7:30–8:30 A.M., is ordered from a menu the night before, and includes your choice of juice, cereal, eggs or French toast, bacon, toast, muffin, or sweet roll, coffee, tea, or milk. Afternoon refreshments are served between 5:00 and 7:00 P.M.

"Delightful B&B in the heart of historic Muncy, beautifully restored and furnished. Picturesque surroundings coupled with the tender care of Mr. and Mrs. Smith make for an unforgettable experience." *(Betty Norman)* Comments appreciated.

Open All year.
Rooms 1 carriage house with private bath, kitchenette, 4 doubles—all with private bath and/or shower, clock, air-conditioning. 1 with TV, desk, fireplace.
Facilities Dining room with fireplace, parlor with piano, sitting room with fireplace, TV, library. Bicycles, patio, off-street parking. Lawn games. Fishing, boating, hiking, cross-country skiing nearby.
Location Central PA. 14 m E of Williamsport. Approx. 10 min. drive from I-80 via I-180. From I-180, take Muncy Main St. exit. Turn left 1 m to inn on right. 3 blocks from center.
Restrictions Traffic noise possible in front room. No smoking. Children over 6.
Credit cards Amex, MC, Visa.

Rates B&B, $125 carriage house, $50–70 double, $50–60 single. Extra person, $10. No tipping.
Extras Limited wheelchair access; suite bathroom specially equipped. Airport pickups, $10.

NAZARETH

Also recommended: In eastern Pennsylvania, a few miles north of Route 22 and Allentown is a **"Classic Victorian"** (35 North New Street, 18094; 610–759–8276), a turn-of-the-century Victorian home with bay windows and a wraparound porch. The house is decorated with period furnishings, Oriental carpets, and lace curtains. Each of the three air-conditioned guest rooms has a private bath. "Elegant furnishings—antiques, candles and flowers. Many delicious breakfast choices, beautifully served on Wedgwood china. Delightful innkeepers, relaxing atmosphere." *(Michelle Silfies)* Nazareth is the oldest Moravian settlement in the U.S.

NEW CUMBERLAND

Farm Fortune ¢   *Tel: 717–774–2683*
204 Limekiln Road, 17070

In 1785, Peter Hursh purchased 490 acres of land for three of his sons, and called the land Farm Fortune. This was the name Chad and Phyllis Combs chose when they restored the house as a B&B and brought it back to its original appearance. Legend says the limestone farmhouse, set high on a hill overlooking Yellow Breeches Creek, was part of the Underground Railroad. Breakfast includes fresh fruit, warm breads, juice, coffee and tea; early or full breakfasts are available with advance notice. In summer, breakfast may be served on the deck overlooking the creek.

"Exquisite antiques complemented by fine reproductions are harmonized to perfection without sacrificing comfort or convenience. Unstinting hospitality." *(J. Preston Fambrough)* "With all the beautiful early American antiques, you feel as if you are staying in a museum—with none of the stuffiness. The Combs are a delightful couple who make their guests feel immediately at home." *(Betty Norman)* "Firm, comfortable mattresses. Breakfast breads were delicious." *(Beverly Malmendier)* "Easy-to-find location between two highways. You can hear traffic, yet the farm is peaceful." *(Elisabeth McLaughlin)* Comments appreciated.

Open All year.
Rooms 4 doubles—2 with private bath, 2 rooms sharing 1 bath. All with air-conditioning. 2 with porches.
Facilities Dining room, family room with walk-in fireplace, terrace, antique shop. 3 acres with tubing, hiking, fishing, picnic area. 10 m to downhill skiing.
Location Across river from Harrisburg. Just off PA Tpke. and I-83. Call for directions.
Restrictions No smoking. No children under 10.
Credit cards Amex, DC, Discover, MC, Visa.
Rates B&B, $65–85 double, $57–77 single. Extra person, $15.

NEW HOPE

See chapter introduction for information on New Hope and Bucks County, as well as additional accommodation suggestions in the general area.

Reader tips: "In spring and summer, we learned, always make reservations in this busy area, both for rooms and dinner. Then enjoy the countryside, where any turn off the main road will bring you by farms and fields." *(LCR)* Also: "Be sure to walk across the bridge to Lambertville for lovely views up and down river, and to explore the New Jersey side." *(MW)* And: "We had one of the finest meals we've ever had at the *Inn at Phillips Mill*. The inn is a lovely old stone building with great ambience—everyone's picture of a Colonial inn. We enjoyed strolling through Lambertville, but thought that New Hope had become too touristy." *(WH)* "The New Hope area is certainly a place in which to experience tourist overwhelm. I would, in future, avoid a weekend visit at all costs." *(LI)*

Also recommended: If you prefer a small hotel atmosphere (and don't mind some street noise from the busy main street), the **Logan Inn** (Ten West Ferry Street, 18938; 215–862–2300) has an ideal in-town location, an easy walk to all restaurants and the playhouse. "Drinks and food readily available in the bar and restaurant—fun places to meet locals and other visitors. We enjoyed being able to walk all over town. Guest rooms are clean, neat, and plain, with good showers, firm beds. Delicious French toast and bacon for breakfast. Owner Gwen Davis was efficient and generous with suggestions, directions, and local chat. No sitting room for overnight guests, regrettably." *(Janeen LaFaver)* B&B double rates for the 16 guest rooms range from $75–150.

Another hotel option is the **Golden Plough Inn** (Peddler's Village, Box 218, Lahaska 18931; 215–794–4004), is a 45-room property offering spacious rooms with canopied and four-poster beds as well as private TV, telephone, refrigerator, and sitting area; many have Jacuzzi tubs and/or gas fireplaces, and B&B double rates range from $95–200. "Our suite had a fireplace, Jacuzzi tub, and Victorian-style furnishings; great staff." *(Sandy Oliver)* "Our room was furnished with a canopy bed and fluffy down comforter; welcoming touches in the room included a fruit-filled basket and a chilled bottle of champagne. The inn is located within Peddler's Village, with over 70 shops." *(Marion Osojnak)*

Information please: The recently renovated **Mansion Inn** (9 South Main Street, P.O. Box 117, 18938; 215–862–1231) is a handsome 1865 Second Empire Victorian home, within walking distance of local shops and restaurants. B&B double rates for the seven guest rooms, each with private bath and telephone, range from $185–205, and include wakeup coffee and newspaper, a full breakfast, afternoon refreshments, turndown service with homemade cookies, and use of the inn's swimming pool. Some rooms have double Jacuzzi tubs, fireplaces, and TVs, and all are elegantly furnished with antiques, fine fabrics and linens.

Listed in previous editions, we need current reports on two well-known and attractive inns, located four miles west of New Hope. **Ash Mill Farm** (Route 202, P.O. Box 202, Holicong 18928; 215–794–5373) and **The Barley Sheaf Farm** (Route 202, Box 10, Holicong 18928; 215–794–5104) are practically across from each other; both are set far back enough from the road to ensure a peaceful quiet setting, and both offer handsome, antique-filled rooms and filling breakfasts. The Barley Sheaf was purchased in 1994 by Veronika and Peter Süess; B&B double rates range from $105–195, including a full breakfast and afternoon treats and refreshments.

For additional area entries, see listings in **Doylestown, Erwinna, Gardenville, Point Pleasant,** and **Wrightstown.**

The Wedgwood Collection of Historic Inns ⛴

111 West Bridge Street, 18938-1461

Tel: 215–862–2570
215–862–2520
Fax: 215–862–2570

Carl Glassman and Nadine (Dinie) Silnutzer opened the Wedgwood in 1982, are continually improving and upgrading their inn. The Wedgwood's most recent addition was personal, however, not architectural—Carl and Dinie's daughter Jessica was born in 1994. Guest rooms are located in three 19th-century buildings: The Wedgwood, Umpleby House next door, and the Aaron Burr House, a short distance away on Bridge Street. Carl points out that "our land was the bivouac site of George Washington's army in 1776, before the famous Christmas Eve crossing of the Delaware." "Carl and Dinie interact easily and frequently with guests, and are very much involved with the details of innkeeping and life in New Hope. They live in a separate house behind the Wedgwood, but there's a resident innkeeper in each of the buildings, and each has its own handsome parlor and dining area. Behind the Wedgwood and Umpleby houses is an inviting backyard with gardens, gazebos, and a guest cottage comfortable for families. Carl claims that the Umbleby House is haunted, and happily regaled us with ghost stories; our favorite room there is the enclosed second-floor sunporch, with windows on three sides and a brass bed with patchwork quilt." *(SWS)*

"The Wedgwood is run with the efficiency of a highly professional operation, yet with warmth and hospitality." *(David & Joanna Sachar)* "Our room in the Aaron Burr House had a king-size mahogany four-poster bed with lots of fluffy pillows." *(Arlene & Hal Pugach)* "We were welcomed with wassail and cookies; dinner recommendations and reservations were made with pleasure." *(Chris Torres)* "We were greeted with delicious chocolate chip cookies and iced tea. After dinner we returned to the living room to read, listen to classical music, munch on apples and cookies, and make ourselves a cup of tea." *(Jean & Leonard Paul)* "Parking is ample and well lighted; we didn't use the car all weekend." *(Denise Stoklosa)*

"Our first room was quite large, beautifully decorated in a mixture of Victorian antiques and country crafts and quilts. We are light sleepers, and asked to move to a quieter room, which was arranged quickly and graciously. Our bathroom was small, but all facilities were new, spotless with great shower pressure and plenty of hot water. Breakfast included ricotta cheese muffins, fresh fruit with yogurt, bran, and terrific coffee." *(Perri & Michael Rappel)* "Terrific strawberry cheese croissants and lemon-poppyseed muffins." *(James Page)*

Open All year.
Rooms 1 cottage, 6 suites, 10 doubles—all with private bath and/or shower, radio, desk, air-conditioning, fan. 9 with gas fireplace. 2 with telephone, TV. Rooms in 4 buildings.
Facilities 3 parlors with fireplaces, 2 dining rooms, 2 sun porches, veranda with hammock. 2 acres with gazebo, lawn games, gardens, cross-country skiing. Club privileges for swimming, tennis.
Location Bucks County. Historic district, 2 blocks from center. From NY, take NJ Turnpike S to Exit 10; take Route 287 N for 15 miles; Rte. 202 S for 30 m over Delaware River Bridge. Take first New Hope exit; follow Rte. 32 S 1 m to traffic light. Turn right on Bridge St. to inn at top of hill on left.
Restrictions Traffic noise in front rooms. No smoking.
Credit cards Amex, MC, Visa.
Rates B&B, $120–185 suite, $80–150 double, $75–95 single. Extra person, $20. 2-3 night holiday/weekend minimum. Hiking/bicycling packages.
Extras Limited wheelchair access. Babysitting. French, Dutch, Spanish, Hebrew spoken. Station pickup. Passover breakfast menu.

The Whitehall Inn
Tel: 215–598–7945
1370 Pineville Road, RD 2, Box 250, 18938

The Whitehall Inn is an elegant country manor house, with high ceilings, wide pine flooring, and wavy-glass windows; it's been owned by Mike and Suella Wass since 1985. Rooms are furnished with antiques, and rates include a multi-course breakfast, beautifully served on fine china, with crystal and sterling. A typical menu includes freshly squeezed orange juice, cranberry poached pears in vanilla custard, buckwheat biscuits with raspberry jam, scones, walnut streusel coffee cake, chilled strawberry soup, and soufflé French toast with sausage. Provided in each guest room are bedtime chocolates, velour robes, homemade rose potpourri, imported toiletries, and a bottle of local wine. "The inn was built circa 1794 and has warm and friendly parlors and inviting porches. Convenient to New Hope with a quiet country location." *(Phyllis Farlow)* "Books with guest-written reviews of area restaurants sit next to sample menus." *(Nancy Wolff)* "The Gerald McGimsey room gets high marks from me, with its antique furnishings, working fireplace, and comfortable four-poster bed. Add to this the double chocolate truffles at bedtime and the outstanding breakfast." *(Betsy Anderson)* "Suella's breakfasts set the pace for a leisurely day ahead, which Mike is more than willing to help you plan. Tea is served each afternoon promptly at 4 P.M., and one can use this time to gather ideas for dinner. Good reading material is abundant in the large living room." *(Elizabeth Sommer)* Reports needed.

Worth noting: "Telephone for information or to make reservations; the inn does not appear to have a brochure."

Open All year.
Rooms 6 doubles—4 with private bath, 2 with maximum of 4 people sharing bath. Most with desk, fireplace.
Facilities Dining room, parlor with fireplace, games, library, pump organ, piano;

sun-room. 12 acres with rose garden, horse farm, swimming pool, tennis court (closed for renovation). Horseback riding/instruction.

Location Bucks County. 3 m from New Hope. Take Hwy. 202 S from New Hope to Lahaska. Go left on Street Rd. to 2nd intersection. Go right on Pineville Rd. for 1.5 m to inn on right.

Restrictions Children over 12. Absolutely no smoking. *Rigid 21-day cancellation policy.*

Credit cards Amex, CB, DC, Discover, MC, Visa.

Rates B&B, $130–190 doubles. 2-3 night weekend/holiday minimum.

Extras Airport/station pickup.

NEW KINGSTON

Kanaga House   *Tel: 717–697–2714*
6940 Carlisle Pike, 17072   717–766–8654

A limestone manor house built in 1775, Kanaga House was bought by the Kretzing family in 1969. Her children grown, owner Mary Kretzing opened her home to B&B guests. The interior is furnished in traditional Colonial style with lovely wood paneling surrounding the many fireplaces.

"The exterior retains its neat stone front and eyebrow windows, while the inside has been lovingly restored and carefully modernized. I stayed in an oversized bedroom with a modern private bath stocked with numerous towels and glycerin soap. The bed was a four-poster and extremely comfortable; the room was tastefully furnished with antiques and knickknacks. The house has a number of inviting sitting areas for relaxing. When asked what I would like for breakfast, I said that I wanted to eat lightly; the next morning, I arrived in the kitchen at the time requested, and was delighted to find fresh baked hot mini-muffins, fruit salad, excellent coffee, fresh juice, and delicious jams. A frame shop is connected to the main house and is run by the innkeeper's son Dave." *(Mark Corigliano)*

Open All year.

Rooms 5 doubles—3 with private bath and/or shower, 2 with a maximum of 4 people sharing bath. All with radio, clock, desk, air-conditioning. 2 with TV, 1 with fireplace.

Facilities Country kitchen, dining room, living room, den, each with fireplace. Den with TV, refrigerator, wet bar. 2 acres with patio, gazebo, gardens, off-street parking, nature sanctuary. Hiking, trout fishing, golf, skiing nearby. 2 m to Appalachian Trail.

Location Central PA. Approx. halfway between Harrisburg & Carlisle. On U.S. Rte. 11, close to PA Tpke & I-81. From PA Tpke (I-76), take Exit 16, Carlisle. Go 3.3 m N on Rte. 11; from I-81 (Exit 17E) go 2.2 m on Rte. 11 N toward Harrisburg. At New Kingston, turn left at 1st house on left (looks like a driveway). Go to stop sign & look straight ahead for B&B.

Restrictions No smoking. Children over 11.

Credit cards Amex, MC, Visa.

Rates B&B, $65–85 double. Extra person, $15.

OXFORD

John Hayes House B&B ¢
8100 Limestone Road, 19363

Tel: 610–932–5347

Built in 1794 of bricks that were used as ballast in English ships, the John Hayes House was first used as a stagecoach stop; in 1850 it served as the Hayes Post Office and general store. In 1989, longtime owners Bill and Melissa Hostetter restored their home as a B&B; furnishings include primitive antiques, hardwood floors, and stenciling. A typical breakfast consists of fresh fruit and juice, an egg casserole, home fries, and home-made sticky buns. The inn's setting is pastoral; the Hostetters also have a working dairy farm, and their land is bordered by Amish farmland and a golf course. "Filled with antiques and folk art. The kitchen is redolent with the aroma of fresh garden herbs. Food is imaginative, tasty, skillfully prepared and served. Friendly and personable proprietors." *(John & Lisa Drozdowski)* "The Hostetter family was welcoming and helpful, making reservations for us at an enjoyable restaurant." *(Marjorie & Henry Zapruder)*

Open All year.
Rooms 3 doubles—2 with private bath, 1 with maximum of 4 people sharing bath. All with telephone, radio, clock, air-conditioning. 1 with desk. TV on request.
Facilities Kitchen with fireplace, dining room, living room, family room with TV/VCR, porch. 1½ acres with herb garden. Wyncote golf course adjacent. Boating, fishing nearby.
Location E PA. Chester County. 28 m SE of Lancaster, 22 m W of Wilmington, 5 N of MD border.
Restrictions No smoking. Children over 11.
Credit cards None accepted.
Rates B&B, $60–75 double, $50 single. Extra person, $15.

PARADISE

For an additional area entry, see listing for the **Oscelola Mill House** in nearby **Gordonville** (adjacent to Intercourse).

Information please: Housed in the carriage house of an old country gentleman's estate and surrounded by Amish farmland, **Frogtown Acres** (44 Frogtown Road, 17562; 717–768–7684) is furnished with antiques, down comforters, and paintings by local artists. "In the morning, you can hear the Amish horse and carriages drive by. Breakfast is served in a glass enclosed porch in the main house where you can look out over the fields. *Witness*, the movie with Harrison Ford, was filmed right down the street." *(Sue Baker)* The $60–70 B&B double rate includes breakfasts of fresh fruit, home-baked goods, and an entrée garnished with fresh herbs from the garden.

In nearby Bird-in-Hand is **The Village Inn of Bird-in-Hand** (2695 Old Philadelphia Pike, P.O. Box 253, Bird-In-Hand, 17505; 717–293–8369), a three-story stone house reminiscent of the Victorian era, with antiques, reproductions, and fresh flowers gracing each of the rooms. The $59–139 B&B double rates include a free two-hour tour of the Amish countryside. "The Bressler Suite was attractive and cozy, with a comfortable feather-bed. Friendly but unobtrusive innkeepers. Extensive continental breakfast buffet served from 7–9 A.M. Walking distance to the appealing shops of this appealing little village." *(Teresa Mulligan)*

Maple Lane Farm B&B ¢ ⁇   *Tel: 717–687–7479*
505 Paradise Lane, 17562

Edwin and Marion Rohrer have owned the Maple Lane Farm for over 25 years, and built a separate house for guests across the lane from their own 200-year-old stone farmhouse. The Rohrers farm 250 acres, and the usual sounds guests hear are the lowing of their dairy cattle and the clip-clop of their Amish neighbor's horses going down the road. Mrs. Rohrer can arrange for guests to visit one of her Old Order Amish neighbors who has quilts for sale. The guest rooms are decorated with quilts, hand-pierced lamp shades, needlework, and stenciling, all done by Mrs. Rohrer, along with poster and canopied beds. The guest parlor, painted white with Williamsburg blue trim, is furnished primarily with Victorian antiques. Breakfast includes fresh fruit, cereal, rolls, breakfast breads, cheese and meat tray, coffee, tea, and juice.

"The Rohrers are helpful, warm, and friendly, yet never intrusive. Rooms are decorated with local crafts, including the lovely quilts. Comfortable sitting room for guests; delicious sticky buns at breakfast. Children enjoy the baby animals and the opportunity to see the cows being milked." *(Doug Campbell)* "My attractive room had lovely views of the nearby farms. Marion drew up a map of local roads and explained the route she enjoys walking through the countryside. Guests are encouraged to come and watch their dairy herd being milked, and to stroll around the farm." *(Jane Doherty)*

Open All year.
Rooms 4 doubles; 2 with full private bath, 2 with maximum of 4 people sharing bath. All with TV, air-conditioning.
Facilities Parlor, guest refrigerator, porch. Spacious lawn with picnic table, play equipment, wading stream. 100-acre working dairy farm with 120 cows. Tennis, golf nearby; 1 m to Strasberg Steam Railroad.
Location Lancaster County, Pennsylvania Dutch country. 10 m SE of Lancaster, 60 m W of Philadelphia. Turn S on Rte. 896 off Rte. 30. Go 3 m to Strasburg. Turn left on Rte. 896 at traffic light and go 1 1/2 m out of town. Turn right at sign for Timberline Lodge onto Paradise Lane.
Restrictions No smoking or drinking.
Credit cards None accepted.
Rates B&B, $45–60 double. Extra person, $8; no charge for children under 3. 2-night weekend minimum.
Extras Crib.

Pequea Creekside Inn ♿
44 Leacock Road, P.O. Box 435, 17562

When you see the sturdy stone construction of the Creekside Inn, built in 1781, you may be reminded of the old lament: "They just don't build 'em like they used to!" Set along Pequea Creek, the Creekside was purchased in 1995 by Cathy and Dennis Zimmerman. Furnishings include four poster beds, locally crafted Amish furniture, and the Zimmerman's long-time collection of antiques. Breakfast menus might consist of oatmeal apple crisp, ham and cheese strata, and lemon poppyseed pound cake; or cranberry pear compote, applesauce pancakes, honey sausage, and pumpkin muffins. Rates also include afternoon tea with homemade sweets.

"Immaculate, warm, and comforting. Our room had a queen-size rice bed and a stone fireplace. Cathy and Dennis were friendly and helpful, helping us select restaurants and offering sightseeing advice. Delicious breakfast of fresh fruit, pancakes, French toast, sausage, and ham." *(Keith & Kim Long)* "We were encouraged to sit in the living room in the evening and socialize with the other guests over tea, coffee, and homemade cakes." *(Mary Seidenberg)* "The Zimmermanns provided helpful insights into the Amish and Mennonite cultures. A duck had chosen the front entrance for her nesting place, adding to the inn's charm." *(Peter Palches)*

Open All year.
Rooms 6 doubles—4 with private bath and/or shower, 2 with maximum of 4 people sharing bath. All with air-conditioning, clock. 2 with fan, fireplace.
Facilities Dining room with fireplace, living room with fireplace, books, games; porch. 2 acres with swings, lawn games.
Location Lancaster County, Pennsylvania Dutch country. 10 m SE of Lancaster, 60 m W of Philadelphia. From 30 E, go left on Singer Ave. Inn on left.
Restrictions No smoking. Traffic noise, small bathroom in 1 room. Children 10 and over.
Credit cards MC, Visa.
Rates B&B, $60–100 double, $49–89 single. Extra person, $10–15. Winter weekend package. 2-3 night weekend/holiday minimum.
Extras Limited wheelchair access.

PHILADELPHIA

Philadelphia has come a long way since W.C. Fields issued his less than complimentary opinions of the city. In addition to fine museums and historical sights, the city now offers many restored neighborhoods, fine shops, and quality restaurants. History buffs will head straight for Independence National Historical Park, a collection of historic buildings including Independence Hall and Congress Hall, then to the Betsy Ross House and Elfreth's Alley, the oldest continuously inhabited street in the country. For more information, call or write the Visitors Center at 1525 Kennedy Boulevard, 19102; 215–636–1666 or 800–537–7676.

Reader tips: "We left our car in the garage and used the 'Philly Phlash' buses, powered by alternative fuel, for sightseeing. These buses make a loop connecting the city's major sights and neighborhoods. The restored century-old Reading Terminal Market is great for lunch; 75 vendors from a variety of ethnic backgrounds sell fresh produce, meats, fish, baked goods, flowers, and merchandise in the historic rail terminal. Our favorites were the wares of Lancaster Country Amish and Mennonite farmers." *(BNS)* And: "For information on free events, pick up a copy of the *Town Crier*, distributed by a man in a tri-cornered hat near the Liberty Bell Pavilion; I discovered a delightful free musical about Ben Franklin. Also noteworthy was my dinner at the 18th century City Tavern at 2nd and Walnut, where the waitstaff dress in period clothes; delicious duck with peach chutney." *(Janet Collinge)*

Also recommended: "I used a reservation service called the **Association of B&Bs of Philadelphia/Valley Forge/Brandywine** (P.O. Box 562, Valley Forge, 19481–0562; 610–783–7838 or 800–344–0123) and was pleased with the arrangements. On one visit I stayed in **Mrs. Ritz' Rooms**, a historic row house not far from Rittenhouse Square. My suite had a sitting room, bedroom, bath, walk-in closet, and refrigerator, with Art Deco collection antique decor. Comfortable and cheery. Vegetarian gourmet breakfast served in an atrium off the kitchen. Friendly, caring, eccentric owner. On another visit, I tried the **Society Hill B&B**, an 1805 Federal-style row house—attractive, comfortable, and decorated with antique architectural components salvaged from historical landmarks. Comfortable bedroom, modern bath, delicious breakfasts." *(Marion Ruben)*

Information please: An appealing, affordable B&B hotel is the **Abigail Adams B&B** (1208 Walnut Street, 19107; 215–546–7336 or 800–887–1776), in a century-old brick building, restored and operated by Robert and Tom Murray. Its 32 guest rooms have private bathrooms, cherry wood Colonial-style furnishings, queen-size four poster beds, cable TV, AM/FM radios, plush towels, and air-conditioning. The location is convenient, a short walk from the convention center, major hospitals, and business, cultural and historic attractions. Suites are $110 per night, doubles $80, including a continental breakfast; parking is $8 daily, and children under 13 stay free.

With just 27 rooms in a restored 1828 hotel overlooking the Delaware River, the **Penn's View Inn** (Front and Market Streets, 19106; 215–922–7600 or 800–331–7634) offers old world elegance in an intimate, distinguished setting. Thoroughly modern guest rooms have Queen Anne reproduction furnishings and state-of-the-art amenities, including terry bathrobes; B&B double rates of $99–175 include a continental breakfast, morning newspaper, and a welcoming glass of wine; some rooms have river views, gas fireplaces, and whirlpool tubs.

For an additional area entry, see **Wayne.**

Chestnut Hill Hotel
8229 Germantown Avenue, 19118

Tel: 215–242–5905
800–628–9744
Fax: 215–242–8778

"The Chestnut Hill Hotel is located in an elegant neighborhood of old stone houses along upper Germantown Avenue, a lovely part of town with upscale shops and excellent restaurants. The guest rooms are spread out among three old buildings, the main inn and small lobby are in the largest building on the corner; the annex occupies the second floor over some shops, and the barn is at the back. We were in room #62, in the delightful old barn. Some of the barn-like features were retained when the building was renovated, including huge wooden beams and an immense gear-like structure with pulleys and ropes. Our room was at the rear of the building and was clean, simply furnished, and quiet. The queen-size bed was firm and comfortable with a skylight just above." *(Mark Menden-hall)* "Our large room in the annex was furnished in attractive Colonial reproductions, including two four-poster beds, a desk, sofa, and chairs, as well as extra pillows and blankets. The bathroom was stocked with a generous supply of thick towels and a wicker basket of shampoo, lotion, and French-milled soap. A charming touch was a small vase of fresh flowers on the vanity. Breakfast, served in a small dining room adjoining the entrance hall, included orange and grapefruit juices, pastries, bagels, English muffins, cream cheese, preserves, and a toaster for do-it-yourself-ers. The hotel's front porch is set with umbrella-shaded tables; the hotel restaurant serves lunch and dinner, and we sat out on the porch for a well prepared and served meal with freshly squeezed lemonade." *(Paul & Kathleen Molinar)*

Open All year.
Rooms 3 suites, 25 doubles—all with private bath and/or shower, telephone, radio, clock, TV, desk, air-conditioning. Rooms in main building, annex, and barn.
Facilities Lobby, breakfast room, conference room. Room service; free parking. Close to Wissahickon Park.
Location NW Philadelphia, about 25 min. drive from center city.
Restrictions Restaurant noise in some rooms in main building. 3 non-smoking rooms.
Credit cards Amex, DC, MC, Visa.
Rates B&B, $120 suite, $92–109 double, $82–99 single.
Extras Wheelchair accessible, some rooms equipped for disabled. Crib.

Independence Park Inn ♿   *Tel:* 215–922–4443
235 Chestnut Street, 19106   800–624–2988
                                      Fax: 215–922–4487

Built in 1856 as a dry goods store, the Independence Park Inn was restored in 1988, and is now affiliated with the Best Western chain. Listed on the National Register of Historic Places, this granite structure is home to a club-like lobby with leather settees and fireplace, where afternoon tea with cucumber sandwiches and cookies are served daily. In back is a glass-enclosed garden courtyard where guests can enjoy a breakfast of fresh fruit and juice, pastries, croissants, and bagels, coffee, and tea, and the morning paper. Guest rooms are comfortably furnished with quality reproductions.

"Our room had a king-size bed with a firm mattress and lamps on both sides of the bed. The writing desk was well stocked, and our large bathroom was supplied with plenty of towels. Guest rooms away from the street are exceptionally quiet for a city hotel, while those facing Chestnut Street have high ceilings and huge windows." *(Diane Wolf)* "Our lovely room facing Chestnut was furnished with Colonial reproductions and attractive window treatments." *(Kathleen & Paul Molinar)* "The delicious breakfast was served under a glass roof. Afternoon tea was offered in the warm and inviting lobby, giving me a chance to meet the other guests." *(Carol Sommers)* "Rooms lovely, refreshing afternoon tea; the hotel was pleasant, convenient, and friendly." *(Celia McCullough)* "Our room was furnished with two queen-sized beds, a love seat, coffee table, TV discreetly hidden in an armoire, chair, and adequate bedside lighting. Ideally located directly across the street from the Visitors' Center, and within easy walking distance of Independence Hall. Helpful manager and front desk staff." *(BNS)*

Area for improvement: "More attention to detail in maintenance and housekeeping."

Open All year.
Rooms 36 suites, doubles—all with full private bath, telephone, radio, TV, desk, air-conditioning.
Facilities Lobby with fireplace, dining room, atrium, meeting rooms. Parking in municipal garage, 1 block away. Health club privileges.
Location Historic Independence Square area, 2 blocks from Independence Mall.
Restrictions Smoking restricted to some guest rooms. Traffic noise in some rooms.
Credit cards Amex, DC, MC, Visa.
Rates B&B, $155 suite, $130–145 double, $120–135 single. Extra person, $5. 10% senior discount.
Extras Wheelchair access. Crib. French, Spanish spoken. Best Western hotel.

The Latham Hotel ♙ ✕

135 South 17th at Walnut Street, 19103

Tel: 215–563–7474
800–LATHAM-1
Fax: 215–563–4034

A small, elegant, European-style hotel, The Latham offers such amenities as nightly turndown service with chocolates, and the Wall Street Journal delivered to your door on weekday mornings. "A return to the friendly atmosphere of The Latham adds to the excitement of being in the city. It is ideally located for shopping, attending the theater and concerts. Rooms are cheerfully decorated with excellent lighting and have been designed with comfort in mind. Special weekend rates include an excellent breakfast." *(Betty Norman)*

Open All year.
Rooms 138 suites, doubles—all with full private bath, telephones with computer/modem hookups, TV, air-conditioning, desk. Some with mini-bar, microwave, safe.
Facilities Lobby, restaurant, bar/lounge. Concierge, business services. Valet parking; garage 1/2 block away. Nearby health club with pool, sauna.
Location 1 block from Rittenhouse Square. Walking distance to historic attractions, business, financial districts. 2 blocks to mass transit.
Restrictions Some non-smoking guest rooms.
Credit cards Amex, CB, DC, Discover, Enroute, MC, Visa.
Rates Room only, $150–180 suite, double, $130–160 single. Extra person, $20. No charge for children under 18. Weekend packages; AAA, corporate rates.
Extras Airport pickups. Several foreign languages spoken.

The Rittenhouse Hotel ♠ ✕ ♿
210 W. Rittenhouse Square, 19103

Overlooking Rittenhouse Square, the Rittenhouse Hotel has one of the best locations in the city. This 6.5 acre park is an oasis of green and quiet, yet is just a few blocks from the Academy of Music, and central to the city's business, cultural and shopping areas. A new 33-story building, the hotel occupies its middle floors; the lower floors are filled with retail and commercial space, while the top floors are home to luxury condominiums. The Rittenhouse has four times earned the AAA five-diamond award for its superior facilities, impeccable service, and highest standards of quality.

Four restaurants are housed here: George Perrier, of Bec Fin fame, has recently opened a French bistro overlooking the square; Tree Tops, serving American regional cuisine; the Cassatt Tea Room, for afternoon tea and evening cocktails, with artwork by Mary Cassatt; and the Boathouse Row Bar, with the casual ambience of an old Schuylkill River rowing club.

"Extraordinary staff and attention to detail, starting with the glorious floral display in front lobby. Our spacious, luxurious room was furnished with two queen-sized beds, several chairs, chest of drawers, armoire with TV/VCR, well-stocked mini-bar, desk, separate dressing area with large mirrored wall, ample closet space with terrycloth robes, and an oversized marble bathroom complete with TV, telephone, scale, hairdryer, make-up mirror, and Neutrogena amenities. We saw several other rooms, some decorated in a feminine, Laura Ashley style, others richly furnished with a more masculine, Ralph Lauren look. The work of four local artists is seen throughout the hotel, depicting local historical sites. The hotel's spa is extremely well-equipped, with state-of-the-art fitness machines, and a skylighted ceiling over the swimming pool." *(BNS)*

"Although rooms overlooking the square have the best view, the others have a pleasant view of the city. Even the least expensive rooms are handsome, with carved mahogany desks and rich upholstery. The weekend rate is a fabulous value." *(Diane Wolf)* "Suite 800 is my favorite—I never want to leave it." *(Kathleen Peters)* "The Boathouse Bar is fun, and the 210 restaurant is superb for its food, staff, and the beauty of the room, overlooking the square. We loved our room, the service, quiet setting, and the beautiful bathroom." *(Dr. Bettyruth Walter)*

Open All year.
Rooms 11 suites, 87 doubles—all with full private bath, telephones, radio, TV/VCR, desk, air-conditioning, fan, mini-bar.
Facilities 4 restaurants, lounge with evening entertainment, health club/spa, sun deck. Valet parking, 24-hour concierge.
Location Downtown between Walnut, Locust, 19th, 20th Sts.
Credit cards All major cards.
Rates Room only, $350–400 suite, $250–275 double. Weekend rate, $150–160. Extra person, $25. Children under 18 free in parents' room. Alc lunch $25, alc dinner, $50.
Extras Wheelchair access; apparatus for hearing impaired. Cribs. French, Spanish, German, Italian, Arabic, Japanese, Russian, Vietnamese spoken. Limo service. Pets with approval.

Shippan Way Inn ¢   *Tel: 215–627–7266*
418 Bainbridge Street, 19147   800–245–4873

A restored 1750 bed and breakfast located near South Street, the Shippen Way Inn appears as an oasis amid this area's many shops, restaurants and nightspots. A wrought-iron gate leads to a walled Colonial herb and rose garden behind the inn's two connected 18th-century houses, one brick, the other frame. Owners Ann Foringer, Homer and Raymond Rhule carefully restored these historic homes in 1989, exposing the original beams. Each guest room is decorated individually; the Stencil Room is furnished with a double pencil-post bed, stenciled walls, and working fireplace, while the third story queen-bedded Dormer Room has a sitting room and a stenciled floor. Access to both is via a narrow winding stairway, adding to the inn's historic authenticity. Breakfast includes fresh-squeezed orange juice, fruit salad, granola, cereal, home-baked goods, and Wolfeman's English muffins, and is served in the garden in good weather. The open kitchen, overlooking the garden, is decorated in yellow, periwinkle, and white, providing a cozy setting in cool weather. Tea or wine and cheese are served each afternoon.

"Great old place, perfect location, satisfactory room. Anne recommended excellent local restaurants. Friendly innkeepers and cat." *(Stephanie Roberts, also BNS)*

Open All year.
Rooms 9 doubles—all with private shower bath, telephone, clock, air-conditioning. 3 with TV, 1 with fireplace.
Facilities Breakfast room, living room with fireplace, walled garden. On-street parking; several parking lots nearby.
Location Downtown Philadelphia. 2 blocks from Society Hill. 6 blocks to Independence Hall.
Restrictions Smoking in living room only. Children 8 and over. Street noise in 3 rooms. Steep staircase.
Credit cards Amex, MC, Visa.
Rates B&B $70–105, double. Extra person, $10. Senior, AAA discount.
Extras Limited Spanish spoken.

The Thomas Bond House   *Tel: 215–923–8523*
129 South Second Street, 19106   800–845–2663
      Fax: 215–923–0504

A 1769 brick home located inside Independence National Historic Park and listed on the National Register of Historic Places, The Thomas Bond House was originally built for Dr. Thomas Bond, who co-founded Pennsylvania Hospital, the first public hospital in the U.S., along with Dr. Benjamin Rush and Benjamin Franklin. The Department of the Interior purchased and restored this building as part of the historic park. In addition to a full complement of modern amenities for both business and pleasure travelers alike, extra soundproofing was installed to reduce street and adjacent room noise. A full breakfast is served on weekends while a continental breakfast is served mid-week. Rates also include afternoon wine and cheese; always available coffee, tea, and soda; and evening turndown service.

"Inviting first impression, from the well-polished brass on the front door and well-manicured exterior to the beautiful, warm lobby. Only one block from the famous Old Original Bookbinders." *(BNS)* "Our room was small but charming; lovely ambience." *(Elaine Bounds)* "Terrific location, close to Society Hill, Old City, Independence Hall, and more. Parking garage next door. Rooms vary in size; ours was large, comfortable and attractive." *(Myra Malkin)* "Well-run and maintained; warm and inviting atmosphere. Warm cookies were set out at night; tea was brought to our suite on request. Breakfast included cereal, fruit, and warm muffins. The innkeeper was friendly and informative, not overbearing." *(Laura Kelly)* "My room was beautifully furnished with Colonial reproductions, a comfortable bed, with big fluffy towels and a hair dryer in the bath. Excellent security system." *(Dorothy Hutchinson)* "Saturday's breakfast was heart-shaped pancakes and scrapple; on Sunday, eggs Benedict and scones, with fresh fruit and orange juice, coffee and tea." *(MP)*

Open All year.
Rooms 2 suites, 10 doubles—all with private bath and/or shower, telephone, radio, TV, air-conditioning. 10 with desk, 3 with whirlpool tub, 2 with gas fireplace.
Facilities 2 dining rooms, parlor with fireplace, library; antique/gift shop. Municipal parking next door. Bicycles.
Location Historic district between Chestnut and Walnut Sts.
Credit cards Amex, MC, Visa.
Rates B&B, $160 suite, $90–130 double. Extra person, $20.

PITTSBURGH

The Priory—A City Inn ♦ ♿
614 Pressley Street, 15212

Tel: 412–231–3338
Fax: 412–231–4838

For 93 years The Priory housed the Bavarian and Benedictine priests and brothers of neighboring St. Mary's Church. In 1986, Ed and Mary Ann Graf restored the building as an inn, decorating the rooms with 19th-century antiques. Rates include breakfast, the weekday paper, and afternoon wine; Joanie Weldon is the general manager.

"Fully endorse existing entry! We were mailed directions and had no trouble finding our way to the inn, in a secluded section on the North Side where many homes are being refurbished—a nice neighborhood stressing its German heritage. Our mini-suite, #104, was furnished with real antiques, and was cool and quiet with central air-conditioning. It overlooked the lovely courtyard with flowers, shade trees and European-style tables and chairs. Antique carved oak furnishings, old silver, and complimentary wine created an inviting ambience in the parlor. A continental buffet breakfast, with lots of choices, was set up adjacent to the spacious dining room." *(Martha Banda)*

"The staff was especially helpful with dinner plans. Most guest rooms are decorated in combinations of navy, burgundy, or peach; they are handsome and elegant—not fussy. Most rooms have either a double- or queen-size white iron bed with brass trim, two or three Victorian armchairs, a table, lace curtains, and high stamped-tin ceilings. Our beautiful suite, #310, had a long and narrow living room with a soft peach leather sofa and two Victorian armchairs. The white tiled bathroom was well supplied with amenities." *(Susan Schwemm)* "Good German restaurants in the area; large city park nearby with aviary and playhouse." *(Jack Johnstone)* "Super clean all over. A sense of silence and peace, almost as if a monk or two might still be praying behind a closed door." *(Mary & Jim Rafferty)*

Open All year.
Rooms 3 suites, 19 doubles, 2 singles—all with private bath and/or shower, telephone, radio, TV, air-conditioning. Some with desk.
Facilities Breakfast room, sitting room with fireplace, library. Courtyard with fountain, outdoor seating. Off-street parking. Park nearby.
Location East Allegheny/Deutschtown. Across 9th St. Bridge, ½ m from center. Close to Warhol Museum, Carnegie Science Center, Natl. Aviary, Public Theater, Children's Museum, Three Rivers Stadium.
Credit cards Amex, DC, Discover, MC, Visa.
Rates B&B, $120–150 suite, $100–130 double, $65 single. Extra person, $10. Weekend rate, $92–120; Corporate rates. 10% AARP discount No charge for children under 7.
Extras Wheelchair access. Free weekday morning limo service to city. Crib, babysitting.

POINT PLEASANT

Tattersall Inn ¢   *Tel: 215–297–8233*
Cafferty and River Road, P.O. Box 569, 18950

Built in 1740, the Tattersall Inn is a plastered stone mansion painted pale lilac with cream trim and deep green shutters, owned by Herb and Gerry Moss since 1985. Rooms are furnished with antiques and decorated with Gerry's paintings and needlework, while the dining room is highlighted by Herb's collection of vintage phonographs. Though on a quiet lane, the Tattersall is only a short walk from a tiny country store where you can buy sandwiches and other picnic supplies, and just a bit farther to Point Pleasant Canoes, where you can rent canoes, rafts, and inner tubes; you travel upstream by bus, then you can float lazily back down to your starting point.

"We enjoyed evenings in front of the crackling fireplace in the gathering room. The Bergs had a selection of herbal teas, wine, cheese and crackers, and peanuts served on an antique wooden table. Excellent homemade muffins, fresh orange juice, good coffee, and interesting conversation among the guests at breakfast." *(Paula Lawrence)* "Surrounded by beautiful shade trees, the Tattersall has four large pillars supporting a balcony that runs the entire length of the second story." *(PBB)* "The baths have good lighting, ample towels, soaps and shampoo; delicious chocolate truffles await you at night. Interesting book of guest comments on area restaurants." *(Richard & Celia Schacher)* "Guest rooms have queen-size beds, with plenty of blankets and pillows; some bathrooms are quite small." *(Debbie Murray)* "Porches are ideal for reading or sipping complimentary afternoon cider and munching snacks." *(Diane Glass)* "The friendly owners are never intrusive, but always have great suggestions of places to see in the area." *(Julie DeMatteo)*

Open All year.
Rooms 2 suites, 4 doubles—all with private bath and/or shower, clock/radio, air-conditioning. Some with desk.
Facilities Dining room, library, common room with fireplace, guest refrigerator, TV, piano; 3 porches. 1½ acres with flower gardens, lawns. Swimming pool, boating, fishing, tubing, playground, hiking, bicycling, cross-country skiing nearby.
Location Bucks County. 8 m NW of New Hope. 2 blocks from village center. Take Rte. 32 to entrance just north of village.
Restrictions No smoking in guest rooms, dining room.
Credit cards Amex, Discover, MC, Visa.
Rates B&B, $94–109 suite, $70–94 double, $60–84 single. Extra person, $15. Senior discounts. 2-3 night weekend/holiday minimum.

READING

For an additional area recommendation, see **Bernville**.

Information please: About five miles northwest of Reading via Route 183 is **The Loom Room** (Old Berntown Road, RD #1, Box 1420, Leesport 19533; 610–926–3217). Dating back to 1815, this farmhouse served as a stagecoach tavern in the 1800s. Today, it is a small B&B and workshop for owner/weaver Mary Smith, and several looms are housed in the 18th century log weaving studio. Breakfast, included in the B&B double rates of $45–50, might consist of stuffed French toast; children under 12 stay free. "Our spacious room had a double and a twin bed, good lighting, country furnishings, and a drop-leaf table where we enjoyed wake-up tea and juice. Later, Gene prepared a delicious breakfast, and he and Mary sat down to eat with us. Plenty to do in the area, from hiking the Appalachian trail, to fishing and boating, to outlet shopping." *(April Burwell)*

The Inn at Centre Park ✕   *Tel:* 610–374–8557
730 Centre Avenue, 19601   800–447–1094
                                                  Fax: 610–374–8725

A Second Empire Victorian home built in 1877, The Inn at Centre Park was restored by Andrea and Michael Smith in 1989. The interior is elaborately detailed with quarter sawn oak and chestnut paneling, extravagantly sculpted plaster work, and beautiful stained glass windows. Though elegantly furnished in period, king- and queen-size beds ensure guests' comfort. Pampering touches include terry robes, bedtime chocolates, and more.

"Our beautiful suite was comfortably furnished with a queen-size bed, a large, immaculate bath with double stained-glass doors opening onto a balcony, a claw-footed tub and separate shower. Delightful owners; Andrea answered our many questions about the house and its restoration, and helped us select a restaurant for dinner. Breakfast found us at a long lace-covered dining room table with the other guests. Cooked by Andrea and served by Michael, it consisted of quiche, potatoes, fruit, hot sticky buns, freshly squeezed orange juice and great coffee." *(Jo-Ann Purser)* Comments appreciated.

Open All year. Restaurant open by reservation Thurs.–Sat. night, Sun. brunch.
Rooms 2 suites, 3 doubles—all with full private bath, telephone, radio, clock, desk, fireplace. 2 with TV, fan. 1 with balcony/deck. 2 rooms in carriage house.
Facilities Dining room, living room with fireplace, family room with TV, library, guest refrigerator, porches. ¾ acre with off-street parking. Hiking, cross-country skiing, fishing, boating, swimming nearby.
Location 60 m NW of Phila. 5 min to all major outlet shopping areas.
Restrictions No smoking. Children welcome in carriage house. BYO wine.
Credit cards MC, Visa.
Rates B&B, $130–160 suite, $85–130 double, $75–120 single. Extra person, $20. Corporate rate weekdays.
Extras Airport/bus station pickups.

SCHELLSBURG

Bedford's Covered Bridge Inn ¢   *Tel:* 814–733–4093
RR 2, Box 196, 15559

A farmhouse built in 1823, Bedford's Covered Bridge Inn is located adjacent to Shawnee State Park, and was restored as a B&B in 1991 by Greg and Martha Lau. Breakfasts of juice, fruit, hot entrée, muffins, breads, and toast are served from 8–9 A.M. on weekdays, until 9:30 on weekends.

"The inn sits next to Shawnee Creek and the Colvin Covered Bridge. All you hear in this quiet country location is the soothing sounds of the water. The homey rooms have comfortable beds, ample blankets, flannel sheets in winter, thick bath towels, and guest soaps. Martha's varied breakfast menu is happily served by Greg; garnishes from the garden bring 'boy-I-sure-didn't-expect-this' smiles to guests' faces, which only broaden after the first bite. Refreshments are served in the afternoon or evening—iced tea, apple cider, or coffee. The smoke house is a small, brick-floored building next to the inn, with a great fireplace, and lit by kerosene lamps. Guests often gather to relax over a glass of their favorite wine. Terrific fishing for bass and trout found just 30 feet away in the spring-fed stream." *(Ken Sepeda)* "A large living room beckons guests to relax in front of the fire. The smoke house has dried herbs and flowers suspended from the ceiling. Hiking trails leave directly from the house, and a large lake nearby provides ample opportunities for water sports in the summer and ice skating in the winter." *(Eric Lien)* "Several good local restaurants in the area. A perfect place for a quiet weekend, walks, nature watching or relaxing on the large, wraparound porch." *(Miriam Lerch)* "Martha and Greg were warm, gracious hosts, informing us of area activities and making dinner reservations." *(Joan Slonaker)*

Open All year.

Rooms 1 2-bedroom cottage with kitchen; 2 suites, 4 doubles—all with private bath and/or shower, radio, clock, air-conditioning. 1 with desk.

Facilities Dining room, living room, library, guest refrigerator, wraparound porch, smokehouse with fireplace. 30 acres with private limestone stream. 15 m of trails on site. Horseshoes, croquet. 2 min. to Shawnee Lake for boating, fishing, swimming, ice skating, sleigh rides. 20 min. to Blue Knob Ski Resort. Next door to Shawnee Park for skiing and hiking. Golf, fly fishing, sporting clays, bicycling nearby.

Location S central PA. 1 ½ hours E of Pittsburgh, 2 ½ hours N of Wash., D.C. 9 m W of Bedford. From I-76, Exit 11 (Bedford), turn right after toll station & go to Bedford business district. Turn right at 2nd light onto Pitt St. (Rte. 30 W). Go approximately 8 m to Schellsburg. 1 block past traffic light, turn left at Mill St. Extension sign. Inn is ½ m on the right.

Restrictions No smoking. No children under 12.

Credit cards Amex, Discover, MC, Visa.

Rates B&B, $95 suite, $75–85 double, $65–75 single. Extra person, $15. Winter packages. 2-night minimum stay holidays, fall foliage, special events.

SCRANTON

Also recommended: *Priscilla Breen* recommends the **Lackawanna Station Hotel** (700 Lackawanna Avenue, 18503; 717–342–8300 or 800–347–6888), an opulent neo-Classical structure built in 1908 and recently renovated, with an elegant lobby of Sienna marble walls and mosaic murals. Rates for the 145 guest rooms range from $89–179; hotel facilities include two restaurants, a health club, an indoor swimming pool and free parking.

SKYTOP

For additional area entries, see listings under **Canadensis**.

Skytop Lodge 🚶 🎿
Route 390, 18357

Tel: 717–595–7401
In PA: 800–422–7SKY
Outside PA: 800–345–7SKY
Fax: 717–595–9618

The natural beauty of the Poconos was scourged twice in modern times, once in the nineteenth century by the logging and leather tanning industries, which left the mountainsides bare of trees, and again, more recently, by much of the tourist industry, which reforested the slopes with gaudy billboards advertising tacky honeymoon havens. In this setting, Skytop is an oasis of old-fashioned elegance and good taste unequaled in the Poconos.

From its handsome stone lodge to its 5,500 wooded acres, all conceivable sports and activities are offered, from a full children's program in the summer to private downhill ski slopes and outstanding cross-country ski trails in winter. There's even a steep toboggan run, which rises high above the lake; when the ice is thick, you shoot down the track and across the frozen surface, slowing down in heaps of hay.

Although some rooms have old-fashioned hotel furnishings, many have been redone in country-style scrubbed pine furniture, comfortable wing chairs, and nature prints, with excellent lighting and newly retiled baths. The lodge and grounds are well maintained, with an airy indoor pool and a handsome outdoor one. The staff is friendly and accommodating, and the food is quite good considering the number of meals prepared daily. My husband enjoyed the old-fashioned 'sporty' golf course, completed in 1928, with its narrow fairways, and my children went charging all over the place with newfound friends, exploring every nook and cranny, trying out every possible activity. The highlights for me were the easy hike up the Trout Stream Trail to Indian Ladder Falls, and the Lodge's rooftop observatory with 35-mile views in all directions. If you're there on a Saturday night, do not miss the 'Grand March,' a longstanding Skytop tradition unchanged for decades." *(SWS)* "Food was abundant, suitable for kids and adults, and the enormous staff functioned smoothly." *(DS)* "The trail system has been expanded, great for our hiking crew." *(SB)* "Even in rainy weather, Skytop provides extensive possibilities, especially for our two boys." *(BNS)*

Suggestion box: "Bring the exercise room up to the level of the other facilities."

Open All year.
Rooms 165 rooms—all with full private bath, telephone, TV, desk, air-conditioning. Most in main lodge, some in neighboring cottages.
Facilities Lobby, dining room, bar/lounge, library, card room, game rooms, porches, exercise room. 5,500 acres with indoor and outdoor swimming pools, wading pool, hot tub, sauna, 7 tennis courts, paddle tennis, lawn bowling, croquet, badminton, archery, miniature golf, bicycling, children's activity program (summer), 18-hole golf course, lake and stream fishing, canoeing, boating, hiking, ice-skating, cross-country & downhill skiing, toboggan run.
Location NE PA, Pocono Mts. Approx. 100 m from NYC & Philadelphia. 1 m N of Canadensis. From I-84, take Exit 7, & take Rte. 390 S approx. 10 m to lodge on left. From I-80, take Exit 49 to Rte. 191 N to Canadensis, then Rte. 390 N to lodge on right.
Credit cards Amex, DC, MC, Visa.
Rates Full board, $270–295 cottage, $330–$395 suite, $240–295 double, $140–160 single. Extra person, $70. 2 children free in parents' room up to age 18 with $15 service charge & 2-night minimum. Extra adult, $70. 15% service. Midweek discounts. Senior, sports, weekend packages.

SLIPPERY ROCK

Information please: Under new ownership as of 1995 is the **Applebutter Inn** (666 Centreville Pike, 16057; 412–794–1844). This farmhouse, built in 1844, was fully renovated in 1988, and a nine-room addition was designed to blend with the original architecture. The handsome result is Colonial in appearance, and the inn is furnished in antiques and reproductions. B&B double rates for the eleven well-equipped guest rooms range from $79–125. The adjacent Wolf Creek School Café, a one-room school house built in 1899, is under separate management.

SOMERSET

The Inn at Georgian Place
800 Georgian Place Drive, 15501

Tel: 814–443–1043
Fax: 814–445–3047

A 22-room Georgian mansion built for a local coal and cattle baron in 1915, The Inn at Georgian Place was restored as an inn in 1993; Jon Knupp is the manager. Oak paneling, ornate fireplaces, gold leaf chandeliers, and an expansive marble foyer reflect the original splendor of the home. Breakfast is served at individual tables in the dining room from 8 to 10 A.M., and includes fresh fruit, muffins, an egg entrée, pancakes or perhaps French toast stuffed with cream cheese and pecans, with bacon, sausage or ham. Afternoon tea, open to the public, is served from 1 to 4 P.M., and cocktails from 1:00–9:00 P.M.; tours are given daily at 1:30 P.M. "Every room is professionally decorated with handsome reproduction furniture, many with king-size beds." *(Janet Payne)* "At tea, we enjoyed a selection of tea sandwiches, scones, and beverages in the bright and sunny dining room." *(Brenda & Anthony Mark Dalessandro)* "Quality renovation. Our luxurious room had a king-size bed, sumptuous pillows, lots of thick towels, and a discreetly hidden color television. On Sunday morning we read the Sunday papers from Washington, New York, and Pittsburgh, whetting our appetites for the main course with freshly squeezed orange juice, fruit, and muffins to die for. Helpful, considerate staff." *(Lester Nauhaus)* Reports appreciated.

Open All year.
Rooms 2 suites, 9 doubles—all with private bath and/or shower, telephone, clock, TV/VCR, desk, air-conditioning.
Facilities Dining room, living room with fireplace, library, verandas. Off-street parking. 15 miles to downhill skiing.
Location S central PA, Somerset County. 60 m E of Pittsburgh. 1 m to center of town. At Exit 10 off I-76, adjacent to Georgian Place Outlet Center.
Restrictions Some nonsmoking rooms. Children over 12.
Credit cards Amex, Discover, MC, Visa.
Rates B&B, $150–165 suite, $85–125 double. Extra person, $10. 10% senior, AAA discount. Afternoon tea, $8.50. Tour, $3.
Extras Local airport/bus station pickups. Pets with approval.

STARLIGHT

The Inn at Starlight Lake ¢ 🏃 ✕ 禾
Route 370, Box 27, 18461

Tel: 717–798–2519
800–248–2519

An inn since 1909, and owned by Judy and Jack McMahon since 1974, The Inn at Starlight Lake is a longstanding favorite of readers looking for a low-key, relaxing getaway at an affordable price. Adult couples are pleased with the quiet atmosphere, yet families are delighted with the child-oriented staff and low-key activities.

"We had a table on the porch overlooking the lake. Perfect martini. Dinner was excellent—black bean soup, salmon with shallot butter and wild rice for me, beef Stroganoff for my husband, generous portions of homemade desserts. Rooms in the inn are rustic and small, although some have newly redone bathrooms; rooms in the cottages are larger." *(Rose & Frank Ciccone)* "The inn is delightfully situated on a winding country road at the base of a mountain, facing a lake. There is a big, welcoming front porch with rocking chairs; a cozy front room with two woodburning stoves and assorted chairs and couches; and a series of charming bedrooms decorated with pretty wallpaper, prints, and antique furniture." *(JC)*

"Our favorites include their wonderful homemade breads and whole-wheat waffles, salads dressed with lemon and pine nut dressing. The soups, full of fresh vegetables, are hearty and delicious, especially welcome in cold weather. The cross-country ski trails are well groomed and marked." *(Micki & Jack Ginsberg)* "The inn is as rustic and informal as your own summer cottage. Still, once you are ensconced in your easy chair in the big lobby living room with a glass of wine in one hand, a good book in the other, you know this is what a holiday is all about." *(Judy Brannen & Larry Machun, also Diane Wolf)* "Judy recommended the comfortable, convenient split-level house adjacent to the inn for our group of four adults and four young children, and offered us a terrific off-season rate. It's dark and starry at night, and all you hear is the peepers." *(John Rounds)*

Open All year.
Rooms 1 suite with double whirlpool bath & private deck; 26 doubles in main house and separate cottages—20 with private bath, 7 with maximum of 4 people sharing bath. 12 rooms in annex. 3-bedroom house also available. Some with Jaccuzi tub, fireplace.
Facilities Restaurant, bar, reading room with fireplace, game room with mini-pool table, ping-pong; TV room. 4 acres with shuffleboard, tennis, biking, hiking, children's play area; cross-country ski trails with lessons and rentals. Starlight Lake for swimming, canoeing, boating, sailing, fishing/fly-fishing school. Riding, golf, downhill skiing nearby.
Location NE PA, Wayne County. Approx. 35 m SE of Binghamton, NY, 35 m NE of Scranton. From NY, take Rte. 17 W to Exit 87 (Hancock NY). Take PA Rte. 191 S to Rte. 370 W to Starlight.
Credit cards MC, Visa.
Rates MAP, $170–200 suite, $110–154 double; $64–94 single. Extra person, $49; children 7–12, $37; children under 7 free (food extra). 12% service. Weekly rates. 2–3 night minimum, July–Aug., Oct., Jan.–Feb., holidays. Theme weekends. Alc lunch, $5–7; alc dinner, $22–40.
Extras Crib, babysitting. Station pickup.

STATE COLLEGE

Carnegie House ✕ ♿
100 Cricklewood Drive, 16803

Tel: 814–234–2424
800–229–5033
Fax: 814–231–1299

Readers who love country inns but are less than thrilled with antique plumbing and wiring are always delighted to find a newly built inn.

Overlooking the 17th hole of Toftrees golf course, Carnegie House bids its guests a Scottish welcome—*Ceud Mile Failte* or 100,000 welcomes. Emulating Scotland's country houses, the owners built this inn in 1994 with many of the same details; hardwood floors, plush Oriental rugs, oak paneling, and roaring fireplaces. Its name pays tribute to Scottish-born American industrialist Andrew Carnegie, whose philanthropy built the library at nearby Penn State. Peter and Helga Schmid, hosts and part-owners, offer a continental breakfast buffet that includes juices, seasonal fruits, homemade granola, baked goods, and a tray of cheeses and meats. Lunch and dinner are served daily in the dining room, with cocktails offered in the Thistle Bar. A recent dinner included an appetizer of wild mushroom caps with herb butter and feta cheese, a salad of baby greens, baked rainbow trout with shrimp salsa, and a pear tart served with fresh almond cream. "The Schmids cannot do enough for you; delicious food elegantly served." *(Mr. & Mrs. William Yoder)* "Wonderful hosts; large rooms, exceptionally decorated; warm, friendly atmosphere in the public rooms; quiet neighborhood; convenient to downtown." *(John Thompson)*

Open All year. Restaurant closed Sun., Mon.

Rooms 2 suites, 20 doubles—all with full private bath, telephone, radio, clock, TV, air-conditioning, fan. 5 with desk, 2 with mini-kitchen, VCR.

Facilities Restaurant, living room, sitting room with fireplace, library with fireplace, bar/lounge, guest laundry, veranda. Fitness trail. Cross country skiing on golf course; 5 m from downhill skiing.

Location Central PA. 88 m N of Harrisburg, 140 m E of Pittsburgh. Take Mt. Nittany Expwy to Toftrees exit; go right onto Toftrees to 1st stop sign. Diagonally across intersection to Carnegie House.

Restrictions Children over 14 preferred. Smoking on veranda, porch.

Credit cards Amex, MC, Visa.

Rates B&B, $225–250 suite, $125–150 double. 2-night minimum Penn State home football weekends. Alc lunch, $12; dinner, $28–35.

Extras Wheelchair access; some bathrooms specially equipped. Airport/bus station pickups. Crib, babysitting. German, French spoken.

STRASBURG

Also recommended: Built in 1973 to replicate an 18th century Williamsburg inn, the **Historic Strasburg Inn** (Route 896, Historic Drive, 17579; 717–687–7691 or 800–872–0201) offers 100 rooms in five buildings on 58 acres of rolling Lancaster countryside. Guest rooms are furnished with Colonial reproductions, detailed with chair rails and crown moldings. A fitness room, game room, heated outdoor pool and public restaurant make this an ideal spot for families. B&B double rates range $55–115, children under 12 stay free, and dogs are welcome in some rooms. "Despite its size, this hotel has a warm atmosphere. It's set far off the road, yet is easily accessible to shops and attractions. Our room was well equipped with double beds, TV, and a modern bath; the reasonable rate included a breakfast of cereal, breads and muffins, fresh fruit and juice." *(Lana Alukonis)*

Limestone Inn   *Tel:* 717–687–8392
33 East Main Street, 17579   800–278–8392

Railroad buffs will want to make Strasburg their Pennsylvania Dutch country headquarters so they can be as close as possible to the Railroad Museum of Pennsylvania, the Strasburg Rail Road Company, and two mini-museums devoted to toy trains. To restore your strength after all that sightseeing, visit the Limestone Inn, built in 1786 and listed on the National Register of Historic Places. Used variously as a private home, post office, and school dormitory, this Georgian stone building with Germanic accents was renovated as an inn in 1986 by Richard and Janet Kennell.

Guest rooms have queen-size beds with locally made Amish quilts. Third-floor rooms, once occupied by the school students, still bear their initials on the wood moldings and doors. Breakfast, served promptly at 8:30 A.M., may include juice, fruit, French toast, ham, muffins, and tea or coffee. "Charming hosts, delightful room, enormous bathroom, comfortable bed, delicious breakfasts. They recommended an excellent restaurant for dinner, where we were treated most cordially. Three-way bulbs in all the lamps are a real plus for readers!" *(Karen Solomon)*

Open All year.
Rooms 5 doubles—all with private bath and/or shower, radio, clock, air-conditioning.
Facilities Dining room, living room with fireplace, stereo, books. ½ acre with garden, swings, lawn games (on request).
Location Lancaster Cty, PA Dutch Country. 160 m SW of NYC, 64 m W of Philadelphia. Historic district. From PA Trpke E, take Exit 20. Take Rte. 72 S into Lancaster, then Rte. 222 S. Go left on Rte. 741 E. Inn at fork of Rte. 741 & Rte. 896.
Restrictions No smoking. Children 12 and over.
Credit cards Amex.
Rates B&B, $75–95. Extra person, $20. 2-night weekend/holiday minimum.

STROUDSBURG

Information please: A 19th century manor house set on 43 wooded acres, **The Inn at Meadowbrook** (Cherry Lane Road, R.D. 7, Box 7651, East Stroudsberg 18301; 717–629–0296 or 800–441–7619) enjoys a quiet country setting in the Poconos. Guest rooms vary in size; some have been decorated with Ralph Lauren fabrics. The Manor House, built in 1842, has large bedrooms with both private and shared baths, while the Mill House offers five bedrooms with private baths. B&B double rates for $75–90, include a full breakfast. The dinner menu includes seafood with linguine, and veal with fontina and prosciutto. The inn has an equestrian center, complete with stables and a large indoor riding area. Other activities include downhill and cross-country skiing, ice skating, bicycling, fishing, swimming, tennis, and outlet shopping in nearby Tannersville.

Located atop its own 150-acre mountain overlooking the town of Stroudsburg, the Pirone family's **Stroudsmoor Country Inn** (P. O. Box

153, 18360; 717—421—6431) offers 30 guest rooms in the main lodge and cottages. Overlooking an outdoor Olympic-size pool, the dining room serves a virtual groaning board of buffet choices at breakfast, lunch, and dinner. The Marketplace, a cluster of country shops, occupies several of the older buildings on the grounds. The Natatorium provides guests with a 40-foot indoor pool and whirlpool spa." The main inn, dating back to 1840, houses the reception area, dining room, a piano lounge, small pub, and 15 guest rooms. A warm feeling is created by the wainscoted walls and fieldstone hearth. Rooms are decorated with country charm, period antiques, and country curtains." *(Carl Zito)* B&B double rates start at $89.

UNION DALE

Also recommended: Approximately 35 miles north of Scranton, close to the Elk Mountain Ski Resort, in the Endless Mountains, is the **Stone Bridge Inn & Restaurant** (RR3 Box 3112, 18470; 717—679—9200). This cluster of steep-roofed buildings offers twelve guest rooms and a restaurant and tavern; the recreational facilities include an indoor swimming pool, tennis courts, horseback riding, and nature walks. "Unique guest rooms, many with a corner fireplace and kitchen facilities; simply furnished and cozy. A continental breakfast of fresh breads, fruits, juices, coffee and tea was served in the lobby. Hardworking owners and staff eager to please." *(Joan Gray)*

UPPER BLACK EDDY

Bridgeton House on the Delaware   *Tel:* 610—982—5856
River Road (Route 32), Box 167, 18972

In 1836, Bridgeton House was built on the banks of the Delaware River, facing the old mill town of Milford, NJ. Originally a private residence, it was later converted to a candy store and bakery, and in 1955, to apartments. In 1981, innkeepers Beatrice and Charles Briggs rescued the building and began its restoration. Seventeen layers of linoleum later, the 100-year-old floorboards came to light, as did the original 1836 fireplace. Soundproofing and private baths were added as part of the renovation process; in 1989 they added a third-floor penthouse. Rooms are decorated with fresh flowers, country antiques and primitives, pottery, quilts, and Oriental and rag rugs. Bea's breakfasts include such goodies as fresh melon, asparagus and cheese omelets, and poppy-seed apple cake.

"Helpful staff, accommodating owners. Mesmerizing views of the Delaware River and the picturesque town of Milford across the bridge." *(David Podehl)* "The highlight of our stay was crossing the bridge over to Milford, for dinner at the Ship Inn." *(PM)* Comments welcome.

Open All year.
Rooms 3 suites, 6 doubles—all with private bath and/or shower, telephone, radio, air-conditioning. Penthouse suite with TV, stereo, deck. Suites with fireplace. 2 bathrooms are quite small.

Facilities Dining room, main room with fireplace, sitting room, library with river views. Swimming, fishing, tubing, rafting, canoeing, boating, sunbathing on riverside terrace. Cross-country skiing, hiking, bicycling nearby.

Location Bucks County; 18 m N of New Hope via Rte. 32 N; 3 1/2 m N of Frenchtown/Uhlerstown bridge. 65 m W of NYC. In village.

Restrictions No smoking. Children over 8 on weekends. Weekday traffic noise in some rooms.

Credit cards Amex, MC, Visa.

Rates B&B, $149–199 suite, $69–149 double. 2-3 night weekend/holiday minimum.

Extras NYC bus stops in village.

VALLEY FORGE

The Amsterdam ¢   *Tel:* 610–983–9620
Mailing address: P.O.Box 1139, Valley Forge, 19482   800–952–1580
Street address: 31 Ridge Road, Route 23, Phoenixville 19460

George Washington's Continental Army suffered through a terrible winter at Valley Forge, but you can absorb American history and retire in considerably greater comfort at this warm and cozy inn. Built circa 1860 and used for many years as a general store on the trade route between Philadelphia and Lancaster, The Amsterdam was renovated as an inn in 1990 by owners Pamela and Ino Vandersteur. Reflecting Ino's native Netherlands, the inn is decorated with Dutch furnishings and paintings, while breakfasts reveal Pamela's Dutch culinary training. In the evening, guests choose when they'd like to have breakfast (served between 8 and 9:30), and can select among French toast, herb scrambled eggs, or the house special—eggs in a mild curried Hollandaise sauce over toast. A continental breakfast is available from 7 to 8 A.M.

"A handsome old home, extensively restored. The Vandersteurs are an interesting and friendly couple." *(Marion Ruben)* "The rooms are decorated in a Dutch motif with many antiques and interesting bric-a-brac. Breakfast was generous and served punctually. Although not allowed in the public areas of the inn, Portia, the family dog, is a well-behaved pet." *(Samuel Glaze)* Comments appreciated

Open All year.

Rooms 1 apartment, 3 doubles—all with full private bath, radio, clock, TV, desk, air-conditioning. 1 with porch. Apartment with kitchen.

Facilities Dining room with wood-burning stove, living room with fireplace, organ, books; porch. Guest refrigerator, microwave. 6-person indoor Jacuzzi room. 1 acre. Fishing, hiking nearby.

Location Chester County. 25 m W of Philadelphia, 5 m N of Valley Forge. From PA Tpke (I-76), take Exit 24 to Valley Forge Natl. Park. From Valley Forge P.O., go 5/8 m on Rte. 23 W through Phoenixville to inn.

Restrictions No smoking. Children over 10.

Credit cards Discover, MC, Visa.

Rates B&B, $75 double, $65 single. Weekly rate in apartment.

Extras Dutch, French, German spoken.

WAYNE

Wayne Hotel 🛏 ✕ ♿
139 East Lancaster Avenue, 19087

Tel: 610–687–5000
800–962–5850
Fax: 610–687–8387

A European-style hotel located on the Main Line outside Philadelphia, the Wayne Hotel is a landmark building furnished with Colonial and Victorian reproductions. Built in 1906, it's owned by Stephen Bajus; Susan Prevost is the long-time manager. Taquet, the hotel's restaurant features French cuisine with an American bistro influence. A continental breakfast of muffins, pastries, juices, coffee and tea is served in the library.

"Lovely old hotel, charming rooms, accommodating manager." *(Ronald Ridgway)* "Clean, comfortable rooms decorated in turn-of-the-century style. Outstanding service; once the staff knew we were avid readers, they made sure we had extra reading lamps." *(Paul Shapero)* "We received a warm welcome from the staff and had an excellent dinner in the restaurant." *(Richard Jackson)*

Open All year.
Rooms 5 suites, 30 doubles—all with private bath and/or shower, telephone, radio, clock, TV, desk, air-conditioning. 3 with refrigerator.
Facilities Restaurant, lobby with fireplace, library, bar/lounge, conference rooms, business services, porches. Off-street parking. Fitness center, swimming pool, jogging, golf nearby.
Location SE PA, 22 m W of Philadelphia. From Philadelphia, take I-76 W to Exit 28A onto I-476 S. Follow to Exit 5-Villanova/Rte. 30. Turn left onto Rte. 30 W (Lancaster Ave.). Go W 1 m to hotel on right. Hotel is 1 blk from Septa Line, Philadelphia commuter railroad.
Restrictions Traffic noise possible in front rooms. No smoking in dining room, some guest rooms.
Credit cards Amex, DC, MC, Visa.
Rates B&B $160 suite, $115–135 double, $105–120 single. Extra person, $10. Children under 12 stay free. Corporate rate, $89–135; weekend rate, $99.
Extras Wheelchair access; bathroom specially equipped. Airport shuttle, $16. Crib, babysitting. French spoken.

WEST CHESTER

Information please: Dating back to the 1830s, the **Duling-Kurtz House** (146 South Whitford Road, Exton 19341; 610–524–1830) offers an interesting balance of old and new. Originally the site of a limestone quarry, lime kilns, sawmill, gristmill, and farm, the property was restored as a restaurant and inn in 1982, with the dining rooms in the main house and the guest rooms in the barn. The two buildings are connected by a covered walkway, lit at night by gas lamps. "Our rooms and breakfasts were adequate, the staff pleasant, but best of all is the restaurant, where we enjoyed several superb meals." *(ML)* B&B double rates for the 13 guest rooms ranges from $55–120. Exton is approximately eight miles north of West Chester.

Faunbrook Victorian Bed and Breakfast Inn ¢   Tel: 610–436–5788
699 West Rosedale Avenue, 19382

An imposing Italianate red-brick mansion built in 1860, Faunbrook has been handsomely restored and decorated in high Victorian style by owners Judi and John Cummings. Inside, this well-proportioned home features carved Honduran mahogany woodwork; a grand staircase handcrafted from walnut trees that grew on the property; and Monticello windows (patterned after Jefferson's invention), which slide up and open onto a wraparound veranda, accented by ornate wrought iron, wicker furniture, and lots of plants. Breakfast specialties include poached eggs, Canadian bacon and melted jack cheese; creamy scrambled eggs served in potato baskets; and hard-cooked eggs in a wine sauce with asparagus and crumbled bacon. Evening sherry is also served.

"A High Victorian treasure, resplendent in its furnishings and decor. Judi is warm, welcoming, and unobtrusive." *(Anita Tuchman)* "Excellent location, near interesting museums and gardens in the Brandywine Valley, close to the pleasant streets of downtown West Chester. Sparkling clean." *(Sarah Henderson)* "Bright and pretty room with a cozy feather bed. A clawfoot tub in the bath with a modern shower; thick, thirsty towels. Wonderful breakfast, well-presented. Judi gave me an informative guided tour. Beautiful plantings around the inn." *(Ellen Kaplan)* "Extremely well preserved building with a fascinating family history. Judi is friendly without being intrusive." *(Mario DePillis, also SWS)*

Open All year.
Rooms 1 suite, 6 doubles—3 with private bath and/or shower, 4 with maximum of 4 sharing bath. All with clock, fan. 5 with air-conditioning, 1 with fireplace.
Facilities Dining room with fireplace, living room with fireplace, grand piano, library with fireplace, books, TV/VCR, sun room, porch. 2 acres with gazebo, off-street parking. Near Brandywine River for canoeing.
Location Brandywine/Chester County. 40 m W of Phila., 20 m N of Wilmington, 10 mins. N of Chadds Ford. Inn is at "V" formed by junction of Rtes. 100/52 & Rosedale Ave.
Restrictions No smoking. Children over 13. Early morning traffic noise possible weekday mornings.
Credit cards None accepted.
Rates B&B, $110 suite, $70–90 double. Extra person, $15.

WHITE HORSE

Fassitt Mansion   Tel: 717–442–3139
6051 Old Philadelphia Pike (Route 340), Gap, 17527   800–653–4139

A Gothic Revival farmhouse built in 1845, the Fassitt Mansion was restored as a B&B in 1989, and was purchased by Tara and Ed Golish in 1992. A "safe house" on the Underground Railroad, the house has a hidden room accessed through a closet. Breakfast menus change daily, but might include cinnamon brioche French toast with fresh fruit and pure maple syrup, bacon or sausage, and homemade coffee cake. Tara serves breakfast in the dining room, with its 12-foot ceilings, or on the front porch in summer.

"Delicious breakfast of Belgian waffles topped with whipped cream and blueberries. Tara arranged for us to have dinner with an Amish family, a highlight of our trip." *(Dorothy Box)* "Thoughtful innkeepers gave us helpful ideas from bicycling to quilting, from history to hot air ballooning." *(Hindrike Jos)* "We loved the front porch with its wicker chairs and views of the beautiful countryside, Amish buggies and cows. Our room had stenciled floors and walls and a wonderful bed with a down comforter. Tara is a warm and generous innkeeper." *(Ron & Eleanor Stauffer)* "Tara and Ed balance their concern for guests' comfort with an unobtrusive, informal manner." *(Chris Sparro & Lisa Alternative)* "Gorgeous sunrises could be seen from our window—no need for blinds or curtains, because no one is around to see in. Our spacious room had twin beds with handmade Amish quilts, a blue and white color bordering the floor and ceiling. Lots of dresser and closet space. Monogrammed towels, plentiful hot water." *(Nancy Rawson)* "Beverages and fruits are always available." *(Lorene Faubert)* "We were there on a chilly evening; when we asked, a fire was lit in the living room fireplace." *(MW)*

Open All year.
Rooms 5 doubles—all with private bath and/or shower, radio, clock, air-conditioning, fan. 3 with fireplace.
Facilities Dining room, living room with fireplace, books; guest refrigerator; porch; lawn games; bicycle tour maps provided (guest brings bike). Tennis, golf nearby.
Location Lancaster County; 16 m E of Lancaster, 20 m W of Exton, 8 m E of Intercourse. From PA Tpke., take Exit 22 (Morgantown). Follow Rte. 10 S to Rte. 340 W. Go 1 m to B&B. From Rte. 30 follow Rte. 10 N to Rte. 340 (Old Phila. Pke.) & go 1 m W.
Restrictions No smoking. No children under 12.
Credit cards MC, Visa.
Rates B&B, $65–110 double. 2 night weekend minimum; $5 surcharge for 1-night stay. Reduced rates for groups or extended stays.

WILKES-BARRE

For a Wilkes-Barre area B&B, see listing under **Dallas**, 10 miles north via Route 309.

WILLIAMSPORT

A major manufacturing center, most people visit Williamsport on business, but more than a few detour to see the home of the Little League World Series, and the Little League Baseball Museum next to the field. Williamsport is located in north central Pennsylvania, 90 miles north of Harrisburg, 60 miles northeast of State College, and 30 miles north of Lewisburg.

Information please: Located on 'Millionaires' Row, the **Snyder House Victorian B&B** (411 West Fourth Street, 17701; 717–494–0835 or 717–326–0411) is decorated with many original furnishings from the circa 1890 house. An antique square grand piano, a baby grand piano, and Victorian pump organ can be found in the music room. A century-old Tiffany grandfather clock chimes in the entrance hall. Owners Elizabeth Snyder-Slothus and Robert Slothus serve a continental breakfast which might include home baked muffins and breads, homemade preserves, fresh fruit, and poached pears. Each of the five guest rooms has a private bath; B&B double rates range from $65–100.

For an additional area entry, see **Muncy**, halfway between I-80 and Williamsport.

The Reighard House ¢   Tel: 717–326–3593
1323 East Third Street, 17701   800–326–8335
           Fax: 717–323–4734

Opened in 1986 as Williamsport's first B&B, the Reighard House is a stone and brick Victorian built in 1905, and has been home to Sue and Bill Reighard since 1976. Rooms are decorated with a mixture of Victorian and more recent furnishings.

"The owners are gracious and friendly, but respect guests' privacy. The common rooms are warm and inviting, and during warm weather the front porch is a frequent gathering place. Each bedroom is decorated with a different color scheme and theme: the Lavender and Lace room has a four-poster canopy bed with a white lace spread, lavender and white accents and wallpaper, purple carpeting, and a full bath with purple towels." *(NB)* "Perfectly clean and well-maintained." *(Keith Forstell)*

"We appreciated the afternoon and evening refreshments and the well-lighted off-street parking." *(Minda Sanders)* "Beds are comfortable, with good reading lights." *(Deirde Byrne)* "Sue's special touches can be seen all around—carefully arranged dried flowers, sherry in the parlor, and little candlesticks lighting each window." *(Sheila Murtland)* "Bob and Sue are always ready with maps, menus from local restaurants, and whatever else a visitor might need." *(Charles & Marilyn Doebler)* "Located in a residential/commercial area adjacent to I-180; highway noise is minimal." *(Mort Sternberg)* "Breakfast included juice, coffee, a fruit plate, pancakes, and sausage. Sherry, soda, and snacks are always available. An assortment of restaurants are within walking distance." *(Karl Wiegers & Christine Zambito)*

Open All year. Closed Dec. 25–Jan. 1.
Rooms 6 doubles—all with private shower and/or bath, telephone, radio, TV, desk, air-conditioning, coffee maker. 2 with fan.
Facilities Living room with piano, library with books, TV/VCR, dining room, guest pantry with microwave, porch. Complimentary YMCA membership for swimming, health club, hot tub. Bicycle path, hiking, hunting, fishing, canoeing, skiing nearby.
Location N central PA. 1 m from center of town.
Restrictions Smoking on first floor only (except dining areas). Traffic noise in front rooms.
Credit cards Amex, CB, DC, MC, Visa.

Rates B&B, $58–78 double, $48–68 single. Extra person, $10; crib, $5.
Extras Airport/station pickup.

WRIGHTSTOWN

Hollileif B&B

Tel: 215–598–3100

677 Durham Road (Route 413), 18940

Owners Richard and Ellen Butkus named their 18th century farmhouse Hollileif (meaning "beloved tree") in honor of the forty-foot holly trees that grace its entrance. Restored in 1989, the rooms of this pre-Revolutionary War dwelling are furnished with antiques, reproductions, and Oriental rugs. Guests might tuck into a breakfast of whipped melon-orange juice, strawberries with almond cream topping, nutmeg muffins, and asparagus turkey omelets. Afternoon treats change with the season: perhaps hot spiced apple wine and chocolate chip Streusel cake in winter, sangria and iced tea with gingerbread and lemon squares in summer; special dietary requirements are accommodated with advance notice. We have heard from many Hollileif guests, all praising the inn's gracious, accommodating hosts, immaculate housekeeping, and superb breakfasts.

"Rooms decorated with Oriental carpets, plants, and such interesting accessories as the antique hand-mirror on our dresser, an old book of love poems, and a pair of spectacles on the bedside table." *(Elaine Nieberding)* "Next to Ellen's sublime breakfasts, we like the backyard hammocks the best." *(E. Michael Desilets)* "Big, fluffy towels in the bath. Grounds were neat and well tended." *(Marilyn & Philip Steitz)* "The Garret Room had a comfortable, firm mattress. Nightly turndown service with chocolates and a decanter of blackberry brandy." *(Maureen Hickey)* "Great attention to detail—from the fresh flowers to the candy and port in our room, and the afternoon baked goods available in the beautiful common room." *(Diane Chaiken)* "Delicious breakfasts of a fruit smoothie, blueberry pancakes with maple butter, strawberry compote, and apple walnut muffins. The innkeepers were charming, delightful, and helpful with restaurant reservations and area suggestions. Wonderful collection of books in living room." *(Betsy and Denny Immergut)*

"Richard and Ellen helped us with our bags, showed us to our room, and left us in complete privacy. Breakfast is a leisurely affair, served by courses at individual tables, with attentive service in the cozy sunlit dining room." *(Jinny Ferguson)* "Classical music plays softly on the stereo system." *(Loretta Wallace)* "Parking is fine with a security light on all night. The owners are attentive to allergies; they will keep their two delightful cats elsewhere if you are allergic." *(Ellen & Joseph Offenstein)*

Open All year.
Rooms 5 doubles—all with private bath and/or shower, clock/radio, air-conditioning. 1 with gas fireplace.
Facilities Dining room with fireplace, living room with fireplace, TV/VCR, games, books; porch. 5½ acres with lawn games, hammocks; lawns, meadows, woods. Nearby Delaware River for fishing, boating, tubing.
Location Bucks County. 5 m W of Washington Crossing, 6 m SW of New Hope. 4 m N of Newtown. 4/10 m S of intersection of Rtes. 232 & 413.

Restrictions Occasional traffic noise in front rooms. No smoking. "Limited accommodations for well-behaved children."
Credit cards Amex, Discover, MC, Visa.
Rates B&B, $85–130.
Extras Some Spanish spoken.

Key to Abbreviations and Symbols

For complete information and explanations, please see the Introduction.

¢ Especially good value for overnight accommodation.
♦ Families welcome. Most (but not all) have cribs, baby-sitting, games, play equipment, and reduced rates for children.
✗ Meals served to public; reservations recommended or required.
⚓ Tennis court and swimming pool and/or lake on grounds. Golf usually on grounds or nearby.
& Limited or full wheelchair access; call for details.
Rates: Range from least expensive room in low season to most expensive room in peak season.
Room only: No meals included; European Plan (EP).
B&B: Bed and breakfast; includes breakfast, sometimes afternoon/evening refreshment.
MAP: Modified American Plan; includes breakfast and dinner.
Full board: Three meals daily.
Alc lunch: À la carte lunch; average price of entrée plus nonalcoholic drink, tax, tip.
Alc dinner: Average price of three-course dinner, including half bottle of house wine, tax, tip.
Prix fixe dinner: Three- to five-course set dinner, excluding wine, tax, tip unless otherwise noted.
Extras: Noted if available. Always confirm in advance. Pets are not permitted unless specified; if you are allergic, ask for details; *most innkeepers have pets.*

Virginia

Lynchburg Mansion Inn, Lynchburg

Few states equal Virginia's importance in the birth of this country. The first permanent English settlement in America was at Jamestown, in 1619. Eight U.S. presidents were born in Virginia; of the founding fathers of the U.S., Washington, Jefferson, Madison, Marshall, Monroe, and Henry were all Virginians. More Civil War battles were fought in Virginia than in any other state; Civil War buffs will want to visit the battle sites. There is much of historical interest for all to explore. The Virginia Division of Tourism has helpful brochures specifically dealing with Virginia history; ask for details when you call or write (see Appendix 3 for address).

Northern Virginia, noted for its historic towns, is known as horse country. The Tidewater area is home to Jamestown, Williamsburg, and Yorktown, plus Virginia Beach. The Eastern Shore is an isolated finger reaching out into the Chesapeake Bay from Maryland—Assateague National Seashore is perhaps its best-known feature. The central and southern portions of the state are rich in history, particularly of the Civil War. In the west, the Shenandoah Valley and Blue Ridge Mountains are where Washingtonians go to cool off, literally and figuratively; the scenery is breathtaking in all four seasons.

Virginia's spa country is located in the Allegheny Mountain Valley towns of Warm Springs, Hot Springs, and White Sulphur Springs, along the West Virginia border. You can soak in medicinal waters, or enjoy the equally recuperative effects of the peaceful mountain air.

Rates do not change seasonally in most locations, but tend to be highest on weekends and lower midweek—for both lodging and meals. If you plan to stay at an inn for three or four nights during the week, be sure to ask if any mid-week discounts apply. Inns within an easy drive of Washington DC range in price from expensive to outrageous, so head to other parts of Virginia if you haven't won the lottery recently.

ABINGDON

A major local attraction is the Barter Theatre, America's longest running professional resident theater company (and also the state theater of Virginia). The theater was named after the original payment to the actors—produce bartered in exchange for theatrical talent. Among the notables who honed their skills here are Thornton Wilder, Gregory Peck, Hume Cronyn, and Patricia Neal. Abingdon is located in southwest Virginia, in the Shenandoah Valley, 133 miles west of Roanoke, and 142 miles north of Knoxville, Tennessee.

Information please: Built in 1832, the **Martha Washington Inn** (150 West Main Street, P.O. Box 1037, 24210; 540—628—3161 or 800—533—1014) has seen numerous changes: first, as a women's college, then as a Civil War hospital, and last as a hotel in the 1930s. Extensively (and expensively) renovated in 1984, the decor combines both antebellum and Victorian decor, with lavish use of gilded trim, velvet and satin furnishings, period reproductions, and antiques. B&B double rates for the 61 guest rooms ranges from $100—125.

If you prefer the atmosphere of a cozy B&B, a good choice might be the **Silversmith Inn** (102 East Main Street, 24210; 540—676—3924), an 1871 house built on the site of Abingdon's first smithy's house. Breakfast includes homemade pastries and special coffees, and evening refreshments are offered as well. In addition to hand-crafted baskets, quilts, and pottery, guests will find bright and cheerful guest rooms simply furnished with antiques and handsome reproduction four-poster beds. B&B double rates for the four guest rooms are $75—85 double, $135 suite.

ALDIE

Little River Inn
Route 50, P.O. Box 116, 22001

Tel: 703—327—6742

After moving his antique shop from Bethesda, Maryland, to Aldie in 1982, Tucker Withers learned that his great-uncle's house was for sale, and decided that he must have it. In the process of making a bid, Tucker discovered that one of the property's outbuildings had been home to his great-grandparents during their last years. "Unknowingly, I'd returned home," he says. Though the house was in poor condition, Tucker fully restored it, adding modern baths and decorating with antiques—quilts, hooked and braided rugs, spool beds, and 19th-century paintings. The inn consists of the main house and a log cabin—built around 1810, the Patent

House—dating to the late 1700s, and the Hill House—a more recent addition with its own herb and boxwood garden.

Tucker's enthusiasm is unlimited: "Aldie's sleepy small-town charms include its many antique stores and its working gristmill, built in 1810. It's protected from urban sprawl by the Bull Run Mountains to the east and prime horse farms to the west. Cyclists love our back roads, and there are eight wineries in the area; nearby Middleburg is known as the 'heart of fox-hunting country.' "

"Breakfast, served at guests' convenience, includes Dutch apple baby pancakes or baked French toast, plus an assortment of juices, locally made sausages, homemade poppy seed muffins or strawberry bread, and, of course, great conversation. For evening snacks Tucker always leaves an assortment of wine, cheese, and other munchies in the kitchen." *(Bob Sanchez)* "Beautiful old quilts and stencilled lamps in every room." *(Elisabeth McLaughlin)* "Delicious breakfasts were delivered to the door of our well-furnished log cabin, complete with a wood-burning fireplace." *(Melinda Early)* "The guest refrigerator was thoughtfully stocked with snacks and beverages." *(Rosemary Grimm)* "Tucker makes you feel like a house guest, not just a 'customer.' " *(Doris Mills)*

Open All year.
Rooms 3 cottages, 5 doubles—5 with full private bath, 3 with maximum of 4 people sharing bath. All with desk, air-conditioning. 3 with fireplace.
Facilities 2 sitting rooms (one with fireplace), dining room; guest refrigerator. 5 acres with gardens, patio, and petting farm. Bull Run Mountain trails nearby.
Location N VA, Loudoun County. 35 m W of Washington, DC, 5 m E of Middleburg. 17 min. from Dulles Airport. From I-495 belt way, take Rte. 66 W to Rte. 50 W 20 miles to Aldie and inn.
Restrictions Children 10 and over.
Credit cards Amex, MC, Visa.
Rates B&B, $135–210 cottage, $80–130 double, $65–125 single. Extra person, $20.

ALEXANDRIA

Morrison House ✕ &.
116 South Alfred Street, 22314

Tel: 703–838–8000
800–367–0800
Fax: 703–684–6283

At first sight, you might assume that the elegant Federal-style Morrison House was built in 1785, not two centuries later when it was constructed by Robert Morrison. A European-style luxury hotel, it is furnished with high-quality period reproduction furnishings, brass and crystal lighting, and elaborately swagged curtains. The inn's dining room offers an intimate setting with an 18th-century decor, while the clubby grill room has leather chairs and a mahogany bar. Both restaurants serve Mediterranean cuisine, featuring the bounty of Tidewater Virginia. Afternoon tea features tea sandwiches, fresh-baked scones with whipped cream and jam, and petits fours.

"Unsurpassed service, from the moment you are greeted at the door by

319

the butler. Lovely furnishings, good food. Thoughtful touches include homemade cookies sent to your room on arrival, and complimentary coffee and tea available until 11:30 A.M. daily." *(Lorraine Cromis)* "Period charm combined with every modern amenity. The bathrooms have lighting designed for putting on makeup—no fluorescents." *(Frank & Dotty Scarfone)* "The perfect base for exploring—an easy walk to the Metro for seeing DC, yet located in Old Town Alexandria, with its safe, neighborhood feel and wonderful shops and restaurants." *(JTD)*

Open All year.
Rooms 3 suites, 42 doubles—all with full private bath, telephone, radio, TV, air-conditioning. Some with ornamental fireplaces.
Facilities Parlor with fireplace, library, restaurants, bar/lounge with fireplace, piano. Nightly entertainment. Concierge service. 24-hr. room service. Health club, pool, tennis, sailing nearby. Indoor valet parking. 8 blocks to Potomac River.
Location Historic Old Town. 2 blocks W of S. Washington St., between King & Prince Sts. Close to Metro station.
Credit cards Amex, DC, MC, Visa.
Rates Room only, $295 suite, $185–205 double. Extra person, $20. Senior, weekend packages; promotional rates. Alc lunch $8–18; alc dinner $19–28.
Extras Limited wheelchair access. Crib, babysitting. French, Spanish, Japanese spoken.

AMHERST

Dulwich Manor Inn ¢ 🏃   *Tel: 804–946–7207*
Route 5, P.O. Box 173A, 24521

Built in 1912 with Flemish bond brick work—in the style of an English estate house, Dulwich Manor has been owned by Bob and Judy Reilly since 1989. Set in the rolling countryside with views of the Blue Ridge mountains, the inn is furnished with antiques and reproductions; beveled glass panels provide a rainbow of light in the entry way and public rooms. Breakfast menus vary daily, but might include cold berry soup, crepes with apple rings, ham, shepherds' potatoes, and homemade breads and muffins; afternoon refreshments are offered as well.

"Judy and Bob make you feel welcome without intruding. We sat on the porch and lawn to enjoy the well-kept grounds and the Virginia air." *(Mr. & Mrs. Frederick Rolkinhagen)* "Set off the main road, making the inn wonderfully secluded. Exquisite breakfast served in the formal dining room." *(Michael & Robin Bastian)* "Wonderful country breakfasts, different each day. The generously sized rooms have large, working windows that flood the space with light." *(Rev. & Mrs. Wayne Harnden)* "Convenient to Appomatox, Appalachian Trail, and Lynchburg." *(Ernie & Helen Copley)* "Spotlessly clean. Spacious common rooms. Great gazebo with hot tub." *(Robert & Ellen Tompkins)*

Open All year.
Rooms 6 doubles—4 with private bath and/or shower, 2 with a maximum of 4 people sharing bath. All guest rooms with radio, air-conditioning. 3 with fireplace, 1 with whirlpool tub.

Facilities Dining room; living room & study with fireplaces; veranda. 5 acres with lawn, gazebo, hot tub. Tennis, golf, children's play equipment nearby. James River nearby for rafting, canoeing. 45 m to Wintergreen ski area.

Location Central VA. 50 m SW of Charlottesville, 15 m N of Lynchburg. 1 m from town. From Rte. 29 turn E on Rte. 60 and go ¼ m to inn.

Restrictions Smoking in study only.

Credit cards None accepted.

Rates B&B, $69–89 double, $64–84 single. Extra adult, $20; extra child under age 12, $5. Midweek senior discount. 2-night weekend minimum, May–Oct.

Extras Airport/station pickups, $5–10.

BEDFORD

With a newly restored downtown and a population of fewer than 6,000 people, Bedford makes a lovely place to overnight when you're traveling the Blue Ridge Parkway along Virginia's western border. It's about 30 miles west of Lynchburg, 100 miles southwest of Charlottesville, and 225 miles southwest of Washington, DC.

Information please: The Peaks of Otter Lodge (Milepost 86, at Route 43, Blue Ridge Parkway, P.O. Box 489, 24523; 540–586–1081 or in VA: 800–542–5927) is an authorized concession of the National Park Service. The Lodge offers motel-style accommodations that blend well with its beautiful lakeside setting. Restaurant specialties include mountain trout, prime rib, and barbecued ribs. "The Peaks of Otter loom above the lodge, and offers a reasonably short but surprisingly challenging climb. Go early to avoid the tourists." *(MG)* Rates for the 62 suites and doubles range from $67–95; children under 16 stay free in parents' room. "Nice lunch, great views." *(BJ Hensley)*

BLACKSBURG/CHRISTIANSBURG

The Oaks B&B　　　　　　　　　　　　　　　　*Tel:* 540–381–1500
311 East Main Street, Christiansburg 24073　　　*Fax:* 540–382–1728

Named for the massive 300-year-old oak trees that shade the many turrets and gables of this 1889 Queen Anne mansion, the building remained in the same family for 90 years. The Oaks was restored in 1989 by Margaret and Tom Ray; in 1994 it was listed on the National Register of Historic Places. Just a few miles from the interstate, the inn is popular with business travelers and visitors to nearby Virginia Tech and Radford University, but is equally appealing to stressed-out city folk who come for the antiquing, wine-tasting, fall foliage, Victorian Christmas, or just to enjoy the New River valley.

The mansion's original high ceilings and tall windows, stained glass, grand staircase, and ornate fireplaces are enhanced by a careful mix of modern and antique furnishings. Breakfast at The Oaks is no less original, with such specialties as curried eggs with shiitake mushrooms, shirred eggs in spinach nests, or whole wheat buttermilk pancakes in praline syrup with toasted pecans and maple cream, accompanied by fresh strawberries and melon, or perhaps poached pears with raspberry currant sauce.

"Wonderfully charming and comfortable, but not overly cute. Our room was spacious; the bathroom functional with a great shower; thickest, fluffiest towels imaginable. Margaret and Tom were delightful, friendly and full of neat stories." *(Gail & Mike Demcsak)* "Margaret's bed covers and window treatments are fantastic. Breakfasts look as good as they taste, with beautiful edible garnishes." *(Rose Ciccone)* "While relaxing on old-fashioned rockers on the large wraparound porch, sherry was served. Gorgeous town, with amazing old homes, pleasant for after-dinner strolls." *(Constance Dehnel)*

Open All year.
Rooms 1 suite, 4 doubles—all with private bath and/or shower, telephone, radio, clock, desk, air-conditioning, fan, refrigerator. 4 with fireplace. 3 with TV. 1 with balcony.
Facilities Dining room, living room, parlor with books; sun room, 2 porches. 1 1/2 acres with hot tub, gazebo, croquet. Tennis, golf, swimming, boating, fishing, hiking nearby.
Location New River Valley. Historic district. 8 m E of Blacksburg (VA Tech.), 26 m W of Roanoke, 26 m N of Blue Ridge Pkwy. From I-81 take Exit 114. From N, turn right; from S, left. Go 2 m to inn.
Restrictions No smoking. Children 14 and over.
Credit cards Amex, Discover, MC, Visa.
Rates B&B, $200–250 suite (for 4), $115–135 double, $75–105 single. Extra person, $15. Weekend packages. 2-3 night weekend minimum for university events.
Extras Airport/station pickups ($20 airport).

CAPE CHARLES

Set near the southwestern tip of Virginia's Eastern Shore, Cape Charles is just a few miles north of the Chesapeake Bay Bridge, 20 miles north of Norfolk/Virginia Beach, and 60 miles south of Chincoteague. Williamsburg is 1 hour away. The town offers golf, tennis, charter boat fishing, antique shops, good seafood restaurants, and charming back roads.

Nottingham Ridge Bed & Breakfast ¢   *Tel:* 804–331–1010
Route 646, Nottingham Ridge Lane, P.O. Box 97-B, 23310

Nottingham Ridge is a classically styled Colonial brick home, built by the Nottingham family in 1975, and surrounded by trees and farm land, with the sandy dunes of Chesapeake Bay to the west. The guest rooms are decorated with antiques, reproductions, and collectibles. Breakfast includes fresh fruit or juice, homemade breads and jams; in the afternoon guests enjoy wine and cheese or cake and coffee.

"We strolled on the beach for hours, discovering shells and treasures, and were rewarded by a brilliant sunset. We were pleased to meet the other guests over afternoon snacks and wine." *(Kenneth Brown & Donna Creedon)* "Bonnie treats every guest like family and makes you feel at home. She is a fine cook with a taste for fresh herbs. A typical day consists of a hearty breakfast, followed by a long walk on a secluded beach, and perhaps a dip in the bay. Nearby are wildlife and nature preserves, art galleries, museums, quaint villages and shopping. Every restaurant Bonnie has told us about has been a winner." *(Steve & Kris Arnold)* "We love Bonnie, Scotty, their B&B and the easygoing lifestyle of the Eastern Shore. Bonnie's delicious breakfasts are served on the back porch with a view of the bay, flowers, and birds, or in the country kitchen." *(Lloyd & Lisa Martin)* "Our favorite room is on the first floor, with a queen-size four poster bed and a water view. Enjoyed the sweet potato biscuits at breakfast." *(DLG)*

Open All year.
Rooms 1 suite, 3 doubles—all with private bath and/or shower, telephone, radio, desk, air-conditioning, fan. TV on request.
Facilities Living room with fireplace, sitting room with fireplace, dining room, screened porch. 17 acres with large private beach on Chesapeake Bay. Hiking, bicycling, birding on grounds. Fishing, golf, tennis nearby.
Location 20 m N of Norfolk, Virginia Beach, 3.5 m N of Bay Bridge-Tunnel. 10 m from town. From Chesapeake Bay Bridge-Tunnel, go 2 m W on Rte. 646 to inn on the bay.
Restrictions No smoking. Children 7 and over.
Credit cards None accepted.
Rates B&B, $85–130 double, $65 single. Extra person, $20.
Extras Airport/station pickups by prior arrangement.

Sunset Inn B&B ¢
108 Bay Avenue, 23310

Tel: 804–331–2424
800–331–3113

A 1915 Victorian located directly on Chesapeake Bay, the Sunset Inn is named for the spectacular sunsets that can be viewed from the porch and common areas. Owners Joyce Tribble and Al Longo restored it as a B&B in 1993; the guest rooms are bright and cheery, most with floral fabrics and delicately patterned fabrics and wallcoverings. The bathrooms have been fully remodeled to ensure that period ambience does not extend to the plumbing. Breakfast is usually served at 9 A.M., and typically includes orange juice, fresh fruit platter, cereals, perhaps home-baked applesauce bread or corn muffins, and such entrées as oven-baked French toast, or sausage, egg, and cheese casserole. Joyce notes that "Birders are very happy here. We are in a major flyway, so birds stop here for food and rest before crossing Chesapeake Bay. Cyclists enjoy our area as well. The land is flat, traffic is light, and the countryside is serene."

"Friendly owners, delicious food, beautiful rooms, with ample lighting and plenty of hot water." *(Judith M. Dellert)* "Our nicely furnished guest room had an immaculate, spacious bathroom—stocked with fluffy towels, bubble bath, and toiletries. Lots of closet space. Al and Joyce were most accommodating, providing us with information on what to see and do. Breakfast times were flexible." *(Brian & Joyce Hickman)* "Agreeable hosts; breakfast was served earlier than usual, at our special request." *(Leone Mendenhall)* "The Victorian room has a large clawfoot tub; the first floor hot tub is also appealing. Sitting on the front porch in the evening looking out over the bay is a pleasure." *(Shandy Baker-Guy)*

Open All year.
Rooms 4 doubles—all with private shower bath or tub, radio, clock, TV, table, air-conditioning, ceiling fan.
Facilities Dining room, living room with TV/VCR, stereo, games; foyer with fireplace, guest refrigerator, sitting room, hot tub, porch. Off-street parking, lawn games, 2 bicycles. Golf, tennis, fishing, birding, bicycling, walking trails nearby.
Location Historic district.
Restrictions No smoking. Children 10 and over.
Credit cards MC, Visa.
Rates B&B, $65–85 double, $60–80 single. Extra person, $15. Tips appreciated. 2-night minimum in season.
Extras Airport/station pickups.

CASTLETON

Blue Knoll Farm

Tel: 540–937–5234

Route 676, 110 Gore Road, 22716

This 19th-century farmhouse, built before the Civil War and expanded at the turn of the century, is set in a scenic valley of Castleton Mountain. Mary and Gil Carlson bought the inn in 1992, and have decorated it with antiques and collectibles acquired during Gil's Navy career. Guests are welcomed with lemonade or iced tea on the porch in summer, hot cider or cocoa by the parlor woodstove in winter, along with brownies or cookies. The breakfast table is set with linen napkins, Battenburg lace place mats, and family silver and china; the meal is served at 9 A.M., and the menu might include pineapple upside-down French toast with Virginia ham, and lemon poppyseed bread.

"Mary greeted us with hot apple cider and cookies. Our neatly furnished room had a bowl of fruit and snacks, as well as a variety of reading material." *(Julie A. Rohrbaugh)* "Surrounded by rolling hills and beautifully maintained grounds. Breakfast treats included blueberry muffins, specially mixed juices, and an egg casserole. Afternoon refreshments and snacks were served when we returned from our outings." *(Teresa Duncan)* "Country solitude, yet close to the antiques shops of Sperryville." *(Bruce Kent Ebel)* "Immaculate and comfortable, decorated with handsome antiques and artwork. Careful attention to detail. My breakfast favorite was the spinach soufflé." *(Brian Claydon)* "Secluded location, yet close to great restaurants." *(Larry Gorenflo)*

"The Meadowview has its own staircase to the main floor, a king-size bed with eyelet pillows, a colorful quilt, plenty of closet space. Windows open to allow in a gentle breeze and the sounds of birds and cows. Delicious breakfast of egg strata with basil, prosciutto and cheese, lime muffins, cantaloupe, and strawberries. Mary and Gil (whom Mary calls the innkeeper-upper since he can fix or build anything) are wonderful hosts without being intrusive." *(Carolyn Myles & Colburn Aker)* "Three porches with old-fashioned swings, rockers, and beautiful views." *(Deborah & Andrew Cohen)*

Open All year.
Rooms 4 doubles—all with private bath and/or shower, air-conditioning. 2 with desk. 1 with fan, fireplace, or whirlpool tub.
Facilities Dining room, breakfast room, parlor with woodstove, 2 porches with swings, deck. 5 1/2 acres with duck pond, walking path; 200-acre farm. Hiking nearby.
Location Shenandoah. 65 m W of Washington, D.C., 15 min. from Little Washington, VA. 15 min. to Skyline Dr. From DC, take Rte. 166 W 22 m to Gainesville, Exit 43 A. Take Rte. 29 S 12 m through Warrenton, take Rte. 211 W 15 m to Ben Venue. Follow Rte. 729 S 4.5 m to T-junction & go left. Continue on 729 for 2 m. Turn right on Rte. 676/Gore Rd. just after Thornton River Bridge. Take 2nd gravel rd. on right, 1/2 m to end.
Restrictions No smoking. No children.
Credit cards MC, Visa.
Rates B&B, $95–125 double, $75–125 single. Extra person, $15. 2-night minimum Oct., some holiday weekends.

CHARLES CITY

North Bend Plantation 🕴
12200 Weyanoke Road, 23030

Tel: 804–829–5176

You've come to the Williamsburg area for a taste of history, and how better to bring it to life than by a staying at a plantation that's been in the Harrison-Ruffin-Copland family since its inception in 1819? North Bend Plantation was built in the Greek Revival style, and served as General Sheridan's headquarters during the Civil War; the surviving breast works are located at the eastern edge of the property. In 1984, Mr. and Mrs. George and Ridgely Copland restored their longtime home as a B&B; Mr. Copland is the great-grandson of Edmund Ruffin, known as the Southerner who fired the first shot of the Civil War at Fort Sumter, and the great-grand nephew of Sarah Harrison (sister of the former U.S. President), for whom the plantation was originally built. The Coplands keep the remaining 850 acres under cultivation, and host a local club's weekend fox hunts during the spring and fall months.

Federal-period mantels and stair carvings survive from the oldest portion of the house, with Greek Revival features predominating in the 1853 remodeling. The house is furnished throughout with antiques—many original to the house, family heirlooms, old and rare books. The Sheridan Room has a queen-size canopy bed that belonged to Edmund Ruffin, and a desk that Sheridan used when he occupied the house. Breakfast, served on crystal and china from the 1850s, might include homemade waffles, cheese omelets, banana pancakes, or eggs and hot biscuits, with country ham, bacon or sausage, juice, coffee, and tea.

"Gracious Virginia hospitality. A rarity in our mobile society, the Coplands convey a genuine feeling of what it means to be rooted to the land and its history, with family ties stretching back through the generations. Beautiful antiques, in a warm and casual setting, with lots of homey touches. Families will enjoy the two connecting bedrooms which make up the suite, complete with a hallway nook set up with children's play kitchen, while both romantics and Civil War buffs should request the Sheridan Room. In most rooms, modern bathrooms have been tucked into corners, while ample heat is provided by gas space heaters set into the fireplaces. Fine dining in a restored historic tavern close by." *(SWS)*

"Sitting on the porch swing with nothing but fields stretching before me, I could imagine what it must have been like a century or more ago. It was fascinating to look though the antique books found throughout the house. I got caught up in the colorful history of Edmund Ruffin, the ancestor in whose bed we slept. Great waffles for breakfast." *(Nancy Sinclair)*

Open All year.

Rooms 1 suite, 3 doubles—all with private bath and/or shower, clock, TV, air-conditioning, ceiling fan. 1 with gas fireplace, 3 with gas space heater.

Facilities Dining room, living room, family room with TV, billiard room, upstairs sunporch with TV; guest refrigerator; porches. 850 acres with swimming pool, lawn games, sandbox, slide. James River borders farm. Tennis, golf nearby.

Location 25 min. W of Williamsburg, 30 min. E of Richmond. From I-64 S, take Laburnum Ave. Exit to Rte. 5. Follow signs for James River Plantations. From I-64 N, take Exit 199. Follow to Rte. 5 W. From Rte. 5, watch for signs for North Bend.

Restrictions No smoking. Children over 6.

Credit cards MC, Visa.

Rates B&B, $130–140 suite, $95–130 double, $85–100 single. 2-night minimum holiday weekends.

Extras Airport/station pickups, $20. Minimal French spoken.

CHARLOTTESVILLE

Charlottesville is best known as the home of Thomas Jefferson's Monticello and the University of Virginia. Other sights of interest include Castle Hill, Ashlawn, Michie Tavern, Court Square, and the nearby Skyline Drive. The best place for information on all these sights is the Thomas Jefferson Visitors' Bureau, located at the intersection of I-64 and Rte. 20 South. The area also offers lakes for boating and swimming; it's a 40-minute drive to downhill and cross-country skiing. Albemarle County is horse country, with many fox hunts and steeplechase events; there's no shortage of golf courses and tennis courts, either.

Charlottesville is 125 miles southwest of Washington, DC, and 75 miles northwest of Richmond.

Information please: Those who prefer a resort atmosphere should be pleased with the well-known **Boar's Head Inn & Sports Club** (Route 250, P.O. Box 5307, 22905; 804–296–2181 or 800–476–1988), offering 174 well-equipped rooms and suites, 3 restaurants, and 55 acres with a full range of sports facilities, including 4 swimming pools, 20 tennis courts (6 indoor), an 18-hole golf course, and more. The location is convenient, just off the freeway, not far from downtown Charlottesville, yet close to Monticello, Ashlawn, Montpelier, and the Virginia wineries. Double rates range from $119–180, and there's no charge for children under 18 in their parents' room; many advantageous package rates are available.

With as much publicity and attention to detail that Sir Bernard Ashley gave to the Inn at Perry Cabin in Maryland, is his latest project, **Keswick Hall** (701 Country Club Drive, Keswick 22947; 804–979–3440 or 800–ASHLEY–1), the transformation of a 1912 Italianate clubhouse into a luxurious 48-room country hotel, as well as a private golf, tennis and fitness club, plus (eventually) a planned residential community. Guest rooms have British antique furnishings and paintings and, not surprisingly, extensive use of Laura Ashley fabrics, wallcoverings and upholstery (no two rooms are alike). Double rates for two people are $195–395 double, $495–645 suite (plus 10% service), and include a country breakfast and traditional English afternoon tea; for an extra fees, guests have access to golf, tennis, fitness center, and an indoor/outdoor pool. Lunch and dinner are served in the hotel's three dining rooms. Truly elegant or haute pretentious? Let us know what you think.

Two miles from Monticello is the **Inn at Monticello** (Highway 20 South, Route 19, Box 112, 22902; 804–979–3593), a country manor house built in the mid-1800s. Each of the five guest rooms has a private bath; some have a fireplace, private porch, or four-poster canopy bed. Double rates range from $110–130, and include a full breakfast.

Nine miles south of Charlottesville is **The Inn at the Crossroads** (Route 2, Box 6, RR 692, North Garden, 22959; 804–979–6452), built in 1820 as a stagecoach tavern. The grounds are especially appealing in summer, when the vistas of the Blue Ridge foothills are enhanced by the inn's flower gardens and the shade of a 150-year-old oak tree. The delicious breakfasts might include baked pears in raspberry cream sauce, spicy apple pancakes, bacon, several kinds of muffins, and orange juice. The five guest rooms share two baths; each has a sink in the room, and the double rate is $65–75.

If the larger inns are full, a call to **Guesthouses B&B, Inc.** (P.O. Box 5737, 22905; 804–979–7264) will help you find a room in a historic Charlottesville area home or your own private cottage. B&B rates range from $60–100, depending on luxury, history, and location.

For additional area recommendations, see **Scottsville**, and **Trevilians.**

Clifton ✗ ♠ ✝ ♿	Tel: 804–971–1800
1296 Clifton Inn Drive, 22901	Fax: 804–971–7098

Stay at Clifton if you'd like to treat yourself to an overnight at a Jeffersonian estate. Set on a cliff overlooking the Rivanna River, Clifton was built in 1799 on land originally part of Shadwell, the Jefferson family estate; Monticello can be seen on a neighboring hill when the trees are bare. Thomas Jefferson gave the land to his eldest daughter, Martha, when she married Thomas Mann Randolph, a future governor of Virginia. Guest rooms have the original pine floors, wall paneling, and working fireplaces, with period decor and quality linens. Early morning coffee is served in the garden room, and breakfast is often served on the back terrace in fine weather. The inn has been owned by Mitch and Emily Willey since 1983; Craig and Donna Hartman have been the chef/innkeepers since 1992.

"The formal parlor was beautifully decorated for Christmas; the inn's fireplaces were lit as soon as the sun had set. The library is more casual, with leather wing chairs and plaid loveseat. The dining room was elegant with linen napery, poinsettias, ivory candles, and Royal Doulton china; there's a terrace dining area as well. The Thomas Jefferson Suite has a living room with comfortable seating, a fireplace and spinet, while the bedroom has a four-poster queen-size bed, good reading lamps, and additional seating. A lovely tray of tea and cookies, cheese, and fruit was brought to our room. The delicious dinner included soup, a salad of baby greens with onion dill bread, raspberry sorbet, roast beef with mushrooms or mahi-mahi with sun-dried tomatoes, and white chocolate Bavarian with strawberry coulis. We were invited to visit the kitchen later on for milk (or tea) and cookies. Breakfast was an equally tasty meal of chèvre cheese omelets with locally made sausage and toasted Sally Lunn bread. Craig Hartmann kindly provided recipes when I asked." *(Rose & Frank Ciccone)*

"Quiet country location down a wooded drive. The grounds combine gardens with 'naturalized' areas, avoiding an overly manicured look. The public rooms have a formal, stately, comfortable, Virginia country atmosphere. Our suite was beautiful and comfortably furnished. Bedroom and bath windows looked out over the valley. Helpful, professional staff." *(JH)* "Heavenly dining area on the glassed-in slate porch. We sipped sherry by the fire while we played a game of checkers. Freshly baked cookies were provided for each guest. Expensive but worth it." *(Judith Barr)*

Suggestion box: "A shelf in our bathroom."

Open All year.
Rooms 7 suites, 7 doubles—all with private bath, radio, clock, air-conditioning, wood-burning fireplace. Telephone on request. 9 rooms in 3 cottages.
Facilities Dining room with fireplace; drawing room with fireplace, grand piano; library with fireplace, books, games; garden room, veranda. Fri., Sat. pre-dinner classical music. 40 acres with river view, gazebo, lake for swimming, tubing, fishing; heated swimming pool, hot tub, tennis court, lawn games, hiking, fishing. Cooking school.
Location 5 m E of town. From I-64, take Exit 124 to Rte. 250 E. Turn right on Rte. 729 (Shadwell). Go S 1/8 m to inn on left.
Restrictions No smoking. Well-supervised children welcome.
Credit cards Amex, DC, MC, Visa.
Rates B&B, $165–225 suite, double. Extra adult, $40. Children's rate. 2-night weekend minimum. Prix fixe dinner $40–50. 18–20% service on meals. Midweek, off-season discount.
Extras Wheelchair access; 1 guest room specially equipped. Crib, babysitting with prior notice.

Silver Thatch Inn
3001 Hollymead Drive, 22901

Tel: 804–978–4686
Fax: 804–973–6156

Built by Hessian soldiers held prisoner on the site during the Revolutionary War, the Silver Thatch has been added onto many times during the past 200 years. Rita and Vince Scoffone bought the inn in 1992, and are doing an admirable job, offering both a high quality dining and lodging experience—no easy task.

Breakfast is served in the country-style sun room, and includes fresh-squeezed orange juice, fruit, cereals and granola, homemade muffins and breads, and coffee. Beverages and snacks are available anytime, "so guests can enjoy a glass of wine or snack at *their* convenience," Vince explains.

The dinner menu changes seasonally but always offers fish and vegetarian entrées; recent menus included such entrées as venison rib chops; lobster, mussels, shrimp, and Andouille sausage in puff pastry; and Cornish hen stuffed with Moroccan lamb sausage and couscous.

"Furnishings were suggestive of Virginia's Colonial period. Impeccable maintenance and housekeeping." *(Kenneth Rivard)* "The restaurant is truly outstanding; bright, fresh, well-seasoned food. Attractive pub and common rooms." *(BB)* "Good location with great trails for running and walking." *(Kim Kurkowski)* "Careful attention to detail; warm, hospitable innkeepers and staff." *(Cynthia Larson)* "Fully endorse existing entry. Beautiful room, The Madison. My husband enjoyed Monday night football in the bar downstairs. Rita was very sweet and referred us to an Italian neighborhood restaurant since their restaurant is closed on Mondays. Delicious fruit and muffins for breakfast." *(Stephanie Roberts)* "Our renovated room was delightful; excellent service." *(Catherine Rhea)*

Open All year. Closed Dec. 24, 25. Restaurant closed Sun., Mon.
Rooms 7 doubles—all with private shower and/or bath, air-conditioning. 4 with fireplace.
Facilities Restaurant, common room, bar/lounge with TV, fireplace. 1½ acres with swimming pool, tennis court. Golf, hiking, biking, fishing nearby.
Location 6 m to town, on Rte. 1520, ⅓ m E of Rte. 29N.
Restrictions No smoking. "The inn is adult-oriented, but well-behaved children welcome."
Credit cards Amex, CB, DC, MC, Visa.
Rates B&B, $110–150 double. Extra person, $25. 2-night minimum in season & holidays. Alc dinner, $40–50.

CHATHAM

Eldon, The Inn at Chatham ¢ ✕ 　　　　　*Tel:* 804–432–0935
Chalk Level Road; Route 1, Box 254 B, 24531

Set among stately white oaks at the foot of the Blue Ridge Mountains, Eldon is a Greek Revival mansion built in 1835. Joy and Bob Lemm restored this former tobacco plantation manor as an inn in 1992, enhancing the grounds with beautiful gardens accented by the work of a local sculptor. Guest rooms are furnished with Empire antiques; beds are dressed in designer linens, and windows provide forest, garden, or mountain views. The Elliott Garden room is fresh in green and white, with a brass and iron queen-size bed and French doors opening to the garden, while the spacious Governor Swanson room is handsome in blue and white, with an unusual canopied cherry "tobacco" bed.

A typical breakfast consists of fresh fruit and juice, perhaps cranberry or zucchini bread, with spinach frittata, artichoke/cheese/egg bake, or waffles with fruit sauce, accompanied by sausage, bacon, or ham. Chef Joel Wesley, a Culinary Institute of America graduate, offers a frequently changing menu with regional specialties. The dinner menu lists such entrées as chicken roasted with lemon, oregano, and honey; duck breast with mushroom risotto; or pork loin stuffed with Mediterranean sausage.

"A well cared-for manor house, decorated with an eclectic blend of antiques, Orientals, and newer pieces. We stayed in the James Whittle room, a spacious queen-bedded room, with a tiny private bath with great lighting and ample shelf space. We enjoyed chatting with Joy on the brick terrace. Fine service and exceptional dinner of shrimp appetizer, mixed salad, and salmon with dill yogurt sauce." *(Peg Bedini)* "Chatham is a charming historic village, with good area antiquing." *(Billie Gill)* "Beautiful formal gardens and a quiet tranquil setting." *(James Alexander)* "Clean and neat, with lots of fluffy towels and warm blankets. Afternoon coffee and bedtime brandy. Lovely music, excellent homemade pastry." *(Lizbeth Logan)*

Open All year. Restaurant closed Mon., Tues.
Rooms 1 suite, 3 doubles—all with private bath and/or shower, radio, clock, air-conditioning. 1 with desk.
Facilities Restaurant with Sat. evening piano entertainment, library with fireplace, 2 parlors with fireplace; porches, patio. 13 acres with English gardens, orchard, fishpond, ice house, smokehouse, stable. Golf, fishing, swimming, boating nearby.
Location SW VA. 65 m N of Durham, NC; 17 m N of Danville. 1/2 m to town center. From US 29 S, go left on Rte. 685 (Chalk Level Road) to inn on left.
Restrictions No smoking; allowed in part of dining room. Children 12 and over.
Credit cards MC, Visa.
Rates B&B, $90–120 suite, $55–70 double. Extra person, $15. Alc dinner, $28–32; Sunday brunch, $10.
Extras Limited wheelchair access (restaurant, public bathroom only).

CHINCOTEAGUE

Chincoteague and Assateague Islands are located at the north end of the Eastern Shore, just south of the Maryland border. They're 180 miles southeast of Washington, DC and 100 miles north of Norfolk. Well known for its wild ponies, the Chincoteague National Wildlife Refuge and the barrier beaches of the Assateague Island National Seashore are popular with visitors.

For other local possibilities, see entries for **New Church** and **Wacha-preague.**

Reader tips: "Most guest rooms at local B&Bs are small; don't plan to spend a lot of time in your room." *(JH)* "I love the beach, but the town is pretty boring." *(JB)*

Information please: The history of **Island Manor House**—formerly The Little Traveler—(4160 Main Street, 23336; 804–336–5436) starts in the 1850s, when the house was built by two local men who eventually married two sisters. The sisters didn't care to live under the same roof, so they split the house in half and moved the front half next door; the houses have been rejoined by a lovely garden room. Purchased in 1991 by Charles Kalmykow and Carol Rogers, the restored houses have been beautifully furnished in antiques. Breakfast, served at individual tables in the dining room or by the courtyard fountain includes fresh fruit, juice, an egg dish, homemade breads, and cakes. Eight rooms are available, and the $69–129 B&B double rates also include a formal afternoon tea.

Miss Molly's Inn
4141 Main Street, 23336

Tel: 804—336—6686
800—221—5620

In 1886, Mr. J.T. Rowley, then known as "The Clam King of the World," built a Victorian home on Chincoteague Island. His daughter, "Miss Molly," was one of the island's best loved citizens, and she lived in the house until the age of 84. Marguerite Henry stayed here while writing *Misty of Chincoteague*, and much of the plot was worked out while rocking on the front porch with Miss Molly and Captain Jack. Today Barbara and David Wiedenheft, who have owned the inn since 1992, note that "Miss Molly's is popular with many young girls (and their mothers) who grew up on Ms. Henry's wild horse stories." In 1995, the Wiedenhefts purchased the former Channel Bass Inn, less than a block away; they have refurbished the rooms, and plan to open a tea room in the former restaurant. A typical breakfast includes orange juice, assorted teas and coffees, fresh fruit salad topped with a yogurt and honey sauce, homemade breads and muffins, bagels with smoked salmon, cream cheese, and onions, and such entrées as spicy eggs with scallions and cheese, crêpes, or spinach quiche.

"Our immaculate room had lots of fluffy pillows, and two large windows with water views. It was warm enough to have breakfast in the gazebo—with fresh flowers everywhere. Tea was served at 5:00 P.M. with the guests seated around the large dining room table with a fire burning in the fireplace, and consisted of raisin scones with raspberry jam and clotted cream. Another day, we were treated to English trifle; the next, chocolate apricot cake." *(Naomi & Bob Halpert)* "Without being intrusive, the innkeepers offered helpful suggestions on meals and activities. The Marguerite Henry room has a comfortable king-size bed, excellent reading lights, and large, soft, fluffy towels and special soaps in the bathroom." *(Carol & Jack Paolini)* "Fabulous breakfasts; we loved rocking on the porch with one of the inn's outdoor cats." *(DLG)*

Open March through New Year's.
Rooms 7 doubles—5 with private bath, 2 rooms share 1 bath. All with radio, clock, air-conditioning.
Facilities Dining room, parlor, living room, books; guest refrigerator; 5 porches. Off-street parking, gazebo, garden.
Location 2 blocks from center. 4 m from wildlife refuge, National Seashore. Go E on VA 175, go left on Main St. Inn 2 blocks on left.
Restrictions No smoking. Street noise in front rooms. Children 8 and over.
Credit cards None accepted.
Rates B&B, $69–145 double, $59–109 single. Extra person, $20. Children's rates. Senior discount midweek. 2-night weekend minimum, April–Sept.
Extras Airport/bus station pickup, $10–30. French, Dutch, German spoken.

The Watson House
4240 Main Street, P.O. Box 905, 23336

Tel: 804—336—1564
800—336—6787

Built in 1898 and extensively renovated in 1992, The Watson House is a family-run B&B, owned by Jacqueline and Tom Derrickson with her parents, Joanne and Dave Snead. Breakfast consists of an egg and meat entrée, hot or cold fruit dish, cereals, breads, pastries, muffins, milk, juice, tea, and coffee; afternoon refreshments are served on the porch. Rooms are simply decorated with Victorian antiques, country furnishings, and wicker pieces, complemented by soft pastel colors and floral print wallpapers.

"Wonderful wraparound porch featuring white wicker furniture, hanging baskets, and pots of pink petunias and geraniums. The little Victorian parlor boasts lovely antiques and a mantel displaying tintypes of the Watson family members. Guests have described their restaurant experiences in a journal; comments are quite entertaining if not necessarily instructive. Breakfasts were excellent, with Jacque and Joanne alternating on the cooking chores. Our first floor room had a delightful little sun room with white wicker furniture and magazines. The sink was in the room, and the toilet and shower were in a little converted closet." *(Sallie Purcell)*

"Spotless house, charming atmosphere, ample parking. Within walking and biking distance of all the sights." *(Sarah Thimmeseti)* "Jo Anne and Tom aren't intrusive, but were always available to answer questions, and suggest activities." *(Robert Keith)* "Afternoon tea was a treat—homemade lemon meringue pie, brownies, cookies, chocolate-covered strawberries, usually offered on the porch." *(Katharine & John Kraeck)* "The Bayview Room is beautifully decorated with antiques and a hunter green and rose decor. The large bathroom has an old-fashioned clawfoot tub great for bubble baths, plus a separate shower." *(Joyce Hoye)*

Open March through Nov.
Rooms 1 3-bedroom cottage, 6 doubles—all with private bath and/or shower, radio, clock, air-conditioning, fan.
Facilities Dining room, living room with TV, stereo; family room, guest refrigerator, porch. Bicycles, beach chairs, towels. Off-street parking.
Location 1/4 to town center.
Restrictions No smoking. Street noise in front rooms. Children 10 and over.
Credit cards MC, Visa.
Rates B&B, $65–105. Extra person, $15. No tipping. 10% senior, AAA discount. 2-3 night weekend/holiday minimum. Off-season 3–7 night discount, midweek. Inquire for cottage rate.

DANVILLE

Gold Leaf Inn
1012 Main Street, 24541   *Tel:* 804–793–1433

When the Gold Leaf Inn was built on Millionaire's Row in 1898, this stately Queen Anne home cost $3,300—which gives you an idea of what an enormous sum a million dollars was in those pre-income tax days. Owners Pam and Jimmy Barbour restored the Gold Leaf as an inn in 1992; rates include a welcome drink, early morning coffee, and breakfasts of fresh fruit, just-baked breads, cinnamon pecan pancakes or perhaps a spiced omelet.

"Comfortable beds; attractive rooms decorated in period. Amenities included fresh flowers, fragrant soaps, and candies. Located in the historic district, the inn sits among many impressive private homes from the same period." *(Lynn Adams)* "We were traveling with a baby, and the Barbours couldn't have been more helpful or accommodating. Spacious rooms; delicious, plentiful food. The Barbours, in addition to being delightful hosts, are also knowledgeable local historians who can provide colorful insights into the area." *(Pete & Heather Trinca)*

Open All year.
Rooms 3 doubles—1 with full private bath, 2 with maximum of 4 people sharing bath. All with clock/radio, air-conditioning, fireplace. 2 with TV, 1 with desk, fan.
Facilities Dining room, living room, den with TV/VCR, books; porch. Office services (computer, fax, copy machine); laundry privileges. Off-street parking, garden, bicycles, croquet.
Location S central VA, at NC border. 60 m N of Greensboro. Millionaire's Row historic district, 2 blocks from downtown. On Main St., roughly across street from Museum of Fine Arts/Sutherlin Mansion.
Restrictions No smoking. Light traffic noise in front room.
Credit cards None accepted.
Rates B&B, $55–65 double. Extra person, $15. Commercial rate.

DILLWYN

Tranquility Farm ₵   *Tel:* 804–392–4456
Rte. 3, Box 174, 23936   800–831–2492

You get an idea of the pace of life at Tranquility Farm when owners Elfriede and Jay Wolford note that a favorite guest activity is watching their black Angus cows and Arabian horses, or having a look at the Wolford's small shiitake mushroom-growing operation. Breakfast includes fresh fruit and juice, a hot entrée, hard rolls, and fresh-baked breads. Rooms in the well-shaded farmhouse are furnished simply with period antiques and reproductions, Oriental rugs, and down comforters.

"Spotless home, with attention given to every detail, including excellent lighting." *(Betty Norman)* "Picture a cozy, white farmhouse tucked in the trees. The Wolfords welcomed us with afternoon tea and cakes. Our room was spotless with country decor and period antiques, plus books, magazines, fluffy towels, live plants, fruit, and a pitcher of ice water. The aroma of freshly baked rolls and blueberry muffins beckoned us to breakfast; we enjoyed a delicious egg and cheese casserole with shiitake mushrooms." *(Jeanne Sanna)* "Excellent breakfast, warm hospitality, a beautiful setting in the Virginia countryside." *(Mrs. Robert Sloan)*

Open All year.
Rooms 1 2-bedroom cottage, 3 doubles—2 with private bath/shower, 2 with maximum of 4 people sharing bath. All with radio, air-conditioning. Cottage with sitting room, kitchen.
Facilities Dining room with piano, living room with TV, fireplace; breakfast room, family room, both with fireplace; enclosed porch. 25 acres of pasture with lawn games. Holiday Lake State Park nearby for swimming, fishing, boating.
Location Central VA, Buckingham County, 60 m W of Richmond, 60 m E of Lynchburg, 50 m S of Charlottesville, 20 m to Appomattox. From Rte. 60 at

Dillwyn, go S on Rte. 15 to Curdsville, then turn W on Rte. 633. At Rte. 635, turn S to farm on right.
Restrictions Smoking permitted in common areas by permission of other guests.
Credit cards None accepted.
Rates B&B, $110–180 cottage (2-day minimum), $50 double, $45 single. Extra person, $7.50.
Extras German spoken.

DRAPER

Claytor Lake Homestead Inn ¢ 👫   *Tel:* 540–980–6777
Route 651, Brown Road, P.O. Box 7, 24324   800–676–LAKE
                                                            Fax: 540–980–8320

Looking at this spacious brick and white-clapboard home, it's hard to imagine that it originated as a two-room log cabin a century ago. Owners Larry and Kathy Nipper learned that the hard way when they renovated the old "Doc Brown House" in 1990. They had to cut a door from the hall into a guest room, and encountered the original outside wall of the cabin in the process—several chain saw blades were much the worse for wear after cutting through the stone-hard foot-thick logs. Rooms are decorated with antiques, as well as period furnishings purchased when the old Hotel Roanoke closed. Breakfast is served from 7–9 P.M. at individual tables in the dining room, overlooking the lake, and includes homemade muffins, biscuits, fruit pancakes, and Virginia country ham. Don and Judy Taylor are the innkeepers.

"Close to one of the ten best biking trails in the U.S." *(Ellie Shick)* "Off the beaten track, yet easily accessible from I-81." *(Roland & Sherry Weaver)* "Beautifully decorated with antiques and family heirlooms." *(William Helms)* "We had a spacious bedroom with a beautiful view of the lake and mountains." *(Patricia & Alan Morrell)* "Breakfast is a wonderful time to share good conversation with the other guests while savoring homemade sausage and pancakes with fresh-picked blackberries." *(Bill & Lynn Reams)* "We rented a boat from the innkeepers, and spent the day swimming and exploring the lake. In the afternoon, we relaxed on the old-fashioned porch swing with glasses of freshly brewed iced tea, as fern baskets swayed in the breeze." *(MW)* "Host was down-home friendly, helpful with dining suggestions." *(George Dunn)*

Open All year.
Rooms 2 suites, 3 doubles—3 with private bath, 2 with a maximum of 4 people sharing bath. All with telephone, radio, TV, desk, air-conditioning. 2 with fan.
Facilities Dining room, living room with fireplace, TV, porch, deck. 7.5 acres on lake with picnic area, private beach, dock, marina, rental boats, fishing. Hiking, bicyling nearby.
Location SW VA, 60 m SW of Roanoke. 10 min. from Pulaski. Take Exit 92 off I-81. Go S on Rte. 658. After Draper Mercantile, turn left on Rte. 651 (Brown Rd.). Go approximately 1 m to inn on left.
Restrictions No smoking.
Credit cards Amex, MC, Visa.

Rates B&B, $55–70 double. Extra person, $10. 2-night weekend minimum holidays, graduations.
Extras Spanish spoken.

FAIRFAX

The Bailiwick Inn ✕ ⟨&⟩
4023 Chain Bridge Road, 22030

Tel: 703–691–2266
800–366–7666
Fax: 703–934–2112

Built in the early 1800s, the Bailiwick Inn is right across the street from the Fairfax Courthouse; both buildings are listed on the National Register of Historic Places. Restored in 1989 at a cost of over $1,600,000, the inn was purchased in 1994 by Bob and Annette Bradley; Holly Snyder is the manager. This elegant small hotel has been lavishly decorated with antiques, reproduction period fabrics, and feather beds. Bedrooms are named for famous and infamous Virginians, and rates include afternoon tea, turndown service with a pillow chocolate, and a breakfast of fresh fruit and juice, homemade breads, and a choice of such entrées as smoked salmon frittata with steamed vegetables, or buttermilk pancakes with baked apple slices and whipped cream. Dinner is a multi-course affair with a choice of four entrées and three desserts; a recent one included a smoked chicken appetizer, black bean soup, wilted spinach salad, lamb with artichokes, and a peach tart with mango sorbet.

"The George Mason Room is richly decorated in shades of green and mauve, with a comfortable queen-size, four-poster feather bed, draped in elegant fabric. Bookshelves filled with an artistic assortment of objets d'art framed the fireplace. Sparkling bathroom with a powerful shower. Breakfast was served at the mahogany Duncan Phyfe table in the dining room from 7:30 to 9:00 A.M. (8:30–10:00 on weekends). Easy walking distance to town; a bus stops in front of the inn and takes passengers to the Vienna Metro Station for the DC train." *(BNS)* "Outstanding meal, deluxe bed, impeccable restoration." *(Deborah Frankel Reese)* "The welcoming innkeepers gave us a tour of the inn, complete with historical anecdotes. We were impressed by the painted tiles, period furnishings, and rich fabrics. Enjoyed the tea served at 4:00 P.M." *(Kathleen Wiedemer)*

Open All year. Restaurant closed Mon., Tues.
Rooms 1 suite, 13 doubles—all with private bath and/or shower, telephone, radio, clock, air-conditioning. 7 with desk, 4 with fireplace, 2 with Jacuzzi tub. TV on request.
Facilities Restaurant, breakfast room, double parlor with 2 fireplaces. Courtyard with fountain, pond, herb garden, arbor. Off-street parking.
Location Historic district. 15 m W of Washington, DC. From Rte. 50 turn S on Rte. 123 (Old Chain Bridge Rd.) Short bus ride from Vienna Metro stop to DC.
Restrictions No smoking.
Credit cards Amex, MC, Visa.
Rates B&B, $295 suite, $130–180 double. Extra person, $20. Prix fixe dinner $45–$55. Murder Mystery weekends.
Extras Wheelchair access.

FLINT HILL

Reader tip: "We had a superb dinner at the **Flint Hill Public House** (Route 522, P.O. Box 605, 22627; 540–675–1700 or 800–551–4142), an interesting building dating back to 1899, and once used as a school house." *(BJ Hensley)* Two queen-bedded guest rooms with private baths are available for $75–95 double, including breakfast, an excellent value in this area.

Caledonia Farm 1812   *Tel:* 540–675–3693
Route 628, Rte. 1, Box 2080, 22627   800–BNB–1812

With the Blue Ridge Mountains in the background and a herd of cattle grazing in nearby pastures, Caledonia Farm offers a bucolic setting. Built of local stone in 1812, this Federal-style home and companion summer kitchen—now a guest cottage—have two-foot thick walls. The beams, mantels, windows and wide pine floors are all original to the house, restored in 1965; Phil Irwin bought the farm in 1967. Guest rooms are simply furnished, accented with antiques. Breakfast is served by candlelight in the gathering room—guests pick the time—and a typical meal will have freshly ground coffee, pastry, fruit, and perhaps made-to-order omelets. Guests are welcomed with refreshments; a tray of goodies is left at bedside in the evening.

"Phil greeted us warmly, offering a glass of wine; his informative library helped immensely in familiarizing ourselves with the area. Some highlights of our visit: cordial but unobtrusive innkeeper; assistance with dinner reservations; fruit, cookies, mints, and liqueur at bedside on our return; delicious eggs Benedict and Virginia sparkling cider at breakfast. We spent the day bicycling, picnicked on the lawn, and had an inspiring view of the Milky Way during our evening walk down the lane." *(Jill Reeves)* "Beautiful home and setting; comfortable suite; great breakfast. Darling cat, 'Clawed.' " *(GR)* Comments appreciated.

Open All year.
Rooms 1 cottage with private bath, 2 doubles sharing 1 bath. All with telephone, radio, desk, air-conditioning, fireplace.
Facilities Breakfast room, living room with fireplace, TV/VCR, fax, piano; 3 porches. 52 acres with pastures, bicycles, lawn games. Afternoon hayride, $20 (for 2).
Location N VA. Rappahannock Cty. 68 m W of Washington, DC; 4 m N of Washington, VA. 1 m from town. From Rte. 211, exit at Washington. Go N on Rte. 628 to inn on left.
Restrictions No smoking. Children 12 and over.
Credit cards Discover, MC, Visa.
Rates B&B, $140 cottage, $80–140 double. *50% surcharge for Sat. only stay.* 2-night holiday, Oct. weekend minimum.

FREDERICKSBURG

Fredericksburg dates back to the early 18th century; it served as an important river port city then, and was a central meeting point for George

Washington, Thomas Jefferson, Patrick Henry, James Monroe, and John Paul Jones. Sights of interest include Mary Washington's home, James Monroe's law office, the Rising Sun Tavern, and the Kenmore plantation house, as well as the town's many craft and antique shops. Surrounding Fredericksburg are a number of major Civil War battlefields, including Chancellorsville, Wilderness, and Spotsylvania.

Fredericksburg is located in northern Virginia, 50 miles south of Washington, DC and 55 miles north of Richmond, just a short distance off the Route 3 East exit of I-95.

Reader tip: "A wonderful town—we planned to drive through, and ended up staying for two nights. We found the townwide hospitality pass for $16 to be extremely worthwhile; ask for a free parking pass. We'd recommend visiting Belmont, Chatham, and the National Military Park. Also fun are the ghost tours. All information is at the visitors' center." *(Larry & BJ Schwartzkopf)*

Also recommended: The **Fredericksburg Colonial Inn** (1707 Princess Anne Street, 22401; 540–371–5666) is within walking distance of the historic district, and offers rooms decorated with antiques and furnished with private baths and air-conditioning, for the modest rate of $55–70. "The regular suites ($65) have a sitting room on one side of the bathroom and the bedroom on the other; family suites have twin sleigh beds instead of the sitting room. Our spacious room had a beautiful king-size four poster bed, with parking just outside the door. The simple breakfast included coffee, tea, milk, orange juice, and delicious banana walnut bread. A pleasant small hotel." *(Larry & BJ Schwartzkopf)*

Information please: Located in the historic district, the **Kenmore Inn** (1200 Princess Anne Street, 22401; 540–371–7622) dates back to 1796. The more expensive of its 14 guest rooms have canopy beds and fireplaces. B&B rates range from $85–150, and its restaurant and pub are popular with locals and readers. "Excellent dinner, accommodations adequate." *(HB)* Comments?

A family-oriented choice in nearby Spotsylvania, 14 miles south of town, is the **Roxbury Mill B&B** (6908 Roxbury Mill Road, Spotsylvania 22553; 540–582–6611). "Our enormous room (900 square feet) had a private bath, a refrigerator and some kitchen facilities, and a private balcony overlooking the river and woods. There's also an appealing screened porch in the common area. The waterfall masks any noise from a road on the other side of the woods, and you feel like you're miles from civilization." *(VE)* Two guest rooms are available, at B&B double rates of $85–150, including a full breakfast. Current reports welcome.

For an additional area entry, see listing for **Renaissance Manor** in **Stafford.**

Richard Johnston Inn   *Tel: 540–899–7606*
711 Caroline Street, 22401

Built in the Federal style in 1787, the Richard Johnston Inn was bought by Susan Thrush in 1992. Guest rooms are furnished with antiques and reproductions: Room #8 has pastel pink walls, hardwood floors, a Victorian oak double bed with high headboard and foot board, and a rose and

337

white star quilt; Room #10 is a spacious suite with wall-to-wall carpeting, soft floral wallcoverings, reproduction furnishings, and two queen-sized beds, plus a separate living room. Breakfast includes assorted baked goods, fresh fruit, juices, tea, and coffee.

"Our cozy and comfortable room was on the top floor. The innkeeper was helpful with dinner suggestions." *(Clara Callahan)* "We enjoyed being right on the main street with second-hand bookstores, craft stores, and antique shops. We enjoyed a candlelight dinner at the Kenmore Inn— good service and food." *(Carole Stover)* "Fully endorse existing entry. Susan is friendly, and served a great breakfast." *(AT)* Reports appreciated.

Area for improvement: "A reading light and table on my side of the bed."

Open All year.
Rooms 2 suites, 7 doubles—all with full private bath, radio, clock, air-conditioning. 8 with desk. 3 with TV. 2 with refrigerator.
Facilities Dining room, living room, family room with TV, books. Courtyard, off-street parking.
Location Historic district. From I-95, take exit for Rte. 3 E. Follow signs to Fredericksburg Visitor Center. Inn is across street.
Restrictions No smoking. "Not suitable for children under 12."
Credit cards Amex, MC, Visa.
Rates B&B, $130 suite, $90–115 double. Extra person, $10.
Extras Train station pickup.

FRONT ROYAL

The northern entry point of the Skyline Drive, Front Royal is also home to the Skyline Caverns, one of the Shenandoah Valley's major caves. Spelunkers will also want to plan visits to the following major caves, as they head south on the Skyline Drive: Shenandoah Caverns, Luray Caverns, Endless Caverns, Grand Caverns, Natural Bridge Caverns, and Dixie Caverns. Front Royal is located 65 miles from Washington, DC.

Chester House Inn   *Tel:* 540–635–3937
43 Chester Street, 22630   800–621–0441

At Chester House, one of the first things that a passerby would notice about this turn-of-the-century home is the boxwood maze in the garden. The care evident in this gardening endeavor is representative of the effort which Ann and Bill Wilson put into their B&B, opened in 1988. Guest rooms are furnished with Sheraton reproduction pieces, Oriental rugs, and crisply ironed linens on the king- and queen-sized beds. Breakfast includes homemade popovers or muffins, juice, cereal, fruit and coffee or tea.

"The expansive public rooms are furnished with antiques, comfortable chairs, period draperies and an interesting art collection. Breakfast was served in the formal dining room with silver service, fine china and crisp linens." *(Susan Guest-McPhail)* "Lots of places to sit, read, and relax, with books and magazines everywhere." *(Frances Taylor)* "Our comfortable room overlooked the beautiful gardens in back. Everything was spotless, the bathroom fixtures new. A basket of quality toiletries was next to our exceptionally large bathtub. The grounds invite exploration, especially the maze. Peaceful, quiet location. Ann and Bill made us feel welcome in every possible way." *(Susan West)*

Open All year.
Rooms 6 doubles—4 with private bath and/or shower, 2 with a maximum of 4 people sharing bath. All with clock/radio, air-conditioning. 2 with fireplace, desk.
Facilities Dining room, living room with fireplace, TV room with fireplace, game room, veranda. 1½ acres with gardens, boxwood maze, fountain, hammock. Off-street parking. Fishing, canoeing, tubing on river nearby. Golf, tennis, horseback riding, wineries nearby.
Location N VA, Warren County. N end of Skyline Dr. 70 m W of Washington, DC. ½ block to center of town.
Restrictions Smoking in TV room only. Children 12 and over.
Credit cards MC, Visa.
Rates B&B, $75–110 double. 2-night minimum some holidays & weekends.

Killahevlin
1401 North Royal Avenue, 22630

Tel: 540–636–7335
800–847–6132
Fax: 540–636–8694

An Edwardian mansion listed on the National Register of Historic Places, Killahevlin reflects the Irish heritage of its current owners, Susan and John Lang, as well as that of the original owner, William Edward Carson, an Irish immigrant. Built in 1905 and named for a castle in Northern Ireland, the stately home is filled with rich wood hues, high-ceilinged rooms, and stained glass transoms. Set on the highest ground in Front Royal, the inn affords lovely views of the Massanutten and Blue Ridge Mountains. Breakfast is served from 8:30 to 10:00 A.M. on fine china and crystal, and includes fresh fruit, just-squeezed orange juice, apple cider, cereal, home-baked breads and muffins, and perhaps Irish-style scrambled eggs and bacon with English muffins. Rates also include beer and wine, served in the inn's private Irish pub.

"Wonderful hospitality; incredible attention to detail. Luxurious bath-rooms, fluffy towels. For dinner, the Langs recommended the Stadt Cafe, a marvelous German restaurant which met our wishes exactly. Sumptuous breakfast of delicious fruit, Belgian waffles and sausages." *(Michael & Florence McKenna)* "Extraordinary on-going renovation." *(SL)* "Ample common areas for both quiet times and sociable ones." *(Andrea Allar)* "Susan greeted us warmly and showed us around the inn. Our spacious suite had a cozy sitting area and fireplace. Best of all was the bathroom, with a marvelous whirlpool tub; the window over the tub offered a view of the mountains. We joined Susan and John for wine and conversation in the Irish pub before dinner. The Langs introduced the guests at breakfast, and conversations soon began around the room." *(Susan Horton)* "The Raspberry Room was immaculate, furnished with antiques, including a French armoire, and two reading chairs, well placed by the window." *(James Van Pelt)*

Open All year.
Rooms 2 suites, 4 doubles—all with full private bath, radio, air-conditioning, fan,

wood-burning fireplace. 2 with desk, TV; 4 with balcony. 2 suites in Tower House. 5 with double whirlpool tub.

Facilities Dining room, living room, pub with TV/VCR, family room with TV/VCR, books. All with fireplaces. 3 acres with gazebos, gardens, lawn games.

Location 1.5 m from town. From DC, take I-66 W to Exit 6. Go left (S) onto Rte. 522/340. Go 2 m (cross 2 bridges); turn left onto 15th St., which dead ends at N. Royal Ave., then go left. Go right at 1st driveway. From I-81, take Exit 300 to I-66 E to Exit 6 & follow directions above.

Restrictions No smoking. Children 12 and over.

Credit cards Amex, Discover, MC, Visa.

Rates B&B, $160 suite, $95–115 double. Extra person, $19–32. 2-night minimum May, Oct., holiday weekends.

GALAX

Information please: A contemporary home overlooking the New River, the **River View B&B** (Route 58, P.O. Box 686, Independence 24348; 540–236–4187 or 800–841–6628) has three guest rooms, each with private bath, and is owned by Rebecca and Ken Ogle. In good weather, Rebecca's breakfasts of baked apple pancakes, sausages, cheese muffins, fresh fruit and juice are served on the deck, with views of the river and forest. Ninety acres are available for hiking, fishing, canoeing, and hunting; B&B double rates are a reasonable $50–70. The Galax/Independence area is in southwestern Virginia, 100 miles southwest of Roanoke, and 120 miles north of Charlotte, North Carolina.

GOSHEN

The Hummingbird Inn ¢
Wood Lane, P.O. Box 147, 24439

Tel: 540–997–9065
800–397–3214
Fax: 540–997–0289

There's a lot to be said for staying at inns just a short ways off the beaten path—quite often the prices are lower, the welcome warmer, and the atmosphere more relaxing. Such a place is the Hummingbird Inn, an easy drive from the Shenandoah's historic towns and major sights. This Victorian Carpenter Gothic villa was built in 1853 and has been owned by Jeremy and Diana Robinson since 1992. It's been an inn since around 1900, and past guests of note included Eleanor Roosevelt, and Ephraim Zimbalist, Sr. Architectural features include wraparound verandas, original pine floors, and a rustic den dating from 1780. Five minutes away is Goshen Pass, a rocky gorge through which the Maury River flows. Breakfast consists of fresh fruit and juice, bacon or sausage, homemade bread, coffee, tea, and milk, accompanied by such entrées as nutmeg-cinnamon French toast, corn pancakes, or cheese omelets. Dinners are prepared with prior notice, and a typical menu includes complimentary wine, soup or salad, chicken with porcini mushrooms, vegetables and potatoes, and chocolate mousse terrine for dessert.

"A great deal of skill and care goes into the excellent meals." *(Paul Matthews)* "Beautifully landscaped grounds. Hosts cater to special needs." *(Carol Kabler)* "Down pillows and comforters; every amenity for the bath including hair dryers." *(Maraly Wagner)* "Wonderful sunroom, porches all around the house; beautifully furnished with comfortable, cozy rooms." *(Bill Rowland)* "Feels as though one is entering an old fashioned English garden with lush plants and colorful blossoms. Beautiful perennial borders, herb and vegetable beds." *(Nick & Jacquie Buch)* "Many birds make their home here, including robins, goldfinches, cedar waxwings, and, of course, hummingbirds. For dinner, Jeremy grilled a perfect steak for my husband; my salmon melted in my mouth." *(Mrs. J.G. Major)* "Immaculate and beautifully decorated with Victorian antiques. Jeremy lit a fire in the family room where there is also plenty of music, movies, books, and so on. Great hiking trails nearby." *(Julia Ruggiere)* "Oriental rugs set off beautiful heart pine flooring; small touches included fresh flowers and potpourri. Comfortable rice bed, with fine-quality cotton sheets and a coordinating comforter." *(Judge & Mrs. Robert K. Dwyer)*

Open All year.
Rooms 5 doubles—all with private bath and/or shower, clock, air-conditioning. 1 with fireplace. 1 with Jacuzzi.
Facilities Dining room, living room, family room with fireplace, TV, stereo; solarium, porch. 1 acre with lawn games, trout stream for fishing, tubing. Tubing, kayaking, canoeing, fishing, hiking, skiing nearby.
Location Shenandoah Valley, 23 m NE of Lexington. From I-64 take Exit 43. Go N on Rte. 780 to Goshen.
Restrictions No smoking. Children 12 and over.
Credit cards Amex, MC, Visa.
Rates B&B, $75–105 double. Extra person, $15. Prix fixe dinner, $27.50 (24 hours notice). Theater packages.

HOT SPRINGS

For additional area entries, see **Warm Springs**.

Information please: An 1899 Queen Anne Victorian, complete with a turret and wraparound porches, the **King's Victorian Inn** (Route 220, Rte. 2, Box 622, 24445; 540–839–3134) is decorated with 18th century reproductions and Oriental carpets. Downtown Hot Springs and the famous Homestead Hotel resort are within walking distance. B&B double rates for the six guest rooms range from $85–150, and include a full breakfast.

IRVINGTON

The Tides Inn 🛏 ✕ 🚭 ♿
King Carter Drive, P.O. Box 480, 22480

Tel: 804–438–5000
800–843–3746
Fax: 804–438–5222

"I relax as soon as I arrive. A greeter meets you at the door, ascertains your needs, and smoothes your way. We arrived just in time for the yacht luncheon cruise, and when we returned, our luggage was in our room and the car was parked. *Miss Ann,* the 127-foot yacht, offers maximum passenger comfort and convenience. The employees are genuinely concerned with your happiness and the guests are friendly. Other favorite moments were spent in some of the inn's lovely public rooms, doing needlework, sipping iced tea, and visiting. Glass walls offer a view of the lawns and gardens sloping down to the Rappahannock River. Our rooms were pleasant, medium-sized, with hotel-style antique reproductions and standard tiled baths. The beds were triple sheeted with down pillows. The twice-daily maid and turndown service was provided without fail while we were at breakfast and dinner. The main building is divided into the Main Wing, the East Wing, and the Garden House; nearly all rooms face the water. The East Wing and the Garden House are newer, with better sound-proofing and in-room TVs. The Windsor House and the Lancaster House are at the rear of the property, and are more luxurious, with balconies and larger bathrooms, some with sunken tubs. The food is excellent, with such selections as lobster Thermidor, veal medallions, and soft-shell crabs." *(Susan W. Schwemm)* "This small resort appeals to families who enjoy tennis, golf, and the beach. Sports-filled days and early nights. Excellent service and first-rate children's programs." *(MDS)* "The cottages are nicest, with large rooms, great baths, and decks overlooking the water." *(Jocelyn Luff)* "Delightful setting on the water, beautifully maintained, excellent food, wonderful outdoor pool, fun cookouts, and trips on the private yacht. The owners take a personal interest in their guests." *(Dorothy Woolman)*

Open Mid-March–Jan. 2.

Rooms 29 suites, 79 doubles, 2 singles in 3 buildings—all with full private bath, telephone, radio, TV, desk, air-conditioning. Some with balcony, terrace. 1 suite with whirlpool tub.

Facilities Dining rooms, living room with fireplace, bar/lounge, TV/VCR, lobby with entertainment nightly, recreation center, gift shop, clothing shops. 25 acres in addition to a 400 acre 18-hole golf course, 4 tennis courts, shuffleboard, croquet, horseshoes, heated saltwater swimming pool, sail and paddle boats, canoes, freshwater fishing, yacht cruises, summer children's program. Complimentary van service to 36-hole championship course 2.5 m away. Valet service.

Location E VA, Tidewater region. 140 m S of Washington, DC. 65 m E of Richmond. 75 m N of Norfolk. From Irvington, go W on Rte. 634 (King Carter Dr.) ¼ m to inn.

Credit cards Amex, MC, Visa.

Rates Full board, $278–650 suite, $260–330 double, $180–230 single. Extra person, $53–60. MAP, $260 suite, $242–296 double, $190–218 single. Family rates. Reduced rates for children under 16; no charge for children under 10. Prix fixe lunch, $12; dinner, $35.

Extras Wheelchair access. Pets permitted by prior arrangement, $5. Crib, babysitting. Airport/station pickups, $90.

Tides Lodge Resort & Country Club

♠ ✕ ✿ ♿

1 St. Andrews Lane, P.O. Box 309, 22480

Tel: 804–438–6000
800–248–4337
Fax: 804–438–5950

The Lodge is an attractive resort, well known for its challenging championship golf course, relaxing atmosphere, good food, comfortable accommodations, and family-friendly atmosphere. A full program of activities is offered daily. Rates include nearly everything except for golf.

A better than one-to-one ratio of staff to guests ensures attentive service. Rooms are furnished in traditional comfort, most with balconies overlooking the river.

"Without exception, every employee is hospitable, friendly and accommodating. Well-maintained facilities; improvements found upon each of our many visits. Delicious Southern cooking, beautifully landscaped grounds; excellent swimming pools, boating facilities, tennis courts, and golf course." *(Leonard Bernstein)* "The beautifully maintained golf course is a traditional Southern course with little water and tall pine trees. It is rarely crowded and offers a spectacular feature—a grass driving range, measuring 75 x 300 yards." *(Allen Mead)*

"E.A. Stephens and his entire staff have created a feeling of welcome, comfort, and relaxation. The beautifully landscaped grounds border on the banks of Carter's Creek, with fantastic views across the marina docks toward the historic Rappahannock River and Chesapeake Bay. The mixture of sail and motor boats and guest rooms bring interesting folks of all sorts, from families to golfers to retirees. My waistline tugs at the thought of their honey buns, their 'anything-you-want breakfasts,' and dinners from a menu that changes daily. Extras include the sunsets seen from the deck of the *Binnacle* and the dinner cruises on the *High Tide II*." *(Norman Block)* "Large, comfortable, immaculate rooms with good reading lights. We watched beautiful sunsets over the water from our private balcony. The hour-long cruise around the coves is well worth the nominal charge." *(Carolyn Myles & Colburn Aker)*

Open Mid-March through Dec.
Rooms 4 suites, 60 doubles—all with full private bath, telephone, TV, desk, radio, balcony, hair dryer, coffee maker. Rooms in 3 buildings.
Facilities Dining room with evening dancing, lobby, game room, bar, pro shop, yacht cruises. 175 acres with 18-hole golf course, 9-hole par-3 course, heated freshwater swimming pool, saltwater pool, sauna, 3 (1 lighted) tennis courts, marina, fishing, boating, sailing, bicycling, putting green, horseshoes, croquet, shuffleboard, exercise room, yacht cruises. Children's programs, playground.
Location E VA. Northern Neck; Tidewater area. 60 m E of Richmond. 8 m from Chesapeake Bay. From Irvington, take Rte. 200 N, go left (W) on Rte. 646, left again on Rte. 709, left again to lodge.
Restrictions No smoking in some guest rooms.
Credit cards MC, Visa.
Rates Room only, $99–139, double, plus $6 service. Extra adult, $20. MAP, $178–208 double, plus $12 service. Extra adult, $60. Children under 18 stay free. Alc lunch, $8–12; alc dinner, $25–30. Golf, honeymoon, midweek packages.
Extras Wheelchair access; some rooms specially equipped. Small pets in some rooms, $8. Crib, babysitting.

LANCASTER

The Inn at Levelfields ¢
Route 3, P.O. Box 216, 22503

Tel: 804–435–6887
800–238–5578

An impressive double-tiered portico and four massive chimneys made the Inn at Levelfields an architectural landmark when it was built in 1857, in the middle of a 1,200-acre plantation. This hip-roofed Georgian Colonial, still an imposing sight amid acres of cultivated land and woods, was completely refurbished in 1984, and furnished with antiques and Oriental rugs by owners Warren and Doris Sadler. Guest rooms have queen- or king-sized beds, and rates include a hearty breakfast and afternoon refreshments.

"Upon arrival we were offered a glass of sherry and shown to our spacious room, with a queen-sized four-poster bed, period bureaus, and a large well lighted sitting area with an 8-by-14-foot Oriental rug." *(John Blewer)* "The bedroom curtains rippling in the breeze, the aromatic boxwood fragrance, and the owners' hospitality were all delightfully Southern." *(Caroline Jackson)* "High ceilings, wide, tall windows; hardwood floors with area rugs; the antique furniture, including big, high beds; and a huge old-fashioned bathroom." *(Lindy Jaouod)* "Outstanding features were the breakfast, for its food, service and table setting, and the innkeepers' attitude—relaxed and smiling." *(JB)* "The plantation home elegantly and simply furnished, without cluttering bric-a-brac to detract from the clean lines and fine woodwork. A quiet atmosphere with friendly, helpful hosts." *(Mrs. LeAnn Williamson Gersh)*

Suggestion box: "A private area or cordless phone for guest phone calls."

Open All year.
Rooms 4 doubles—all with private bath and/or shower, air-conditioning, fan, fireplace. 2 with desk. 1 with balcony.
Facilities 2 dining rooms with fireplace, library with fireplace, TV. 54 acres with swimming pool, garden, stream. Golf, fishing, sailing nearby.
Location Lancaster Co., Northern Neck, 125 m SE of Washington D.C., 75 m E of Richmond. From Rte. 17 go E on Rte 33. 7 m E of Saluda, turn left on Rte. 3. Cross Rappahanock River Bridge to Kilmarnock. Inn is 5 m W of Kilmarnock on right.
Restrictions Children 12 and over.
Credit cards MC, Visa.
Rates B&B, $85 double, $55 single. Extra person, $10.

LEESBURG

Founded in 1758, Leesburg has a rich and varied history. President Madison and his cabinet fled here during the War of 1812, when British troops torched Washington, D.C. The fourth battle of the Civil War was fought here, now marked by Ball's Bluff cemetery—the smallest national cemetery in the country. Many of Leesburg's beautiful Colonial homes have been preserved along its brick-lined streets, and a number of them are now restaurants, antique shops, and inns. Nearby are two plantations worth touring: Oatlands and Morven Park. Leesburg is located in Loudoun County—Hunt Country—in northeast Virginia, 35 miles northwest of Washington, D.C., via Route 7, and just 14 miles from Dulles International Airport.

Note: Parking is a problem in Leesburg. Plan to drop off your luggage, then park at the city lot and forget about driving during your stay.

Information please: We'd like more reports on the historic **Norris House Inn** (108 Loudoun Street SW, 22075; 703–777–1806 or 800–644–1806), a Federal-style home built in 1806. The six guest rooms (which share three bathrooms) are appointed with Colonial elegance. B&B double rates of $90–135 (lower midweek off-season) include afternoon wine, cider, or iced tea, and a full breakfast served before a crackling fire in the dining room. "Beautifully restored; furnished with antiques. The shared bath was fully modern and immaculate. Hospitality and food was great." *(Cynthia Raines)*

For a more rural setting, **Fleetwood Farm** (Route 1, Box 306-A, Leesburg 22075; 703–327–4325) offers two guest rooms with fireplaces, antiques, and handmade quilts in a farmhouse dating from 1754. The $110–135 rates include a full breakfast and afternoon refreshments. Guests are welcome to explore the grounds, visit the flock of sheep, have a game of horseshoes or croquet, or borrow the canoe. "The larger downstairs room has a private Jacuzzi and an antique rope bed. Thoughtful extras included fluffy robes and a variety of toiletries. We played horseshoes, relaxed in the hammock, and returned from dinner to find our bed turned down with chocolates. Breakfast was delicious—grapefruit, apple pancakes, bacon, coffee, and juice." *(VS)*

LEXINGTON

Lexington is a nineteenth-century town with a handsome historic district and the homes of both Robert E. Lee and Stonewall Jackson; Washington and Lee University and Virginia Military Institute are also located here. Nearby attractions include Natural Bridge and the Blue Ridge Parkway.

Lexington is in the Shenandoah Valley, in the western part of Virginia, 54 miles northeast of Roanoke, and 69 miles southwest of Charlottesville.

Reader tip: "Lexington is pretty, friendly, and one of the most interesting historic towns we've visited. The Visitors' Center is expansive and lovely, the staff knowledgeable. The two colleges—Virginia Military Institute and Washington & Lee—are totally different but both are 'must-sees'. The Robert E. Lee Chapel and George Marshall Museum are fascinating, as is Stonewall Jackson's home. Natural Bridge is touristy, but the bridge itself is worth seeing." *(Peg Bedini)*

For additional area entries, see listings for the **Hummingbird Inn** in **Goshen,** and the **Oak Spring Farm** in **Raphine**.

Brierley Hill　　　　　　　　　　　*Tel:* 540–464–8421
Borden Road, Rte. 6, Box 21, 24450　　　　800–422–4925
　　　　　　　　　　　　　　　　　　Fax: 540–464–8925

Imagine tucking into a breakfast of cornmeal pancakes, Grand Marnier French toast, or perhaps fresh herb omelets, accompanied by fresh fruit, home-baked oat bran bread, and hot apple turnovers. Now place this tempting feast on a nicely set table on the veranda of the Brierley Hill B&B, where you can watch the morning mists rise from the Shenandoah

Valley, with the Blue Ridge Mountains on the horizon. How fast can you pack?

Built in 1993 as a B&B by Carole and Barry Speton, Brierley Hill offers spacious guest rooms handsomely decorated in soothing colors, antique furnishings, four-poster and canopy queen- and king-size beds with firm mattresses and Laura Ashley linens, and Oriental rugs on the hardwood floors. In addition to breakfast (served from 8 to 9 A.M.), rates also include afternoon tea. Dinners are served at 7 P.M. by candlelight in the dining room, before the blazing fire; a typical menu might consist of curried carrot soup, salad, salmon with leeks and white wine, and chocolate apricot torte.

"A fine B&B with lovely decor, exemplary and personable hosts. The spectacular morning views were a highlight. Breakfast was delicious and beautifully served." *(Andrew Hollinger)* "Typical of Carole's attention to detail was the way the floral cream pitcher coordinated with the floral tablecloth. Homey atmosphere, magnificent setting." *(SMC)* "Immaculate housekeeping, lovely lavender scent, fine linens, and good cooking." *(LBW)*

Open All year. Dinner Thurs.–Sun.

Rooms 1 suite, 5 doubles—all with private bath and/or shower; 1 with whirlpool tub. All with radio, clock, air-conditioning, fan. 2 with TV, desk, wood-burning fireplace. 1 with refrigerator, deck.

Facilities Dining/breakfast room with fireplace, living room with fireplace, TV room, guest refrigerator, porch, veranda. 8 acres with gardens. Horseback riding, trap shooting by arrangement.

Location $1^1/2$ m to historic district. From I-81 S, take Exit 188B, Rte. 60 W. Drive 3 m to Lexington & continue on 60 W (Nelson St.). Go left on Borden Rd; continue 1 m to inn. From I-81 N, take Exit 191 to Rte. 64 W. Take Exit 55 to Rte. 11 S to Business Lexington, past VMI & Washington & Lee to Nelson St. (second light) & go right (W) to Borden Rd., then as above.

Restrictions No smoking. Children 14 and older.

Credit cards Amex, DC, MC, Visa.

Rates B&B, $115–130 suite, $75–100 double. Extra person, $20. 10% senior discount midweek; 10% AAA discount. 2-night weekend minimum, May, Sept., Oct. Prix fixe dinner, $25 by reservation. Dinner, theater packages.

Lavender Hill Farm ¢

Route 631, RR 1, Box 515, 24450

Tel: 540–464–5877
800–446–4240

For many travelers, it's enough that the Lavender Hill Farm offers comfortable accommodations, gracious innkeepers, delicious food, and a peaceful country farm setting, complete with sheep and goats. But for those who'd like a little something more, owners Cindy and Colin Smith offer horseback riding packages in cooperation with Deb Sensabaugh of Virginia Mountain Outfitters. You can spend the day following trails through the Blue Ridge Mountains, then return to the inn in time for a hot shower and one of Colin's delicious dinners.

Built in 1790, Lavender Hill Farm was totally restored in 1991 by the Smiths. Guest rooms are airy and light, furnished simply with country antiques, comfortable furnishings, English lace curtains, and Cindy's watercolors. Colin, retired from the British Air Force, is the inn's chef, and prepares breakfasts of stuffed French toast or dishes made with organic eggs; homemade breads and jams; sausage or bacon, cereals, locally produced honey, and locally roasted coffee, including espresso and cappucino. A recent dinner menu included black and white mushroom soup, Venetian orange salad, Cornish game hen, herbed potatoes, snow peas, with chocolate mousse cake for dessert.

"English innkeeper Colin Smith and his artistic American wife, Cindy, create a warm, welcoming atmosphere. We awakened to the bleating of sheep and breakfast aromas wafting up the stairs. Colin's delicious dinners are made with herbs and vegetables right out of his garden. In early spring, breakfast is occasionally interrupted when Colin needs to repair to the barn to assist in the birthing of lambs; guests are invited to watch. Later, we watched them frolic in the fields." *(Kitty Weaver, also Susan Tapley)* "Both breakfast and dinner were fine. Good food and clean accommodations." *(BJ Hensley)*

Open All year.
Rooms 1 suite, 2 doubles—all with private bath and/or shower, ceiling fan, air-conditioning, clock.
Facilities Dining room with fireplace; living room with TV/VCR, stereo, books, games; porch. Wool spinning demonstrations on request. 20 acres with stream for fishing. Hiking, biking, swimming, canoeing, tubing nearby. Horseback riding, theater packages available.
Location From I-81 N or S, take I-64 W at Lexington to Exit 50 for Kerrs Creek (2nd exit after leaving I-81). Go left off exit ramp onto Rte. 623. Go left at stop sign on 60 E. Immediate left onto Rte. 631. Go 1.2 m to farm on left.
Restrictions No smoking.
Credit cards Discover, MC, Visa.
Rates B&B, $70–110 suite (2–4 people), $60–70 double, $50–60 single. Extra person, $15. Senior discount, 5-night discount. 2-night minimum special events, holiday weekends. Prix fixe dinner, $24 (by reservation). 2-night horseback riding packages, $250.

Llewellyn Lodge ¢

603 South Main Street (Route 11 South), 24450

Tel: 540–463–3235
800–882–1145

Ellen Roberts opened the Llewellyn Lodge as a B&B in her eclectically furnished 1930s-era home in 1985; the guest rooms were refurbished in 1993. Guests are welcomed with a refreshing drink, and breakfast is cooked to order from 8–9:30 A.M. at the dining room table for eight.

"Ellen and John go out of their way to make you feel at home; enjoyed visiting on the front porch." *(R. Sidney Cauthorn)* "Immaculate guest rooms, simply, but nicely decorated." *(Jean Little)* "Delicious breakfast choice of eggs, omelets, Belgian waffles, pancakes." *(Billie Pavich)* "Lighting, heating, plumbing, cleanliness, parking were all excellent. Relaxed atmosphere with good conversation." *(Scott & Ann Withrow)* "Much useful advice about what to see and where to eat." *(John Parker-Jones)* "Spotless, with extra-firm beds." *(Emily Murphy)* "Convenient location—quiet, yet within easy walking distance of town." *(Joy Thompson)* "My room was a bit small but was well furnished. Breakfast was well prepared and served in a dining room with views of the neighborhood." *(James Utt)* Reports welcome.

Open All year.
Rooms 6 doubles—all with private bath and/or shower, radio, air-conditioning, ceiling fan. 1 with TV, 1 with desk.
Facilities Living room with fireplace, dining room, TV room. Patio, picnic table. Maury River & Goshen Pass nearby for swimming, fishing; hiking, horseback riding on the 7-mile Chessie Nature Trail. Golf, tennis nearby.
Location 8-min. walk to historic district. From I-81, take Rte. 11 S to inn.
Restrictions No smoking in dining room or guest rooms. No children under 10.
Credit cards Amex, MC, Visa.
Rates B&B, $70–85 double, $65–80 single. Extra person, $10. $5 senior discount.
Extras Bus station pickups.

LOCUST DALE

The Inn at Meander Plantation

James Madison Highway, U.S. Route 15, HCR 5, Box 460A, 22948

Tel: 540–672–4912
Fax: 540–672–4912

Could there be a better way to get a feel for Virginia's history than to stay in a manor house on a working plantation dating from 1766? To enjoy quiet conversation or a book in a parlor where both Jefferson and La-fayette were frequent visitors? A three-story white brick Georgian man-sion with an expansive columned front porch, The Inn at Meander Plantation has a brick archway connecting the main house to the summer kitchen, said to have been designed by Thomas Jefferson. After days spent exploring Montpelier and Monticello, Chancellorville or Charlottesville, guests can relax on the rocking chairs on the two-story back porches and enjoy the sun setting over the Blue Ridge Mountains. Guest rooms are furnished with antiques, period reproductions, and queen- or king-size beds; one is done in deep begonia pink with Battenburg lace, another in hunter green with crisp white accents. The inn was purchased in 1991 by Suzanne Thomas, Suzie Blanchard and Bob Blanchard, who also operate a horse farm on the grounds.

Breakfast is usually served at 9 A.M. in either the formal dining room or in the arched breezeway on sunny mornings. A typical menu might consist of cantaloupe with mint; cornbread with sausage, mushrooms and sun-dried tomatoes; herbed scrambled eggs; tomatoes with basil; sugar-cured ham; and poppyseed muffins with homemade preserves; equally tempting dinners are available by advance reservation.

"Outstanding setting; gracious, friendly hosts. Rooms are spacious, clean, and furnished with lovely antiques. Bathrooms have been redone with modern plumbing." *(Helgi Shuford)* "The owners have done an incred-ible amount of work; every room seems freshly painted, linens are new, bathrooms updated, beds comfortable—especially the high four-posters. Cordial hosts; even the dog and cat welcome guests." *(Anne Wright)* "Suzie Blanchard is a superb cook; breakfasts could not have been more delicious or more attractively served." *(Charles Wikle)*

Open All year. Closed Christmas Day.
Rooms 2 suites, 3 doubles—all with full private bath, radio, clock, air-condition-ing. Some with desk, fireplace, refrigerator, veranda. TV, telephone on request.

Facilities Dining room, living room with fireplace, reception room with baby grand piano, guest refrigerator, porches. 80 acres with lawn games, hammock, gardens, woods; borders river for rafting, fishing, tubing (poles, tubes provided). Golf nearby.

Location 70 M SW of Washington DC, 35 m NE of Charlottesville; 9 m S of Culpeper, 6 m N of Orange. On W side U.S. Rte. 15, approx. halfway between Orange & Culpeper.

Restrictions No smoking.

Credit cards MC, Visa.

Rates B&B, $165–175 suite, $95–130 double. Extra person, $15. Tips appreciated. 2-night minimum Oct. weekends & holidays. Prix fixe dinner by advance reservation, $39. Business, weekly rates. Holiday weekend packages.

Extras Station pickups, $10.

LURAY

Also recommended: Two lodging concessions are located on the Skyline Drive, within Shenandoah National Park, **Big Meadows Lodge** at Milepost 51.3, and **Skyland Lodge**, at Milepost 41.7. Both can be reached through ARA Virginia Skyline Company, P.O. Box 727, 22835; 800–999–4714, 540–999–2211, in-season, or 540–743–5108, off-season. Big Meadows is open from mid-May through October; Skylands is open from March through mid-December. Reservations for either must be made months in advance. Big Meadows takes its name from its setting on a high plateau looking down over the Shenandoah Valley. The rustic main lodge is built of wormy chestnut with floors of flagstone and oak; a dining room and bar provide local cuisine and beverages. Miles of hiking trails provide breathtaking views, cool waterfalls, and fields of wildflowers; tours by horse drawn wagon are also available. Evening campfire programs are provided for both entertainment and information. "Well worth the small difference for a room with a mountain view in the actual lodge; upstairs rooms are quieter. Rooms are basic, but clean and comfortable; strong water pressure in the shower. The food is homestyle and tasty; try the turkey and gravy with mashed potatoes. Sign your name on the reservation list when the restaurant opens, then relax in a rocking chair in the sitting room, while you wait to be called. Don't miss the ranger's talk at the amphitheater near the lodge in the evening after dinner." (Jill Reeves) "No problem with the lack of air-conditioning in July—the altitude meant night temperatures were fine for good sleeping." (Ellsworth Morey) Rates range from $60–117.

For an additional area entry, see **Stanley**.

LYNCHBURG

Lynchburg is located in the foothills of the Blue Ridge Mountains, 15 miles east of the Parkway, three hours southwest of Washington, DC, 50 miles east of Roanoke, and 60 miles southwest of Charlottesville. The city was built along the banks of the James River, and was a Confederate supply base during the Civil War. Lynchburg, Randolph-Macon, and Sweet Briar colleges are based here.

Reader tip: "Getting around Lynchburg is confusing for the uninitiated; make sure you have specific directions from your innkeeper."

Federal Crest Inn
1101 Federal Street, 24504

Tel: 804–845–6155
800–818–6155

A classic brick Georgian Revival home built in 1909, the Federal Crest inn was opened in 1995 by Ann and Phil Ripley, and features the original woodwork, moldings, mahogany pocket doors, and leaded glass windows. Rates include tea and home-baked chocolate chip cookies on arrival, night snack baskets, and breakfasts served between 7:30 and 9:30 A.M. A typical menu might consist of grapefruit broiled with brown sugar, just-baked blueberry muffins, omelets with hash brown potatoes, baked apples, and homemade biscuits. Guest rooms are named for Virginia trees, with queen-size canopy or poster beds. The pink and white blossoms of the Dogwood room complement the yards of white lace framing the iron canopy bed, while the Blue Spruce room has a mahogany queen-size bed and a double Jacuzzi tub with a wall mural of the Blue Ridge Mountains.

"Classy yet cozy, ideal for relaxed pampering." *(Susan Tracy)* "Ann and Phil have thought of everything to make their guests comfortable, from the down comforter on the bed to the terry bathrobe waiting for me after showering. The coffee and juice set on the landing outside my room was a perfect wakeup." *(Kathy Jenkins)*

Open All year.
Rooms 2 suites, 3 doubles—all with private bath and/or shower, radio, clock, air-conditioning. 2 with TV, 3 with desk, gas fireplace, enclosed porch; 1 with double whirlpool tub.
Facilities Dining room, living room with fireplace, TV/VCR; library with books, games; guest pantry, Fifties Cafe, gift shop. 1 acre with off-street parking, lawn games, bicycles.
Location Federal Hill historic district; 6 block from center. Take Rte. 29 Expressway & exit at Main St. Go to 11th St. & turn left. Go 6 blocks to Federal & 11th. Inn is red brick home on left corner.
Restrictions No smoking. Children 10 and over.
Credit cards Amex, MC, Visa.
Rates B&B, $85–115 suite, $55–95 double. Extra person, $15. 5% senior, AAA discount. 2-night weekend minimum, May, Oct. Prix fixe lunch, $8; dinner, $12; advance notice; 15% service. Dinner weekend packages.
Extras Airport/station pickups, $10.

Langhorne Manor 🏃
313 Washington Street, 24504

Tel: 804–846–4667
800–851–1466

While recycling newspapers and bottles is undoubtedly important, perhaps the ultimate in recycling is returning the remains of a once-beautiful house to its original elegance. A 27-room neoclassical mansion built in 1850, Langhorne Manor sat boarded up and abandoned when Jaime and Jaynee Acevedo first saw it in 1987. The mansion's restoration, still in progress, has produced handsome rooms decorated with mahogany and walnut furnishings, crystal and brass chandeliers, and yards of lace, moiré, and damask. Breakfasts are served at guests' convenience; perhaps poached pears with apricot lime sauce; Scottish scones with currants; whole grain apple pancakes with homemade blackberry syrup; and thick slab bacon, garnished with fresh pineapple, kiwi, and grapes.

"Wonderful hospitality and comfortable furnishings. Good location close to main road and local attractions. Excellent breakfast including edible flowers from the garden. Resident proprietors Jaime and Jaynee Acevedo are accommodating to children, arranging for babysitters and special kid-sized breakfast." *(Laurie G. Ford)* "Outstanding food, wonderful hosts, great ambience." *(Charles Guggenheimer)*

Open All year.
Rooms 1 suite, 3 doubles—all with private bath and/or shower, telephone, radio, clock, air-conditioning, fan. 2 with TV, desk.
Facilities Breakfast room, living room, parlor, music room with games, gathering room, art gallery. 6/10 acre with off-street parking, swing set. YMCA next door for swimming.
Location Diamond Hill historic district; 5 blocks to center. From Rte. 29S, exit at Bus. 29. Cross James River. Turn left at third traffic light onto Church & go right onto Washington. From Rte. 29 N, take Main St. exit (towards downtown). Immediate left onto Pearl. Right onto Church, left onto Washington.
Restrictions Train whistle audible in 2 rooms. No smoking. Infants and children over 5 welcome.
Credit cards Amex, Discover, MC, Visa.
Rates B&B, $95–115 suite, $80–105 double, $65–90 single. Extra adult, $15; extra child, $10. 10% senior, AAA discount. 2-night weekend minimum May, Oct. Picnic lunches; prix fixe dinner, $15–30.
Extras Airport/station pickup. Crib, babysitting with notice. Spanish spoken.

Lynchburg Mansion Inn
405 Madison Street, 24504

Tel: 804–528–5400
800–352–1199

When it comes to B&Bs, there are mansions and then there are *mansions*. At 9,000 square feet, this imposing Spanish Georgian mansion, built in 1914, clearly falls into the latter category. Constructed for the then princely sum of $86,000, the mansion has massive concrete front steps rising to the huge six columned entry portico. The front door opens onto the 50-foot grand hall with soaring ceilings and restored cherry columns and wainscoting. Chopped up into apartments in the late 1950s, it was restored to its original glory by Bob and Mauranna Sherman in 1990. Guest room decor varies from the Victorian-style Gilliam Room, with a mahogany four-poster bed, a rose-strewn comforter, plump pillows, and billowing lace, to the light and airy Country French Room done in crisp Laura Ashley fabrics with a bleached four-poster bed and immense armoire. Breakfast, served in a formal dining room on fine china, crystal, and silver, might consist of honey-roasted fruits, muffins and crumpets, peach French toast, asparagus omelet, or broccoli bacon quiche, accompanied by ham, local sausage, or bacon. It's served starting at 7 A.M. on weekdays, and generally around 8:30 or 9:00 on weekends.

"Spacious, well-equipped suite. A short jaunt took us to a hot tub. Coffee and juice delivered to your room; a full family-style breakfast served thirty minutes later. Lots of reading materials and good bedside

351

lighting made this a restful get-away." *(Christine DeSantis)* "Spanish Colonial Revival with Chinese Chippendale details, best describes this magnificent edifice, built by mining heir James Gilliam, who clearly subscribed to the philosophy that 'more is more.' The inn was decorated professionally and guest rooms and baths are thoughtfully furnished with every necessity for a comfortable stay. Extensive Edwardian paneling has been preserved on the ground floor." *(Kristina Taylor)* "Top-of-the-line from enormous towels to satin-soft sheets to fantastic breakfast." *(Ali & Jon Matheson)*

Open All year.
Rooms 1 suite, 3 doubles—all with private bath and/or shower, telephone, radio, clock, TV, air-conditioning. 3 with desk, 3 with fireplace; suite with refrigerator, microwave, veranda.
Facilities Dining room, living room with fireplace, piano; library with fireplace. ½ acre with off-street parking, hot tub.
Location Garland Hill Historic District. From Rte. 29, take Exit Main Street (downtown). Continue on Main St. until 5th St. (Business Rte. 29). Go left on 5th St. Go right on Madison St. Inn on left.
Restrictions No smoking.
Credit cards Amex, MC, Visa.
Rates B&B, $119 suite, $89–99 double, $84–94 single. Extra person, $20. Children under 8, free. 10% senior, 10% AAA discount; corporate rates. 2-night weekend minimum in Oct., May.

The Madison House B&B ¢ 413 Madison Street, 24504

Tel: 804–528–1503
800–828–6422

Lynchburg's first B&B, The Madison House is a combination of Eastlake and Italianate architecture, and was restored as a B&B in 1990 by Irene and Dale Smith. Its "painted lady" exterior is yellow with dark green trim, plus touches of coral, gold, and purple. The mansion, built in 1880 for a tobacco baron, features original porcelain bathroom fixtures, crystal chandeliers, a peacock stained glass window in one of the parlors, and a gigantic gold leaf over-mantel mirror in another. Antiques highlight the guest room decor, from the antique vanity and king-size canopy bed of the Gold Room to the 1830s hand-carved mahogany bed and a Civil War-era dresser of the Rose Room. The focal point of the dining room is an 1850s English banquet table, where the Smiths serve breakfasts of cinnamon coffee, orange juice, fresh fruit, homemade muffins and French puffs, and such entrées as Swiss oven omelets, quiche with Southern fried potatoes, or French toast with Vermont maple syrup. Rates also include afternoon tea, served at 4:00 P.M. with such home-baked treats as chocolate chip cake, blueberry cake, chocolate torte, ginger cake, Irish soda bread, or English scones.

"Irene prepared a light breakfast for us at 7:00 A.M. when we were in town for a ten-mile race." *(Col. & Mrs. M.W. Smiley)* "Exquisitely furnished and decorated—nothing is spared to ensure guests' comfort." *(Coleen & Joe Bennett)* "Breakfast was delicious and appealing." *(Simeon & Helen Stidham)* "Afternoon tea was a highlight of my stay; warm hospitality, splendid conversation." *(GR)*

Open All year.
Rooms 1 suite, 3 doubles—all with private bath and/or shower, telephone, radio, clock, TV, air-conditioning. 3 with fireplace. 1 with desk, porch.
Facilities Dining room with fireplace, 2 parlors with fireplace, piano, stereo, books; library, guest refrigerator; porch. Off-street parking. Golf, boating, fishing, hiking, skiing nearby.
Location Garland Hill Historic District. From Expy Rte. 29, take Main St. downtown Exit (1A). Take Main to 5th St. Go left on 5th, for four blocks. Go right on Madison. 1st house on left.
Restrictions Traffic noise in one room. No smoking. No children.
Credit cards Amex, MC, Visa.
Rates B&B, $109 suite, $79–89 double, $69 single. Extra person, $10. 2-night weekend minimum in May, Oct.
Extras Airport/station pick-ups, $5 per person.

MIDDLEBURG

Middleburg is located in northeastern Virginia, in Loudoun County—Horse Country. It's just 50 minutes west of Washington, DC, and 22 miles west of Dulles International Airport. Although readers are unanimous in their praise of the town's charms, such convenience doesn't come cheap, and rates are high.

Reader tip: The town of Middleburg is most appealing, and the surrounding countryside lovely, with rolling hills and thoroughbred horse farms." *(BH)* "The numerous shops and galleries are attended by gracious and helpful shopkeepers." *(GA)*

Information please: The **Middleburg Inn and Guest Suites** (105 West Washington Street, 22117; 540–687–3115; 800–432–6125) offers five elegantly furnished suites and doubles—all with canopy bed, private bath, telephone, and cable TV. Rates range from $130–195; guests are referred to the neighboring **Red Fox Inn**'s main dining room for a complimentary breakfast.

For additional area entries, see listings under **Aldie** and **Paris**.

Middleburg Country Inn 🏃   *Tel:* 540–687–6082
209 East Washington Street, Box 2065, 22117   800–262–6082
                                            Fax: 540–687–5603

Dating back to 1820, the Middleburg Country Inn served as an Episcopal rectory for 150 years; Susan and John Pettibone purchased it in 1987 and opened it as an inn in 1990. Each room (with king- or queen-size canopy bed) is furnished in the color, period and style suggested by the home of a favorite son of Virginia. A breakfast of blueberry or apple spice waffles, eggs any style, and home-baked cakes, plus fresh fruit or freshly squeezed orange juice, is served from 8:00–10:30 in the dining room, or on the veranda in good weather. Guests can help themselves to coffee, tea, soft drinks, and baked goods set out in the parlor during the day. At 7:00 P.M., a four-course prix fixe dinner is served.

"Well-maintained, with comfortable beds and clean bathrooms. Breakfast was excellent with a large number of choices." *(W.F. Ogden)* "Greeted warmly at this cozy, quaint inn. Fine meals, good wine from local vineyards, good service." *(Michelle & Al Hendricks)* "We were welcomed with freshly baked cookies, brownies, and iced tea—perfect for a hot summer day. Our hosts provided information on wine tastings and tours, and other area activities." *(Allison & Brian Schultz)* "Our room, 'Monticello,' offered excellent lighting for reading, a comfortable sitting area, and a comfortable bed." *(DH)* "Fine food; quiet, peaceful accommodations." *(Kathleen Pilcher)*

Open All year.
Rooms 2 suites, 6 doubles—all with full private bath, telephone, TV/VCR, fireplace, air-conditioning. Suites with Jacuzzi tub.
Facilities Dining room, living room with fireplace, TV/VCR, book/tape library; veranda. ½ acre with hot tub. Off-street parking.
Location On Rte. 50, 3 blocks from center.
Restrictions Traffic noise in 3 front rooms; "no complaints so far."
Credit cards Amex, MC, Visa.
Rates MAP, $225–275 suite, $145–195 double. B&B rates midweek. Corporate discount.
Extras Crib, babysitting. French, Spanish spoken.

The Red Fox Inn and Tavern ✖

2 East Washington Street
P.O. 385, 22117

Tel: 540–687–6301
Outside VA: 800–223–1728
Fax: 540–687–6053

In 1728, Joseph Chinn built this tavern, known then as Chinn's Ordinary. During the Civil War, the tavern also served as a hospital; the pine bar in the Tap Room was made from an operating table. The name was changed to the Red Fox in 1937, and in 1976, Turner Reuter, Jr. took over the inn and began a major renovation effort. The nearby Stray Fox Inn and McConnell House date back to the 19th century and are decorated with period reproductions; guests preferring a quieter atmosphere should request rooms in either one.

"Our lovely room was pleasantly furnished with reproduction pieces. A *Washington Post* was left outside our door each morning; a dish of chocolate truffles and fresh fruit slices awaited by our bedside each night." *(Barbara Hornbach)* "Offers the privacy of a small hotel. Our suite, the Glenwood, had an entry hall, separate bedroom and sitting room. The food was excellent, especially the black bean soup with sausage." *(Reid Mitchell)* "Our fourth floor room at the Red Fox was up a steep, narrow staircase. It's easy to bang one's head on the low door frames, but our exceptionally spacious quarters made it well worth the effort. We had a large bathroom with ample plush towels and soaps, lots of hot water, and a full-length mirror. Across the hall was the sitting room with a full-size desk, comfy couch, current magazines, wine for purchase, a huge closet with real hangers, and good lighting. Our spacious bedroom was decorated with an antique dresser, night tables on either side of the queen-size four poster bed, two comfy chairs, and another massive closet with extra pillows and blankets. The beds were firm and comfy with soft sheets and pillows. A breakfast tray of fresh-baked coffee cake, tea, coffee, and juice was brought to our room. We had an outstanding dinner at the tavern, with a tender filet mignon, and tasty roast chicken. The peanut soup is a must. Superb service." *(Perri & Mike Rappel)* Reports needed.

Open All year.
Rooms 9 suites, 15 doubles in 5 buildings—all with private bath and/or shower, telephone, radio, TV, desk, air-conditioning. Most with canopy bed; 9 with fireplace. 1 suite with screened porch. 17 rooms at Stray Fox Inn, McConnell House.
Facilities Restaurant, bar, pub, terraces. Riding lessons, ballooning trips, equestrian events and activities nearby.
Location Center of town.
Restrictions Weekend restaurant noise at Stray Fox.
Credit cards Amex, DC, Discover, MC, Visa.
Rates B&B, $150–225 suite, $135–155 double. Extra person, $25. Alc lunch, $15; alc dinner, $40–50; smaller portions for children under 12.
Extras Limited wheelchair access. Crib, cot, by advance notice, $10–25.

MIDDLETOWN

Wayside Inn Since 1797 🛏 ✗
7783 Main Street, 22645

Tel: 540–869–1797
Fax: 540–869–1797

The Wayside served as a stagecoach stop through much of the 19th century. Since it was used by soldiers from both the North and South during the Civil War, it was saved from destruction when Stonewall Jackson's famous Valley Campaign swept past only a few miles away. The two side wings and the third floor date to the early 1900s, when owner Samuel Rhodes changed the inn's name to the Wayside. Meals feature Colonial-era favorites—peanut soup, spoon bread, prime rib, country ham, pan-fried chicken, served with fresh vegetables and homemade breads and dessert. "We give Wayside the highest recommendation; wonderfully friendly staff, great ambience, fully modern bathrooms, good food—starting with a large glass of freshly squeezed orange juice at breakfast." *(Mary Littlejohn)* "Excellent food, friendly staff; toured rooms—clean, comfortable, nice antiques." *(Jane Beck)* "We slept in a high rope bed, and our bath had bars of lavendar soap and lots of thick new towels. Beautiful antique-filled dining rooms serving original Colonial foods." *(Mrs. Peter Payne)*

Open All year.
Rooms 2 suites, 22 doubles—all with private bath and/or shower, telephone, TV, desk, air-conditioning. 1 with balcony/deck. 5 rooms in guest house, sharing two baths.
Facilities 3 dining rooms, sun-room, sitting room, den with TV, library, bar/lounge with VCR, stereo; conference/seminar facilities. 20 acres with patio, gazebo. Hiking, swimming, fishing, boating, golfing, downhill skiing nearby.
Location 75 m W of Washington, D.C. 13 m S of Winchester. In-town location. From I-81, take Middletown Exit 302 & follow Rte. 11 S to town.
Restrictions Light sleepers should request rooms in back. No smoking in dining areas.
Credit cards Amex, DC, Discover, MC, Visa.
Rates Room only, $110–125 suite, $70–100 double. Extra person, $20. Children

under 16 stay free. 10% AAA, AARP, senior discount. Full breakfast, $3–7. Alc lunch, $5–8; alc dinner, $25.

Extras Crib. Babysitting by arrangment. French spoken.

MONTEREY

At the turn of the century, travelers journeyed to the mountains of western Virginia to enjoy the cool climate and spring waters. Monterey is a village of 300 people and is surrounded by three million acres of National Forest.

Information please: Built as a resort in 1904, the **Highland Inn** (Main Street, P.O. Box 40, 24465; 540–468–2143) is listed on the National Register of Historic Places. In its heyday, guests ranged from Henry Ford and Harvey Firestone to Eric Rommel (the "Desert Fox"), who stayed in the hotel in the late 1930s when researching the battle tactics of Confederate General Stonewall Jackson. A three-story frame Victorian with a two-story porch, the Highland has 17 guest rooms simply furnished with Victorian antiques and collectibles; some have four-poster and canopy beds. The B&B rates of $50–80 include a light continental breakfast, and the reasonably priced restaurant is open Wednesday through Saturday for dinner and Sunday for brunch.

NELLYSFORD

Information please: Built by a mill owner in 1913, **The Meander Inn** (Routes 612 & 613, 22958; 804–361–1121) offers a peaceful farm setting and lovely views of the Rockfish River and the surrounding woods and mountains. Guest rooms are furnished with either Victorian or country antiques, four-poster or twin sleigh beds. Early risers can fetch the morning eggs from the hen house and bring the horses their breakfast grain. Breakfast varies daily, but might include eggs scrambled with ham, feta cheese, and scallions, plus herbed red potatoes, English muffins, banana bread, fresh fruit and juice. Double rates for the five doubles, all with private bath, range from $60–90.

The Mark Addy   *Tel:* 804–361–1101
Route 613 West, Rte. 1, Box 375, 22958   800–278–2154

John Maddox, who manages the inn purchased in 1993 by his mother, Joanne Maddox, is using his experience as a chef, antiques expert, and theatre director, to good effect at the Mark Addy. Named for Joanne's parents (John's grandparents), the inn is furnished with Victorian antiques. Breakfasts reflect John's catering background; perhaps blueberry-stuffed French toast and fresh pears with blue cheese and pecans, or hot cinnamon grapefruit and an egg and cheese strata with ham and apples. Dinners are available by reservation; a recent menu included crab in pastry, coq au vin, herb-roasted potatoes, spinach and pea timbales, salad with blood oranges, and a chocolate truffle loaf.

"Magnificent mountain setting; beautiful views. Friendly owners, yet ample privacy. An atmosphere of quiet elegance and relaxation." *(Dave & Cindy Slawson)* "Therapeutic Jacuzzi after a day of skiing. Best of all are the 'power' breakfasts, different each day." *(Steven Faber)* "Exceptional care and attention to detail. Every facet of our stay, from the check-in and tour of the antique-filled rooms to the mouth-watering breakfasts was perfect. The innkeepers accommodated our vegetarian preferences, arranged for flowers to enhance the romance of our room, and were knowledgeable about local restaurants and sites. The Mimosa Room was exquisitely decorated with an Oriental silkscreen, miniature carvings and delicate wood furniture. The chocolate truffles and cordials left at our bedside were a wonderful touch." *(Mark Faherty & Stephanie Herold)*

Open All year.
Rooms 1 suite, 8 doubles—all with private bath and/or shower, clock, air-conditioning, ceiling fan. 3 with double whirlpool tub, 4 with balcony/deck, 2 with radio.
Facilities Dining room, breakfast room, living room, sittting room with TV/VCR, stereo, library; guest refrigerator. Porches, veranda, deck, hammock. 12.5 acres with off-street parking. Near Lake Nelson and James River. 9 m to Wintergreen for downhill skiing. 9 m to Appalachian Trail.
Location Nelson County, Rockfish Valley. 30 m SW of Charlottesville. From Charlottesville, go W on Rte. 250 for 15 m; go S (left) on Rte. 151 for 9.8 m; go W (right) on Rte. 613 to inn immediately on right.
Restrictions No smoking. Children 12 and over.
Credit cards MC, Visa.
Rates B&B, $125–135 suite, $90–115 double, $90–105 single. Extra person, $25. Midweek senior discount. Packages. 2-night weekend minimum, Oct., holidays. Prix fixe lunch, $20; dinner, $35.
Extras Wheelchair access. Train station pickup, $27.50. Airport pickup, $30. Crib. German spoken; some French, Spanish.

Trillium House ✗ ⚮

Wintergreen Drive,
P.O. Box 280, 22958

Tel: 804–325–9126
800–325–9126
Fax: 804–325–1099

Wintergreen is a beautiful four-season mountain resort community of 10,000 acres. Ed and Betty Dinwiddie designed and built Trillium in 1983, for people who prefer a country inn with easy resort access. Nineteenth-century antiques, reproductions, and contemporary furniture make up the decor.

"The inn has a lovely arched window over the entrance, and lots of wood used inside and out. Just inside the front door is the main living area; a library is located upstairs in a quiet loft setting, and downstairs is a TV room with large-screen television. The spacious guest rooms are simply but comfortably furnished, with such amenities as fluffy towels and scented soaps. We found the weekend dinners to be tasty and a good value; breakfast was hearty and plentiful. Good features include parking facilities, ski racks, great showers, and perfect location for skiing." *(CBG)* "The breakfast room overlooks the trees and golf course; closer to the window are bird feeders attracting numerous and varied birds. The Dinwiddies do everything possible to see that every guest is comfortable." *(Corbin White)*

"Just as described. The twice-daily towel service and evening turndown were a treat. Always a bowl of fresh fruit and a filled candy dish in the sitting room. Dinner on Friday night was delicious; although the tables were set with linen and candles, the atmosphere was casual and relaxing." *(Amy Peritsky)* "We had a relaxing family-style dinnner here. Great location for skiing in winter, golf in summer. Nice owners; friendly, homey common areas." *(Laurie Ford)*

Open All year. Closed Dec. 24, 25. Dining room open Fri., Sat. (single entrée, seating at 7:30 P.M.).

Rooms 2 suites, 10 doubles—all with full private bath, telephone, air-conditioning. Some with desk. TV on request.

Facilities Restaurant, living room, library, garden room, TV room with VCR, woodstove. 1½ acres with gazebo, wildflower garden. Wintergreen resort activities ($8 per person & up): swimming pools, exercise spa, tennis courts, golf, hiking, fishing, canoeing, horseback riding, downhill skiing.

Location NW VA; Blue Ridge Mts. 3 hrs. SW of Washington, DC. Between mileposts 13 & 14 on Blue Ridge Parkway. From Charlottesville, take I-64 W to Crozet Exit 107. Take 250 W to Rte. 151 & turn left. Follow 151 S 14 m & turn right onto 664 & go 4.5 miles to entry. From entry gate follow Wintergreen Dr. 3 ½ m to inn on left.

Restrictions No smoking in dining room.

Credit cards MC, Visa.

Rates B&B, $120–150 suite, $90–105 double, $85–100 single. Extra person, $35. 2–3 day peak/holiday weekend minimum. Prix fixe dinner, $25–35.

Extras Wheelchair access. Airport/station pickup, cost varies. Crib; babysitting by prior arrangement.

NEW CHURCH

The Garden and the Sea Inn
Rte. 710, Box 1A, 23415
Mailing address: P.O. Box 275

Tel: 804–824–0672

Whether it needs it or not, you can probably give an old inn a total makeover every 100 years or so. Built as a tavern in 1802, this building was enlarged into a Victorian country home in 1901, complete with gables, gingerbread trim, and stained glass windows. Some 90 years later, it was restored as a full-service country inn decorated with country Victorian furnishings. In 1993, an adjacent 1870s farm house was renovated to provide additional guest rooms. Owners since 1994, Tom and Sara Baker share the innkeeping responsibilities; Tom, a graduate of the Culinary Institute of America, is the chef, while Sara handles the guest accommodations. House specialties include shrimp with bourbon cream sauce, or a melange of sea scallops and oysters with tomatoes and mushrooms. Continental breakfast is served either in the dining room overlooking the gardens or on the garden patio beside the lily pond and fountains. The color scheme effectively varies soft mauves, blues, ivory, and moss green tones. Some antiques, swagged and puffed window treatments, flowered chintz fabrics, and Oriental rugs complete the look. One guest room is done in wicker, another has an unusual wrought iron bed and matching makeup table; modern bathrooms are large and well-equipped. "Charming rooms, exceptional food." *(DLG)* More reports welcome.

Open April 1–Thanksgiving weekend.

Rooms 5 doubles—all with full private bath, air-conditioning, ceiling fan. 2 with bidet, 3 with whirlpool tub. 3 rooms in Garden House.

Facilities Restaurant, parlor, library, guest kitchen, screened & unscreened porches. Tennis, golf, beaches, fishing, swimming nearby. Off-street parking.

Location Eastern Shore. 3 hrs. from Washington, DC, Baltimore, MD, Richmond, VA. 12 m W of Chincoteague. From N, take Rte. 13 S to New Church; 1 m past the MD-VA state line turn right at First Virginia Bank (Rte. 710) to inn on right. From S, take Rte. 13 N to New Church. 2 m N of Rte. 175 turn left at First Virginia Bank (Rte. 710) to inn on right.

Restrictions Smoking in parlor only.

Credit cards Amex, Discover, MC, Visa.

Rates B&B, $85–155 double. Extra person, $15. 2–3 night minimum holidays, June–mid-Sept. weekends. Romance packages. Prix fixe dinner, $27–34; alc dinner, $35–40.

Extras Restaurant wheelchair accessible. Airport pickups. Pets with advance permission and damage deposit.

NEW MARKET

Information please: Just off I-81, 16 miles west of Luray is the **Red Shutter Farmhouse** (Route 1, Box 376, New Market 22844; 540–740–4281), dating back to 1790. Rates for the five guest rooms range from $65–70, and include a full breakfast, served in the log cabin dining room. The inn occupies 20 rural acres, and sits at the base of Massanutten Mountain. "Quiet and peaceful, clean and cheery. George and Juanita Miller are gracious owners, and her pancakes are terrific. Our favorite is the Blue Room, with a gas fireplace." *(JM)*

NOKESVILLE

Also recommended: In northeastern Virginia, one hour west of Washington, near the Manasses National Battlefield, is the **Shiloh Bed and Breakfast** (13520 Carriage Ford Road, 22123; 703–594–2664). One suite has a view of the freshwater bass-filled lake and meadows beyond, the other has a private garden patio with hot tub. Each has a private bath, sitting area, microwave and refrigerator. A full breakfast and welcoming refreshments are included in the $95–130 double rates. "Romantic, private, lovely setting, cordial hospitality, delicious breakfasts." *(Lori Hamilton, and others)*

NORFOLK

A prominent port from the 1700s to the present, Norfolk, home to the Norfolk Naval Base, has recently restored and revitalized its historic business and residential areas, starting with the Waterside complex, a new convention center, as well as several other projects.

The Page House Inn
323 Fairfax Avenue, 23507

Tel: 804–625–5033
Fax: 804–623–9451

A typical B&B restoration involves stripping paint and wallpaper, pulling up layers of linoleum, and pulling down false ceilings and walls to reveal the hidden treasures beneath. At the Page House, an 1899 Georgian Revival brick mansion, years of decay and abandonment ensured that there was little left to uncover. When Stephanie and Ezio Di Belardino bought the then-condemned Page House in 1990, an enormous challenge awaited them. Stephanie battled the zoning board for months, while Ezio—a master craftsman—set up shop in the kitchen to mill the golden oak woodwork—moldings, banisters, balustrades, cornices, and more—that now highlights the house; he also installed central air-conditioning and private baths. The stunning staircase soars three stories to the rooftop skylight. Guest rooms are furnished with antiques and fine art, some with canopy beds. A breakfast of fresh-squeezed orange juice and home-baked breads is served on fine china, with crystal and silver. Cappuccino and freshly baked cookies are offered each afternoon from 4 to 6 P.M. in the drawing room. The inn is located in the Ghent Historic District, originally developed in the late 19th century as an exclusive residential neighborhood. Badly rundown after World War II, it's now been regentrified with beautifully restored homes, gardens, and quiet tree-lined streets.

"Gorgeous place, extraordinary renovation; cordial hosts." *(Lars Nilsson)* "Delicious food; appreciated the 24-hour availability of refreshments. Immaculate rooms, beautifully decorated." *(S. Gulley)* "Stephanie is a gracious hostess, providing good advice about local attractions." *(Karl & Linda Warmbrod)*

Open All year. Closed Christmas week.
Rooms 2 suites, 4 doubles—all with full private bath, telephone, radio, clock, TV, desk, air-conditioning. 3 with fireplace, 2 with wet bar/refrigerator, whirlpool tub.
Facilities Living room with fireplace, dining room with fireplace, TV room with VCR, books, fireplace; 2nd & 3rd floor sitting areas, 2 unscreened porches. Off-street parking. 20 min. to ocean beaches, fishing.
Location Ghent Historic District. Adjacent to Chrysler Art Museum. Walking distance to cultural attractions & downtown financial district. From I-64, take exit for I-264 to downtown Norfolk. Merging into I-264, stay left & follow signs for Waterside Dr. Waterside becomes Bousch St. after Town Point Park. From Bousch, turn left on Olney Rd., then left again at Mowbray Arch. Go 1 block, then right on Fairfax to inn on left.
Restrictions No smoking. Children over 12.
Credit cards MC, Visa.
Rates B&B, $130–145 suite, $80–120 double. 2-night minimum some weekends, holidays. Corporate rates.
Extras Italian, some Spanish spoken.

ORANGE

Orange is in north central Virginia, 60 miles southwest of Washington, DC, midway between Fredericksburg and Charlottesville. It's 30 miles northwest of Charlottesville, and 5 miles from Montpelier. From Washington, DC, take I-495 to I-66 west to Route 29 south. Take the Orange exit of Route 29 to Route 15 to Orange.

Reader tip: "This area is rich in history. Montpelier, home of James and Dolley Madison, is 10 minutes away and is now open to the public. Ash Lawn (President James Monroe's home) is about 30 minutes away." *(Carolyn Myles)*

For an additional area entry, see **Locust Dale.**

The Hidden Inn
249 Caroline Street, 22960

Tel: 540–672–3625
800–841–1253
Fax: 540–672–5029

Ray and Barbara Lonick bought the Hidden Inn in 1987, and describe it as being a particular favorite with "couples from the Washington, D.C., area who are looking for a romantic getaway. Our inn is quiet and cozy, with wicker pieces on the verandas; Oriental rugs in the public rooms; silver, and lace tablecloths in the dining room. Our color scheme is rose, white, and light blue, with lots of fresh flowers." The decor is largely Victorian, and most rooms have brass or canopy queen-size beds. Breakfast is served from 8–9:30 A.M. (until 10:00 A.M. on weekends) and might include granola, corn muffins with strawberry jam, grits, eggs, fried apples, ham, and toast, while the single-entrée dinner offering might consist of artichokes Romano, carrot orange soup, green salad, beef filet in wine sauce with wild rice and asparagus, and Oreo cookie cheesecake for dessert.

"Generous, delicious breakfasts; each day a new menu. Mid-day tea with homemade pastries." *(Jane Gawron)* "Thirty minutes from Skyline Drive and several Civil War battlefields. Innkeepers kept us informed of all the nearby events." *(Jim Kasoff)* "We slept in brass twin beds; they placed chocolates on our pillow at night. Friendly owners, good service— quiet and peaceful atmosphere." *(Arlyne Craighead)* Reports welcome.

Open All year. Closed Christmas.
Rooms 10 doubles, 2 cottages—all with private bath and/or shower, air-conditioning, radio, clock. Some with double Jacuzzi tub, telephone, TV, desk, ceiling fan, fireplace, refrigerator, veranda. Rooms in 4 buildings.
Facilities Dining room, 2 living rooms with fireplace, TV; wraparound verandas. 6 acres with vegetable, rose gardens, gazebo, croquet, horseshoes, and badminton. Swimming, fishing, boating, tennis, golf nearby.
Location N central VA. 30 m N of Charlottesville, 5 m from Montpelier. 3 blocks from center. From Washington, DC, take I-495 to I-66 W to Rte. 29 S. Take Orange exit off Rte. 29 S to Rte. 15 to Orange.
Restrictions Morning train might disturb light sleepers. No smoking.
Credit cards Amex, MC, Visa.

Rates B&B, $79–159 double, $59–79 single. Extra person, $20. 2-night weekend minimum. Prix fixe dinner $35, plus 15% service. Candlelight picnic dinners, $55 for two.
Extras Station pickups. Spanish spoken. Babysitting.

Holladay House
155 West Main Street, 22960

Tel: 703–540–4893
800–358–4422
Fax: 540–672–3028

When Doc Holladay bought this 1830 Federal-style house in 1899 as his home and office, he used an innovative speaking tube to communicate with his patients. Nowadays, if you'd like to talk to his grandson Pete Holladay and his wife Phebe, all you need to do is call their toll-free number to arrange a restorative visit to this welcoming B&B. The large, comfortable guest rooms are furnished with family pieces and Phebe's artwork, each with a sitting area. Breakfast is served at guests' convenience, at a table in their room or in the dining room, and may include freshly squeezed orange juice, coffee or tea, a fruit plate, homemade biscuits or muffins, and perhaps an apple puff or baked eggs with cheese and tomatoes.

"The decor includes contemporary and traditional art, crisply ironed linens, soft antique quilts, and fresh-cut flowers. My room had a wonderful, firm bed, pure white towels and linens, a cozy loveseat, a fine assortment of books and magazines, proper lighting, and interesting decorative accessories. The bathroom was new, and well supplied with toiletries. The covered deck, overlooking the yard, invites peaceful retreat at any hour. I relaxed in the wooden swinging settee, enjoying the beautiful perennial gardens." *(Kristen Stevens)* "Real Southern comfort and hospitality." *(Marian Johns)* "Pete's breakfasts are outstanding." *(Beverly & Morris Marley)* "Pete and Phebe helped with dinner reservations and directions." *(Paula Onet)* "This beautiful house fronts right on the sidewalk, so we were amazed by their big, beautiful back yard, with gardens and flowering trees." *(MW)*

Suggestion box: "Reading lamps and tables needed on both sides of the bed." And: "Better lighting in the parking area."

Open All year. Closed Thanksgiving, Christmas.
Rooms 2 suites, 4 doubles—all with private bath and/or shower, radio, clock. 5 with desk, air-conditioning. Some with fan, TV.
Facilities Dining room, living room, TV room with books, guest refrigerator, porch with swing. Large backyard with gardens, off-street parking. Fishing, hiking nearby.
Location 2 blocks from town center, intersection Main St. & Rte. 20.
Restrictions Occasional traffic noise in front rooms. No smoking in guest rooms. Children 10 and over in suite.
Credit cards Discover, MC, Visa.
Rates B&B, $185 suite, $75–120 double, $75–115 single. Extra person, $25. 2-night Oct. weekend minimum. Corporate rate midweek.

The Shadows ¢
14291 Constitution Highway, 22960

Tel: 540–672–5057

A restored 1913 stone Craftsman-style farmhouse, this inn sits on a hilltop in the shadows of old cedar trees, and was originally built as a hunting lodge. The Shadows is owned by Barbara and Pat Loffredo, who have been welcoming B&B guests since 1987. Rooms are furnished with antiques, lace curtains and designer bed linens; some bathrooms have claw foot tubs.

"The Peach Room, with a firm, comfortable king-sized bed and armoire, was not large but not cramped. Our private bathroom was in the hall, adjacent to the bedroom, and had a large shower, ample hot water, strong water pressure, good lighting and a wide window sill convenient for toiletries." *(Carolyn Myles)* "The Victorian Room was furnished with a white iron and brass bed, beautiful ruffled sheets and comforter." *(Dana Abdella)* "The Rocking Horse cabin is rustic but modernized, furnished with antiques; it has a bedroom, a sitting room, and small bathroom. Barbara sat and chatted with us during our breakfast of poached pears with Grand Marnier sauce, fruit, juice, coffee, and cheese-stuffed French toast with sausages." *(Chris Zambito & Karl Wiegers)* "Delicious vegetable omelet, hash browns, and ham for breakfast." *(Nance Lieberman)* Reports needed.

Open All year.
Rooms 2 cottages, 4 doubles—all with private bath and/or shower, air-conditioning. 4 with ceiling fan, 1 with porch. Cottages with gas fireplace or deck.
Facilities Breakfast room, living room with fireplace, library; porch with swing. 44 acres with gazebo, gardens, fish pond, woodland. 10 min to lake for fishing, boating.
Location Central VA. 1 m SW of town on Rte. 20 S. From Washington, D.C., take I-95 to Rte. 3W Fredericksburg. Then 3W to Rte. 20S into Orange. Follow Rte. 20S out of Orange ¾ m to the Shadows on right. From Charlottesville, 28 m NE of Charlottesville on Rte. 20, 3 m past Montpelier. From Richmond, 90 min from Richmond via I-64 to Rte. 15N.
Restrictions No smoking. Children 13 and over.
Credit cards MC, Visa.
Rates B&B, $100–110 cottage, $80–95 double. Extra person, $20. 2-night holiday/weekend minimum.
Extras Airport/station pickups.

Willow Grove Inn ✕
14079 Plantation Way, 22960

Tel: 540–672–5982
800–WG9–1778
Fax: 540–672–3674

The strong influence of Thomas Jefferson's preference for classic Greek architecture can clearly be seen at the Willow Grove Inn, with its imposing center pediment and four supporting Doric columns. The house dates back to the 1770s, and was originally built in the Federal style, but a brick addition, completed in the early 1800s, doubled its size and gave the house its present look. Now listed on the National Historic Register, and owned by Angela Mulloy since 1987, the house and grounds have been fully restored to their original beauty. Antique furnishings grace the inside, and rolling lawns, formal gardens, magnolias, and willow trees abound outside. The breakfast menu includes a choice of omelets with vegetables, cheese, and bacon; multi-grain waffles with blueberry compote, and homemade muesli with fresh fruit and honey yogurt. Dinner menus reflect the season; favorite entrées include cornmeal-crusted trout; marinated breast of duck; and smoked chicken with wild mushrooms.

"Each room or suite is named after a president born in Virginia, and furnishings reflect the era of his term in office. The Washington room is enormous, with six windows, a splendid bed with lots of pillows, and working fireplace. The bathroom was equally large with a huge old bath, a sink, and shower. Thoughtful touches included an array of lotions, creams, soaps and shampoos, as well as sparkling water set out with wine glasses. Breakfast, brought to our room at the time requested, was a splendid spread of fresh fruit, yogurt, granola, coffee, and fresh-from-the-oven muffins." *(Ellie Freidus)*

"There is nothing like settling down in a beautiful antique bed, heaped high with pillows and a down comforter, after a superb dinner." *(Sandra Hunter, also Philip J. Tarnoff)* "In the morning, coffee and muffins were brought up to our room, and then we went downstairs for tasty omelets with fresh vegetables and cheese." *(HJ)* "Even more than the delicious food and attractive decor, is the warmth, friendliness, humor, enthusiasm, and good service of Angela and her staff." *(Madeleine Adams)* "The downstairs bar with its stone walls and entertaining bartender, adds to the fun." *(C.E. Myers)* Reports appreciated.

Open All year. Restaurant closed Mon–Wed.
Rooms 2 2-bedroom suites, 3 doubles—all with private bath and/or shower, desk, air-conditioning. 3 rooms with fireplace. Telephone on request.
Facilities Restaurant with fireplace, music on weekends; tavern, music room, TV room. 37 acres with formal gardens, barns, outbuildings.
Location 95 m SW of Washington, D.C., 40 m NE of Charlottesville. On Rte. 15, N of Orange.
Credit cards None accepted.
Rates B&B, $95–165 suite, double. Extra person, $20. MAP, $195–255 suite, double. Children's rate. Prix fixe brunch, $16. Alc dinner, $35; 15% service. MAP required for one-night stay.
Extras Pets by arrangement. Crib; babysitting by arrangement.

PARIS

The Ashby Inn ✕   *Tel: 540–592–3900*
Route 759, Route 1, Box 2A, 22130   *Fax: 540–592–3781*

Once called Pun'kinville, this tiny village took a small step toward sophistication when the Marquis de Lafayette came to visit in the early 1800s; it was renamed Paris in his honor. The inn dates to 1829, and has been restored by John and Roma Sherman with its Federalist spirit very much intact. Guest rooms are decorated with early 18th-century antiques and reproductions, including hand-painted wardrobes, quilts and coverlets, rag and Oriental rugs and blanket chests; all overlook a hillside where Black Angus cattle and white-tailed deer graze. The original basement kitchen, with walnut beams and stone fireplace, is now a taproom, while two upper rooms and an enclosed porch contain the inn's restaurant. The menu is limited, concentrating on seasonal foods like asparagus, shad, raspberries, soft shell crab, and game. Breads and pastas are homemade, much of the produce is homegrown, and backfin crabcakes are a speciality. Area activities include horse shows, races, and stable tours, wine touring in the nearby vineyards, hiking along the Appalachian trail, riding, and antiquing.

"Our large room was furnished rather sparely but in excellent taste—some simple antiques, two comfortable chairs, a big rag rug, and carefully chosen pictures. The food is good, with lots of game and well-prepared vegetables. The breakfast of juice, fruit, muffins, eggs, sausage or bacon, and potatoes, served between 8:30 and 10 A.M., was excellent." *(Carolyn Mathiasen)*

"Each guest room is decorated with a different theme in mind—Victorian, Colonial, Fireplace room, and so on; the Victorian is my favorite." *(Saeed Aminzadeh)* "Great service and food, with the owner taking a personal interest. Comfortable third floor East Dormer room." *(James Gould)* "Charming atmosphere. We ate outdoors under a large awning." *(Hopie Welliver)* "We splurged on one of the Schoolhouse rooms, 60 steps from the main inn. The room had its own wood-burning fireplace, as well as a stunning view of the Virginia hills." *(Brian Donaldson)* Comments appreciated.

Open All year. Restaurant closed Mon., Tues.; brunch only, major holidays.
Rooms 4 suites in Schoolhouse, 6 doubles—8 with private shower and/or bath, 2 with sink in room share 1 bath. All with air-conditioning. 5 with balcony/porch. 4 suites with fireplace, telephone, TV.
Facilities Restaurant, library/sitting room with fireplace, taproom, patio, garden. Hiking, riding, antiquing nearby.
Location N VA, Hunt Country, Blue Ridge foothills. 60 m W of Washington, DC. From I-495 (Beltway), take Rte. 66 W to Exit 23 (Delaplane/Paris). Go 7.5 m N on Rte. 17, then left on Rte. 701 into village. From Middleburg, take Rte. 50 W. 3 m W of Upperville, turn left on Rte. 759 (1st left after light). Paris located at intersection of Rtes. 17 & 50; inn is at intersection of Rtes. 701 & 759.
Restrictions Smoking restricted in dining rooms, guest rooms. Children 11 and over.
Credit cards MC, Visa.
Rates B&B, $175 suite, $90–150 double, single. Extra person, $20. $15–25 surcharge for Sat. only stay in some rooms. Alc dinner, $30.
Extras Wheelchair access to dining. Babysitting. Spanish spoken.

PULASKI

The Count Pulaski B&B and Gardens
821 North Jefferson Avenue, 24301

Tel: 540–980–1163
800–980–1163

Pulaski and its only B&B are named in honor of Count Casimir Pulaski, who fought and died as one of George Washington's generals during the Revolutionary War. Built in 1910, this red brick home was fully renovated as a B&B in 1993 by Flo Stevenson and her husband, William Struhs. The decor includes antiques, oil paintings, and accessories gathered from the 40 foreign countries where Florence has traveled; guest rooms are simply furnished with floral comforters and matching curtains, with queen-, king-, or twin-size beds. Breakfast is served at guests' convenience, at the Hepplewhite table in the dining room, on Wedgwood, Lenox, or Haviland china, with sterling silver, crystal, fresh flowers, lighted candles, and soft music, and includes fresh fruit and juice, a hot entrée, and several breads.

"Flo Stevenson is a lovely lady, excellent cook, and an interesting personality." *(Betty Sadler)* "Charming decor, careful attention to detail; close to wonderful lake, parks, and hiking trails." *(Lynne Clawson)* "Beautiful old home built in the early 1900s, filled with antiques and the innkeeper's artwork. Charming town with fine old homes and antique shops. Flo is an excellent hostess and storyteller." *(Martha Eddings)*

Open All year.
Rooms 1 suite, 2 doubles—all with full private bath, telephone, radio, clock, desk, air-conditioning, ceiling fan. 1 with gas fireplace.
Facilities Dining room, living room with fireplace, piano; sunroom with fireplace, TV, books, guest refrigerator; porch. ½ acre with garden, off-street parking, indoor bicycle storage.
Location SW VA. 50 m S of Roanoke on I-81. Historic district, 5 blocks from center. From I-81 S, take Exit 94 to Rte. 99 2 m to town. Cross Washington Ave & go right on next street, Jefferson to inn on left corner. From I-81 N, take Exit 89B into town on Washington Ave. Turn left at 2nd left, & go right on Jefferson to inn on left.
Restrictions No smoking. Children not encouraged.
Credit cards MC, Visa.
Rates B&B, $75 suite, double; $60 single. Extra person, $20. 2-night minimum graduation, major fall weekends. Murder mystery weekends.

RAPHINE

Oak Spring Farm & Vineyard ¢   *Tel: 540–377–2398*
Route 2, Box 356, 24472

Listed on the National Register of Historic Places, Oak Spring Farm was built in 1826, and was in need of total restoration; fortunately the farm had only three owners in its lifetime, so much of the original structure was still intact. The property itself has many interesting aspects: some of the farm is leased to the Natural Bridge Petting Zoo, so a herd of friendly burros are frequently in residence; it is a registered archaeological Indian site; and it has a 5-acre vineyard with both table and wine grapes grown for area wineries.

The Tichenors have decorated the house with an eclectic mix of antiques, artwork, and accessories collected during Jim's military career. Breakfasts feature fresh-ground coffee, just-squeezed orange juice, and homemade jams and jellies, with different menus every day: perhaps fruit soup, bran muffins, pineapple nut bread, and maple oat banana bread.

"Wonderful, caring, knowledgeable hosts; well-maintained B&B in a peaceful, rural setting; clean, comfortable room; delicious food and pleasant company at breakfast." *(Steve Schneider)* "The Victorian room has an antique walnut bed and large bathroom with both a tub and separate stall shower. The views from our bedroom were of the flowering orchard and vineyard, and the cows and burros grazing in the meadow beyond." *(CD)* 'Spacious and well-decorated Victorian home. Our spotless room had interesting reading materials, and with chocolates left with evening turndown. The owners were helpful with restaurant recommendations." *(Anne Mickel)* At press time, we learned that the inn had been sold to John and Celeste Woods.

Open All year.
Rooms 3 doubles—all with full private bath, air-conditioning.
Facilities Living room with fireplace, dining room, sitting room, porch with swing. 40 acres with barn, pasture, vineyards, gardens, hiking trails. Horseback riding, canoe trips.
Location Central VA, Blue Ridge foothills. 50 m W of Charlottesville, 20 m S of Staunton, 14 m NE of Lexington. 7 m from Blue Ridge Parkway. From I-81 take Exit 54 and follow Rte. 606 E to Steele's Tavern. Turn right on Rte. 11 and proceed to next crossroad and turn left on CR 706. Inn is 50 yds. on the right.
Restrictions No smoking. No children under 16.
Credit cards MC, Visa.
Rates B&B, $63–73 double, $53–63 single. Extra person, $15. No tipping.
Extras Station pickups. Some German, French spoken.

RICHMOND

Richmond has had a dramatic history—including such high points as Patrick Henry's famous "Give me liberty or give me death" speech in 1775, the attack by the British not long after, and its tenure as the capital of the Confederacy from 1861 to 1865. The city is still home to several churches of significant historic interest, and a number of historic James River plantations lie within an easy drive, as does the Richmond National Battlefield Park. Also of interest are the Museum and White House of the Confederacy, the Edgar Allan Poe Museum, and other museums devoted to science and fine art. If you're visiting Richmond on a weekend, take the Cultural Link Trolley, connecting most hotels with the city's major attractions; ride all day for only $2.

Reader tips: "Several B&Bs are located in the Church Hill district, a charming enclave surrounded by poor inner-city neighborhoods. The area is 12 blocks from downtown, and night-time strolls are definitely *not* recommended." More positively: "Great dinner at the Strawberry Street Cafe in the Fan District—try the crab soup; reasonably priced, a Richmond landmark for decades." *(FD)*

Richmond is in the eastern part of the state, 106 miles south of Washington, D.C., and 50 miles west of Williamsburg.

Also recommended: A bit large for a full entry with 274 rooms, **The Jefferson** (Franklin & Adams Streets, 23220; 804–788–8000 or 800–424–8014) is an elaborate Beaux-Arts structure built in 1895. Meticulously restored in 1986 at a cost of $35 million, it's listed on the National Register of Historic Places. Even if you can't stay overnight, stop by to see the stained glass dome and Tiffany side windows in The Palm Court lobby, and the magnificent marbled two-story Rotunda. "The atmosphere is gracious and the staff is attentive to your needs. Lemaire Restaurant serves breakfast, lunch and dinner; they also serve a fabulous Sunday brunch in the rotunda." *(Elizabeth Sommer)* "A super experience." *(BJ Hensley)* Rates range from $140–180 double, $225–375 suite; ask about the reasonable weekend, summer, and senior rates.

Information please: Known best for its food, **Mr. Patrick Henry's Inn** (2300 East Broad Street, 23223; 804–644–1322 or 800–932–2654), offers a cozy tavern for pub fare, a skylit lunchroom where the full breakfasts and noon-time meals are served, and a more formal restaurant, offering French-accented cuisine. Accommodations are available in four suites, decorated traditionally with period reproductions; B&B rates are $95–135.

The **Commonwealth Park Suites Hotel** (Ninth & Bank Streets, P.O. Box 455, 23203; 804–343–7300 or 800–343–7302) offers 49 luxurious guest rooms, furnished with 18th-century mahogany reproductions, accented with Oriental rugs and brass chandeliers. Double rates range from $85–155, with suites up to $245.

Abbie Hill Guest Lodging ¢

P.O. Box 4503, 23220

Tel: 804–355–5855
Fax: 804–355–5855

A B&B in a turn-of-the-century Federal townhouse, long-time owners Bill and Barbara Fleming report that "our guests seem to enjoy the high ceilings, period decor, and huge old-fashioned bathrooms supplied with heaps of thirsty white towels. Our grandmothers were the source of most of the furnishings and we even have some of their handmade quilts." A full breakfast is served from 7:30–8:30, with a continental breakfast tray available after 9 A.M. for "sleepyheads."

"Convenient location, gracious accommodations, welcoming owners. Delightful seasonal and holiday accents." *(Joan Nelson)* "Clean, airy rooms in a residential area full of shops and restaurants, just a short drive from the financial district." *(Norm Topf)* "Our room had a four-poster bed, fireplace, and large dressing/sitting room. The white bathroom was elegant with heaps of coral pink towels. Barbara's blueberry muffins were mouthwatering and Bill's scrambled eggs exceptional." *(Julie May)* "Many thoughtful details: bowls of fruit, personalized soaps, area maps, and magazines. Wonderful homemade blueberry pancakes served in the magnificent dining room." *(CR)* "Barbara and Bill are a delightful and unpretentious couple dedicated to the comfort and well-being of their guests." *(Gwen Jones)*

Open All year.
Rooms 1 suite, 2 doubles—1 with private bath, 2 with a maximum of 4 people sharing 1 bath. All with radio, clock, air-conditioning, fan. 2 with fireplace, TV, desk, 1 with balcony.
Facilities Dining room with fireplace, piano; parlor with fireplace, games, books, TV; guest pantry, refrigerator, laundry; porch, deck. Limited off-street parking.
Location Historic Fan district. 2½ m from Exit 14, I-95. Turn right on North Blvd. and continue to Broad St. Turn left and go to 2200 block. Turn right on Allison; take Monument Ave. to 3rd house on right.
Restrictions Traffic noise in front room. No smoking. Children 12 and over.
Credit cards Amex, DC, Discover, MC, Visa.
Rates B&B, $85–105 suite, $75–85 double, $55–75 single. Extra person, $15. $5 service charge. Tipping accepted. Weekly rates. Honeymoon packages. 2-night holiday weekend minimum.
Extras Airport/station pickups, $18.

Berkeley Hotel ✕   *Tel:* 804–780–1300
1200 East Cary Street, 23210   *Fax:* 804–343–1885

The Berkeley is an elegant, small hotel built in 1988 with handsome period decor and a style that gives it the feel of an earlier era. It's located in Shockoe Slip, the city's 19th century warehouse district, and home to the Farmers Market—one of the country's oldest—offering fresh produce and local crafts. Today this area is also home to antique shops and boutiques, comedy clubs and restaurants. The hotel's dining room offers such entrées as salmon with spinach and leeks, veal with endive and fennel, and pork sirloin with cabbage and apple fritters.

"Exceptionally pleasant, helpful, efficient staff; the housekeepers take great pride in their fine work. Presentation in the dining room is outstanding; the menu reflects a blend of local and exotic ingredients, and the service is attentive but not hovering." *(Dianne McCarty)* "Excellent location, with six restaurants in a two-block area, including The Tobacco Co.—one of Richmond's best—directly across the street. Staff attentive and efficient." *(JSL)*

"Guest rooms are decorated in soft shades of beige, taupe, teal, blue, and rose, and accented with floral bedspreads and draperies. My favorite room, #307—called an Executive Parlor—had three windows, with a love seat, king-size bed, desk and chair, corner table, and two armchairs; the bathroom was huge, with a double shower stall, a separate tub, and a wide marble sink vanity. Some rooms on the upper floors have connecting tile terraces that overlook the Shockoe district." *(SHW)*

Open All year.
Rooms 55 doubles—all with full private bath, telephone, TV, radio, air-conditioning, desk, coffee maker.
Facilities Lobby, restaurant, valet parking, business services. Fitness center nearby.
Location Historic Shockoe Slip District, at corner of 12th St. 2 blocks to Capitol.
Credit cards Amex, DC, Discover, MC, Visa.
Rates Room only, $154 double, $128 single. $99–134 weekend rate. Alc dinner, $30.
Extras Wheelchair access. Downtown shuttle.

The Emmanuel Hutzler House/Bensonhouse   *Tel:* 804–353–6900
2036 Monument Avenue, 23220   804–355–4885
              Fax: 804–342–6027

The Emmanuel Hutzler House, built as a grand private residence in 1914 by the youngest son of a prosperous dry goods merchant, stands proudly with the other architecturally distinctive houses on Monument Avenue. Owners Lyn Benson and John Richardson opened this B&B in 1992, after years of renovation. The natural mahogany paneling, leaded glass windows, interior columns and coffered beam ceiling of this 8,000-square foot house are complemented by colors, fabrics, and wallpapers that create a welcoming atmosphere. Robinett's Suite is a peach-colored room with cream-colored moldings, a marble fireplace, triple bow window, four-poster queen-size bed, antique sofa, and cherry dresser, and double

Jacuzzi. Henrietta's Room is done in deep green with cream-colored moldings and a tiled fireplace.

"Beautifully furnished rooms with antiques, crystal chandeliers, marble fireplace, tapestries, and queen-sized beds. Parking is never a problem due to Lyn and John's knowledge of their guests' schedules and willingness to shuffle cars. Breakfasts are customized to the likes and dislikes of individual guests; the apricot/walnut bread is a favorite. Beverages are always available, day or night, and the hospitality of the hosts extends to restaurant suggestions, directions, and more." *(Stephanie Underwood)* "Warm, hospitable owners who take care of every detail. Immaculate housekeeping; good location and facilities for both business and leisure travelers. Good for sleeping; no noise from the other rooms." *(Ronna Brenneman)* "Vibrant yet soothing decor. The simple but tasty breakfast was different each day: first we had an egg casserole with juice and coffee; next we had French toast and bacon. In residence is a wonderful enormous gray cat. The owners also run a B&B reservation service covering central and Eastern Virginia." *(Michele Mikesell)*

Open All year.
Rooms 2 suites, 2 doubles—all with private bath and/or shower, telephone, radio, clock, TV, air-conditioning. 2 with desk, fireplace. 1 with whirlpool tub.
Facilities Foyer, living room with fireplace, dining room, guest kitchen. Lighted off-street parking.
Location 3.5 m from downtown.
Restrictions Traffic noise in some rooms. No smoking. Children 13 and over.
Credit cards Amex, Discover, MC, Visa.
Rates B&B, $110–135 suite, $89–95 double. Extra person, $15. 2-night minimum, special event and holiday weekends.

Linden Row ✕
100 East Franklin Street, 23219

Tel: 804–783–7000
800–348–RICH
Fax: 804–648–7504

The famous people associated with historic buildings often hold as much interest as the architecture itself. In the case of Linden Row, Edgar Allan Poe was inspired by the lovely gardens around which these homes were built; Irene and Nancy Langhorne, students at a school in the row, went on to become famous as the Gibson Girl and Lady Astor respectively; and Mary Johnston, best-selling author at the turn of the century, lived here too.

Built in 1847 and listed on National Register of Historic Places, the hotel is comprised of seven restored red brick Greek Revival townhouses. The many original interior features include marble mantelpieces, pocket doors, and chandeliers. Furnishings include authentic late Empire and early Victorian pieces, as well as quality reproductions. Guest rooms are located in the original townhouses; the garden courtyard area has restored dependencies with the smaller rooms. The hotel restaurant serves traditional favorites "with a French flair." Rates include a wine and cheese reception from 5–7 P.M., continental buffet breakfast, and daily newspaper. Jeanette Weir is the long-time manager.

"Staff were wonderful, very helpful. Rooms clean and nicely decorated.

Nice front lobby and brick courtyard with fountains. Breakfast good, but basic." *(M.W. Midkiff)* "My spacious room had antique reproduction furnishings and two queen-size beds. To reach it from the main lobby, I followed a covered gallery along the courtyard; a separate key is provided for the outside door. The hotel's location was both convenient and quiet." *(Bob Schwemm)*

Open All year.

Rooms 6 suites, 64 doubles—all with full private bath, telephone, radio, clock, TV, air-conditioning, desk. 16 rooms in back garden carriage house.

Facilities Restaurant, parlor with fireplace, bar. Meeting room, full business services; courtyard garden. Valet parking. Free use of YMCA swimming pool, fitness center.

Location Franklin at 1st St. Walking distance to State Capitol, Shockoe Slip, financial district, etc. From I-95 S or I-64 E, take Exit 13. Left on Leigh St., right on Belvidere St. Left on Franklin St., left on 2nd St., left on Grace St., left on 1st St. From I-95 N, take Exit 9a onto I-95 Downtown Expressway. Exit Rte. 60, Canal St. Turn right at 2nd, left on Grace, left on 1st. From airport, take I-64 W & exit onto 5th St. Right on Grace, left on 1st to inn.

Restrictions Non-smoking rooms available.

Credit cards Amex, DC, Discover, MC, Visa.

Rates B&B, $137–145 suite, $112–135 double, $97–120 single. Extra person, $10. AAA, senior discount. Alc lunch, $10; alc dinner, $30–50.

Extras Wheelchair access; bathroom specially equipped. French, Italian spoken. Free shuttle to downtown, business districts.

SCOTTSVILLE

In the Monticello wine region, Scottsville combines a closeness to such historical points of interest as Ashlawn, Monticello, and the University of Virginia, with a variety of local attractions: numerous historic sights and antique shops, as well as canoeing, tubing, and fishing on the James River, plus winery tours and hiking. Scottsville is located in Albemarle County, of central Virginia. It's 17 miles south of Charlottesville.

Information please: Originally from England, owners Jennie and Chris Cook have furnished **Lennox Farm** (Rte. 1, Box 261, 24590; 804–286–3010) with 19th century English antiques. Their inn sits on 80 acres of pasture and woodland; the oldest part of the house dates back to 1795, the most recent, to 1963. The B&B double rate for the four air-conditioned guest rooms is $100, including a full English breakfast; supper is available for $25 per person by arrangement.

Chester B&B   *Tel:* 804–286–3960
2783 James River Road, Route 726, 24590

Imagine that a friend of a friend invited you to spend a few days in his Greek Revival mansion, built in 1847 and surrounded by equally venerable plantings. Imagine further that two gracious hosts await to make your visit as pleasant as possible. This is much the atmosphere that Gordon Anderson and Dick Shaffer have created in the many years that they've owned Chester. In addition to a breakfast of fresh fruit and juice, eggs, pancakes, and Virginia sausage, guests may enjoy wine, beer, soft drinks, tea, or coffee at any time. Dinners are served as well, and guests feel that the delightful food and conversation are the highlight of their stay. Chester is furnished throughout with antiques, Oriental rugs, and objets d'art, while the grounds have in excess of 50 different varieties of trees and shrubs.

"We were graciously greeted by Gordon and Dick; they offered us drinks and showed us to our room—beautifully furnished with a high four-poster bed, good lighting, night stands and a dresser. The fireplace was laid with wood and ready to light." *(Kelly & Michael Warkoczeski)* "Guests having dinner are expected to say so early in the day so the hosts can shop for the delicious meal. Cocktails and dinner are convivial, and the conversation lively, sparked both by the wide range of guests and their interests, and the hosts' own interests and knowledge. Gordon and Dick have firm opinions and do not hesitate to express them." *(John Hyland III)* "The owners' dogs (Russian wolfhounds) are friendly, perfectly well-behaved, and beautiful." *(Gary Blonston)*

"Dietary restrictions were no problem, and when I requested glasses, Dick brought me a beautiful crystal set (no Dixie cups here)." *(Ali Marie Matheson)* "Dick and Gordon's hospitality is unparalleled—even to our canine companion. Dinner was hearty and excellent; Cornish game hen, accompanied by a lovely Virginia wine, followed by a luscious orange soufflée." *(Julie Marx & Jeff Thompson)*

Open All year.
Rooms 5 doubles—1 with full private bath, 4 rooms share 2 baths. All with radio, fan, central air-conditioning. 4 with fireplace. 1 with desk.
Facilities Dining room with fireplace, living room with fireplace, Library with TV/VCR, stereo; lounge, porches. 7 acres with pond, picnic area, croquet, dog kennel, gardens. Bicycles. River for fishing, boating nearby.
Location Central VA, Albemarle County. 17 m S of Charlottesville, in Monticello wine region. From I-64/VA Hwy. 20 (Charlottesville-Monticello) S on Hwy. 20 for 17 m, right on State Route 726 (James River Rd.), 2½ blocks.
Restrictions Children 8 and over. Occasional barking from dog kennel. Hosts smoke.
Credit cards Amex.
Rates B&B, $65–115 double. Extra person, $20. Prix fixe dinner with wine, $30, by advance reservation.
Extras Limited wheelchair access. Airport/station pickups. Pets by arrangement.

SMITH MOUNTAIN LAKE

Information please: The Manor at Taylor's Store (Route 1, Box 533, Wirtz, 24184; 540–721–3951 or 800–248–6267) dates to the early 1800s, and was originally part of a tobacco plantation. Lee and Mary Lynn Tucker bought the property in 1986, and have fully restored it as a B&B. A heart-healthy breakfast is served, with a hot entrée—perhaps baked peach puffs or whole wheat pancakes—plus a buffet of fresh fruit, yogurt, granola, nuts, and home-baked breads. Rates for the six guest rooms range from $80–125. "We enjoyed an early morning walk to the ponds, fields and woods behind the house and stopped to pet the Newfoundlands in their pen." *(Dick & Erna Loerch)* "The lower level area with a pool table, hot tub, large-screen TV with VCR, and more is a big plus." *(Debbie Murray)* Current reports?

SPERRYVILLE

Sperryville is located in northern Virginia, in Rappahannock County. It's 1½ hours west of Washington, DC and 45 miles north of Charlottesville. From DC, take I-495 to Route 66 West, then exit on Route 29. Go south to Warrenton and turn west on Route 211. Go past "little" Washington to Sperryville.

Also recommended: Eleven miles south of Sperryville is **Dulaney Hollow** (Hwy 231, Star Route 2, Box 215, Etlan 22719; 540–923–4470), a turn-of the century guest house. Four guest rooms and two rustic cottages are available, at B&B rates of $60–80. "A charming old farmhouse located just 90 minutes from DC. Laid-back hosts are helpful and friendly. Decorated with a down-to-earth country character, the house offers an interesting blend of antiques, from priceless quilts to creative gadgets. Breakfast included waffles, fresh berries, ham biscuits, homemade apple butter, and jams. The property is spacious with a small pond and old barns full of antiques. It's fun to take a stroll with their two friendly dogs and look out at the distant Blue Ridge mountains. A quiet, relaxed, affordable place to stay." *(Jill Reeves)*

Information please: An 1880s farmhouse, the **Apple Hill Farm** (Route 612, 117 Old Hollow Road, 22740; 540–987–9454) is close to good hiking, and is just as convenient for lazy porch sitting. The three guest rooms are furnished with antiques, down comforters, rocking chairs, and collectibles. The $95–135 rates include breakfast of eggs Benedict or perhaps apple pancakes.

STAFFORD

Renaissance Manor B&B and Art Gallery 🏃   Tel: 540–720–3785
2247 Courthouse Road, 22554   800–720–3784
     Fax: 540–720–3785

Renaissance Manor is convenient to all that northern Virginia has to offer, including George Washington's home, Mount Vernon—the inspiration for the inn's design. Renaissance Manor was built in 1991 and has a 3,000-square-foot center section reserved for guests, with two symmetrical wings. Innkeepers Deneen and Joe Bernard and their two young children reside in one of the two wings. The glassed-in connecting breezeways and common areas also serve as art galleries, displaying the work of local artists and craftsmen. High ceilings with ornate frieze trim and oak hardwood floors give the inn a period feel; the shades of teal and cranberry in the decor were inspired by those at Mt. Vernon. Guest rooms are furnished with some antiques and quality reproductions, one with a king-size four poster bed, others with queen-size canopy or sleigh beds.

"The William Shakespeare Room is decorated in soft peach tones with white lace curtains and lovely antiques. A crystal decanter of sherry with cordial glasses added a welcoming touch. We relaxed before the living room fireplace, reading from the excellent book collection. Breakfast included homemade blueberry and walnut-date muffins, melon, strawberries, assorted yogurts, cereals, hot coffee and tea, served on beautiful bone china and silver." *(Sandra Rogers)* "We were greeted at the door with a warm smile and a cold glass of lemonade." *(Patricia Reger)* "The tree-lined country road that follows the river is appealing for those who like to walk or run." *(Sharon Frichtl)* "The George Washington Suite has a king-sized four-poster bed, sofa, two Queen Anne chairs and a fireplace; the large bathroom has a glassed-in shower and an antique clawfoot tub." *(Ali Marie Matheson)*

Suggestion box: "Better lighting in the parking lot and bathrooms." And: "A reading light on my side of the bed."

Open All year.
Rooms 2 suites, 6 doubles—4 with private bath and/or shower, 2 with a maximum of 4 people sharing bath. All with clock, air-conditioning, ceiling fan. 1 with fireplace. 1 with Jacuzzi.
Facilities Dining room, living room with fireplace, stereo; library; porch. 3 acres with brick patio, gardens, windmill, children's swing set, gazebo, lawn games, fountain. 1 m to marina (Potomac River), water sports. 1 m to train station.
Location N VA. 8 m N of Fredericksburg, 40 m S of DC. From I-95, take Stafford exit 140, & go E on Courthouse Rd. (Rte. 630). Watch for fence & windmill.
Restrictions No smoking.
Credit cards Amex, MC, Visa.
Rates B&B, $125–150 suite, $55–95 double. Children free in same room.
Extras Train/boat pickup. German spoken.

STANLEY

Also recommended: About a mile from Jordan Hollow Farm is a restored early 1800s two-story farmhouse, **The Brumback House at Oak Mountain Farm** (Route 689, Rte. 2, Box 249, 22851; 540–778–2331 or 800–296–2331). A full kitchen and bathroom, TV and VCR, living room with fireplace and sofabed, two double-bedded rooms upstairs, a front porch with rockers, and an upper deck with outdoor furniture make the house a good choice for families. "Beautiful setting at the base of the Blue Ridge foothills, with a panoramic vista across the Shenandoah Valley. Hiking trails start right behind the house. Kids can watch the cows, play on the rope swing or run amongst the trees of the Christmas tree farm." *(SV)* Rates for the guesthouse are $200 for two nights, $500 for a week.

Jordan Hollow Farm Inn ¢ 🏃 ♿   *Tel:* 540–778–2285
Virginia Route 626, Route 2, Box 375, 22851   *Fax:* 540–778–1759

Jordan Hollow is a horse farm, where plenty of horses are available for riding or "just looking." The dining rooms, where breakfast and dinner are served, are in the 200-year-old farmhouse. Guest rooms are located in two separate lodges built in 1983 and 1990, and are simply furnished with country touches. Marley and Jetze Beers have owned and run the farm since 1979. The dinner menu offers a choice of entrées—perhaps veal piccata, chicken Dijon, and pink salmon cakes. Dessert lovers will appreciate such sweets as apple crisp with whipped cream, double chocolate torte, and lemon nut cake.

"Comfortable, well-decorated rooms, friendly staff, fabulous food. The kids have a great time in the game room, walking on the hills behind the inn, playing with the cats—even helping to catch escapee goats! Shenandoah National Park, Luray Caverns, Shenandoah River canoe trips are all nearby for extra family fun." *(Marguerite Garfield)* "The inn gives you the feeling of living on a farm with lazy cats all around, sheep and horses, and, especially the bullfrog serenade at night outside the window. Our homey room had antique furnishings and rocking chairs on the porch." *(Carol Holmes)*

"Verdant hills and glens, green meadows sparkling with wildflowers, and horses grazing. We wandered in the barns, roamed the pastures, ate well, and sipped drinks in the friendly bar/recreation room. We took trail rides through the lovely countryside on their well-trained mounts, hiked in the adjacent Shenandoah National Park, and relaxed on the lawn, reading and playing with the resident kittens." *(SG)* "Three horses, which had foaled recently, were out in paddocks where the guests could watch them. The old farmhouse's small dining rooms are decorated nicely in country calico, antiques, and African artifacts." *(MD)* "Dinner included warm fresh bread, homemade soup, salad, and rib eye steak seasoned with fresh herbs." *(Sarah & Mark Fredrick)* "The inn is well maintained, with constant improvements." *(Lucy Kiekebusch-Steinitz)*

Open All year.
Rooms 21 doubles—all with private bath and/or shower, telephone, desk, air-conditioning. 4 with gas fireplace, whirlpool tub, porch.
Facilities Restaurant, bar/lounge/pub/game room, books. 145 acres with swimming pool, horseback riding, carriage lessons/rides, walking/birding trails. Shenandoah River nearby for canoeing, fishing. Golf, tennis nearby. Cross-country, downhill skiing 15–30 min.
Location N VA, Shenandoah Valley. 2 hrs. W of Washington, DC, NW of Richmond, VA. 6 m S of Luray. From Luray, take Rte. 340-Bus. S 6 m. Go left on Rte. 624, left again on Rte. 689, right on Rte. 626, follow signs.
Restrictions No smoking in barn.
Credit cards Amex, CB, DC, Discover, MC, Visa.
Rates MAP, $140–180 double, $115–155 single. Children 5–16, $15; over 17, $35. Trail rides, $25 per hour; riding, carriage-driving packages.
Extras Wheelchair access; guest room/bath equipped for disabled. German, Dutch, some French spoken. Cribs, babysitting. Horses boarded.

STAUNTON

In easy reach of many area sights, Staunton is a popular base for touring the Shenandoah Mountains. Staunton itself has undergone considerable renovation of its historic downtown. In addition to the birthplace of Woodrow Wilson, the Museum of American Frontier Culture has opened recently.

Reader tip: "Staunton is full of narrow one-way streets, and it's hard to look for a particular address and still maneuver if you are driving during the afternoon rush; be sure to get specific directions. Staunton is a lovely town in which to walk if you can handle the hills. Woodrow Wilson's birthplace is beautifully restored and is well worth a visit." *(Peg Bedini)*

Information please: About 25 miles north of Staunton via I-81 is the **Joshua Wilton House** (412 South Main Street, Harrisonburg 22801; 540–434–4464), an 1883 Victorian mansion within walking distance of the local historic district and James Madison University. Five well-furnished double rooms (each with private bath and telephone) are available at this elegant inn; the $85–95 rates include an afternoon beverage and a full breakfast. Two menus are offered in the acclaimed restaurant, one for formal dining, another in the Cafe for moderately priced meals. Local ingredients are a key to the cuisine, with such entrées as roast lamb with mustard and herbs, grilled pork loin, and risotto with morel mushrooms.

About halfway between Staunton and Harrisonburg is the **Inn at Keezletown Road** (Route 276, Keezletown Road, Rte. 1, Box 14, Weyers Cave, 24486; 540–234–0644), a century-old Victorian home with views of the Blue Ridge Mountains. Each of the four guest rooms has a queen- or king-size bed, private bath, and antique decor; the B&B double rates range from $75–85. Owners Sandy and Alan Inabinet serve a full country breakfast, including freshly laid eggs from their own chickens. A formal herb garden and a goldfish pond compliment the grounds.

For additional area recommendations, see entries for **Lamb's Gate** in **Swoope**, and the **Iris Inn** in **Waynesboro**.

Belle Grae Inn ✕ ♿

515 West Frederick Street, 24401

Tel: 540–886–5151
Fax: 540–886–6641

Restored by owner Michael Organ in 1983, the Belle Grae is a brick Victorian mansion with white gingerbread trim. In addition to accommodations in adjacent homes, the Belle Grae offers formal dining in the "Old Inn" and casual dining in the bistro. A full, innkeepers' choice breakfast served from 7:30 to 9:00 with seating at individual tables.

"Room #1 was delightful, with a little sitting area and lovely antique furnishings. Thoughtful touches included the sherry in our room and soothing bath salts. Quiet location; welcoming fire in the living room fireplace, good breakfast of bacon and eggs, pancakes, and muffins." *(Sally & George Brooks, Dot Martz)* "Parking behind the house is ample, and gives you a nice stroll through the beautifully landscaped garden and terrace area. The dining rooms are lovely, with tables set with crystal and silver, while the bistro area is more informal and open." *(Patricia DeMonte)*

"Well situated for a walking tour of historic Staunton. Our room had an attractive bedroom and tiny bathroom. Breakfast is served in the bistro, a 60s-style extension to the main house, with nice views of the lawn with squirrels scampering about." *(Ellie Freidus)* "We occupied a suite on the third floor of a house on a slope above the mansion. It had a gas fireplace, period furniture, and comfortable bed. The room opened out onto a balcony with a nice view of the city." *(Joseph Savino)* Comments welcome.

Worth noting: "Room #6 was simply furnished, lacked reading lights and had a noisy location over the office."

Open All year. Restaurant closed Dec. 24, 25, 26.
Rooms 2 cottages, 5 suites, 10 doubles—all with private bath and/or shower, desk, air-conditioning, fan. Some with telephone, TV, gas fireplace, balcony. 2 with refrigerator. Rooms in 9 buildings surrounding restaurant.
Facilities Restaurant with fireplace, bistro with piano music weekends, parlor with fireplace, music room, TV room, gift shop, veranda, courtyard. 1⅓ acres with garden, hot tub, gazebo, lawn games, off-street parking. 4 blocks to tennis, golf, indoor pool.
Location Take Exit 222 off I-81 (follow signs to Woodrow Wilson Birthplace). Take 250 W to 254 W (Frederick St.) to inn on right.
Restrictions No smoking in rooms. Children over 10. Street noise in 4 rooms.
Credit cards Amex, MC, Visa.
Rates B&B, $109–149 suite, cottage; $69–119 double. Extra person, $25. Weekday senior, AAA discount. Bistro dinner, $10; alc dinner, $30. 15% service/tax. Tipping welcome. 2-night weekend minimum April, May, Oct., Nov., & holidays.
Extras Wheelchair access; 3 rooms specially equipped. Spanish spoken.

Frederick House ¢ ♠ ✕

28 North New Street, 24401

Tel: 540–885–4220
800–334–5575

Composed of five connected town houses built between 1810 and 1910, The Frederick House has been owned by Joe and Evy Harman since 1984, who have furnished it simply with antiques and reproductions. New in 1996 are a cottage ideal for families, and an additional building with six one- and two-bedroom suites, all with kitchens. Breakfast is served in the inn's Chumley's Tearoom and includes fresh fruit, homemade bread, and such choices as apple raisin quiche, ham and cheese pie, granola with yogurt, or waffles and syrup.

"Upon arrival, we were greeted by Joe Harman, who answered our questions, got us checked in, then helped us carry the luggage to our suite, which was complete with a small sitting room with a gas fireplace. Breakfast offered quite a few choices; everything we tried was wonderful with fresh herbs from the Harman's garden." *(Debbie Rindfleisch)* "Our immaculate room was decorated with antiques, attractive stenciling, and pretty wallpaper. Delicious breakfasts are served in a bright, cheery setting and often include stimulating conversation with the friendly and accommodating Harmans." *(Carole Coleman)* "Our breakfast favorite was the waffle with pineapple and warm syrup, presented beautifully with fresh melon, kiwi, and strawberries." *(Nancy Goddard)* "Our children were made to feel truly welcome. The downtown location, ideal for walking tours, is convenient to good restaurants and shops." *(CC)* "Impressive smoke detecting and automatic emergency light systems. Extremely quiet air-conditioning. Many good restaurants within walking distance." *(Peg & Ben Bedini)*

Open All year.
Rooms 1 cottage, 12 suites, 8 doubles—all with private bath and/or shower,

telephone, radio, TV, desk, air-conditioning, ceiling fan. 6 with deck, kitchenette. 2 with gas fireplace. Rooms in 7 buildings.

Facilities Dining room, living room with TV, books; laundry service; gift shop. Off-street parking, gardens. Athletic club with indoor heated swimming pool adjacent.

Location Town center. From I-81 take Exit for Rte. 250 W. Go right on Rte. 11 (Coalter St.) Go left on Frederick St. to inn on left. Across from Mary Baldwin College.

Restrictions No smoking. Traffic noise in some rooms.

Credit cards Amex, DC, Discover, MC, Visa.

Rates B&B $65–95 suite, $65–95 double. $55–85 single. Extra person, $25. Senior discount. Inquire for cottage, kitchen suite rates.

Extras Airport/bus station pickup. Crib.

The Sampson Eagon Inn ¢
238 East Beverley Street, 24401

Tel: 540–886–8200
800–597–9722

Although any inngoer will enjoy the exceptionally handsome and comfortable accommodations provided by Frank and Laura Mattingly at the circa 1840 Sampson Eagon Inn, lovers of antiques and historic homes will be particularly fascinated. The Mattinglys explain that "collecting is a passion for us, ranging from formal American Federal and Empire to Victorian furniture." Solid masonry walls and thick carpets provide a quiet, private environment in each room. The spacious guest rooms have a sitting area, queen-size antique canopy bed with reading lamps and tables on both sides, and antique furnishings; shades of ivory, soft blue, or gold provide a soothing color scheme. Breakfast includes juice, fresh fruit compote with lemon-yogurt sauce, coffee, tea, hot chocolate, tea breads, cereal, and such entrées as Grand Marnier soufflée pancakes, Kahlua pecan Belgian waffles, French toast with strawberry sauce, or an omelet to order, with bacon, country sausage, or ham.

"Lovely, affordable luxury. Our room had a beautiful Delft tile decorative fireplace. Meissen plates adorned the ivory walls; the blue and white theme carried through to the canopy and Roman-style shades. A love seat at the foot of the bed faced a butler's tray which held a large bottle of lemon/lime spring water, two goblets, an ice bucket, and magazines. A magnificent leaded glass window graced the spotless bathroom. A guest refrigerator, stocked with mineral water and juices, was tucked in a corner at the end of the second floor hallway. Bookcases held a variety of magazines, books, and sundries—from a hair dryer to antacid tablets. For breakfast, we were treated to Frank's baked apples and Laura's Grand Marnier soufflée pancakes and sausage." *(Rose Ciccone)*

"Beautiful antiques, lace curtains, stained glass windows, crown moldings, hardwood floors, green plants, and a gorgeous winding staircase. Frank and Laura assist guests with directions to local attractions, restaurants, and shops. Wonderful breakfasts were served on fine china and silver, with juice in crystal goblets. A down-filled comforter, feather pillows, and cotton eyelet lace sheets ensured a restful sleep. The innkeepers turn down your bed, draw the curtains, and leave candy on the bedside table." *(Pam Sungren)* "Good air-conditioning, great VCR library, flashlight on night stand, magnifying mirror in bathroom, coffee for early risers, fresh flowers in room, touch keypad system." *(Patsy Berry)*

Open All year.
Rooms 2 suites, 3 doubles—all with bath and/or shower, telephone, clock, TV/VCR, desk, air-conditioning. 1 with fan.
Facilities Dining room, living room, library, videotape collection, guest refrigerator; porch. Off-street parking.
Location Gospel Hill Historic District; adjacent to Woodrow Wilson birthplace. 2 blocks to town center. From I-81, take Exit 222. Follow Rte. 250 to Staunton. Go right at Rte. 11 (Coalter St.) Go through stop light. Inn on left.
Restrictions No smoking. Children 12 and over.
Credit cards None accepted.
Rates B&B, $99 suite, $85 double. Extra person, $15. 2-night weekend minimum May, Sept., Oct.

Thornrose House at Gypsy Hill ¢   *Tel: 540–885–7026*
531 Thornrose Avenue, 24401

A gracious Georgian style brick home, built in 1912, Thornrose House was purchased in 1992 by Suzanne and Otis Huston. Guests can relax in the rockers on the wraparound veranda, stroll under the vine-covered pergolas, or play golf or tennis in Gypsy Hill Park across the street. Guest rooms are handsomely furnished with Oriental rugs on hardwood floors, four-poster beds with bedside tables and lamps, and ample comfortable seating. Rates include afternoon tea and a breakfast of fresh fruit, and muffins, with pancakes, waffles, or perhaps an egg dish.

"A comfortable home with a wonderful porch and backyard garden. Exceptional breakfasts, different each day; we especially enjoyed the French toast and delicious Birchermuesli—a Swiss oat cereal with fresh fruit and yogurt." *(Doug & Val Kloeb)* "Gracious, hospitable innkeepers. Spotless, comfortable rooms, with good lighting for reading in bed. Ice, fruit, and cookies were always available in the dining room." *(Freda Mazer)* "The resident cats, Guilford and Sylvester, are delightful pets. Convenient location." *(Marilu Townsend)*

Open All year.
Rooms 5 doubles—all with private bath and/or shower, radio, clock, air-conditioning. Some with fan, desk.
Facilities Dining room with fireplace, living room with fireplace, piano, TV; upstairs sitting room, wraparound veranda. 1 acre with gardens, pergolas, off-street parking, lawn games. 300-acre Gypsy Hill Park across street for swimming, golf, tennis.
Location Shenendoah Valley. 8–10 blocks from downtown historic area. Next door to Statler Complex. From I-81 N, take Exit 222 & follow Rte. 250 W for 3.2 m. Turn left on Thornrose Ave. to 4th house on left. From I-81 S, take Exit 225. Go W on VA 275 (Woodrow Wilson Pkwy), then go left (S) on Rte. 11, bearing right onto Business Rte. 11 (Augusta St.). Go right on Rte. 250 W, then left on Thornrose.
Restrictions No smoking. No children under 5. Some traffic noise possible in front rooms.
Credit cards None accepted.

Rates B&B, $55–75 double, $45–65 single. Extra person, $15. 2-night weekend minimum in May & Oct.
Extras Station pickups.

STEELES TAVERN

Information please: Midway between Lexington and Staunton and just five minutes from the Blue Ridge Parkway is the **Sugar Tree Inn** (Highway 56, Steeles Tavern, 24476; 540–377–2197), set on 28 wooded acres, threaded with nature trails. The main lodge has a long porch lined with rocking chairs, a living area with a massive two-story stone fireplace and hand-hewn beams, and a glass-walled dining room overlooking a meadow. Rates for the eleven guest rooms range from $90–120. Guest rooms are in three buildings, each with a woodburning fireplace and a private bath; some have a VCR and double whirlpool tub. Owners Sarah and Hal Davis serve a breakfast of fruit, cereals, rolls, breakfast meats and hot entrées; light suppers are served on weekdays, with more elaborate meals on weekends.

Another possibility is the five guest room **Steeles Tavern Manor** (Highway 11, P.O. Box 39, 24476; 540–377–6444) situated on 55 acres with a stocked pond for fishing. A romantic candlelight breakfast and afternoon tea are included in the $75–140 rates.

STRASBURG

Information please: Seven miles west of Front Royal is the century-old **Hotel Strasburg** (201 Holliday Street, 22657; 540–465–9191). Once a major pottery-making center, the town is now better known for the Strasburg Emporium, an enormous warehouse crammed with antiques. The hotel's furnishings are antique, and rooms vary widely in size. Almost all the furnishings are for sale, with a price list on the dresser. Rates for the 29 rooms (all with private bath, suites with Jacuzzi tub) range from $70–80 for a double, $100–150 for a suite. The hotel restaurant is open for breakfast, lunch and dinner. "Quaint, filled with lovely antiques, wonderful dinner, skimpy weekday breakfast." *(DK)* Comments welcome.

SWOOPE

Lambsgate B&B ¢ **♦**　　　　　　　　　　　*Tel:* 540–337–6929
Routes 254 & 833, RR 1, Box 63, 24479

Lambsgate is a restored 1818 red brick farmhouse, owned since 1984 by Daniel and Elizabeth Fannon. Rooms are cheerfully furnished with antiques, collectibles, and handmade quilts. Elizabeth notes that guests enjoy "our pastoral surroundings, the opportunities for hiking and bicycling nearby, the comfortable, informal accommodations, and the convenience of being so close to Staunton and the interstate."

"Small extras made our visit most pleasant, including fresh flowers inside and out, old-fashioned embroidered pillowcases, great smelling soaps, comfortable chairs, and a variety of reading materials." *(Donna Julian)* "Fresh, plentiful breakfast of ginger pancakes with a luscious peach sauce." *(Kay Jones)* "Our spacious room had a beautiful view of Eliot Knob (second highest mountain in the valley) and the Alleghenies. Elizabeth and Dan Fannon run a lamb farm and both are full of lambing stories that animal lovers are sure to enjoy. Country ham with red-eye gravy and grits are Dan's breakfast specialties." *(Lynn Bachenberg)* "Accomplished, gracious hosts. Dan's bran muffins and homemade peach and strawberry preserves were delicious." *(Sharon Downing)* "When you sit on the front porch to watch the spectacular sunsets, the whispering sounds of a nearby stream and the distant jingling of the sheep bells dissolve stress. We liked the wooden floors, solid furniture, warm quilts handmade by Mrs. Fannon, and the sheepskin rugs at either side of the bed." *(J. A. Bowyer)*

Open All year.
Rooms 3 doubles share 1 bath. All with radio, ceiling fan.
Facilities Dining room, living room, porch with swing. 7 acres with sheep, lambs; river for fishing (poles provided). Hiking nearby.
Location Western VA, near W VA border. Shenandoah Valley. 8 m W of I-81, 6 m W of Staunton. From Staunton, go W on Rte. 254, turn right on Rte. 833 to B&B on right.
Restrictions No smoking. Traffic noise in some rooms.
Credit cards None accepted.
Rates B&B, $55 double, $44 single, including tax, service. Extra child, $10. No tipping. Discount for 5-night stay. 20% family discount for children in second room.
Extras Crib.

TREVILIANS

Prospect Hill Plantation Inn ✖
State Highway 613, Rte. Box 430, 23093

Tel: 540—967—0844
800—277—0844
Fax: 540—967—0102

Prospect Hill dates back to 1699; by 1840, when William Overton was the owner, the plantation covered over 1,500 acres. The family fortunes were reduced after the Civil War, and the Overtons began taking in paying guests from the city. In 1880 they expanded the Manor House and slave quarters to accommodate visitors on a regular basis; today the number of overnight guests has remained small, although up to 75 can be served at dinner. Rooms at Prospect Hill, in the main house and in various outbuildings, are decorated with antiques and handmade quilts. A full breakfast is served in your room, and dinner is a leisurely four-course meal, served at 7 P.M. weekdays, at 8 on weekends. Mireille and Bill Sheehan have owned Prospect Hill since 1977; son Michael is the innkeeper and chef.

"Our rustic room, the Summer Kitchen, was one of the separate outbuildings (one of the oldest on the property), with a large fireplace, sitting

381

area in front of the fireplace, and modern bath with a double Jacuzzi. A fire was already set and ready to light, homemade cookies and a small bottle of wine stood on a table with flowers and fresh fruit (even in winter), cold drinks were available in the small refrigerator, and coffee and tea could be made in the room in the morning. We went to the main house, just up the walk, for dinner and were seated in front of a cozy fire. The chef, Michael Sheehan, gave the assembled guests a detailed description of the gourmet delights that were to follow, including the recommended wine. The dinner did not disappoint in either taste or presentation. The next morning, once again we sat in front of the fire and enjoyed waffles and marvelous sausage." *(Betsy Madero)*

"The grounds are lovely to explore; there is a graveyard on the property where the slaves were buried." *(Pat Drake)* "Many of the charming accommodations are located in restored dependencies on the grounds, offering a romantic setting and much privacy." *(Joan Reid)* "We stayed in Pansey's Cottage. A load of wood on the front porch supplied us for the weekend. The sitting room with a stocked refrigerator and stereo provided hours of reflection while looking out over the pasture at the pond and mountains." *(Marcia Hostetler)*

Open All year. Closed Christmas.
Rooms 3 suites, 10 doubles—all with private bath and/or shower, radio, desk, air-conditioning, fan, fireplace, refrigerator, deck. Some with double whirlpool tub. 5 rooms in main house, 8 in 6 outbuildings.
Facilities 4 dining rooms, 3 with fireplaces; 2 sitting rooms, 1 with fireplace; library; veranda. 40 acres with 10-acre arboretum, swimming pool, hammocks, benches. Lake Anna for fishing, boating. James River for tubing, canoeing. 45 min. to Skyline Drive. Golf, ballooning nearby.
Location N central VA. Approx. 15 m E of Charlottesville, 90 m SW of Washington, DC. From Charlottesville, take Rte. 250 E 12 m to Zions Crossroads. Go 1 m E to Rte. 613, turn left & go 3 m to inn on left. From Washington, DC, take I-495 W to I-66 to Gainesville, VA. Go S on Rte. 29 to Culpeper. Continue S on Rte 15 to Zions Crossroads. Go left on Rte. 250. Go E 1 m to Rte. 613. Turn left & go 3 m to inn on left.
Restrictions No smoking in dining rooms.
Credit cards Discover, MC, Visa.
Rates MAP, $300–325 suite, $200–300 double. Inquire about extra person, midweek rates. Prix fixe dinner, $30.
Extras French spoken.

VIRGINIA BEACH

Barclay Cottage B&B   *Tel: 804–422–1956*
400 16th Street, 23451

Two blocks from the beach, the century-year old Barclay Cottage is, according to owners Peter and Claire Catanese, "one of the last true beach cottages at Virginia Beach, with wraparound verandas on both the first and second floors." Breakfast at 9 A.M. is served at a leisurely pace: perhaps strawberries, bananas, and kiwi with yogurt; home-baked cinnamon buns; and baked French toast with maple syrup and bacon or sausage, plus juice and hot beverages. Rates also include afternoon lemonade or espresso. Guest rooms are simply furnished with quilt-topped brass, iron, or sleigh beds, with Oriental or braided rugs.

"Lovely rooms, delicious breakfasts, delightful hosts, Peter and Claire, who loaned us chairs and a beach umbrella." *(Ellen Montemarano)* "Our modest room was nicely decorated. We had to leave early, but Peter offered to leave out muffins and cereal for us." *(Stephanie Roberts)*

Open March 1–Oct. 31.
Rooms 6 doubles—2 with private bath and/or shower. 4 with a maximum of 4 people sharing bath. All with clock, air-conditioning. 4 with fan, 1 with radio.
Facilities Dining room, living room with fireplace, TV, games, guest refrigerator. Wraparound two-story verandas. Beach chairs. Off-street parking for 6 cars; terrace, horseshoe court, putting green. 2 blocks to beach, $1/2$ m to boating, fishing.
Location SE VA. 18 m SE of Norfolk. 2 blocks from center of town. At corner of Artic & 16th.
Restrictions No smoking. No children. Some street noise.
Credit cards Amex, MC, Visa.
Rates B&B, $40–90 double. Senior discount. 2-3 night minimum.

WACHAPREAGUE

Reader tip: "A quiet town with a delicious seafood restaurant at the marina. No beach, but a beautiful tidal marshland along the channel which wanders among the barrier islands." *(Lori Sampson)*

Information please: For a quiet, inexpensive Eastern Shore getaway, consider the **Burton House and Hart's Harbor House B&Bs** (11 Brooklyn Street, P.O. Box 182, 23480; 804–787–4560), owned by fifth generation Wachapreague natives, Pat, Tom, and Mike Hart. Two adjacent century-old homes, ten guest rooms and four cabins offer clean, comfortable accommodations at rates of $65–75, including a full breakfast and afternoon tea, often served on the screened gazebo porch. Wachapreague is located 28 miles south of Chincoteague.

WARM SPRINGS

A historic town nestled at the base of Little Mountain in the Alleghenies, Warm Springs offers pleasant streets lined with beautiful old buildings, and makes a good base for exploring the area's natural beauty—and of course, for taking the baths here, or at nearby Hot Springs. The town lies along a mill stream, on a quiet loop of Old Mill and Old Germantown roads, about four blocks removed from U.S. Highway 220, a heavily traveled commercial route, which runs just outside of town. Warm Springs is located in western Virginia, about 10 miles from the West Virginia border.

Reader tip: "The village of Warm Springs offers a charming museum, Gristmill Square for evening dining and shopping, and the famous Warm Springs Pools, complete with separate 19th century bath houses for men and women. There's serious hiking available just a mile or so away on Warm Springs Mountain. Just five miles south is the famous Homestead and complex of shops, restaurants, golf courses and ski area." *(Peggy Davis)*

Information please: About 15 miles to the east of Warm Springs, in Millboro, is the **Fort Lewis Lodge** (HCR 3, Box 21A, Millboro 24460; 540–925–2314). This reasonably priced country lodge is located on 3,200 acres in the Allegheny Highlands and adjoining George Washington National Forest. It encompasses a Black Angus cattle farm, complete with 1850s gristmill and a renovated silo with glassed-in observation tower. The lodge building, built by owners John and Caryl Cowden, provides scenic views from both the gathering room and the large deck; the guest rooms have handcrafted cherry and oak furniture accented with quilts, country plaid blankets, and rag rugs. John reports that "guests enjoy miles of marked hiking trails, bicycling on country roads, river fishing for trout and small-mouth bass, wildlife observation, and great home cooking." Double rates of $130–180 include breakfast and dinner; blueberry pancakes are a breakfast favorite, while dinners feature their own beef, lamb, or fish. Families are most welcome; the Cowden's kids will happily invite young guests to join them for farm chores like collecting eggs.

For an additional area entry, see **Hot Springs.**

Anderson Cottage B&B ¢ 👭

Old Germantown Road, P.O. Box 176, 24484

Tel: 540–839–2975
Fax: 540–839–3058

Anderson Cottage was originally a four-room log tavern, opened around 1790. With changes made over the years, it reached its present configuration around 1840, became a school for girls and later, a summer inn. A separate brick kitchen (now the cottage) was added in the 1820s. Owner Jean Randolph Bruns explains that "Anderson Cottage has been in our family since the 1870s; the furnishings, pictures, and books are all family pieces. Our B&B is not an elegant or splendid inn—it's a comfortable place for reading and porch sitting with grand scenery all around. Our family-style buffet breakfast is served around 9 A.M. The meal consists of juice, a fruit plate with vanilla yogurt, sausage with sage seasoning, stewed apples, pancakes with maple syrup or scrambled eggs with chives and cream cheese, biscuits and homemade preserves. Sometimes guests become so engrossed in conversation that I have to remind them that 'there's a lovely day going on outside!' Most guests help clear the table, so I really think they feel at home here. Guests' privacy is totally respected; other than breakfast, there is no pressure on anyone to be part of a group. The Warm Springs Pools are a ½ mile away, and the warm stream from them flows through the back yard, to the delight of small children."

"Bookshelves line the walls of each room and comfortable chairs with reading lamps are everywhere. A large coffee urn in the kitchen allows early risers to sip coffee while Jean cooks breakfast and chats. Her homemade biscuits are wonderful." *(Alice Forbes)* "Our visits start with conversation and an ice-cold drink on the spacious porch, listening to the waters from the warm springs rush gently over stones nearby. Jean has family pictures on the walls, old books on the shelves, and ice or coffee for the asking. If charm, history, and privacy are your cup of tea, the pot is brewing here." *(Peggy Davis)* "A wonderful place because of the woman who owns it, the house itself, and the surrounding landscape. Jean is a delightful, well-informed, well-traveled, well-read lady who loves this house and is happy to share it and its history with guests. The wide-plank floors go this way, the door jams go that. The porch has several old rocking chairs that look across the lawn. On a cool morning the mist comes off the stream and makes a painfully beautiful scene." *(Caitrine Callison)* "Immaculately clean. Friendly, non-intrusive innkeepers." *(Amy Wasserman Klein)*

Open Cottage all year. Main house, March–Nov.
Rooms 1 2-bedroom, 2-bath cottage; 2 suites, 2 doubles—3 with private bath, 1 with shared bath. All with desk. Some with fireplace, refrigerator, deck.
Facilities Dining room with fireplace and piano, living room with games; porch. 2 acres with stream, swing set, lawn games. Hiking, skiing nearby.
Location Western VA. Allegheny Highlands. From Staunton, take Rte. 254 W to Buffalo Gap (becomes Rte. 42); continue to Millboro Springs. Then take Rte. 39 to Warm Springs. Go left on Old Germantown Rd. (Rte. 692) to 4th house on left. From Roanoke take I-81 N to Rte. 220 N Warm Springs. Go left on Rte. 619, right on Rte. 645. Go right on Old Germantown Rd. to 3rd house on right.
Restrictions No smoking in guest rooms. No children in main house.
Credit cards None accepted.
Rates B&B, $110 cottage, $80–90 suite, $60–70 double. Extra adult, $10; extra child, $5.
Extras Airport pickup. Crib.

Meadow Lane Lodge 🕇🕇   *Tel: 540–839–5959*
Route 39, Star Rte. A, Box 110, 24484

If you want to get away from crowds when you're on vacation, you'll love Meadow Lane Lodge, which accommodates fewer than thirty guests on its 1,600 acres. Built in 1920, Meadow Lane was opened as an inn in 1979 by owners Philip and Catherine Hirsh; Cheryl and Steve Hooley are the innkeepers. Surrounded by the George Washington National Forest, the lodge offers miles of hiking trails and a two-mile stretch of the Jackson River for catch-and-release fly-fishing. A short stroll brings guests to an overlook deck with spectacular views of the valley and the Allegheny Mountains. When company is desired, the Great Room's twin stone fireplaces are favorite gathering places. Breakfast is served in the dining room between 8:15 and 9:30 A.M., and varies each day, but typically consists of fresh fruit and juice, yogurt, and cereal, plus omelets, French toast, or pancakes, with grits, homefries, bacon, sausage, or trout. On Saturday nights in season, guests share tables and enjoy a set dinner menu.

"A narrow lane takes you from the main road to the inn, through trees and meadows filled with wildflowers. We arrived after dark and could see only the light of our little cabin. The next morning I stepped out onto our porch and was truly amazed by what I saw. To the right, separated by several fields, was a white barn and flocks of chickens, guinea hens, and sheep. To the left were the Allegheny Mountains, partially enshrouded in mist. Our small cabin had a tiny kitchen where we cooked our own dinners. At dusk, we watched deer grazing in the meadow. The innkeepers are friendly and attentive to guests' needs; the ladies who make breakfast cook everything to perfection." *(Carolyn Kulisheck)*

Open All year. Prix fixe dinner, Sat., April–Oct.
Rooms 3 cottages, 6 suites, 5 doubles—all with private bath and/or shower, clock, desk, fan. Some with TV, telephone, air-conditioning, refrigerator, fireplace, porch, kitchenette.
Facilities Breakfast room, common room with two fireplaces, porch. 1,600 acres with swimming pool, hiking, tennis court, croquet court, river for fly fishing, canoeing, swimming hole. Mountain bikes, fly rods rented. Golf nearby.
Location Follow Rte. 39 (Lewis Memorial Hwy) 4 m W of Warm Springs & turn at lodge sign. Approx. 10 min. to Warm Springs, Hot Springs, Homestead.
Restrictions No smoking. Children over 6.
Credit cards Amex, MC, Visa.
Rates B&B, $125–255 cottage, $115–145 suite, $105–115 double. Extra adult, $25; child under 15, $15. Picnic lunch with 24 hrs. notice. 2-night weekend minimum. Prix fixe dinner, $30–35.
Extras Crib, babysitting.

WASHINGTON

The tiny town of Washington (population 158) was laid out by George Washington over 250 years ago; the street names are unchanged. It is home to several quality gift, craft, and antique stores. Known as Little Washington, it is located in Northern Virginia, in Rappahannock County. It's 60 miles west of Washington, D.C., 13 miles east of the Skyline Drive, and ½ hour west of Warrentown.

Regrettably, the success of the Inn at Little Washington has had an inflationary ripple effect on the prices of most area inns. Expect to pay about double what you'd pay elsewhere in Virginia for an overnight in this area, especially on Saturday night.

Information please: A well-known restaurant and five guest-room inn, the **Bleu Rock Inn** (12567 Lee Highway, 22747; 540–987–3190 or 800–537–3652) is owned by Bernard and Jean Campagne, also owners of La Bergerie Restaurant in Alexandria. "Upon arrival, we were shown to our room on the ground floor (with its own private entrance) and offered something to drink. Wonderful dinner, accompanied by a bottle of wine from the Bleu Rock vineyards. Breakfast was equally spectacular as dinner with freshly squeezed orange juice, fresh fruit, biscuits, and smoked trout with shirred eggs and Amaretto French toast. An early morning walk around the pond, stables and vineyards was relaxing and refreshing." *(Lana Alukonis)* Another reader was equally pleased with the food, but found his room to be noisy. B&B double rates are $125–150, with a midweek off-season rate of $89.

Set atop Menefee Mountain (elevation 1,043 feet), **Sycamore Hill** (Route 1, Box 978, 22747; 540–675–3046) is a contemporary stone house with lots of windows and a 63-foot veranda enjoying the views of meadows and woodland, gardens and mountains. The three guest rooms are handsomely decorated with an eclectic touch; the Wagners' interest in Oriental art is evident. Double rates of $100–140 include breakfast, which might consist of sourdough French toast, stuffed pears, or apple soufflé.

For additional area entries, see listing for **Blue Knoll Farm** in **Castleton,** and **Caledonia Farm** in **Flint Hill.**

The Foster-Harris House
189 Main Street, P.O. Box 333, 22747

Tel: 540–675–3757
800–666–0153

No, George Washington didn't sleep here! But, in 1749, he did survey the land the Foster-Harris House sits on. The home itself was built much later—in 1901, and was home to the village's first indoor bathroom. Phyllis Marriott bought the inn in 1992, and has furnished the rooms with queen-size beds, and both Victorian antiques and American folk art. Views of the Blue Ridge Mountains can be enjoyed from many room, which are stocked with specialty towels and linens, bathrobes and down comforters. Breakfast menus vary, but might include orange juice, fresh fruit, corn bread, dried cherry muffins, and an egg and cheese soufflé, and bacon.

"Phyllis is a thoughtful innkeeper—helpful yet not intrusive. My comfortable room had an inviting reading area, exquisite bed linens, and a spotless bathroom. The hearty Virginia breakfast included fresh melon, muffins, and baked French toast." *(Mary Ann Kuhn)* "Fantastic water pressure in the shower; bright rooms; friendly, kind innkeeper; extremely clean." *(Linoa Sen Usoi)*

Open All year.
Rooms 1 suite with woodstove, double whirlpool tub; 3 doubles—all with full private bath, air-conditioning.
Facilities Dining room, living room/parlor with fireplace; porch with swing, laundry. 1 acre with on-site parking for 6 cars. Fishing, boating nearby.
Location 65 m W of Washington, D.C. In-town location. From Warrenton, take Rte. 211 W 25 m. Go right at 1st entrance to Washington. Go to stop sign. Turn left. Go to last house on right.
Restrictions No smoking. Children 10 and over.
Credit cards Discover, MC, Visa.
Rates B&B, $135 suite, $95–115 double. Extra person $20. Midweek discount.

The Inn at Little Washington ✕
Middle and Main Streets, P.O. Box 300, 22747

Tel: 540–675–3800
Fax: 540–675–3100

Not long after Patrick O'Connell and Reinhardt Lynch opened their Little Washington restaurant in 1978, a Washington, DC, food critic described it as "the best restaurant within a 100-mile radius of Washington." Since then, the inn has received accolades from every conceivable source, including five diamond/star ratings from AAA and Mobil. Despite steep surcharges, advance reservations for weekends are needed well in advance, especially in the fall. Given the hoopla, guest expectations run as high as the prices, and reader feedback indicates that most feel it's worth it for the ultimate experience. Use the advance lead time to budget for your excursion (or just take out a second mortgage), so when you get to the inn, you won't have to think about money at all. Some feel it's worthwhile to go the whole nine yards and reserve one of the suites for the most extravagant evening of all. Guest rooms are lavishly decorated with English fabrics, elaborate wallcoverings, *faux* marble painting, an-

387

tiques, and all possible amenities. Rooms vary in size, design, decor and style as well as price; the least expensive are compact, while the suites are extremely spacious.

A recent dinner menu selection included caviar on potato crisps, rockfish with grilled radicchio, veal and sweetbreads with country ham, braised rabbit in apple cider sauce, and a pecan tart with caramel ice cream. These are tough decisions, though, so you might want to arrange for a tasting dinner instead; ask when you make reservations. Breakfasts, served from 8–10:30 A.M., are no less tempting; rates include a continental breakfast, but à la carte possibilities might include a wild mushroom omelet with sausage and potatoes, or pan-fried trout, with thick-sliced bacon and eggs scrambled with smoked salmon.

"We had dessert in the beautiful landscaped garden, serenaded by the local tree frogs." *(Pamela Young)* "We stayed in the 'cheapest' room, and though it was small, it was outstanding in all other regards." *(Carol Blodgett)* "We stayed in the suite across the street above the inn's antique shop, with a living room, bedroom with king-size bed, kitchen, sitting room with twin bed, and bath. Exquisite fabrics, wall paper, and antiques. We were pampered beyond our wildest imaginations." *(Richard & Sheri DeBro)* "Like walking into the pages of *Architectural Digest.* Decor is astonishing—lovely William Morris papers and English fabrics. Staff is youthful, quiet, abundant, and well-trained." *(Deborah Reese)* "The richly appointed dining room is decorated in deep colors of maroon and dark blue. Yards and yards of fabric made up the thick, dark curtains. Plates were garnished with edible flowers." *(Hopie Welliver)*

Open All year. Closed Tues. except May, Oct. Closed Christmas.
Rooms 2 duplex suites, 8 doubles—all with private bath and/or shower, desk. Suites, with balcony, across street.
Facilities Restaurant, sitting rooms, covered garden terrace with fountains.
Location Center of town. From Washington D.C., take I-66 W to exit 10-A Gainseville (22 m from Beltway). Follow 29 S to Warrenton (12 m). In Warrenton, take 211 W for 23 m. Turn right on 211 Business to Washington. Inn is ½ m on right.
Restrictions Children 10 and over.
Credit cards MC, Visa.
Rates B&B, $390–490 suite, $240–370 double. $100 surcharge Oct., also Fridays, holidays. $150 surcharge Saturdays. Extra person, $40. Prix fixe dinner, $70 (Sun.–Fri.); $90 Sat. Full breakfast, $10–20 extra. Service additional.

WAYNESBORO

The Iris Inn   ♿
191 Chinquapin Drive, 22980

Tel: 540–943–1991

A contemporary structure built in 1991, The Iris Inn combines the best of old and new. Wayne and Iris Karl built their inn on a wooded tract on the western slope of the Blue Ridge Mountains, overlooking the Shenandoah Valley. Though clearly a modern building, it reinterprets many elements of traditional central Virginia architecture; wraparound porches, cupola, and a standing seam metal roof. The inn's interior also creates an appealing balance of tradition and innovation. While the spacious guest rooms are decorated with 18th century reproductions, family pieces, and antiques, the inn's main gathering room has the feel of a modern lodge, with a cathedral ceiling that rises three stories, floor-to-ceiling windows, and 28-foot fieldstone fireplace. Best of all are the realistic murals painted by a Virginia wildlife artist, from the raccoons perched on the door frame to the floor-to-ceiling woodland scene in the breakfast area, complete with deer, woodchuck, and bunnies. Beverages are served here at arrival time, and the "bottomless" cookie jar is a round-the-clock temptation. "Wide porches with rockers beckoned us to come relax and enjoy the view. In addition to the wonderful wildlife paintings, the great room has a large fireplace—warm and welcoming on a chilly day. Iris and Karl always have time for their guests and are a great source of information on restaurants and sights. Wonderful breakfasts of fresh fruit, orange juice, and homemade muffins are followed by a delectable entrée—perhaps an egg dish, mushroom in puff pastry, or an artichoke-spinach casserole. Served in the great room at tables for four or six, guests have an opportunity to meet the other guests. You are never hurried, but set your own pace for the day's activities." *(Frank & Doris Sutton)*

"Rooms are provided with everything you could want, from the terry robes to the chilled sodas in your individual refrigerator." *(Diane Johnson)* "The Bird Room is decorated with birdcages, bird wallpaper and paintings, and is charming, yet not overdone. Our room had a private door to the garden, making it handy to slip to the hot tub without going through the common area." *(Carolyn Myles)*

Open All year.
Rooms 1 apartment with kitchenette, 6 doubles—all with private bath and/or shower, radio, clock, TV, air-conditioning, refrigerator. 6 with fan, balcony. All with telephone jack; phone on request. 1 with double whirlpool tub.
Facilities Great room with fireplace, breakfast area, games, books, piano; deck. 21½ acres with hot tub. Downhill skiing, hiking nearby.
Location NW VA. 24 m W of Charlottesville, 12 m E of Staunton. 2 m from town. From I-64, take Exit 96 (Waynesboro-Lyndhurst). Go S on Rte. 624 toward Lyndhurst for ¹⁄₁₀ m. Go left on Chinquapin Dr. to inn on left ³⁄₁₀ m.
Restrictions No smoking. Children in apartment only.
Credit cards MC, Visa.
Rates B&B, $75–100 double. Extra person, $20. 2-night weekend minimum. Corporate rates.
Extras Wheelchair access; 1 bathroom specially equipped. Waynesboro Airport pickup.

WHITE POST

L'Auberge Provençale ✗
Rte. 340 South, P.O. Box 119, 22663

Tel: 540–837–1375
800–638–1702
Fax: 540–837–2004

For a touch of southern France in northern Virginia, L'Auberge Provençale is an excellent choice for both food and accommodation. In 1980, fourth-generation chef and owner Alain Borel and his wife Celeste bought this 1750s stone farmhouse, first renovating the downstairs for their restaurant. Over the next seven years, they added a wing with guest rooms and a sunny breakfast room where the full breakfast is served. Guest rooms are eclectically decorated with French art and fabrics, Victorian wicker, and Federal reproductions. One of Chef Borel's recent dinners included fois gras with mango and ginger; scallops with baby shrimp and thyme; and raspberry brown butter tart with sabayon.

"Like staying at a friend's well-appointed country house. Our bedroom had random-width floors and a four-poster bed, with a profusion of pictures, fresh flowers and plants, wooden carvings and magazines. If only one's friends served food as good as that of gracious chef-owner Alain Borel. My first course was a mousse of scallops with beurre blanc sauce; my next course was a dish made famous in a Parisian 3-star restaurant—lobster with vanilla butter sauce—shelled and then reshaped, served with asparagus and the thinnest French beans. My husband had a salad of sweetbreads and wild mushrooms, followed by pigeonneaux with local morels and tarragon. The inn is on the way to the Blue Ridge Mountains and Skyline Drive; you could spend the day hiking in the mountains, then retire to the inn for dinner and the night. We sat on the porch and gazed at fields of cows, rolling green countryside and the blue hills beyond." *(Carolyn Mathiasen)* "Rooms are warm and inviting, but it's the food that gets our rave reviews—from the poached pears and wonderful breads, muffins, and croissants at breakfast, to the lobster and turkey entrées at dinner, to the delicate crème brulée for dessert." *(MF)* "Marvelous food, excellent wine list, charming dining rooms. Our French-style guest room had white wicker appointments. Breakfast just as good—maybe better—than dinner." *(Ernie & Happy Copley, also Miryam Prosper)*

Open Feb. 14 through Dec. 31. Restaurant closed Mon. & Tues.
Rooms 1 suite, 9 doubles—all with private bath and/or shower, air-conditioning. 5 with fireplace, 1 with balcony. 7 rooms in separate building.
Facilities Restaurant, bar, sitting room. 8.5 acres with gardens. Golf, canoeing nearby. 15 min. to downhill skiing. Off-street parking.
Location NW VA, Clarke County. 65 m SW of Washington, DC, 9 m to Winchester. Take I-66 W to Exit 5. Go N on Rte. 17 for 9 m to Rte. 50 and turn left. At 1st traffic light turn left on Rte. 340. Go 1 m to inn on right.
Restrictions Children 11 and over.
Credit cards MC, Visa.
Rates B&B, $165–190 suite, $120–165 double, $100–145 single. Extra person, $25. Tipping encouraged. Prix fixe dinner, $55. 10% senior discount midweek.
Extras Wheelchair access. Airport pickup, $60. French, Spanish spoken.

WILLIAMSBURG

Williamsburg was selected as the new Colonial capital of Virginia when it became clear that the original capital at Jamestown was disease-ridden and undefensible. It was planned and built starting in 1700 by Governor Francis Nicholson, and grew rapidly. In 1780, the capital was moved again, this time to Richmond. Williamsburg continued as the county seat and as the home of William and Mary College and the Public Hospital for the Insane. Fortunately, a large number of 18th-century houses survived, and, in 1926, the Reverend W.A.R. Goodwin persuaded John D. Rockefeller, Jr., to finance the city's restoration. Today, the historic area is operated by the nonprofit Colonial Williamsburg Foundation. All visits to Colonial Williamsburg should begin at the Visitor's Center, for full information on what to see and do.

Over one million visitors come to Williamsburg every year. Remember that Williamsburg is very hot and crowded in the summer; late fall or early spring are probably the best times to visit. If you do visit in the warm weather, try to walk or jog through the restoration early in the morning (around 6 A.M.), before the crowds arrive. Although the weather can be chilly and damp, special programs and reduced-rate packages are available from January to early March, and the lack of crowds does much to compensate.

Williamsburg is located 155 miles south of Washington, D.C., and 50 miles southeast of Richmond. Most of the town's B&Bs are on either Richmond Road or Jamestown Road, both of which border William and Mary College and which meet in a "V" at Duke of Gloucester Street at Colonial Williamsburg; the lower the house number, the closer the B&B to the restored area. All houses are set quite close to the street; expect some traffic noise in all if staying in rooms at the front of an inn, plus occasional noise from parties at William and Mary on some fall and spring weekends.

Also recommended—B&Bs: Several appealing B&Bs—all on Richmond Road— are within an easy walk of Colonial Williamsburg. The **Homestay B&B** (517 Richmond Road, 23185; 804–229–7468 or 800–836–7468) is an affordable choice in an excellent location. "Of the three guest rooms, I thought the most appealing is the one with the lovely garden mural behind the king-size bed. Warm and welcoming owners." (SWS)

Jamestown Road also offers some good choices within walking distance of Colonial Williamsburg, across from the William and Mary campus. The **Candlewick Inn B&B** (800 Jamestown Road, 23185; 804–253–8693 or 800–418–4949) offers three guest rooms, each with a private bath. Guest rooms are decorated with uncluttered country Colonial charm, with lace-canopy quilt-topped beds. Guest can relax with a book or a game before the common room fireplace, or on the screened porch. The $85–95 B&B double rates includes breakfasts of pancakes, sausage, fried apples, coffee cake, juice, and coffee, served from 8:30–9:30 A.M. on the antique plank table in the dining room.

Williamsburg's most romantic B&B is the **Liberty Rose** (1022 Jamestown Road, 23185; 804–253–1260), just over a mile from the historic area. Richly decorated with a lush collection of English, French, and Victorian antiques, the B&B double rates range from $105–175, including a full breakfast.

Received just as we were going to press was an enthusiastic recommendation for the **Indian Springs B&B** (330 Indian Springs Road, 23185; 804–220–0726 or 800–262–9165), just off Jamestown Road, and a good choice for families. Owned by Paul and Kelly Supplee, a young couple with two children, a dog and a cat, this B&B offers garden level guest rooms; common areas are on the first floor, and the family lives on the second floor. Three suites and one cottage are available for $90–125, including a full breakfast of fruit, juice, muffins, ham, waffles, and fried potatoes. "The guest rooms are clean, airy, and comfortable, with country-style decor. The two king suites and adjacent cottage are furnished with feather beds and quilts. A large porch area, outside the rooms, provides guests with a view of the beautifully landscaped grounds, including a small stream running behind the house. Amenities were abundant—from filled ice buckets to umbrellas." *(Larry & BJ Schwartzkopf)*

Also recommended—resort: We've received fine reports on the **Kingsmill Resort** (1010 Kingsmill Road, 23185; 804–253–1703 or 800–832–5665), a conference center and condominium complex on the James River, owned by the Anheuser-Busch company. It's two miles from Colonial Williamsburg, and close to Busch Gardens—an ideal family choice. In fact, the resort offers special children's programs during the summer months, plus a shuttle bus to these popular spots. "This well-maintained resort has 13 tennis courts, two 18-hole golf courses, a marina on the James River, rental bikes, a well-equipped sports club with indoor and outdoor swimming pools, Nautilus equipment, and racquetball; and a stocked fishing pond, with boats and equipment. Condos are built of gray cedar, blending well with the surrounding pine forests. Our spacious unit was done in Williamsburg style, with Queen Anne reproductions; others may reflect the differing tastes of the owners. Daily maid service, triple-sheeted beds, enormous plush towels, and bathroom amenities provided hotel-style comfort. We had an excellent dinner in the Riverview Dining Room, and enjoyed a sumptuous buffet breakfast in the Bray Dining Room. The staff was extremely accommodating, patient, and friendly." *(SHW, also SWS)*

Information please: A two-story Colonial with a gambrel roof and wraparound porch, the **Fox Grape B&B** (701 Monumental Avenue, 23185; 804–229–6914 or 800–292–3699) has four guest rooms with private baths. Owners Pat and Robert Orendorff have decorated the inn with Colonial and Victorian reproductions, some antiques, duck decoys, and Pat's cross-stitching. "A short walk to the restored area; clean room, comfortable bed, large bath with plenty of fresh towels; modest breakfast." *(MJS)* B&B double rates are $78–84.

A blissfully peaceful escape, just 25 miles northeast of Williamsburg via the Colonial Parkway and Route 17 is **The Willows Bed and Breakfast** (5344 Roanes Wharf Road, Gloucester 23061; 804–693–4066). Owners Ted and Angela Kristensen, both alumni from Colonial Williamsburg—he as a certified executive chef, and she as concierge—have decorated their B&B with old family pieces reflecting their Danish and English backgrounds, respectively. The four guest rooms are found in an 1890s Victorian farmhouse, and a restored country store. The $75–85 double rate includes a breakfast of Danish country omelets, home-baked breads and muffins, and custom-blended coffee. Each guest room has a queen-size bed, private bath, and color TV.

For an additional area recommendation, see **North Bend Plantation** in **Charles City**.

The Cedars B&B 🏠
616 Jamestown Road, 23185

Tel: 804–229–3591
800–296–3591

Built in 1930 of 200-year-old brick, The Cedars was owned by a doctor's family with seven children, each of whom would be attending the College of William and Mary, across the street. Opened as a guest house in 1940, it was purchased by Carol, Jim, and Brona Malecha in 1993. Breakfasts are served in the airy, brick-walled sunporch, at individual tables. In addition to cereal, assorted toasting breads and muffins, and fresh fruit, the menu also includes such entrées as oatmeal pudding with sausages and apples, a grits casserole with Virginia ham biscuits, or smoked salmon flan with dried fruit compote,

"Attractively decorated with quality antiques and reproductions, including four poster or canopy beds and Oriental rugs in most rooms. Pleasant, energetic, hands-on owners." *(SWS)* "Marvelous breakfasts—even for non-breakfast eaters. We requested and were given the recipe for their delicious French toast. Our room was clean, comfortable, and attractive. Relaxing atmosphere; careful attention to detail." *(GR)* Reports appreciated.

Open All year.
Rooms 1 cottage, 2 suites, 8 doubles—all with private bath and/or shower, radio, clock, air-conditioning. Most with ceiling fan. 2 with desk, fireplace; 1 with TV.
Facilities Breakfast room with games, living room with fireplace, books. ½ acre with off-street parking.
Location 40 m E of Richmond. ½ m from historic district.
Restrictions No smoking.
Credit cards MC, Visa.
Rates B&B, $125–180 suite, cottage; $95–165 double. Extra person, $15. 2-night holiday weekend minimum.
Extras Airport/station pickups. Crib. Babysitting. German spoken.

Colonial Capital B&B
501 Richmond Road, 23185

Tel: 804–229–0233
800–776–0570
Fax: 804–253–7667

Barbara and Phil Craig restored this Colonial Revival home, built in 1926, to its original charm in 1989. Each guest room has a canopy bed, and most have delicately flowered wallpapers. Rates include breakfast and afternoon tea and wine. Guests are delighted with Barbara's breakfasts, which include fresh fruit and juice, and a hot entrée; she notes that her baked French toast with strawberries, raised-dough waffles, and the ham and cheese breakfast soufflé are among the favorites.

"The Craigs are extremely warm and hospitable; I loved their dry Southern humor. Welcoming living room, with beautiful red velvet chairs flanking the fireplace. Breakfast is usually served in the dining room and at the round table in the sunny breakfast room at 8:30, and is different each day; Barbara is careful to ask about personal preferences. Phil ensures that your coffee cup is never empty, and decaf is always available. Guests eat in dining room, or at the round table in the sunny breakfast room. I stayed in the York Room, done in soft yellow and Williamsburg blue—comfortable and soothing—with a handsome canopy bed with a firm mattress and good linens. A large closet and dresser provided ample storage space; spacious bathroom. Good lighting throughout, including a reading light at the comfortable wing chair. A fine choice for families or honeymooning couples is the attic suite, charmingly tucked under the eaves, yet still spacious and airy. Its large living room has TV/VCR, plus two built-in window seats that can be made up as children's beds. Great location, easy walk to historic area. At the end of a busy day, Phil was always ready to offer a refreshing glass of (surprisingly good) Virginia wine." *(SWS)*

"From Phil assisting with our bags upon arrival, to help with restaurant reservations, to Barbara quietly fixing us coffee and rolls for our 6 A.M. departure, they couldn't do enough for us." *(Nancy Dew)* "We were greeted with a warm smile, a glass of iced tea, a tour of the Craig's inviting home and a friendly lick on the hand from their placid golden retriever." *(Donna & Bob Cowdrey)* "Thoughtful attention to my food allergies." *(WJG)*

Open All year.
Rooms 1 suite, 4 doubles—all with private bath and/or shower, telephone, air-conditioning. 1 with radio. Suite with TV/VCR.
Facilities Dining room, living room with fireplace, TV/VCR, stereo, books, games; breakfast room, screened porch, deck, patio. Bicycles. Off-street parking on site.
Location 3 blocks from historic area; across street from Wm & Mary. From I-64, take Exit 238. Go ½m & turn right onto Rte. 132 S. Follow signs to Wmsburg. Bus. & College of Wm. & Mary. Rte. 132 becomes Henry St. After railroad tracks, turn right at light onto Lafayette St. Take Lafayette to Virginia Ave.(4th on left), & turn left. Inn is at 2nd block on right, at corner of Richmond Rd.
Restrictions No smoking. Occasional noise from alumni house across st; football stadium nearby. "Well behaved children over 6 welcome."
Credit cards Amex, Discover, MC, Visa.
Rates B&B, $100–125 suite, $76–115 double, $60–92 single. Extra person, $16–20. 2-night weekend minimum high season, also holidays.
Extras Airport/station pickups

War Hill Inn 🛉
4560 Long Hill Road, 23188

Tel: 804–565–0248
800–743–0248

Like much of Colonial Williamsburg, the War Hill Inn is not as old as it looks; it was constructed in 1968 under the direction of an architect from Colonial Williamsburg. Long time owners Bill and Shirley Lee built their inn of old bricks and woodwork salvaged from historic buildings. While the trees to make the living room paneling were cut right on the farm, many of the materials came from the Pennsylvania Dutch Country. The wide heart-pine floors came from an old school, the stairs from a Lutheran church, and the overhead beams from a nearby barn; the fireplace mantel in the family room is about 200 years old. The cottage exterior is a replica of a Colonial Williamsburg kitchen. A restful contrast to the bustle of the main tourist areas, this B&B overlooks fruit orchards and the Lee's herds of grazing Black Angus cattle.

"Quiet, peaceful setting, far from the road, yet just minutes from the historic area and outlet shopping. Comfortable, pleasantly furnished accommodations." *(SWS)* "Delicious breakfast served at 8:30 A.M. in the dining room. An easy drive to the Visitors' Center, where we picked up the shuttle to Colonial Williamsburg. For dinner, Shirley recommended Giuseppi's, a nearby Italian restaurant where we enjoyed a tasty meal. Looking out over a field of grazing cattle, watching the bluebirds in their house, swinging or playing soccer in the yard, and talking to Bill about his years as a veterinarian made for a delightfully pleasant weekend retreat." *(Jill Reeves)* "The full Southern breakfasts were fabulous, but the best part of our stay were the hosts. Bill and Shirley Lee were just as warm and inviting as their inn." *(Lee Richman)* "Bill Lee is a retired veterinarian, who also runs an active cattle breeding farm. The cottage is beautifully furnished and private." *(MC)*

Open All year.
Rooms 2-bedroom cottage, 1 suite, 3 doubles—all with private bath and/or shower, air-conditioning, TV. Cottage with whirlpool tub.
Facilities Living room, dining room, family room with fireplace. 32 acres with fruit orchard, cattle barn.
Location 3 m from Historic Williamsburg. From I-64 take Exit 234. Go W on Rte. 646 to Rte. 60 (Richmond Rd.). Go E 1 m to Olde Towne Rd. Go right 1 1/2 m to Long Hill Rd. Go right 8/10 m to inn on right.
Restrictions No smoking.
Credit cards Amex, MC, Visa.
Rates B&B, $70–110. Extra person, $15.
Extras Portable crib.

Williamsburg Inn 🛏 ✕ 🐾 ♿

Frances Street, P.O. Box B, 23187

Tel: 804–229–1000
800–HISTORY

The Colonial Williamsburg Foundation owns and operates 1,000 rooms spread over seven different lodging establishments, including the Williamsburg Inn, the Williamsburg Lodge, the Colonial Houses, the Woodlands, Providence Hall, and the Governor's Inn (call the toll-free phone number above for information on all of them). A key asset of all of these lodgings is their location, enabling you to stroll the grounds in the early morning or evening, after the crowds have dispersed. The Inn and the Colonial Houses are most highly recommended, with the Colonial Houses way ahead as the first choice of most respondents. *Susan Schwemm* recommends: "Carefully outline your needs, because each Colonial house is different—large or small bedroom, living room or not, fireplace, porch or garden, type of beds, and so on—then the staff can match a house with your needs." At check-in, ask for details on afternoon tea, discounts, and reservations, and read the information packet carefully.

Here's a sample of the reader feedback received:

The Inn: The Williamsburg Inn is a well-known full-service luxury hotel, with high standards, and corresponding rates. Elegant rooms have muted Schumacher fabrics, original paintings and prints, and brass candlestick lamps. "The inviting public rooms overlook a patio facing the golf course; the gift shops are appealing." *(Elizabeth Sommer)* "Outstanding buffet breakfast, with fresh fruit and granola, hot dishes and fresh-baked muffins and pastries. Afternoon tea in the East Lounge was accompanied by a pianist, and on Friday, we had a lovely evening in the Regency Room, complete with dancing. Dinner included lobster and crab bisque, veal noisettes, and an excellent selection from the dessert cart. The staff was friendly and helpful." *(Alex & Beryl Williams)*

Worth noting: "Our first-floor room overlooking the patio was lovely, but lacked privacy."

The Colonial Houses: "Furnishings in the Colonial Houses are antique reproductions, as is the artwork. Floors are hardwood, with woven rag rugs. Most have fireplaces and TVs; bathrooms are well-equipped with thick towels and amenities, although many are tucked up under the eaves. Some are authentically cramped. All are within a four-square-block walk of the Williamsburg Inn. Nowhere else can you see the fife & drum corps coming down the street and past your front door without having to reserve your square foot of curbside. On a hot day, it's particularly pleasant to stop by 'your house' for a cold drink, the bathroom, or a dose of conditioned air." *(SHW)* "We rented the second floor of a small house on Duke of Gloucester Street. The spacious room and bath were appropriately decorated, but the best part came in the evening, when we could step out the door of our little home and walk throughout the town, looking into the shops and buildings and pretending to be an actual part of this marvelous 18th-century town." *(Jack & Sue Lane)* "We stayed in the Chiswell-Bucktrout Kitchen (in Colonial times, kitchens were often in separate buildings), and found it charming, comfortable, and wonderfully convenient. It had a large closet/pantry, brick floor, with a little courtyard. The windows were authentically small, which made it a bit dark, but otherwise it was absolutely delightful." *(Dianne Crawford)* "All houses are discreetly marked and one needs a map (provided at check-in) to decipher what is where. One of the staff escorts you to your 'house' and settles you in." *(Elizabeth Sommer)* "Our tavern room faced the rear of the building and was quieter than those facing Francis Street." *(HW)*

The Motor House: "Delightfully clean. Easy walking distance to local transportation to all events and meals." *(Robert Rieger)*

Providence Hall: "Our spacious room in this contemporary lodge had a king-size bed, pull-out queen-size sofa, and a terrace overlooking the tennis court. Two lovely swimming pools. Breakfasts in the Regency Room were good, the service adequate. A relaxing getaway." *(Lorraine Cromis)*

The Woodlands: "A contemporary resort on wooded grounds, with suites perfect for families." *(Anne Wichman)*

Open All year.
Rooms 25 suites, 210 doubles—all with full private bath, telephone, radio, TV, desk, air-conditioning.
Facilities Restaurant, 4 lobbies, 2 cocktail lounges, library. Music nightly, dancing weekends. 200 acres. 2 swimming pools, 8 tennis courts, golf, lawn bowling green, summer children's program, fitness center with lap pool.
Location Center of town.
Credit cards Amex, MC, Visa.
Rates Room only, $425–650 suite, $245–280 double. Extra person, $12. Alc breakfast, $6–16; alc lunch, $17; alc dinner, $65. 20% service. Special packages. Rates at Colonial Homes, approx. $99–145. Other hotels $60–225. Children under 12, free.

Extras Wheelchair access. Station pickup. Crib, babysitting. French, German, Spanish, Italian spoken.

Williamsburg Sampler B&B
922 Jamestown Road, 23185

Tel: 804–253–0398
800–722–1169

Helen and Ike Sisane are the energetic owners of the Williamsburg Sampler, a three-story 18th century plantation-style red brick Colonial Revival built in 1976. The decor includes Ethan Allen and Thomasville reproductions, Queen Anne wing chairs, and is highlighted by their collections of pewter, framed samplers, Helen's hand-crafted woodwork, and antiques. The guest rooms have king- or queen-size rice-carved four poster beds. Ike's breakfasts include fresh fruit and juice, waffles, quiche, French toast, or Western eggs, plus sausage or bacon, potatoes, biscuits, muffins, Danish, and coffee.

"Thoughtful touches included early morning breakfasts, dinner reservations, use of the garden hose to rinse off our car. Our room had a bowl of fruit, dish of candy and supply of thirsty towels—all renewed daily." *(Elaine & George St. John, also Martha Jeffries)* "The authentic samplers were finely stitched and intriguing. The bathroom lighting was bright and practical, the bed linens beautiful and in keeping with the period. Breakfast kept us well-fueled for sightseeing. We enjoyed Helen's sampler collection and her own beautifully crafted wooden cabinets and accessories. Ike was gracious and welcoming from our arrival until our departure." *(Mrs. & Mr. William Owen, also SWS)*

Open All year.
Rooms 2 suites, 2 doubles—all with private bath and shower, air-conditioning, fan, TV.
Facilities Living room, dining room, den, common room with piano, TV/VCR, books; porches, deck. Off-street parking.
Location From I-64, take Exit 242A to Rte. 199 W. At 4th traffic light, make right turn on to Jamestown Rd. Go ⁹/₁₀ m to inn on right.
Restrictions No smoking. Children 12 and over.
Credit cards None accepted.
Rates B&B, $140 suite, $90 double. 2-night weekend/holiday minimum.
Extras Airport/station pickups.

WOODSTOCK

Woodstock is located in the Shenandoah Valley of northern Virginia, 90 miles west of Washington, DC. From Washington, take I-66 west to I-81. Then take I-81 south to Woodstock. Take Exit 72, then follow Route 42 east into Woodstock.

Reader tips: "The area is full of historic sites, caverns, antique shops, national parks, wineries, and recreational activities. The view from Massanutten Tower is truly magnificent, with the seven bends of the Shenandoah River spread out below." *(Joy & John McCauley)* Also: "The Shenandoah River provides excellent fishing—either wading, fishing from the bank, or from your own boat. A scenic area walk includes a swinging bridge which spans the river." *(Phyllis & Bill Ponn)* And: "The Spring House served simple but well-prepared fresh food at very reasonable prices." *(AW)*

The Country Fare ¢
402 North Main Street, 22664

Tel: 540—459—4828

Built in 1772 of log and brick, The Country Fare served as a hospital during the Civil War. The inn is a cozy B&B restored in Williamsburg colors and wallpapers, with hand-stenciled designs throughout. Rooms are decorated with a mix of antiques and country collectibles, reflecting owner Bette Hallgren's interest in crafts. Rates include a breakfast of fresh fruit and juice, homemade breads and biscuits served on old family china and silver.

"Bette Hallgren makes one feel truly welcome. She is a gracious innkeeper who provides just the right reading material for a quiet evening, and balanced with lively conversation over breakfast. We swung gently on the old-fashioned upstairs porch swing, and strolled along the village streets, absorbing the 'Old South' atmosphere." *(Burt Weston)* "Bette's bread pudding is the best!" *(Jan Lundquist)* "Nana's Room has hand-printed stencils on the furniture, hardwood floors (sloping slightly), and crisp linens. A simple, warm and inviting retreat." *(Judilynn Niedercorn)* "A haven of solitude, charm, and serenity; spacious antique-filled rooms." *(Bud & Barbara Linder)*

Open All year.
Rooms 3 doubles—1 with private shower, 2 with maximum of 4 sharing bath. All with radio, air-conditioning, ceiling fan. 1 with desk.
Facilities Dining room, living room both with fireplace, screened porch with rockers, swing; patio. Shenandoah River nearby for fishing. Off-street parking.
Location Walking distance to village.
Restrictions No smoking.
Credit cards Visa.
Rates B&B, $45—65 double, $35 single. Extra person, $10. 2-night fall holiday/weekend minimum.
Extras Airport pickup by prior arrangement. Porta-crib.

The Inn at Narrow Passage ⚑
U.S. 11 South, P.O. Box 608, 22664

Tel: 540—459—8000
Fax: 540—459—8001

Long before Shenandoah Valley travelers rolled down Interstate 81, stagecoaches bumped their way along the Wilderness Road, past what is now known as The Inn at Narrow Passage, site of Indian raids and, in 1862, the headquarters of Stonewall Jackson. Portions of the inn date back to 1740, although some guest rooms are housed in a recent addition. The inn was restored by Ellen and Ed Markel in 1984, who exposed the original log construction and pine floors. They've furnished the inn with Colonial reproductions and queen-size canopy beds.

"Relaxed, rustic atmosphere; charming, friendly hosts. A pleasure to return on a hot afternoon to find pitchers of fresh lemonade and iced tea waiting on the veranda." *(Julie Day)* "Rocking chairs on the porch beckoned me to try them out. Ellen offered directions and advice on local eateries." *(Paul Bramel)* "Inviting common room, with a warm fire and inviting atmosphere. Ed pointed out area attractions, including a relaxing walk along a country road following the river, complete with friendly neighborhood dogs. Breakfast consisted of fresh fruit and French toast, accompanied by conversations with Ed. Our room in the annex—the last one available—had two double beds and white walls." *(JK)* "Visit the Woodstock Tower, offering a beautiful view of the seven bends of the Shenendoah River. Stonewall Jackson's Room is perfect in winter, with rustic log walls and a wood-burning fireplace." *(Donna Seery)* "Grounds are spacious, well-kept and beautifully landscaped." *(Holly Liss)*

Open All year. Closed Christmas.
Rooms 12 doubles—10 with private bath and/or shower, 2 with a maximum of 4 people sharing bath. All with radio, air-conditioning. Some with desk, fireplace.
Facilities Living room with fireplace, dining room with fireplace, porch. Country store. 5 acres on Shenandoah River with fishing. Water sports, hiking, horseback riding, vineyards, caverns, battlefields nearby. 30 min. to downhill skiing at Bryce Mt.
Location N VA, Shenandoah Valley. 90 m W of Washington, DC. From Washington, take I-66 W to I-81. Take I-81 S to Exit 283, Rte. 11. Go S 2 m S to inn at corner of Rte. 11 & Rte. 672.
Restrictions Traffic noise possible in some rooms. No smoking in guest rooms.
Credit cards MC, Visa.
Rates B&B, $85–110 double. Extra person, $10. 2-night minimum holiday, Oct. weekends.
Extras Cribs.

Free copy of *INNroads* newsletter

Want to stay up-to-date on our latest finds? Send a business-size, self-addressed, stamped envelope with 55 cents postage and we'll send you the latest issue, *free!* While you're at it, why not enclose a report on any inns you've recently visited? Use the forms at the back of the book or your own stationery.

West Virginia

Thomas Shepherd Inn, Shepherdstown

West Virginia is a rural, mountainous state, with areas of great beauty. Most of our listings are in the Eastern Panhandle, a region of historic interest and natural attractions. Because this area is only a 60- to 90-minute drive from Washington, D.C., and Baltimore, MD, it is particularly popular on weekends. Rates are most often highest Friday and Saturday nights, and can be substantially lower midweek. Rates don't usually vary much with the seasons, although October is generally the most popular period.

The rest of the state is also worth exploring, particularly if you have time to drive the backroads and "hollers." Look for rugged scenery, traditional Appalachian crafts, fall foliage that challenges New England's, and towns with names such as "Odd," "Man," "Hometown" and "Paw Paw."

Note: In a number of entries, 800–CALL–WVA is listed as the toll-free number; after dialing it, request the specific inn you're contacting.

BERKELEY SPRINGS

"We this day called at Ye Famed Warm Springs," says the March 18, 1748, journal entry of sixteen-year-old George Washington, who was traveling with a Virginia surveying group. He was referring to the warm mineral waters of what is now called Berkeley Springs, the nation's oldest spa. These days the spa offers a full range of mineral baths and massage, as well as a regular swimming pool. Other sights of interest include nearby Prospect Peak, with a three-state view; Cacapon State Park, with a lake for swimming and boating, and an eighteen-hole Robert Trent Jones golf course; hiking and riding on Cacapon Mountain; Berkeley Castle; and the historic Chesapeake and Ohio Canal Tunnel in Paw Paw, completed in 1850.

Berkeley Springs is located in the Eastern Panhandle region of West Virginia, 100 miles west of Washington, D.C., and Baltimore, MD, and 165 miles southwest of Philadelphia, PA.

Reader tips: "Berkeley Springs State Park has an outdoor swimming pool, health club, Roman soaking baths which are filled with 750 gallons of heated natural spring water, and a professional massage staff. My half-hour soak in a private Roman bath, followed by a quiet shower and a half-hour massage, was a wonderful experience and a top value." *(SHW)*

Information please: We'd like current reports on **The Country Inn** (207 South Washington Street, Route 522, 25411; 304–258–2210 or 800–822–6630), built in 1932 in a brick Colonial style. The Country Inn West was built in 1985 at the rear of the older hotel, and contains luxury motel-style rooms; the older building has been refurbished, with most smaller rooms being combined into suites. The 70 guest rooms are comfortable, with a mixture of period and contemporary decor; most have private baths. "The building which houses the restaurant and guest rooms stands as an oasis in the center of town. Porches with white wicker chairs evoke its Southern charm. The menu selections were creative and well prepared—as good or better than you would find in any major city." *(Jean Wright)* Double rates are $37–85; suites are $90–145. Additional comments?

Highlawn Inn ¢

304 Market Street, 25411

Tel: 304–258–5700

The Highlawn is a turn-of-the-century Victorian home, owned by Sandy Kauffman and Timothy Miller. Guests enjoy relaxing on the Highlawn's porch rockers, with a lovely view overlooking the town. An additional four rooms are located in "Aunt Pearl's" Victorian house next door, each with a queen-sized bed.

"Sandy and Tim treated us as guests in their own home, and made reservations at the baths and with an excellent masseuse. Breakfast included cherry tarts made with homegrown fruit, and wonderful French toast." *(Angela Mauran)* "Sandy Kauffman and Tim Miller are exceptionally friendly, considerate, and helpful. The inn's distance from the main street ensures a peaceful, quiet setting, enhanced by the ample soundproofing between rooms. Despite its hilltop location, shower pressure is excellent, with ample hot water. Coffee, tea, and spring water are always available in the small parlor; there's also a larger sitting room and breakfast area. All rooms have antique furnishings, window air conditioners, luggage racks, and a brass shelf with hangers for garment bags. Rooms are wallpapered in small prints and stripes; lace and potpourri touches are everywhere. My favorite room is #3, which is large and elegant, with a huge carved walnut bed, a sitting area, and a wonderful nook with windows on three sides." *(SHW)*

"Upon arrival, you are generally greeted by one of the cats, who are often found on the huge wraparound porch, with lovely wicker furniture for reading and relaxing. The beds are delightfully firm and the pillows perfect. Delectable dishes of homemade breads and pastries, locally grown apples for cider and apple butter; egg casseroles, vegetables from the garden, dried and fresh fruit, oatmeal-apple crisp, country bacon and sausage, and plenty of coffee and tea." *(Connie Guy)* "Hard to believe that low-fat cooking could taste so good." *(Carol Vodra)* "Bright, clean, spacious rooms." *(Patricia Wood)*

Open All year.
Rooms 10 doubles—all with private bath and/or shower, TV, air-conditioning. 2 with private porch. 4 rooms in adjacent building.
Facilities Sitting room with fireplace, games, books, puzzles; parlor; wraparound veranda with porch swings, rockers. ¾ acre with gardens, paths. 9 m to Cacapon State Park for golf, tennis, hiking, swimming.
Location 3 blocks from center, 3 blocks to Berkeley Springs Mineral Baths. From I-70, I-81, take Rte. 522 to Market St. At the top of the hill on the left is the inn.
Restrictions No children.
Credit cards MC, Visa.
Rates B&B, $98 suite, $70–98 double. Prix fixe dinner, Sat night, May–Oct.; holiday weekends year-round, $35.

CASS

Information please: Back in 1911, West Virginia led the nation with over 3,000 miles of logging railroad line. Only 11 miles remain—in Cass, West Virginia at the Cass Scenic Railroad State Park, an authentic operating museum of lumber railroading. Located in what was formerly the park superintendent's house, **The Shay Inn** (Box 46, 24927; 304–456–4652) offers four guest rooms, each decorated with country antiques. B&B double rates of $45–55 include a full breakfast.

CHARLESTON

Historic Charleston Bed and Breakfast ¢   *Tel:* 304–345–8156
114 Elizabeth Street, 25311   800–CALL–WVA

Charleston's first B&B, this American Foursquare home was built in 1905 and was restored by Bob and Jean Lambert in 1991. Guest rooms are furnished in delicate florals with some antiques, and each has a sitting area.

"Perfectly located for anyone with business at the state capitol. Jean and Bob provide a relaxing atmosphere with the entire second floor reserved for guests. The living room provides a place to sit and visit with other guests or to watch television. Breakfast is served in the dining room on fine china around 8 or 8:30 each morning, and might typically include Belgian waffles with fresh strawberries and freshly whipped cream, plus eggs, bacon, juice, and coffee. All of Jean's breakfasts are first-rate; you will never go hungry." *(Ann Christoffersen)*

Open All year.
Rooms 3 doubles—all with private bath and/or shower, clock, desk, air-conditioning, fan.
Facilities Dining room with fireplace, living room with fireplace, TV; sunporch with books, porch. Off-street parking.
Location W WVA. Historic district. 1 block W of State Capitol, Culture Center. 1¼ m to Civic Center. From I-77 & I-64, take Exit 99 (State Capitol) & turn S. Go 3 blocks to Quarrier St. & go right to inn at corner of Elizabeth & Quarrier.
Restrictions No smoking.
Credit cards Amex, MC, Visa.
Rates B&B, $70–75 double, $65 single. Extra person, $10. 6% senior discount.

CHARLES TOWN

Charles Town is home to the Charles Town Races and the Old Opera House. Harper's Ferry National Historic Park and Antietam Battlefield are both nearby. Area activities include bicycling, hiking, horseback riding, whitewater rafting, outlet shopping, and horse and car racing. Charles Town is located on the Eastern Panhandle, 70 miles west of both Washington, D.C., and Baltimore, MD.

Information please: Although high rates make it a special-occasion splurge, many feel that the **Hillbrook Inn** (Route 13, RR 2, Box 152, 25414; 304–725–4223) is worth the considerable expense for exceptional dining and accommodations in a handsome and rambling mansion, half-timbered with many chimneys, gables, and leaded-glass windows. Off-season packages are somewhat more affordable. Weekend MAP rates for the five guest rooms begin at $370 for two people ($240 midweek). Comments?

The Cottonwood Inn ¢   *Tel:* 304–725–3371
Route 2, Box 61-S, 25414   *Fax:* 304–728–4763

The Cottonwood is a Federalist-era (circa 1800) farmhouse, decorated with antiques and period reproductions. Restored as an inn in 1976, this long-time reader favorite was purchased by Joe and Barbara Sobol in 1995, who moved from here from Shreveport, Louisiana. They've enhanced the inn's decor with their collections of clocks and antique and contemporary quilts (Barbara is an avid quilter). Breakfast is served from 8:30 to 10 A.M., and consists of fresh fruit and juice, home-baked lemon muffins or perhaps apple coffee cake, and such entrées as puff pastry filled with ham and cheese, or an egg, cheese, and sausage casserole. Initial guest comments compliment the Sobel's gracious hospitality, but the reports quoted below predate their ownership; new reports are needed.

"This beautifully and tastefully decorated farmhouse is immaculate; each uncluttered guest room has a different color scheme and personality." *(Peg & Ben Bedini)* "The living room is a quiet, warm place to sit and read." *(Elizabeth Ingles)* "Though not far from town, this inn is really out in the country—even the driveway is long and winding. The inn is spotless and quiet, with creaky floors, thin doors, and thick walls. Even though all rooms on our floor were occupied, I heard no noise from other guests. The living room is lined with book shelves; the wide-board pine floors are covered by blue hooked area rugs with a flower design; the woodwork is painted Wedgwood blue. The focal point of the dining room is the original arched brick cooking fireplace. Room #2—the original master bedroom—is by far the largest and nicest guest room, with three windows to the front and side, as well as a white brick fireplace. A sleigh bed sits between the front windows, and a rose velvet love seat faces the fireplace." *(SHW)* "We awakened each morning to the sounds of the birds singing and the creek babbling." *(Carla Baldwin)*

Open All year.
Rooms 6 doubles—all with private bath and/or shower, TV, air-conditioning. 3 with desk, 1 with fireplace.
Facilities Living room, dining room, both with fireplace; library. Porch with swing. 6 acres with stream, picnic area, pavilion. Fishing, swimming, boating on Shenandoah & Potomac rivers nearby.
Location 6 m S of Charles Town. From Charles Town, take Rte. 9 S. Go 2.5 m to Kabletown Rd., turn right. Go 3.2 m to Mill La., turn right. 1/4m to inn.
Restrictions No smoking.
Credit cards Amex, MC, Visa.
Rates B&B, $75–105 double. Extra person, $10. 2-night minimum holiday, craft festival weekends.

Washington House Inn ¢

216 South George Street, 25414

Tel: 304–725–7923
800–297–6957

"George Washington didn't sleep here—but his relatives did," report innkeepers Mel and Nina Vogel. "Descendants of his brothers John Augustine and Samuel built the house in 1899. It is a Queen Anne Victorian home with a three-story turret and a wraparound porch."

"The Victorian architecture, antique furnishings, carved oak mantels, and spacious guest rooms were greatly enhanced by warm hospitality. Nina is an ideal innkeeper: pleasant, relaxed, knowledgeable, and a great cook. Before our arrival she sent us area literature, checked what entertainment was available, and made dinner suggestions and reservations. The house was remarkably clean; even the towels had a lovely scent. Each of the guest rooms is color-coordinated, and lovely quilts decorate the walls. The third floor Dormer room is incredibly spacious, with lots of windows, and a large bathroom. The Garret room, across the hall, was equally large.

"The wonderful breakfasts were different each day. Fresh fruit with tasty vanilla sauce and home-baked blueberry or apple bran muffins were followed by carmelized French toast; stuffed French toast with cream cheese and strawberry jam; or an egg, sausage, mushroom and cheese casserole. A bowl of fresh fruit, homemade cookies, and coffee and tea were always available. We loved the relaxing swing on the veranda." *(Ruth Ann McCay)*

Open All year.
Rooms 6 doubles—all with private bath and/or shower, air-conditioning. Some with fireplace, ceiling fan.

Facilities Parlor with fireplace, dining room with fireplace, 2nd floor lounge with TV, 3rd floor sitting area, wraparound porch with swings. 3 blocks to museum.
Location In town.
Restrictions No smoking.
Credit cards None accepted.
Rates B&B, $70–95 double. 10% discount on 4th night.

DAVIS

Davis is located in the Potomac Highlands, and is a center for skiing in winter, and rafting, fishing, and hiking the rest of the year. About 10 miles south of the Maryland border, Davis is located 167 miles west of Washington, D.C., 210 miles northwest of Richmond, and 123 miles south of Pittsburgh.

Also recommended: A bit large for a full entry with 250 guest rooms and 23 cabins is the **Canaan Valley Resort & Conference Center** (Rt. 1, Box 330, 26260; 304–866–4121 or 800–622–4121), located in Canaan Valley State Park. A golf course, tennis courts, indoor/outdoor pools, downhill skiing, cross-country skiing, ice skating, and fitness center give it year-round appeal. "A modern hotel with clean, comfortable rooms, and a relaxed atmosphere—a great place to bring the kids. Wonderful hillside views from the dining room. Food was exceptional and reasonably priced, with lots of homemade items. Make reservations early for the better rooms." *(Jill Reeves)* Double rates range from $55–79.

Information please: A boarding house built in 1896, **Bright Morning B&B** (William Avenue, P.O. Box 576, 26260; 304–259–5119) was restored as a B&B in 1988. The 18 guest rooms (all with private bath) are furnished with double beds, quilts, country antiques, and colorful rugs. Breakfast includes a choice of eggs, hot cakes, French toast, sausage gravy with biscuits, plus bacon, ham, or sausage. A full range of hot and cold sandwiches are served for lunch, while dinner (by reservation) offers a salad bar, soups, steaks and seafood, pasta, and desserts. Double rates are $55–65.

Blackwater Falls Lodge ¢ 🛏 ✕ 🏹   *Tel:* 304–259–5216
P.O. Box 490, 26260   800–CALL–WVA

Blackwater Lodge sits on the south rim of the Blackwater Falls gorge. The falls are over 60 feet high, while the gorge drops down over 500 feet. The lodge offers sweeping views of the densely forested gorge.

"Comfortable, clean accommodations. Charming, rustic, family-oriented atmosphere. Ample portions of country-style food in the restaurant; we also enjoyed eating in town. The morning buffet was plentiful and satisfying; the cinnamon rolls were a treat. At dinner, stick with traditional favorites like the ham dinner with beans. Many great activities: mountain biking on the many trails, hiking, and taking the kids to the nature center. Deer roam freely on the lawn. Attractive landscaping; the views of the river and tree-covered hillsides create a sense of peace and relaxation." *(Jill Reeves)*

Suggestion box: "Find an alternative to the strong-smelling disinfectant now used."

Open All year.

Rooms 55 doubles—all with full private bath, telephone, TV, air-conditioning. 25 cabins with fireplace, heating, private shower bath, kitchenette. Some with radio.

Facilities Restaurant, gift shop, game room, lobby with fireplace. Nature program, hiking, biking, swimming, boating, tennis courts, volleyball court, 25 km. cross-country ski trails, ice skating, toboggan run, horseback riding. Golf, downhill skiing nearby.

Location Take US 33 N to Harmon, then WV Rte. 32 N. Southbound, take US Rte. 219 to Thomas, then Rte. 32 S.

Credit cards Amex, MC, Visa.

Rates Room only, $75–90 cabin (for 2); 1-week minimum early June through Labor Day, $418 (for 2); extra person, $4–5. Room only, $65–80 suite, $50–65 double, $40–57 single. Extra person, $6; children under 12 free. 10% senior discount in cabins. Skiing, rafting packages.

Extras Crib.

DURBIN

Information please: Thirty miles southeast of Elkins is the historic **Cheat Mountain Club** (Box 28, Durbin, 26264; 304–456–4627), built in 1887 as an exclusive retreat for industrialists such as Henry Ford and Harvey Firestone. Located on the banks of the Shavers Fork River, at an elevation of 4,000 feet and surrounded by the 900,000-acre Monongahela National Forest, the hand-hewn spruce log interior creates a rustic, restful atmosphere. Seven doubles, two singles, and a third-floor bunk room share separate men's and women's baths. Dining specialties include hearty soups and stews, home-baked breads and muffins, and bonfire picnics with all the trimmings. In addition to three meals a day, the $160–200 double rate (children half-price in parents' room) includes fly fishing, swimming, canoeing, kayaking, rafting, biking, lawn games, volleyball, soccer, and cross-country skiing. Guide services are available for catch-and-release fishing and deer, bear, grouse, snowshoe hare, and turkey hunting in season.

ELKINS

The town of Elkins is surrounded by opportunities to delve deeper into West Virginian highlands and wilderness: the Monongahela National Forest, Bickle Knob, Cheat River, and Otter Creek Wilderness areas are close at hand; not much farther away are Canaan Valley and Blackwater Falls state parks, Spruce Knob, Seneca Rocks, and Dolly Sods Wilderness areas. If that isn't enough to consider for hiking, sightseeing or skiing, Elkins is also home to Davis & Elkins College and the annual Augusta Heritage Arts & Crafts Workshops.

For additional area options, see **Cass, Davis, Durbin, Huttonsville,** and **Valley Head.**

Tunnel Mountain B&B ¢
Route 1, Box 59-1, 26241

Tel: 304–636–1684

Tunnel Mountain B&B, purchased in 1990 by Anne and Paul Beardslee, is a contemporary, Colonial-style home, built of fieldstone and clapboard, and paneled inside with pine and wormy chestnut. The house is decorated with family antiques, handmade comforters, crafts and collectibles. Breakfast includes fresh fruit and juice, and such entrées as pecan cinnamon waffles, tropical French toast, or blueberry pancakes; during the five-week summer Augusta Heritage Festival, a continental breakfast is offered.

"Anne and Paul are gracious, outgoing, sincere people, sensitive to their guests' needs." *(Ann & Phil Case)* "Our favorite room is the wormy chestnut attic room on the third floor with a spectacular view of the sunrise." *(Sterling & Brenda Mays)* "The inn's hiking trail leads through the woods to a meadow, offering spectacular valley and mountain views." *(Dean Graham)* "We watched ten deer come out of the woods to feed on corn that Paul set out for them. The largest guest room has a gorgeous antique canopy bed, and another has a Civil War-era rope bed. Anne's breakfasts are a real treat and Paul grinds the coffee; Anne happily accommodated a diabetic's diet. They advised us about local attractions and restaurants, and invited us into their kitchen for an evening cup of coffee while Anne worked on one of her many craft projects." *(Jim Bolinger)* "Spacious, well-maintained rooms." *(Nancy Drinkwine)*

Open All year.
Rooms 3 doubles—all with private bath and/or shower, TV, air-conditioning.
Facilities Dining room, living room with fireplace, porch. 5 acres with patio, walking/skiing trails. Swimming, tennis, golf nearby. 1½ m to Monongahela Nat. Forest, Cheat River for water sports. 30 m to downhill, cross-country skiing.
Location NE WV, Potomac Highlands. 4 hrs. W of Washington, D.C. 4 m E of Elkins on Rte. 33.
Restrictions No smoking in common areas.
Credit cards None accepted.
Rates $65 double, $55 single. Extra person, $15. Holiday/weekend minimum. AARP discount.
Extras Station pickup.

GERRARDSTOWN

Gerrardstown's Prospect Hill ¢
Route 51, P.O. Box 135, 25420

Tel: 304–229–3346

This red brick Georgian mansion—with four towering chimneys—rests at the foot of North Mountain and is surrounded by fields and orchards, with a pond and a waterfall. Once the home of William Wilson—a member of Thomas Jefferson's cabinet—the house now belongs to Hazel and Charles Hudock, who have been welcoming B&B guests since 1978.

"I felt at ease from the moment I entered. Hazel had made a fresh apple pie and had a big slice waiting for me. In my cottage, even the fire was laid and ready to light. Hazel directed me to wonderful trails for hiking and mountain biking." *(John Galvin)* "After an inexpensive but delicious dinner in town, we settled by the fireplace with hot apple cider to play gin rummy." *(STR)* "Hazel's country breakfasts are highlighted by her apple pancakes with sour cream and syrup." *(Tim Learman)* "The main house is filled with art, books, and antiques of an astonishing variety— from marvelous furniture to museum-quality photographs and a mural depicting early American life. Our room was beautifully decorated with a charming quilt, scatter rugs, and a small couch before the fireplace. We breakfasted on omelets, fruit salad, biscuits, jam, baked apples, and wonderful coffee." *(Teresa Garcia & Bill Ahearn)*

"Breakfast is served from 8 to 9 A.M. in the dining room, which has a fine crystal chandelier, and a built-in floor-to-ceiling corner cupboard. The spacious Gold Room has a four poster queen-size rice bed, overstuffed couch, and high-quality antique furnishings; its huge bathroom has two marble sinks and a large square tiled tub and shower combination. One of the Flemish bond brick slave quarters has been remodeled as a guest cottage with more modest furnishings, and would be a good choice for a family." *(SHW)*

Open All year.
Rooms 1 cottage, 2 doubles—all with private bath and/or shower, radio, TV, air-conditioning, fan, fireplace. Cottage with kitchen.
Facilities Dining room with fireplace, living room with fireplace, TV. 225 acres with pond for fishing, walking trails, farmland. Hiking, bicycling, climbing, tennis, golf nearby.
Location E Panhandle. 10 m S of Martinsburg. From I-81 take Rte. 51 W 3 1/2 m W to Gerrardstown. Inn on left.
Restrictions No smoking in guest rooms. Children in cottage only.
Credit cards MC, Visa.
Rates B&B, $85–95 suite, double. Extra person, $20.
Extras Crib.

HUTTONSVILLE

Hutton House B&B ¢ 🏃   *Tel: 304–335–6701*
Routes 250 & 219, P.O. Box 88, 26273

At Hutton House, (unlike many B&Bs) schedules are created by individual guests—not the innkeepers. Loretta Murray and Dean Ahren, who restored this 1898 Queen Anne Victorian home in 1988, report that "there is no set time or plan for anything here. Guests are offered food and drink at any time of the day or evening. Guests are invited into the kitchen to get their morning coffee. They meet one another and sit down as friends rather than as strangers. Sometimes group events spontaneously occur, from pumpkin carving to guest-prepared gourmet dinners. The inn features elaborate windows—each with 29 panes of glass, original oak woodwork, arched pocket doors, and period furnishings. Creative breakfasts are served at the dining room table. A recent menu included pineapple sorbet, apricot-stuffed French toast, and turkey ham stir-fried with green peppers and snow peas.

"Graciously restored, clean and well-appointed. Upper story windows offer panoramic views of the Tygart Valley and gently rolling hills. In summer, we relaxed on the porch with a glass of wine; in winter, we took hot spiced cider and freshly baked cookies to our room. Breakfast is served when you want it—from early morning if you have a ski trip—to much later if you want to sleep in." *(JA)* "Beautifully refinished winding oak staircase, with lovely lace curtains and antiques. They've even 'gold-leafed' the top of the three-story turret. Guest rooms have antique furnishings and comfortable beds with comforters. Coffee is ready each morning for early birds, and breakfast is served on beautiful pink Depression glass dishes. We had baked pears, stuffed French toast with maple syrup from their own trees, and potatoes with basil. Loretta and Dean are there to help you have a wonderful time. If that means leaving you alone to enjoy the solitude, they respect that. If you want to sit around the table and swap recipes, that's fine too." *(Madison & Pamela Gartman)*

Open All year.
Rooms 6 doubles—all with private shower and/or bath. 2 with desk, 1 with double whirlpool tub, 1 with air-conditioning.
Facilities Living room, dining room, family room with TV, guest refrigerator, porch. 2 acres with lawn games, gardens, hiking. 45 min. to skiing, state forests.
Location NE WV, Laurel Mts. 150 m NE of Charleston, 160 m S of Pittsburgh, PA. 17 m S of Elkins.
Restrictions No smoking. "Could have traffic noise in front rooms but have had no complaints."
Credit cards MC, Visa.
Rates B&B, $60–75 double, $45–60 single. Extra person, $12. 2-night minimum holiday, festival weekends.

LEWISBURG

The General Lewis Inn ¢ ✕ ♿ ♦   *Tel:* 304–645–2600
301 East Washington Street, 24901   800–628–4454
                                   Fax: 304–645–2600

Listed on the National Register of Historic Places, Lewisburg is associated with both the Revolutionary and Civil wars. The inn is composed of a home built in 1834 housing the inn's restaurant and lobby, and the main section of the inn, which dates to 1929.

"The exterior of the inn is a long, lovely white-pillared affair." *(MFD)* "Antiques lovers will enjoy both the inn and the charming town of Lewisburg." *(Betty Norman)* "An attractive rural hotel with an eclectic collection of Civil War memorabilia. Rooms are small and plain but adequate; for warmth and charm you can relax in a corner of the living room with its roaring fire, comfortable chairs, and good reading lamps. Drinks are served there, and we found the staff to be exceptionally friendly and attentive. The adjoining dining room is pretty and the service good." *(Judith Brannen & Larry Machum)* "Accessible to area resorts, but much more reasonably priced. The town is just down the hill and fun to explore." *(Janet Levy)* "Excellent location, near Greenbriar, with great antique collection." *(Don Burd)*

Open All year.
Rooms 2 suites, 23 doubles—all with full private bath, telephone, radio, TV, air-conditioning. Some with desk.
Facilities Restaurant, parlor with puzzles, games, books; porch with rocking chairs. Pioneer items & stagecoach on display. 1 acre with gardens. Fishing, swimming, white-water rafting, hiking, golf, tennis nearby.
Location SE WV. 103 m E of Charleston, WV, 72 m W of Lexington, VA. Historic district. 2 blocks to center. From I-64 Lewisburg Exit, go S on Rte. 219 to 1st traffic light (Washington St.), then left 2 blocks.
Restrictions No smoking. Minimal interior soundproofing.
Credit cards Amex, MC, Visa.
Rates Room only, $88–106 suite, $60–88 double. Extra person, $10. Alc breakfast, $4–7; alc lunch, $8; alc dinner, $22. No charge for child under 3.
Extras Wheelchair access; 1 room specially equipped. Airport/station pickup. Crib, pets, $10.

MARTINSBURG

Martinsburg prospered with the coming of the railroad in the 1850s; fruit orchards and woolen mills became its principal businesses. Although the apples are still growing strong, the textile business has faded. More recently, several old woolen mills have been refitted as outlet centers, especially popular with shoppers at Christmas. Outdoor activities include hiking, golf, tennis, canoeing and white water rafting, and exploring the area's historic sites.

Martinsburg is located in the eastern West Virginia panhandle, 75 miles northwest of Washington D.C., and 75 miles west of Baltimore.

Aspen Hall
405 Boyd Avenue, 25401

Tel: 304–263–4385

If you're among the many who feel that "they don't build 'em the way they used to," your suspicions will be confirmed on arrival at Aspen Hall, a 200-year-old Georgian-style home with limestone walls two feet thick. Listed on the National Register of Historic Places, it was authentically restored in 1989 by LouAnne and Gordon Claucherty. Now shaded by giant locust trees, the original 20-by-20-foot building was constructed by Quakers in the 1740s, and was protected by George Washington's troops during the French and Indian War. The larger Georgian section was added in 1788, and the building was further expanded in 1900. Guest rooms are decorated with queen-size lace canopy beds, rosewood and mahogany antiques. Collections and prints in each room add interest—perhaps century-old hats and gloves, or photograph albums with pictures of Civil War soldiers. A typical breakfast might include banana slush, sour cream coffee cake, garden quiche, sausage and fried apples; or fresh fruit, English muffin bread with homemade preserves, herb flower omelet, and potato pancakes. Tea is served each afternoon from 3 to 5 P.M.

"Breakfast was plentiful and delicious. Friendly, helpful, unobtrusive hosts." *(Susan de Jong)* "LouAnne and Gordon obviously love what they do; many delightful small touches." *(Rebecca Polis)* "Convenient to good restaurants, rich history, the Potomac River, and shopping outlets. Gordon, a skillful, self-taught renovator, has restored the house to its former state; LouAnne is an artist, and has decorated and painted the house befitting its character." *(Janice Muse)* "Our hosts made dinner recommendations and reservations and told us about the area." *(Beverly & Alan Feldman)* "Delicious hot cranberry bake. The grounds are delightful to explore, with a stream and the remains of the old mill." *(DN)* "The enormous Stewart Room has pine floors with Oriental rugs, three floor-to-ceiling windows, and an arched canopy rice bed. The inn has a lovely setting at the far end of a street that can most charitably be called transitional; persevere to the end; you won't be sorry." *(SHW)*

Open Feb. 10 - Dec. 24.
Rooms 5 doubles—all with private bath and/or shower, radio, desk, air-conditioning. 1 with woodburning fireplace.
Facilities Dining room with fireplace, 2 parlors with piano, stereo, TV, library. Porch with hammock; terrace. 4 acres with gardens, gazebo, swing, horseshoes, trout fishing stream.
Location 5 blocks from center. From I-81, take King St. exit. Go N (left) on Raleigh, E (right) on Race St., N (left) on Boyd Ave. to inn at end of street.
Restrictions No smoking. No children under 12. Some train noise.
Credit cards MC, Visa.
Rates B&B, $95–110 double. Extra person, $40. 10% AARP discount.
Extras Station pickup.

MORGANTOWN

Morgantown is in northern West Virginia, 70 miles south of Pittsburgh, and is the home of the University of West Virginia.

Information please: Built in 1927 as a school, Chestnut Ridge Commons (1000 Stewartstown Road, 26505; 304–598–9595 or 800–CALL–WVA) is located in a quiet residential area. Breakfast includes homemade muffins and a breakfast casserole; late-night snacks are provided. "Beautifully decorated guest rooms; excellent lighting; my favorites were numbers two and four; ample common areas for guests to gather and relax; there's even an exercise room." *(John & Lillie Galvin)* B&B double rates for the five guest rooms range from $60–100, including private bath, telephone, and TV. Comments appreciated.

PETERSBURG

Located in the Potomac Highlands, area activities include swimming, canoeing, fishing, and rafting in the South Branch of the Potomac River, as well as hiking and rock climbing at Seneca Rocks National Recreation Area, and other state parks.

Information please: About 15 miles north is the **McMechen House Inn** (109 North Main Street, Moorefield 26836; 800–298–2466). Dating back to 1855, this Federal/Greek Revival home served alternately as

Union and Confederate headquarters during the Civil War. Decorated with period antiques, the inn has seven guest rooms; B&B double rates range from $60–85, including a full, homemade breakfast.

Smoke Hole Lodge ¢ 👫
P.O. Box 953, 26847

For a truly remote escape, consider the isolated Smoke Hole Lodge. Owner Edward Stifel III picks up his guests and drives them to the lodge he built in 1981 and rebuilt after the floods of 1985. There is neither electricity nor telephones, and the lodge runs on kerosene, wood, and bottled gas. "We usually don't have more than eight guests on the place," explains Ed. "That's all we can comfortably handle and still provide a good measure of personalized attention. Well-behaved kids? We love 'em. We have a cat, cows, chickens, and geese. Deer abound, and occasionally a bear wanders through the area. What to bring? Let the romantic in you bring an enthusiasm for life, an ear for the song of nature, a heart to soar with the hawk and a sense of inquiry toward your fellow beings. We have no tennis courts or golf courses; we do, however, offer good food and lodging in an intimate mountain wilderness environment including our three-mile frontage on the South Branch of the Potomac River. People who want nature and serenity love our place. Excellent photographic opportunities."

"During the hour-long trip to the lodge, Ed's four-wheel-drive vehicle bumps and bounces up steep mountain roads, through streams and beneath a dense forest canopy. With luck you will spot deer, perhaps a bear, and pass Ed's prize-winning Angus cattle. The inn is nestled in a deep valley, and views from the rooms, deck and porch are spectacular. Inside, the polished wood floors are spotless. The rooms, while simply furnished, are more than adequate; water comes from a clear mountain stream and bottled gas provides an ample supply of hot water. Food is simple, pleasant, and filling. In the morning guests perform chores such as collecting eggs and hand-feeding trout in the stream's quiet pools. On hot days you can tube the rapids or sit in the shallows. After dinner Ed lights kerosene lamps throughout the inn (bring your own flashlight) while guests gather on the rocking chairs to talk and count shooting stars." *(Joe & Sheila Schmidt)* "Hiking in complete solitude for miles and miles; hearty home cooking served at meals presided over by the innkeeper—an eminent conversationalist." *(Michelle Magee)*

Open Early May–Oct.
Rooms 2 dorms, 5 doubles—all with private shower bath, desk.
Facilities Dining room, living room with fireplace; library, kitchen, guest laundry; porch. 1,500 acres with wildlife, river for swimming, fishing (with license), tubing; hiking.
Location 12 m S of Petersburg. "Indescribable" directions. Transportation provided to/from lodge. 5 m on dirt access rd.; 4-wheel drive only.
Restrictions No smoking in kitchen.
Credit cards None accepted.
Rates Full board, $175 double, $95 single. Extra person, $80. Children under 4, free. 2-night minimum. Group discounts.
Extras Airport/train station pickups. Some pets allowed.

ROMNEY

Hampshire House 1884 ¢   *Tel: 304–822–7171*
165 North Grafton, 26757

The Hampshire House 1884, a restored 19th century brick Federal-style home, is owned by Jane and Scott Simmons. The renovation process included the installation of central heat, air-conditioning, sound-proofing materials, and modern bathrooms, balanced with decor and furnishings from the Rococo, Renaissance, and Eastlake styles, all popular in 1884. Dinners are available by advance reservation; a sample menu might include cream of leek soup, chicken with couscous, salad, steamed vegetables, and apple pie.

"Comfortable, clean, attractive old house in tip-top condition. Jane is sensitive to travelers' needs and is a delight to visit with; we sat on the front porch sipping cider and listening to the mockingbirds' serenade." *(Steve Schneider)* "Upon arrival we were offered a choice of wine, cider, coffee, or freshly squeezed grape juice. The upstairs common room had games, magazines, and an extensive library. Breakfast offerings included omelets, pecan and blueberry pancakes or waffles, plus bacon or sausage, and plenty of hot, fresh coffee. The location is perfect for a walking exploration of town." *(Ray & Corrine Erickson)* "Easy access to some of West Virginia's finest scenery, including Romney itself, West Virginia's oldest town." *(Waldemar & Beth Scherer)* "Pleasant music during breakfast—I enjoyed dining at a private table." *(John Lane)*

Open All year.
Rooms 5 doubles—all with full private bath, telephone, radio, TV, air-conditioning. 3 with desk, fireplace.
Facilities Dining room, tea room, living room, family room with fireplace, books, pump organ, TV/VCR, games; massage therapist. Guitar, banjo music occasionally. Covered veranda, patio, off-street parking. Tennis, golf, canoeing, horseback riding nearby.
Location NE WV, Eastern Panhandle. 2½ hrs. W of Washington, DC, 1 hr. W of Winchester, VA. 1½ blocks N on Grafton St. off Rte. 50.
Restrictions No smoking.
Credit cards Amex, DC, Discovery, MC, Visa.
Rates B&B, $80 double, $50 single. Extra person, $15. MAP, $95 double, $70 single. Extra person, $15. 10% discount for stays over 3 nights. 15% service on meals. Prix fixe lunch, $9; dinner, $23.
Extras Airport/station pickup, fee charged by distance.

SHEPHERDSTOWN

Shepherdstown, West Virginia's oldest community, was founded in 1730. Area attractions include the Old Opera House in Charles Town, Harper's Ferry, Antietam Battlefield, and the races at Charles Town and Summit Point; golf, tennis, horseback riding, white-water rafting and canoeing, and jogging and walking on the old C&O Towpath across the Potomac River.

Shepherdstown is in the upper Shenandoah Valley of the Eastern Panhandle, at the Maryland border. It's 8 miles from Harper's Ferry and 4 from Antietam Battlefield. Washington, D.C., and Baltimore, MD, are an hour and a half away by car. From Washington, take I-270 to Frederick bypass, then onto I-70 to Exit 49. Turn left at Route 34 in Boonsboro to Shepherdstown.

Information please: Although too small for a full entry, a charming choice is **Stonebrake Cottage** (Box 1612, Shepherd Grade Road, 25443; 304–876–6607), a Victorian English-style three-bedroom, three-bath cottage furnished with country antiques, peacefully located on a 145-acre farm. Owners Anne and Dennis Small notes that "when the cottage is rented, the entire cottage belongs to that group, whether there are two or six in the party." Breakfast supplies include homemade blueberry muffins, fresh fruit, juice, milk, English muffins, eggs, jelly, coffee, and cereals; mints and a carafe of wine is also provided. Double rates are $80–90, with $25 for each additional person. "The Smalls live nearby at Stonebrake Farm. Anne's warm welcome, thoughtful concern for her guests, and knowledge of the area make her a delightful host." *(Eileen Yago)*

For an additional area entry, see **Sharpsburg, Maryland**.

Bavarian Inn and Lodge 🏃 ✕ 🎿   *Tel:* 304–876–2551
Route 1, Box 30, 25443

The Bavarian Inn includes a handsome stone Colonial building, constructed as a private residence in 1930 and converted to an inn in 1962; in 1981 four adjacent chalet-style structures were added. The guest rooms are luxuriously decorated with oak furniture and canopied beds; all have tiled fireplaces and balconies overlooking the Potomac. The Bavarian theme in food and accommodation was introduced by innkeeper/owner Erwin Asam, originally from Munich.

"An elegant treat with a casual and friendly atmosphere. Decorated with antique furnishings, our room had dormer windows, an alcove and a private balcony with a spectacular view of the Potomac. Meals are reasonable and rewarding." *(Michaelene McWhinney)*

"Noted especially for the original German dishes served in the elegant restaurant, the menu also provides wild game entrées and an extensive wine list." *(Natalie & Jonathan Birbeck)* "The furnishings are a mix of German oak and early American oak reproductions." *(Sally Sieracki)* "Good dinner, especially the crab cakes." *(Karen Hughes)* "We enjoyed our clean, well-maintained chalet suite, just as pictured on the brochure. Shepherdstown is a delightful town to explore." *(Joseph Savino)*

Open All year.
Rooms 35 suites, 37 doubles—all with private bath, telephone, TV, radio, desk, air-conditioning, balcony. Most with queen-size canopy bed, gas fireplace. Suites with whirlpool tub. Guest rooms in 4 separate chalets.
Facilities Restaurant, bar, conference room, gift shop. Live music in bar/lounge Fri. and Sat. nights. 11 acres with exercise room, gazebo, heated swimming pool, tennis court. Golf nearby. Jogging on C&O towpath across river, whitewater rafting/canoeing.

Location In town.
Restrictions Smoking restricted in some areas.
Credit cards Amex, CB, DC, MC, Visa. Checks preferred for deposit.
Rates Room only, $105–145 suite, $75–125 double. Extra person, $10. 2-night holiday weekend minimum. Alc breakfast, $4–8; alc lunch, $6–10; alc dinner, $12–25.
Extras Wheelchair access. Crib, babysitting. German, French, Spanish spoken.

The Thomas Shepherd Inn

Tel: 304–876–3715

300 West German Street, P.O. Box 1162, 25443

The Thomas Shepherd Inn was built as a parsonage in 1868, and was restored in 1984 as a B&B. A long-time reader favorite, it was purchased in 1989 by Margaret Perry. This white brick Victorian home, with wide plank floors and a real double parlor, is elegantly furnished with period antiques, old prints, and Oriental rugs. Margaret prepares an imaginative array of breakfast dishes: perhaps warm apple soup with creme fraîche, blueberry sour cream pancakes, eggs Benedict, or ricotta pancakes with sage sausage.

"The inn is wonderfully decorated with post-Civil War antiques; I especially enjoyed the atmosphere of the living room and the sherry, lemonade, and snacks served there by Margaret." *(Pat Cunningham)* "We stayed in a lovely, comfortable room with a double spool bed. The polished pine floor was covered with area rugs; in front of the small fireplace were two armchairs and a coffee table." *(Heather & Charles Rories)* "The decor is not fussy or cluttered; there are plenty of antiques but you don't have to worry about tripping over them. Our favorite room was #6, at the back of the house for quiet, with a canopied bed." *(Nancy Debevoise)* "Margaret thoughtfully took care of our Saturday night dinner reservations for us in advance." *(KLH)* "Though located at the intersection of two busy streets, we've never been bothered by traffic noise. At the back of the house is a small, well-shaded second floor porch with rocking chairs, overlooking the garden. Breakfast is served at 9 A.M.; guests gather beforehand in the living room to chat over coffee and tea." *(Jeremiah & Dorothy Reilly)* "Our large, quiet room had a four-poster bed, comfortable chairs with reading lamps, and a pretty bathroom. Outstanding breakfast of orange juice, baked spiced pears, cheese-stuffed French toast, bacon, pumpkin muffins, and coffee—delicious and filling." *(Judith Brannen & Larry Machum)* "Shepherdstown is a good base from which to explore the area and offers two fine dining restaurants, unusual in such a small town." *(Sally Sieracki)*

Open All year.
Rooms 7 doubles—all with private bath and/or shower, central air-conditioning.
Facilities 2 dining rooms; living room with fireplace; library with TV; porch. Golf, fishing, white-water rafting, canoeing, hiking, bicycling nearby. 1 m to cross-country skiing.
Location Historic district. Walking distance to shops, restaurants.
Restrictions No smoking. Well-behaved children over 12.
Credit cards Amex, Discover, MC, Visa; plus 5% service charge.
Rates B&B, $85–115 double. Extra person, $20. 5% senior, AARP discount. Corporate rates midweek. $10 surcharge for 1-night weekend stay; 2-night week-

end/holiday minimum if Sat. included. With 24-hr notice: picnic lunch, $12; dinner, $20–30.

VALLEY HEAD

Nakiska Chalet B&B   *Tel:* 304–339–6309
HC 73, Box 24, 26294   800–225–5982

When Doug and Joyce Cooper retired to Valley Head in 1993, they brought an appreciation for Native American spirituality, nurtured during earlier years in western Canada. It was a natural for them to name their B&B "Nakiska" Chalet (meaning "where friends meet"). This A-frame chalet, built in 1982, has a three-story wall of windows facing the peaceful rolling hills, where turkey and deer roam. "In mild weather," Joyce reports, "guests can stay in the huge teepee, supported by western lodgepole pine." The comfortable decor is accented by the twig furniture Doug makes; the floral sofas in front of the massive stone fireplace create an inviting gathering spot. A typical breakfast, served from 7:30 to 9 A.M., might include a brandied orange cup, baked eggs with basil, sausage, and cinnamon rolls.

"We sat at the large breakfast table, looking out to the mountains, enjoying Joyce's creative breakfasts of puffed pancakes." *(Joan Carroll)* "Cozy, secluded atmosphere." *(Mistie Tolley)* "The Coopers' warmth and friendliness makes you feel as if you've been friends for years. Creativity in room design and incredible food add to this B&Bs charm." *(Corianne Carroll)* "We loved the warmth of the open fireplace in the great room." *(Genia Adams)*

Open All year.
Rooms 3 doubles—1 with private bath, 2 with a maximum of 4 persons sharing bath. All with clock. 1 with radio.
Facilities Breakfast room, great room with fireplace, stereo, books, games; deck. Twig furniture workshops. 11 acres with hot tub, cross-country skiing, hiking. 10 m to downhill skiing.
Location E WVA. Randolph County. 35 m S of Elkins. From Elkins, take Rte. 219 S to Valley Head/Rte. 15 junction. Continue 5 m on Rte. 219 to Mingo Flats Rd. Turn right & go 1.7 m to Dry Branch Rd. Turn right & go ½ to inn on right.
Restrictions No smoking.
Credit cards None accepted.
Rates B&B, $66–77 double (including tax). Extra person, $11. 2-night holiday minimum.

WHEELING

Information please: An 1892 townhouse on Wheeling's "Millionaire's Row," **The Eckhart House** (810 Main Street, Wheeling 26003; 304–232–5439) offers two charming guest rooms, with private bath, air-conditioning, and double or twin beds. The 18-room building also houses an interior design studio and gift shop. Double rates of $75 include a continental breakfast. Three additional rooms are available across the street at the Christian Hess House; both are part of the Victorian Wheeling Landmarks Foundation tour of homes. Within walking distance is the historic Center Market, Independence Hall, Wheeling Downs, and West Virginia's answer to the Grand Old Opry, the WWVA Jamboree. Comments?

WHITE SULPHUR SPRINGS

The James Wylie House B&B ¢ **ⅈ**   *Tel:* 304–536–9444
208 East Main Street, 24986   800–870–1613

White Sulphur Springs has been a popular resort since the late 1700s, and is best known for the luxurious (five-star, five-diamond) 700-room Greenbrier resort. If you'd like to experience all the area has to offer (but haven't yet hit the lotto), consider a stay at The James Wylie House, a three-story red brick Georgian Colonial-style dwelling dating back to 1819, and listed on the National Register of Historic Places. When Cheryl and Joe Griffith bought this abandoned house in 1988, the decor consisted of birds' nests and graffiti, the walls and paneling covered with endless coats of paint. The 200-year-old log cabin behind the main house (complete with musket holes in the walls) had lost all the chinking between its foot-wide handhewn timbers, and its handsome river rock fireplace was close to collapse. After endless renovation work, guests are welcomed to bright and spacious rooms, with gleaming wide-plank pine floors, original brass chandeliers, and an appealing, uncluttered decor of simple country antiques. Breakfast is served between 8 and 9 A.M. in the dining room; complimentary beverages are available all day.

"Cheryl graciously greeted us at the door and offered drinks and help with our luggage; we sipped freshly-made lemonade, garnished with mint. Our second floor room had a double bed (firm mattress), a rocking chair, bureau, window air-conditioner, and several antiques, including a hobby horse and a school desk. Breakfast featured a fresh fruit cup, delicious French toast, bacon, fresh orange juice, and coffee. Cheryl joined us for conversation that ranged from the history of the house to contemporary issues." *(Mark & Brenda Dalessandro)* "The log cabin was perfect for our family; my daughter felt like she was living in an episode from *Little House on the Prairie.*" *(MW)*

Open All year.
Rooms 1 cabin, 3 doubles—all with private bath and/or shower, radio, clock, TV, air-conditioning, fan. 3 with telephone. 2 with desk. Cabin with fireplace, kitchenette.
Facilities Dining room, living room with piano; family room with TV/VCR; porch. Guest refrigerator. 1.5 acres with off-street parking, swing set, lawn games. Tennis courts, boating, fishing, rafting, skiing, hiking nearby.
Location S WV. 100 m SE of Charleston. 200 m SW of DC. From I-64 W, take Exit 181. Go W on Rte. 60 for 9/10 m. Inn on right of Castle Drive. From I-64 E, take Exit 175. Go E on Rte. 60 for 4 m. Inn on left of Castle Drive.

Restrictions No smoking. "Families with children under age 6 welcome in cabin."
Credit cards Amex, MC, Visa.
Rates B&B, $100–120 cabin; $70 double, $65 single. Extra person, $10. Tipping encouraged. Breakfast for cabin guests, $5 extra, with advance notice.
Extras Airport/station pick-up, $10–20. Babysitting.

Key to Abbreviations and Symbols

For complete information and explanations, please see the Introduction.

¢ Especially good value for overnight accommodation.

♦ Families welcome. Most (but not all) have cribs, baby-sitting, games, play equipment, and reduced rates for children.

✕ Meals served to public; reservations recommended or required.

♦ Tennis court and swimming pool and/or lake on grounds. Golf usually on grounds or nearby.

♿ Limited or full wheelchair access; call for details.

Rates: Range from least expensive room in low season to most expensive room in peak season.

Room only: No meals included; European Plan (EP).

B&B: Bed and breakfast; includes breakfast, sometimes afternoon/evening refreshment.

MAP: Modified American Plan; includes breakfast and dinner.

Full board: Three meals daily.

Alc lunch: À la carte lunch; average price of entrée plus nonalcoholic drink, tax, tip.

Alc dinner: Average price of three-course dinner, including half bottle of house wine, tax, tip.

Prix fixe dinner: Three- to five-course set dinner, excluding wine, tax, tip unless otherwise noted.

Extras: Noted if available. Always confirm in advance. Pets are not permitted unless specified; if you are allergic, ask for details; *most innkeepers have pets.*

Appendix

STATE AND PROVINCIAL TOURIST OFFICES

Listed here are the addresses and telephone numbers for the tourist offices of the Middle Atlantic states covered in this book. When you write or call one of these offices, be sure to request a map of the state and a calendar of events. If you will be visiting a particular city or region, or if you have any special interests, be sure to specify this as well.

Delaware Tourism Office
99 Kings Highway
P.O. Box 1401
Dover, Delaware 19903
302–739–4271 or 800–441–8846

Washington, D.C., Convention and
    Visitors' Assoc.
Suite 600 1212, New York Avenue,
    N.W.
Washington, D.C. 20005
202–789–7000

Maryland Office of Tourist
    Development
217 E. Redwood Street
Baltimore, Maryland 21202
410–333–6611 or 800–543–1036

New Jersey Division of Travel and
    Tourism
C.N. 826, 20 West Beach Street
Trenton, New Jersey 08625
609–292–2470 or 800–JERSEY–7

New York State Division of Tourism
1 Commerce Plaza
Albany, New York 12245
518–474–4116 or 800–225–5697

Pennsylvania Office of Travel
    Marketing
Department of Commerce
453 Forum Building
Harrisburg, Pennsylvania 17120
717–787–5453 or 800–847–4872 or
    717–232–8880 (B&B information
    only)

Virginia Division of Tourism
1021 East Cary Street
14th Floor
Richmond, Virginia 23219
804–786–4484 or 800–VISIT–VA or
    800–262–1293 (B&B information
    only)

West Virginia Department of
    Commerce
Travel & Tourism Division
1900 Canal Boulevard East
Building 6, Room B-564
Charleston, West Virginia 25305
304–558–2286 or 800–CALL WVA

MAPS

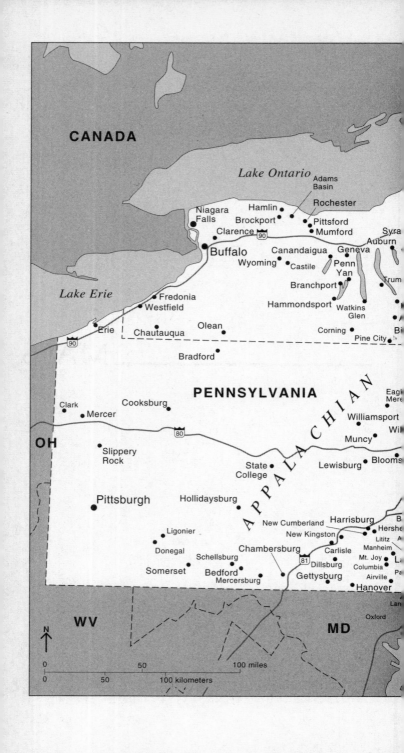

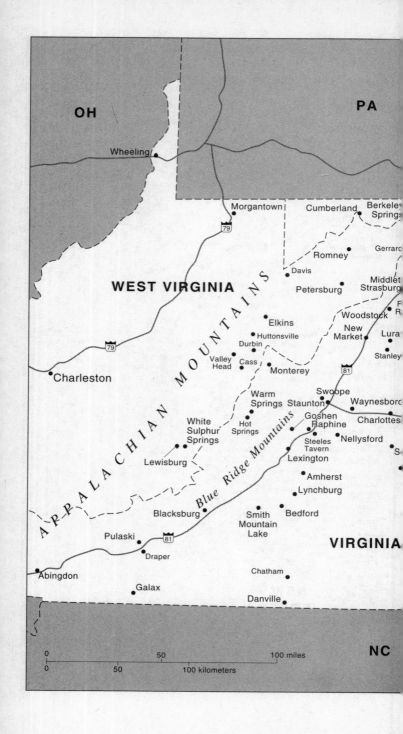

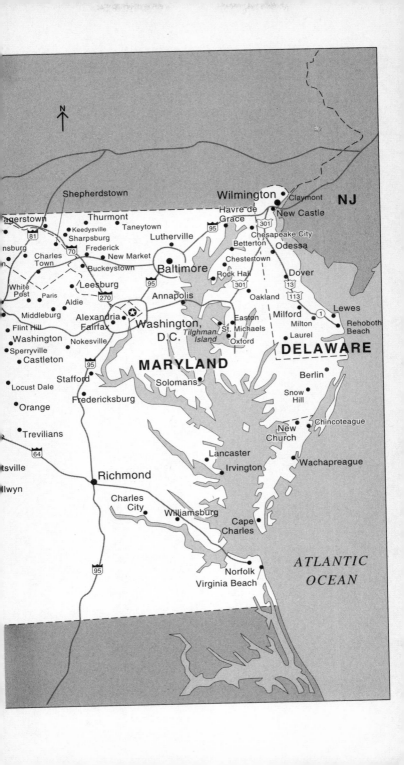

Index of Accommodations

Hotel/Inn Report Forms

The report forms on the following pages may be used to endorse or critique an existing entry or to nominate a hotel or inn that you feel deserves inclusion in the next edition. Don't feel you must restrict yourself to the space available; feel free to use your own stationery. All nominations (each on a separate piece of paper, if possible) should include your name and address, the name and location of the hotel or inn, when you have stayed there, and for how long. Please report only on establishments you have visited in the last eighteen months, unless you are sure that standards have not dropped since your stay. Please be as specific as possible, and critical where appropriate, about the character of the building, the public rooms, the accommodations, the meals, the service, the nightlife, the grounds, and the general atmosphere of the inn and the attitude of its owners. Comments about area restaurants and sights are also appreciated.

Don't feel you need to write at length. A report that merely verifies the accuracy of existing listings is extremely helpful, i.e., "Visited XYZ Inn and found it just as described." There is no need to bother with prices or with routine information about the number of rooms and facilities, although a sample brochure is very helpful for new recommendations.

On the other hand, don't apologize for writing a long report. Although space does not permit us to quote them in toto, the small details provided about furnishings, atmosphere, and cuisine can really make a description come alive, illuminating the special flavor of a particular inn or hotel. Remember that we will again be awarding free copies to our most helpful respondents—last year we mailed over 500 books.

Please note that we print only the names of respondents, never addresses. Those making negative observations are not identified. Although we must always have your full name and address, we will be happy to print your initials, or a pseudonym, if you prefer.

These report forms may also be used, if you wish, to recommend good hotels in Europe to our equivalent publication, *Europe's Wonderful Little Hotels & Inns* (published in Europe as *The Good Hotel Guide*). Reports should be sent to *Europe's Wonderful Little Hotels & Inns*, St. Martin's Press, 175 Fifth Avenue, New York, NY 10010; to P.O. Box 150, Riverside, CT 06878; or directly to *The Good Hotel Guide*, 61 Clarendon Road, London W11 4JE. Readers in the UK can send their letters postage-free to *The Good Hotel Guide*, Freepost, London W11 4 BR.

To: *America's Wonderful Little Hotels & Inns,*
    P.O. Box 150, Riverside, CT 06878

Name of hotel——————————————————————————

Address——————————————————————————————

Telephone—————————————————————————————

Date of most recent visit——————— Duration of visit———————

☐ New recommendation   ☐ Comment on existing entry

Please be as specific as possible about furnishings, atmosphere, service, and cuisine. If reporting on an existing entry, please tell us whether you thought it accurate. Unless you tell us not to, we shall assume that we may publish your name in the next edition. Thank you very much for writing; use your own stationery if preferred:

I am not connected with the management/owners.
I would stay here again if returning to the area.   ☐ yes   ☐ no
Have you written to us before?   ☐ yes   ☐ no

Signed————————————————————————————————

Name—————————————————————————————————
                        (Please print)

Address————————————————————————————————
                        (Please print)

MA96/7

To: *America's Wonderful Little Hotels & Inns,*
   P.O. Box 150, Riverside, CT 06878

Name of hotel _____

Address _____

Telephone _____

Date of most recent visit _____ Duration of visit _____

☐ New recommendation   ☐ Comment on existing entry

Please be as specific as possible about furnishings, atmosphere, service, and cuisine. If reporting on an existing entry, please tell us whether you thought it accurate. Unless you tell us not to, we shall assume that we may publish your name in the next edition. Thank you very much for writing; use your own stationery if preferred:

I am not connected with the management/owners.
I would stay here again if returning to the area.   ☐ yes   ☐ no
Have you written to us before?   ☐ yes   ☐ no

Signed _____

Name _____
                          (Please print)

Address _____
                          (Please print)

_____

MA96/7

To: *America's Wonderful Little Hotels & Inns*,
   P.O. Box 150, Riverside, CT 06878

Name of hotel_____

Address_____

Telephone_____

Date of most recent visit_____ Duration of visit_____

☐ New recommendation   ☐ Comment on existing entry

Please be as specific as possible about furnishings, atmosphere, service, and cuisine. If reporting on an existing entry, please tell us whether you thought it accurate. Unless you tell us not to, we shall assume that we may publish your name in the next edition. Thank you very much for writing; use your own stationery if preferred:

I am not connected with the management/owners.
I would stay here again if returning to the area.   ☐ yes   ☐ no
Have you written to us before?   ☐ yes   ☐ no

Signed_____

Name_____
                         (Please print)

Address_____
                         (Please print)

MA96/7

To: *America's Wonderful Little Hotels & Inns,*
   P.O. Box 150, Riverside, CT 06878

Name of hotel_____

Address_____

Telephone_____

Date of most recent visit_____ Duration of visit_____

☐ New recommendation   ☐ Comment on existing entry

Please be as specific as possible about furnishings, atmosphere, service, and cuisine. If reporting on an existing entry, please tell us whether you thought it accurate. Unless you tell us not to, we shall assume that we may publish your name in the next edition. Thank you very much for writing; use your own stationery if preferred:

I am not connected with the management/owners.
I would stay here again if returning to the area.   ☐ yes   ☐ no
Have you written to us before?   ☐ yes   ☐ no

Signed_____

Name_____
                              (Please print)

Address_____
                              (Please print)

_____

MA96/7